SOCIAL PROBLEMS

SECOND EDITION

SOCIAL PROBLEMS

JOSEPH JULIAN
University of Nebraska

PRENTICE-HALL, INC., Englewood Cliffs, New Jersey

Library of Congress Cataloging in Publication Data

Julian, Joseph.
  Social problems.

  Includes bibliographies and indexes.
    1. Sociology. 2. Social problems. 3. United
States—Social conditions. I. Title.
HM51.J84 1977   309.1'73   76-44252
ISBN 0-13-816736-2

Printed in the United States of America

10 9 8 7 6 5 4 3 2 1

Photo credits: cover, Nicholas Foster/The Image Bank;
p. 1, Joel Gordon; p. 25, Charles Harbutt/
Magnum; p. 79, Frederick De Van/
Nancy Palmer; p. 133, Jan Lukas/Photo
Researchers; p. 187, Courtesy of Storer Broadcasting
Company. Photo by Cailer/Resnick; p. 223, Bruce
Davidson/Magnum; p. 271, Charles Gatewood; p. 313,
Suva/DPI; p. 357, Ken Heyman; p. 387,
Bruce Roberts/Photo Researchers; p. 429,
Charles Gatewood; p. 477, Sven Simm/Katherine
Young; p. 511, Ken Heyman; p. 541,
Arthur Tress/Magnum.

PRENTICE-HALL INTERNATIONAL, INC., *London*
PRENTICE-HALL OF AUSTRALIA, PTY. LTD., *Sydney*
PRENTICE-HALL OF CANADA, LTD., *Toronto*
PRENTICE-HALL OF INDIA PRIVATE LIMITED, *New Delhi*
PRENTICE-HALL OF JAPAN, INC., *Tokyo*
PRENTICE-HALL OF SOUTHEAST ASIA (PTE.) LTD., *Singapore*
WHITEHALL BOOKS LIMITED, *Wellington, New Zealand*

CONTENTS

PREFACE   xv

1 THE SOCIOLOGICAL APPROACH
TO SOCIAL PROBLEMS   1

How Does a Social Condition
  Become a Social Problem?   3
Assumptions About Social Problems   5
The Study of Social Problems:
  Related Disciplines   8
The Sociological Perspective   11
  Useful deviance and social change   14
Five Perspectives on Social Problems   15
  The social pathology perspective   16
  The social disorganization perspective   17
  The value conflict perspective   18
  The deviant behavior perspective   18
  The labeling perspective   19

v

Organization of the Book   21
Summary   22
Bibliography   23

2 PHYSICAL AND MENTAL HEALTH   25

Problems of Physical Health   28
    Inequality in access to health services   29
    The high cost of health   30
    The problems of unnecessary
        or harmful treatment   35
The Roots of Health Problems   38
    General problems   38
    The problems of poverty   39
Social Policy and Action   41
    Alternative provider organizations   41
    Alternative financing systems   42
    Improving the existing system   43
Prospects   44
Problems of Mental Health   46
The Nature of Mental Disorders   46
Classification of Mental Disorders   51
    The illness model   51
    Labeling theory   52
Mental Disorder and Social Structure   54
    Social class and mental disorder   55
    Urbanization   59
    Other social factors   60
The Treatment of Mental Disorders   62
    The historical background   62
    Modern approaches   64
    The organization of treatment   67
Prospects   74
Summary   75
Bibliography   76

3 PROBLEMS OF CHEMICAL DEPENDENCY   79

What is a Drug?   81
The Abuse of Legal Drugs   82
Alcohol Use and Abuse   84
    Problem drinkers and alcoholics   85
    The ethnic factor   86
    Who drinks?   87
    Drinking among young people   88

Social Problems Related to Alcohol 89
    Health 89
    Drinking and driving 90
    Alcohol and arrest rates 91
    Effects on the family 93
    Skid row alcoholics 93
Social Control 94
    Treatment and rehabilitation 95
    Alcoholics Anonymous 95
    Antabuse programs 96
    Community programs 97
    Company programs 98
    Educational programs 98
Drug Use and Abuse 99
    Marijuana 100
    The opiates 107
    Hallucinogens 110
    Amphetamines 111
    Barbiturates 113
Social Problems Related to Drug Abuse 114
    Drugs and the law 115
    Drug use and crime 117
Social Control 119
    Rehabilitation programs 119
    The British system 123
    Educational programs 125
    Revision of drug laws 126
Prospects 127
Summary 128
Bibliography 130

4 CRIME AND CRIMINALS 133

The Nature of Crime 137
Types of Crime and Criminals 139
    Violent personal crime 140
    Occasional property crime 141
    Occupational (white-collar) crime 141
    Political crime 146
    Public order crime 147
    Conventional crime 147
    Organized crime 148
    Professional crime 152
    Juvenile delinquency 153
Conditions and Causes of Crime 154
Explanations of Crime (Sociological Theories) 158

Group-supported crime   159
Anomie approach   160
Delinquent subcultures   161
Lower-class culture and delinquency   164
Social Control   165
Retribution-deterrence   165
Rehabilitation   167
Prevention   173
Criminal and juvenile justice reforms   175
Prospects   181
Summary   183
Bibliography   185

5 VIOLENCE   **187**

A historical perspective   190
The Concepts of Violence   191
Explanations for Violence   193
The biological viewpoint   193
Frustration-aggression and
   control theories   195
Subculture of violence   195
Media influence   197
Domestic Violence   199
Criminal violence   200
Civil disturbances   205
Social Action and Domestic Violence   209
Regulation   209
Social reforms   212
War   214
Explanations of war   215
Prevention of war   217
Prospects   219
Summary   220
Bibliography   221

6 AFFLUENCE AND POVERTY   **223**

The Affluent Few   225
The rich get richer . . .   227
. . . At the expense of the poor   228
The Nature of Affluence   229
The perpetuation of wealth   229
Who are the affluent?   231
Affluence and Corporatism   233
The corporation-politician connection   233

The corporate-military connection   235
The Significance of Affluence and Poverty   237
The Nature of Poverty   240
The fixed income approach   240
The relative income approach   241
Who are the Poor?   242
The elderly poor   242
Poverty and family structure   243
Poverty and minorities   245
Poverty and spatial distribution   246
Concomitants of Poverty   248
Health care   248
Education   250
Housing   251
Justice   252
Explanations of Poverty   253
The cultural explanation   254
The situational approach   255
The cultural-situational approach   256
The adaptation approach   257
The value-stretch concept   258
Employment, Unemployment, and Welfare   259
Work and the poor   259
The poor on welfare   260
Social Action   262
Employment and economic growth   263
Income maintenance programs   264
Prospects   266
Summary   267
Bibliography   269

7   PREJUDICE AND DISCRIMINATION   **271**

The Meaning of Minority   275
Dominance and subordination   276
Prejudice and Discrimination Defined   276
Prejudice and Discrimination: Sources   278
Psychological needs   278
Socialization and social structure   280
Institutionalized Discrimination   282
Education   283
Housing   290
Employment   294
Social justice   296
**Some Consequences of Prejudice and
Discrimination**   299

Social Action   304
     Manpower training programs   305
     Head start   305
Prospects   308
Summary   309
Bibliography   310

8   SEX ROLES AND INEQUALITY   313

Origins of Traditional Sex Roles   315
     The requirements of hunting and
        gathering societies   317
     The threat and use of force by men   318
     The Freudian theory of anatomical
        destiny   319
The Rise of Feminism   320
     Industrialization   321
     The feminist movement   322
     The need for equality   324
The Nature of Sexism   327
     Stereotyping   328
     Job opportunities and salaries   329
     Legal, civil, and economic rights   332
Sexism, Social Class, and Race   334
     Black women   335
     Puertorriqueñas   336
     Native women   337
     Chicana women   338
     Asian women   339
Sources of Sexism   339
     Socialization   339
     Education   340
     Family   342
     Psychiatric medicine   343
     Language and the media   344
     Organized religion   345
     Government   346
     The legal system   347
Social Action   348
     Changes in child-rearing practices   348
     Changes in the educational process   350
     Changes in the legal system   351
Prospects   352
Summary   353
Bibliography   354

9 YOUTH, AGE, AND INEQUALITY   357

Who Are the Young and Elderly?   359
> Who are the young?   359
> Who are the elderly?   361
> Similarities between the young and
>   the elderly   362

Agism: Prejudice and Discrimination against
the Young and the Old   364
> The minority position of young people   364
> The aged as a minority   366
> Social Security: A special form of agism   370

Some Consequences of Agism   372
> For the young   372
> For the elderly   374
> For both the young and old   375

Social Policy and Prospects   376
> For the young   376
> For the elderly   378
> For the elderly and the young   382

Summary   384
Bibliography   385

10 FAMILY PROBLEMS   387

Kinship Units   389
> Adequate family functioning   389
> Family happiness and working wives   391
> Family happiness and children   392
> The black family   393

Problems within Traditional Families   395
> Child abuse   395
> Illegitimacy   400
> Divorce   405
> Family problems of the aged   414

Alternative Kinship Units   417
> The two-partner family   417
> The communal family   419

Prospects   425
Summary   426
Bibliography   427

11 PROBLEMS IN HUMAN SEXUALITY   429

Origins of Today's Attitudes   432
> Formal study of human sexual conduct   433

The Varieties of Human Sexuality 435
Classifying Problems in Human Sexuality 437
Defining sexual social problems 437
Sex crimes 437
Types of sexual social problems 439
Homosexuality 442
Subcultural aspects of homosexuality 449
Lesbianism 450
Social control 453
Prostitution 455
Reasons for prostitution 458
The prostitute subculture 463
Social control 464
Pornography 465
Prospects 471
Summary 473
Bibliography 474

12 WORK 477

Trends 480
The increase in white-collar workers 481
Specialization 481
An employee society 482
Age and sex composition of the
labor force 482
Problem Aspects of Work 483
Unemployment 485
Automation 489
Job satisfaction 493
More leisure time 497
Social Action 501
Paraprofessionals 501
The four-day work week 503
Flexible work hours 505
The use of leisure time 506
Prospects 506
Summary 508
Bibliography 509

13 THE POPULATION CRISIS 511

Scope of the Population Problem 513
Population growth 515
The Effects of Population Growth 517

Population problems in
   industrial countries   517
Population problems in
   agrarian countries   519
Attitudes toward Population Control   527
  Religious attitudes   529
Population Control Programs—
  Voluntary or Compulsory   530
  The voluntary approach   531
  Compulsory birth control   532
  Population control programs in
    the advanced nations   533
  Population control in
    the developing nations   534
Prospects   536
Summary   538
Bibliography   539

14   THE ENVIRONMENTAL CRISIS   541

Dimensions of the Problem   543
  Air pollution   544
  Water pollution   547
  Nonrenewable resources and
    solid waste disposal   551
  Land degradation   553
  Other hazards   554
Origins of the Problem   558
Social Action   565
  Educating the public   565
  Recycling   566
  Technology assessment   567
  Legislation   569
  Population control   570
  Creating the future   570
Prospects   571
Summary   572
Bibliography   573

NAME INDEX   574

SUBJECT INDEX   578

PREFACE

This book represents an effort to present a progressive, comprehensive, and engaging approach to contemporary social problems. Its goal is to provide the student with a conceptual framework, a way of looking at social problems. We systematically discuss the sociological perspective on social problems and try to convey a great deal of the information generated by the research of outstanding sociologists and others. We have been eclectic in our approach and explore different points of view among sociologists. We have also tried to indicate what the most current thinking is with regard to these problems.

ORGANIZATION

The chapter sequence reflects a broad approach to social problems, following a logical micro to macro (individual to global) pattern that acknowledges the fact that most social problems are interrelated and can be approached from several points of view. The chapters have been constructed to be sufficiently self-contained so that they may be used in a variety of sequences, although of course some chapters are more closely related than others.

In early chapters we focus on relatively individual behaviors, such as drug use or crime. Of course, the social institutions and other environmental factors affecting these behaviors are noted and described. Chapters in the middle of the book focus on inequality and discrimination in discussions of such topics as poverty, prejudice, sexism, and age discrimination. We make every attempt to indicate the effects of large-scale discrimination on individuals as well as to deal with the concept of institutional "isms"—institutional racism, institutional sexism, and agism. In later chapters we discuss problems common to many societies, such as those relating to family, sexuality, and work. In the final chapters, on population and environment, we focus on matters of global significance. It seemed best to discuss each subject in a separate chapter in order to deal with it comprehensively and in depth. We have tried to indicate points at which different problems overlap and how these problems are interrelated.

While there is a flexible organization for the book as a whole, within each chapter a clear structure is utilized as much as possible in order to maintain a logical flow to the material. First, we explore the nature of the problem. Then we discuss the various explanations for the causes of the problem. From there, we move to a discussion of social control and social action—that is, the ways in which the problem might be dealt with or eliminated. Finally, we explore the prospects for dealing with the problem within the next few years.

The latter two sections, on social control and on future prospects, are particularly important. We are all aware of the many problems that face us and their constantly changing nature. It is important for students to understand that these problems are complex, but we also believe strongly in this book that it is important for students to think in terms of what can be done about social problems. More than other social problems texts, we look at the possibilities for social action (or social control) and the prospects of each problem in the near future.

PEDAGOGICAL DEVICES

We have tried to present the material in such a way as to be most helpful to students and teachers alike. Each problem is discussed in a well-organized and readable manner. As much as possible, we have deemphasized sociological terminology. Our treatment of each problem is analytical as well as descriptive, and we have included the most up-to-date findings available.

We have also included carefully selected illustrative material—photographs, tables, and graphs. The photographs were chosen primarily for their functional value, to clarify points which are difficult to make verbally. The tables and graphs were also selected to clarify or expand certain points made in the text.

At the end of each chapter, there is a concise chapter summary which distills and reviews the important concepts of the chapter. There is also a bibliography which may be used as a suggested reading list. Both important classical works and the most up-to-date books in the field are included.

SUPPLEMENTAL AIDS

The text is accompanied by a Study Guide and Workbook, an Instructor's Manual, and a Test Item File. The Workbook is designed to help students review and understand the key concepts of each chapter and how they are interrelated. Each chapter in the Workbook features a detailed review outline, a series of self-test review questions, and an "Applications" section that helps students apply their knowledge to real-life situations. Each of the self-test review questions is keyed to a specific page in the text, so that students will find it convenient to review unfamiliar material.

The Instructor's Manual provides chapter outlines, additional material for classroom discussion, suggested topics for papers and research projects, and a series of essay questions based on the material in the text. A new feature of this edition is the annotated list of popular and educational films that appears at the end of each chapter. The separate Test Item File contains short-answer questions keyed to specific pages in the text.

CHANGES IN THE SECOND EDITION

The response to the first edition has been gratifying. Much of the feedback from colleagues, teachers, and students has been constructive and has been put to good use. This second edition represents a continuing effort to present a contemporary social problems text. To this end, wholesale updating has taken place, along with some changes and a few additions. For greater flexibility, the chapter sequence has been changed. Chapter summaries have been added for better comprehension and easier review. Increased chapter cross-referencing will make it easier for students to grasp the interrelatedness of social problems.

Two brand new chapters have been prepared for this second edition: Chapter Eight ("Sex Roles and Inequality") and Chapter Nine ("Youth, Age, and Inequality"). The new, separate chapter on sexism in this edition is designed to raise the consciousness of those who are not fully aware of the subordination of women in American society. We have also added a chapter on "agism." For many of us, being young and growing old are stressful life stages. We think Chapter Nine is an engaging, perhaps unique, discussion of agism today.

Each of the remaining chapters was updated and underwent at least minor revisions. Six chapters were significantly revised. Chapter One ("The Sociological Approach to Social Problems") now includes a section on the positive aspects of deviance and the various sociological approaches to social problems. The physical health half of Chapter Two ("Physical and Mental Health") is totally new. The handling of problems associated with drugs in Chapter Three has been broadened to deal more generally with problems of chemical dependency, especially in terms of legal drugs. Chapter Four ("Crime and Criminals") is a combination of two chapters from the first edition and stresses the diversity of types of criminal offenders and the sociopolitical nature of crime. The nature and problems of affluence in our country are greatly expanded in Chapter Six ("Affluence and Poverty"). Finally, Chapter Eleven ("Problems in

Human Sexuality") discusses more fully the origins and complexity of current sexual attitudes.

ACKNOWLEDGMENTS

Writing a textbook, especially in the area of social problems, is a major effort that requires the special talents and hard work of the people directly involved as well as the help of many others. In the first edition there were Virginia Hoitsma, Sarah Parker, Vincent Covello, Karen Reixach, and Janet Brunoski. Of course this revision involved a number of people also. The opinions and teaching experience of users of the first edition were solicited, and their many suggestions were quite helpful. In addition, reviews and critiques were obtained from specialists in the various fields. I would like to thank the prior users of the book for their help, especially Joseph W. Rogers. I would also like to thank, for their valuable comments and suggestions, Joan Acker, James Carey, John Conklin, Joe Feagin, Erich Goode, Arlie Hochschild, Joan Huber, Carol Kronus, Peter Manning, Anthony Orum, Carolyn Perrucci, Alexander Rysman, Constantina Safilios-Rothschild, David Schulz, Donald Warren, and Mary Jo Deegan. I owe a special debt of gratitude to Don C. Gibbons, friend, colleague, and former mentor for, among other things, his cogent critique of the crime chapter. This book is a better book because of the criticisms, advice, and suggestions of all these people. Of course, any problems in the book associated with errors of fact or errors of interpretation, should be labeled mine.

In addition to the assistance of my colleagues in sociology, this project has had the help of a team of publishing specialists, people with research, editorial, and writing skills. I want to thank Ron Csuha, Jane Kidwell, Barbara Keating, Jean Karlen, and Margaret Roller for performing superior research work. At Prentice-Hall, I want to thank Patricia McDermott and Ed Stanford as production editor and sociology editor respectively. And I would especially like to thank Sheldon Czapnik, who collaborated on this revision, for his invaluable help and his enormous capacity for just plain hard work.

Saving the best for last, I would like to once again pay tribute to Lynn Julian, who is still my main partner, and to two other partners, Jeff Julian and Jay Julian.

JOSEPH JULIAN

SOCIAL PROBLEMS

1

THE SOCIOLOGICAL APPROACH TO SOCIAL PROBLEMS

An old woman sits in a home for the aged, staring at the TV set all day long. Two or three times a month her married son stops in to visit her. Last Christmas she spent the day with her daughter's family. She is not sick, but she cannot live alone. Neither of her children seems anxious to have her live with them. They contribute what money they can to supplement her Social Security and enable her to be here at a private old-age home. She feels lonely and isolated from the rest of the world.

The city of San Francisco decides, in the interests of equal educational opportunity for all of its children, to bus students from ethnically segregated districts to integrated schools. The Chinese minority in the city protest strenuously. They claim that busing in effect discriminates against them in that it will tend to undermine their special way of life.

Medical missionaries and health officers dedicate their lives to the service of underdeveloped peoples. Medicine, surgery, sanitation are introduced. The death rate falls dramatically. Babies live, grow up, marry. Men and women who once would have died at 35 live to the age of 50 or 60. Suddenly there are too many people. The farms have been divided up too many times; the pastures are eroded from overgrazing. The new national governments struggle to increase production fast enough just to keep up with the mushrooming population. To get ahead of it—to raise the standard of living for more than a tiny minority—seems beyond hope.

After World War II, the U.S. government, concerned about the hostile stance of the U.S.S.R., concludes that for the sake of national defense the United States must oppose Communism at every point. Money is appropriated for weapons research; organizations are funded to counter

Soviet propaganda; an intelligence network is set up; armed forces are kept in readiness. Thirty years later the arms race is costing the nation billions of dollars yearly; thousands of Americans have died in an undeclared war in a small, remote Asian country; and political opinion on the subject of national defense has become severely polarized.

On June 17, 1972, burglars were discovered breaking into the Democratic party headquarters in Washington's Watergate complex. Investigation of the event and its attempted cover-up culminated more than two years later in the forced resignation of President Nixon and the imprisonment of his aides on charges of conspiracy, perjury, and obstruction of justice. Subsequent congressional investigations, sparked in part by the Watergate affair, revealed extensive evidence of illegal corporate contributions to political campaigns; CIA involvement in attempts to assassinate foreign leaders; and FBI harassment of U.S. citizens.

In the late nineteenth century, unskilled factory laborers often worked twelve hours a day, seven days a week. Eighty or ninety years later, after bitter battles in the streets and in governmental chambers, the eight-hour day and five-day week have become standard, and the four-day week is being tried. Sociologists are becoming aware of a potential problem new in the history of the world: in a relatively few years, large numbers of ordinary people may have more leisure time than they know how to use.

HOW DOES A SOCIAL CONDITION BECOME A SOCIAL PROBLEM?

We have just cited some examples of what most of us would agree are problems in our society. It is not clear, however, how these problems and others like them have come to be regarded as something we should solve or alleviate. Just when did the isolation of the aged in our society change from a "condition" to be deplored from afar to a "social problem" society should reform? What caused us to view corruption among elected officials as something we should punish and prevent rather than as something we should accept or at least tolerate?

The answer to this is quite simple, even though the process which it involves is complex. Conditions become "social problems" when society decides that they should be improved. In order for a social condition to become a social problem, a significant number of people—or a number of significant people—must agree both that this condition violates an accepted value or standard *and* that it should be eliminated, resolved, or remedied through collective action.

The critical point is that for a social problem to exist, there must be both an "objective" and a "subjective" element. The objective part is the condition itself; the subjective part is the belief that the condition should be changed. The process by which this subjective belief arises is a complex one, involving those individual and historical forces that affect the evolution of a society's values.

Until the eighteenth century, for example, the great mass of people labored in poor conditions, worked long hours at arduous tasks for other people, lived in poor conditions, and died at early ages, often of terrible diseases—and no one considered these to be "social problems." Most people accepted them as a natural and inevitable condition of life, decreed by a divine providence which they would some day understand and appreciate. However, as philosophers like Locke and Rousseau developed the democratic theory that every person was created equal to every other person, and as others acquired the scientific knowledge which enabled them to improve their environment, people everywhere began to reassess their living conditions. In France and England, certain "enlightened" individuals began to preach that poverty was not inevitable, but was the result of an unjust aristocratic system, and that it could be alleviated by the democratic reorganization of society, the redistribution of wealth, and the determination of a person's station in life by his or her own merit rather than by his or her parents' social position.

Although this awareness began in the late eighteenth century, at a time when the possible powers of human reason were being explored as never before, similar reassessments are always being made. These changes in judgment often take place when what has been considered a "misfortune" suddenly appears as an "injustice"—when a significant number of people realize that a certain condition has a social or institutional cause. Prior to the nineteenth century poverty was considered a misfortune because people felt helpless to do anything about it. They could lament it, bemoan it, write plays, poems, and tragedies about it—even alleviate it in particular cases—but they could not prevent it. Poverty was God's will, a result of humanity's original sin, a stroke of fate, bad fortune. It was only when people began to believe that they could rearrange society and provide better living conditions that they were able to reconceive poverty as being not a misfortune but an injustice. Unfortunately, even today there are people who continue to hold the earlier view.

However, it is not only old misfortunes which become new social problems as the growth of knowledge and technology makes us more able to change existing conditions. Even what was once considered a desirable social norm may take on a negative appearance. The position of women furnishes a good example. In the day when most work had to be done by hand and there were few labor-saving devices, it was accepted as a social norm that the work of procuring food and other necessities was principally a man's responsibility, and the care of home and children, which usually required somewhat less physical strength, was a woman's. As society changed, the nature of outside work also changed, and the realm of business came to be known as man's world, while woman's place was still in the home. But with the growth of technology and the increased prevalence of outside child-care agencies—schools, recreational facilities, and others—the practical need for women to stay at home was lessened, while changes in the education of women made them less willing to stay there. Thus the norm began to look less acceptable. Today a substantial part of society regards the traditional restrictions on women's participation in the business world as constituting a social problem and urges investigation of hiring practices, provisions of day care, equal pay for equal work, and other measures designed to alleviate it. Thus a practice which was once socially valuable has now become, in the eyes of many, a social liability.

ASSUMPTIONS ABOUT SOCIAL PROBLEMS

People have their own ways of looking at things, their own points of view. That is to say, all of us make certain assumptions as to what the world is all about. These assumptions give us a framework for understanding our experience, for making some kind of coherent sense out of all the different things that happen to us and around us; and they help us decide how to respond. Sometimes, of course, we begin to discover that our point of view no longer supplies us with a useful framework, and then we may change it.

Likewise, when sociologists look at social problems, they make certain basic assumptions about why things happen as they do. These assumptions, or premises—described below—give them a starting point for studying even some very complicated problems:

Social problems are to some extent the results of indirect and unexpected effects of acceptable patterns of behavior.

There are numerous examples of this phenomenon. The so-called population explosion is one. Having many children has been a valued practice in many places for a long time, and for most of that time it was a real necessity. Throughout most of history, men and women have been producing offspring in great numbers, hoping that perhaps some of them might survive to adulthood. But now, because we have discovered ways of sustaining most human life, most societies suddenly have more than enough people. Certain countries, such as India, have far more than they can feed properly, and demographers warn that many other nations will soon face similar problems. In fact, many demographers predict that unless universal birth control is instituted soon, by the year 2000 the earth will have more people than it can provide for. This population problem involves more than a question of food supply, although severe malnutrition has usually been endemic in heavily overcrowded countries. Clean air, adequate housing, education, employment, and the whole intangible but real thing we call "quality of life" are also involved. Consequently, what was once a revered norm (having many children) has suddenly turned into a social problem.

Or consider the use of insecticides. At one time these chemicals were regarded as a great boon to farmers and consumers, since they destroyed insects and helped to preserve crops. With them, farmers could produce more food for more people at less cost than ever before. In view of this, it seemed obvious that a farmer ought to use insecticides.

Recently, however, ecologists have demonstrated that some insecticides destroy the soil, damage plants, and taint the food produced by these plants. Insecticides have, therefore, created new problems—for the farmers who now depend on them to protect their crops, for the consumers who have been eating the foods affected by them, for the government, which must decide whether to restrict their use and prohibit the sale of certain foods, and for the scientists who must find substances to replace them and ways to undo whatever harm they have caused. Once again, what was considered a beneficial innovation has actually created new and unexpected problems.

This will give some idea of the way in which many social problems arise—not because of bad deeds, bad people, or even bad luck, but as unintended consequences of widely accepted and often expected ways of doing things, particularly as these interact with subsequent technological change. While many religions and philosophies have viewed the existence of problems such as crime and poverty as the result of an "evil" or weak people (the "bad seed" idea), this can no longer be accepted as an adequate explanation.

In fact, not only are social problems not usually caused by evil intent, they may even be the result of extremely well meaning actions. For example, Prohibition laws (outlawing the sale of liquor) were passed in the 1920s in order to protect people from the "evils" of alcohol. But, as it turned out, Prohibition in effect promoted bootlegging and the rise of modern organized crime.

Why do people with good intentions tend to create problems, or cause others to do so? The answer gives us our second premise:

A certain social structure and culture induce most people to conform, but can also cause some people to deviate.

A major element in the social structure of the United States, for instance, is that of property rights, and this is associated with the perennial problem of the haves and the have-nots. We regard it as possible and legitimate for a person to become the owner of some portion of the land, money, or other goods of society; and we consider that such ownership confers a right to keep this property, or to dispose of it in any way the owner chooses, subject to certain socially determined limitations. Some ways of acquiring property are socially approved—a person works to earn money, buys a car from a dealer, grows vegetables on his or her own land, writes a book and copyrights it. Certain other ways are considered deviant—a person takes a car without the owner's consent, or sells stock by making fraudulent claims about the company's profits.

Probably most people in the United States conform in general to the established pattern regarding property rights. They may stretch the limits occasionally—a little deceit, an occasional "liberation" of a bit of company property—but not beyond the degree which society is willing to tolerate. The average middle-class wage-earner wants to own a house; he or she is willing to work at a steady job and pay interest on a mortgage in order to buy it; and he or she claims the right to remodel it, enlarge it, or sell it, once it is bought.

But some people are unable, and/or unwilling, to acquire property by the approved means. They may be unable to find work which pays an adequate salary, or they may have too many children, high medical bills, and/or other expenses which eat up their earnings. These people may turn to deviant means of obtaining money and goods. Thus we have the shoplifter, the embezzler, the burglar, the mugger, the armed robber— all deviant from cultural norms, yet in a sense all created by the cultural pattern.

In this connection, it is worth noting that what is deviant behavior in the eyes of one group within a society may be approved, or at least tolerated, by another. What a middle-class merchant calls stealing may be "taking" to lower-class youngsters who reason that they need the object more than the merchant does.

This leads to a third premise:

Every social structure or society is composed of different categories of people who have similar levels of income, amounts of education, ethnic background, and occupations. These various groups constitute "strata" or layers of society. Persons in different strata experience problems differently and are therefore likely to understand them differently.

In other words, one's attitude toward a problem will be influenced by one's background, education, level of income, occupation, and personal experience. Since a person may occupy more than one position (one may be a middle-class Jewish lawyer or an upper-class Protestant lawyer), his or her attitude is seldom wholly determined by any of these factors. The chances are that a person earning $50,000 per year will react differently to the problems of the ghetto slums than will the person who lives in one; but a Jewish corporation president may have the same attitude toward Israel as his or her Jewish secretary.

Moreover, people's attitude toward a certain problem may change when they move from one position to another. In their study of the Polish people in Chicago, Thomas and Znaniecki [1] pointed out that years ago most Chicago residents considered the Polish people (then a poorly paid immigrant group) a threat to law, order, and middle-class morality, since they had an unusually high rate of delinquency and crime. However, now that the same Polish people have achieved well-paying jobs, suburban homes, and social respectability, they in turn are similarly hostile toward the poor blacks who now occupy ghetto areas of the city. The same thing has happened with many other ethnic groups—Italian, Irish, and Russian—all of whom today react to black and Spanish-American ghetto residents very much as white Anglo-Saxon Protestants once reacted to them and their parents.

Consequently, in order to assess people's attitudes toward social problems, one should consider their social background and previous experience. These factors not only affect the way in which they understand a particular problem, they also influence the solution which they will propose to remedy it. And this leads to our fourth major premise:

People in different social strata propose different solutions to social problems. Since these solutions usually favor their particular interests and values, it is often difficult to reach agreement on or to implement a solution to a given problem.

Any number of common events in today's world illustrate this premise. If the problem is one of improved housing for the poor, it is likely that the poor themselves will favor public financing and scatter-site housing in middle-class neighborhoods, while the residents of these neighborhoods, fearful of crime, new taxes, and the decline of property values, will argue for private financing and the rebuilding of present poverty areas. Or, on a college campus, students may demand open admission of minority applicants, regardless of academic qualifications, as a means of raising minority status, while the administration maintains that the

[1] William I. Thomas and Florian Znaniecki, *The Polish Peasant in Europe and America.* New York: Octagon, 1971.

same end will best be accomplished by holding minority students to the same standards required of others.

In other situations, a group may actually prefer *not* to see certain problems solved, since it may benefit from the existence and perpetuation of these problems. Many landlords, for example, benefit from housing shortages among the poor and even middle classes, because the existence of such a shortage allows them to impose high rents without providing adequate (and costly) service.

The above premises imply two vital points. First, every social structure has potential to generate social problems. Moreover, new patterns may create new problems and new deviations. Second, a good deal of a person's behavior, perception, and attitude is influenced by his or her social position. Consequently, the environment and background of the groups involved are significant factors in the origin and elimination of social problems.

THE STUDY OF SOCIAL PROBLEMS: RELATED DISCIPLINES

Many persons other than sociologists have concerned themselves with social problems. Philosophers since antiquity have speculated as to the causes of social problems and offered solutions; religious leaders, philanthropists, revolutionaries, and writers have striven to lessen the suffering of individuals or groups. It is impossible to consider here all the theories, or all the ways in which people have worked for social improvement. We will instead discuss the various approaches to social problems of some of the disciplines within the social sciences. History, political science, economics, social psychology, anthropology, and even biology all share to some extent with sociology the analysis of human behavior, and each sees a given problem from a somewhat different point of view.

History. History is the study of the past, and it is usually concerned more with the explicit detail and sequence of events than with their causes and interrelations, which are the concerns of sociology. The material history gathers can be used as data, however, for the study of such causes and interrelations, and this study constitutes the field of historical sociology. But even in seeking to understand present social problems, a knowledge of their historical background, or of the forms which social institutions took in earlier times, can be helpful.

For instance, historical factors can be seen to have played an important part in shaping the present position of black Americans. The very fact that black people were once, typically, slaves, has made it very difficult for us—not only whites but even blacks—to free ourselves from a derogatory view of them. In addition, any number of specific factors enter in. The peculiar character of the English law of slavery, which treated the slave as wholly dehumanized property; the technological developments which created a rapidly expanding market for cheap, slave-grown cotton; the widespread fear of slave revolts, which led to severe legal restrictions even on freed slaves; the whole course of post–Civil War economic and political developments in the South—all of these need to be recognized if we are to understand why black Americans have for so long been second-class citizens in their own country, and why they have often been not only poor and uneducated, but "shiftless," "improvident," and dogged by a high crime rate. The environment of the past, and the self-image developed during the past, are important factors in creating the situation of the present. For these and other reasons, historians can make enormous contributions to our study and understanding of social problems.

Cultural Anthropology. Cultural anthropology studies the social organization and development of primitive societies past and present. It is closely related to sociology, since many of the same techniques can be used in both fields, and the findings of cultural anthropologists in regard to primitive and traditional cultures shed light on related phenomena in more complex modern societies.

Suicide is one of the modern social problems about which anthropologists have contributed some insights. It has been shown that suicide rates vary from one culture to another, and that societies differ in their attitudes toward suicide—some regard it as laudable, some absolutely forbid it or cannot even conceive of it. Some societies have had a place for ritual suicide—the Japanese *hara-kiri,* the Indian *suttee,* and even older forms in which kings or religious leaders killed themselves, or accepted death, to ensure some needed good fortune for the people. On the basis of these anthropological observations, students of today's society can recognize that calling suicide a product of modern life, city life, or technological and depersonalized culture, as is sometimes done, is overly simplistic.

The role of women in society is a subject of particular interest today, and here the anthropologists have much to contribute, for they can report on the position of women in widely differing cultures around the globe. Their studies show that women seem to occupy a generally subordinate position in most societies, but that in some cases they exercise a certain amount of authority. A particularly interesting subordinate pattern appears in a study of village life in Taiwan in 1959–1960.[2] In the village of Peihotien, the only careers for a woman were those of wife and prostitute. Children were valued largely on the basis of what they could contribute to the family, and so a girl, who would normally be marrying into another household at about the age when she began to be economically useful, was considered rather a liability. Poor families frequently gave or sold their infant daughters to others who would adopt them as future wives for their sons.

A wife's status in the world depended entirely on her husband's family, and on her ability to bear sons. If not adopted in infancy, she married into a home in which she was a stranger and a servant. Only when she had borne a son did she begin to be really a member of the family.

If a daughter did not marry, it was usually because she was needed to support her parents. There were a few paying jobs available to young

[2] Margery Wolf, *The House of Lim: A Study of a Chinese Farm Family.* Englewood Cliffs, N.J.: Prentice-Hall (ACC), 1960.

women, such as working in a small local factory. But the only way a girl could earn a substantial income was by becoming a prostitute. She could do this and remain respectable so long as she carried on her professional activities outside the village and turned over most of her earnings to her parents. She could dress better and eat better than most of the villagers. She might even marry, later on, into a quite respectable family, since there was a tendency to feel that such a woman was less likely than most to be unfaithful after marriage. Nevertheless, few ever took up the prostitute's life except out of necessity.

On the other hand, among some Pacific island peoples, women have been found to hold positions of almost chiefly dignity, and in some societies family descent is reckoned through the female line. Cross-cultural comparisons, made possible by anthropological studies, thus bear on the question of how much the relative positions of women and men are the result of nature, and how much they are created by social convention.

Psychology and Social Psychology. Psychology deals with human mental and emotional processes, focusing primarily on individual experience. It is rooted in biology, and has always had a more strongly experimental nature than the other social sciences. An understanding of the psychological pressures underlying individual responses to societal pressures can often be illuminating with regard to social attitudes and behavior. Some studies have been done, for instance, of the childhood experiences of parents who are child abusers. A few apparently significant patterns have been found; it appears that parents who are child abusers were themselves beaten, neglected, or otherwise abused as children. Knowledge of such factors can shed light on child abuse as a social, as well as an individual, problem.

Social psychology, the study of the ways in which the psychological processes, behavior, and personalities of individuals influence, or are influenced by, social processes and social settings, is of particular value in regard to social problems. For instance, intensive studies have been done of the personality dynamics of anti-minority prejudice—anti-Semitism, white racism—and a certain "authoritarian" personality type has emerged. Authoritarian personalities have little insight into their own behavior and feelings, and try to stifle or deny their emotions. Unable to admit to themselves their hatred, resentment, or fear of their parents or other childhood authority figures, they project these emotions onto others, and become submissive toward, or even fearful of, those with authority over them, and harshly aggressive toward those beneath them.

Other anti-minority prejudice appears to be a function of social conformity on the part of those whose need to be liked and approved of is strong. In this case, as in that of the authoritarian personality, prejudice and discrimination stem from and fulfill a personal need.

Other studies have investigated the psychological characteristics of youth protest. Some correlation has been indicated between leftist activists and permissive, mother-dominated families on the one hand, and between conservative activists and authoritarian, father-dominated families on the other, but the evidence is far from conclusive. Family differences have also been suggested between the politically radical and the culturally renunciatory ("hippie," "dropout") types of protester against "the establishment." This field of study is still so new that many of the findings remain tentative.

Biology. The relationship of biological inheritance and biological processes to social behavior has long been a subject of speculation, and the annals of prejudice are rich in supposed biological justifications. For instance, it is customary, if incorrect, to regard lower-class ethnic minorities as being especially highly sexed—to believe that they "breed like rabbits," that they constantly lust after sexual activity, and so on. Actually, it is quite reasonable to conceive of a biological influence on behavior, but difficult to establish scientific proof of it. For example, it has been suggested that certain non-Caucasian peoples, including the American Indian, may suffer from an inherited genetic vulnerability to the effects of alcohol, and may therefore be more likely than Caucasians, under given circumstances, to become alcoholics. But since it is difficult to find situations in which all conditions except heredity are the same for Caucasians and Indians, this thesis has been impossible to prove.

One social problem area in which the possibility of biological influence has been systematically investigated is that of criminal behavior. In the nineteenth century the Italian Cesare Lombroso developed a theory of the "born criminal"—that certain people are born with traits which predispose them to criminal activity, and that such people can usually be recognized by their bestial appearance. In its original form, the theory was too simplistic and could not ultimately be maintained. More recently, some studies have found that men with a genetic disorder known as the XYY syndrome (in which they possess an extra Y chromosome) are somewhat overrepresented in prison populations. This does not necessarily mean that all victims of the disorder will become criminals (most do not); it may be, however, that such individuals will be unduly sensitive to environmental factors that encourage crime.

In general, then, it can be said that possible biological influences on specific types of social behavior are worth investigating and may turn out to be significant but that as yet we have very little hard data as to the nature and importance of such influences.

Thus we see that there are numerous approaches to the study of social problems, besides that of sociology. Rather than regard them as rivals, to be championed against one another in a kind of party spirit, as is sometimes done, it is necessary to take all approaches into account, if the fullest possible understanding of social problems, and an adequately comprehensive attack on them, are to be achieved.

THE SOCIOLOGICAL PERSPECTIVE

Social problems directly or indirectly affect all our lives—and some of them do serious damage to segments of our society. Sociologists, as well as other social scientists, are trying to determine in what respects our society works satisfactorily and in what respects it fails. The hope is that this will contribute to ways of intervening in problem situations so that the quality of life can be improved for everyone.

Sociology is a relatively young discipline. Its particular focus is on people's social behavior and social organization. Unlike psychology, which deals primarily with the individual, sociology studies *patterned social relationships,* how they are maintained and how they change. For instance, sociologists might study protest movements on college campuses. They would try to discover the patterns of relationship within protest groups (do the groups have strong leadership? are they loosely or tightly organized? how do they arrive at decisions? how do they handle dissent?), and the relationships between these groups and others, such as college administration and police (is hostility expected? how is it expressed? what mechanisms of communication are employed?). They would ask about the roles—the patterns of expected behavior—of groups and individuals in these relationships, and about the ways in which the roles and relationships originate and change in response to surrounding social forces. They would not be particularly concerned, though, with the psychological motivations of individual participants nor with the features unique to the situation of one particular group.

While sociology is concerned with social behavior patterns in general, the study of social problems is concerned primarily with behavior which departs from established norms (deviance) and with social structures which experience disruption and conflict to the extent that individual and collective goals are not being achieved. For instance, a student of social problems might try to determine why, in a society with the highest standard of living in the world, over 30 million people are living in poverty, or why, in a society which stresses a high level of education, many highly educated people are unable to find employment. Through the collection of data on such phenomena, the student hopes to contribute to the means of remedying the situation and making it possible for a greater number of citizens to lead personally satisfying lives. In addition, he or she hopes to obtain insight about human behavior in varying conditions which will illuminate general sociological questions.

Drug addiction, for example, has become one of the most persistent and oppressive problems in the United States. Among other things, the continued abuse of narcotic drugs often destroys individual initiative, self-control, and sometimes even life itself; moreover, it is linked with large-scale organized crime. A number of approaches have been developed to fight the problem. A religious teacher might preach that using drugs is spiritually debilitating; a lawmaker might impose severe penalties on the user or dealer; a journalist might do a news feature on the number of addicts who are arrested and jailed each year, or the number who die from the effects of drugs; and a writer or filmmaker might portray the terrifying and torturous aspects of addiction. Sociologists attempt to discover the causes and effects of addiction by analyzing its manifestations in certain groups of people under various sociocultural conditions. By so doing, they hope society will obtain a realistic and accurate view of the drug problem and will be able to make informed decisions about it.

Drug abuse is only one example of the many types of so-called deviant behavior to be found in any society. The term "deviant" carries for some people unfortunate connotations of sickness, craziness, or unnaturalness, which are not intended in the sociological meaning of the word. Hence it may be useful here to give some idea of what sociologists mean when they speak of deviance.

Fundamentally, deviant behavior is simply behavior which varies from some accepted norm, in whatever direction and for whatever reason. The father of modern sociology, Emile Durkheim, postulated that no society could be completely free from deviant or even criminal behavior. All of us will, at some time or other, deviate from some behavioral norm, either by choice or by necessity, and most of us will not, as a result, be labeled as deviants. On the other hand, almost no one will deviate from all norms, and few will deviate from any norm all the time. The embezzler may be a faithful marriage partner, and the prostitute may be quite conventional in all respects save occupation. Deviance and conformity, then, are not generalized traits—a person is not wholly "normal" or wholly "deviant."

Nor does society react to deviance with perfect consistency. Deviance from the norm is usually tolerated within certain limits; only when those limits are exceeded is the label "deviant" applied. Consider drinking, for example: in most cultures, moderate drinking is accepted and approved. People can drink a little more than the accepted norm, and can even get drunk once in a while, without being called alcoholics or drunkards. But if they begin getting drunk two or three times a week, they have passed the allowable limits, and will be labeled alcoholics. An additional factor in society's judgment will be the degree to which these people adhere to other norms. If they are frequently absent from work, appear dirty and unshaven in public, or are arrested for disorderly conduct, they are more likely to be considered alcoholics than if they manage to remain neat, punctual, and courteous, even though they may be similarly dependent on alcohol.

Furthermore, it is usually possible to deviate by overconformity as well as by nonconformity. In a business office, there is often one employee who observes all the rules so minutely as to be somewhat of a nuisance. In most cases overconforming deviants are probably more easily tolerated than the nonconforming deviants, since they usually cause less trouble— teetotalers may pose minor problems at a party, but they are not likely to cause the breakup of their families.

We see, then, that deviance and normality, or deviant and normal persons, cannot be set opposite each other as mutually exclusive absolutes. Deviance is part of a behavioral continuum, shading into both ends of normality, and the boundaries between them are exceedingly flexible.

It should be pointed out, too, that both the norms and the degree of tolerance for deviation vary considerably from society to society and from time to time. What is considered promiscuous behavior in the United States may not be so considered in Sweden; and a degree of dependence on narcotic drugs which would be labeled abuse in the 1970s might have passed as necessary treatment for poor health in 1910. And, as we indicated earlier, the norms of any given social structure tend to foster deviance in certain respects, as the means of attaining approved goals are unequally distributed among the society's members. Just as a society which places a high value on property may promote crimes against property, so one which is especially concerned about female chastity may have a high incidence of rape and prostitution; and one which exalts education may cause those without the approved educational background to patronize "diploma mills" or use other fraudulent, or even violent, means to attain the ends to which education is supposed to lead. In order to understand what a society regards as deviant behavior, therefore, the sociologist must study the norms of that society and the values supporting them.

It is important to note that deviant behavior under some circumstances can have constructive consequences for society, a number of which have been identified by Cohen.[3] For example, we live today in a society dominated by complex organizations which prescribe a bewildering variety of rules and procedures for us to follow. On many occasions these become overly time-consuming and counterproductive. It may be necessary to circumvent these rules if effective action is to be taken. Cutting a class to study for an upcoming exam or staying home from work to complete an assignment are minor examples of deviance that is constructive.

USEFUL DEVIANCE AND SOCIAL CHANGE

Occasional deviance may also offer a kind of safety-valve contribution to society. There is usually some frustration incurred by individuals in curbing their own desires to conform to society's rules. Over time, such frustrations may accumulate to dangerous levels. Thus in all social systems, large or small, there is occasional deviance which expresses and relieves such frustrations. As a matter of fact, all societies provide periodic recognized occasions (sometimes called "saturnalia" by anthropologists) during which the normal rules of conduct are temporarily suspended. A minor, familiar example would be snowball or water balloon fights on college campuses. Sometimes people are hurt and property is damaged in these episodes. However, formal complaints are seldom lodged by the authorities, since the behavior is defined as letting off steam rather than as an attempt to destroy the organization within which the behavior occurs. On a more complex level, prostitution is a form of deviance that can be useful to society because it provides for extramarital sex (for those who feel they need it) without really threatening the institutions of marriage and the family.

Kai Erikson has pointed out that one of the most important functions of deviance in any organization or society is to clarify norms.[4] People do not learn about acceptable behavior by memorizing lists of rules; they learn by "testing the limits" themselves or by watching what happens to others. Most children, for example, experiment with stealing at least once, but when their parents scold or punish them for it they quickly give it up. Some children may not even attempt stealing after observing the punishment given by the parent to a brother or sister for stealing. In either case, they learned what society will or will not tolerate by seeing the consequences of deviant behavior. On a much larger scale, institutions in society often go through elaborate procedures (such as the media publicity and courtroom rituals that accompany criminal trials) to identify and label deviants. These often serve to mark the boundaries of permissible behavior for society. Finally, deviant acts also may promote

[3] Albert K. Cohen, *Deviance and Control*. Englewood Cliffs, N.J.: Prentice-Hall, 1966.
[4] Kai T. Erikson, "Notes on the sociology of deviance." *Social Problems* 9 (Spring 1962):307–314.

group cohesiveness and solidarity in that they cause members of the group to perceive such acts as a common threat.

It is important to note that society's strong interest in identifying deviants results in an unfortunate consequence: people who are labeled as deviants often remain stigmatized long after the label has lost whatever validity it may have had. For example, ex-convicts or former mental patients often encounter many forms of discrimination after their release from an institution.

Deviance can also serve an important function for society by signaling to its members that certain rules are not just or reasonable. For example, strains caused by unmet needs or blocked access to the means of success may become severe; resulting deviance may be an important signal of social discontent. Rosa Parks refused to relinquish her seat to a white man on an Alabama bus, a gross violation of Southern etiquette in the 1950s; yet this black woman's act sparked the Montgomery bus boycott that brought Dr. Martin Luther King, Jr., to national prominence and was an important landmark in the civil rights movement. Similarly, one of the useful outcomes of the campus protests of the 1960s was that they led to clearer policy statements governing disruptions, the academic tradition of dissent, and the basic right of free speech. The liberalization of divorce laws, the gradual acceptance of premarital sex, and the growing equality between the sexes are other examples of changes that have occurred in our society as a result of widespread deviance from traditional standards of acceptable behavior. Thus deviance can be one of the factors that bring about needed changes in the organization of society.

FIVE PERSPECTIVES ON SOCIAL PROBLEMS

Sociology, as we have suggested, is a science committed to the study of social behavior and social organization. Because it is still a young science, it does not yet possess a solid set of propositions and laws comparable to those used by physicists and other natural scientists. Instead, sociologists have a frame of reference which guides them in their study of human behavior. This orientation is reflected in the premises which we discussed earlier, and which contain two basic postulates: first, that certain kinds of social problems may be an inevitable, but unplanned, development of *any* social organization; second, that people in different social strata react to these problems differently and propose different solutions. One implication of these postulates is that many problems can be alleviated by a reorganization of the social structure which has generated them.

Guided by these assumptions, sociologists try to establish comprehensive theories of human social behavior which will enable them to understand the nature of societies. Since the knowledge that guides them is often recent and frequently fragmented, such theories must still be considered as empirical generalizations rather than as scientific laws. These generalizations are based on repeated observations of certain behavior (for instance, that official juvenile delinquency rates are often higher in low-income than in middle- and upper-income areas). By testing the generalizations in other situations (for instance, by studying the relationship between juvenile delinquency and poverty in many societies), then, sociologists try to develop a set of laws and principles which will explain how and why social problems occur.

In the section that follows we describe five of the most significant sociological perspectives for the study of social problems.[5] Each theory emphasizes a different aspect of a social problem and offers differing explanations of why social problems occur and how they may be alleviated (see Table 1-1).

THE SOCIAL PATHOLOGY PERSPECTIVE

As we pointed out earlier, the idea that it is possible to correct social problems is relatively new—throughout most of history people had generally considered misery to be a permanent part of the human condition. In the United States, the new perception that the conditions of society could be improved arose after the Civil War. Coincidentally, a host of urban problems appeared at the same time, brought about by industrialization, the immigration from farms to cities, and a large influx of European immigrants. Early sociologists, impressed by the success of the scientific method in technical fields, attempted to develop a scientific approach to the study and solution of these social problems.

The premises of the sociological theory developed by these sociologists were rooted in the "organic analogy." This analogy held that human society, like the human body, is a vast organism, all of whose complex, interrelated parts should work together for the health and stability of the whole. Social problems, then, arise when either individuals or social institutions fail to keep pace with changing conditions and thereby disrupt the healthy operation of the social organism. Such individuals or institutions were considered "sick" (hence the term "social pathology"). For example, the European immigrants who failed to adjust to American urban life were considered to be a source of "illness," at least insofar as they affected the health of their adopted society. Underlying this concept of illness was the concept of morality: social problems ultimately violated the moral expectations of social order and progress.

Early social pathologists tended to focus on individuals as the source of society's problems. They felt problem individuals are those who could not be properly socialized or who rejected society's values and beliefs because of some innate defect. Modern social pathologists tend to focus more on defects in society and its institutions. In other words, it is immoral societies that produce immoral individuals, who in turn may become the source of social problems.

The consequences of social problems, according to social pathology theorists, are increases in the cost of maintaining social order; if left unsolved, social problems may also lead to a gradual dehumanization of society. Because they felt social problems resulted from innate defects in individuals, early social pathologists recommended eugenics programs to prevent the transmission of these defects to succeeding generations. Modern social pathologists focus on changing the morals of individuals

[5] The following discussion is based on Earl Rubington and Martin S. Weinberg, eds., *The Study of Social Problems: Five Perspectives.* New York: Oxford University Press, 1971. There are, of course, alternative ways of discussing sociological perspectives on social problems. See, for example, Amitai Etzioni, *Social Problems.* Englewood Cliffs, N.J.: Prentice-Hall, 1976.

TABLE 1-1 Five Perspectives on Social Problems

Perspective	Definition	Causes	Conditions	Consequences	Solutions
Social pathology	Violation of moral expectations	Failure in socialization Can't be taught, or rejects values and beliefs	Innate defects—immoral properties of individuals or societies	Costly Dehumanizing	Eugenics Moralizing individuals Education
Social disorganization	Failure in expectations Normlessness Culture conflict	Social change—disharmony	Anything technical, social, etc.) that causes change	Personal stress and disorganization System change or failure	Equilibrate parts of system (slow down technology, for example)
Value conflict	Any conditions incompatible with values	Value conflict	Competition and contact	Costly—sacrifice of values	Consensus Trading Power
Deviant behavior	Departure from norms	Learning and being committed to deviant ways	Restricted conventional means Accessible deviant means Restricted societal ends	Many possible consequences depending on nature of illegitimate world	Resocialization Increase legitimate means and ends
Labeling	Conditions under which society defines social problems	Awareness	When labeler stands to gain	Reordering relations Secondary deviance	Change definitions Take profit out of labeling

Source: Earl Rubington and Martin S. Weinberg, eds., *The Study of Social Problems: Five Perspectives.* New York: Oxford University Press, 1971.

and societies. Thus they emphasize education as the solution to social problems.

THE SOCIAL DISORGANIZATION PERSPECTIVE

Immigration, urbanization, and industrialization increased rapidly after World War I. Many new arrivals to the cities failed to adapt to urban life. European immigrants, rural whites, and Southern blacks were often crowded together in small areas. Often they had difficulties in acquiring the language, manners, and norms of the dominant urban culture. Many who did manage to acclimate themselves to the city discovered they could still be discriminated against because of their religion or race. Others lost their jobs because technological advances made their skills obsolete. Under these conditions, many groups formed their own subcultures or devised other means of coping. The rates of alcoholism, drug addiction, mental illness, crime, and delinquency rose drastically. Some sociologists of the time believed the social pathology perspective could not adequately explain the widespread existence of these social problems. They developed new concepts that eventually became known as the social disorganization perspective.

This new perspective viewed society as being organized by a set of expectations or rules. Social disorganization, according to this theory, results when these expectations fail. This failure can be manifested in three major ways—through *normlessness,* when people have no rules that tell them how to behave; through *culture conflict,* when people feel trapped by a contradictory set of rules; and through *breakdown,* when obedience to a set of rules results in no rewards or in punishment. Rapid social change, for example, might make traditional standards of behavior obsolete without providing new standards (normlessness). The children of foreign immigrants might feel trapped between the expectations of their parents' culture and the expectations of their new society (culture conflict). Blacks might experience a failure in expectations when they do well in school but encounter job discrimination (breakdown).

The stress experienced by the victims of social disorganization may result in a form of "personal disorganization," such as drug addiction or crime. The social system as a whole also feels the force of disorganization, and may respond by changing its rules, by keeping contradictory rules in force, or by breaking down. The process of disorganization can be halted or reversed by isolating its cause and correcting it. For example, technological change can be slowed down until members of society can formulate new rules and expectations.

THE VALUE CONFLICT PERSPECTIVE

The value conflict perspective arose after the experiences of the Depression and World War II, when the need was felt to make sociology more objective and more useful to society. According to value conflict theorists, previous concepts of "sickness" or "social expectations" were largely subjective. They point out that deviance from the rules is not necessarily due to the failure of the individual or of society's rules: after all, what is problematic to the larger society may well be normal or justifiable to a particular group. Thus value conflict theorists define social problems simply as "conditions that are incompatible with group values." [6] They add that such problems are normal, because in a complex society there are many groups whose interests and values are bound to differ.

Social problems, then, according to value conflict theory, occur when groups with different values come into contact with each other and compete. For example, the interest of landlords lies in raising revenues; the interest of tenants lies in keeping rents low. If the landlords try to raise rents too high, conflict will result. The consequences of conflict can be costly: groups become polarized, and higher goals (compromise) may be sacrificed for lower goals (victory). Conflicts are generally settled in one of three ways—through consensus, trading, or power. For example, landlords and tenants may agree that a smaller rent increase is justified (consensus); tenants may require that landlords do less for their buildings in return for a lower rent increase (trading); or, finally, landlords might evict tenants who do not pay the demanded rent increase (power).

THE DEVIANT BEHAVIOR PERSPECTIVE

The deviant behavior perspective was and still is one of the most influential perspectives for the study of social problems. It was developed for two main reasons. First, previous theories of social problems proved to be too broad to be useful for empirical research. It was more practical,

[6] Rubington and Weinberg, p. 86.

or at least easier, to study people who deviated from accepted norms—such as hobos or delinquents—than to study "morals," "rules," or "groups." Second, many sociologists felt the need to explain why higher rates of deviance seemed to exist among certain groups and certain positions of the social structure, and why certain individuals in these groups or social positions became deviant and others did not.

Social problems, according to the deviant behavior perspective, are defined as behaviors or conditions that are deviant. They arise when the legitimate means of achieving cultural goals are blocked. For example, working-class youngsters whose employment opportunities are limited may form delinquent subcultures as a way of obtaining and maintaining status in their group. Not all individuals with limited legitimate opportunities will become deviant, however; they must also have access to deviant means of behavior. If delinquency is admired in their group, for example, and if their friends are delinquent, then they will have many opportunities to become deviant themselves.

Deviant behavior can have many possible consequences to society, depending on the specific nature of the deviance. (Some of these consequences, such as fear of crime, are obvious.) The best way to reduce deviance is to "resocialize" deviants by increasing their contacts with accepted patterns of behavior.[7] The social system must also be made less rigid, so that legitimate opportunities and goals become more accessible.

The labeling perspective is the most recent major sociological approach to the study of social problems. It questions many of the assumptions made by other sociological theorists. Other perspectives take for granted that phenomena such as poverty, delinquency, addiction, and crime will be defined as social problems. They are concerned with explaining why and under what conditions such problems occur. Labeling theorists feel that accepted definitions of deviance or social problems are subjective. They are interested in explaining why and under what conditions certain acts and situations came to be defined as problematic or deviant.

THE LABELING PERSPECTIVE

Implicit in the labeling perspective is the idea that the label "deviant" tells more about the society applying it than about the act or individual to which it is applied. For example, in certain societies homosexuality is a far more accepted phenomenon than it is in our own. To labeling theorists, this suggests that there are forces in American society which benefit from the labeling of homosexuals as deviant (for example, institutions which profit from the strong emphasis in America on marital and family ties). Similarly, the same supposedly deviant acts are not always judged in the same way—prison sentences for black criminals, for instance, tend to be longer than sentences for white criminals who commit the same crimes. To labeling theorists, this suggests something about the distribution of power in our society. In short, according to labeling theory the difference between deviant people and nondeviant people is not what they do but how society reacts to what they do.

Thus, to labeling theorists, social problems are conditions under which certain behaviors or situations become defined as social problems. The cause of a social problem is simply society's awareness that a certain behavior or situation exists. (Obviously, society could not react to some-

[7] Rubington and Weinberg, p. 127.

thing it knows nothing about.) The condition under which the behavior or situation becomes a social problem is when one can profit in some way by applying the label "problematic" or "deviant" to it. When such labeling occurs, society suffers in two ways. First, one group unfairly achieves power over another group—"deviants" have their opportunities limited and may become subject to ostracism or arrest. Second, individuals labeled as deviant may accept this definition of themselves; the label may then have the effect of a self-fulfilling prophecy. These individuals may increase the number and variety of their deviant acts in order to reinforce their new roles as deviants. For example, a person labeled as a drug addict may adopt what is popularly considered to be a drug addict's life style—by resisting employment or treatment, engaging in crime, and so on. (Sociologists call this elaboration on the original deviant act "secondary deviance.")

The solutions to social problems, according to labeling theory, lie in changing the definitions of what is considered deviant and in taking the profit out of labeling.[8] Accepting a greater variety of acts and situations as normal will automatically eliminate these acts or situations as objects of concern. (The legalization of marijuana use in some states is an example of how changing the definition of deviance removes a social problem.) Similarly, discouraging the tendency to impose labels for one's own gain or satisfaction will reduce the labeling process and in effect cause former problems to become less significant. Communism, for example, was an issue of great concern to the United States in the 1950s; many individuals achieved popularity or power by misapplying the label "Communist" to others. When it became clear that the label was being misapplied and that monolithic Communism was not a realistic threat, the Communist label lost its significance—the "social problem" of internal Communist influence all but disappeared.

Each of the above perspectives attempts to supply a coherent explanation for the existence of social problems. Considering the differences among them, however, it is not surprising that these perspectives have had different effects on the discipline of sociology. The social pathology perspective has proved to be of limited usefulness in generating empirical research; its concepts of "sickness" and "morality" are too subjective to be meaningful to many sociologists. Where moral considerations are paramount, however, the social pathology perspective can still be applied. For example, in modern times this perspective has provided a meaningful way of looking at extreme or pathological conditions in our world, such as the existence of concentration camps or the widespread indifference to mass starvation.

The social disorganization perspective developed when there was a need to explain the specific problems of the day more successfully than the social pathology perspective explained them. When the United States was undergoing rapid social change and social problems seemed localized among immigrant groups, disorganization was a useful concept. Later sociologists criticized the value judgment inherent in the term "disorganization" and pointed out that a diverse society is not necessarily a disorganized one. Today the social disorganization perspective is best used

[8] Rubington and Weinberg, p. 169.

in the study of the effects of rapid industrialization on technologically underdeveloped societies.

The value conflict approach was and is felt by many sociologists to be of limited relevance because it is difficult to demonstrate its validity for most social problems. Where the values of contending groups are clearly a factor in causing a problem, the value conflict perspective is of course highly applicable. The so-called generation gap, for example, more often than not has its basis in a conflict of values.

Of the five, the deviant behavior perspective, as suggested earlier, has sparked the greatest amount of research. It was developed when there was widespread agreement as to what constituted a social problem and also when there was a need for practical solutions to social problems. Indeed, many of the social programs of the 1960s and 1970s were based on the concepts of the deviant behavior perspective and on the research generated by these concepts. For example, laws requiring busing in order to achieve educational equality were based on research (now being questioned) that suggested black students would learn more in an integrated setting.

The labeling perspective developed as a counterweight to several of the other perspectives in that it stressed the subjective nature of labels like "immoral" or "deviant" and described how such labels could aggravate social problems. Because it represents a relatively new approach to the study of social problems (and indeed is rather controversial among sociologists), it is not yet certain how great its impact will be. It has already proved useful in discussing areas that do not involve clearly defined values or norms, such as drug use, mental illness, and sexual behavior. It should be noted that many of the fundamental social problems we will be discussing in this book have their origin in a multiplicity of causes. They may require the application of several sociological perspectives in order to be completely understood and resolved. For this reason in this book we take an eclectic approach to the study of social problems, and use those perspectives that seem to most reasonably apply to each specific problem.

ORGANIZATION OF THE BOOK

Sociologists have become increasingly aware of the interdependence of many social problems. In this volume, therefore, we do not group chapters according to the traditional divisions of deviant behavior and social disorganization. Instead, our chapter sequence follows a logical "micro" to "macro" pattern that suggests the interrelationships of social problems and offers both teachers and students maximum flexibility in the use of the text. In early chapters, for example, we focus on individual behaviors such as drug use or crime. Of course, the societal factors affecting these behaviors are noted and described. The middle section of the book focuses on discriminatory social institutions and norms, with chapters on such topics as prejudice, sexism, and age discrimination. We make every attempt, however, to indicate the effects of large-scale discrimination on individuals. In later chapters we discuss problems common to many societies, such as those relating to family, sexuality, and work.

In the final chapters on population and environment we focus on matters of global significance. It seemed best to discuss each subject in a separate chapter in order to deal with it comprehensively and in depth. We have tried to indicate the points at which different problems overlap and how these problems are interrelated.

In order to make the book easier to use, the organization of each chapter follows a fairly consistent pattern: (1) the specific aspects of the problem which is to be considered; (2) the important sociological theories or hypotheses relating to it; (3) factors that seem to correlate with it; (4) possible means of intervention to control or alleviate the problem; (5) prospects for the near future—that is, how the problem seems likely to develop in the next few years; and (6) a concise summary that reviews the essential concepts and facts of the chapter. There is also a comprehensive bibliography at the end of each chapter that can be used as a study and research aid.

SUMMARY

Social problems are conditions in society that are widely regarded as needing improvement or remedy. The idea that something can or should be done about social problems is a relatively recent development, coinciding with the evolution of enlightened philosophical concepts and the scientific revolution.

Conditions defined as social problems vary from society to society and with changes in a society. Certain generalizations about social problems can be made, however: They often result unexpectedly from acceptable patterns of behavior (such as having large families resulting in overpopulation); they may arise as a result of accepted social principles (such as the desirability of private property, which may cause poor people to steal); they are likely to be perceived differently by people in different layers of society; and solutions proposed for them are likely to reflect the interests of the people offering the solutions. Thus the social and cultural environments of groups or individuals are important factors in the origin and elimination of social problems.

Several disciplines in the social sciences, other than sociology, contribute to our understanding of social problems. *History* can help us understand what factors in the past led to present conditions. *Cultural anthropology* can tell us how our own problems differ from or are similar to problems in other societies. *Psychology* and *social psychology* can help us understand how individual experiences and personality types can affect the incidence of social problems. Finally, *biology* can offer insight into how individuals can be naturally disposed to behaviors that society considers problematic.

Sociology focuses generally on people's social behavior and social organization. The study of social problems focuses specifically on behavior that departs from established norms (*deviance*) and on social organizations that experience difficulties to the extent that their goals are not being achieved. Sociologists attempt to determine why these problems occur and how they can best be remedied. Though they often study so-called deviant behavior, sociologists are aware that both "deviant" and "normal" behaviors are difficult to isolate and that deviance often has constructive consequences, such as clarifying social norms and bringing about necessary changes in society.

Five theoretical sociological perspectives for the study of social problems have been identified. They are the *social pathology* perspective, which sees social problems as violating society's moral expectations; the *social disorganization* perspective, which stresses the failure of rules as a source of social problems; the *value conflict* perspective, which considers problems to be "conditions incompatible with social values"; the *deviant behavior* perspective, which focuses on acts or conditions that deviate from social norms; and the *labeling* perspective, which is concerned with the conditions under which society defines social problems. Each perspective generally offers insights into different kinds of social problems. When social problems have many, complex causes, however, several perspectives may apply.

BIBLIOGRAPHY

Bates, Alan P. *The Sociological Enterprise*. Boston: Houghton Mifflin, 1967.

Becker, Howard S. *Outsiders: Studies in the Sociology of Deviance*. New York: Free Press, 1963.

————, ed. *Social Problems: A Modern Approach*. New York: Wiley, 1966.

Bell, Robert R. *Social Deviance*. Homewood, Ill.: Dorsey Press, 1971.

Berger, Peter L. *Invitation to Sociology: A Humanistic Perspective*. New York: Overlook Press, 1973.

Clinard, Marshal B. *The Sociology of Deviant Behavior*. 4th ed. New York: Holt, Rinehart and Winston, 1974.

Cohen, Albert K. *Deviance and Control*. Englewood Cliffs, N.J.: Prentice-Hall, 1966.

Dinitz, Simon, *et al.*, eds. *Deviance*. New York: Oxford University Press, 1969.

Douglas, Jack D., ed. *Observations of Deviance*. New York: Random House, 1971.

Elliot, Mabel A., and Merril, Francis E. *Social Disorganization*. 4th ed. New York: Harper, 1961.

Freeman, Howard E., and Kurtz, Norman R., eds. *America's Troubles*. 2nd ed. Englewood Cliffs, N.J.: Prentice-Hall, 1973.

Gouldner, Alvin W., and Miller, S. M., eds. *Applied Sociology*. New York: Free Press, 1965.

Hornstein, Harvey, *et al.*, eds. *Social Intervention*. New York: Free Press, 1971.

Inkeles, Alex, ed. *What Is Sociology? An Introduction to the Discipline and Profession*. Englewood Cliffs, N.J.: Prentice-Hall, 1964.

Lindenfeld, Frank. *Radical Perspective on Social Problems*. 2nd ed. London: Macmillan, 1973.

Merton, Robert K. "Social structure and anomie." *American Sociological Review* 3 (October 1938): 672–682.

Offenbacher, Deborah I., and Poster, Constance, eds. *Social Problems and Social Policy*. Englewood Cliffs, N.J.: Prentice-Hall, 1970.

Perrucci, Robert, and Pilisuk, Marc, eds. *The Triple Revolution Emerging*. Boston: Little, Brown, 1971.

Rosenberg, Bernard, *et al.*, eds. *Mass Society in Crisis*. 2nd ed. New York: Macmillan, 1971.

Schur, Edwin. *Labeling Deviant Behavior*. New York: Harper & Row, 1971.

Sutherland, Edwin H., and Cressey, Donald R. *Criminology*. 9th ed. Philadelphia: Lippincott, 1974.

2

PHYSICAL AND MENTAL HEALTH

- In the past ten years, physical health care spending has tripled.
- Nearly one-third of the hospitals in the United States fail to meet minimum standards of safety and adequacy.
- An estimated 40,000 people die each year in the United States as a result of unnecessary or harmful medical treatment.
- About 5 million people in the United States are treated for mental illness each year, about 25 percent of the total estimated to need such treatment.
- There are about 800,000 people in the nation's 500 mental hospitals; an estimated 250,000 of these are untreated, harmless, and able to function on their own.

Health is a basic requirement of all societies. If societies are to survive and perpetuate themselves, their members must attain and maintain some degree of health. However, precise definitions of health and illness vary from society to society. As Saxon Graham has stated,

In some underdeveloped societies, the malaise and apathetic approach to life associated with infestation by certain parasites is a normal condition of life and is not considered a state of disease as it would be in urban middle and upper classes (but not necessarily in the rural lower classes) of the U.S. Similarly, a "touch of the liver," a bacterial enteritis, is a common complaint, but not necessarily an illness, in France. In the middle-class urban U.S. . . . the gastric and intestinal symptoms so loosely defined in France are unusual and avoided wherever possible. The mere question of the presence or absence of a diseased state is answered in terms of the expectations in the culture.[1]

In the United States, there can be little question that health and happiness are among our most highly prized values. "To your health" is a

[1] Saxon, Graham, "Sociological aspects of health and illness." In R. E. L. Faris, ed., *Handbook of Modern Sociology*. Chicago: Rand McNally, 1965, pp. 310–311.

common toast; "Have a happy and healthy New Year" is a common year-end expression. As Lerner put it, "One indication of the importance of health in our society is the enormity of the industry which has developed to maintain it." [2] The health industry today employs some 4.5 million people and accounts for 8 percent of the gross national product. Americans spent over $115 billion on health care in 1975, 10 percent more than the previous year and almost four times as much as in 1960.[3]

Most of us, in fact, have come to consider proper medical care as one of our basic human rights rather than as a privilege. However, this was not always the case. As late as 1967, for example, the president of the American Medical Association maintained that health care was a privilege, not a right—implying that good health should be available only to those of us who can afford it. Today, however, health care has come to be viewed by most citizens and a substantial number of physicians as a community resource, rather than as a commodity to be bought and sold. Like education, which was once a matter of private enterprise but in the nineteenth century began to come under public control, physical and mental health fields are under increasing pressure to meet our needs in an efficient, effective, and equitable manner. As a result, federal legislation has established, as public policy, the definition of health care as a right. A 1966 health law amendment, for example, stated in part:

The Congress declares that fulfillment of our national purpose depends on promoting and assuring the highest level of health attainable for every person . . .[4]

If Americans spend large amounts of money on health care; if there exist large numbers of health personnel; if a philosophy of health care has developed that considers proper health a right of every citizen—why then is health care in the United States, as Richard Nixon once described it, in a state of "massive crisis"? [5] The fact is that although our health care resources have the *potential* for delivering the highest-quality care to all citizens, in *actuality* they leave a great deal to be desired. One reason for this is that our health resources are designed largely to *treat* disorders rather than to *prevent* them from occurring. Few of us, for example, receive reminders from our physicians that we are due for an annual checkup (the way we might from our dentists). The emphasis on treatment violates the common-sense notion that "an ounce of prevention is worth a pound of cure." It also makes medical care a much more problematic and expensive affair. As a result, many of us—and not only the poor or disadvantaged—feel mentally or physically unfit much of the time.

In addition, health care services are not distributed equally. As Lerner put it, medical care is still "a scarce product . . . rationed by society according to the individual's ability to pay." [6] Thus illness and disability

[2] Monroe Lerner, "Health as a social problem." In Erwin Smigel, ed., *Handbook on the Study of Social Problems.* Chicago: Rand McNally, 1971, p. 295.

[3] "Health care in America: Progress—and problems." *U.S. News & World Report,* June 16, 1975, pp. 50–51.

[4] Lerner, pp. 297–298.

[5] Quoted in "Health care: Supply, demand, and politics." *Time,* June 7, 1971, p. 93.

[6] Lerner, p. 287.

are much more common among the poor than among the more affluent, while at the same time only the affluent have sufficient access to proper medical care. Finally, costs for health care, including health insurance, are extremely high and are continuing to increase sharply. The result is that even among the middle class many individuals are not protected against the cost of a debilitating illness, and many individuals cannot afford even the most essential medical services.

In this chapter we will discuss these and other problems of America's health care resources in greater detail. We will concentrate in the first part of the chapter on physical health problems, and in the second part more extensively on mental health problems. We will also try to describe why and how these problems developed, and what can be done to help remedy them.

PROBLEMS OF PHYSICAL HEALTH

Many aspects and achievements of America's health care resources are admirable. A large portion of our more than 7,000 hospitals are among the most modern in the world, and our more than 360,000 physicians are among the most rigorously trained. Many diseases, such as polio, have been all but eliminated; and advances in medical technology suggest that means of prevention or cures for other diseases will eventually be found.

Despite these impressive facts, however, we are not as healthy as we could or should be. For example, our life expectancy is twenty-second in the world, and our infant mortality rate is higher than that of fourteen other countries.[7] Death rates from heart disease in the United States are by far the highest in the world, and cancer incidence and death rates are among the highest. Maternal death rates (death per 1,000 mothers due to childbirth or related causes) also rank high in the United States, compared to other industrialized nations.

Part of this comparatively poor health picture has less to do with our health resources than with the way we live. The growing number of people in sedentary occupations, the preponderance of fattening, non-nutritious foods in our diet, and the widespread lack of proper exercise have undoubtedly contributed to our high incidence of heart disease and other ailments. Similarly, it is highly probable that environmental pollution (see Chapter 14) and cigarette smoking contribute to our already high and still rising cancer incidence. There can be little doubt, however, that many of our health problems are worsened considerably because of the kind of medical care that is—or is not—made available. As two analysts of our health care resources stated:

Every day three million Americans go out in search of medical care. Some find it; others do not. Some are helped by it; others are not. Another twenty million Americans probably ought to enter the daily search for medical

[7] *United Nations Demographic Yearbook, 1974.* New York: United Nations, 1975; see also *New York Times,* January 13, 1976, p. 1.

help, but are not healthy enough, rich enough, or enterprising enough to try.[8]

In short, there is a wide gap between the ideal of equal access for all to the best possible health care and the health care that is actually available or obtained.

The use and availability of medical care are directly related to socio-economic class and race. The racial aspect is most directly illustrated by a comparison of life expectancy for whites and nonwhites: on the average the life expectancy for whites is about 5 years longer than that for non-whites. In addition, the infant death rate for nonwhites is almost twice that of whites.[9] More generally, nonwhites suffer proportionately more from almost every illness than whites; and because they are less likely to have been immunized, nonwhites suffer higher rates of death from infectious diseases. Such differences cannot be ascribed to income differences alone, since even when income is the same, death rates are still higher for nonwhites.[10]

INEQUALITY IN ACCESS TO HEALTH SERVICES

From a socioeconomic point of view, there is a strong relationship between membership in a lower class and higher rates of illness. People in the lower classes tend to feel sicker and have higher rates of untreated illness than those in the middle and upper classes.[11] They also tend to be disabled more frequently and for longer periods than the nonpoor.[12] Furthermore, mortality rates for almost all diseases are higher among the lower classes.[13] For example, contrary to the popular belief that top executives have higher rates of heart disease because their jobs are stressful, the highest rates of heart disease actually occur among the lowest salaried; the lowest rates occur among top-level managers and executives.[14] Low-income women, both black and white, are four times more likely than their more affluent sisters to die in childbirth.[15]

What factors account for these disparities in health? Perhaps primary among them is the fact that, as Seham points out,

for the most part, delivery of health care services is geared to the upper- and middle-class culture because these services take on all the qualities of a

[8] Barbara Ehrenreich and John Ehrenreich, *The American Health Empire.* New York: Vintage Books, 1971, p. 3.

[9] *New York Times,* January 13, 1976, p. 1.

[10] Max Seham, *Blacks and American Medical Care.* Minneapolis: University of Minnesota Press, 1973, p. 10.

[11] Patricia L. Kendall and George G. Reader, "Contributions of sociology to medicine." In Howard E. Freeman *et al.,* eds., *Handbook of Medical Sociology,* Englewood Cliffs, N.J.: Prentice-Hall, 1972, pp. 6–7.

[12] "Profile of American health." *Public Health Reports,* November–December 1974, p. 505.

[13] Aaron Antonovsky, "Class and the chance for life." In Lee Rainwater, ed., *Inequality and Justice.* Chicago: Aldine, 1974.

[14] Saxon Graham and Leo G. Reeder, "Social factors in the chronic illnesses." In *Handbook of Medical Sociology,* pp. 95–96.

[15] Irving Block, *The Health of the Poor.* New York: Public Affairs Committee, 1969, p. 4.

commodity for sale and the affluent are the preferred and often the only market. This is especially true in the preventive areas.[16]

Thus, for example, a large portion of the high infant mortality rate among the poor is due to their high incidence of infectious diseases. Unlike those in the middle and upper classes, poor parents simply cannot afford a private or family physician who will make sure their infant is properly immunized. In all age groups, the health of the poor is adversely affected by their inability to afford private, high-quality medical care. As Lerner states, the illnesses of the poor "are much more likely to remain untreated and, consequently, to increase in severity, because the poor generally remain outside the private medical-care system." [17] Not only are the poor unable to afford proper care, they also have no care available in most of their own neighborhoods. Rural or poor urban areas characteristically suffer from a severe shortage of physicians and a lack of other medical services.

When poor people do seek treatment for an illness—often only when a crisis situation is reached [18]—they tend to visit a clinic rather than a private physician. Usually, they must travel at some cost and inconvenience to the nearest facility. At the clinic, they receive the most impersonal kind of treatment, often waiting many hours in crowded waiting rooms and seeing different physicians on successive visits. Thus a trusting relationship with a physician is never established, and their health care becomes fragmented. Furthermore, physicians at the clinic almost always come from a white, middle- or upper-class background that differs markedly from that of poor whites, blacks, and Spanish-speaking peoples. And, as Seham put it,

In general, health professionals have little—if any—understanding of the life style of the poor. For a doctor to advise a patient who is living in poverty to increase his intake in protein,without helping him to work out how to do it, is useless. Similarly, to suggest to a working mother that she come to the clinic for weekly treatments, when the clinic hours coincide with her working hours, is tantamount to not providing treatment at all.[19]

In sum, poor people, white and black, are shut off from private medical care by their inability to pay for it. They become distrustful of public health clinics, however, and avoid them as long as possible. This lack of proper medical care leads to higher rates of illness and death among the poor and nonwhite. It is for this reason that class or race, in the words of one observer, "influences one's chances of staying alive." [20]

From 1959 to 1968, health costs increased by 45 percent even though the cost of living increased by only 20 percent. By 1976, health care costs had increased another 55 percent (see Figure 2-1), again more than

THE HIGH COST OF HEALTH

[16] Seham, p. 20.
[17] Lerner, pp. 308–309.
[18] Lee Rainwater, "The lower class: Health, illness, and medical institutions." In Rainwater, *Inequality and Justice*, pp. 179–189.
[19] Seham, pp. 22–23.
[20] Antonovsky, p. 177.

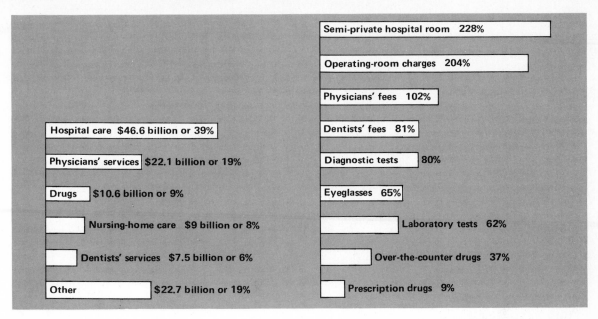

Hospital care $46.6 billion or 39%

Physicians' services $22.1 billion or 19%

Drugs $10.6 billion or 9%

Nursing-home care $9 billion or 8%

Dentists' services $7.5 billion or 6%

Other $22.7 billion or 19%

Semi-private hospital room 228%

Operating-room charges 204%

Physicians' fees 102%

Dentists' fees 81%

Diagnostic tests 80%

Eyeglasses 65%

Laboratory tests 62%

Over-the-counter drugs 37%

Prescription drugs 9%

FIGURE 2-1
(Left) United States
Medical Expenditures
(Fiscal Year 1975);
(Right) The Increase
in Medical Costs
(from 1965 through
1975)

Note: Totals are inexact
because of rounding.

Sources: U.S. Department
of Health, Education, and
Welfare. *Research and
Statistics Note,* no. (SSA)
76-11701, p. 3, and *Social
Security Bulletin,* March
1976, vol. 39, no. 3, p. 69.

the increase in the cost of living.[21] Today, hospital and physician costs are rising almost twice as fast as the overall inflation rate. We are spending about $530 per person for health care each year, whereas in 1960 our average annual health bill was $142. One example of a cost increase: In 1965, hospital costs for the delivery of a baby averaged $225; in 1975, the average cost was about $800. Paralleling this rise in the cost of health services, fees for health insurance have also increased dramatically.[22]

Hospitals. Why have health costs risen so sharply? Hospital charges have gone up much more than any other aspect of medical care, and they account for some 40 percent of all health costs. The average cost of a day in the hospital is now over $110 nationwide. The use of technologically advanced—and expensive—equipment, and the increases in wages won by hospital workers account for some of the rise in hospital fees. More significant, however, have been inefficient hospital management and the fact that hospitals—unlike other businesses—feel no need to keep costs down.

Inefficient hospital management is responsible, in a number of ways, for many unnecessary health care expenses. Patients and physicians are discouraged from using hospitals on an outpatient basis (no overnight stay), even though as much as one-third of hospital procedures could be performed as effectively—and much more economically—in this way. Also, few hospitals offer self-care facilities for patients undergoing limited

[21] "The plight of the U.S. patient." *Time,* February 21, 1969, p. 54; and "Health care in America," pp. 52–53.
[22] "Health care in America," p. 53; and Barbara Cooper *et al.,* "National health expenditures." *Social Security Bulletin,* February 1974.

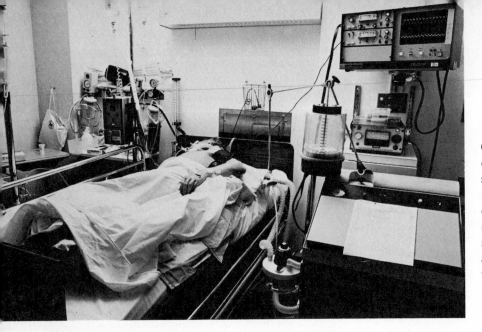

One reason health costs have risen sharply is that technologically advanced equipment is very expensive. The use of such equipment has also tended to increase the impersonalization of health care.
Joel Gordon

tests or procedures, who can look after themselves; nor do hospitals offer their communities preventive services that will keep many health problems from arising. In addition, hospitals in a given area often compete with one another over which facility has the most prestigious and costly equipment. This usually results in the duplication of expensive, seldom-used equipment, the costs of which are passed on to every patient.[23]

Another important consideration is the fact that hospitals, like most health services, do not operate according to normal patterns of supply and demand. People use medical care because they need to; they cannot reduce the costs of care by avoiding treatment. Thus the fees for health services are controlled by the suppliers—hospitals, physicians, and drug companies—rather than by consumers. People must either pay what health care costs or go without health care.

This already unequal situation has been further biased in favor of health service providers by public and private health insurance programs. Blue Cross, for example, which provides hospital insurance, was originally designed to protect people against the high and often sudden costs of hospital care through the prepayment of low premiums, and to ensure that hospital fees would get paid. The system proved so successful, however, that hospitals were able to raise their fees at will, assured that Blue Cross would then pass costs on to the consumer by raising the premiums. The result was increasingly high premiums for those covered by Blue Cross. (Blue Shield, which offered similar coverage for physicians' fees, followed much the same pattern of development.) Furthermore, until recently, Blue Cross would not pay medical expenses incurred during outpatient care; it actually became cheaper for a patient to be hospitalized than to be treated and sent home. In consequence, alternatives to hos-

[23] U.S. Department of HEW, *Toward a Systematic Analysis of Health Care in the United States.* Washington, D.C.: U.S. Government Printing Office, 1972.

pitalization, such as preventive medicine and outpatient care, were never fully developed.[24]

Physicians. Over the past 30 years, physicians have had the highest median income of any occupational group. Since 1958, physicians' fees have more than doubled and they now cost the nation some $20 billion annually. As we have already suggested, one factor in this increase has been the part played by Blue Shield and other insurance programs. Physicians have felt no need to reduce their costs, since the nature of their occupation assures them a steady supply of patients, and medical insurance guarantees that their bills will be paid.

Another factor is the shortage of physicians, which developed during a time when the demand for medical services increased. In 1950, for example, there were about 109 physicians providing private patient care for every 100,000 people in the United States; today, though the total number of physicians relative to population has increased, only 95 physicians per 100,000 people are providing private care.[25] The remaining physicians either work in hospitals or enter fields such as research or teaching. The shortage is particularly acute in the less populated areas of the country and in poorer urban areas. In all areas, however, doctors find increasing demand for their services, and are able to raise their fees.

The growing willingness of many patients to sue if they feel they have

In some areas of the country, the physician shortage is so acute that communities must advertise for physicians. This sign appears along a highway only about 50 miles from Chicago.
Paul Sequeira/Photo Researchers

[24] Sylvia A. Law, *Blue Cross: What Went Wrong?* New Haven, Conn.: Yale University Press, 1974.
[25] U.S. Department of HEW, *The Supply of Health Manpower*. Washington, D.C.: U.S. Government Printing Office, December 1974.

been badly treated—perhaps reflecting the rise of the consumer movement—and the tendency of juries to award large sums in malpractice
cases have also had an impact on physicians' fees. Most physicians are
required by law to carry malpractice insurance, and premiums for such
insurance range from $3,000 to $35,000 annually. (The highest premiums are paid by anesthesiologists, whose job is considered to carry the
greatest risk.) Needless to say, the costs of these premiums are passed
on to the consumer in the form of higher physicians' fees.

Perhaps the greatest cause of the increase in physicians' fees, however,
has been the growing tendency toward specialization. Of the nation's
360,000 physicians, over 85 percent are in a specialty and only about
14 percent are in general practice. (This compares to about 30 percent
who were general practitioners in 1960.)[26] One reason for this growth
in specialization is, of course, the increase in medical knowledge. Physicians today can become competent only in increasingly limited areas,
and so tend to specialize. Another reason, however, is the fact that
specialists receive more income than general practitioners, because it is
assumed that their longer training and expertise entitle them to higher
fees. Thus while GPs have annual incomes of over $40,000, specialists
receive close to $60,000 a year. The extra income comes directly from
patient fees. Specialization also increases costs in another way: patients
are forced to consult a number of physicians for a variety of ailments,
instead of being able to see one physician for all of them. These repeated
visits to different physicians multiply the cost of treatment many times.
One additional side effect is that medical care becomes fragmented and
impersonal, because the patient rarely establishes a long-term relationship with one physician.

Health Insurance. The high cost of medical services has made some
form of health insurance a necessity for all except the wealthy. Poor
people cannot afford even out-of-pocket expenses for the most minimal
care; and while middle-income individuals can pay most ordinary expenses, a severe or prolonged illness can ruin them financially.

Hospitalization insurance is held by more than 90 percent of families
with incomes of $10,000 or more; fewer than 54 percent of poor families,
however, who are likely to need health care the most, are so covered.[27]
Middle-income persons generally carry private (rather than public)
health insurance policies, but almost all of these have a number of shortcomings. To begin with, the premiums are expensive, and their cost has
been increasing steadily. There is usually a high deductible—the dollar
amount a subscriber must pay toward hospital (or physician) costs
before the insurer takes over. There is almost always a ceiling in payments, so that subscribers are not really covered for a truly catastrophic
illness. Finally, those whose policies are job connected find that they are
left with no coverage should they leave their jobs. In practical terms, the
result is that private insurance plans—including Blue Cross and Blue
Shield—pay only about 35 percent of all medical expenses. Thus, as

[26] *The Supply of Health Manpower,* p. 17.
[27] U.S. Department of HEW, *Medical Care Expenditures, Prices, and Costs.*
Washington, D.C.: U.S. Government Printing Office, September 1973.

health and insurance costs increase, middle-income persons pay higher sums—and larger portions of their incomes—for medical care.[28] And despite their insurance coverage, such persons can still be wiped out financially during a serious illness.

Two programs designed to help the medically needy obtain health care—Medicare and Medicaid—were passed by Congress in 1965. Medicare is a public health insurance program paid for by Social Security taxes. It is designed to partially cover the medical expenses of those over 65. Those over 65 who are ineligible for Medicare may voluntarily enroll in the program by paying premiums. Medicaid is an assistance program financed from federal and state tax revenues. It is designed to pay the medical costs of those unable to afford even basic health care. Though these programs have been important and helpful to many Americans, there are many problems associated with them.

For example, the cost of Medicare premiums when the program first started in 1966 was $3.00 a month; today the cost is $7.20 a month. The deductible in 1966 for hospitalization was $40; today the deductible is over $100—often beyond the reach of the indigent elderly. Enrollees in the Medicare program must also pay the first $25 of costs per day after 60 days' hospitalization, and the first $50 of costs per day after 90 days' hospitalization. Thus a prolonged illness—which is most likely to strike the elderly—can bring financial disaster to even middle-income persons.

The major problems with Medicaid have been a lack of sufficient funds to cover all the needy, and the existence of red tape that prevents the poor from taking full advantage of the program. Many states have not provided sufficient funds to match federal contributions to their Medicaid programs. As a result, poor people in many areas have little or no coverage. Also, Medicaid programs are administered in most areas by local welfare departments, which are under pressure to keep costs down. These departments have imposed complex and time-consuming requirements for Medicaid that discourage poor people from applying for aid.[29]

Medicare and Medicaid have also been a major factor in the rise in health costs, because they have sharply increased the demand for health services. Moreover, the maximum fees that Medicare set for specific health services (Medicaid offers blanket coverage) became the minimum that physicians and hospitals were willing to charge—driving up the costs of care still further. The costs of Medicare have also increased as a result of the many abuses it has suffered by physicians, hospitals, and nursing homes. For example, patients are frequently—and unnecessarily—sent from one specialist to another so that each physician can bill the government. It has been estimated that such overcharges totalled $27 million over a 5-year period.[30]

In a significant number of cases, patients receive treatment that is either unnecessary or harmful to their health or even their lives. Sometimes this treatment is psychologically harmful—that is, it is provided in such a way as to make the patient feel abused and resentful. Members of minorities

THE PROBLEMS OF UNNECESSARY OR HARMFUL TREATMENT

[28] "Plight of the U.S. patient"; and *Analysis of Health Care in the United States.*
[29] Lerner, pp. 312–313; and "Health care: Supply, demand, and politics," p. 87.
[30] "Health care in America," p. 51.

and women are often mistreated in just this way. As one analysis of the American health system stated:

Since blacks are assumed to be less sensitive than white patients, they get less privacy. Since blacks are assumed to be more ignorant than whites, they get less by way of explanation of what is happening to them. And since they are assumed to be irresponsible and forgetful, they are more likely to be given a drastic, one-shot treatment, instead of a prolonged regimen of drugs, or a restricted diet. . . . Women are assumed to be incapable of understanding complex technological explanations, so they are not given any. Women are assumed to be emotional and "difficult," so they are often classified as neurotic well before physical illness has been ruled out. (Note how many tranquilizer ads in medical journals depict women, rather than men, as likely customers.) And women are assumed to be vain, so they are the special prey of the paramedical dieting, cosmetics, and plastic surgery businesses.[31]

Many other forms of mistreatment are physically harmful, however, and result in death. Several studies have found, for example, that about 2.4 million unnecessary operations are performed each year. (The largest groups of such operations are hysterectomies and tonsillectomies, of which 260,000 and 500,000, respectively, are estimated to be unnecessary.) Of these, at least 11,900 result in the death of the patient. These deaths would have been avoided had the unnecessary surgery not been performed.[32] There are also 30,000 deaths each year caused directly by reactions to antibiotics and other prescribed drugs. Such bad reactions also cause some 300,000 side effects that result in hospitalization. Thus the overprescription of antibiotics and other drugs is in itself a major cause of illness and death in the United States.[33]

Considering the high level of training required of physicians and the many modern health facilities that exist, why does such shocking mistreatment occur? Perhaps the most important reason is that physicians are not required to keep up with medical knowledge once they leave school. No state in the nation requires a relicensing examination of its physicians. Once a physician is licensed, he or she need never read another medical text or journal, or attend a medical conference, in order to remain in practice. Conservative estimates are that about 16,000 practicing physicians, or almost 5 percent of the total, are incompetent.[34]

This bad situation is worsened by the fact that few states have an agency where incompetence can be reported and acted upon. Furthermore, because patients rarely know that they are being poorly treated, the responsibility for reporting incompetence lies with other physicians. Yet most physicians are reluctant to report on their colleagues, even when they know that these colleagues are endangering their patients'

[31] *The American Health Empire,* pp. 14, 16.
[32] "Incompetent surgery is found not isolated." *New York Times,* January 27, 1976, pp. 1 ff.
[33] "Thousands a year killed by faulty prescriptions." *New York Times,* January 28, 1976, pp. 1 ff.
[34] Unfit doctors create worry in profession." *New York Times,* January 29, 1976, pp. 1 ff.

Surgery			
14 million non-emergency operations annually	of which	2.38 million deemed unnecessary	during which	11,900 people died
Antibiotics			
6 billion doses estimated consumed in United States	of which	22 percent of these deemed unnecessary	during which	10,000 fatal and near-fatal reactions to antibiotics occurred
Regulation of Doctors			
320,000 licensed physicians in United States	of which	16,000 deemed incompetent or unfit	of these	66 licenses revoked each year, on the average, in the United States

Source: New York Times, January 26, 1976, p. 20. ©1976 by The New York Times Company. Reprinted by permission.

TABLE 2-1
Indications of Medical Incompetence in the United States

lives. The result is that on the average only about 72 doctors (in recent years) a year lose their license for incompetence—a tiny fraction of the total that is believed to exist.[35]

The large number of deaths due directly to surgery are largely a reflection of the fact that much of the surgery performed in the United States is unnecessary. Americans have the highest rate of elective (optional) surgery in the world; they undergo about 14.4 million such operations in a year. Yet, it has been estimated that one-fifth of all elective surgery is not in the patient's best interests. No surgical procedure is without its risks. Even in a simple operation such as a tonsillectomy, approximately 2 out of every 1,000 patients die; and the death rate for more complex operations is much higher. If an excessive number of operations are performed, proportionally more patients die. (See Table 2-1.)

Why is the rate of surgery so high in the United States? One reason is simply that there are too many surgeons. In fact, it has been estimated that there are 22,000 more physicians who do surgery than are necessary. Since their livelihood depends on performing operations, surgeons are less likely to recommend a nonsurgical treatment to a patient. This is demonstrated by studies that show that rates of surgery are higher in those states that have proportionately more surgeons, and lower where there are proportionately fewer surgeons. Presumably, patients in those states with less surgery are finding other forms of treatment. Another, related, reason for excess surgery is the American system of fee-for-service. Because most surgeons—and physicians—are paid each time they treat a patient, they are encouraged to see and treat as many patients as they can. Often, patients do not receive the individual attention they need. The result is that more surgeries are performed, sometimes with less than adequate carefulness. For example, studies by the Department of Health, Education, and Welfare and the Social Security

[35] "Few doctors ever report colleague's incompetence." *New York Times*, January 29, 1976, pp. 1 ff.

Administration found that patients covered by fee-for-service insurance plans such as Blue Cross were undergoing significantly higher rates of surgery than patients covered by prepaid plans.[36]

THE ROOTS OF HEALTH PROBLEMS

GENERAL PROBLEMS

Most of the problems we have described in this chapter so far can be traced to the fact that this country has no unified health care delivery system. In fact, the United States is the only industrialized nation without such a system. Great Britain, for example, pays most of its physicians a salary from general tax revenues. Because these physicians do not earn fees for service, they can afford to emphasize the preventive rather than the treatment aspects of health care. Moreover, there is less need for them to practice only in affluent areas; thus health care is more equitably distributed. Patients, for their part, pay only a special tax for all the health services they need. They can afford to see a physician when they want to, and they do not have to worry that a major illness will ruin them financially.[37]

The weaknesses of the American system, such as it is, have been described in a report to Congress by the Health Services and Mental Health Administration:

Composed as it is of several hundred thousand more or less independent provider units, the existing system lacks effective planning and coordination which, in varying degrees, has resulted in:
  —duplication of costly facilities, equipment and patient record systems, increasing the costs of health care.
  —maldistribution of medical resources, with relative abundance in affluent urban areas and shortages in the poorer urban and rural areas.
  —lack of comprehensiveness and continuity of care.
Current legal restrictions on medical practice, particularly licensing laws, tend to discourage use of paramedical personnel for tasks that now require scarce and expensive professional time.

The emphasis on fee or charge-per-service in less than a totally free market combined with the greater amount of insurance for inpatient than for outpatient care apparently tends to:
  —encourage consumers and physicians to substitute hospital for ambulatory care, with the resultant higher costs.
  —encourage providers to over-prescribe or supply services that are marginal or not needed.
  —deter consumers from seeking relatively inexpensive care in the early stages of illness at the risk of requiring more expensive care later on. . . .

The pervasive influence of the medical profession over almost all facets of the health care delivery process, including the management of hospitals and admission policies of medical schools, has tended to make the health system more responsive to the interests of the profession than to the needs of consumers.[38]

[36] "Incompetent surgery is found not isolated."
[37] See *Health Services in Britain.* New York: British Information Services, 1974.
[38] *Analysis of Health Care in the United States,* pp. 5–6.

The "pervasive influence of the medical profession" described in the report is exemplified by the role played by the American Medical Association (AMA) in limiting the number of physicians in this country. In the last part of the nineteenth century, the AMA prevailed upon state legislatures to set up stringent licensing requirements for all physicians. More often than not, these requirements took the form of examinations prepared, administered, and judged by other physicians. The result was that the proportion of physicians to population began to decline. During the first part of the twentieth century, the AMA was able to limit the number of medical schools by ensuring that licensing standards for the schools were increased. In addition, the number of admissions to these schools was severely limited.[39] A major outcome of these actions by the AMA was that the physician shortage became a critical problem in the United States. Moreover, because the demand for physicians was so much greater than the supply, physicians were able to achieve a virtual monopoly on health care delivery and raise fees almost at will.[40]

The development of private insurance plans like Blue Cross and Blue Shield and the passage of federal Medicaid and Medicare legislation were originally intended to solve many of the problems and inequities of the American health care system. However, these plans, as we have already suggested, have in many instances compounded the difficulties that already exist. In the words of one analysis, "They are at one and the same time the major cause of the runaway costs of the medical system, and a major source of power defending the status quo and preventing major reorganizations of the medical care system from occurring." These plans leave control of the system in the hands of health care suppliers: it is the physicians and hospitals that decide what and how much treatment each patient needs. Moreover, it is the physicians and the hospitals that decide how much to charge; there are no restrictions on fees, because the insurance plans guarantee that they will be paid no matter how inflated they are. Thus the costs of health care keep going up. And as the above analysis noted,

Meanwhile, in the face of rising health care costs, the cost of . . . health insurance has soared, too. As a result, an increasing number of people fall into no man's land—too rich for Medicaid, too young for Medicare, too poor to buy private health insurance, and certainly too poor to pay hospital bills.[41]

We have already suggested that lack of access to proper medical care causes higher rates of illness and death among the poor. Antonovsky, in his analysis of the relationship between class and illness, suggests that the problem of access has become even more significant for the health of the poor than in the past. Until the early part of the twentieth century, the ill health of the poor was due largely to the effects of infectious diseases, which were rampant among the poor because of the crowded, unsanitary, and debilitating conditions in which they were forced to live. Though these conditions have not changed a great deal, medical science today is able to control and cure infectious diseases much more effec-

THE PROBLEMS OF POVERTY

[39] Lerner, p. 302.

[40] See R. Kessel, "Price discrimination in medicine." *Journal of Law and Economics* 1 (1958):20–53.

[41] Ehrenreich and Ehrenreich, pp. 130–132.

Poor people tend to be ill and disabled more frequently and for longer periods of time than the more affluent.
Ken Heyman

tively. Thus, except among the extremely poor (who rarely receive medical attention) and among the infants of the poor (who are usually in a weakened condition), infectious diseases by themselves no longer account for the tremendous differences in health between the poor and the nonpoor. Instead, as Antonovsky stated,

Access to good medical care, preventive medical action, health knowledge, and limitation of delay in seeking treatment have become increasingly important in combating mortality, as chronic diseases have become the chief health enemy in the developed world. In these areas, lower class people may well be at a disadvantage.[42]

Antonovsky predicted, in fact, that as control of the chronic diseases (cancer, for example) became more important, the differences between

[42] Antonovsky, p. 178.

the health of the poor and the nonpoor would increase—that is, that the poor would have still higher rates of illness and death compared to the nonpoor.

Lee Rainwater, in his analysis of the relationship of class to ill health, suggests that lack of access to medical care is not the only factor that affects the health of the poor. To Rainwater, just being poor is a condition that promotes poor health. The poor, for example, cannot afford the right foods, and so their bodies are likely to be in a weakened condition. They often live in the most polluted areas, and so are susceptible to respiratory diseases. They cannot afford proper housing, and so are exposed to disease-carrying refuse and rodents. Perhaps most important, the lives of the poor are filled with stress—they are always worried about getting enough money to pay for essential needs. Such long-term stress can cause a variety of illnesses, physical and mental. It also makes it difficult to react to minor signs of ill health. A cough, for example, is likely to be dismissed when one is preoccupied with getting enough food to eat. It is only if the cough worsens considerably that the individual will visit a clinic, and by then it may be too late. Rainwater also cites studies that indicate that the poor feel middle-aged before the nonpoor do. As such, the poor are more likely to accept illness and disability as somehow natural—even in their thirties—than the nonpoor. Finally, the poor are treated with contempt and hostility by the physicians and personnel that they encounter. They are therefore more likely to avoid professional treatment—either of a preventive or curative nature—and become ill more frequently and remain ill for a longer period of time.[43] (See Chapter 6 for an additional discussion of poverty and health.)

SOCIAL POLICY AND ACTION

Suggestions for solving some of the problems of the health care system focus largely on two areas: so-called alternative provider organizations and alternative health financing plans. Implicit in almost all proposals is an expansion of the government's role in supervising and financing health services.

Health Maintenance Organizations. Two of the major problems of the present health care system are its lack of emphasis on preventive medicine and its high cost. Health Maintenance Organizations (HMOs) are designed to deal with both these problems. Subscribers pay a fixed annual sum (in installments); in return they get comprehensive medical care, with a major stress on preventive services. Immunizations, vaccinations, checkups, and diagnostic procedures such as X-rays are provided routinely. More extensive care, such as hospitalization, is also made available. Thus HMOs provide an entire range of health services at a reasonable cost. Because of their emphasis on prevention and early detection of illness, HMOs are also likely to reduce the need for extensive treatment. For example, one study found that enrollees in HMOs spend

ALTERNATIVE PROVIDER ORGANIZATIONS

[43] Rainwater, pp. 179–187.

less than half as much time in hospitals as those with traditional health insurance plans. For reasons such as these, Congress passed the Health Maintenance Organization Act in 1973. It provided funds for the creation of HMOs and made it obligatory for employers to offer HMOs (where available) as alternatives to their usual employee health plans. Unfortunately, HMOs have still not been adequately funded and popularized; thus, though they offer many advantages, their number is still small.[44]

Planned Regional Health Systems. This alternative would eliminate most free-market aspects of health care delivery. Modeled after such systems as the National Health Service of Great Britain, a centrally planned regional health system would provide the entire range of health services on demand, instead of for a fee. The system would be financed by government subsidies and business and employee taxes. A regional planning council would distribute and supervise all health services in a given region. Individuals would go to their local medical center for basic health care; more specialized services, such as hospitalization, would be provided in a regional center.

Advocates of such a system see it as a way to make health care equally available to all. Medical facilities would not be concentrated in only affluent areas, but would be distributed strictly by population. Because they would not have to pay a fee for each visit to a physician or hospital, poor people could afford all the care they needed. Also, because physicians and hospitals would be paid fixed fees by the government for their services, the cost of the system would remain low. Finally, since health care would be available on demand, individuals would be encouraged to take advantage of preventive medicine, such as inoculations and checkups. The major disadvantages of such a system are that people's choice of physicians would be limited, since they would have to report to their local center, and that a two-level system could develop if the more affluent continued to use private sources of medical care. It is also likely that there would be tremendous resistance on the part of physicians and hospitals if implementation of such a system were attempted in this country.[45]

For all their limitations, Medicare and Medicaid were significant landmarks in the drive toward providing health care for all citizens. Medicare, by offering government-financed health services to the elderly, reinforced the idea that health care was a right, not a privilege. Medicaid, by setting standards of "medical indigency," acknowledged that people who were not officially defined as poor could nevertheless be unable to afford medical care.[46]

We have already suggested, however, that both Medicare and Medicaid leave much to be desired. In the mid-1970s a number of bills that attempt to fill in existing gaps in the financing of health services were proposed. The Long-Ribicoff bill, if passed, would provide federal financing in the

ALTERNATIVE
FINANCING SYSTEMS

[44] Mary Costello, "Health maintenance organizations." *Editorial Research Reports,* August 9, 1974, pp. 603–619.
[45] *Analysis of Health Care in the United States,* pp. 6–8.
[46] Lerner, pp. 311–312.

event of catastrophic illness; it would supplement existing health insurance plans by paying all medical costs above $2,000. However, while the passage of such a bill would prevent bankruptcy in the event of an illness, it would do nothing to solve the basic problem of all health insurance plans: how to keep medical costs down. In effect, the Long-Ribicoff bill simply guarantees that physicians and hospitals will be paid whatever they charge; the financial ability of the patient will become a totally irrelevant factor in determining fees.

A more comprehensive national health insurance system was proposed in the Kennedy-Griffiths bill. This bill provides that the government would pay from 50 to 70 percent of all health services (including psychiatric treatment). It would be financed in much the same way as Social Security, with a special tax on employees and employers. Some form of cost-control would be instituted: hospitals, for example, would be required to work within an annual budget, and physicians would have to accept a fee for each patient, rather than a fee for each service. Other, similar proposals favor expansion of Medicare to include every citizen. However, it has been estimated that medical care under such plans would cost consumers even more than they are paying now.[47] For this reason, most impartial observers of health care in the United States favor eliminating the fee-for-service system almost entirely and substituting a system based on prepayment or some form of national health insurance, such as we described above.

It is probable that the present system of health care delivery will require a major overhaul before its inefficiency, inequality, and ineptitude can be effectively eliminated. Certain preliminary steps can be taken, however, to improve the system as it now exists:

IMPROVING THE EXISTING SYSTEM

1. Outpatient facilities in hospitals can be expanded, so that illnesses will be detected and treated earlier.
2. More medical schools can be built, and more people can be accepted into them, so that there will be an adequate supply of physicians.
3. Medical schools can be encouraged—perhaps through federal subsidies—to graduate more general practitioners, so that the reliance on impersonal and expensive specialists can be reduced.
4. Physicians, through special training, can be made more sensitive to the needs of poor people and minorities. In addition, greater numbers of minority group students can be accepted into and graduated from medical schools. In these ways the poor would be less likely to avoid the medical treatment they need. At present, because of cutbacks in government funding, medical schools are accepting fewer non-female minority students. The reduction in available scholarship aid has also made minority recruitment difficult.
5. Public and private insurance agencies can adopt a more critical stance with regard to physician and hospital fees. They can refuse to pay unreasonable charges, and they can set lower maximum payments for services.
6. Physicians can be permitted to advertise their fees, in much the same way that drugstores can now advertise prescription prices.

[47] "Health care: Supply, demand, and politics," p. 88.

7. Patients can participate more actively in their own health care—seeking a second opinion if surgery is recommended by their physician, for example, or questioning their physician if a treatment seems inappropriate or too expensive.

Additional proposals involve improving the quality of health care. For example, Senator Edward M. Kennedy has suggested that physicians all over the United States be required to take a national relicensing exam every three or four years. This will make it necessary for physicians to keep up with advances in medical knowledge. It will also make it easier to keep incompetent physicians from practicing.

One important step toward the monitoring of physicians' performance was taken in 1973, when Professional Standards Review Organizations (PSROs) were set up by federal amendments to the Social Security Act. The legislation provided that, starting in 1976, review boards composed of physicians would review the treatment given to all Medicare and Medicaid patients. Any physician who treats such patients may have to register with a local PSRO; the PSRO approves or disapproves the physician's treatment of these patients. If a less expensive form of treatment can be used, the PSRO suggests it; thus costs are kept down. In addition, because the PSRO is made up entirely of physicians, proper treatment of Medicare and Medicaid patients has become much more likely.

Increasing the number of medical groups, which at present are scattered throughout the country, would also do much to reduce costs and the possibility of mistreatment. A medical group generally consists of a general practitioner or internist working and sharing facilities with a number of different specialists. Members of the group share the expenses of overhead and equipment. Thus they can afford to charge lower fees. And because the physicians work together, they tend to monitor and learn from each other, reducing the chance of malpractice.

PROSPECTS

As this book goes to press, it is not yet clear which, if any, of the health bills before Congress will pass. There is, however, widespread agreement that the health system needs to be reformed; and some new form of health financing—either through national health insurance or through a prepayment system—will probably become a reality soon. There is also a belated recognition on the part of the AMA that the shortage of general practitioners must be ended. As a result, medical schools are beginning to graduate more GPs. Whether there will be enough of them to meet the need remains to be seen.

It is likely, in any case, that health and health care will be social problems for the foreseeable future. Aspects of the American life style that contribute to illness—such as the existence of pollution—will not be eradicated overnight. And even if health services are made available to all, class and racial inequality in health will continue to exist. So long as poor people and those who suffer the effects of discrimination are deprived in every other area of life, they will be deprived of health: it is difficult for those who live outside the mainstream of society, with limited access to food, shelter, and comfort, to maintain optimum levels of physical and emotional health. No health care system, however equitable and efficient, can cure the ills caused by poverty, prejudice, and discrimination.

One problem of recent origin that has begun to receive much-needed attention is the problem of controlling our new power over health and the life span. Advances in medical technology have caused many complex ethical questions to be raised: How should a limited number of organ transplants be allocated? Should abortion be mandatory if genetic defects are detected in the fetus? Who decides when to terminate life-prolonging efforts, or, in the common, inelegant phrase, when to "pull the plug"? If machines can keep people breathing and their hearts beating indefinitely, when does death occur? Under what conditions, if any, can experimentation on human subjects be allowed? It is obvious that new codes and guidelines will have to be developed to cope with these new issues. At present, no clear standards for the medical and research industries exist in many complex, delicate areas. Experts testifying before a congressional committee in 1973 recommended that a national board of ethics be created to supervise all federally funded research on human subjects. Others suggest that local ethics boards be created to supervise the medical and research practices within a local area.[48] Physicians and researchers strongly resist such suggestions, however, fearing that they will lose the freedom that they now have. It is therefore likely that a code of ethics, if one is developed, will come from within professional medical societies rather than from any regulatory agency.

Another issue that has become more prominent in recent years is our treatment of the dying. Kübler-Ross has described this treatment well:

One of the most important facts is that dying nowadays is more gruesome in many ways, namely, more lonely, mechanical, dehumanizing. . . . Dying becomes lonely and impersonal because the patient is often taken out of his familiar environment and rushed to an emergency room. . . . He will be surrounded by many nurses, orderlies, interns, residents, a lab technician perhaps who will take some blood, an electrocardiogram technician who takes the cardiogram. He may be moved to X-ray and he will overhear opinions of his condition and discussions and questions to members of the family. He slowly but surely is beginning to be treated like a thing. He is no longer a person. Decisions are made often without his opinion. If he tries to rebel he will be sedated. . . .

He may cry for rest, peace, and dignity, but he will get infusions, transfusions, a heart machine, or tracheotomy if necessary. He may want one single person to stop for one single minute so that he can ask one single question— but he will get a dozen people around the clock, all busily preoccupied with his heart rate, pulse, electrocardiogram or pulmonary functions, his secretions or excretions but not with him as a human being. . . . Is this approach our way to cope with and repress the anxieties that a . . . critically ill patient evokes in us? [49]

[48] See Amitai Etzioni, *Genetic Fix*. New York: Macmillan, 1973.
[49] Elizabeth Kübler-Ross, *On Death and Dying*. New York: Macmillan, 1969, pp. 8–9.

To Kübler-Ross, such treatment is counterproductive, especially when it has ceased to have any meaningful function, as with terminally ill patients. She recommends that the dying be treated with much more sensitivity and frankness, and wherever possible be permitted to die at home amid familiar surroundings. Such suggestions have encountered great (though by no means total) opposition on the part of physicians and hospital administrations; a few medical schools, however, have instituted courses on "death education" to make their students more sensitive to the needs of the dying. More extensive changes in the treatment of the critically ill will probably depend on widespread changes in society's attitude toward death itself, namely, a greater acceptance of the fact that death is unavoidable and a greater willingness to discuss death openly rather than pretend it does not exist.

PROBLEMS OF MENTAL HEALTH

The problems of physical health we have discussed seem serious and widespread. But mental illness, afflicting at least 10 percent of the population, is "America's primary health problem," according to the National Institute of Mental Health. Every year more than four million people, including perhaps half a million children, are treated for some kind of mental disorder. Nearly half of these people are hospitalized, either in mental or in general hospitals. Some are discharged after a brief stay; some are long-term, chronic patients; some will be hospitalized until they die. Over 2 million patients are treated in outpatient clinics or by psychologists and psychiatrists in private practice.[50] Some 15 million more who are not under treatment at all suffer from some degree of mental disorder, often unrecognized as such. The total cost of all this, in tax money, private fees, losses to business through employee illness, and other expenses, is estimated to be well over 20 billion dollars per year.[51]

Clearly, mental health is a problem we cannot afford to neglect. It has not been ignored in professional circles: research as to its causes, and experiments in developing more effective treatment, have been going on for over a hundred years. But until recently, efforts at systematic, concerted programs foundered because of public fear, ignorance, and apathy. Few wanted to know about the problem or were willing to spend the necessary money to solve it. But in recent years public awareness of the possibilities for helping the mentally ill has grown, aided by television programs, magazine articles, and books dealing with various aspects of mental health.

THE NATURE OF MENTAL DISORDERS

Some of the language of mental disorder has become a familiar part of the lay vocabulary. We use the terms "neurotic," "psychotic," "paranoid," and perhaps "psychosomatic" to express judgments, usually unfavorable,

[50] U.S. Bureau of the Census, *Statistical Abstract of the United States, 1975.* Washington, D.C.: U.S. Government Printing Office, 1976, p. 82.
[51] *The High Cost of Mental Illness* (pamphlet). New York: National Association for Mental Health, n.d.

about the behavior of other people. Those who, we feel, are convinced that their co-workers are out to get them are paranoid; others who keep their teenage children home from school every time they sneeze are neurotic. Sometimes we substitute more general colloquial terms, such as "spaced out," "uptight," or simply "sick." In general, whatever the terms we use, we are apt to have only a rather vague idea as to their precise meaning.

In part, this imprecision reflects an empirical fact—that mental disorders are often very difficult to diagnose exactly. Whereas a large percentage of physical illnesses are known to have agreed-upon determinants whose presence can be revealed by objective tests, the identification of mental disorders depends largely on behavioral symptoms, and on the relative importance assigned to them by the person making the diagnosis. In a few cases, it is true, a specific disorder has been found to have a specific organic cause. However, for the most part there is less consensus with regard to mental disorders. Furthermore, an erroneous medical diagnosis does not, in many instances, have the same consequence as an erroneous psychiatric diagnosis. A person who is told that the diagnosis of heart disease was incorrect feels relieved. But a person who is told that the diagnosis of schizophrenia was incorrect often still remains labeled as mentally ill, no matter what the doctor says. Moreover, the diagnosis of mental illness—correct or incorrect—carries a greater stigma than a diagnosis of physical illness. Senator Thomas Eagleton, for example, was forced by public demand to forego his candidacy for vice-president in 1972 after it was revealed that he had undergone shock treatments for depression; Franklin Roosevelt on the other hand, was elected president four times even though he had polio.

This is not to say that diagnosis of mental disorders is useless or impossible. Practical experience has shown that certain sets of symptoms seem to occur together, and numerous tests have been developed that can indicate a patient's underlying motivations. With the aid of these, plus personal sensitivity and patience, trained, experienced, and skilled practitioners can often learn a great deal about a patient's problems. But in the nature of the process, much more depends on the orientation of the practitioners than is usually thought to be true in the case of medical doctors. How do these practitioners decide which symptoms are significant? For that matter, how do they decide what *is* a symptom? What, fundamentally, do they believe mental disorder is?

There are two, and perhaps three, different ways to answer this last question, and each has its implications for prevention and treatment.

Mental Illness. The most familiar school of thought holds that a mental disorder is properly considered an illness. That is, a mental disorder is primarily a disturbance of the individual's normal personality system analogous to the disturbance of the physiological system by physical disease, and is to be remedied primarily by treatment of the individual. Attention is centered on the pathology—the anxieties, hostilities, maladjustments, and other tensions underlying abnormal behavior—and the aim of treatment is to relieve or remove these personal tensions, on the assumption that once this is done, patients will be able to function adequately in their external lives.

The illness concept or medical model of mental disorder arose in reaction to the older notion that the mentally disturbed were mad, possessed, perhaps blameworthy, to be locked up, beaten, or killed. It made possible serious and scientific investigation of possible causes and cures of mental disorder, and underlay the development of practically all the systems of mental health care and therapeutic treatment in existence today—systems which are still largely in the hands of medically oriented personnel. It has helped to lessen, at least among the sophisticated, the stigma and shame of mental disorder, since, after all, "illness can happen to anyone."

Nevertheless, the concept of mental disorder as "illness" has certain disadvantages. In concentrating on individuals and their immediate environment (often their childhood environment), it tends to disregard the wider social environment as a possible major source of difficulty. In addition, especially for hospitalized patients, it can lead to impractical criteria of "recovery"—people may have gained considerable insight into their inner tensions, but still prove unable to function adequately when they return to the outer tensions of a perhaps unsatisfactory home, job, or society. Conversely, people who no longer have any abnormal behavioral symptoms may be kept hospitalized because it is felt that their "illness" may resurface.

Deviance. The concept of mental disorder as illness holds that something about the individual is abnormal; that the fundamental trouble is in his or her interior emotional makeup, which was twisted, repressed, or otherwise wrongly developed as a result of genetic or chemical factors or events in early life. While this seems to provide a satisfactory explanation of some mental disorder, there has gradually developed a feeling that other factors need to be taken into account, especially the pressures exerted at all stages of life by the wider society. Out of this has grown the view that mental disorder represents a departure from certain institutionalized expectations of society—that it is a form of social deviance or maladjustment.

It is worthwhile to point out the slightly differing implications of the two terms "maladjustment" and "deviance." The first, with "mal-," which means "bad," built into it, immediately assumes the rightness of the norms being violated; it is in the violators that something is wrong, something that is perhaps not their fault but that for their own sakes needs to be corrected, "readjusted." The notion of deviance is much more dependent on how society regards the particular norms that have been violated. Here the idea of *residual deviance,* formulated by Thomas Scheff, may be useful. According to Scheff,[52] most social conventions are recognized as being such, and their violation carries fairly clear, often moral, labels: people who steal another's wallet are thieves; people who act haughtily toward lower-class persons are snobbish; and so on. But there is a large residual area of social convention that is so completely taken for granted that it is assumed to be more or less part of human nature. In Scheff's example, it seems natural for people holding a conversation to face each other, rather than to look away. Violation of these norms is frightening to society, because it seems contrary to human

---

[52] Thomas J. Scheff, "The role of the mentally ill and the dynamics of mental disorder." *Sociometry* (1963):436–453.

nature—there is no reason for it. After all, it is perfectly "natural" for wallet-thieves to want money; they merely take the illegal way to get it. But what natural reason could there be for someone to stare at the ceiling while talking to people, or to retreat to the far side of the room and shout at them? There must be something wrong with such people—they must have mental problems.

Scheff's suggestion is that this residual deviance occurs in many, even most, people at one time or another, and usually goes away without treatment. What causes it, in some cases, to become a stabilized mental disorder is that *society decides to label it as such*. When this happens, the *role* of "mentally ill person" is offered to deviants. Since they are often confused and frightened by their own behavior during a time of stress, and by other people's reactions to it, they are apt to be particularly impressionable, and may accept the offered role. Once this happens, it becomes difficult for them to change their behavior and return to the "normal" role.

While Scheff admits that his theory is not fully developed, he does cite in support of it certain evidence from the military:

The experience of battlefield psychiatrists can be interpreted to support the hypothesis that residual deviance is usually transitory. Glass reports that combat neurosis is often self-terminating if the soldier is kept with his unit and given only the most superficial medical attention. . . . [But] soldiers who are removed from their unit to a hospital . . . often go on to become chronically impaired. That is, their deviance is stabilized by the labeling process, which is implicit in their removal and hospitalization.

If this is so, then behavior that is considered to show mental disorder will vary from one society or culture to another. More important, mental disorder may actually be caused by some of the attempts to cure it. As Levine and Levine point out, commenting on Scheff:

The mental health professions, and psychiatry in particular, are viewed as contributing to the development of mental illness by providing the doctor role. In effect, by treating a patient in a separate treating institution, the doctors certify that the patient is indeed a patient and is indeed mentally ill.

A further implication of Scheff's thesis, again brought out by Levine and Levine, is that by regarding residual deviance as evidence of mental illness, the psychiatrist may be creating personal conflict and attempting to hold up social change.

Not only is the mental health professional the one who identifies the deviant; in the very doing he confirms the validity of the social norm violated. . . . In periods of relative social stability, there may be little problem in the mental health professional acting to confirm societal norms. However, in periods of acute social change, the mental health professional may contribute to the exacerbation of the dislocations people endure by becoming part of the process which induces and maintains cultural lag. The mental health professional may be confirming social norms which no longer have validity in terms of the way people actually live in a changing society.[53]

[53] Murray Levine and Adeline Levine, "The climate of change." In Murray Levine and Adeline Levine, *A Social History of Helping Services: Clinic, Court, School, and Community*. Englewood Cliffs, N.J.: Prentice-Hall, 1970.

The point of the concept of mental disorder as deviance, then, is that such disorder may be the function of an individual's inability to comply with societal expectations, and of the label which society attaches to persons who deviate.

Problems in Living. A third approach to the nature of mental disorder is offered by Thomas Szasz, a psychiatrist who has stirred up considerable controversy in the field with his contention that mental illness is a myth. By this, as he explains in "The Myth of Mental Illness," he means not that the social and psychological disturbances commonly called mental illness do not exist, but that it is dangerously misleading to call them illnesses. Rather, he believes, they should be regarded as manifestations of unresolved problems in living.

We have failed to accept the simple fact that human relations are inherently fraught with difficulties and that to make them even relatively harmonious requires much patience and hard work. . . . Instead of calling attention to conflicting human needs, aspirations, and values, the notion of mental illness provides an amoral and impersonal "thing" (an "illness") as an explanation for *problems in living.*

Szasz's basic concern is an important one, for it has to do with justice and individual liberty. As he sees it, a diagnosis of mental disorder involves a value judgment, based on the behavioral norms held by the psychiatrist; and to call it illness is to "create a situation in which, it is claimed, psychosocial, ethical, and/or legal deviations can be corrected by (so-called) medical action."[54]

Not only is this logically absurd, claims Szasz, it is dangerous. In a further article, "Justice in the Therapeutic State," he discusses the divergent concepts of the Legal State and the Therapeutic State. The business of the Legal State is "the maintenance of peace through a system of just laws justly administered." Insofar as it is true to its nature, the Legal State has no claim on the individual beyond what is set down in the law; for the rest, what the citizen does is none of the State's business. By contrast:

In the scientific-technological conception of the State, therapy is only a means, not an end. The goal of the Therapeutic State is universal health, or at least unfailing relief from suffering. This untroubled state of man and society is a quintessential feature of the medical-therapeutic perspective on politics. Conflict among individuals, and especially between the individual and the State, is invariably seen as a symptom of "illness" or psychopathology, and the primary function of the State is accordingly the removal of such conflict by "therapy"—"therapy" imposed by force, if necessary. It is not difficult to recognize in this imagery of the Therapeutic State the old Inquisitorial, or the more recent Totalitarian, concept of the State, now clothed in the garb of psychiatric treatment.[55]

[54] Thomas S. Szasz, "The myth of mental illness." *American Psychologist* 15 (1960):5–12.
[55] Thomas S. Szasz, "Justice in the therapeutic state." *Comprehensive Psychiatry* 11 (1970):433–444.

In short, Szasz believes, liberty can be unwittingly sacrificed by a too great concern for the "cure" of "mental illness."

CLASSIFICATION OF MENTAL DISORDERS

There have been many attempts to classify mental disorders, but none of the systems thus far offered has been fully satisfactory. As was pointed out above, diagnosis of these disorders is a complicated matter, depending largely on the surface evidence of emotional and behavioral symptoms, which rarely occur in clear-cut, easily distinguishable patterns. The traditional medical model of mental illness distinguishes certain major categories, in which different types of emotional disturbances are grouped. Labeling theory, on the other hand, sees such categories as value-laden; that is, they reflect the biases of those who make up these categories, rather than any objective set of behaviors. We will discuss both schools of thought below.

THE ILLNESS MODEL

Here we shall briefly describe four of the major categories in the illness model: *neurosis,* a condition of considerable anxiety and distress, but one which can usually be healed without hospitalization; *psychosis,* a condition of severe impairment and of the rejection of reality; *organic psychosis,* caused by damage to the nervous system; and *psychosomatic illness,* in which actual physical illness is caused by psychological disturbance.

Neurosis. The term "neurosis" refers to a general type of disorder in which the individual suffers from severe anxiety but continues to try to function in the real world, usually through the use of various subterfuges or defense mechanisms. The line between neurosis and the ordinary defensive mechanisms of a functionally healthy person is a fine one, and probably no two diagnosticians would draw it at the same point. In general, neurotic persons need some help in order to operate acceptably in their ordinary environment. They are usually aware that their behavior is somewhat inappropriate, and have some understanding of the reason why, or at least are somewhat open to such understanding. In attempting to cope with their deep-seated anxiety, they may have adopted behavior which severely hampers them in normal activities—such as constant hand-washing or repeated, objectively needless checking and rechecking of minor calculations—or they may have developed a phobia, a persistent fear of some object or situation. Less frequently, they may develop more severe symptoms, such as amnesia.

Neurotic anxiety seems to originate from childhood experiences, although it may not reveal itself fully until individuals encounter the new demands of adult life. If the adults upon whom young children are dependent, or the surroundings in which they are placed, are such as to teach them that reality is painful, unreliable, and incomprehensible, or that they themselves are bad or worthless, their capacity for self-confidence, achievement, and comfortable relationships with other people is likely to be fundamentally undermined. Later, if the pressure of the underlying anxiety becomes too great, they may seek professional help. However, most persons who are neurotic never seek treatment, because they can usually still function somewhat realistically.[56]

Psychosis. Psychosis is a condition in which a person's mental functioning is severely impaired. Here, too, individuals seldom fit a standard pattern exactly; there are several types of psychoses, each encompassing several kinds of behavior. *Schizophrenia,* the most common, varies considerably among individuals in its symptoms. Schizophrenic persons may withdraw from reality or distort it to suit themselves; their emotional responses may be either apathetic or inappropriate and inconsistent; their thought and speech may be disorganized, and they may make bizarre associations of ideas; they may suffer from delusions or hallucinations; they may believe that they, or a part of them, is nonexistent or dead. One or another type of symptom may predominate at different times in a single individual. *Manic-depressive illness* is another form of psychosis in which the individual shows moods of extreme excitement or depression.

Organic Psychoses. This is psychotic behavior resulting not from some emotional difficulty but from damage to the central nervous system. One of the most common forms is *senile psychosis,* which is believed to result from the diminished oxygen supply to the brain associated with cerebral arteriosclerosis in advanced age. *Alcoholic psychosis,* often found in long-term alcoholics, is another organic psychosis. In rare cases, infection or tumor of the brain, or repeated injury to the head, may cause organic psychosis.

Psychosomatic Illness. Probably because of the physical tension created by fear and anxiety, or because of the chemical secretions induced in the body by these emotions, continued emotional stress can result in physical illness. These psychosomatic disorders involve real organic harm. Common forms are headaches, stomachaches, backaches, ulcers, high blood pressure, and allergies. They may be learned, perhaps unconsciously, as defenses against specific threats; thus a person who dislikes parties but does not quite want to recognize the fact may develop a headache whenever a party threatens. It is sometimes difficult for a physician to know whether a given disorder is primarily physical or mental in its origin, for psychosomatic illness is not always accompanied by clear neurotic symptoms.

LABELING THEORY

As we noted at the beginning of this chapter, some physical illnesses may be culturally defined; this is even truer for mental disorders. The medical model assumes that patients present symptoms, that those symptoms comprise diagnosable categories of mental illness, and that we may thus distinguish the mentally healthy from the mentally unhealthy. But there is a growing belief that at least some psychiatric diagnoses of mental illness are pigeonholes into which certain behaviors are arbitrarily placed.[57] To Szasz, for example, the customary psychiatric diagnoses are not distinct categories of diseases, but rather labels describing behavior

[56] John A. Clausen, "The sociology of mental disorder." In Freeman *et al.,* p. 172.
[57] See T. R. Sarbin, *Psychology Today,* vol. 6, no. 18 (1972); and E. Schur, *American Journal of Sociology,* vol. 75, no. 309 (1969).

that is contrary to accepted social and psychological norms.[58] As Scheff put it,

The separation of the members of a society along the axis of sanity and insanity is largely a product of social rather than medical or scientific selection. Virtually all persons who are proposed by members of the community (or by public agencies such as the police) are accepted for treatment. The medical "examinations" that supposedly determine whether the candidate is sane or insane are, as a rule, peremptory and ritualistic. The actual goal in most of these examinations . . . seems not to be *whether* the candidate is mentally ill, but *which* illness he has.[59]

The diagnosis of schizophrenia, according to labeling theorists, has been particularly misused. The origins and causes of schizophrenia are largely unknown; most explanations are the subjects of disagreement and controversy. Furthermore, the symptoms which are supposed to indicate schizophrenia are, as we have seen, somewhat vague and variable. Yet, schizophrenia is today the most widely used diagnosis for serious mental illness. To labeling theorists, this suggests that the diagnosis of schizophrenia (and, by implication, many other diagnoses of mental illness) tends to reflect the cultural values of those who apply it rather than accurate scientific analysis. Individuals are not "schizophrenic," in the sense that they manifest symptoms of a disease. More likely than not, they are simply "rule-breakers," violating commonly accepted standards of behavior. For example, people who never talk to anyone else might in another society be tolerated and even accepted. In our own society, however, such people might well come to the attention of public agencies, and they might even be hospitalized as mentally ill. Applying the label "schizophrenic" or "mentally ill" thus is one of the ways a society can reinforce its own values and norms.

The problem with labeling people as mentally ill is threefold: First, such labels result in a certain rigidity of thinking. Behaviors that might otherwise be tolerated or even seen as interesting become defined as "sick." Moreover, these behaviors come to be regarded as something to be eliminated rather than as something to be understood. Second, the use and acceptance of such labels give public agencies the right to incarcerate people, sometimes against their will. Third—and this is the crucial point in labeling theory—labeling people as mentally ill may cause these people to accept this definition of themselves and never give up their roles as rule-breakers. In Scheff's words,

Rule breaking will generally be transitory (as when the stress causing rule breaking is removed . . .), compensated for, or channeled into some socially acceptable form. If, however, labeling occurs (that is, if the rule breaker is segregated as a stigmatized deviant), the rule breaking . . . may be stabilized; thus, the offender, through the agency of labeling, is launched on a career of "chronic mental illness." [60]

[58] T. Szasz, *The Myth of Mental Illness: Foundations of a Theory of Mental Illness.* Rev. ed. New York: Harper & Row, 1974.

[59] Thomas J. Scheff, "On reason and sanity: Some political implications of psychiatric thought." In Thomas J. Scheff, ed., *Labeling Madness.* Englewood Cliffs, N.J.: Prentice-Hall, 1975, pp. 16–17.

[60] Thomas J. Scheff, "Schizophrenia as ideology." In Scheff, pp. 5–12.

Many studies have demonstrated the influence of societal factors on a diagnosis of mental illness and the vagueness of such a diagnosis. Rosenhan, in a study we shall describe more fully later, found that psychologists and psychiatrists on the staffs of several mental hsopitals were unable to determine accurately which of the people they interviewed were mentally healthy or unhealthy.[61] Greenley found that the attitudes of the families of patients in a mental hospital were critical factors in how the illnesses of these patients were defined. If the family insisted that the patient be released, the psychiatrist in charge would generally agree. The patient, upon discharge, would then be defined in the doctor's conversation and in official records as "well enough to leave." Where there were no pressures for a patient to be released, the patient generally remained in the hospital for a longer period. He or she became defined as "too sick to leave." [62]

Along the same lines, Temerlin found that a person who is labeled as mentally ill tends to be regarded that way whatever the true nature of his or her condition. In this study, a professional actor was given a psychiatrist-prepared script of a psychological interview in which he described himself and his life in normally healthy terms. The taped interview was played for various groups of those treating the mentally disturbed in several hospitals and clinics. Before the tape was played, a prominent psychiatrist remarked to selected groups of listeners that the patient on the tape was "a very interesting man because he looks neurotic, but actually is quite psychotic." Of those hearing this suggestion, 60 percent of psychiatrists, 28 percent of clinical psychologists, and 11 percent of graduate student interns diagnosed various psychoses; no similar diagnoses were offered by control groups not hearing this suggestion. The strong effect of the prestige suggestion upon psychiatrists in the study indicates the strength of their professional identification with the prestige colleague, but may also, as Temerlin comments, be a problem due to "the nature of the concept of mental illness itself." [63]

MENTAL DISORDER AND SOCIAL STRUCTURE

Sociologists try to investigate the relationship between social factors and the incidence of mental disorders. For instance: Is mental disorder associated with social class? Does it occur more frequently in urban centers than in rural areas or suburbs? Among what age group is it most prevalent? Would changes in social conditions preclude or alleviate certain mental disorders?

The study of these relationships, however, is complicated by the difficulty of ascertaining the prevalence of mental disorder. We can count

[61] D. L. Rosenhan, "On being insane in insane places." *Science,* vol. 179, no. 4070 (January 19, 1973):250–258.
[62] James R. Greenley, "Alternative views of the psychiatrist's role." *Social Problems,* vol. 20, no. 2 (Fall 1972).
[63] Maurice K. Temerlin, "Suggestion effects in psychiatric diagnosis." In Scheff, pp. 46–54.

the number of patients in mental hospitals, and, somewhat less accurately, those receiving treatment in clinics and other outpatient facilities. It is far more difficult to obtain reliable statistics as to the number being treated in private practice. Moreover, any number of persons who would qualify as emotionally disturbed are not under treatment at all, and so do not appear in most estimates of mental disorders. Consequently, any statistics on treated mental disorder must be regarded as providing only a very rough estimate of the total number of people suffering from such problems. Nevertheless, sociologists have been able to establish a number of tentative conclusions about the relationship between mental disorders and social structure.

SOCIAL CLASS AND
MENTAL DISORDER

Much scientific knowledge has its origins in folk wisdom and common sense, and long before sociologists began to make systematic studies of social conditions and mental disorder, the connection between the two had been recognized by writers, artists, social workers, and many others concerned with the human condition. However, it was only in the 1930s that a serious sociological study of this relationship began; and while the results are not in perfect agreement, they offer some useful information.

One of the earliest studies, carried out in 1938 by Faris and Dunham,[64] reported on the residential pattern for 35,000 hospitalized mental patients from the city of Chicago. It was found that the highest rates of mental disorder occurred in the areas near the center of the city, where the population was poor, of very mixed background, and highly mobile. While this number included many cases of organic psychosis, due to syphilis and alcoholism in the "skid row" districts, it also included a significantly high rate of schizophrenia throughout the area. Conversely, the lowest rates of mental disorder were found in stable residential areas of higher socioeconomic status. Manic-depressive psychoses, however, were more randomly distributed than schizophrenia. The authors concluded that the seriously disorganized character of life in the central city was largely responsible for the high incidence of personal disorganization and mental illness.

A later study, by Hollingshead and Redlich,[65] sought to determine the relationship between social class and treated mental illness in New Haven, Connecticut. Whereas Faris and Dunham had studied only hospitalized patients, Hollingshead and Redlich obtained reasonably complete data on clinic and private patients as well. Using a socioeconomic scale running from class I (highest) to class V (lowest), they determined that the *incidence* (rate of occurrence in a year of new cases) and *prevalence* (number of cases existing on a given date) of psychosis were significantly higher in class V than in the other four classes. Schizophrenia was the most common psychosis in all classes, but it was especially prevalent in class V. However, as Redlich later pointed out, the study also revealed that the types of treatment and opportunities

---

[64] Robert E. L. Faris and H. Warren Dunham, *Mental Disorders in Urban Areas*. Chicago: University of Chicago Press, 1938.
[65] August B. Hollingshead and Frederick C. Redlich, *Social Class and Mental Illness: A Community Study*. New York: Wiley, 1958.

for rehabilitation available to the lower classes were much less satisfactory than those for the upper classes, and this may have contributed to the proliferation of schizophrenia in class V. Another possible factor is brought out by Miller and Mishler in commenting on the Hollingshead-Redlich study: they cite evidence that "the same set of presenting symptoms is diagnosed as more severe when the patient is perceived . . . to be a working class person than when he is seen as middle class." [66] Such inconsistency in diagnosis could have inflated the figures for class V. (See Figure 2-2.)

A third study, by William Rushing,[67] tended to confirm this relationship between mental disorder and social class. This study includes a relatively large number of cases occurring over an extended time interval, and thus overcomes some of the shortcomings of earlier, more limited investigations. Rushing studied 4,650 males admitted for the first time to mental hospitals in Washington, D.C., between 1954 and 1956. He found that the rate of hospitalization for lower-class males was higher than that for all others; that hospitalization varied inversely with class; and that while the rate increased steadily with each drop in social class, the increase from the next-to-lowest to the lowest class was disproportionately large. Rushing considered that the high incidence in the lowest class might be explained by the fact that people of low socioeconomic status are most frequently in contact with the courts, welfare workers, and other officials who are in a position to refer them for hospitalization; moreover, they are less likely to be protected, tolerated, or financially supported by their families, to whom they have become a burden.

All of these studies, then, are in agreement that psychosis in general, and schizophrenia in particular, are much more common at the lowest socioeconomic level than elsewhere. However, they do not indicate whether most of these schizophrenics originated in class V, or whether they drifted down to it as their disorder increased. In other words, they fail to make clear whether low socioeconomic status is primarily a cause or an effect of serious mental disorder. One other study bears on this point.

The Midtown Manhattan Study, by Srole and Langer and their associates,[68] went beyond treatment data to include a random sample of 1,660 adult residents of Manhattan's midtown area. They found that almost 23 percent were significantly impaired in mental functions, including many persons not under treatment. One of the factors investigated was the socioeconomic status, not only of the subjects, but also of their parents. It was found that, among subjects judged to be seriously impaired in their mental functioning, twice as many had lower-class as upper-class parents. Among those judged to be well, more than twice as many had upper-class parents. This suggests a definite influence of socioeconomic status on the mental health of the developing child.

---

[66] See S. M. Miller and Elliot G. Mishler, "Social class, mental illness, and American psychiatry: An expository review." *Milbank Memorial Fund Quarterly* 37 (April 1959):1–26.

[67] William Rushing, "Two patterns in the relationship between social class and mental hospitalization." *American Sociological Review* 34 (August 1969):533–541.

[68] Leo Srole *et al., Mental Health in the Metropolis: The Midtown Manhattan Study.* Rev. ed. New York: Harper & Row, 1975.

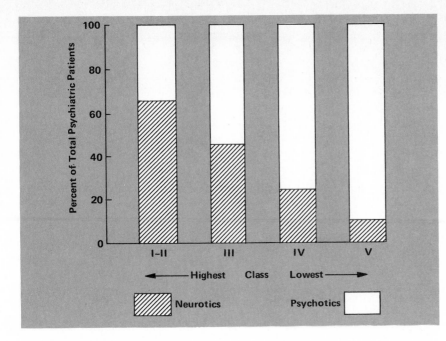

FIGURE 2-2
Percentage of
Neurotics and
Psychotics Among
Total Psychiatric
Patients, by Class

Source: August B. Hollingshead and Frederick C.
Redlich, *Social Class and
Mental Illness: A Com-
munity Study.* New York:
Wiley, 1958. Reprinted
by permission.

One question that has interested sociologists is the effect of social mobility—movement from one socioeconomic level to another—on the incidence of mental disorders. The Midtown Manhattan Study suggested a stronger relationship of downward than of upward mobility to severe mental disorder. However, in a research review, Kleiner and Parker [69] distinguish between *social mobility* (actual achieved mobility of the individual) and *mobility orientation* (the discrepancy between the individual's aspirations and actual status). They suggest that orientation is significantly more related to mental disorder than mobility alone. Presumably, individuals who feel they should have attained a higher (or a lower) status are more likely to become disturbed than those who accept their status, whatever it may be. Kleiner and Parker caution, however, that unrealistic aspirations (high or low) may be a result of mental disorder as well as a cause of it. They suggest that more research is needed to make clearer the relationship between social mobility and mental disorder.

Social Class and Treatment. We have already mentioned Rushing's speculation that lower-class patients are more likely to be hospitalized, because they are more often in contact with the courts, welfare workers, and others who are likely to think in terms of treatment by hospitalization. The Hollingshead-Redlich study seems to support this: in the lowest class, 52 percent of the psychotic patients were referred for treatment by the police and courts and 20 percent by social agencies; whereas in the highest class over 70 percent were referred by themselves or by family and friends. The conclusion drawn by the authors is that

[69] Robert J. Kleiner and Seymour Parker, "Goal striving, social status, and mental disorder." *American Sociological Review* 28 (April 1963):169–203.

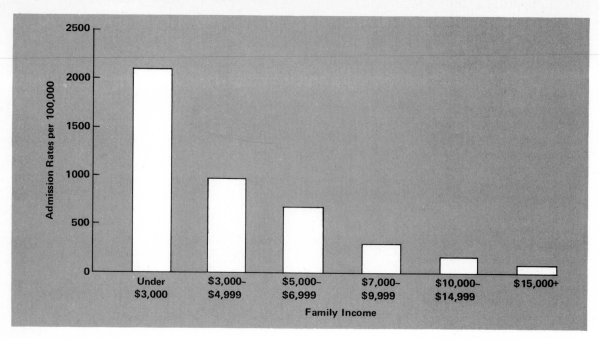

FIGURE 2-3
Annual Admission
Rates to Outpatient
Psychiatric Services
by Family Income

*Source: Statistical Note
#47.* National Institute of
Mental Health, Survey and
Reports Section, Biometry
Branch.

there is a definite tendency to induce disturbed persons in Classes I and II to
see a psychiatrist in more gentle and "insightful" ways than is the practice
in Class IV and especially in Class V, where direct, authoritative, compulsory,
and at times, coercively brutal methods were used.[70]

Even when lower-class individuals actively seek treatment, their socioeconomic position may be against them. A study by Myers and Schaffer
of class differences in a community clinic illustrates this. The clinic in
question, which treated mainly neurotics, had a system of nominal and
scaled fees, so that, in theory, it should have been equally available to
persons at all levels. And, in fact, persons from all but class I did apply
for treatment. However, of the class V persons who applied, only about
one-third were recommended for acceptance by the interviewing staff,
compared to about four-fifths in class IV and nine-tenths in classes II
and III. In addition, lower-class individuals who were accepted were
likely to be treated for shorter periods of time and by less-qualified
personnel—psychiatrists in training, or medical students taking a four-
week course—than were the upper-class patients. Myers and Schaffer
suggest that some of this may have resulted from communication and
value differences—that the psychiatrists, who were mainly from classes I
and II, found it difficult to relate effectively to class IV and V patients.
The staff is reported to have found that these applicants were often "not
psychologically minded" or "lacked motivation for psychotherapy." The
authors suggest that "perhaps psychiatrists need to acquire new symbols
and values in dealing with lower-class patients; or perhaps new ap-

[70] Hollingshead and Redlich.

proaches are necessary to bring psychotherapy to such persons."[71] (See Figure 2-3.)

It is not unreasonable to suppose that such class differences in treatment would affect recovery rate. A ten-year follow-up of the Hollingshead-Redlich study by Myers, Bean, and Pepper[72] reported on the 1960 treatment status of all patients included in the original sample. It was found that among those who had been hospitalized in 1950, more lower-class than upper-class individuals were still hospitalized in 1960. Particularly low rates of release were found for those who had received primarily custodial care, and for state hospital, as opposed to private or veterans' hospital, inmates. Lower-class individuals, of course, are likely to fall into the categories with low rates of release. The authors also suggest that social factors in the community are partly responsible for the different release rates: middle- and upper-class families are more apt to have available resources for consultation and outpatient treatment of family members who still require some amount of care and supervision, and may therefore be more willing to take them back.

It seems clear that whether or not lower-class persons are in greater danger of becoming emotionally disturbed, once they have become so, their chances for quality treatment and eventual recovery are substantially lower than those of their upper- and middle-class counterparts.

URBANIZATION

Cities have always had a rather bad press in America. It is one of our cultural predispositions to believe that most of what ails city dwellers can be remedied by getting them off the streets and into the country. Hence it is not surprising that we tend to assume a connection between city life and mental disorder. Unfortunately, there has so far been very little comparative research on mental disorder in urban and non-urban areas, so that no conclusive test of the assumption is yet available. Investigation is rendered more difficult by the fact that mental disorder is more likely to be diagnosed and treated where facilities are readily accessible—which usually means in and around cities. Studies of treated mental disorder, therefore, can only be used with great caution for city-country comparison.

The Midtown Manhattan Study, the major urban study dealing with how mental disorder is distributed among a general population, did reveal a high percentage of disturbance within an adult sample. Only about 18 percent of the respondents were rated as "well"; roughly 60 percent showed mild to moderate symptoms of disorder, and slightly over 20 percent were significantly impaired in their functioning. However, a study by Eaton and Weil[73] of the rural Hutterite communities

[71] Jerome K. Meyers and Leslie Schaffer, "Social stratification and psychiatric practice: A study of an outpatient clinic." *American Sociological Review* 19 (June 1954):307–310.

[72] Jerome K. Meyers, Lee L. Bean, and Max P. Pepper, "Social class and psychiatric disorders: A ten year follow-up." *Journal of Health and Social Behavior* (Summer 1965):74–79.

[73] Joseph W. Eaton and Robert J. Weil, *Culture and Mental Disorders.* New York: Free Press, 1955.

of Montana, the Dakotas, and Canada did not reveal an especially low percentage, as might have been expected. The rate of severe mental illness among the Hutterites, a homogeneous and closely knit Anabaptist group with strong European roots, was about equal to the rate of hospitalized mental illness in New York State. In a comparison with studies of the incidence of mental disorder in ten other groups, the Hutterites ranked third. They did differ from the usual urban group in having a higher proportion of manic-depressive than schizophrenic individuals; and they tended to care for their mentally ill at home rather than placing them in hospitals.

Other studies have suggested that it is not urban life *per se,* but the deteriorated quality of life which often develops in the central city that creates a high level of mental disorder. Freedman investigated the effects of crowding on the performance and behavior of individuals. The reported experiment involved intense crowding of small groups of people for a few hours at a time, and the author warns that the effects of the less intense long-term crowding characteristic of city life have not yet been proved to be the same. Nevertheless, the results are interesting. Performance of the subjects on various tasks was unaffected by the degree of crowding. Behavior, on the other hand, was affected—but in precisely opposite ways for men and women. Men became more competitive and more negative in their judgments and reactions to other people, in the crowded situation; women, in the same situation, became less competitive, more intimate and friendly. When the results for men and women were combined, there was no significant statistical effect of crowding. On the basis of this last finding, Freedman concludes that the emotionally harmful effects of urban life are a consequence not so much of crowded living in itself as of the environmental difficulties which crowding usually brings with it—dirt, noise, transportation problems, inadequate housing, and so on.[74]

OTHER SOCIAL FACTORS

Other factors which have been investigated for their relationship to mental disorder include race and sex. Thus studies have found, for example, that there are proportionately about 33 percent more blacks in mental hospitals than whites.[75] In large part such differences can be explained in terms of factors we have already described: Blacks (and poor people, a large part of whom are black) are much more likely to be seen as requiring hospitalization rather than whites, who are seen as best suited for psychotherapy. Blacks are also much more likely to come into contact with social agencies, including mental health officials. Finally, blacks are more likely than whites to live in the deprived urban environments cited earlier by Freedman.

Scott's review of research on the social-psychological correlates of mental illness [76] mentions findings that blacks have a higher incidence

[74] Jonathan Freedman, "The effects of crowding on human performance and social behavior." In F. J. McGuigan and Paul J. Woods, eds., *Contemporary Studies in Psychology.* Englewood Cliffs, N.J.: Prentice-Hall, 1972.

[75] Seham, p. 11.

[76] William A. Scott, "Social psychological correlates of mental illness and mental health." *Psychological Bulletin* 55 (March 1958):65, 72–87.

of psychosis than whites, but that among blacks there is less association between psychosis and low-prestige occupations. The different relationship between occupational status and psychosis for blacks and for whites in America can be explained in part by a lesser importance attached to upward social mobility in the traditional black society. After all, when most middle-class jobs were closed to blacks by the very fact of their color, black people with any steady job could feel they were proving their worth fairly well. However, most blacks today are refusing to accept the lower rank so long assigned to them by American culture, and are aspiring to opportunities long enjoyed by the dominant white majority. It may be expected that some types of disorder will increase among blacks as their aspirations outstrip their present achievements, pushing them to strive for ever better education, jobs, and social acceptance. And some of the most successfully mobile blacks may suffer most, by being cut off from their black-culture background.

Seymour Leventman [77] anticipates that something of this sort will actually take place. Leventman discusses the difference between the relatively impersonal, functionally oriented mass society of modern times and the more organic, ethnically based, familial-religious minority group. He feels that a critical factor in the change from the one to the other is the ability of members of minorities to break free of caste-like job limitations, such as the assignment of blacks to domestic or unskilled labor. Once they have done this, they begin to acquire a status based on occupation rather than on ethnic background, and to take on more of the characteristics of the general society of people at a similar social and economic level. Consequently, both the stresses they encounter and the interpretations placed by others on their actions will begin to change, and among the results will be a change in their pattern of mental disorder.

Only half humorously, Leventman predicts that as blacks become more self-aware and gain more economic and social freedom, they will be able to choose more "prestigeful" mental disorders—neuroses, character disorders, psychosomatic illnesses—instead of the old "lower-class" psychoses. Then, he concludes, with these illnesses and a full stock of standard mass-society anxieties, blacks "will know they have truly 'made it.'" Of course, the validity of these predictions depends on the assumption that the main structure, the dominant mass-society pattern and middle-class ideals, of American society will remain the same, and that blacks and other minority group members will accommodate themselves to it. In view of some of the new ideas and movements of recent years, this may not be an entirely safe assumption.

Women and Mental Disorders. According to Phyllis Chesler,[78] women have much higher rates of admission to mental hospitals than men, and women also have much higher rates of depression. Chesler suggests that the nature and incidence of mental disorder among women are a reflection of women's secondary status and restricted roles in our society.

[77] Seymour Leventman, "Race and mental illness in mass society." *Social Problems* 16 (Summer 1968):73–78.
[78] Phyllis Chesler, *Women and Madness*. New York: Avon, 1972.

Women are expected to conform to rigidly defined standards of behavior —to be passive, dependent, and emotional, for example, in accordance with traditional feminine roles. Women are therefore more likely than men to find their roles restrictive, and to become depressed if they cannot conform to them. Also, because the range of behaviors they are permitted is narrow, women are more likely than men to behave in ways that are considered unacceptable—especially to other men. Since mental health professionals are predominantly male, women who behave in non-traditional ways are therefore more likely to be defined as mentally disturbed. (See also Chapter 8.)

Chesler cites one study in which mental health clinicians were asked to identify healthy male traits, healthy female traits, and healthy adult traits. It was found that the majority of clinicians hold different standards of mental health for men and women, and that these standards followed traditional sex-role stereotypes. Thus, healthy women were considered to be those who were unaggressive, submissive, excitable, and vain. Other studies cited by Chesler confirm that such attitudes are indeed acted upon by mental health professionals. For example, it was found that the major difference between female ex-mental patients who were rehospitalized and those who were not was that the rehospitalized patients had refused to perform their domestic "duties"—cleaning, cooking, and the like. Females were also found more likely to be labeled as schizophrenics for behavior that was considered acceptable for men.

In a study of depression among middle-aged women, Bart [79] found that women who accepted their traditional female roles became depressed when these roles were no longer useful—when children grew up and left home, for example. It is likely that as the social climate changes, fewer women will feel the need to fulfill traditional expectations. We can then anticipate, to paraphrase Leventman, that women, too, will be able to choose more prestigious mental disorders, and will then "know they have truly 'made it.'" Again, however, this may not be an entirely safe assumption.

THE TREATMENT OF MENTAL DISORDERS

Having considered the nature and some of the causes of mental disorder, we turn now to the matter of treatment—the principal techniques, and the social institutions through which these are made available. A brief sketch of the history of mental health care will enable us to understand the picture today.

It is only recently that mental disturbance has been considered an "illness" which could be cured. In the Middle Ages people looked upon mental aberration as a sign from God, a symptom of demonic power, or evidence of the supernatural. These attitudes continued for centuries,

THE HISTORICAL BACKGROUND

[79] Pauline B. Bart, "Depression in middle-aged women." In Vivian Gormick and Barbara K. Moran, eds., *Woman in Sexist Society*. New York: Basic Books, 1971, pp. 163–186.

with the mentally deranged being displayed for amusement, locked up in prisons, or left to starve in streets and fields.

Change began with the innovations of Philippe Pinel, a French physician who, during the French Revolution, removed the chains of asylum inmates and showed that they would respond to kindness and consideration. Pinel's treatment of the mentally deranged inspired the creation of a number of "moral treatment" centers throughout Europe and America, but the vast majority of the insane continued to be locked up as before.

Reform in the United States began with the work of Dorothea Dix, a New England humanitarian who led the fight for the establishment of state-supported mental hospitals, first in New England and then in other areas. With growing numbers of inmates, however, the hospitals which were established tended to become prisonlike institutions designed to protect the public from the mentally disturbed and the latter from each other and even from themselves. The next major impetus to reform came from Clifford Beers, whose depressing experience as a mental patient in a New Haven hospital led him to work for the reform of mental institutions and treatment. By publicizing his own harrowing trials in the mental hospital, in *A Mind That Found Itself,* Beers [80] won public support for reform and engineered the establishment of the National Committee for Mental Hygiene in 1909.

The emergence of professional social casework in the 1920s gave further impetus to public support of mental health care. But it was the depression of the 1930s which forced the recognition that mental disorder could not be explained simply as individual maladjustment to a good social order—that unhealthy social forces were themselves partly to blame. This view was aided by the theoretical work of the psychiatrist Harry Stack Sullivan and his followers. Whereas earlier psychiatrists had sought the cause of mental disorder wholly within the individual, Sullivan held that mental disorder is basically a disturbance of interpersonal relationships, and is thus social in origin.[81]

During World War II, psychiatrists were frequently called upon to treat soldiers suffering from breakdown under the stresses of combat, and to screen out in advance those who would be unable to function under stress. As psychiatrists became an important national asset—necessary for the war effort and crucial for the rehabilitation of soldiers who had suffered during the war—the government began to appropriate more funds for mental health and to set up more organizations for the study and treatment of mental disorder. In 1946 the National Mental Health Act was passed, and three years later the National Institute of Mental Health was established. Since then, federal funds have increasingly been available to support research and training and to help subsidize the establishment of community mental health services. State funds, also expanded, have been used largely to improve the facilities and staffs of the state mental hospitals.

---

[80] Clifford W. Beers, *A Mind That Found Itself: An Autobiography.* Doubleday: New York, 1948.

[81] See, for example, Harry Stack Sullivan, *The Interpersonal Theory of Psychiatry.* New York: Norton, 1963; and *Clinical Studies in Psychiatry,* New York: Norton, 1956.

The question in recent years has, in fact, been as much one of how to spend allotted funds as of whether or not to allot them. While most money after World War II was spent on psychiatric research and the construction of mental hospitals, more attention and funds are now being directed toward the establishment of community mental health centers and outpatient clinics. These centers reflect an increased awareness that society in general and the community in particular may be instrumental in both aggravating and alleviating the mental disorders of many patients. They focus attention upon the social causes or ramifications of the disturbance, and seek to reintegrate patients with their communities through short periods of hospitalization and subsequent outpatient care.

MODERN APPROACHES

The scientific treatment of mental disorder began with attention to the individual sufferer. And despite our more recent realization of the importance of social factors, the traditional individual methods, and variations of them, continue to be employed, whether in the hospital-and-private-office framework or in the context of the new community orientation. We shall look briefly at several of the main techniques of therapy, and then consider the treatment structure itself, and some of the ways in which it can facilitate or impede the patient's recovery. It should be stressed that most modern therapists do not restrict themselves to any one school or approach, but rather use a variety of methods to suit the special needs of each patient.

Psychotherapy. Most of the major types of treatment fall into the general category of psychotherapy. Individuals are helped to understand the underlying reasons for their troubles, and then, in the light of this understanding, to work out a solution. The process is guided by means of some form of personal interaction, usually between patient and therapist, but sometimes also among patients in small groups (group therapy).

The classic system of psychotherapy is *psychoanalysis*. Developed by Sigmund Freud in the late nineteenth century, psychoanalysis seeks to uncover the unconscious motives, memories, and fears which may prevent a person from functioning happily and achieving his or her desired goals. During a series of analytic sessions, patients are encouraged to say whatever comes into their mind, report on their dreams, and explore other avenues of discovery. In this way, the analyst hopes to discover those desires and thoughts which are being repressed by the conscious mind and causing conflict. Once uncovered, they can be rationally examined and understood, and patients can learn to direct the underlying drives into acceptable channels.

Client-centered or nondirective therapy was developed by Carl Rogers in the 1940s. Whereas Freud believed that the treatment of mental disorder requires an uncovering of deeply buried motives and past experiences, and that the patient needs a great deal of expert help and information over a long period of time to accomplish this, Rogers tended to concentrate more on the client's present problems. He also assumed that when given the opportunity and allowed to proceed at their own pace, people who are willing to keep trying can solve their own emotional problems. Therefore, in this system, the patient takes the initiative, chooses the topic and direction, and sets the pace of the therapy session. The role of the therapist is to rephrase the patient's statements, thus clarifying his or her thoughts and feelings and providing a supportive atmosphere. Given this support, the creative and integrative powers of the individual can do the rest. Client-centered therapy generally works best with persons who are reasonably strongly motivated.

Whereas nondirective therapy leaves the initiative almost completely to the patient, *directive therapy* assigns it very actively to the therapist. Directive therapy is actually not so much a technique as an approach— the idea that therapists should use every legitimate means to teach, lead, and influence the patient in accordance with the therapist's understanding of the problem. This may mean explaining to patients the meaning and causes of their behavior; it may involve changing, or instructing them to change, the outward conditions of their lives, so as to facilitate learning new behavior patterns; it may entail the use of techniques such as hypnosis and behavior modification (see below). The goal is still insight for patients into their condition, but the major responsibility has been taken over by the therapist. Directive therapy may get results more quickly than psychoanalysis or the nondirective approach, and it may be useful with less verbal patients.

Group therapy is a recent and popular innovation. It is designed to provide a situation in which individuals can interact with other people, discover the needs and experiences they share, help and be helped, without fear of being rejected or condemned. Therapy groups usually consist of from eight to ten people, meeting together with the therapist once or twice a week, and the atmosphere is generally nondirective. Sometimes special techniques may be employed—physical contact to build up a warm emotional atmosphere, or psychodrama, in which patients assume different roles in order to act out repressed feelings connected with difficult events in their lives, or to explore alternative ways of reacting to situations.

Therapy groups are usually composed of people with relatively similar problems. Some organizations formed to deal with common problems use a modified group-therapy approach—Synanon, Alcoholics Anonymous, Weight Watchers. A very recent and promising application is in family therapy—the treatment of disturbed individuals within their families, so that not only the diagnosed problem but the unsatisfactory interpersonal situation which contributed to it may be resolved.

Hypnosis, Shock Treatment, and Chemotherapy. *Hypnosis* is sometimes used to aid patients in remembering deeply repressed material that they are otherwise unable to recall; this technique is used when it appears that a specific repressed memory may be preventing a patient's positive response to psychotherapy, or by practitioners who have a particular interest in this technique. *Shock treatment,* developed during the 1930s, was particularly helpful for deeply depressed and some schizophrenic patients. An electric shock is administered, which produces a brief convulsion and a short period of unconsciousness. While such treatments will sometimes result in quite dramatic relief of severe depression, shock therapy is frightening to many persons, and can be dangerous.

More recently, it has been largely supplanted by *chemotherapy,* the use of drugs for specific purposes. After World War II sodium pentothal was used on veterans suffering from "shell shock," combat-associated breakdown, to aid them in recalling traumatic events that had been repressed. In the 1950s, *tranquilizers* came to be used to calm intensely excited or overactive patients. Stronger tranquilizers (such as chlorpromazine, or Thorazine) can sometimes be of particular value with schizophrenics, while milder tranquilizers (such as meprobamate, or Miltown) can help less troubled people to relax. *Antidepressants* are used with patients who are withdrawn, apathetic, or deeply depressed. None of these drugs in itself cures mental disorder; rather, by easing the intensity of emotional reaction, they allow patients to use their faculties and to respond better to the therapist. In some cases they enable them to remain at home and receive outpatient therapy instead of being committed to a mental hospital. However, there is a tendency on the part of many patients to overuse such medication. Also, medication is too often prescribed, instead of using other therapies. While medication may make patients more manageable in the short run, the substitution of a temporary palliative for effective treatment accomplishes little, if anything, in the long run. (See Chapter 3.)

Behavior Modification. The theory behind psychotherapy holds that unacceptable behavior is the result of a maladjusted personality. Another school of thought takes the reverse position—that behavior is the cause,

Historically, the mentally disturbed have been treated inhumanely. This painting depicts an early advocate of humane treatment for the mentally ill, Philippe Pinel, releasing the chained inmates of an eighteenth-century insane asylum.
Courtesy of National Library of Medicine

personality the result. Somehow individuals have learned—have been conditioned—to respond in an unsatisfactory manner, and this has prevented them from relating in a healthy manner to their social environment. Thus a child may have been taught always to behave aggressively, or always to be silent and withdrawn. If the child can learn a more effective pattern of behavior toward other people, he or she will have a better chance of having normal relationships and a healthy personality. Therapy, then, according to this approach, is a matter of learning—in fact, it is reconditioning.

The behavior therapist may use any one of a number of learning techniques in order to replace the patient's maladaptive behavior with more useful responses. Fearful and anxious behavior can be dealt with by *desensitization*—that is, by strengthening a natural response which cannot coexist with fear and anxiety. Usually the patient is taught first to relax, and then to practice relaxing while in closer and closer proximity to the feared object or situation. Eventually the fear reaction is overcome by the stronger habit of relaxation.

Another method used in behavior modification is *reinforcement.* This is based on the idea that if patients learn that behaving in a certain way will gain them a desired reward, their impulse toward that behavior is reinforced. Eventually they will be able to maintain the behavior without the reward. Reinforcement techniques have been used very successfully in some mental hospitals: A system of jobs or behaviors, such as washing dishes, is set up, with a clearly specified reward in the form of tokens for the performance of each task. The tokens can be exchanged for rewards, ranging from a pack of cigarettes to weekends at home. Patients gain satisfaction and grow in self-confidence as they find that they can earn tokens and privileges.

A third behavior modification technique is *modeling,* or imitation, in which the individual is shown someone else doing the desired thing and encouraged to imitate the model. In a number of experiments, persons with phobic fears of snakes or of dogs have been successfully treated in this way. Modeling works particularly well with children, who are still young enough that they naturally learn many things by imitation.

Mental Hospitals. From the time of Pinel until well into the twentieth century, mental health care meant, in practice, mental hospitals. The insane were to be sheltered within protecting institutions from the buffets of a hostile world, kept from harming themselves or others, and given such help and treatment as might be available. Administrators of some of the early hospitals were aware of the importance of individual care and a positive atmosphere. Charles Dickens, describing one small New England "retreat" which he visited in 1842, speaks "of the evening lectures and concerts, of the gardening, fishing, and hunting, of the availability of horses and carriages for drives in the country," and concludes, "It is obvious that one great factor of this system is the inculcation and encouragement, even among such unhappy persons, of a decent self-respect." [82]

THE ORGANIZATION OF TREATMENT

82 Harold L. Raush with Charlotte L. Raush, *The Halfway House Movement: A Search for Sanity.* Englewood Cliffs, N.J.: Prentice-Hall (ACC), 1968, pp. 3–4, 11.

Such an approach was possible in an era of small private hospitals. As the government began to take over responsibility for the care of the mentally disturbed, the ideal of a "retreat" remained. Hospitals were built in secluded spots, and surrounded by high walls and locked gates. Within the walls, all the patient's needs were to be provided for. But the purpose of the hospital was not merely to protect patients from society and if possible to cure them; it was also to protect society from the patients. The old stereotype of the "raving lunatic" persisted, and imperceptibly security came to be treated as more important than therapy. The insane were safely tucked away, no longer disturbing the rest of society; and, as usually happens in human affairs, out of sight was largely out of mind.

In the interest of economy and efficiency, there eventually developed the system of enormous hospitals, each housing several thousand patients, staffed largely by aides whose main job was to keep things under control, and run on as low a budget as a state legislature could reasonably supply. One fairly typical "modern" hospital was described [83] as having 3,500 patients and a total staff of 707, not including the psychiatrists. Nearly all the psychiatrists, including the superintendent, were foreign-born, and many were handicapped by a very poor knowledge of English. Of the rest of the staff, 594 were aides, none with more than rudimentary training in modern treatment procedures. The rest included nurses, social workers, activities workers, and a small staff of clinical psychologists. The operating budget of the hospital was about $5.25 per patient per day. Under these circumstances, and despite efforts at improvement, it was quite impossible for the majority of the patients to receive more than minimal treatment and routine custodial care.

Staffing such hospitals is a perennial problem. Salaries are usually low, conditions of work are often unattractive or discouraging, and professionally trained personnel are understandably tempted to go to private hospitals, clinics, or into private practice, where the rewards, both in money and in visible therapeutic achievement, are greater. Considering the number of years of training which go into the making of a clinical psychologist, a psychiatrist, or any other fully qualified mental health care professional, it is small wonder that most of them prefer to work where they can feel they are "really accomplishing something." Consequently, public institutions must depend heavily on partially trained personnel, and particularly on the attendants, or nursing aides. These attendants, though not fully qualified, are the persons most constantly in contact with the patients, and typically control most aspects of their daily lives, including access to doctors.

It is also becoming increasingly clear that the design of many of these older buildings may actually do emotional harm to patients. All of us are affected by our surroundings, and mental patients are no exception. High ceilings, endless labyrinthine corridors, huge wards lined with rows of matching beds, lack of color, lack of privacy—all may tend to increase depression or disturbance and undo the benefits of therapy.

For this reason, mental hospitals now being built often aim at a

---

[83] Donald R. Peterson, "The study of a social system: Elba State Hospital." In Donald R. Peterson, *The Clinical Study of Social Behavior*. Englewood Cliffs, N.J.: Prentice-Hall (ACC), 1968, pp. 202–220.

maximum degree of flexibility, while incorporating current insights into the needs of those suffering from mental disorders. Construction is low and open: space is planned to allow for small-group relationships and a variety of normal and constructive activities, and to provide the necessary minimum of security without creating a prison atmosphere. However, building mental hospitals entails enormous expense; and since the problems of the institutionalized mentally ill do not have a high priority in our society, a sufficient number of new hospitals are not being built.

The need for proper staff is also beginning to be faced, if only in a minimal way. In a 1972 decision, a federal district court laid down minimum guidelines for two Alabama institutions which, if followed, would result in a ratio of about four staff members to every five patients, as compared with about one to five in the midwestern hospital described earlier. If such guidelines are implemented, and if they become usual, the future prospects of the public-hospital mental patient will be considerably improved.

While state and county hospitals account for the great majority of institutionalized mental patients in the United States, a substantial number are cared for by the Veterans Administration in its own large hospitals, and by psychiatric units in many general hospitals, and a much smaller number in private hospitals. The private facilities present an almost total contrast to the public institutions. They are usually small, well staffed, and oriented toward intensive, short-term treatment. Unfortunately, most of them are, unavoidably, expensive. Most families of mentally disturbed persons simply cannot afford to pay the fees of such institutions. (However, Medicaid has enabled some lower-income patients to be treated in these facilities.) Perhaps the greatest value of the private hospital is in the area of research and training, because concepts and methods developed here, where numbers are small and organization flexible, can be applied eventually to improving the situation in other, larger hospitals.

But there is a growing body of evidence that hospitalization may not always be the best solution, even in good hospitals and for the psychotic patient. Long-term studies of patients have shown that those who do not improve enough to be discharged fairly soon are likely to remain for a long time, if not indefinitely. In part this results from the hospital inadequacies already discussed, but in part it seems to be a consequence of the very fact of hospitalization. This is the position taken by Erving Goffman, who developed the concept of the "total institution." Goffman defines a total institution as

a place of residence and work where a large number of like-situated individuals, cut off from the wider society for an appreciable period of time, together lead an enclosed, formally administered round of life.[84]

Such institutions include mental hospitals, prisons, convents and monasteries of the traditional sort, army posts, ships, boarding schools, and various other establishments. Goffman believes that every organization or institution tends, to a certain extent, to try to force people into a mold,

[84] Erving Goffman, *Asylums: Essays on the Social Situation of Mental Patients and Other Inmates.* Garden City, N.Y.: Doubleday, 1961, p. xiii.

So long as patients do not cause trouble, they may be left largely to their own devices in the bare wards of many huge, understaffed mental institutions.
Jerry Cooke/Photo Researchers

to shape them to the purposes of the institution; but that the total institution, just because inmates are subject to it all the time and in all aspects of their lives, is able to do this shaping and molding to a degree much more complete and profound than other, partial institutions. This may have serious harmful effects on people's sense of self, and consequently on their ability to function outside the total institution.

The social setting, interpersonal interactions, and physical setting of people's lives, Goffman points out, form the basic material out of which they construct their sense of self. In the mental hospital, all of these factors tend to downgrade them—to impress upon them their inadequacy, their failure, and their incompetence as adults and to deprive them of any way to assert their individuality. This results from a number of factors in the hospital situation. One of these is the perennial need for economy in most hospitals—the hospital can be run much more cheaply, for instance, if patients wear uniform clothing, live in quarters with uniform furnishings, and follow a regimented program of activities. The custodial function of the hospital is another factor, since patients can be managed much more easily if they are rendered docile and unassertive

—if they can be brought to accept the staff's idea of what is good for them. Finally, the official psychiatric emphasis of the hospital works in the same direction, since the fundamental medical justification for the patients' commitment requires that they be considered sick and unable to function satisfactorily in the outside community—an assumption that Goffman would challenge in a substantial number of cases. Since the psychiatric approach to treatment requires the inmates' cooperation, they must be induced to take the hospital's view of themselves; and this entails an interpretation of their past lives as a process of failure, of becoming sick. Any act of self-assertion or of rebellion against the institutional arrangements will probably be interpreted as further evidence of illness, and patients will be expected to take that view of it themselves. Release from the hospital is often contingent upon their acceptance, or apparent acceptance, of the official interpretation of their hospital and prehospital life. Finally, Goffman believes, the social stigma of being in a mental hospital can tend to further alienate the patients from society, leading them in some cases to be unwilling to leave the hospital even when they could be released. In short, Goffman concludes that in most cases the probability is high that hospitalization will do more harm than good.

The Rosenhan study mentioned earlier in this chapter sheds light on the conditions within mental hospitals and, in addition, raises provocative questions about the criteria that are used for accepting and releasing patients. Eight "pseudopatients" arrived at the admissions office of several hospitals complaining that they had heard voices speaking words like "hollow" and "thud." These symptoms were selected because there was no record of any such symptoms in psychological literature. Beyond falsifying symptoms, name, vocation, and employment, the pseudopatients were entirely truthful about their personal lives. All were immediately admitted to the hospitals, most having been diagnosed as schizophrenic; once admitted, the pseudopatients never again complained about voices and behaved in an entirely normal manner. Nevertheless, none of the hospital staff discovered that the pseudopatients were sane; many of the real patients, however, detected the subterfuge almost immediately, and assumed the pseudopatients were journalists or researchers. When the pseudopatients were released, it was with a diagnosis of "schizophrenia in remission"—that is, they were not considered sane or even cured, but simply as no longer manifesting any symptoms. In a follow-up study, a hospital that had heard of these findings was told that over a period of three months, some pseudopatients were going to attempt to gain admission into the hospital. Staff members were asked to judge which applicants to the hospital were faking illness. Over this three-month period, at least 41 patients were judged to be pseudopatients. In fact, none were.

The results of this study were widely cited as evidence of the labeling theory, in that the diagnosis of illness—or health—was applied regardless of the actual condition of the patient. But it is what the pseudopatients observed while in the hospital that interests us here. Though staff members were helpful and even dedicated, their behavior toward the patients left much to be desired. As much as possible, staff members were kept apart from patients, behind a glass enclosure. Psychiatrists, in particular, almost never appeared on the wards. When staff members were approached by pseudopatients with questions, their most common responses were to ignore the questions or to mumble something—avoiding eye contact all the while—and quickly move on. Patients were sometimes punished excessively for misbehavior, and in one case a patient was beaten. The entire atmosphere was characterized, in Rosenhan's words, by "powerlessness and depersonalization."

Patients do, of course, contrive all sorts of ways to defend themselves against self-destroying influences. One common though harmful way is for patients to retreat into an inner "fantasy life" which more or less shuts out outer circumstances and events. Some recent reforms in hospital procedures have been aimed at dealing with the problems caused by hospitalization, and progress has been made. But a more revolutionary development is the idea, made practical by the existence of therapeutic drugs, that mentally disordered persons should be treated in their own community, within as nearly normal a pattern of everyday life as possible. This brings us to the growing field of what is known as community psychology.

Community Psychology. Outpatient treatment for mental disorders is far from new, but until recently it has been largely confined to the milder, neurotic disorders, and, in considerable degree, to the middle and upper classes. As a rule, the tendency in the past, particularly among private practitioners and to a lesser extent in clinics and group services, has been to treat the patient in relative isolation from the social situation. This is not to say that therapists have ignored the importance of the social situation, but that, perhaps under the influence of the generally accepted "illness" concept of mental disorder, they have usually waited for the individual patient to come to them, and have then considered the disturbed state of affairs within that patient to be their main concern. Cowen [85] speaks of "a mental health orientation that begins at the point of pathology and focuses on subsequent rehabilitation." While treatment within this approach has been of help to many people, it has certain practical disadvantages as a means of large-scale mental health care:

1. People do not usually seek help until disorders are fairly far advanced. By this time, treatment will be more lengthy and costly than if the trouble had been caught early.
2. The one-to-one pattern of treatment necessitated by most conventional therapy—one therapist seeing one patient at a time—sharply limits the number of people who can be helped.
3. The poor are usually discouraged from seeking help, often by the cost, but more fundamentally by a failure to see it as at all relevant to their needs. Given the high incidence of serious mental disorder among the poor, this is a major drawback.

Reiff, in this connection, points out that a basic difference of orientation is involved:

[85] Emory L. Cowen, "Emergent approaches to mental health problems: An overview and directions for future work." In Emory L. Cowen, Elmer A. Gardner, and Melvin Zax, *Emergent Approaches to Mental Health Problems.* Englewood Cliffs, N.J.: Prentice-Hall, 1967, pp. 389–445.

The fundamental justification and aim of most psychotherapy today is self-actualization. . . . For the most part, disturbed middle-class patients see themselves as *victims of their own selves*. Low-income people, on the other hand . . . see themselves as *victims of circumstances*. . . . They have to believe that they can play a role in determining what happens to them. Thus, *self-determination* rather than self-actualization is a more realistic and meaningful goal for them.[86]

If such self-determination is to be achieved, action in the community is needed. The poor will have time enough to worry about their psyches when they no longer need to worry so much about rats, chronic unemployment, high street crime, bad schools, and condescending welfare workers.

The community psychology movement seems to have arisen from two basic sources: the awareness that social conditions and institutions must be taken into account in dealing with individual mental health problems; and the idea that the psychologist or psychiatrist should be able to contribute something useful to the understanding and solution of social problems. So far, most of the action taken has related to the first of these. The establishment by Congress in 1955 of the Joint Commission on Mental Health and Mental Illness provided support for studies in the field, and the Mental Health Facilities Act in 1963 made available funds for the building, and later for the staffing, of comprehensive community mental health centers throughout the nation. The guidelines laid down for these centers provided for a wide range of mental health care within the community and for coordination with, and consultative assistance to, other community agencies. Unfortunately, the "illness model" was still strong: the Joint Commission's central concern was defined as being with treatment rather than with prevention, and closely related problems such as alcoholism, juvenile delinquency, and mental retardation were largely ignored. Similarly, in the community mental health centers so far established, "traditional services tend to be emphasized, rather than preventative and consultative roles," [87] and there have been complaints of long waiting lists, lack of community orientation and control, and poor relationships between the centers and the communities they serve. An important part of the trouble is that community psychology, and that narrower part of it which is community mental health, are so new that the theory is still being shaped, and techniques for translating theory into practical action are few and little known. Consequently the professionals must rely on what they already know, and the community mental health center inevitably tends to drift into the old, medical, individual-treatment pattern.

Nevertheless, there are certain encouraging developments. In Caplan's technique of mental health consultation,[88] psychologists or other profes-

[86] Robert Reiff, "Mental health manpower and institutional change." In Cowen, Gardner, and Zax.
[87] See Ira Iscoe and Charles D. Spielberger, "The emerging field of community psychology." In Ira Iscoe and Charles D. Spielberger, eds., *Community Psychology: Perspectives in Training and Research*. Englewood Cliffs, N.J.: Prentice-Hall (ACC), 1970.
[88] See, for example, G. Caplan, *Principles of Preventive Psychiatry*. New York: Basic Books, 1964. See also discussion in Cowen, Gardner, and Zax, pp. 412–415.

sionals spend much of their time in consultation with community care-givers—the doctors, teachers, clergy, law enforcement personnel, and others who by virtue of their professional roles are most likely to be in contact with people who need help. These people are apt to encounter problems of mental disorder at a very early stage, and if they are taught to recognize them and are provided with information and resources, they can often handle such early problems themselves, or refer them to professional therapists before they become serious and chronic. In addition, they may be able to contribute valuable knowledge from their own professional fields, once they are encouraged to see themselves as participants in the mental health care process.

At the other end of the treatment continuum are ex-mental patients discharged from a hospital and attempting to reestablish themselves in the community. Especially if they have been hospitalized for a long time and in a large custodial-type institution, they may need considerable help in relearning the skills of everyday life and social contact in the ordinary world. To help meet this need, various expedients are being tried, one of the most interesting of which is the halfway house. This is a small residential community, usually under private auspices and most often in an urban area, in which over a period of some weeks or months ex-patients are helped to make the transition from hospital to normal life. They may receive therapy from a psychiatrist, may be trained for a job and helped to obtain or keep one, and in any case get needed practice in fitting into a community where behavior is not subject to hospital regulations.

PROSPECTS

Mental disorder has probably existed since the beginning of time, and in today's crowded, complicated, high-pressure world it persists, possibly to a more serious degree. But the nature of the problem has changed. Where once insanity was a mysterious, incomprehensible affliction, and its victims were written off as hopeless cases, to be pitied or abused according to the custom of the society, today mental disorder is known to have understandable (though not yet fully understood) causes and a substantial chance of prevention and cure. The modern frustration arises because many of those causes are recognized as being so deeply rooted in human social organization, so interwoven with economic and political institutions, that any attempt to deal with them at a fundamental level is bound to have frightening effects on the status quo and may well create new dislocations with their accompanying ill effects—not to mention the sheer cost in dollars and cents. Nonetheless, recent decades have seen a dramatic increase in awareness of these problems and in attempts to meet them at all levels of government, as well as by private agencies. Much of the effort is going into training and treatment of a fairly traditional medical pattern, but innovative experiments are also under way, and the need for an interdisciplinary, community-wide approach is being recognized. In particular, the realization is growing that effective mental health care for the poor requires new concepts and techniques.

One sign that attitudes toward the mentally ill are beginning to change was the 1975 Supreme Court decision that mental patients cannot be held in institutions against their will if they are not dangerous and are capable of surviving on their own. The decision represented a new awareness that the mentally ill have legitimate civil rights that must be protected and that mental illness does not, of itself, imply an inability to function within the community.

But, even today, much of the knowledge about mental illness remains the province of a relative few, and a great many people still tend to regard such disorders as alien, frightening, and shameful. Consequently it is hard for them to sympathize with new approaches to treatment. Where the psychologist sees a mentally ill individual who could be treated in the community, many persons see a dangerous lunatic who must be "put away" to protect other people; where the professional sees a depressed neurotic in need of understanding and psychotherapy, the public may see a weakling who needs to stop sponging off other people and get to work. Conversely, where some sociologists see nonconformity, many psychiatrists and psychologists see mental disorder. And where the sociologist sees people trapped in a slum environment which predisposes them to mental disorder, riots, and crime, too many honestly worried citizens see unreasonable demands, unwillingness to work, and the influence of outside agitators. An effective attack on mental disorder in our society must include—perhaps must begin with—an enormous amount of reeducation. Only as the majority of American citizens gain some real understanding of what mental disorder is, and why it happens, are they likely to assume the responsibility for dealing with it. A major responsibility of sociology is to build this understanding.

SUMMARY

Health is a basic requirement of all societies, though definitions of health and illness vary. In the United States, health is a highly prized value. However, medical care in the United States has traditionally been a product available at a price through private enterprise, and has only recently come to be regarded as a right rather than a privilege.

Nevertheless, gross disparities continue to exist in the use and availability of health services. Members of minorities and the poor have considerably higher rates of illness and death than white people and the more affluent. Even the more affluent individuals have problems obtaining quality health care, however. Hospital, physician, and health insurance costs have increased enormously, and much of the medical treatment that is provided is unnecessary or harmful. In large part these problems exist because the nation has no unified health care system, as exists in all other industrialized nations. Suggestions for solving the problems of health care focus on alternative provider organizations, such as Health Maintenance Organizations, and alternative financing systems.

Mental illness is "America's primary health problem." But only about 25 percent of those with some mental problem receive treatment. Traditional definitions of mental disorder favor the "medical model" of mental illness, seeing disturbance of the personality system as analogous to the disturbance of the physiological system by physical disease. Major categories of illness in the medical model include neurosis, psychosis, organic psychosis, and psychosomatic illness. The social deviance model of Scheff and others holds that the disturbed individual is departing from certain societally defined norms of behavior, but that "rule-breaking" behavior is not illness. Still another concept for understanding the nature of mental disorders ascribes them to problems in living. According to Szasz, human relations are inherently difficult and inevitably involve interpersonal conflicts; by defining problems of adjustment as symptoms of "illness," we may impose therapy by force and deprive individuals of liberty.

Labeling theory holds that behaviors cannot be categorized in the same clear-cut way that physical symptoms can be. It suggests that if deviant behavior is overlooked, it is likely to be transitory, but if it is publicly labeled, it may become stabilized.

The relationships of social variables—socioeconomic class, urbanization, race, and sex—to the incidence of mental disorders have been investigated in numerous studies, and some correlations have been found. It has also been found that similar symptoms may receive different diagnosis and treatment according to the socioeconomic status and sex of the patient.

While in the past hospitalization was the major form of treatment for the mentally disturbed, most treatment today involves psychotherapy in any of several forms; increasingly, chemotherapy is being used as an adjunct. The more severely impaired are still hospitalized, however, usually in large, impersonal, and inadequately staffed institutions. But there is a new trend toward community treatment, which encourages patients to resume their daily lives in the community and to continue care on an outpatient basis.

BIBLIOGRAPHY

Chesler, Phyllis. *Women and Madness*. New York: Avon, 1972.

Cowen, Emory L., Gardner, Elmer A., and Zax, Melvin. *Emergent Approaches to Mental Health Problems*. Englewood Cliffs, N.J.: Prentice-Hall (ACC), 1967.

Driver, Edwin D. *The Sociology and Anthropology of Mental Illness: A Reference Guide*. Amherst: University of Massachusetts Press, 1972.

Ehrenreich, Barbara, and Ehrenreich, John. *The American Health Empire*. New York: Vintage Books, 1971.

Faris, Robert E. L., and Dunham, H. Warren. *Mental Disorders in Urban Areas*. Chicago: University of Chicago Press, 1939.

Freeman, Howard E., *et al. Handbook of Medical Sociology*. Englewood Cliffs, N.J.: Prentice-Hall, 1972.

Friedson, Eliot. *The Profession of Medicine*. New York: Dodd, Mead & Co., 1968.

Goffman, Erving. *Asylums: Essays in the Social Situation of Mental Patients and Other Inmates*. Garden City, N.Y.: Doubleday, 1961.

Hollingshead, August B., and Redlich, Frederick C. *Social Class and Mental Illness*. New York: Wiley, 1958.

Jaco, E. G., ed. *Patients, Physicians, and Illness*. 2nd ed. New York: Free Press, 1972.

Jones, Kathleen. *History of the Mental Health Services*. London: Routledge & Kegan Paul, 1972.

Lowenthal, Marjorie, *et al. Aging and Mental Disorder in San Francisco*. San Francisco: Jossey-Bass, 1967.

Mechanic, David. *Medical Sociology*. New York: Free Press, 1968.

————. *Mental Health and Social Policy*. Englewood Cliffs, N.J.: Prentice-Hall, 1969.

Pasamanick, Benjamin, Scarpitti. Frank R., and Dinitz, Simon. *Schizophrenics in the Community: An Experimental Study in the Prevention of Hospitalization*. Englewood Cliffs, N.J.: Prentice-Hall (ACC), 1967.

Rose, Arnold M. *Mental Health and Mental Disorder: A Sociological Approach*. New York: Norton, 1955.

Rosen, George. *Madness in Society: Chapters in the Historical Sociology of Mental Illness*. London: Routledge & Kegan Paul, 1968.

Scheff, Thomas. *Being Mentally Ill: A Sociological Theory*. Chicago: Aldine, 1966.

————. *Mental Illness and Social Processes*. New York: Harper & Row, 1967.

————, ed. *Labeling Madness*. Englewood Cliffs, N.J.: Prentice-Hall, 1975.

Seham, Max. *Blacks and American Medical Care*. Minneapolis: University of Minnesota Press, 1973.

Srole, Leo, *et al. Mental Health in the Metropolis: The Midtown Manhattan Study*. Rev. ed. New York: Harper & Row, 1975.

Stevens, Rosemary. *American Medicine and the Public Interest*. New Haven: Yale University Press, 1971.

Szasz, Thomas. *The Myth of Mental Illness*. Rev. ed. New York: Harper & Row, 1974.

U.S. Department of HEW. *Toward a Systematic Analysis of Health Care in the United States*. Washington, D.C.: U.S. Government Printing Office, 1972.

Weinberg, S. Kirson. *The Sociology of Mental Disorders*. Chicago: Aldine, 1967.

Wilson, Robert Neal. *The Sociology of Health—An Introduction*. New York: Random House, 1970.

3

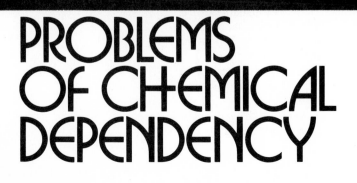

PROBLEMS
OF CHEMICAL
DEPENDENCY

- 24 to 30 million Americans have used marijuana at least once.
- The average American drinker consumes almost 3 gallons of absolute alcohol a year.
- 70 percent of all U.S. prescriptions are for psychoactive compounds.
- The economic cost of alcoholism is over $25 billion per year.

Ours is a drug-using society. To ease pain, to increase alertness, to relax tension, to lose weight, to fight depression, to prevent pregnancy, Americans of all ages and at all socioeconomic levels consume vast quantities of chemical substances every year. Most of these drugs are socially acceptable, and most people use them for socially acceptable purposes. Alcohol is a drug, as are caffeine and nicotine, and these are commonly and widely used as simple aids to sociability and ordinary activity. But some drugs, and some uses of other drugs, are socially defined as unacceptable, and it is these which are believed to constitute the "drug problem."

The uses and abuse of alcohol and other drugs are treated together in this chapter for a number of reasons. For one thing, as has been said, alcohol is, pharmacologically, a drug, although it is not usually called such. In its personal and social effects, alcohol abuse is probably more harmful than abuse of less socially accepted drugs. Alcohol and other drugs offer satisfactions which make them attractive to many people, but both can be habit-forming, sometimes with destructive consequences to users as well as to nonusers. And in both cases there are controversies over the causes, consequences, and moral implications of use.

The rationale determining the acceptability of a given drug is often less than logical. Frequently a drug favored by the dominant culture is approved, while another, associated with a subculture, is outlawed. Meyers, among others, has pointed out that

the effects of marijuana, both operationally and in its mechanism of action, correspond . . . to those of other sedatives and anesthetics, especially alcohol. . . . One is driven to the conclusion that the differences between the dominant attitudes and consequent laws toward marijuana and alcohol are unrelated to the pharmacological effects of the drugs but are due to a conflict between the mores of the dominant and one or more of the subcultures in this country.[1]

Along the same lines, a poll taken by the National Institute on Alcohol Abuse and Alcoholism found that a majority of parents considered hard liquor less dangerous to the future health and safety of their children than most drugs, and only 16 percent believed it was a greater threat than marijuana. A survey by the National Commission on Marihuana and Drug Abuse found that alcohol was regarded as a drug by only 39 percent of adults and 34 percent of young people.[2] As Chafetz put it, "Non-alcoholic drugs are somehow foreign and frightening, because their use, except as medicine, is not yet accepted as part of the mainstream of American culture. Alcohol, on the other hand, is so common a drug that we tend to ignore it—and its victims—as we have done for far too long." [3]

Other observers have noted that increased drug use in the 1960s coincided with a period of cultural ferment—political disturbances, sexual freedom—involving young people especially. Increasingly adults from the dominant culture consider youth itself as "a separate and separable" cultural subgroup, and while alcohol use is "interpreted as part of growing up, as an act of socialization, [some drug use] is viewed as 'growing away' rather than growing up." [4] Similarly, excessive use of amphetamines and barbiturates, drugs which have long been common among the middle and upper classes, has until recently been regarded with much less concern than even occasional use of heroin, which has been typically a lower-class drug—despite the fact that authorities regard abuse of the former drugs as more widespread and more dangerous.

WHAT IS A DRUG?

From a strictly pharmacological viewpoint a drug is simply any substance which chemically alters the structure or function of a living organism. However, so inclusive a definition encompasses everything from food, vitamins, and hormones to laxatives, snake and mosquito venom, anti-

---

[1] Frederick H. Meyers, "Pharmacological effects of marijuana." In David E. Smith, ed., *The New Social Drug*. Englewood Cliffs, N.J.: Prentice-Hall, 1970, p. 39.
[2] Sandra Stencel, "Resurgence of alcoholism." *Editorial Research Reports* 2 (December 26, 1973):990–991.
[3] Morris E. Chafetz, in U.S. Department of HEW, *Alcohol and Alcoholism*. Rockville, Md.: National Institute on Alcohol Abuse and Alcoholism, 1972, p. iii.
[4] Joseph R. Gusfield, "The (f)utility of knowledge?: The relation of social science to public policy toward drugs." *Annals of the American Academy of Political and Social Science* 417 (January 1975):1–15.

perspirants, insecticides, and air pollutants. Obviously, this definition is so broad as to be of little practical value. Definitions which depend on context are more useful. For instance, in the medical sense, a drug may be any substance prescribed by a physician or manufactured expressly for the purpose of relieving pain or for treating and preventing disease. In the sociolegal context, "drug" is a term for habit-forming substances which directly affect the brain or nervous system. More precisely, it refers to any chemical substance which affects bodily function, mood, perception, or consciousness; which has a potential for misuse; and which may be harmful to the individual or society.

Although this last definition is more satisfactory for our purposes than the original, broad one, it fails to take into account the social bias which traditionally has determined what is labeled as a drug. When society has for centuries made use of a habit-forming substance, this substance may not be classified as a drug, even if it has been scientifically proven to be harmful. Alcohol and tobacco (nicotine) are cases in point.

THE ABUSE OF LEGAL DRUGS

We can define drug abuse as the use of unacceptable drugs and the excessive or inappropriate use of acceptable drugs so that physical or psychological harm can result. (See also the discussion of drug dependence later in the chapter.) From this definition, there can be little question that the abuse of legal drugs—even excluding alcohol—causes more harm than the abuse of illegal drugs.

The most widely abused of all drugs is aspirin. About 27 million pounds of aspirin—several billion tablets—are consumed each year in the United States. Aspirin is often taken in excessive dosages for every physical or mental discomfort, real or imagined. However, it is far from harmless, and, in fact, can and does cause ulcers, gastrointestinal bleeding, and other ailments. Many other substances that can be obtained without a prescription are also widely abused. The American preoccupation with "regularity," for example, causes millions of people to use laxatives unnecessarily, with resultant harm to their digestive systems. Also, the fear that they are not getting enough vitamins causes many people to take excessive doses of vitamin supplements; yet, large doses of vitamins A and D are toxic.

More serious is the abuse of drugs that require a doctor's prescription, because these are often more powerful—and potentially more harmful—in their effects. Over 1.5 billion drug prescriptions, averaging 20 per family, are filled each year. These drugs often have side effects that many physicians ignore or are unaware of. For example, one study has found that up to 75 percent of physicians learn about a new drug from the manufacturer's advertisements; from 50 to 60 percent of these physicians are convinced by the advertisements alone to prescribe the drug to their patients.[5] The result: about 1.5 million Americans are admitted to

[5] Harry F. Dowling, *Medicines for Man*. New York: Knopf, 1970.

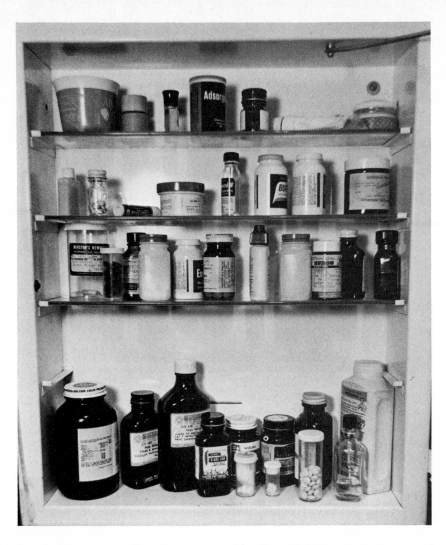

The abuse of legal
drugs is often kept
private and hidden, but
exists on a far wider
scale than the abuse
of illegal drugs.
Sepp Seitz/Magnum

hospitals every year because of drug side effects.[6] Other consequences of
overprescribed drugs are even more disturbing. It has been estimated, for
example, that the overuse of antibiotics in the United States has created
new, resistant strains of bacteria that cause from 50,000 to 100,000
deaths each year.[7] The overuse of tranquilizers like Valium, the overprescription of amphetamines and barbiturates (discussed later), the forced
feeding of mental patients with powerful tranquilizers to keep them
sedated for the convenience of their caretakers, and the unnecessary use of
drugs like Ritalin or amphetamines to treat "hyperactive" children are
some other disturbing examples of legal drug abuse.

[6] Richard Burack, *The New Handbook of Prescription Drugs*. New York: Random
House, 1970.
[7] Henry E. Simms and Paul D. Stolley, "This is medical progress?" *Journal of the
American Medical Association* (March 1974).

Perhaps the main reason so many legal drugs are abused is that they are so available. For example, of the approximately 50 barbiturates on the market today, only about 6 are needed for medical purposes. The remainder are created by a variety of drug companies simply to increase sales. The pervasive advertising of drugs is also a causative factor in drug abuse. Drug companies spend one-fourth of their income on advertising, trying to convince consumers that there is something wrong with them—that they take too long to fall asleep, for example, or are too tense—and then suggesting that using drugs will solve these problems. The result is that many people use unnecessary drugs excessively, and others with serious ailments fail to seek treatment. Finally, the common desire for convenient, short-term solutions to problems may lead to excessive drug use. For many people, taking (or offering) a pill is simply easier than working a problem out or learning to live with it. It is safe to say that the easy availability of drugs, the persistent advertising of drugs, and the popular desire for instant cures for symptoms or difficulties create an atmosphere in which the abuse of legal *and* illegal drugs is more likely to take place.

ALCOHOL USE AND ABUSE

It is one of the cultural peculiarities of our society that the problems specific to alcohol—chronic inebriation, "skid row" vagrancy, drunken driving—arouse less interest and concern than abuse of other drugs. In part, as we have already suggested, this is because alcohol—in contrast to other drugs—is thoroughly integrated into Western mores. It may also be better adapted to the life style of our complex society, since, in addition to relieving tensions and lessening sexual and aggressive inhibitions, it seems to facilitate interpersonal relationships, at least superficially, whereas other drug experiences, even in groups, are often a highly private matter.

It has been estimated that the "Average American Drinker" consumes 2.69 gallons of absolute alcohol in the course of a year. This represents the equivalent of a total annual consumption of 2.61 gallons of whiskey, 2.25 gallons of wine, and 27.49 gallons of beer per person.[8] For some of America's 95 million drinkers, the use of alcohol is a normal, pleasant, sociable activity; for others it is a spur to enable them to work, or a sedative to calm them down, or a kind of anesthetic to dull the pain of living. For still others it seriously impedes normal functioning and creates major problems in living, both for themselves and for those closely associated with them.

Our society approaches alcohol with mixed feelings. On the one hand, it is a creator of warmth and "high spirits," an aid to interpersonal harmony and agreement ("happy hour," "Let's drink to that"). It has long been used in informal rituals (such as Christmas eggnog) and formal rituals (wine as the blood of Christ), and has been important to

[8] *Statistics on Consumption of Alcohol and on Alcoholism.* New Brunswick, N.J.: Rutgers Center of Alcohol Studies, 1974, p. 4.

the economy of many nations. The growing and harvesting of grapes, grain, and other crops, and the brewing, fermenting, distilling, and sale of alcoholic beverages therefrom have utilized much agricultural land, and provided laborers with employment, businesses with trade, and nations with revenue from heavy taxation of alcohol.

On the other hand, the problems created by the abuse of alcohol have been staggering: public drunkenness and disorderly behavior, traffic and industrial accidents, poor social functioning, broken marriages, and exacerbation of poverty, mental and physical illness, crime, and suicide.

PROBLEM DRINKERS AND ALCOHOLICS

There are an estimated 4 million problem drinkers and 5 million alcoholics in the United States; some 75 percent of them are men, the remaining 25 percent women.[9] Almost one out of every ten persons who consume some kind of alcoholic beverage, then, is afflicted with problem drinking or alcoholism. Yet the terms "problem drinking" and "alcoholism" elude clear-cut definition. According to sociologist Robert Straus, a distinction should be drawn between addictive and non-addictive alcoholism.[10] Non-addictive alcoholics may be chronic drinkers, who drink to the point of stupefaction and whose frequent imbibing interferes with their health, interpersonal relationships, and economic functioning. Nevertheless, they are not addicted to alcohol. The roots of their drinking are usually psychological or social, and its goal is to help them escape reality. Alcohol produces the desired oblivion and euphoria. Thus, they may be said to be problem drinkers, rather than alcoholics.

In contrast, alcohol addicts have an uncontrollable need to achieve a peak of intoxication, and if, before they reach it, the supply of alcohol becomes exhausted, they will develop acute withdrawal symptoms, resembling those experienced by narcotics addicts—uncontrollable trembling, nausea, rapid heartbeat, and heavy perspiration. In some varieties of alcohol addiction, individuals may experience bodily symptoms after abstaining for as little as one day; and in fact, alcohol withdrawal is even more likely to result in death than narcotics withdrawal.

Alcoholism may develop after ten or more years of problem drinking, but many alcoholics go directly from total abstinence into chronic alcoholism. In some cases, it is believed, this may be due to biochemical predisposition. For example, a genetic cause for alcoholism was suggested by the results of a study in Denmark of men who had been adopted and raised apart from their biological parents. It was found that of the men whose biological parents were alcoholic, there were significantly more with a history of drinking problems and psychiatric treatment, and higher divorce rates, than among the adopted men in a matched control group.[11] Most authorities believe, however, that a single cause for problem drinking or alcoholism is rare. Instead, it is believed that a complex variety of physiological, psychological, and sociological factors is involved.

[9] Stencel, p. 989.
[10] Robert Straus, "Alcohol and alcoholism." In Robert K. Merton and Robert Nisbet, eds., *Contemporary Social Problems*. 3rd ed. New York: Harcourt Brace Jovanovich, 1971, pp. 247–248.
[11] Donald W. Goodwin *et al.* "Alcohol problems in adoptees raised apart from alcoholic biological parents." *Archives of General Psychiatry* 28 (February 1973): 238–243.

According to one study, the person who develops a drinking problem is most likely to be one who:

(1) responds to beverage alcohol in a certain way, perhaps physiologically determined, by experiencing intense relief and relaxation, and who (2) has certain personality characteristics, such as difficulty in dealing with and overcoming depression, frustration, and anxiety, and who (3) is a member of a culture in which there is both pressure to drink and culturally induced guilt and confusion regarding what kinds of drinking behavior are appropriate.[12]

THE ETHNIC FACTOR

Fermented grape juice has for thousands of years been a staple in the diets of the people inhabiting the Mediterranean region. Even today most of the countries on the rim of the Mediterranean have a strong tradition of accompanying food with wine. And in Jewish families, wine is part of the weekly Sabbath and yearly Passover rituals. In northern Europe, beer and hard cider are traditional. The Orient has rice wine, the tropics palm wine, orange beer, and other quick-fermented beverages; nomadic herdspeople of the past sometimes made use of fermented mare's milk. Scarcely any society, past or present, has been without some form of alcoholic beverage. Of the world's major religions, only the Islamic religion does not incorporate wine into rituals and even expressly forbids its social use.

Among some groups, these beverages are normally drunk in moderate amounts at meals. Among others, the custom is to drink after meals, or independently of them, and perhaps to drunkenness. It is the latter custom which seems most conducive to the development of alcoholism, as is illustrated by comparison of U.S. Jews and Italians, who customarily drink with meals and in the home, and U.S. Irish, who are more likely to drink outside the home and/or not at meals. Among the former, a majority of adults use alcohol and report having done so since childhood, but the rate of alcoholism is quite low; while among the latter, childhood drinking is less likely, and alcoholism rates are much higher.[13]

This correlation between familial drinking patterns and alcoholism rates has been found to hold true for other groups as well. For ethnic groups in which drinking habits are established by cultural custom, alcohol abuse is rare. But in those groups with ambivalent attitudes toward alcohol, including American Protestants, alcoholism rates are high: in particular, drinkers from those groups in which alcohol is seldom used are most likely to encounter problems.[14] In general, when children grow up with routine, comfortable, intrafamilial exposure to alcohol, they are very unlikely to become excessive drinkers later on.

It is interesting that in the United States generational status is becoming as important as ethnic background in determining drinking patterns. Among first-generation Italian-Americans, for example, frequent and

[12] Report of the Cooperative Commission on the Study of Alcoholism. In Stencel, pp. 1001–1002.
[13] U.S. Department of HEW, *Alcohol and Health*. Rockville, Md.: Public Health Service, 1974, pp. 15–16.
[14] Chafetz, pp. 10, 16.

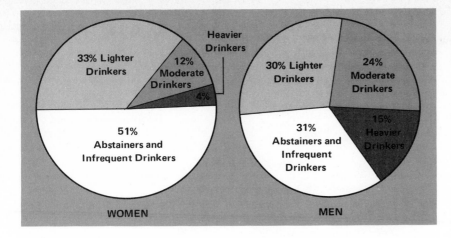

FIGURE 3-1
Percentage of Drinkers and Types of Drinkers, by Sex

Lighter drinkers—less than 0.22 oz. absolute alcohol daily. Moderate drinkers—between 0.22 and 1 oz. absolute alcohol daily. Heavier drinkers—over 1 oz. absolute alcohol daily.

Source: U.S. Department of HEW, *Alcohol and Health.* Rockville, Md.: Public Health Service, 1974, p. 9.

even daily wine drinking is customary, but there are few alcohol-related problems; later generations have higher rates of heavy drinking and favor drinks of high alcoholic content.[15]

A study published by the Department of Health, Education and Welfare [16] lists some of the characteristics of the American drinker (see Figures 3-1 and 3-2). Age, sex, ethnic and religious background, education, occupation, and place of residence all seem to be related to whether, how much, and how an individual will use alcohol. For instance, heavy drinking among men is most common at ages 30 to 34 and 45 to 49, among women at ages 21 to 24 and 45 to 49. Men of the youngest age group for which data are available, 18- to 20-year-olds, are heavier drinkers than 21- to 24-year-olds. In general, older people drink less, even if they have been drinkers when young.

WHO DRINKS?

The proportion of adult women who drink has been increasing steadily for the last thirty years. According to National Institute of Mental Health estimates, in the 1950s one out of every six alcoholics was a woman; now it is one out of every four. However, even these figures may be understated, especially for non–working women who can more easily disguise their habit.[17]

In regard to socioeconomic status, drinking appears to be most frequent among young men at the highest socioeconomic level and least frequent among older women at the lowest level. However, the higher socioeconomic classes drink to excess less often. Heavier escape drinking is found at the lower socioeconomic levels and among young people.[18]

Occupationally, business and professional men rank high on heavy drinking, farmers low. However, among women, service workers have

[15] *Alcohol and Health,* p. 15.
[16] *First Special Report to the U.S. Congress on Alcohol and Health,* U.S. Department of HEW, December 1971.
[17] *Alcohol and Health,* pp. 13, 15.
[18] Gary L. Albrecht, "The alcoholism process: A social learning viewpoint." In Peter G. Bourne and Ruth Fox, eds., *Alcoholism: Progress in Research and Treatment.* New York: Academic Press, 1973, pp. 26–27.

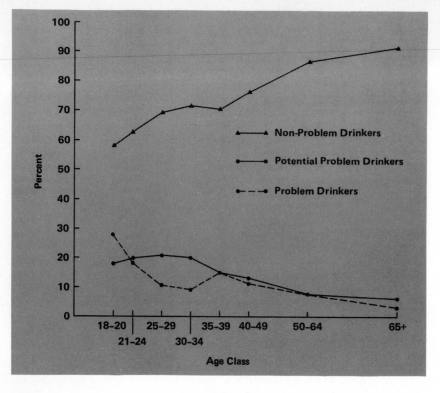

FIGURE 3-2
Drinkers, Problem
Drinkers, and Potential
Problem Drinkers

Source: U.S. Department of
HEW, *Alcohol and Health.*
Rockville, Md.: Public
Health Service, 1974, p. 27.

the highest proportion of heavy drinkers. Religiously, regular churchgoers drink less than nonchurchgoers; Jews and Episcopalians are highest, conservative and fundamentalist Protestants lowest. But Jews have a low proportion of heavy and escape drinkers, and more Catholics than others are both drinkers and heavy drinkers. Regionally, the South has a below-average proportion of drinkers, which may correlate both with rural and small-town status, and with the more conservative religious affiliations of the "Bible Belt." There are no significant racial differences in drinking behavior.[19]

DRINKING AMONG YOUNG PEOPLE

Many observers have noted that alcohol use—and abuse—is increasing among young people. "The switch is on," says Chafetz. "Youths are moving from a wide range of other drugs to the most devastating drug—the one most widely misused of all—alcohol." [20] Yankelovich, in a recent survey, found twice as many drinkers as other drug users among all students—58 percent of high school and 79 percent of college students use alcohol regularly.[21]

More comprehensive are the results of a 1975 study made for the National Institute of Alcohol Abuse and Alcoholism. Of 13,000 youths in 450 schools throughout the country, 28 percent had drinking problems

[19] *Alcohol and Health,* pp. 17–18; and see Albrecht.
[20] "Alcoholism: New victims, new treatment." *Time,* April 22, 1974, p. 75.
[21] Daniel Yankelovich, "How students control their drug crisis." *Psychology Today* (October 1975):39.

—being drunk at least four times in the previous year or being in trouble with peers or superiors because of drinking twice during the previous year. One-fourth of the 13-year-olds surveyed were already moderate drinkers. The study also found that boys drank more often and more heavily than girls, and that children of drinking parents tended to drink more frequently.[22]

It has been estimated that there are 450,000 alcoholics under age 21 in the United States. They differ from the average adolescent drinkers in that they drink more often, in larger amounts, and usually for the specific purpose of getting "bombed" or drunk; they are more likely to display aggressive or destructive behavior, to drink alone, and to have severe emotional problems.[23] Among the reasons adduced for the increasing popularity of alcohol among the young are: a shortage of high-quality narcotics; the fact that alcohol is cheaper and easier to obtain than other drugs, and that it gives a satisfactory "high"; revised laws lowering the legal drinking age; and heavy advertisement of sweetened "pop" wines. Many young people use alcoholic beverages along with other drugs, a particularly dangerous practice since the alcohol-drug combination may be synergistic; that is, both together may have an effect that is more harmful than the effects of either one used separately.

Adolescents drink, as do their elders, to be sociable, to relieve tension, and also because it is an accepted social custom. As Albrecht points out, "Both their peer group and the adult society that they are being socialized to enter encourage and reward drinking behavior. Learning to drink for the adolescent is but present and anticipatory socialization. . . . The major influences on whether or not the individual drinks are the principal agents of socialization in his life, his parents and his peers." This analysis is borne out by the results of a study in which over 30 percent of adolescents reported that friends were the most important influence on their drinking, and 50 percent said that "going along with the group" was the primary reason for teenage drinking.[24]

Drinking behavior in teenagers and youth may also serve as an attempt to assert adulthood, and to flout adult authority. Like any other behavior so motivated, it is likely to be most valued when most sternly disapproved —which is probably why excessive drinking among college students is most likely in colleges which adopt a severely prohibitory attitude toward alcohol. As teenage drinking behavior increases and becomes conspicuous and detrimental, it is bound to arouse increased public concern among those who have thus far ignored or accepted it.

SOCIAL PROBLEMS RELATED TO ALCOHOL

Alcoholics have a life expectancy that is, on the average, 10 to 12 years **HEALTH**
shorter than nonalcoholics. There are several reasons for this. First, alcohol contains a substantial number of calories, but no vital nutrients

[22] "School study calls 28% of teen-agers 'problem' drinkers." *New York Times,* November 21, 1975, p. 45.
[23] See Stencel.
[24] Albrecht, pp. 30–31.

except water; thus, alcoholics generally have a reduced appetite for nutritious food, and inevitably suffer from vitamin deficiencies. As a result, they have lowered resistance to infectious diseases. Second, over a period of time large amounts of alcohol destroy liver cells and cause them to be replaced by scar tissue. This condition (cirrhosis of the liver) is one of the most frequent causes of death (13,000 a year) in this country. Heavy drinking also contributes to a wide range of heart ailments, and there is some evidence that alcohol contributes to the incidence of cancer. Finally, some studies indicate that alcohol is implicated in about one-fourth of all suicides, or over 5,000 deaths annually. It is interesting that there is some evidence that, for unknown reasons, the life expectancy for light-to-moderate drinkers exceeds even that of total abstainers.[25]

The statistical connection between alcohol and driving accidents is staggering. Wherever studies have been undertaken to measure the alcoholic level of drivers involved in accidents, the same distressing conclusions are reached. Alcohol is a factor in about 50 percent of all fatal vehicular accidents and serious automobile accident injuries. That is, alcohol is implicated in almost 30,000 deaths and half a million serious injuries resulting from auto accidents each year. (See Figure 3-3.) The rate among young drivers is even higher—60 percent of highway fatalities for drivers age 16 to 24 are alcohol-related. In addition, about one-third of the pedestrians fatally injured by automobiles are intoxicated at the time of death.[26]

Other studies have shown that the dimensions of the problem may be even greater. For example, statistics released by the Secretary of Trans-

DRINKING AND DRIVING

[25] *Alcohol and Health.*
[26] Chafetz, p. 10; "Alcoholism: New victims, new treatment." *Time,* p. 75; and *Alcohol and Health,* pp. 128, 132.

FIGURE 3-3
Results of Selected
Surveys on the Rela-
tionship Between
Drinking and Traffic
Accidents

California Surveys	Illinois Surveys
53% of drivers killed in accidents had over 0.09% blood alcohol content.[1]	44% of drivers killed had been drinking— 75% had over 0.10% blood alcohol content.
2 out of 3 drivers killed had been drinking—3 out of 5 had over 0.10% blood alcohol content.	Increased probability of accident; blood alcohol content vs. sobriety. 0.06% ·········· 2 times 0.10% ·········· 6 times 0.15% ········· 25 times
Wisconsin Surveys	Indiana Surveys

[1] A 1-oz. serving of 45 percent alcohol will produce a blood alcohol content of between 0.015 to 0.02 percent.

Source: Facts About America's #1 Safety Problem. National Council on Alcoholism, 1971.

portation, based on investigations conducted over a number of years, indicate that at least 800,000 traffic accidents a year are the result of drinking.[27] One study of fatal motor accidents in New York showed that the blood-alcohol level of 75 percent of the drivers was above 0.1 percent. A study of drivers and pedestrians involved in fatal accidents in California during one year similarly demonstrated that alcohol contributed to the death toll. Alcohol levels of more than 0.1 percent were found in 53 percent of the drivers and 32 percent of the pedestrians.[28]

The prosecution of persons involved in accidents attributable to alcohol is seriously hampered by the general attitude toward drink. An Indiana report asserts that juries are found to be reluctant to render guilty verdicts in drunken-driving cases because the jurors themselves identify and sympathize with the defendant. Even when drunken-driving laws are rigidly enforced, however, the problem is not always solved; in some European countries, for example, vigorous attempts by the governments to curb drunken driving have met with little success. The attitude that it is acceptable to drive after drinking is apparently too widespread for law enforcement to have much effect.

In a recent year the FBI reported that 1,765,281 arrests, or about a third of the national total, involved drunkenness or an offense related to excessive drinking.[29] However, these criminal acts were minor, involving breaches of the peace, disorderly conduct, vagrancy, and so on. In arrests for major crimes, drunkenness generally does not appear in the charges, yet alcohol is often a factor in the criminal act.

Thus, among 588 cases of homicide in Philadelphia, alcohol was found

**ALCOHOL AND
ARREST RATES**

[27] *Alcohol and Highway Safety: A Report to the Congress from the Secretary of Transportation.* Washington, D.C.: U.S. Department of Transportation, 1968.
[28] Chafetz, p. 11.
[29] Stencel, p. 998.

in either the victim, the offender, or, more often, both, in 64 percent of the cases. Likewise, among 100 male sex offenders in another study, "8 percent were chronic alcohlics, and 35 percent were drinking at the time of the offense." The rates for drinking in relation to skilled property crimes, such as forgery, appear to be somewhat lower than for violent and sexually related crimes.[30]

Other studies have shown that alcohol was used by at least half of offenders directly prior to their committing homicide and other assaultive offenses; that alcohol was a factor in 67 percent of sexual crimes against children and 39 percent of sexually aggressive acts against women. Still other studies have indicated that young people who used alcohol were responsible for significantly more crimes of assault than their nondrinking peers; and that the use of alcohol correlated significantly with other forms of antisocial behavior, such as poor school attendance, unsatisfactory work records, and excessive fighting.[31] (See also Chapter 5.)

The reasons for the high correlation of drinking with arrests for serious crimes are not fully understood. It has been pointed out that alcohol, by removing some inhibitions, may lead persons to behave as they would not ordinarily do. Likewise, as with other drugs, the need to obtain supplies may lead to theft or other property crimes, sometimes with violence, such as a store holdup. Since chronic alcoholics may be unable to hold jobs, their financial difficulties are compounded, perhaps increasing the temptation to commit crimes.

Also, the values and self-concepts of chronic heavy drinkers are apt to change as their condition progresses. They are more likely to associate with delinquent or criminal persons, and these associations may make it easier for them to imagine themselves committing criminal acts.

It is also possible that excessive drinking may not be the cause of crime but an effect of other underlying conditions, such as disordered social environments. As the President's Commission on Law Enforcement and Administration of Justice has said:

At the very least a criminal outcome is the consequence of alcohol . . .
plus personality, plus group or subcultural membership plus opportunity
plus drinking circumstances plus other events. Even this addictive scheme is
insufficient, for the likelihood is one of interplay or interaction with differing
outcomes each time one element in the drama of conduct is altered.

Finally . . . one does not know that the relationship now shown between
alcohol use and crime is not, in fact, a relationship between being caught
and being a drinker rather than in being a criminal and being a drinker.[32]

In addition to its involvement in serious crime, alcoholism creates another problem by straining the law-enforcement machinery, with the processing of petty offenders. In terms of cost to the taxpayer, the expense

---

[30] *Task Force Report: Drunkenness. Annotations, Consultants' Papers, and Related Materials.* The President's Commission on Law Enforcement and Administration of Justice. Washington, D.C.: U.S. Government Printing Office, 1967, pp. 40–41.

[31] National Commission on Marihuana and Drug Abuse, *Drug Use in America: Problem in Perspective.* Second Report. Washington, D.C.: U.S. Government Printing Office, March 1973, p. 157.

[32] *Task Force Report: Drunkenness,* p. 43.

of arrest, trial, and incarceration of offenders amounts to billions of dollars each year. And many of these arrests involve only a small segment of the community—the neighborhood drunk or derelict—who may be repeatedly arrested and imprisoned in the course of the year.

EFFECTS ON THE FAMILY

If the only victims of alcoholism were the alcoholics themselves, the social effects would be serious enough. But others, especially the families of alcoholics, suffer as well. The emotional effect, which is part of any family crisis, is heightened when the crisis itself is socially defined as shameful. Fire, illness, and accident are tragedies that cannot be helped; but alcoholism somehow reflects on the people affected by it. The children of an alcoholic parent frequently develop severe physical and emotional illness, and the family often breaks up through divorce or desertion. The alcoholic parent may eventually become unable to provide support, and poverty may ensue. (See Chapter 10.)

If the families of alcoholics attempt to stand by them and help them overcome their condition, certain typical stages of adjustment are likely to occur. These stages were examined by Joan K. Jackson in a study of the families of alcoholic men.[33] She found that the first stage was a denial by all concerned that the problem existed, an attempt to explain away excessive drinking as somehow being normal behavior. When this ceased to be possible, it was followed by a series of attempts to eliminate the problem, and then by progressive family disorganization. At some point the wife began to take over the husband's roles, and gradually a reorganization, with the alcoholic husband more or less excluded, took place. Eventually, in some cases, it appeared necessary to separate from the husband, and a further degree of reorganization occurred. Finally, if the husband obtained help and succeeded in bringing his alcoholism under control, there came the stage of reintegrating him into the family, with the new redefinition of roles and the groping after renewed trust and confidence which this entailed. Not all families complete this cycle, and even in those which do, permanent scars may remain.

SKID ROW ALCOHOLICS

Contrary to popular belief, only about 5 percent of all alcoholics and problem drinkers are in the "skid row" category. Most alcoholics appear to be average individuals with jobs and families.[34] A number of theories have been advanced by sociologists to explain the differences between individuals who become alcoholics in the anonymity of skid row, and alcoholics who stay at home in their usual setting. Skid row alcoholics clearly wish to divorce themselves from their past in addition to following their inclination to drink. Howard M. Bahr concludes that neither alcohol nor the lack of a home or family is the central factor impelling a person to become a skid row alcoholic. Rather, the cause is a "lack of social affiliation," a feeling which usually preceded by a long time the actual decision.[35] Skid row derelicts are persons with a great need to escape the

[33] Joan K. Jackson, "The adjustment of the family to alcoholism." *Marriage and Family Living* 18 (November 1956):358–370.
[34] Stencel, p. 989.
[35] Howard M. Bahr, *Homelessness and Disaffiliation.* New York: Columbia University Press, 1968.

realities of social living—an escape which chronic drinking can, for a time, provide.

In a sample study of men who were repeatedly arrested for inebriation, disorderly conduct, vagrancy, and other similar offenses, about 96 percent of the offenders were either not married or had broken marriages, compared with 11 percent of the total male population of the United States. In addition, offenders were educationally disadvantaged. Seventy percent had not gone beyond eighth grade. Sixty-eight percent were unskilled workers. Many were accustomed to institutionalized living and semiprotective environments such as the Civilian Conservation Corps, the Army, the railroad gang, lumber and fruit camps, or Salvation Army and similar shelters. They had become habituated to dependent living.

The chronic drunkenness offender is the product of a limited environment and a man who has never attained more than a minimum of integration in society. He is and has always been at the bottom of the social and economic ladder; he is isolated, uprooted, unattached, disorganized, demoralized and homeless, and it is in this context that he drinks to excess. As such, admittedly through his own behavior, he is the least respected member of the community, and his treatment by the community has, at best, been negative and expedient. He has never attained, or has lost, the necessary respect and sense of human dignity on which any successful program of treatment and rehabilitation must be based.[36]

"Skid row" alcoholics constitute only a small percentage of alcoholics, but because of their visibility and low status, account for a high percentage of those arrested for drunkenness.
Charles Gatewood

For the most part, towns and cities have been satisfied to make skid row the province of the police, who cart off the alcoholics to jail to sleep off a stupor or to receive a 30-day jail sentence. This was conceived as a proper course both to remove a menace from the community and to protect the derelict. However, the legality of this treatment was challenged in a number of court cases in the late 1960s, mainly on the ground that criminal prosecution for public intoxication constituted "cruel and unusual" punishment and was, therefore, a violation of the person's constitutional rights. While the Supreme Court subsequently denied that there was a constitutional basis for the challenges, the lower court actions had the effect of focusing attention on the problem. In 1967 three commissions studying aspects of this problem recommended that public health approaches to public drunkenness should be substituted for criminal statutes, which were not only possibly unconstitutional but ineffective, inhumane, and expensive as well.

SOCIAL CONTROL

Because of the many facets of human motivation and the diverse social conditions leading to alcoholism and excessive drinking, these problems are complex and no one solution can be applied to all cases. It is suspected that repeated arrests of chronic inebriates merely perpetuate a deviancy-reinforcement, or "revolving door," cycle. An offender is arrested, processed, released, then arrested again, possibly only hours

[36] *Task Force Report: Drunkenness*, pp. 11–13.

after his or her release. Each such arrest, involving police, court, and correctional time, costs the public more than $50, and may actually contribute to an excessive drinker becoming an alcoholic and encourage the inebriate to act out secondary deviances.[37]

It is increasingly being recognized that alcoholism is a sickness, with a variety of psychological as well as physiological components, and that by means of an equal variety of treatments it is possible to rehabilitate, although not completely cure, large numbers of chronic inebriates. There have been nonpunitive attempts—some more successful than others—to assist alcoholics to overcome their addiction or habituation and to create alternatives to enable alcoholism-prone individuals to handle disturbing emotions and anxieties.

TREATMENT AND REHABILITATION

This represents a significant shift of public opinion in the last few years. Not long ago the alcoholic was considered an outcast, untreatable (and therefore not to be treated), intractable, and, if he or she happened to be in one's family, unacknowledged. It is now believed that,

No miracle cure, no equivalent of the Salk vaccine is in sight for the alcoholic, and none is ever likely to be found . . . [but] for every one of the many alcoholisms there is at least one treatment or combination of treatments that offers a good chance of cure.[38]

One reflection of this changed attitude was the Comprehensive Alcohol Abuse and Alcoholism Prevention, Treatment and Rehabilitation Act of 1970, which created both the National Institute on Alcohol Abuse and Alcoholism to coordinate federal activities and the National Advisory Council on Alcohol Abuse and Alcoholism to recommend national policy. The act provided more immediate aids as well, such as grants to individual states for developing comprehensive programs on alcoholism, grants and contracts for specific projects on prevention and treatment, and incentives for private hospitals admitting patients with alcohol-related problems.

Traditionally, hospitals have offered little beyond immediate "drying out" and release of the specifically alcoholic patient, or treatment of a specific medical problem but not its alcoholic cause. This too is in process of change. The American Hospital Association is actually advocating alcoholism programs that would be available in the nation's general hospitals during regular medical care, and is attempting to utilize the resources of general hospitals in community systems of alcoholic treatment.[39] Unfortunately, many hospitals still do not provide such care for alcoholics, and most health insurance programs do not yet cover this illness.

Unquestionably, the most dramatic successes in coping with alcoholism belong to Alcoholics Anonymous. The effectiveness of this group in reforming individuals is based on what amounts to a conversion, a profound and quasi-religious phenomenon. Alcoholics are led to this experi-

ALCOHOLICS ANONYMOUS

37 *Task Force Report: Drunkenness,* pp. 8–9.
38 "Alcoholism: New victims, new treatment." *Time,* p. 78.
39 *Alcohol and Health,* p. 148.

ence by a fellowship with other individuals like themselves, some of whom have already mastered their problem, while others are in the process of mastering it.

Alcoholics Anonymous insists that drinkers face their shortcomings and the realities of life and, when possible, make amends to persons they have injured or aggrieved in the past. At the same time, the movement concentrates on building up the alcoholics' self-esteem and reassuring them of their basic worth as human beings. Since its founding in 1935, the group has evolved a technique by which reformed alcoholics give support and comfort to the drinker attempting rehabilitation. This support is available to the alcoholic during crises when he or she feels in danger of a relapse to drinking.

Estimates of membership vary from half to three-quarters of a million, in up to 12,000 groups in the United States. Over twenty-five groups have been created to deal specifically with the growing number of teenage and young adult drinkers.[40] In addition, AA has spawned Al-Anon, a program to aid the nonalcoholic spouse, and Alateen, to help the children of alcoholics with their common problems of understanding the sick family member and coping with their own troubling emotions. The alcoholic family member need not be a participant in Alcoholics Anonymous for relatives to participate in these offshoot programs, which grew from the recognition that an entire family is psychologically involved in the alcohol-related problems of any one of its members.

Alcoholics Anonymous appears to be the most successful large-scale program for dealing with alcoholism. It is essential, according to AA precepts, for addicts to acknowledge their lack of control over alcohol and completely abstain from all alcoholic beverages. This approach sees alcoholism as a kind of "allergy" in which even one drink can produce "an intolerable craving for more." [41] While precise figures are not available, it seems that more than half of those who join the group with serious intentions are rehabilitated.[42] The voluntary character of the program probably has something to do with this; whether the AA approach—particularly its insistence on total abstinence—could successfully be applied to all alcoholics is difficult to say.

ANTABUSE PROGRAMS

Antabuse, a drug developed in Copenhagen in 1947, is one of the newer weapons against alcoholism. It is a prescription drug that sensitizes the patient's system so that consuming even a small quantity of alcohol results in strong and uncomfortable physical symptoms. Drinkers become intensely flushed, their pulse quickens, and they feel nauseated.

Before beginning treatment with Antabuse, an alcoholic is detoxified. Then the drug is administered to the patient for several consecutive days, along with doses of alcohol. The patient continues to take the drug for several more days, and at the close of the period another dose of alcohol is administered. The trial doses of alcohol condition the patient to recognizing the relationship between drinking and the unpleasant effects.

[40] Stencel, pp. 992, 1003–1004.
[41] From the AA credo, in Stencel, p. 1004.
[42] Morris E. Chafetz and Harold W. Demone, Jr., *Alcoholism and Society*. New York: Oxford University Press, 1962.

Other techniques similar in principle depend on different nausea-producing drugs, or on electric shock, to condition the patient against alcohol; this basic process is variously known as aversion therapy or behavior conditioning.

Antabuse, which the World Health Organization has named disulfiram, has so far gained only limited acceptance in the treatment of alcoholics. Critics claim that it is too narrow in its range of effectiveness, and that the personality problems of the drinker are neglected. It is also claimed that the drug is ineffective with persons suspicious of treatment and those exhibiting psychotic tendencies. Nevertheless, in the hands of a skilled practitioner it is a useful tool.

Sanford Billet regards Antabuse as part of a total treatment program including psychotherapy, drug therapy, and vocational and social rehabilitation. He believes that Antabuse, by providing a concrete, immediate reason not to drink, helps the patient to stop drinking entirely so that he or she is better able to make constructive use of all phases of the treatment program. In a sample study, 64 percent of the alcoholics who used Antabuse (together with the rehabilitation program) improved "markedly"; 35 percent improved "moderately." Without Antabuse (but with the rehabilitation program), 31 percent improved "markedly" and 42 percent improved "moderately." [43]

COMMUNITY PROGRAMS

The problem drinker or alcoholic who receives medical help while remaining part of a family unit usually responds better than the one who is institutionalized. In community-care programs, many of which are being set up, not only the problem drinkers and alcoholics, but also the family members are treated. The approach here is similar to that used in family therapy in community mental health programs (see Chapter 2). The need to deal with the problem drinker's or alcoholic's family, both in their attitude toward the patient and in their own adjustment, is an essential part of the therapy. In addition to getting medical help, problem drinkers and alcoholics need to develop a healthy image of themselves and their families as well as a feeling of security about them. Consultations with the families are used to persuade patients that they are trusted and respected—feelings they must develop if they are to obtain satisfaction from a nondrinking life.

Since the vast majority of problem drinkers and alcoholics are still living with their families and working, rehabilitation is often the goal of treatment, instead of total abstinence. The National Institute of Alcohol Abuse and Alcoholism considers this goal achieved "when the patient maintains or reestablishes a good family life and work record, and a respectable position in the community, and is able to control . . . drinking *most of the time*." The institute reports that "a successful outcome can be expected in at least 60 percent, and some therapists have reported success in 70 or 80 percent, depending on the motivation and intelligence of the patient and his determination to get well; the competence of the therapists; the availability of hospital or clinic facilities and tranquilizers

[43] Sanford L. Billet, "Antabuse therapy." In Ronald J. Cantanzaro, *Alcoholism: The Total Treatment Approach.* Springfield, Ill.: Charles C Thomas, 1968, pp. 167–174.

and other drugs; and the strong support of family, employer, and community." [44] One relatively new development on the community level is the establishment of transitional intermediate care facilities, from which problem drinkers and alcoholics undergoing rehabilitation can re-enter community life while remaining in a supportive environment.

COMPANY PROGRAMS

Another relatively new development, and one that has been demonstrably successful, is for companies to sponsor alcohol treatment programs for their employees. The aims of such programs are twofold: early identification of a drinking problem and therapeutic intervention before it is too late. Company programs have met with some resistance on the part of employees who resented an invasion of their privacy or being stigmatized as alcoholics. However, successful programs have overcome these objections by not appearing to be specifically geared to alcoholism, but by making counseling by a social worker-therapist available to deal with personal problems as they surface. As problems are identified, they can be referred to appropriate community resources. Since there is no stigma attached to a worker's seeking help or being called in for a conference under such multipronged programs, they have met with notable success.

It is estimated that problem drinkers in business and industry may have a rehabilitation rate as high as 80 percent. An important factor in that rate is the motivation of the worker to remain in the community and to retain his or her job.[45]

EDUCATIONAL PROGRAMS

Alcohol education, like drug education, is most helpful when it imparts accurate information instead of exploiting fears and overdramatizing effects. Because of recent evidence that adolescents have begun drinking at younger ages and that peers and the family are decisive in determining drinking attitudes and behavior in young people, information programs on alcohol have been started in many elementary schools and high schools.

Rupert Wilkinson points out that changes in public attitude can accomplish much in the prevention of alcoholism, and stresses the potential importance of advertising in this regard. He suggests the need to shift the direction of advertising campaigns for alcoholic beverages away from the present themes in which alcoholic drink symbolizes virility and romance, thus investing alcohol with a special mystique. Advertising, he holds, should show drinking in a family setting, as a natural part of home life. In this way the myths of alcohol use could be eliminated.[46]

The most significant education programs, however, should try not only to demythologize alcohol and disseminate information about its effects, but also to change the public attitudes toward problem drinking and alcoholism. For too long we have emphasized the abuse of illegal drugs and ignored "the most serious drug problem facing this country today" [47] —the problem of alcohol abuse. Only when we achieve greater under-

[44] Chafetz, p. 17.
[45] Chafetz, p. 28; and *Alcohol and Health*, p. 154.
[46] Rupert Wilkinson, *The Prevention of Drinking Problems: Alcohol Control and Cultural Influence*. New York: Oxford University Press, 1970.
[47] *Drug Use in America*, p. 142.

standing of how widespread and harmful alcohol abuse is, and learn to regard alcohol abusers as people needing help rather than as outcasts, will we begin to make significant headway toward solving the problems of alcohol use in our society.

DRUG USE AND ABUSE

Like the term "drug," the term "addiction" is used rather loosely to denote any habitual or frequent use of a drug, with or without dependence on it. In fact, the process of addiction is a complex phenomenon involving the drug user's physical and psychological condition, the type of drug being used, the amount being taken, and the frequency with which the drug is being used. Similarly, precise degrees of dependence are difficult to define because of the physiological and psychological complexity of drug use. Nevertheless, a limited consensus has developed among some experts and certain definitions are considered acceptable: physical dependence occurs when the body has adjusted to the presence of a drug and will suffer pain, discomfort, or illness—the symptoms of withdrawal—if the use of the drug is discontinued. The word "addiction" is used to describe physical dependence. Psychological dependence occurs when an individual comes to rely on a drug for the feelings of well-being it produces. The word "habituation" is sometimes used to mean psychological dependence.

Other experts prefer not to make the distinctions between physical and psychological dependence, since these are so often interrelated. Also, words like "addiction" have come to be defined in the public mind as something alien or evil. These experts prefer to characterize the compulsion to use a drug simply as "drug dependence," without attempting to define its physical and psychological components.

It is important to note that not all drug use is considered drug abuse, in the sense that an individual's health is impaired. A person suffering from an illness that required treatment with morphine, for instance, might be addicted but would not be considered an abuser. In a survey of drug use among students, Yankelovich found it most useful to distinguish between nonusers, regular users, and abusers.[48] About 58 percent of high school and college students were nonusers of illegal drugs, and about a third used illegal drugs (usually marijuana) regularly, generally on social occasions; fewer than 10 percent manifested an inordinate preoccupation with and a dependence on drug use.

Most adult Americans are users of drugs; many use a wide variety of drugs frequently; and the appellation "drug user" might justly be applied to nearly all of us. A survey of regular and occasional users of both legal and illegal drugs—persons not chronically dependent on drugs—showed a correlation of broad drug experience with higher education, high average income, and liberal or independent political beliefs. From the group with the least drug experience to that with the most intensive drug use, there was a steady shift up the social scale, as well as increased

---

[48] See Yankelovich.

education, a higher divorce rate, a lower average age, and a higher proportion of white persons.[49]

With the exception of the opiates and alcohol, precise knowledge is lacking about the rate of use of mind-altering drugs, the kinds of users, and the dosages and effects of long-term ingestion. In some instances, the pharmacological properties and effects of these drugs on the individual are not fully understood. Thus a definitive judgment on the risks and dangers involved is not always possible. Nevertheless, some general statements can be made. (See Table 3-1.)

MARIJUANA

While those who regard every young person as a regular user of marijuana are evidently exaggerating the facts, there is no question that marijuana use is widespread. Yankelovich found that 64 percent of college students and 48 percent of high school students had experimented at least once or twice with marijuana and that 41 percent of the former and 26 percent of the latter considered themselves regular users. Eight percent of college students and 6 percent of high school students smoked marijuana daily.[50] Another study showed that 22 percent of 14- and 15-year-olds used marijuana in 1974, more than double the 10 percent rate of only two years earlier.[51]

The National Commission on Marihuana and Drug Abuse, on the basis of one survey,[52] estimated that 15 percent of Americans aged 18 and over have used marijuana at least once; of those people who have not themselves tried marijuana, nearly half of the adults and slightly over half of the younger group know someone who has.

Since such surveys depend on self-report by individuals about illegal behavior, it is quite possible that the true percentage of drug use is somewhat higher than these figures suggest. But it is apparent, in any case, that the degree of frequency of use varies widely. Nowlis, in her book on drug use on college campuses,[53] distinguishes three categories of users: (1) the *experimenters,* who have tried one or more drugs, usually marijuana or LSD, once or twice; (2) the *users,* who use one or more drugs occasionally; and (3) the *heads,* for whom drug use is the dominating activity of their lives. To lump together and condemn persons in all of these categories, as is sometimes done by the popular media and the opponents of drug use, is to obscure the true issues.

A generation or two ago, the drug most favored by students and young adults seems to have been alcohol, and there were many who regarded college drinking as a fairly serious social problem. About a decade ago the concern shifted to those drugs legally designated as narcotics, and

---

[49] Richard H. Blum *et al., Society and Drugs: Social and Cultural Observations.* San Francisco: Jossey-Bass, pp. 272–275.

[50] See Yankelovich.

[51] Nancy Hicks, "Drug use called up among youths." *New York Times,* October 2, 1975.

[52] *Marihuana: A Signal of Misunderstanding.* The Official Report of the National Commission on Marihuana and Drug Abuse. New York: New American Library, 1972, p. 38.

[53] Helen H. Nowlis, *Drugs on the College Campus.* New York: Doubleday, 1969, p. 62.

some social scientists believed that marijuana in particular was becoming a replacement drug for alcohol, being used by a generation developing new ways of expressing itself. But it is now apparent that marijuana did not replace alcohol, but was adopted in addition to, and frequently along with, alcohol. In fact, as stated earlier, alcohol use is twice as prevalent as illegal drug taking among all students.

Probably because of the illegal status of marijuana and other mood-altering drugs, their use during the 1960s became almost the hallmark of that group of young people who were rebelling against existing social norms—rebelling far more deeply than the earlier alcohol generation usually did. Today, however, the popularity of marijuana among young people is due in general to the fact that, like alcohol, it is a social drug. It is generally used as part of group activity, and apparently contributes to a heightened feeling of warmth and unity among the persons present. In fact, in some circles, the student who abstains from marijuana use is likely to encounter considerable social pressure.

It appears that the marijuana neophyte normally has to be helped to recognize and appreciate the pleasurable sensations of the drug, as well as to master the technique of smoking it. Becker, in a classic study of this process, reports that "the novice does not usually get high the first time he smokes marijuana, and several attempts are usually necessary to induce this state." Many of his informants said that they failed to recognize the signs of being "high" until these were identified for them by fellow marijuana smokers. As one admitted, "It was only after the second time I got high that I realized I was high the first time." Furthermore, initially they sometimes found the sensations unpleasant—they felt sick, frightened, or dizzy. It was the reassurance and interpretation provided by more practiced smokers which eventually enabled them to enjoy the experience and therefore to continue use of the drug.[54]

Marijuana has been used in various societies for some 5,000 years. Because of its mind-altering characteristics, it is classified pharmacologically as a hallucinogen. It produces a relatively mild, pleasurable sense of euphoria and well-being, rather than the very pronounced "high" of the opiates.

Marijuana is made by shredding the flower and stem of the Indian hemp plant, or *Cannabis sativa*. It can be mixed with food and eaten, or boiled and the tea drunk. But it has the fastest effects when smoked, in cigarettes usually called "joints," or "jays," and it is most commonly used this way. The smoke is not exhaled in quite the same way as the ordinary cigarette smoke, but is instead held in the lungs for a short period of time.

Moments after the smoke has been inhaled, distinctive symptoms appear. The commonly encountered physical effects are dryness of the mouth and pharynx, an irritation in the throat, and exaggerated sensitivity to visual, aural, and tactile stimuli. This sensitivity is probably a factor in smokers' feelings that they are more aware of their surroundings and more open to other people than in their normal state. Other changes are an increase in the pulse and heartbeat and a reddening of the eyes.

Marijuana smokers generally must be taught to recognize the sensations caused by the drug before they can enjoy using it.
Bob Combs/Photo Researchers

[54] Howard S. Becker, *Outsiders: Studies in the Sociology of Deviance.* New York: Free Press, 1963, pp. 46, 51.

TABLE 3-1 Major Substances Used for Mind Alteration

Name of Drug	Slang Names (Current and Past)	Usual Adult Single Dose	Duration of Action (Hours)	Medical Uses (Present and Projected)	Risk of, Potential for	
					Tolerance	Physical Dependence
Alcohol (beer, wine, vodka, whiskey, gin, etc.)	Hard stuff, booze, drink, suds, cocktail	1–2 oz 12 oz (beer) 4 oz (wine)	2–4	None	Yes	Moderate
Nicotine (cigarettes, cigars, snuffs, tobacco)	Fags, weed, coffin pegs	1–2 cigarettes	1–2	None. Recommended against because even small quantities are poisonous	Yes	Maybe
Sedatives-hypnotics (chiefly sleeping pills)			4–8	Tension, insomnia, neurosis	Yes	High
Alcohol						
Barbiturates	Downers, goof-balls					
Nembutal	Yellow jackets	50–100 mg				
Seconal	Reds					
Phenobarbital	Phennies			Epilepsy		
Chloral hydrate		250–500 mg				
Doriden		500 mg				
Miltown, Equanil		300 mg				
Quaalude, Sopor		500 mg				
Valium						
Stimulants			4–12	Narcolepsy, fatigue, sleepiness. No longer recommended for obesity.	Yes	Maybe
Caffeine						
Nicotine						
Amphetamines	Uppers, pep pills					
Benzedrine	Bennies	2.5–5 mg				
Dexedrine	Dexies			Hyperactive children		
Methedrine	Speed, meth					
Ritalin		10 mg		Obesity		
Preludin		25 mg		Obesity		
Tenuate		25 mg				
Tepanil		25 mg				
Cocaine	Coke, snow	1–2 snorts	2–4	Local anesthetic (now rarely prescribed)		
Narcotics			4–6	Severe pain	Yes	High
Opiates						
Heroin	H, junk, shit, smack, horse	1 bag, balloon, or paper				
Morphine		15 mg				
Opium (paregoric)		12 pellets		Diarrhea		
Codeine		32–64 mg				
Synthetics						
Methadone		5–10 mg	12–24	Heroin addiction		
Demerol		50–100 mg	4–6			
Percodan		5 mg				
Cough syrups		1 tsp–2 oz				
Romilar, Hycodan, Cheracol, etc.)				Cough		

Source: Joel Fort and Christopher T. Cory, *American Drugstore.* Boston: Little, Brown, 1975, p. 40.

Reason Drug is Used and Abused	Short-Term Effects of Average Dose	Long-Term Effects of Frequent or Heavy Use	Laws and Public Policy
Relaxation, getting high (euphoria), conformity, overavailability, advertising	Central nervous system (CNS) depressant, drowsiness, decreased alertness and inhibitions, driving accidents	Impaired coordination and judgment, drowsiness to stupor, permanent liver and brain damage, obesity, violence, addiction, death	Fully available legally for use and sale except for mild criminal penalties (usually not enforced) for those under 18 or 21. Powerful lobby, legally advertised with token exceptions. Large black market to avoid taxes. Not classified as drug.
Relaxation (stimulation), ritual, conformity, over-availability, advertising, boredom	CNS stimulant, increased wakefulness. Also body poison and air pollutant	Heart attack, stroke, lung cancer, bronchitis, emphysema, high mortality of newborn offspring, fire, pollution, death	Fully available legally for use and sale except for mild criminal penalties (usually not enforced) for those under 18 or 21. Powerful lobby, legally advertised with token exceptions. Large black market to avoid taxes. Not classified as drug.
Relaxation or sleep, over-prescription by physicians, getting high, drug-company promotion	CNS depressant, sedation, drowsiness, sleep, decreased alertness and inhibitions	Impaired coordination and judgment, drowsiness to stupor, confusion, addiction, suicide	Readily available in unlimited amounts by medical prescription, which can be obtained from more than one doctor and refilled 5 times in 6 months. Other manufacture, sale, and possession prohibited by federal and state "dangerous drug" laws. Large illicit traffic (black market). Moderate penalties.
Relief of fatigue or sleepiness, overprescription by physicians, getting high, drug-company promotion	CNS stimulant, increased alertness (wakefulness) and decreased fatigue, reduced hunger, restlessness	Sleeplessness, weight loss and malnutrition, irritability, delusions, and hallucinations (toxic psychosis)	Generally available by medical prescription. Advertised and promoted to doctors (except cocaine). Other distribution and possession barred by federal and state "dangerous drug" laws (except codeine, which is covered by narcotic laws). Medium black market. Moderate to severe penalties.
Relief of pain, cough, or diarrhea; elimination of withdrawal symptoms; getting high; wide distribution by organized crime and government officials in S.E. Asia, Turkey, and Mexico	CNS depressant, sedation, drowsiness, analgesia, decreased alertness and inhibitions	Constipation, decreased hunger and weight, temporary impotency or sterility, addiction, accidental death from overdose, social stigmatization and frequent criminality as a result of public policy (not a drug effect)	Available by special narcotics prescription from physicians (except heroin, which is not used medically in U.S.) and in cough syrups sold over the counter. Other production, sale, and possession banned by U.S. and state narcotic laws. Extensive illicit traffic. Severe penalties.

TABLE 3-1 Major Substances Used for Mind Alteration *(Cont.)*

Name of Drug	Slang Names (Current and Past)	Usual Adult Single Dose	Duration of Action (Hours)	Medical Uses (Present and Projected)	Risk of, Potential for	
					Physical Tolerance	Dependence
Psychedelics (hallucinogens)				Alcoholism, narcotic addiction, and emotional adjustment of dying persons	Yes	No
LSD	Acid	150–250 mcg	10–12			
Mescaline (peyote)	Cactus	350 mg	12–24			
Psilocybin	Mushrooms	25 mcg	6–8			
STP–MDA						
DMT–DET						
Scopolamine (belladona)						
Tranquilizers				Schizophrenia, agitation, anxiety, vomiting	No	No
Phenothiazines		500–600 mg				
Thorazine		2–5 mg	6–12			
Stelazine		20–60 mg				
Prolixin						
Thioxanthenes						
Butyrophenones						
Benzodiazephines		5–10 mg				
Librium			4–8	Tension		
Valium						
Antidepressants			12–24	Severe depression	No	No
Imipramines						
Elavil		50 mg				
Tofranil		50 mg				
MAO inhibitors						
Nardil		15 mg				
Lithium		600 mg				
Amphetamines						
Miscellaneous				None	Maybe	No
Inhalants		1–2 sniffs				
Glue, solvents,			2			
gasoline, aerosols			1			
Nitrous oxide	Gas	Variable	1			
Carbon dioxide						
(built up through						
rapid breathing)	Gas	Variable	4–6			
Amyl nitrate	Popper	1 ampule				
Over-the-counter						
pseudo-sedative and						
sleep drugs		1 pill				
Compoz						
Sleepeze						
Nutmeg	Spice	Variable	1–2			
Cannabis sativa				Glaucoma, asthma, depression, loss of appetite, high blood pressure, headache, alcoholism	No	No
Marijuana	Pot, grass, weed	1 cigarette	2–4			
Hashish (charas)	Hash	1 cake or pipe	2–8			
Caffeine			2–4	Fatigue, sleeplessness, coma	Yes	No
Coffee, tea	Java					
Cola drinks	Coke					
No-Doz, Tirend						
APC, Excedrin	Headache pills			Headache		

Reason Drug is Used and Abused	Short-Term Effects of Average Dose	Long-Term Effects of Frequent or Heavy Use	Laws and Public Policy
Mind expansion, perceptual changes, mystical experience, problem solving	Intense visual and other sensory experiences, rapid flow of thoughts, mood changes, anxiety or panic	Hallucinations, delusions (acute psychosis), confusion, impaired judgment	Unavailable legally except from U.S. government to a very few mental researchers and for use by Indians (peyote). Otherwise prohibited by federal and state "dangerous drug" laws. Medium illicit traffic. Moderate penalties.
Relaxation, relief of agitation, hallucinations or delusions, prescription by physicians	Easing of anxiety or tensions, improved functioning, suppression of neurotic or psychotic symptoms	Destruction of blood cells, jaundice (liver damage), hypertension, skin rash, blurred vision, decreased initiative (apathy), muscle stiffness, convulsions	Readily available for physicians prescribing for indefinite periods. Advertised and promoted to doctors. Negligible black market.
Relief of depression (to feel normal), prescription by physicians	Improved mood and functioning, more energy	Destruction of blood cells, jaundice (liver damage), hypertension, skin rash, blurred vision, decreased initiative (apathy), muscle stiffness, convulsions	Readily available for physicians prescribing for indefinite periods. Advertised and promoted to doctors. Negligible black market.
Getting high, relaxation, substitute for other substances, overavailability	CNS depressant, drowsiness, impaired coordination and judgment. Over-the-counter drugs provide mainly a placebo effect as the combination used is almost inactive	Liver or kidney damage, hallucinations, confusion, death	Most are fully available to all ages. Some restrictions on airplane glue, nitrous oxide, and amyl nitrite. Not considered drugs. Not usually covered by criminal laws.
Relaxation, getting high, conformity, ready availability, reaction to distortions about its dangers	Mixed CNS effects, increased appetite, decreased alertness and inhibitions, changed time perspective	Acute (short-lived) panic or or hallucinations, bronchitis	Unavailable by medical prescription. Cultivation, sale, and possession prohibited by U.S. and state laws. Enormous black market; not much enforcement.
Increased alertness, relaxation (stimulation) conformity (custom), ready availability, work break, boredom, advertising	CNS stimulant, increased wakefulness, reduction of fatigue	Insomnia, restlessness, stomach irritation	Fully available for use and sale to children and adults. No civil or criminal penalties. Not classified as drug.

Appetite is usually stimulated, and one's sense of time may also be affected. Physical, emotional, and mental effects vary with the potency of the marijuana, the dose taken, the individual's past history and present mental state, the setting in which the drug is taken, and the individual's anticipation of a "high."

For some time, heated debates about the hazards of long-term marijuana use have been raging, and there appears to be no end in sight. Some studies that apparently show lowered male hormone levels, brain damage, and other ill effects as a result of marijuana use have been questioned on the grounds of poor research techniques and methodology. In one often-cited hormone-level study, for example, all of the 10 marijuana-smoking subjects had used LSD, and most had been on amphetamines and/or other drugs as well; there is an obvious question of whether these drugs, or the multiple-drug combination, would be responsible for any long-range ill effects.

One study by the National Institute of Mental Health analyzed the effects of long-term marijuana smoking in Jamaica, where many heavy users smoke at least eight "spliffs" (a more potent marijuana cigarette than the typical American joint) a day. The researchers found that field workers expended more energy after smoking a spliff than before, but appeared to accomplish less actual work. They noted "no significant physical abnormality" attributable to the drug in any of the smokers or in the control group. Neither were there significant chromosome abnormalities or differences in brain-wave recordings. When the long-term marijuana users were deprived of the drug for two or three days, there were no "demonstrable intellectual or ability deficits. . . . there is no evidence . . . of brain damage." At worst, the Jamaica study indicates, there may be impaired lung function due to smoke (marijuana or tobacco) inhalation. A number of additional studies tend to support these findings.[55]

One of the public's greatest fears about marijuana is that its use will lead to the use of other drugs (the "stepping-stone" theory). This appears to be a myth. Persons are most likely to become multidrug users as a result of peer pressure, not because of the effects of one specific drug. If any drug is associated with the use of others, including marijuana, it is tobacco, followed closely by alcohol. Many studies have revealed a close association between the use of tobacco and, to a lesser extent, of alcohol, and the use of marijuana and other mind-altering drugs. In fact, some studies indicate that marijuana users tend to have parents who use tobacco or alcohol, while marijuana abstainers tend to have been raised by parents who use no drugs.[56] It should be emphasized that although many opiate users may at some time have used marijuana, the overwhelming majority of marijuana users do not progress to other drugs. In particular, no causal relationship has been shown to exist between marijuana use and subsequent heroin use.[57]

[55] Edward M. Brecher and the Editors of Consumer Reports, "Marijuana: The health questions." *Consumer Reports,* March 1975, pp. 143–149.
[56] See, for example, the articles by Denise Kendal *et al.* in *Journal of Social Issues,* vol. 30, no. 2 (1974) and *Journal of Health and Social Behavior,* vol. 15, no. 4 (December 1974).
[57] *Marihuana: A Signal of Misunderstanding,* p. 109.

Despite a general lack of convincing data on the ill effects of marijuana, the drug continues to be outlawed. It was first introduced in the United States in 1920, and its general use was made illegal by the federal government in 1937. Subsequently every state enacted statutes forbidding its use. However, in recent years there has been some modification of the legal approach to marijuana. By 1977, six states—Oregon, Alaska, Maine, Ohio, Colorado, and California—had decriminalized marijuana, typically reducing penalties to a moderate fine for possession of small amounts of the drug, and making possession a misdemeanor or civil offense instead of a criminal act. Other states were considering similar legislation.

The recognition of a need for reform was due in part to the greatly widening marijuana constituency, which now includes students, suburbanites, and numerous other middle- and upper-class individuals. When the dominant culture viewed drug users as members of a troublesome minority, harsh penalties were legislated. But when use by middle-class youth increased, and marijuana gained some acceptance among a segment of the adult population as well, modification of punitive laws became inevitable. In fact, data from various surveys of marijuana use suggest that up to 30 million people in the United States have tried marijuana at least once. For reasons such as these, even the federal government is deemphasizing its efforts to control marijuana use.

THE OPIATES

Opium has been known, and in some instances esteemed, for many centuries. It is derived from certain species of poppy and is the source of heroin, morphine, paregoric, and codeine, some of which are still widely used medically.

Early in the nineteenth century, physicians came to recognize that opium and morphine not only had therapeutic and pain-killing properties, but also caused physical and psychic dependency. It was observed that after taking the drug over a period of time, a person could no longer enjoy a feeling of normalcy and well-being without it. Also, the dosage had to be gradually increased. The individual was addicted, or "hooked."

Heroin, a refined form of morphine, was introduced about 1898. At first it was hailed as a breakthrough, a drug with all the advantages of morphine and none of the addiction-producing characteristics. The medical profession soon recognized its mistake, but by then the illegal traffic in the drug had begun.

In the 1960s, most heroin reaching America was grown in Turkey and processed and distributed in Marseilles. A joint French-American campaign disrupted "The French Connection" in 1971, at about the same time as an agreement between the United States and Turkey resulted in a ban on the growing of opium poppies in that country. The immediate result was a shortage of heroin, creating panic among addicts and resulting in, among other effects, substantial voluntary enrollment in addiction treatment programs. The estimated number of heroin addicts dropped from about 600,000 in 1970 to 300,000 or less in early 1974, and officials were predicting that addiction rates would be permanently lowered. However, by 1975 crude brown heroin from Mexico began appearing in the border cities of the Southwest: "Mexican brown" and heroin from Southeast Asia replaced Turkish heroin (even after the ban on poppy cultivation in Turkey had been lifted). Soon, addiction rates were back to their previous elevated levels.[58] It is important to note, however, that there are many more heroin users than addicts. For example, one recent study estimated that about 1.5 million people between the ages of 12 and 18 have tried heroin at least once.[59]

In contrast to the use of marijuana, use of heroin is essentially an individual activity. Neophytes may need to be shown how to prepare and inject heroin, or how to "snort" it, but once they have learned, they seem to derive no particular benefit from the presence of others.

The chief method of administering heroin is by injection into a vein, or "mainlining." Heroin can also be taken orally or sniffed, but it has a more immediate and more powerful effect when injected. Contrary to popular opinion, few addicts experience a sudden intense feeling of pleasure, or "rush," when using heroin. Instead, the user may feel calmed, relieved of tensions and anxieties, and enjoy a sense of self-esteem and composure. A typical reaction from an addict is that heroin "makes my troubles roll off my mind." Because heroin slows the functioning of parts of the brain, the addict's appetite and sex drive tend to be dulled; and after the initial euphoria he or she becomes lethargic and stuporous. Thus addicts are responsible for few rapes or aggressive crimes not connected with theft.

The acknowledged relationship of crime to heroin addiction results not from the addict's state when influenced by the drug, but from his or her suffering when without it. After about 18 hours' abstention, withdrawal symptoms set in, and these typically entail acute physical agony—chills, nausea, heavy sweating, sharp abdominal and leg cramps, diarrhea, convulsions, rapid weight loss, and general exhaustion. Once having experienced withdrawal symptoms, the addict will do almost anything to avoid a repetition of the experience; and since a single day's supply of heroin may cost an addict anywhere from $20 to $100, most of his or her waking hours must usually be devoted to obtaining it. In addition, because addicts are seldom employable, it is almost impossible for most of them to support their habits without resorting to illegal means, usually crimes against property (see Table 3-2).

The typical known addict probably is under 30, lives in an urban area, has serious health problems, and can anticipate a greatly shortened life expectancy. In addition to hepatitis and other infections often caused by the intravenous injections, the heroin addict frequently suffers from malnutrition.

It has usually been thought that heroin use is most common at the lower socioeconomic levels. However, at least one recent study has obtained data which raise some questions on this point. In a survey of two neighborhoods in Brooklyn, New York, researchers found that

heroin addiction is still concentrated in slum communities . . . but . . . the percentage of those with high school or college training who reported heroin

Mainlining heroin induces first euphoria, then a kind of numbness. Although users are almost always enchanted by friends, they afterwards become loners, oblivious to social interaction as long as they are high.
Dan McCoy/Black Star

[58] Bernard Weinraub, "Amsterdam called center of heroin traffic." *New York Times,* November 16, 1975, p. 2; and Martin Kasindorf, "By the time it gets to Phoenix." *New York Times Magazine,* October 26, 1975, pp. 18ff; and *U.S. News & World Report,* June 30, 1975, p. 29.

[59] Selma Mushkin, "Politics and economics of government response to drug abuse." *Annals of the American Academy of Political and Social Science* 417 (January 1975).

		TABLE 3-2
Shoplifting	22.5%	Sources of Funds
Burglary	19.0	for Heroin
Pickpocketing	5.4	
Larceny	7.4	
Robbery	3.4	
Confidence games	4.7	
Prostitution	30.7	
Welfare	3.0	
Other, legal sources	3.9	
	100.0%	

Source: S. Mushkin, "Politics and economics of government response to drug abuse." *Annals of the American Academy of Political and Social Science* 417 (January 1975): 30.

use in their families was double that of those who had only grade-school educations.

Those with blue-collar occupations or annual incomes less than $6,000 had distinctly less heroin use in their families than those with white-collar occupations or incomes greater than $6,000.[60]

According to Dr. Robert L. DuPont, director of the National Institute for Drug Abuse, "Heroin used to be an East Coast problem, and there was a lot of truth to the saying that half of all American addicts were in New York. This is no longer the case. The fastest-growing use of intravenous drugs has been among suburban and nonminority groups—although there is still a higher rate of use among minorities and the poor." By 1975 it was estimated that there were 8,400 heroin addicts in Phoenix, Arizona, a predominantly middle- and upper-class city where 80 percent of the population are Anglo whites; and such middle-class, Middle American cities as Denver, Jackson, Omaha, and Des Moines were cited as experiencing rapidly growing opiate use. One survey indicated that one in every 12 high school seniors in Phoenix has used heroin, morphine, or cocaine. A local anti-addiction agency in that city had many teachers and lawyers among its clientele.[61]

Typically, the middle-class user is introduced to the narcotic at a party by a well-meaning friend. A minority of users, estimated at perhaps 20 percent, are apparently able to use the drug without becoming addicted.[62] Many of these are wealthy, and can support their habit without resorting to crime. Others are able, for long periods of time at least, to continue working at high-paying jobs. According to DuPont, "Between 20 and 30 percent of the people entering treatment centers have jobs when they come in." An observer of the drug scene in Phoenix says, "People in the middle class can function better on a dope habit than working-class people, even in their jobs. We've had some people function for 20 years in the community without being detected." This phenomenon, according to Kasindorf, "raises a troubling question: Is narcotic addiction itself

[60] *New York Times,* July 23, 1972.
[61] Kasindorf, pp. 18, 20.
[62] Other studies suggest that only 1 in 10 heroin users is an addict; see Hicks.

debitating, or are only the poor debilitated by what they have to go through to pay for it?" [63]

A hallucinogen—what in popular terms is called a "psychedelic" drug—is a substance which causes a distortion of reality so that the subject will often "see" or "hear" something which is not objectively there. The best known hallucinogen probably is the synthetic alkaloid D-lysergic acid diethylamide, usually referred to as LSD. Hallucinogens are present in many plants—cactus, tree barks, flower seeds, and various species of mushrooms—and have a long history of use in many parts of the world, especially by nonliterate, relatively isolated societies. South and North American Indian groups and Siberian tribes have long utilized hallucinogens in religious and mystical rituals. In fact, mescaline, a substance occurring naturally in the peyote cactus, is legally available to the Native American Church, for which it is one of their sacraments.

At least one, and perhaps two, million Americans had used LSD by the end of the 1960s. It seemed to appeal primarily to persons of middle- and upper-middle-class background, students, avant-garde artists, and persons interested in Zen Buddhism, other Oriental religions, and/or religious "enlightenment." However, Ashley observes that, "unlike heroin, LSD never gained much of a following in the black ghettoes. Heroin permits the user to ignore his immediate environment, whereas LSD makes him more sensitive to it." [64]

A common word used to describe the LSD experience is "mind-expanding." A constellation of sensory changes typically forms part of the experience. Colors seem unnaturally bright, objects appear to expand, contract, or move, and the user loses his or her normal sense of time. Some LSD users report feeling as if they are no longer earthbound and have the ability to fly and soar. It is believed that under the influence of LSD the transmission of nerve impulses becomes scrambled so that music may be perceived in visual terms and color as an olfactory sensation. However, the hallucinations of the LSD user have been described as largely pseudo-hallucinations; that is, the individual is rarely deluded into accepting the fantasies as realities. He or she is usually aware that they are a purely subjective experience induced by the drug.[65]

Until the early 1960s LSD was unknown outside of medical circles, where it had found some application as a diagnostic tool. It has been used to draw out patients with severe mental disorders, and as a psychotherapeutic aid in treatment of neurotic, alcoholic, and terminal cancer patients. In the case of cancer patients, for example, there have been varying degrees of successful use, and no negative experiences. "What seemed to happen was that the patients were so engrossed in thinking about their LSD experience and so interested in talking about it to others that they paid much less attention to their pain." [66] Despite its potential for medical use, however, LSD is rarely used therapeutically. As a result

[63] Kasindorf, pp. 26–28.
[64] Richard Ashley, "The other side of LSD." *New York Times Magazine,* October 19, 1975, p. 48.
[65] Nowlis, p. 104.
[66] Ashley, p. 44.

of highly publicized negative experiences, government regulations and red tape make it extremely difficult at present for researchers to obtain the drug even for experimental purposes.

The most common hazards reported from LSD usage are: "bad trips," in which the user experiences a panic due to fear of insanity; lack of judgment or rational control, which may lead the user into physical danger; excessive subjectivity when the "trip" is over; and suspected organic impairment, either of the brain or of the chromosome structure. Up to 1969, there were over 100 "bad trip" victims a year admitted to one New York hospital alone. This rate has fallen off substantially, leading some investigators to conclude that LSD use has declined. Other observers, however, feel that LSD is as popular as ever, but that people are better informed about and prepared for its effects, and are therefore less likely to have a bad experience. It is also possible that the typical street product in recent years has been less potent and offered in doses too small to bring on a full response or lead to adverse reactions.

Ashley sums up the medical facts as they are presently known:

. . . no human deaths have been reported from LSD's pharmacological action, even though doses of several thousand micrograms have been recorded. . . . There has, however, been one verified coronary attack and two suspected attacks that occurred during LSD sessions, and one asthmatic patient died of acute asthma 12 hours after his third session.

There have also been reports that LSD damages white-bloodcell chromosomes [but other] agents—including coffee, aspirin, X-rays and fever—cause the same kind of damage . . . and [white-bloodcell chromosome damage is not the same as] genetic damage. Subsequent studies of babies born to LSD users showed that birth defects were no more common among them than among the offspring of nonusers.

. . . tests have turned up no evidence of major brain damage in heavy users and no conclusive evidence of subtle damage.

As yet there is no evidence to support the contention that LSD creates a physical dependency, nor that most experimenters with the drug develop a psychological craving for it. LSD-induced psychosis has been described, but there are no adequate data which would consistently link the occurrence of a psychotic reaction or mental illness with the use of LSD. Some studies indicate that those who had serious adverse reactions to LSD had preexisting mental problems.[67]

AMPHETAMINES

Drugs of the amphetamine family are popularly called "ups" or "uppers" because of their stimulating effect. They are usually safe when properly used; and, unlike marijuana and heroin, they are perfectly legal when prescribed by a physician. As a result, many people first become dependent on them through medical use. For example, drivers working on long-haul truck routes obtain prescriptions for a supply of amphetamine tablets so that they can safely negotiate a long trip. They become accustomed to the lift, the energetic and spunky feeling, which the amphetamines give them. They become habitual users. Or overweight individuals seeking to slim down are given amphetamines by their doctors.

[67] Ashley, pp. 48–50, 59.

They soon find that the pills also help them to get through a grueling daily schedule of activities with greater buoyancy and self-confidence. They, too, become users, continuing to take amphetamines long after they cease to be medically indicated.

A serious social problem is posed by extensive adolescent use of amphetamines. A study of colleges and other schools showed that amphetamines ranked among the most widely used drugs, following alcohol and marijuana.[68]

Amphetamines are usually taken orally, in tablet, capsule, or powder form. But they can also be "snorted" or injected. Injecting the drug intravenously, or "speeding," produces the most powerful impact and can cause the greatest harm. Though unlikely, an overdose may result in coma, with the possibility of brain damage or even death. There are other dangers as well. The speeder may develop serum hepatitis, abscesses, long-term personality disorders, and psychotic states. This "amphetamine psychosis" is particularly likely to occur with long-term, high-dose use. Secondary effects of continued use of amphetamines may include skin lesions, respiratory problems, and acute gastrointestinal discomfort.

Chemically, the amphetamines are a family of stimulants including benzedrine, dexedrine, and methedrine. They are related to adrenalin, a homone normally secreted by the adrenal gland, which stimulates the central nervous system. The organic effects of the amphetamines can be far-reaching. The acceleration of metabolic action causes the fat stored in the body tissues to be burned up; there is a stepped-up heartbeat, respiratory stimulation, inability to sleep, and reduction of appetite. Other psychological and physical effects vary, depending on the user. Among some users, for example, amphetamines are believed to have hallucinogenic effects. Most subjects experience a feeling of greater strength, euphoria, and elation. Their ability to concentrate and express themselves verbally is enhanced.[69]

Continued amphetamine use is generally thought to create psychological dependence. Upon abrupt withdrawal, the person accustomed to a heavy dosage may plunge into a suicidal depression. Even with lower levels of habituation, giving up the drug is extremely difficult because, to the person deprived of it, life becomes a dismal routine. Medical opinion long held that amphetamines were not addictive, because withdrawal did not produce the syndrome familiar to withdrawal from other drugs. It is now recognized, however, that amphetamine withdrawal is accompanied by its own distinctive syndrome: apathy, decreased activity, and sleep disturbances. There is, then, some evidence of a physical dependence potential.[70]

Although amphetamines are widely available on the illegal market,

[68] Louis G. Richards, "Patterns and extent of abuse." In J. R. Wittenborn *et al.*, eds., *Drugs and Youth*. Springfield, Ill.: Charles C Thomas, 1969, p. 142.

[69] Leslie Grinspoon and Peter Hedbloom, *The Speed Culture*. Cambridge, Mass.: Harvard University Press, 1975.

[70] National Clearinghouse for Drug Abuse Information, *Amphetamine*. Rockville, Md.: Alcohol, Drug Abuse, and Mental Health Administration, Report Series 28, No. 1, February 1974, pp. 9–10.

the only legitimate access to them has been via a doctor's prescription. Until mid-1970, amphetamines were used extensively in treating epilepsy, narcolepsy (persistent attacks of sleepiness), Parkinson's disease, depression, certain personality disorders, and, as noted above, for the control of weight, bladder ailments, and excessive fatigue. At that time, however, the widespread abuse of amphetamines became apparent, and they were placed under stricter federal controls. At present the Food and Drug Administration restricts the legal use to narcolepsy, hyperkinesis (marked overactivity and underachievement in children), and short-term weight reduction. The appetite-depressant effects of amphetamines have been found to last only for four to six weeks. (It was because patients developed tolerance to the drug so rapidly that its use was frequently abused.) Since they are effective as weight-reducing aids for this short period only, and since overeating is generally a psychological problem and not a physical one, amphetamines are being prescribed less frequently today.

BARBITURATES

Barbiturates are depressants of the central nervous system that are derived from barbituric acid. The first sleep-producing barbiturate was introduced in 1903, and more soon followed. Today there are some 2,500 known barbiturates. Of those ordinarily available on the legitimate market, over a dozen are widely used medications.

Barbiturates are drugs of enormous versatility. By themselves and in combination with other drugs, they are used in treating temporary insomnia, epilepsy, and high blood pressure, and in relaxing patients before and after surgery. They are also valuable tools in the diagnosis and treatment of mental disorders. But, as in the case of amphetamines, the potential for misuse is great, so that mere possession without a prescription is unlawful.

Production statistics alone are highly informative about barbiturate use in the United States. Over 400 tons—3.6 billion average doses—of barbiturates are manufactured in the country each year. According to Blum, "Enough barbiturates . . . are manufactured every year in the United States to provide thirty or forty doses for every man, woman, and child." [71]

Prolonged barbiturate use and high dosage can result in a physical dependency with symptoms similar to those of heroin addiction. Indeed, many drug experts are convinced that barbiturate addiction is even more dangerous, and more resistant to treatment and cure, than is heroin addiction. A barbiturate addict deprived of the drug frequently experiences a range of symptoms which include cramps, nausea, delirium, and convulsions. Abrupt withdrawal can even result in death.

In addition, barbiturate overdose may cause poisoning, with convulsions, coma, and sometimes death. In fact, in the United States barbiturates are a leading cause of accidental deaths by poisoning. One of the reasons for this high total is the fact that barbiturates tend to heighten the effect of alcohol, sometimes with toxic results. Also, persons who take the drug to induce sleep may, if the first dose is not quickly effective, become confused as to how many pills they have taken, and take too many.

[71] Blum *et al.,* p. 242.

Taken in moderate doses, barbiturates, like alcohol, are mildly dis-inhibiting. However, reports of other personality changes show no consistent patterns. Sometimes the barbiturate user is calmed and relaxed —reactions normally associated with a depressant—but sometimes he or she becomes convivial and lively instead.

Frequently, individuals will develop a habit of using both ampheta-mines and barbiturates, together or in alternation. The combination amphetamine-barbiturate users are persons for whom the normal rhythm of life, the alternation of rest and wakefulness, has become meaningless. It has been replaced by the chemical cycling of consciousness through "ups"—amphetamines—and "downs"—barbiturates. However, such chemical regulation of activity, if prolonged, usually results in the indi-viduals' physical and psychological deterioration.

SOCIAL PROBLEMS RELATED TO DRUG ABUSE

The drug problem traced to its very roots stands out as chiefly a "people problem." It centers on the people in the streets who use the drugs, and the people in the halls of government who are empowered to make the laws and judgments affecting drug users.

A consideration of present attitudes and beliefs about drugs and drug control suggests a number of rather basic questions:

» Has society's attitude toward the drug problem adequately taken into account the differences between drug users and abusers?
» Has sufficient thought been given to the fact that drug use and abuse have existed throughout human history? Is the desire to escape reality a legitimate human need?
» Is a society historically based upon the principles of individual initia-tive, productivity, moderation, self-restraint, and deferred pleasure in the best position to deal rationally with behavior that is self-gratifying or escapist? Should we always consider the individual who takes drugs without medical consultation to be either physically or psychologically ill? Do people have the right to control their own destinies?
» When does the government have a legitimate right to interfere in personal affairs and define permissible and proscribed behavior? And who are the judges?

As these questions indicate, concern about drugs is integrally related to judgments about human nature and human behavior; the role of social institutions and the responsibilities of social control; the rights of the individuals against their obligations to society; and definitions of danger, safety, risk, and abuse.

There exists more than a suspicion that drugs can make people lose control over their lives—a possibility recognized by those who favor drug use as well as by those who oppose it. In the oral tradition of the counter-culture, this is known as "getting wasted," which produces "dead freaks," "zombies," useless to themselves, to society at large, and even to their own society. There is also, on the other hand, the belief among some drug users that a more widespread use of drugs, particularly marijuana, could reduce some of our social problems (such as war or aggression).

Most drug use is not aimed toward solving social problems; nor does it inevitably result in a "wasted" life. It is a fact, however, that in recent years young people have tended to use drugs more than adults and with increasing frequency. "Figures for alcohol, tobacco and marijuana use show basically the same pattern: Use peaks at the 18–21 age bracket, levels off for a while and then falls off sharply. The fall-off for marijuana use comes at a younger age, the mid-30s, than for alcohol and tobacco use, the mid-40s, because it has not been widely used as long." [72] Further, young people tend to experiment with a number of different substances. High school students are more likely than college students, only a few years older, "to have regular highs from psychedelics (LSD), barbiturates, cocaine, and even heroin as well as marijuana, several times a month at least. Further, young people do not try drugs *instead* of alcohol, but in addition to it." [73]

Drug use is increasing among adults too. One side effect of the medico-pharmacological advances of the last half-century is that we have become a nation of drug takers and "pill poppers." For every ailment we bring to the physician, we expect to be given a prescription with an implicit promise of a speedy recovery. In a strange perversion of our "unalienable right" to the "pursuit of happiness," we demand instant cures and instant gratification. Advertising, especially on television and in magazines, touts "immediate relief" for everything from mild headache to severe arthritis. And, as Kramer has pointed out, television itself is analogous to the drug experience: "Both depend on 'turning on' and passively waiting for something beautiful to happen." [74]

The increased use of drugs as a means of escape by all segments of the population may indicate the larger problem of society's failure to provide its members with the ability to face and comprehend change, or to cope with minor as well as major problems. It may also indicate society's failure to provide its members with meaningful activities or values, a failure which for some necessitates the search for such values outside the mainstream of society.

DRUGS AND THE LAW

How effective is legal drug control? The answers to that question seem to be discouraging. Through the years drug laws have proliferated, the penalties have become harsher, and the number of drug users has steadily increased. Now we have reached a point at which drug offenses severely tax an overburdened police and judicial system and penal institutions are already unbearably overcrowded. In every federal and state jail, drug offenders comprise a large proportion of the population. In the most recent year for which statistics are available, there were about 630,000 arrests for drug-law violations. Some two-thirds of these were marijuana-related. [75]

Often the punishment for drug offenses is unduly severe. As Nowlis states: "Drug legislation makes possession of a 'potentially dangerous'

[72] See Hicks.
[73] Yankelovich, pp. 39–41.
[74] E. H. Kramer, in F. Earle Barcus and Susan M. Jankowski, "Drugs and the mass media." *Annals of the American Academy of Political and Social Science* 417 (January 1975):88.
[75] Richard S. Schroeder, "Marijuana and the law." *Editorial Research Reports* (February 21, 1975):124.

substance a crime with penalties in some cases equivalent to or in excess of those for such criminal acts as grand larceny and second degree murder." [76] In some states the penalties for selling or even giving a small quantity of marijuana to another person may be as high as 25 years, or even life imprisonment, for the first offense. Such disproportionate harshness not only creates injustice for the individuals sentenced, but tends to discredit the entire criminal law system in the eyes of many who recognize the injustice, whether or not they are themselves users of illegal drugs.

The earliest attempt to control addictive drugs in the United States was the Harrison Act, passed by Congress in 1914. This provided for strict regulation of the sale, use, and transfer of opium, coca, and coca products, with possession of drugs declared unlawful except in the instances where it could be shown that the drugs had "legitimate medical purposes." For the first time, narcotics distribution was strictly controlled by the government, specifically by the Narcotics Division of the Treasury Department, an agency vigilant and zealous in hunting down and prosecuting violators. The right of the government to control drug use was further reinforced by a series of Supreme Court decisions. Soon, legitimate sources for procuring drugs dried up, and addicts had little recourse but to turn to illicit dealers. By 1925 the illicit drug trade had grown so much that more legislation was considered necessary, and a series of measures designed to strengthen and expand the Harrison Act followed.

In addition to more stringent laws, penalties too were made stiffer. Twice in the 1950s, when the fact of increasing drug use became apparent, Congress reacted. In 1951, minimum federal prison sentences were established for all narcotics and marijuana violations, ranging from two years for first offenders to ten years for third offenders. Again, in 1956, the growing magnitude of the drug problem spurred Congress to increase federal sentences for illegal sale or importation of drugs to a mandatory five years for the first offense and ten years for the second. State laws generally were modeled on federal legislation.

More recently, there was the Comprehensive Drug Abuse Prevention and Control Act of 1970, which established schedules of controlled substances in order of their potential abuse. Manufacturers and distributors of such substances must register annually with the Attorney-General, who also determines annual production quotas for certain drugs. By decreasing the amount of drugs manufactured and in inventory, these provisions attempt to decrease the amount of legally produced drugs available for diversion into illegal channels. [77] The Drug Abuse Treatment Act of 1972 was primarily concerned with the health aspects of drug abuse; federal funds, for example, now support community treatment centers serving an estimated 300,000 addicts. [78] And in 1973 a separate National Institute on Drug Abuse was established within the newly reorganized

[76] Nowlis, p. 51.
[77] Oakley S. Ray, *Drugs, Society and Human Behavior*. St. Louis: C. V. Mosby, 1974, pp. 26–27.
[78] *U.S. News & World Report,* June 30, 1975, p. 29.

Alcohol, Drug Abuse and Mental Health Administration of the Public Health Service. It is estimated that federal expenditures for all drug-abuse–related activities was $754 million in 1975, and that total state expenditures may well have been equal to that amount.[79] However, enforcement and treatment are still carried out to a considerable extent under the aegis of the federal government.

Until recently, the principal theme running through all this legislation has been its punitive character—the state's function is to punish, not to prevent or treat. Though campaign after campaign was being lost in the struggle with drugs, the legislators seemed unable to try any other approach. In fact, general ignorance of the real physical and social effects of drugs, and the irrational fear of them which resulted, probably made any course other than uncompromising, severe punishment of offenders politically impossible.

Increasingly, however, punitive legislation is proving unworkable. It is now clear that punishing offenders does not get at the basic problem. Most of the present drug laws are based on an outdated and inadequate knowledge of the scientific and social aspects of drug abuse. When the Harrison Act was passed, it was at least excusable for legislators to think that penalties would have a deterrent effect, but today it is much less so. If nothing else, we have the parallel example of Prohibition, which proved almost totally unworkable and resulted in the growth of large-scale organized crime. Similarly, laws making it difficult for addicts to acquire drugs have been responsible for the enormous growth of the illicit drug trade.

Our national inability to approach the problem of drug abuse except by repression stems in part from the ignorance of the real nature and effects of drugs, aided and abetted by a certain amount of media sensationalism. Perhaps more deeply, it stems from a not very precisely defined feeling that the drug revolution may be a manifestation of an extremely basic challenge to our way of life and even our national existence. This may or may not be true, but so long as we think it is true, we are probably going to react with a certain degree of panic and irrationality. Clearly, accurate knowledge, and intelligent dissemination of knowledge, would seem to be prime necessities.

Of even greater importance to the workability of drug laws—or for that matter any law—is the support and compliance of the population. All across America, on college campuses and in industrial centers, in large and small communities, the beliefs, mores, and values incorporated in traditional drug laws are either being challenged or undergoing dramatic revision. This trend has been reflected in the liberalized laws passed by many states, as well as in individual behavior choices.

If punishment is to have any deterrent effect on illegal drug use, it must include not only the user and the small-scale dealer, but the major distributors as well—those operating at the highest levels of drug importation and manufacture. Drugs filter down through many levels and many hands before they reach the neighborhood distributor. The pushers trans-

DRUG USE AND CRIME

79 Mushkin, p. 28.

acting business with junkies are more than likely to be addicts themselves and the lowest people in the hierarchy. The drug trade earns them money or a share of drugs to support their own habit. Top syndicate figures, however—the real money-makers in the business—are rarely arrested. At recent hearings of a Senate subcommittee, investigators testified that 90 percent of arrests by federal agents were of low-level pushers, instead of the drug traffic instigators. In addition, it was charged that the use of undercover agents to buy drugs and arrest sellers fostered corruption and in fact often stimulated the illegal drug market.[80]

The nature of drug-related crimes varies with the drug involved. According to the National Commission on Marihuana and Drug Abuse, "The only crimes which can be directly attributed to marihuana-using behavior are those resulting from the use, possession or transfer of an illegal substance," and neither marijuana nor low to moderate doses of barbiturates are likely to cause aggressive behavior, "although high dose use of [barbiturates] has been known to cause irritability and unpredictably violent behavior in some individuals." Amphetamine users, however, seem disproportionately involved in violent crimes such as robberies and assaults, and it was possible "that these crimes were directly attributable to acute reactions of the drug." Supporting evidence comes from Japan, where a limited period of amphetamine use during the mid-1950s was associated with a rise in violent crimes, which decreased markedly when amphetamine use diminished.[81]

Heroin, however, is the drug most frequently associated with criminal behavior of various kinds. According to the National Commission on Marihuana and Drug Abuse,

The available data indicate that most known opiate (primarily heroin) dependent persons had long histories of delinquent or criminal behavior prior to their being identified as drug users, that opiate use becomes a further expression of delinquent tendencies.

Thus, heroin users tend to be persons with histories of illegal activity. The question of the extent to which heroin addiction bears a cause-and-effect relationship to crime is addressed by a number of studies, which focus on the addict's necessity to resort to crime in order to support his or her heroin habit. Most note that the crimes committed for this purpose generally tend to be nonviolent, money-making crimes such as shoplifting. More significant, perhaps, is the indirect evidence indicating "that when the drug users are active in a therapeutic program and presumably not using heroin, criminal activity decreases. That is, when heroin use decreases either by treatment or other means, criminal behavior is also said to decrease." In sum, heroin users tend to engage in money-acquisitive crimes, "most of which are directly related to supporting the drug habit," but that "the available evidence indicates that [they] are significantly less likely to commit homicide, rape, and assault than are users of alcohol, amphetamines, and barbiturates.[82]

[80] *U.S. News & World Report*, p. 29.
[81] *Drug Use in America*, pp. 158–161.
[82] *Drug Use in America*, pp. 161–163.

SOCIAL CONTROL

Efforts to rehabilitate narcotics addicts have been impeded by the attitude "once an addict, always an addict." Until very recently, statistical evidence supported the pessimists, and the prospects for returning detoxified addicts to normal living were bleak and discouraging. As we have already suggested, however, it is likely that the social milieu in which addicts find themselves contributes significantly to their continued drug use. For example, one study of American soldiers in Vietnam who were addicted to heroin indicates that most were able to kick their habits rather easily when they returned home.[83] Drug use, as DuPont has noted, does not necessarily follow a predictable process from experimentation to addiction, but incorporates a wide range of behavior that includes "experimentation, occasional use, regular use, and heavy use." [84] The factors that cause different individuals to fall into different categories of use are many and complex, and efforts to rehabilitate addicts have not always addressed themselves to the full range of problems with which addicts may be confronted. Furthermore, different types of therapeutic programs may be more successful than others for different types of addicts. The various programs described here represent relatively recent attempts to address the problems of addicts more fully.

Something similar to the community supervision idea has taken shape recently in the development of self-help addict communities, staffed by nonprofessionals and semiprofessionals, as well as professionals. The theoretical groundwork for the community treatment technique was laid by Dr. Maxwell Jones, who enlarged upon the germinal concept which he borrowed from Alcoholics Anonymous. Jones advocated group therapy and communal living for addicts so that all of the experiences of daily life would be shared in an atmosphere of constant supportive group interaction.

REHABILITATION PROGRAMS

Synanon. The first community formed to implement this idea was a West Coast group called Synanon, founded in 1958 by addict-members mainly for the treatment of drug addicts and, to a limited extent, of alcoholics. Synanon has, paradoxically, a more rigid daily structure than that of a hospital or clinic. The members rise at 6:30 each morning, and embark on a tightly planned schedule that keeps them fully engaged throughout the day. The purpose is not only for members to be kept occupied, but for their activities to take place in a setting that requires them to interact with other addicts all the time.

Synanon's approach differs from that of a hospital in another sense. The distinctions in roles and functions which in a hospital environment set apart the patient from the therapist, the patient from the doctor, and the patient from the administrator are absent in Synanon. A member of the Synanon community can and does act in all these roles simultane-

---

[83] Study reported by Kasindorf, p. 30.
[84] See Hicks.

ously. A detoxified addict will be thrust into many roles as soon as he or she is capable of handling them.

The most crucial and valuable component of Synanon is its unique form of psychotherapy, which in recent years has become more widely known through similar practices by encounter groups. Much more than in traditional group therapy, Synanon's sessions are uninhibited semi-public confessionals. As a way of getting in touch with their feelings, the participants are free to express their rage and hostility quite openly, even toward others in the group, as long as they stop short of physical aggression.

Daytop Village and Phoenix House. The Synanon experiment has been the prototype for Daytop Village and the Phoenix House, both of which have adapted the Synanon experience to their particular needs. Daytop has the reputation of being a free and more open community than Synanon. Synanon members, for example, are heavily dependent on their community and remain attached to it for many years, which appears to be consistent with the goals of their program. Daytop, on the other hand, encourages independence, and the addict is educated to function without ties to the Daytop community.

The first Phoenix House community was organized in 1967 under a government program and as part of the New York City Addiction Services Agency. It relied to a large extent on former addicts trained as therapists to serve in its facilities, in the belief that ex-addicts are better qualified than traditional therapists to understand the addict's problems. For one thing, they provide the addict with evidence that addiction is curable. Furthermore, ex-addicts, being familiar with the language and pattern of thinking distinctive to the addict's world, function as a cultural bridge between the addict and the Phoenix House professional staff. Finally, being members of the patient's peer group, they can penetrate the protective shell with which most addicts surround themselves from the authority of the "straights" and the influence of the outside world. Even counseling is often viewed by the addict as a form of authority and an imposition of control to be resisted. Key concepts of the Phoenix House program, as defined by Dr. Efren Ramirez, who has headed the city's addiction programs are: (1) an addict, unless psychotic, must be held responsible for his or her own behavior and be forced to face the realities he or she may wish to evade; and (2) treatment should not be directed only at the problem of physical dependence, but must seek to cure the psychological weaknesses of the addict as well.[85]

Methadone Maintenance. Methadone, a synthetic narcotic, has been extensively tested as a possible means of treatment for heroin addiction, and is now in regular use in a number of programs. It is similar enough to heroin that it satisfies the addict's physical craving, preventing the agony of withdrawal symptoms and the bleak depression of abstinence,

[85] Philip H. Connel, "Treatment of narcotic and non-narcotic drug dependence: The need for research." In R. Phillipson, ed., *Modern Trends in Drug Dependence and Alcoholism.* Englewood Cliffs, N.J.: Prentice-Hall (ACC), 1970, p. 33.

Here addicts partici-
pate in a free-wheeling
group therapy session
at Daytop Village, one
of the more successful
rehabilitation centers.
Rocky Weldon

but, unlike heroin, it does not induce a high. Consequently, an addict using methadone can continue to function more or less normally in the community. However, the drug is unlikely to be acceptable to those addicts who seek a high, if heroin is available.[86]

Methadone is addictive, and its proponents do not claim that it constitutes a cure. Rather, it offers a "maintenance" treatment for addicts who prove unresponsive to other types of therapy. But many, including even addicts enrolled in programs, believe that methadone keeps addicts dependent on drugs, and is therefore useful only as a short-term solution to get them away from heroin. Methadone treatment is also regarded, especially by both addict and non-addict minority group members, as a means of social control being imposed on them by the majority culture. However, these ambivalent attitudes toward methadone treatment apparently are not significant deterrents to potential clients. According to one survey, the major reasons cited by addicts for not entering treatment earlier were their inability to recognize their heroin addiction and the absence of treatment facilities in the immediate neighborhood. As Brown, Benn, and Jansen put it, "When the addict recognizes and is concerned about heroin dependence, his problems are too intense for ideological considerations. There is the clinic, the street, the jail, or the morgue. In that context the clinic becomes at least an acceptable alternative." [87]

Methadone is legally available only through approved programs, and in the early stages of such programs addicts are required to report to the treatment center for their daily dosage. Unfortunately, a black market in methadone seems to have developed as some heroin addicts discovered that the drug could tide them over periods when they are unable to obtain heroin, and others perhaps attempted self-treatment outside of established programs. An overdose of methadone, as with heroin, can be fatal, and a number of methadone-related deaths have been reported. Consequently, methadone maintenance programs have come under fire from various quarters.[88] Nevertheless, it has been estimated that at least 85,000 persons are now being treated with methadone, a substantial number of them under federally funded programs.

Narcotic Antagonists. Narcotics users who are weaned from the physical addiction will often experience a psychological craving for drugs as soon as they return to their previous environment. The need to overcome this problem led scientists to develop narcotic antagonists, substances which prevent the euphoria ordinarily produced by the opiates.

Two of the best-known opiate antagonists are Cyclazocine and Naloxone. The more widely tested rehabilitation technique is based on Cyclazocine, a synthetic analgesic which can be administered orally in liquid form, capsules, or tablets. However, undesirable side effects were reported

---

[86] Richard Brotman and Fredric Suffet, "The concept of prevention and its limitations." *Annals of the American Academy of Political and Social Science* 417 (January 1974):53–65.

[87] Barry S. Brown, Gloria J. Benn, and Donald R. Jansen, "Methadone maintenance: Some client opinions." *American Journal of Psychiatry* 132 (June 1975): 623–628.

[88] See, for example, *New York Times,* May 16, 18, 25, 1972.

in the use of Cyclazocine, and this provided the stimulus for developing Naloxone. In a number of tests the latter has shown some promise as a means of therapy. By negating the positive sensations achieved by heroin, the narcotic antagonists help motivated addicts to overcome their psychological conditioning to the drug.

In addition, researchers at the University of Chicago studying heroin-saturated muscle cells have reported the discovery of an agent that might be able to confer immunity against the effects of heroin. This substance stimulates the production of antibodies that specifically combat the effects of the drug. However, there are a number of problems involved in its use, including the most important question of selecting those to be immunized. Furthermore, those so immunized would also lose the ability to respond to common opium-based pain killers.[89]

Community Programs. Halfway houses are another means of attacking the high relapse rate of addicts who, detoxified and physically cured, are returned from institutional life to the community. Through the halfway house, individuals are able to re-enter the community gradually and at their own pace. This buffers the shock of moving from a protective institutional environment to the much greater freedom of the outside world.

One of the most elaborate halfway house programs is that of the already-mentioned Phoenix House. Here, in moving from the supervised environment to the open community, the former addict passes through a five-stage transitional program. The gradual reintegration into everyday life takes place in a Re-Entry House to which addicts who have completed their treatment are transferred. Educational facilities are part of the Re-Entry House program and include training in vocational skills and preparation for those who wish to undertake professional education.

Ever since drugs first became a social problem in this century, the British approach has contrasted sharply with the American. The British avoided branding drug addicts as criminals and treated their condition as a disease requiring therapy. From this difference in fundamental attitudes, there developed a totally different set of legal practices and government policies. As early as 1926, a British government advisory committee issued a report which recommended: "With few exceptions, addiction to morphine and heroin should be regarded as a manifestation of a morbid state, and not as a mere form of vicious indulgence." [90]

An erroneous but generally held notion assumes that the British system permits an addict access to an unlimited supply of narcotics. Actually, the British government takes every precaution to strictly regulate the possession and distribution of opiates and of a number of other drugs. Until recently such drugs could be prescribed by any licensed medical practitioner, but detailed records were required, and physicians found guilty of deliberate overprescribing or of diverting drugs to illegal use were liable to severe penalties—fine, imprisonment, and loss of license.

In the 1960s the rate of opiate addiction in Britain began to climb

THE BRITISH SYSTEM

---

[89] "Blocking the effects of heroin." *Science Digest* (April 1975):27.
[90] Ministry of Health, Departmental Committee on Morphine and Heroin Addiction, *Report*. London: His Majesty's Stationery Office, 1926, p. 31.

An addict in England
has come to his local
clinic for his legal
heroin dose.
Mary Ellen Mark/
Woodfin Camp
& Associates

sharply, and a government committee, the Brain Committee, was con-
vened to study and report on the reasons and possible solution. The committee concluded that overprescription and the activities of a few medical
charlatans were largely, though not wholly, responsible for the spread
of addiction. It recommended that a system of government-run clinics be
established, and that only these clinics be authorized to prescribe heroin.
Such a system was inaugurated in 1968.

The program, under which physicians must notify the government of
any patients suspected of being addicted, applies to narcotics—heroin,
morphine, and cocaine—only, and does not affect marijuana, amphetamine, barbiturate, or hallucinogen users. British addiction peaked in
1968 with 1,476 new cases in the first year of compulsory notification.
By 1970, it was clear that the upward spiral of heroin addiction had been
curbed, with the first decrease in the annual addiction total in a decade.
In 1974, the latest year for which figures are available, only 777 previously unknown, out of a total number of 1,769 cases, were reported;
at the end of that year, 1,555 addicts were in treatment.[91]

No one believes that the clinics are the whole answer to Britain's
heroin problem, but clearly they do a great deal to contain it. Addicts

[91] *The Prevention and Treatment of Drug Dependence in Britain.* New York:
British Information Services, 1973, pp. 4–6.

who are registered with a clinic can obtain a supply of heroin or methadone legally and at reasonable prices; and because all known addicts are listed with one central authority (the Home Office), it is difficult for them to register with more than one clinic and obtain extra supplies for resale or excessive personal use.

The advent of methadone is partly responsible for the drop in heroin use. Unlike heroin, methadone is still available from private physicians, and methadone addiction is on the rise. While previously known addicts are given National Health Service prescriptions for heroin, new cases are being given methadone.[92] However, the increase in methadone use is not sufficient to cancel out the reduction in heroin use. Barbiturates and amphetamines, as in the United States, also enter the picture, especially as most British addicts appear to be multidrug users. Nevertheless, the total rate of addiction and of associated problems is evidently far lower than in the United States.

Granted that the British system has not succeeded in eradicating addiction and drug-related crime, certain facts are worthy of note:

» The black market in hard drugs is far smaller and less lucrative in Britain than in the United States.
» British addicts have a lower rate of arrests for nondrug crimes than do their United States counterparts. Since British addicts can get drugs at reasonable prices, they have less need to steal in order to support their habit.
» More British addicts are able to hold on to jobs and live fairly normal lives than is true of their United States counterparts. British estimates of employment rate among registered addicts range as high as 50 percent.

If official statistics are any guide, the British drug problem is minuscule compared with that of the United States. Thus, while it is not certain that the British system would work here—and considerable controversy has focused on this question—there is no doubt that it is worth studying. The basic philosophy behind it seems to have spared the country many of the consequences traceable to a punitive approach, and for that reason alone it merits our respectful attention.

EDUCATIONAL PROGRAMS

Much drug education in the past has concentrated on scare tactics, painting a lurid picture of the terrible consequences of drug abuse. The theory behind this was that an emphasis on the demoralizing, sordid, and negative side of drugs would frighten people away from experimenting with them. The alarmist approach, however, has a long record of failures, especially in dealing with the young. Emotional appeals of this type often discredit educators, destroying their credibility; and they have a reverse impact, arousing curiosity about the forbidden experience. They also conflict with the facts presented by friends or gained from firsthand experience, as well as with the present tendency among young people toward greater freedom and self-determination.

Perhaps the most damaging aspect of this approach is the tendency of the educator to exaggerate every possible ill effect and to ignore or deny

[92] Kasindorf, p. 36.

the positive features of drug taking, so that the student is in effect told not to understand but only to fear. When the National Coordinating Council on Drug Education evaluated 220 films on drug use, 84 percent of them were judged to be inaccurate, unscientific, and psychologically unsound. The basic concept of using education as an anti-drug tool assumes that informed people will usually not choose a destructive course of action; however, in practice, people often believe they are invulnerable to risk.[93]

A sound drug-education program requires an objective presentation of all the available information about the drugs under consideration. To a greater extent than many educators suspect, students today are knowledgeable and sophisticated about drugs and easily detect unbalanced or incorrect information.

While a rational approach to drug education is still in the early stages, some encouraging things are happening. A number of curriculum guides for teachers, texts, and audiovisual materials are now available; some states have mandated the addition of drug-education courses to the standard curriculum at various grade levels; and the federal government has established grants to aid the states in teacher training. It may be that the scare approach is on its way out, and that in the not too distant future children will learn about drugs in ways which they can believe.

Another way to ease the drug problem is to revise drug laws so that they deal with the issues realistically and consistently. So far, the most insistent demands for reform have centered on marijuana. It is increasingly recognized that marijuana should not logically be classified with the far more dangerous hard drugs, and many, even those who do not favor its legalization, are tending to support a lessening of the penalties for its possession and sale.

In fact, some revision has taken place.[94] Even the 1972 report of the National Commission on Marihuana and Drug Abuse, recommended changes in both federal and state laws. Under these recommendations, for instance, the private possession of marijuana for personal use would no longer be an offense, nor would the distribution of small amounts without profit to the distributor. Public use would be a criminal offense, but the maximum penalty would be a fine of $100; cultivation and distribution for profit would remain felonies, however. Persons would be held responsible for actions committed while under the influence of marijuana, and driving while under the influence would be a misdemeanor subject to fine, imprisonment, and suspension of license.[95] While these recommendations still contain inconsistencies, they represent a considerable advance over previous government thinking; and, as mentioned earlier, similar laws have already been adopted by several states and are under consideration in others.

Even with regard to the hard drugs, in recent years there have been a number of advocates of law revision, though few have gone so far as

REVISION OF DRUG LAWS

93 Brotman and Suffet, p. 60.
94 See, for example, "Marijuana: The legal question." *Consumer Reports,* April 1975, pp. 265–266.
95 *Marihuana: A Signal of Misunderstanding,* pp. 190–195.

to call for complete legalization of these drugs. One argument for legalization is that if heroin were available through some sort of legitimate channel, the price would go down, and addicts would no longer be forced into violent crime to support their habits; the British system is cited in support of this position. On the other hand, there is the fear that ease of supply would tempt many more people to experiment and perhaps to become addicted.

In some of our large cities, the question of legality is in a sense being bypassed. Although free heroin, on the British pattern, is not yet available to addicts, in many places treatment programs are available. Possession of heroin is still a crime, but an individual can admit to being an addict, and seek treatment, without risking arrest or commitment to an institution. While such programs are still largely experimental, and are presenting some problems of their own, their existence nevertheless suggests that in practice, if not in legal theory, there is a growing willingness to regard drug addiction as a sociomedical, not simply a criminal, problem. Brotman and Suffet, for example, conclude that "because of the prevalence of recreational patterns of moderate drug use . . . the prevention of all illicit drug use is not an achievable goal," and that we should "adjust our goals and focus our preventive efforts primarily on high-risk patterns of use—on those patterns, that is, where drug involvement demonstrably and significantly increases the chances of self-harm." [96]

The whole subject remains controversial, often with political overtones, and it is evident that we are a long way from achieving a national consensus on this highly emotional subject. Even if there were some generally accepted principles, the multiple causes and variety of patterns of drug use make it likely that the drug problem, even if it can be reduced, can never be completely solved.

PROSPECTS

Although Prohibition has been repealed, the kind of thinking which engendered it is still very much in evidence. Chronic drinkers are still being thrown into the tank to "dry out"; people are still being arrested for possession of a marijuana cigarette; drug addicts are still receiving heavy jail sentences. What is worse is that, in many places in the United States, treatment is still limited to the incarceration prescribed by the law.

The scope of the problem is not small: even rough estimates count several hundred thousand narcotic addicts, from 2 to 2.5 million chronic users of barbiturates or other sedatives, perhaps as many as 5 million people taking oral amphetamines without prescription,[97] and some 9 million with severe alcohol-related problems. Obviously, previously attempted solutions have not worked, and reform is in order. Surveys have found no consistent relationship between excessive drinking in a given

[96] Brotman and Suffet, pp. 53, 64.
[97] Bertram S. Brown, "Drugs and public health: Issues and answers." *Annals of the American Academy of Political and Social Science* 417 (January 1975):110ff.

area, and the rate of sale of alcoholic beverages or the number of liquor stores in the same area. It is evident that whatever legal measures have been taken to control drug and alcohol abuse have little relationship to the extent and nature of abuse and addiction problems. Moral persuasion and scare tactics have likewise been unavailing. Our laws must, therefore, begin to operate as rehabilitative instruments. We can no longer ignore the fact that a punitive approach to social problems does not work—and this is especially true for drug- and alcohol-related problems. It is simply not realistic to treat a drug or alcohol abuser as a criminal. Unless the situation that created the problem is eliminated, and unless he or she receives extensive rehabilitative treatment, the addict cannot change.

Suggested changes in federal and state drug laws have already been discussed. Analogous changes in the method of handling alcoholics have been proposed in a model program offered by the President's Commission on Law Enforcement and Administration of Justice. The commission recommends:

1. Routine medical evaluation of all individuals suspected of intoxication and taken into custody by the police
2. Routine training of police officers in handling public intoxication cases
3. Repeal of drunkenness statutes
4. Establishment of detoxification stations
5. Development of effective referral systems from detoxification stations to other community resources for treating alcoholics, e.g., outpatient clinics, domiciliaries, community houses, social centers
6. Development or strengthening of treatment programs within correctional institutions
7. Incorporation of special treatment for alcoholic offenders in parole and probation services
8. Federal action in the area of alcoholism control [98]

Programs of drug-abuse education and workshops in the field have been organized by the National Institute of Mental Health, and through the National Institute of Drug Abuse and the National Institute of Alcohol Abuse and Alcoholism. These should be expanded to better inform the public and to train more workers in this area. Changes in health insurance coverage to recognize the definition of alcoholism—and drug abuse in general—as an illness would make various treatments more accessible. It would seem that our hopes for the future lie with preventive education and humane psychotherapy rather than with fear- and anger-arousing prohibitions and punishments. It is likely to be some time, however, before most citizens learn to regard alcohol and other drug abuses as primarily a sociomedical problem rather than a legal or a moral one.

SUMMARY

A *drug* is any chemical substance that affects bodily function, mood, perceptions, or consciousness. Which drugs are and are not legal in a society often depends on cultural bias, rather than on an objective analysis of the effects of each drug.

[98] *Task Force Report: Drunkenness*, p. 17.

Drug abuse is the use of unacceptable drugs and the excessive or inappropriate use of acceptable drugs so that harm can result. Alcohol is an example of legal drugs that are widely and harmfully abused.

Problem drinking or alcoholism may be associated with a number of physiological, psychological, and ethnic factors. There has been a recent increase in the number of alcohol abusers among young people. Social problems related to alcohol abuse include the facts that alcoholics have a shortened life expectancy, alcohol is implicated in about half of all automobile accident fatalities and injuries, alcohol correlates highly with commission of serious crimes, and alcoholism often leads to broken families. Contrary to popular belief, only about 5 percent of alcoholics are in the "skid row" category.

Treatment for alcoholics has not been widely available, because of the traditional view of the alcoholic as an outcast. There are some indications that this attitude is beginning to change. The most successful treatment program for alcoholics thus far appears to be *Alcoholics Anonymous,* which combines a group therapy approach with an insistence on total abstinence from alcohol use. Other therapeutic efforts include *Antabuse programs, community programs,* and *company programs.* Educational programs attempt to prevent alcohol-related problems from arising.

Physical dependence, or addiction, occurs when the body experiences withdrawal if the use of a drug is discontinued. Psychological dependence, or habituation, occurs when the individual needs to use a drug for the feelings of well-being it engenders but is not addicted to it. There is considerable evidence that only a small portion of drug users are dependent on drugs.

Marijuana is generally smoked on social occasions, causing increased sensitivity to one's surroundings. There is little or no evidence that marijuana causes physical harm or leads to heroin use.

Unlike marijuana use, *heroin* use is largely an individual activity. It does not generally produce a euphoric "rush," but rather a feeling of calm and well-being. Thus heroin addicts are not likely to commit aggressive crimes unconnected with theft. Because heroin withdrawal is a painful process, however, addicts will steal to enable them to obtain the drug. There is evidence that heroin use among middle- and upper-class people has increased.

While some "bad trips" have been associated with the use of hallucinogens, particularly LSD, there is little evidence that they are physically harmful. In fact, they have some possible medical applications.

Amphetamines are stimulants that are widely abused. Heavy or prolonged use may do extensive physical and psychological damage. The body quickly builds up a tolerance for the drug, and there is evidence that it is addictive. *Barbiturates* are depressants that can also cause addiction. Both barbiturate overdose and withdrawal can result in death. Barbiturates are particularly dangerous when used in conjunction with alcohol.

Despite the proliferation of drug laws, drug use among young people and adults is widespread and increasing. The criminal justice system and penal institutions have been severely overburdened. From the Harrison Act of 1914 to the Comprehensive Drug Abuse Prevention and Control Act of 1970, the emphasis of the government has been on punishment rather than on prevention and treatment of abuse.

Drug rehabilitation programs that have proved relatively effective include those of Synanon, Daytop Village, and Phoenix Houses. Though they differ in some respects, they are similar in their focus on the psychological problems of addicts. The use of a synthetic narcotic, *methadone,* enables many addicts to function in society; however, it keeps the addict drug-dependent. *Narcotic antagonists,* which block the effects of heroin, are also available but are not widely used.

The British approach to the drug problem contrasts sharply with that of the United States, in that it views the addict as ill rather than criminal. Under strict guidelines, addicts can obtain heroin or methadone at nominal cost. Though it is unclear how well the British system would work with the much more extensive drug problem in the United States, it has apparently reduced the illicit drug trade, the drug-related crime rate, and the number of unemployed addicts.

BIBLIOGRAPHY

Bejerot, Nils. *Addiction and Society*. Springfield, Ill.: Charles C Thomas, 1970.

Blum, Richard H., *et al. Society and Drugs*. San Francisco: Jossey-Bass, 1969.

Cahalan, Don. *Problem Drinkers: A National Survey*. San Francisco: Jossey-Bass, 1970.

————, Cisin, Ira H., and Crossley, Helen M. *American Drinking Practices: A National Study of Drinking Behavior and Attitudes*. New Brunswick, N.J.: Journal of Studies on Alcohol, 1969.

Cortina, Frank M. *Stroke a Slain Warrior*. New York: Columbia University Press, 1971.

Duster, Troy S. *The Legislation of Morality: Law, Drugs, and Moral Judgment*. New York: Free Press, 1972.

Fort, Joel. *The Pleasure Seekers: The Drug Crisis, Youth and Society*. Indianapolis: Bobbs-Merrill, 1969.

Geller, Allen, and Boas, Maxwell. *The Drug Beat*. New York: Cowles, 1969.

Goode, Erich. *The Marijuana Smoker*. New York: Basic Books, 1970.

Grinspoon, Lester. *Marijuana Reconsidered*. Cambridge, Mass.: Harvard University Press, 1971.

Houser, Norman W., and Richmond, Julius B. *Drugs: Facts on Their Use and Abuse*. New York: Lothrop, Lee, and Shepard, 1969.

McGrath, John H., and Scarpitti, Frank R. *Youth and Drugs: Perspectives on a Social Problem*. Glenview, Ill.: Scott, Foresman, 1970.

Marihuana: A Signal of Misunderstanding. First Report of the Commission on Marihuana and Drug Abuse. Washington, D.C.: U.S. Government Printing Office, 1972.

National Commission on Marihuana and Drug Abuse. *Drug Use in America: Problem in Perspective*. Washington, D.C.: U.S. Government Printing Office, 1973.

Nowlis, Helen H. *Drugs on the College Campus*. Garden City, N.Y.: Doubleday, 1969.

Ray, Oakley S. *Drugs, Society, and Human Behavior*. St. Louis: C. V. Mosby, 1972.

Russo, J. Robert, ed. *Amphetamine Abuse*. Springfield, Ill.: Charles C Thomas, 1972.

U.S. Department of HEW. *Alcohol and Health*. Rockville, Md.: Public Health Service, 1974.

Westman, Wesley C. *The Drug Epidemic: What It Means and How to Combat It*. New York: Dial, 1970.

Whitney, Elizabeth D., ed. *World Dialogue on Alcohol and Drug Dependence*. Boston: Beacon, 1970.

Winick, Charles. *The Sociological Aspects of Drug Dependence*. Cleveland: CRC Press, 1974.

Wittenborn, J. R., Brill, Henry, Smith, Jean Paul, and Wittenborn, Sarah A. *Drugs and Youth: Proceedings of the Rutgers Symposium on Drug Abuse*. Springfield, Ill.: Charles C Thomas, 1970.

4

CRIME AND
CRIMINALS

- Over 10 million serious crimes were reported in 1975:
    463,000 robberies (taking property by force)
    3,232,000 burglaries (taking property from a home, un-seen)
    5,855,000 larcenies (taking property in general)
    993,000 auto thefts
- In a recent year, 71 percent of all persons convicted of auto theft were imprisoned for an average of three years, but only 16 percent of those convicted of securities fraud were sent to prison, and then only for an average of 19 months.
- Theft by employees, suppliers, and competitors forces companies to increase the costs of goods and services by 15 percent.
- In one survey, 4 out of 7 businesspersons reported that they would violate a code of ethics if they could avoid detection.
- For every 100 reported crimes,
    20 persons are arrested
    14 persons are charged
    7 persons are referred to juvenile court
    2 persons are acquitted
    1 person is fined
    1 person is found guilty of a lesser offense
    3 persons are placed on probation
    3 persons are imprisoned

The issue of law and order has assumed tremendous importance in America today: crime is widely considered to be one of our most pressing social problems. It is important to realize, however, that at least some crime has existed in almost all societies. As French sociologist Emile Durkheim pointed out, wherever there are people and laws, there are crime and criminals:

Crime is present not only in the majority of societies of one particular species but in all societies of all types. There is no society that is not confronted with the problem of criminality. Its form changes; the acts thus characterized are not the same everywhere; but, everywhere and always, there have been men who have behaved in such a way as to draw upon themselves penal repression. . . . From the beginning of the [nineteenth] century, statistics enable us to follow the course of criminality. It has everywhere increased. . . . What is normal, simply, is the existence of criminality.[1]

[1] Emile Durkheim, *Rules of Sociological Method*. 8th ed. trans. S. A. Solvay and J. H. Mueller, ed. G. E. G. Catlin. Glencoe, Ill.: Free Press, 1950, p. 65.

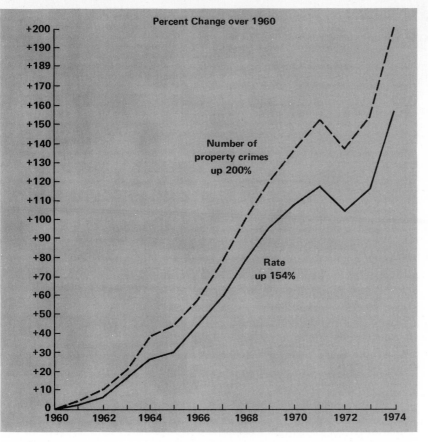

Percent Change over 1960

Number of
property crimes
up 200%

Rate
up 154%

FIGURE 4-1
Crimes Against
Property: 1960–1974

Limited to burglary, larceny
$50 and over, and auto theft.

Source: U.S. Department of
Justice, *Uniform Crime
Reports.* Washington, D.C.:
U.S. Government Printing
Office, November 17, 1975,
p. 55.

It is generally agreed that serious, violent crime has reached alarming proportions in the United States today, but the extent of the increase remains in doubt. One survey of five large U.S. cities revealed that the actual rates for violent personal and property crime were several times higher than the official rates presented in the FBI's *Uniform Crime Reports,* which are based on crimes reported to the police. A great many people do not tell the police that they have been victims of crime because they feel that nothing can be done about it or that the crime was unimportant.[2]

However, the official statistics tell a grim enough story: Although improved methods for the collection of data have added somewhat to the reported increase, the crime rate has doubled in the last fourteen years; it rose 18 percent between 1973 and 1974 alone, and another 9 percent by the end of 1975.[3] (See Figure 4-1.) Official statistics, of course, do not tell the whole story. For example, it has never been easy to assess

[2] Law Enforcement Assistance Administration (LEAA) study reported in UPI dispatch, April 15, 1974.
[3] U.S. Department of Justice, *Uniform Crime Reports.* Washington, D.C.: U.S. Government Printing Office, November 17, 1975, and March 25, 1976.

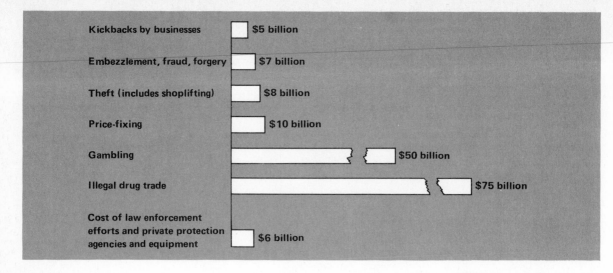

Kickbacks by businesses — $5 billion

Embezzlement, fraud, forgery — $7 billion

Theft (includes shoplifting) — $8 billion

Price-fixing — $10 billion

Gambling — $50 billion

Illegal drug trade — $75 billion

Cost of law enforcement efforts and private protection agencies and equipment — $6 billion

FIGURE 4-2
Estimated Annual
Dollar Cost of
Selected Crimes

Sources: U.S. News and World Report, December 16, 1974, p. 32; and Thomas Plate, *Crime Pays!* New York: Simon & Schuster, 1975.

the extent of organized and occupational crime with any substantial accuracy. However, recent exposures of government and business scandals show that these types of crime are far more widespread and pervasive than had been realized. (See Figure 4-2.)

Not only has crime itself increased, but the fear of crime, especially in large cities, is significantly affecting the life styles of many people. As the President's Commission on Law Enforcement and the Administration of Justice observed in its report, "The existence of crime, the talk about crime, the reports of crime, and the fear of crime have eroded the basic quality of life for many Americans." [4] For example, a Gallup Poll reported that about 67 percent of the women sampled were afraid to leave their homes at night.[5] A public opinion poll by the Law Enforcement Assistance Administration revealed that 41 percent of the population believed that there was an area near their place of residence where they would feel unsafe walking alone at night; 51 percent of the households surveyed contained a gun, and most of these guns were kept for personal protection.[6]

Meanwhile, the crime rates continued to rise, and youth gangs, relatively moribund in the 1960s, have reappeared in our cities. Some knowledgeable people in the field believe that the problem has reached crisis proportions, and the claim by the President's Commission that "America can control crime if it will" sometimes appears highly optimistic. At the very least, there are some serious questions to be asked about why crime occurs, why there is so much of it today, and what we can and should be doing about it.

[4] The President's Commission on Law Enforcement and the Administration of Justice, *The Challenge of Crime in a Free Society.* Washington, D.C.: U.S. Government Printing Office, 1967, p. v.

[5] *The Gallup Opinion Index—Political, Social and Economic Trends,* Report no. 82, April 1972.

[6] LEAA, *Sourcebook of Criminal Justice Statistics.* Washington, D.C.: U.S. Government Printing Office, 1975, pp. 172, 183–85.

THE NATURE OF CRIME

Crime is defined as an act or omission of an act for which the state can apply sanctions. The criminal law, a subdivision of the rules governing society, prohibits certain acts and prescribes punishments to be meted out to violators. Confusion frequently arises from the fact that although the criminal law prescribes certain rules for living in society, not all violations of social rules are violations of criminal laws. For example, a swimmer's failure to come to the aid of a drowning person would not constitute a criminal act, although it might be considered a moral wrong. Many acts which are regarded as morally wrong are not mentioned in the criminal law but are considered civil offenses. Under civil law—which deals with those noncriminal acts committed by one individual which injure another—the state, as an agent of society, acts as an arbitrator between the aggrieved party and the offender. An example of a civil case occurs when a person whose car was destroyed in an accident brings suit against the driver who was responsible in order to recover the cost of the damages. The driver who is judged responsible for the accident is not considered a criminal unless he or she can be shown to have broken one of the criminal laws, as, for instance, to have been driving while intoxicated. Further confusion results from changes in social attitudes, which usually precede changes in the criminal law. Old laws still "on the books" continue to make some acts criminal which are no longer considered wrong by society (such as kissing one's wife on the sabbath).

One problem with the legal definition of crime is that it ignores the effect of social values in determining what laws are to be enforced. Although judges and prosecutors use criminal law to determine the criminality of certain acts, the very act of applying the law involves issues of class interest and political power: one group imposes its will on another by enforcing its definition of illegality on the powerless. For example, authorities are not nearly as anxious to enforce laws against consumer fraud as they are to enforce laws against the use of certain drugs, because consumer fraud is often perpetrated by powerful business interests that have a strong influence in federal and state legislatures. The drug user, on the other hand, usually has little power or public support.

The history of vagrancy laws is another example of how groups in power create and enforce laws to protect their own interests:

Vagrancy laws emerged in order to provide landowners with a supply of cheap labor. When this group no longer needed cheap labor and were no longer powerful, the laws fell into disuse. Similarly, when the interests of a new power class—e.g., the mercantile class—were threatened, the vagrancy statutes were reactivated and appropriately altered to reflect the desires and needs of this group. Finally, the use of vagrancy laws in contemporary society to keep bums and other undesirables off the streets, or at least out of respectable neighborhoods, suggests the influence of middle-class desires and power to shape criminal laws.[7]

In practice the definition of criminality also largely depends on what the police believe criminal behavior to be. Given the thousands of laws that exist at any time, the police have a wide power of discretion over

[7] Clayton A. Hartjen, *Crime and Criminalization.* New York: Praeger, 1974, p. 29.

which laws to ignore, which to enforce, and how strongly to enforce them. This discretionary power, in turn, offers the police many opportunities to exercise their own concept of lawful behavior in their decisions as to what citizen's complaint needs attention, whom to arrest, and who to release.[8]

In a two-year study of two groups of adolescents in the same high school, William Chambliss examined how the biases of the local police and community members affected their reactions to and treatment of middle- and lower-class delinquents, and how the behavior and appearance of the delinquents themselves determined the kind of treatment and response they received.[9]

A group of middle- and upper-middle-class boys—the "Saints"—had been truant almost every day of the period they were studied. They had vandalized houses and harassed citizens and the police; they drove recklessly, drank excessively, and openly cheated on exams. Yet only twice in the two years were members of the Saints stopped by a police officer; even then, arrangements were made so that nothing appeared on their school records. Many of them received school distinctions. Teachers and school officials were blind to any acts that might be called delinquent and expected these boys to succeed in life.

The group called the "Roughnecks," on the other hand, were all from lower-class families. They had no money for clothes or cars, and in general could not maintain the same kind of physical appearance as the Saints. Where the Saints had cars and could "sow their wild oats" in parts of town where they were not known, the Roughnecks were confined to an area where they could be easily recognized, and therefore they established a reputation for being delinquent. They did relatively poorly in school.

The demeanor of the two groups of boys differed markedly whenever they were apprehended by the police. When caught, the Saints were apologetic, penitent, and generally respectful of middle-class values; they were therefore treated as harmless pranksters. The Roughnecks were openly hostile and disdainful toward the police and were therefore labeled by the police as "deviant." Chambliss found that the adult careers of the two groups followed the community's conceptions. Almost all of the Saints went on to college and white-collar careers, while most of the Roughnecks either went on to low-status jobs or became criminals.

An important fact to be noted about the Roughnecks and about lower socioeconomic classes in general is that the visibility of their "illegal" behavior works to their great disadvantage in their confrontations with the police and the criminal justice system. Crowded living conditions may predispose inhabitants of the ghetto to drink, gamble, fight, and take drugs more or less in public, where they can be seen easily by neighbors and the authorities. Members of the middle class, on the other hand, own private houses and automobiles in which to indulge in the same activities, but out of sight of neighbors and the law. These conditions reinforce the idea in the minds of middle-class authorities that most present-day crime and delinquency are lower-class phenomena.

---

[8] Hartjen, p. 84.
[9] William Chambliss, "The Saints and the roughnecks." *Society,* vol. 2, no. 11 (November–December 1973):24–31.

The relationship between lower social class and criminality, therefore, is complex and not very clear.[10] It does appear that lower-class persons, especially lower-class members of minority groups, are more likely to be arrested, indicted, convicted, and imprisoned for any given offense than are members of the middle and upper classes.

In addition to police and court bias, two other factors enter into this predominance of lower-class persons in the official statistics of crime. The first is the fact that in our society lower-income people have neither the money nor, often, the knowledge to hire a competent lawyer, to invoke habeas corpus, or to construct an adequate defense. They cannot raise bail or bond money easily, and their lack of substantial real property or jobs often leads a judge to fix bail at a level high enough to keep them in jail, on the ground that the accused does not have strong enough ties to the area to keep him in it until the trial. Second, the authorities have reasoned—until quite recently—that it is better for the accused to be taken out of the ghetto and afforded the opportunity to be "rehabilitated" or "retrained" within the facilities of a prison or training school. Although the administrators of the system may have felt that they were acting humanely, society at large, and the person sentenced to such rehabilitation, have always viewed it as a stigmatizing punishment, which may in fact preclude later resumption of employment or social opportunities.

The rich and powerful, on the other hand, have been quite well insulated from such stigma. They are so seldom sent to prison that when one of them is finally jailed for stealing—by fraud, embezzlement, or tax evasion—often millions more than the cleverest bank bandit, it makes nationwide headlines. Some sociologists, noting the difficulty of obtaining accurate information on the rate of such occupational crime, have contended that, since the upper classes constitute such a small proportion of the total population and the actual incidence of occupational crime is greater than official statistics reflect, the upper classes may actually have a higher rate of crime than the lower classes.[11] It will be helpful to bear these facts in mind in the following discussion on the various types of crime.

TYPES OF CRIME AND CRIMINALS

Most of us tend to think of crime in an overgeneralized way, and to have stereotypic notions about criminals. We usually speak of the "crime problem" without really specifying which crimes we mean; and we tend to label those who break laws as "criminals," without stopping to think that they are not law violators all the time. Professional thieves, for example, might well behave in quite traditional ways outside their occupation, and juvenile delinquents might well give up all lawbreaking behavior once they become adults. The very words "crime" and "criminal" are so broad

---

[10] William Chambliss, *Criminal Law in Action.* Santa Barbara, Calif.: Hamilton, 1975, p. 135. See also Gwynn Nettler, *Explaining Crime.* New York: McGraw-Hill, 1973, and Don C. Gibbons, *Delinquent Behavior,* 2nd ed. Englewood Cliffs, N.J.: Prentice-Hall, 1976.

[11] Walter C. Reckless, *The Crime Problem.* 5th ed. Englewood Cliffs, N.J.: Prentice-Hall, 1973.

as to be of limited use in describing certain acts or persons. Actually, criminal acts and lawbreakers are almost as varied as non-criminal acts and law-abiders. No one term can encompass the wide range of behaviors that are illegal, nor can one term meaningfully describe people who are lawbreakers.

In this section we shall review nine major types of crime and criminals. Eight of these have been classified by sociologists Marshall B. Clinard and Richard Quinney in their book on criminal behavior.[12] Clinard and Quinney have separated the categories of criminal behavior according to how great a part criminal activity plays in people's lives; that is, whether or not these individuals see themselves as criminals, and the extent to which they commit themselves to a life of crime. Such distinctions are useful, because they help sociologists understand why and how different law-breaking behaviors occur. The eight major categories of crime and lawbreakers as defined by Clinard and Quinney are (1) violent personal; (2) occasional property; (3) occupational (white-collar); (4) political; (5) public order; (6) conventional; (7) organized; and (8) professional. In our discussion we shall add a ninth category: juvenile delinquency. We shall look at each of these types and examine what kinds of activity they involve and where the individuals who commit them fit into the picture of criminality. Two kinds of activity—occupational and organized crime—will receive more extensive treatment because their social costs probably exceed the social costs of all the others combined.

VIOLENT PERSONAL CRIME

This category of crime includes assault, robbery, and the various forms of homicide—acts in which physical injury is inflicted or implied. Legally such acts are crimes because in most cultures they violate every citizen's right to life and to conduct his or her daily affairs in personal safety.[13] Although robbery occurs most often between strangers, murders are usually the result of a violent personal dispute between friends or relatives, both of whom are prone to use violence to settle their differences:

If only one responds in a dispute, it is not likely to become violent; likewise, if only one of the disputants is accustomed to the use of violence and the other is not, the dispute is likely to end only in verbal argument. On the other hand, when a cultural norm is defined as calling for violence by a person in social interplay with another who harbors the same response, serious altercations, fist fights, physical assaults with weapons, and violent domestic quarrels, all of which may end in murder, may result. . . . Consequently, the victim by being a contributor to the circular reaction of an argument increasing in its physical intensity, may precipitate his own injury or death.[14]

It has been customary, therefore, to think of murders and aggravated assaults as unpremeditated acts and not as the result of criminal life styles or purposes. Violent behavior of this kind has usually been attributed

---

[12] Marshall B. Clinard and Richard Quinney, *Criminal Behavior Systems: A Typology*. New York: Holt, Rinehart and Winston, 1967.
[13] Richard Quinney, *The Social Reality of Crime*. Boston: Little, Brown, 1970, pp. 249–252.
[14] Clinard and Quinney, p. 27.

more to cultural conditioning, and the offenders have been portrayed as normally law-abiding persons who are not likely to be engaged in other criminal activities. However, in recent years there has been a disturbing increase in violent crime between strangers; for example, 34 percent of New York City's murder victims in 1974 were killed by someone they did not know, and it has been estimated that 65 percent of all violent crimes are directed at strangers.[15] (The subject of violent crimes is discussed comprehensively in Chapter 5, "Violence.")

OCCASIONAL PROPERTY CRIME

Crimes of this type include vandalism, check forgery, shoplifting, and some kinds of auto theft; they are crimes in the legal sense because they violate society's belief in the sanctity of private property. Vandals, check forgers, shoplifters, and other such offenders are usually naive and unsophisticated in their operations, most of them having no knowledge of professional criminal skills. Because occasional offenders commit their crimes only at irregular intervals, they are not apt to associate with those who make crime a way of life. Non-professional shoplifters, for example, consider themselves to be respectable, generally law-abiding working people or homemakers, who steal articles from stores only for their own purposes. They excuse their behavior on the grounds that what they steal has relatively little value and that the "victim" is usually a large, impersonal organization such as a chain store, which can easily replace the stolen article.[16]

Neither non-professional shoplifters nor non-professional check forgers are likely to have a criminal record. They, together with vandals and car thieves, are usually isolated individuals who work alone and are not part of any criminal subculture; none of them seeks to earn a living by their activities.

OCCUPATIONAL (WHITE-COLLAR) CRIME

The phenomenon of occupational crime was first defined and popularized by the sociologist Edwin H. Sutherland, first in a 1940 article, and then in his book *White Collar Crime*.[17] He analyzed the behavior of people who break the law as part of their normal business activities: corporation directors, who use their inside knowledge of the market to sell large blocks of stock at a tremendous profit; accountants who juggle the books to conceal the several hundred dollars of company money they have pocketed; stores which raise the list price of a $20 dress to $40, in order to offer it as a "sale" item at $28; firms which make false statements about their profits in order to avoid paying taxes. Such crime can occur in the medical, legal, and other professions as well, as when a doctor submits a fraudulent accident report, or charges a patient for unnecessary and unrequested treatment. Such acts tend to be ignored by society: they rarely come to the attention of the criminal courts, and even when they do, they are rarely judged by the same criteria as are applied to other criminal activities.

[15] "The crime wave." *Time,* June 30, 1975, pp. 10–11.
[16] Quinney, pp. 252–253.
[17] Edwin H. Sutherland, "White-collar criminality." *American Sociological Review* 5 (February 1940):1–12; and *White Collar Crime.* New York: Holt, Rinehart and Winston, 1961.

Since Sutherland described it, the category of occupational crime has been broadened to include such disparate acts as embezzlement, fraud in its various forms, false advertising, fee-splitting, labor violations, price-fixing, antitrust violations, and black-market activity. In this section we shall concentrate on embezzlement, fraud (mostly antitrust violations and consumer fraud), and the wide range of business and government crimes. Frequently, there is also a strong connection between organized crime and corrupt government officials; this will be discussed in the section on organized crime.

The occupational offender is far removed from the popular stereotype of a criminal. Few of us think that a conservatively dressed Wall Street lawyer or stockbroker who catches the 8:34 train each morning from the suburbs to get to his or her well-paying, high-status job in the city is likely to be engaged in illegal activities. Because of such persons' respectable appearance, it is difficult for most people to think of these offenders as criminals. In fact, occupational offenders often think of themselves as respectable citizens and do everything they can to avoid being labeled as lawbreakers, even by themselves. Most embezzlers, for example, use elaborate rationalizations to explain their actions, seeing embezzling as a kind of secret "borrowing." [18]

Sutherland offered his own explanation of what makes people break the law. His theory of "differential association" asserts that occupational criminality, like other systematic criminality, is a behavior learned through frequent direct or indirect association with those who already practice it, and lack of frequent contact with law-abiding behavior. (We discuss this theory later in this chapter.) Thus, those who become occupational criminals may do so simply by getting into businesses or occupations where their colleagues regard certain kinds of crime as the standard way of conducting business.

Embezzlement. Embezzlement, or theft by an employee from his or her employer, is usually committed by otherwise law-abiding persons in the course of their employment. Embezzlement occurs at all levels of business, from a clerk stealing from the petty cash to a vice-president stealing large sums of investment money; it makes use of a variety of techniques and involves widely varying amounts of money. It has been estimated that no more than 1 percent of all cases of embezzlement result in criminal action.[19] Most cases are not detected, and companies are often unwilling to prosecute for fear of bad publicity. One conservative estimate is that losses due to embezzlement exceed $4 million every working day.

A now-classic study of embezzlers was done by Donald Cressey, in his book *Other People's Money*.[20] Cressey interviewed convicted financial trust violators in prison, and found that there were three basic conditions that had to be present before people turned to embezzlement. First,

The illegal acts associated with the Watergate break-in and its cover-up seem to support the theory that occupational criminality is behavior learned through association with those who already practice it. Here, former Presidential Assistant John Ehrlichman testifies before the Senate Watergate Committee. Wide World Photos

[18] Quinney, pp. 253–256.
[19] Edwin M. Schur, *Our Criminal Society*. Englewood Cliffs, N.J.: Prentice-Hall, 1969, p. 171.
[20] Donald R. Cressey, *Other People's Money: A Study in the Social Psychology of Embezzlement*. Reprint of 1953 ed. Montclair, N.J.: Patterson Smith, 1973.

employees had to have a financial problem they were unable to share with others. Second, they had to have the opportunity to steal. Finally, and to Cressey this was the most crucial consideration, they had to be able to find a formula in words to rationalize the fact that they were not really committing a criminal act—such as "I'm just borrowing a little to tide me over." In this way embezzlers could feel that their actions would have society's understanding.

Fraud. Fraud is the obtaining of money or property under false pretenses. It can occur at any level of business, and in any type of business relationship. A citizen defrauds the government by evading the payment of his or her income tax; a butcher defrauds a customer by charging the price of a pound for fifteen ounces of hamburger; an industry defrauds the public when members agree to hold prices at an artificially high level. The cost of fraud may run from a few cents to millions of dollars, and the methods may be as crude as to require no more than a thumb on the scales or as sophisticated as to require the coordinated efforts of dozens of lawyers, executives, and government officials.

Fraud has been a part of business life for so long that there is a standard Latin warning against it—*caveat emptor,* "Let the buyer beware." However, some observers feel that it is especially prevalent in America today, and that the values most characteristic of American business—competition, selling, risk-taking, persuasion—tend to encourage it. It is perhaps worth noting in this regard that professional confidence men and women, whose livelihood depends on their ability to find respectable potential victims willing to take a chance on a dishonest deal, generally consider American businesspeople as their best "marks." [21]

It is impossible here to go into all the kinds of fraud to be found in our society. We shall consider two—antitrust violation and consumer fraud—in some detail, and look briefly at the area of business-government fraud.

Antitrust Violations. In the latter part of the nineteenth century, the Industrial Revolution entered a period of rapid mergers and monopolies. Powerful industrial magnates, striving to make and sell as much as possible at the highest possible price for the lowest possible cost, saw the attractive chance of controlling so much of the market for a particular product that they could set prices as they chose, unhampered by competition. The consequences to the public were serious enough to force passage, in 1890, of the Sherman Anti-Trust Act, which declared that

every contract, combination in the form of trust or otherwise, or conspiracy, in restraint of trade or commerce among the several States, or with foreign nations, is hereby declared to be illegal . . . [and that] every person who shall monopolize . . . or conspire . . . to monopolize any part of . . . trade or commerce . . . shall be deemed guilty of a misdemeanor.[22]

Penalties were established in the form of fines (up to $5,000 per violation) and imprisonment (up to one year). Exactly what was meant by "trust," "monopoly," and "restraint" was left to the courts to decide;

[21] Schur, *Our Criminal Society,* p. 182.
[22] *U.S. Statutes at Large.* Vol. XXVI, p. 209.

nevertheless, over the next decade or so, and particularly under President Theodore Roosevelt, many of the established monopolies were broken up.

Later on new types of merger were tried, and then a variety of "agreements," "arrangements," and "understandings" aimed at achieving some sort of monopoly without openly violating the Anti-Trust Act. The Justice Department's antitrust division has never been large enough to follow up on all the suspected cases of monopolistic practice, and when it has won convictions, the penalties imposed have seldom been severe enough to constitute a serious deterrent. Convicted individuals have rarely been jailed, and even the maximum fine (now raised to $50,000 per violation) is hardly more than petty cash to a modern large corporation. Whatever the law may say, American opinion in general, for several generations at least, has not regarded antitrust crimes on a level with property crimes such as burglary.

Consumer Fraud. The term "consumer fraud" is usually applied to cases of cheating in direct transactions between retail buyer and seller. Common examples are shortweighted food packages, failure to put required information on credit contracts, mislabeling of meat so that a customer buys ground chuck for the price of sirloin, and unnecessary auto repairs. It has been estimated that $1 billion is spent annually on worthless goods and services, and that consumer losses from fraudulent repair and other rackets amount to many more billions of dollars each year.[23]

Consumer fraud bears most heavily on the poor. For one thing, ghetto stores consistently charge higher prices for a given type of merchandise than do stores in more affluent neighborhoods, and often the merchandise is of poorer quality. Since the poor are often unaware of the possibility of comparative shopping or are unable for one reason or another to shop outside their own neighborhoods, they are trapped by these inflated prices. And since, for many of them, English is not their native tongue, and they have no practical access to accurate information about their rights as citizens and as consumers, it is difficult for them to complain effectively even when they know they are being cheated.

Many abuses to which the poor in particular are subject involve credit. By definition, poor individuals are poor credit risks and have a hard time getting credit from reputable firms. Consequently, they may be forced to borrow money from a neighborhood "loan shark" at highly inflated interest rates. Likewise, if they wish to buy furniture or appliances on the installment plan—and this is one of the biggest businesses in ghetto areas—they are apt to turn to a neighborhood store or door-to-door peddler offering "easy credit." The credit may be easy in the beginning, but the costs in the end are usually excessive. (See Table 4-1.)

Business-Government Crime. An area of occupational crime which has been receiving increased attention in recent years is generally known as business-government crime. It can be either the misuse of government funds by business organizations, with or without the collusion of government officials; or it can take the form of corporate bribes to legislators to further the corporation's interests. (See also Chapter 6.) There have

[23] "White collar crime: Huge economic and moral drain." *Congressional Quarterly,* May 7, 1971, p. 1049.

TABLE 4-1
Cost of Appliances
According to Type
of Source

Appliance	Bureaucratic Sources			Traditional Sources	
	Discount House	Department Store	Chain Store	Neighborhood Dealer	Peddler
Television:					
Percent high price	8	22	31	53	67
Phonograph:					
Percent over $200	14	46	51	51	55
Washing machine:					
Percent over $230	30	50	29	54	87
Percent over $300	10	14	8	36	87

Source: David Caplovitz, *The Poor Pay More.* New York: Free Press, 1967, Table 6–4, p. 85.

also been cases of elected officials extorting money from corporations in return for votes for legislation favorable to the corporation's interests. In some cases, the actions are clearly illegal, and when they come to light, scandals and prosecutions ensue; in others they occupy a gray area of irresponsibility, in which no one seems to have committed a crime, but something about the proceedings is felt to be wrong.

In the past few decades an enormous amount of government money, particularly federal money, has been poured into numerous projects—housing, urban renewal, job training, education, health. The money goes to states, municipalities, or business firms, through allotment or contract, and then presumably is spent for the designated purposes. Unfortunately, in some cases the availability of so much cash seems to offer an irresistible temptation to some of the people through whose hands it passes, and considerable sums are periodically revealed to have been siphoned off into private pockets. Recent housing-fraud scandals are a case in point. One common type of fraud, involving the sale of used housing under a mortgage insured by the Federal Housing Authority, was investigated by the Justice Department in 1972. The original purpose of the Federal Housing Authority program was to enable low-income persons to buy their own homes. The fraud process, as described by a Justice Department official to a congressional subcommittee, works as follows:

To obtain [F.H.A. insurance] an appraisal must be made by a housing administration inspector, who assigns a value to the house as of the time it was bought by the speculator and a "restored value" after certain designated repairs have been made.

"The ideal situation requires a 'friendly' appraiser, either an F.H.A. staff appraiser who is bribed, or a fee appraiser . . . who will perform the favor on a reciprocal basis," Mr. Peterson said. "However, the scheme need not die because of an honest appraisal. The scheme could then operate through an unscrupulous contractor or tradesman, who will certify that repairs have been made when they have not been made. A second party to the scheme is a mortgage company which will submit the documents to F.H.A. for mortgage insurance, the mortgage company having knowledge of the true condition and worth of the property.

"Shortly after moving in, the new homeowner is faced with repairs he cannot afford," Mr. Peterson said, adding: "He soon abandons the property and the F.H.A. finds itself in possession of another inner-city dwelling. The property is then placed in the hands of an area management broker, a local real estate agent designated by F.H.A. as their agent, to rehabilitate and resell the property. Depending upon the honesty of the broker, the cycle may well begin again." [24]

Given the amounts of money involved, and the far-flung nature of many government programs, it is hard to see how adequate control over their administration can best be maintained. Nevertheless, the degree to which some speculators have apparently profited from the public purse, at the expense of the needy, is frightening.

The issue of corporate involvement in federal elections came to light in the scandals surrounding the re-election of Richard M. Nixon in 1972. Although it has been illegal since 1907 for corporations to give money to any politician's campaign for federal office, at least seven large U.S. corporations admitted to having contributed amounts ranging from $30,000 to $100,000 to the 1972 Nixon re-election campaign. The money was funneled indirectly to the campaign committee through foreign branches or subsidiaries of the corporations, or by having company employees hand over special "bonuses" to several Nixon re-election committees. [25] Other business-government crimes involved American businesses and foreign governments. The Lockheed Corporation, for example, admitted in 1975 that it had spent at least $22 million in bribes in attempts to win sales of its products overseas.

POLITICAL CRIME

Political offenses include such activities as "treason, sedition, and civil disobedience." In the eyes of the state these activities threaten the existing social order, and if allowed to go unchecked, they would do serious harm to a country's governmental structure. The offenders, of course, far from seeing themselves or their actions as criminal, consider their law violations to be in the service of purposes and ideals higher than the state's. [26]

The best-known examples of this kind of offense came into national prominence in the 1960s and early 1970s with the rise of the black civil rights movement and the development of widespread opposition to U.S. involvement in the Vietnam War. Protest groups defined the existing social structure and political institutions as illegitimate and engaged in such activities as sit-ins, draft-card burnings, draft evasions, and marches. Even when such actions are legal (such as a protest demonstration), they may become viewed or dealt with as illegal because of their political nature. The arrests of black and white protesters in the South during the early days of the civil rights movement, and the killing of students protesting the war in Cambodia at Kent State University in Ohio, were government responses to a perceived threat against the social order. [27]

[24] *New York Times,* May 8, 1972.
[25] "Why it was better to give than . . . ." *Time,* November 26, 1973, p. 18.
[26] Quinney, pp. 256–259.
[27] See, for example, *The Report of the President's Commission on Campus Unrest.* Washington, D.C.: U.S. Government Printing Office, 1970, pp. 282, 449.

In sheer numbers, public order offenders constitute the largest category of what society chooses to regard as criminals, their activities outnumbering by far all other types of reported crime. Public order offenses include prostitution, homosexuality, gambling, drug addiction, drunkenness, vagrancy, disorderly conduct, and traffic violations. Prostitution, gambling, homosexuality, and drug use, and possibly drunkenness and vagrancy, are often called "victimless crimes" because these activities cause no physical harm or injury to anyone but the offenders themselves. Society regards them as crimes because they violate the sense of order in the community, but allows a certain measure of toleration in the case of gambling and prostitution.[28] (See Chapter 11.)

Public order offenders rarely consider themselves criminals, nor do they think of what they do as crimes. The behavior and activities of prostitutes, homosexuals, and drug users, however, tend to isolate and segregate them from others; and some, such as drug users, may find themselves drawn into criminal roles. The law defines certain drug use as illegal, and so users may come to see themselves as being outside the mainstream of society. In addition, they may be forced to commit other criminal acts in order to pay for drugs. In this way, criminal laws can have the unintended side effect of expanding and promoting criminal behavior. (See Chapters 1 and 3 for further discussion of this topic.)

Conventional offenders are most often young adults, in their twenties, who commit robbery, larceny, burglary, and gang theft as a way of life. Their criminal offenses usually begin during their adolescence as members of juvenile gangs, where they join other truants from school to routinely vandalize property and fight in the streets. As juvenile offenders they are not organized or skillful enough to avoid arrest and conviction, and by young adulthood they have compiled a police record and may have spent time in prison.[29]

Conventional offenders could be called "semiprofessionals" because they are not as sophisticated in criminal techniques as organized and professional criminals, and move only by degrees into a criminal life. For this reason, the development of their self-concepts as criminals and their identification with crime are only gradual. However, by the time they have built up a criminal record, they have usually made a fairly strong identification with criminality. The criminal record itself is society's way of permanently defining these offenders as criminals, and once so defined, these individuals find it almost impossible to re-enter the mainstream of society and are more likely to continue their criminal activities.

Since only a small percent of known conventional crime results in arrest, the odds of being caught are lowered to the point where most offenders of this type readily believe that crime does pay. Their relative success in a criminal career leads them away from a conventional way of life. In addition, the life of a successful criminal has a certain excitement. As James Q. Wilson puts it:

One works at crime at one's convenience, enjoys the esteem of colleagues who think a "straight" job is stupid and skill at stealing is commendable, looks

PUBLIC ORDER CRIME

CONVENTIONAL CRIME

28 Quinney, pp. 259–264.
29 Quinney, pp. 264–267.

forward to the occasional "big score" that may make further work unnecessary for weeks, and relishes the risk and adventure associated with theft. The money value . . . of all these benefits is hard to estimate but is almost certainly far larger than what either public or private employers could offer to unskilled or semi-skilled young workers.[30]

And because they associate mostly with other criminals, they develop a kind of camaraderie and point of view that does not value the benefits of law-abiding behavior.

Surprisingly, some conventional criminals give up crime by the time they are in their late twenties and early thirties for reasons that are still not clear to criminologists. Perhaps they marry and have to support families, and it may be that they find this more rewarding than their previous life. In the relatively low incidence of conventional criminality among older adults, family responsibilities seem to be a more powerful factor than rehabilitation or fear of getting caught.

The groups we usually think of as representing organized crime tend to be large and diversified regional, or even national, bodies. They may organize initially to carry on a particular crime, such as illicit drug traffic, extortion, prostitution, or gambling. Later they may seek to control this activity within a given city or neighborhood, destroying or taking over the competition. Eventually they may expand into other types of crime, and may arrange to protect their members from arrest through intimidation or bribery of public officials.

ORGANIZED CRIME

A major element which distinguishes organized from other crime is that organized crime is a system in which illegal activities are carried out not haphazardly, but as part of a rational plan devised by a large organization which is seeking to maximize its overall profit. In order to operate most efficiently, organized crime relies on division of labor, and has numerous, diverse roles which must be performed. (However, there is some controversy over how structured organized crime is.[31])

A second major characteristic of organized crime, and one which it shares with some other types of crime, is that instead of being wholly predatory—like burglary, which involves only taking from victims—the syndicate supplies goods and services which a large segment of the public wants but cannot obtain legally. Without the public's desire for gambling, for loans of money not available from legitimate sources, for drugs, organized crime's base would collapse.

The Scope of the Problem. Many people think of organized crime as something remote from them, belonging more to fiction and movies than to everyday reality. This tendency is fostered by mass media accounts of individual racketeers who are invariably referred to by their "in" names (for example, "Crazy Joe Gallo"). This makes it seem as if organized crime is just a matter of a few television-style gangsters. Robert F. Kennedy noted and deplored this tendency:

[30] James Q. Wilson, "Lock 'em up and other thoughts on crime." *New York Times Magazine,* March 9, 1975, p. 20.
[31] See, for example, Francis Ianni and Elizabeth Ianni, *A Family Business.* New York: Russell Sage Foundation, 1972.

One reason efforts to control organized crime have been hampered is because the public tends to have a romanticized view of it. Here, in a scene from "The Godfather," a parent asks the local syndicate boss to avenge him on his daughter's attackers. The film was one of the highest grossing pictures of all time.
Wide World Photos

The racketeer is not someone dressed in a black shirt, white tie, and diamond stick pin, whose activities affect only a remote underworld circle. He is more likely to be outfitted in a gray flannel suit and his influence is more likely to be as far-reaching as that of an important industrialist. The American public may not see him, but that makes the racketeer's power for evil in our society even greater. Lacking the direct confrontation with the racketeer, the American citizen fails to see the reason for alarm. The reason, decidedly, exists.[32]

Organized crime gets its initial huge profits from supplying illegal goods and services to segments of the American public. Its major source of profit, and in many cases the original activity of the syndicate or its parent gang, is its gambling operations—lotteries, "numbers," off-track betting, illegal casinos, and dice games. Some of these can be located anywhere—in a tenement, on business premises, in a restaurant or garage. Much illegal gambling in the United States today is controlled by organized crime, operating through elaborate hierarchies in which money is filtered from the small operator who takes the customer's bet through several other levels until it finally reaches the organization's main offices. This complex system protects the higher-ups, whose identity remains concealed from those below. Centralized organization of gambling also increases efficiency, enlarges markets, provides a systematized method of paying graft to public officials, and makes it possible to avoid large losses by providing money to operators so that they can "lay off" on bets (i.e., cover themselves against losses by making counterbalancing bets). It is

[32] In Donald R. Cressey, *Theft of the Nation: The Structure of Organized Crime in America.* New York: Harper & Row, 1969, p. xiii.

estimated that syndicate profits from gambling amount to $6 or $7 billion a year.[33]

The second highest source of revenue for organized crime is loan-sharking, the lending of money at interest rates above the legal limit. Illegal interest rates can go as high as 150 percent *a week,* and over 20 percent is standard. Through its profits from gambling operations, syndicated crime always has a large supply of cash to lend, and it can ensure repayment by the threat of violence. Most loans are to gamblers who need money to pay off debts, drug users, and small businesses unable to obtain credit from legitimate sources. It is estimated that profits from loan-sharking are in the multibillion-dollar range.

The narcotics trade is organized crime's third major source of revenue. Its direct dealings in narcotics are probably limited to importation from abroad and wholesale distribution in the United States. Lower-level operations are left to others, since they are considered to involve too much risk. Organized crime probably gets about $5 billion in profits each year from the narcotics trade.[34]

One use which organized crime makes of its huge profits from these illegitimate activities is to expand into legitimate businesses. This expansion benefits organized crime in many ways. For one thing, legitimate businesses serve as useful tax covers for syndicate members. They also confer a certain respectable status in the community. Finally, legitimate businesses serve as another source of profit—particularly since the syndicate, using its ready reserves of cash and threats of force, can temporarily lower prices to drive competitors out of business, employ strong-arm tactics to obtain customers, and in other ways implement business policies outside the law.

Direct investment is only one of several ways in which organized crime gets into legitimate businesses. It can accept business interests in lieu of money as payment for a loan or gambling debt. It can foreclose usurious loans in which businesses were put up as collateral. It can use extortion, demanding that a legitimate business pay tribute for the privilege of remaining open. The tribute can be in the form of a demand that the business buy all its supplies from companies controlled by organized crime—thus assuring markets for those companies.[35]

Organized crime is also deeply involved in labor racketeering. By infiltrating labor unions, for example, organized crime gains access to union funds; it may also get into a position to make profitable deals with management by ensuring labor peace or by threatening a strike. Thus a *New York Times* story of May 9, 1972 described investigations which revealed that criminal infiltration into the New York City meat industry had inflated retail meat prices by as much as 15 percent. Possible collusion between key industry and union figures was suggested, but

the daily operation is rather straightforward. Representatives of both the retail and wholesale outfits are approached by racketeers who make it clear

[33] *Challenge of Crime,* p. 189.
[34] "The losing battle against crime in America." *U.S. News and World Report,* December 16, 1974, p. 39.
[35] Charles Grutzner, "How to lock out the Mafia." *Harvard Business Review* (March–April 1970):45–58.

that unless they inflate their prices and hand over the extra money, their companies will no longer be able to stay in business because of severe labor troubles.

Through its involvement in a wide range of businesses, both legal and illegal, syndicated crime inflicts major costs on our economy. These costs include higher prices for goods through the establishment of monopolies; lower-quality goods; the forced closing of businesses, with resulting unemployment; and manipulation of stock market prices. Through infiltration of labor unions, thousands of workers are defrauded and denied the benefits of true union representation. Through the narcotics trade, the drug problems of cities are intensified and perpetuated. Finally, through corruption of public officials—a necessary adjunct to its other operations—syndicated crime helps to raise the general tax burden and has a detrimental effect on overall law enforcement and on the democratic process.

Organized Crime and Corruption. Organized crime could not continue to flourish without paying off key public officials. By corrupting such officials—police, district attorneys, mayors, judges, legislators—organized crime seeks to ensure that laws which would hamper its enterprises are either not passed or not enforced.

As is stressed in the report of the President's Commission on Law Enforcement and the Administration of Justice, the harm which can result from government corruption is greater today than ever before because government regulation affects an increasing range of business and private activities. Thus the corrupter can gain control over more matters which closely affect every citizen.[36]

There are various methods of corrupting officials. Bribes can be given directly, or in the form of a share of the profits from illegal operations. Officials can be placed under obligation by means of gifts or favors—a trip to Florida, a campaign contribution, the promise of voter support. Threats can be made to support opponents in campaigns, or blackmail may be used. Sometimes officials are corrupted after taking office; sometimes people are placed in office who are already associated with the syndicate.

The corruption occurs on all levels of government, from police officers to high elected officials. It is especially effective to reach the latter, as they are in a position to quell attempts by overzealous lower personnel to enforce the laws against syndicate activities. For example, if the cooperation of the police chief can be obtained, any police officer who tries to arrest gamblers may be shifted to another assignment or passed over for promotions and salary raises. Other officers will quickly learn from this example.

The occasional exposé in the media or by a special investigative agency gives a vivid description of how the corruption process works and of the huge payoffs involved. In the borough of Brooklyn in New York City, for example, some 37 members of a plainclothes Public Morals Squad

[36] *Challenge of Crime*, p. 191.

were indicted in 1972 after they were discovered to have taken payoffs amounting to a quarter of a million dollars annually from gambling establishments in four Brooklyn precincts. The group was so well organized that it even provided severance pay for members reassigned to other divisions and insurance to cover legal expenses if a member was caught.[37]

The ramifications of political corruption in a community's life are well illustrated in Gardiner's study of "Wincanton." [38] The city was known for years as a wide-open center for gambling and vice, under a local syndicate. Bookmaking, numbers, pinball machines, and dice games flourished; bootleg whiskey was manufactured and sold; brothels catered to men from all over the state.

The head of the syndicate protected his lucrative empire by means of a well-organized system of corruption, based on two simple principles: "Pay top personnel as much as necessary to keep them happy (and quiet), and pay something to as many others as possible to implicate them in in the system and to keep them from talking." Payments totaling some $2,400 per week went to about fifteen key local and state officials, including the mayor, the police chief, some judges, state legislators, members of the city council, and a few others. Christmas gifts and political campaign contributions went to many more.

In addition to direct payment, the syndicate bought the cooperation of some officials by helping them arrange corrupt activities of their own. Kickbacks on city contracts and equipment purchases became standard. Although the syndicate head went to jail on tax evasion charges, the syndicate continued to function, and it was not until a year later, when the police chief was caught perjuring himself before a grand jury and hastily "blew the whistle" on his confederates, that the golden structure fell apart and an active reform administration was elected.

Professional criminals are the ones we read about in many traditional detective novels or see on television: the expert safe-cracker with sensitive fingers, the sharp customer in Cartier's who switches diamonds so quickly the clerk does not notice, and the counterfeiters working under bright lights in the basement of a respectable shop. However, this class of criminals also includes the less glamorous pickpockets, full-time shoplifters, check forgers, truck hijackers, fencers of stolen goods, and blackmailers.[39]

Professional criminals are dedicated to a life of crime; they earn their living by it and pride themselves on their accomplishments. They are not often caught, and when they are, they can usually manage to have the charges dropped or have the sentence reduced to a comfortable term. Meyer Lansky, a particularly successful thief (who was also a top

PROFESSIONAL CRIME

[37] *New York Times,* May 3, 1972.

[38] John A. Gardiner, with the assistance of David J. Olsen, "Gambling and political corruption." In *Task Force Report—Organized Crime: Annotations and Consultants' Papers,* President's Commission on Law Enforcement and the Administration of Justice. Washington, D.C.: U.S. Government Printing Office, 1967, pp. 61–79.

[39] Quinney, pp. 270–273.

figure in a national crime syndicate hierarchy) spent only three months and sixteen days in jail out of a criminal career that spanned over fifty years.[40] These are the most highly evolved of all criminals, and they are the most sophisticated and skilled in their working methods; they rarely have to resort to physical violence.

Many professional criminals come from higher social strata than most individuals who get arrested for criminal activities. They often begin as typical employees who work for companies, hotels, and restaurants, and keep their criminal life as a sideline. Eventually, their criminal careers develop to the point where they make their living almost entirely by illegal activities. This phase usually starts at a time of life when conventional criminals are giving up crime. Confidence people often persist in their occupation until old age. As Quinney put it, "Unemployment occasioned by old age does not seem to be a problem of con men; age ripens their skills, insights, and wit, and it also increases the confidence they inspire in their victims." [41] Most professional criminals enjoy long, uninterrupted careers because through experience they become skilled at avoiding arrest. They often justify their activities by claiming that they are simply capitalizing on the fact that all people are dishonest and would most likely be full-time criminals if they had the chance and sufficient ability.

JUVENILE DELINQUENCY

According to official statistics, children under 15 commit more crime than all adults over 25, and some authorities claim that a relatively small group of juveniles commits over half the crime in the United States.[42] The statistics also show young people under 18 committing 10 percent of all murders and 45 percent of all robberies, rapes, and assaults. The highest proportion of arrests occurs among 13- to 14-year-olds, with over 399,500 arrests in 1974, 6.5 percent of the total.[43]

There is, however, considerable variation in the types of crime committed by the different age groups, and these statistics must be examined closely. The great bulk of delinquent acts are *status offenses*—acts that would not be illegal if performed by adults. They include "running away from home, being incorrigible, ungovernable, and beyond the control of parents, being truant, [and] engaging in sexual relations." [44] Many juveniles, therefore, are judged to be delinquent for behavior and actions that would be legal if they were only a few years older.

Historically, children have been presumed to lack the "criminal intent" necessary to the commission of willful crimes. Because of this, juvenile law was designed primarily to protect and redirect young offenders, rather than to punish them. It allows judges a wide range in dealing with youthful offenders brought before them, so that they can choose the approach which will be most helpful, rather than impose a more or less

[40] Thomas Plate, *Crime Pays!* New York: Simon & Schuster, 1975.
[41] Quinney, p. 273.
[42] "Children and the law." *Newsweek,* September 8, 1975, p. 66; see also Wilson, "Lock 'em up."
[43] *Uniform Crime Reports,* pp. 18–19, 186.
[44] Paul Lerman, "Delinquents without crime." *Trans-action,* July–August 1971, p. 252.

predetermined sentence. But in recent years there has been increasing dissatisfaction with the practical workings of the juvenile law. Some contend that authorities and law enforcers have too much latitude over how to construe juvenile behavior, and that standards differ too greatly between communities. Most juvenile officials continue to be concerned over such matters as "female sexuality, male braggadocio, and disrespect of adult authority," and capitalize on the ambiguity of terms such as "incorrigible" and "ungovernable" in order to jail any young person whom they think needs correction.[45] (See also Chapter 9.)

Because of inadequate facilities and insufficiently trained judges and other personnel, the correctional action taken with regard to the young offender often amounts only to a trial and a prison sentence, though the records may speak of "hearings" and a "training school." In addition, these are frequently imposed without benefit of the elementary constitutional rights guaranteed to the adult offender—the right to counsel, the right to be confronted with witnesses and to cross-examine them, the right to a trial by jury. In 1967 the issue reached the Supreme Court in the important *Gault* case, in which a boy who had participated in a lewd telephone call was committed to a state "industrial school" for what could have been a maximum of six years. The court held that, in a case where commitment to a state institution and consequent curtailment of freedom is a possible result, the juvenile is entitled to the same rights of due process as an adult.[46]

CONDITIONS AND CAUSES OF CRIME

Criminologists and sociologists have offered a variety of sociocultural explanations which may account for the prevalence of crime. For example, it has been said that countries that give their citizens a large degree of personal freedom have the greatest incidence of deviant or criminal behavior. Emile Durkheim, on the other hand, pointed out that a high crime rate is almost always the product of rapid economic development and social change. A sudden rise in prosperity and technology creates what he called "overweening ambition"—that is, people develop unreasonably high expectations for themselves. In their rush for material gain, some play by the rules while others ignore them.[47] And it is true that the educational and economic system of the United States promotes an enthusiastic desire for wealth, which can create lawbreaking attitudes and an emphasis on personal attainment at the expense of others.

Other students of criminal behavior see this country's uniquely high crime rate as being fostered by its cultural heterogeneity. Countries with culturally homogeneous populations, such as England and Japan, have relatively low crime rates; London, for example, reported only 113

[45] Lerman, "Delinquents without crime," p. 253.
[46] President's Commission on Law Enforcement and the Administration of Justice, *Task Force Report: Juvenile Delinquency and Youth Crime.* Washington, D.C.: U.S. Government Printing Office, 1967.
[47] In "The crime wave," p. 14.

murders and 135 rapes in a recent year, while New York City had 1,690 murders and 3,735 rapes.[48] Generally, the low crime rates of homogeneous countries and communities are a result of social bonds and a sense of collectivity. The majority of citizens share the same cultural values and ethnic backgrounds. (This suggests one reason why crime rates in the United States tend to be higher in cities than in more homogeneous rural communities.) The people share more or less the same idea of what a criminal act is and what is appropriate and law-abiding behavior. The police, as representatives of the citizens, will not be as ready to apply criminal sanctions in homogeneous communities as they would in heterogenous communities. Instead, they will tend to handle much law-violating behavior on an informal basis and make fewer arrests.[49]

Still other authorities believe that the high prevalence of crime in the United States is due to demographic, economic, and social factors. Demographic factors have swelled the numbers of youth in the 14- to 24-age group: In 1950 there were only 24 million individuals in the United States in this age group; in 1960, 27 million; and by 1975 there were over 44 million. Over 80 percent of the people arrested for property crime, which includes burglary, larceny, and auto theft, are under 25 years of age. This same under-25 age group accounts for almost 58 percent of all arrests.

Social factors relative to crime are reflected in the fact that far more men than women are charged with the commission of crimes. As women have begun to gain equal rights in industrialized countries, the ratio of male to female arrests has decreased, but men are still in the lead in most categories (except prostitution and runaways). In the United States, although the number of female arrests is increasing about 7 percent faster than male arrests, over 7 million men are arrested annually, compared to over 1 million females.[50] The reason for this situation seems to lie in the different patterns of socialization for men and women. Men in our society have traditionally been brought up to be more aggressive, even violent, than women. They have therefore been more likely to commit certain kinds of crimes. Females, as a rule, have also been regarded more protectively by both the police and the courts. Thus they have been less likely to be arrested, and if arrested, less likely to be punished. It can be expected that both crime statistics and the attitudes of the criminal justice system will gradually reflect contemporary changes in the patterns of socialization for men and women.

All studies of crime based on official statistics have shown a high incidence of crime among the lower socioeconomic classes, and particularly among blacks, Puerto Ricans, and American Indians. We have already suggested, however, that lower-class persons, and especially lower-class minority group members, have a much higher chance of coming into conflict with the established justice system than the more affluent (particularly if they are nonwhite). In fact, Chambliss and Nagasawa, in their study of delinquents, concluded that "official statistics are so misleading that they are virtually useless as indications of actual deviance in the

---

[48] *New York Times Magazine,* April 13, 1975, pp. 69–70.
[49] Quinney, Chapter 4.
[50] *Uniform Crime Reports.*

population." These authors have suggested that the demeanor of different groups, the visibility of the offenses, and the bias of police and courts give rise to official rates of crime and delinquency that are "a complete distortion of the actual incidence." [51]

Others suggest that the higher official rates of property and personal violent crimes among minority groups reflect the fact that unemployment among these groups, especially among their teenage members, is catastrophically high, ranging up to 40 percent. This point of view suggests that social and economic factors have intertwined to produce a great mass of people who feel they have no stake in society. As one journalist has written, there has developed "something like a permanent underclass, not so much exploited as left behind—an economic substratum unable to rise by unskilled labor that is no longer in demand, unable to compete in a highly organized technological society, heavily damaged by being in cities, . . . and embittered by evidence all around of its hopeless disadvantage." [52]

The continuing disintegration of family and community life and the relentless presentation of violence in the mass media have also been seen as reinforcing, if not causing, much present-day antisocial behavior. According to the director of the Fortune Society, an organization of ex-convicts, most convicts have a childhood history full of physical abuse and neglect, and many have spent their childhoods in homes, orphanages, and reformatories where physical punishment was given out as a matter of course.[53] Physical abuse of children creates in them a basic personality structure that is marked by hostility, anger, and indifference to others. It alienates children from other people and the community and brutalizes them to the point where they have a diminished capacity to feel guilt.[54] (See Chapter 10.) The decline in authority of traditional institutions, and the pervasive presence of violence on television and in newspapers (see Chapter 5), may also have reduced the likelihood that an individual will be discouraged from committing a criminal act.

What are some of the social and economic factors that lead to widespread public toleration and outright acceptance of occupational crime? One key attitude, in the case of crimes such as price-fixing and other instances of corporate collusion, is probably the feeling that government has no business regulating such matters in the first place. As one General Electric executive convicted of price-fixing maintained, "Sure, collusion was illegal, but it wasn't unethical." [55] Our nineteenth-century principles of rugged individualism and laissez-faire, however unsuitable to the vastly more intricate economic world of the twentieth century, remain precious to many people, and when conditions are favorable, they easily persuade themselves to act on them, whatever the law may require. It may also be that otherwise honest people will perform illegal acts they know are

[51] William J. Chambliss and Richard H. Nagasawa, "On the validity of official statistics: A comparative study of White, Black, and Japanese high-school boys." *Social Forces* (Winter 1969):71–77.
[52] Tom Wicker, *A Time to Die.* New York: Quadrangle, 1975.
[53] *New York Times Magazine,* April 13, 1975, p. 72.
[54] "The crime wave," p. 17.
[55] In Ralph Nader and Mark Green, "Crime in the suites." *New Republic,* April 29, 1972, pp. 17–18.

wrong, because of the pressures to which they are subjected in their lines of business.

Again, in modern American society, deception is, to a large degree, taken for granted. This is particularly apparent in the field of advertising. We are so accustomed to advertisements which promise us heaven in some form or other for the price of a bottle of shampoo or a pack of cigarettes, and TV promotions of wonderful toys which turn out, after being paid for, to be cheap plastic junk, that we scarcely see anything improper about them. In fact, advertisements of an earlier day, giving only straightforward information and ending with some such modest claim as, "The most economical one on the market," are reprinted on shopping bags and dress fabrics as a nostalgic joke. Yet, as Schur points out, "modern mass advertising at its heart represents a kind of institutionalization of deception and misrepresentation." [56] Certainly we seem to assume that a certain amount of deception is to be expected in business and in government, and this expectation may well constitute a self-fulfilling prophecy— that is, by expecting people to try to deceive each other, we create an atmosphere which eventually encourages them to do so.

Another related element is that much-discussed American characteristic, materialism, or the profit motive. Whether or not Americans are prepared, as is sometimes asserted, to "sell their souls for a buck," there is little doubt that many of us find profit hard to resist. We take for granted that it is natural and right for someone in business to want to increase his or her income, for a company to maximize its profits; and if in order to do so the company finds it necessary to pollute a river or cooperate with a labor racketeer, our protests are muted and apologetic. The fact that a practice is profitable, that it increases sales, leads to growth, puts more products on the market, creates jobs, or otherwise adds something to a gross national product which must always be larger this year than last, seems to be a justification so powerful as to override moral, ecological, and even safety objections with extraordinary ease. This is not a matter of some conspiracy of wicked, scheming business barons plotting international destruction in the secrecy of their luxurious executive suites—as once people blamed the arms manufacturers for fomenting World War I—but rather a widespread assumption, seldom seriously examined by the great majority of people.

Organized crime is also strongly interrelated with American values, culture, and institutions. For one thing, it depends on the willingness of millions of Americans—from retired individuals who place an occasional bet to businesspeople who knowingly accept criminal loans—to buy goods and services which they know are illegal.

Second, organized crime is furthered by the willingness of thousands of "respectable" people in business and professions to deal with it in order to make a personal profit—the corporation official who accepts the services of labor racketeers, the lawyers and accountants who offer their expertise to organized crime for the fees involved.

There are other ways in which organized crime is tied to American society. Many of the syndicate's recruits and workers, without whom the organization could not maintain itself effectively, have come from

[56] Schur, *Our Criminal Society,* p. 168.

minority and immigrant groups living in the inner city. It has been pointed out that for these groups organized crime has provided the only evident means of social mobility—because society has failed to provide other, legitimate avenues of opportunity.[57] Salerno points out the effect of the "successful" criminal on ghetto youth:

To them he has "made it"; he has "beat the system" by being associated with organized criminal activities. The dope peddler, the gambling operator, and the loan shark—without the benefit of education and without the demands of gainful employment—can drive the expensive auto, dress well, and manifest affluence. This is regarded by youth as perhaps the only opportunity for "breaking out" of the slums.[58]

So long as the more visible signs of organized crime, such as drug pushers and houses of prostitution, stay in ghettos, "respectable" Americans who use some of the services of organized crime for their own profit seem to be willing to ignore the consequences of their dealings.

Organized crime also relies on the corruptibility of government officials, on their willingness to suspend law enforcement in exchange for campaign funds or private kickbacks. In fact, such corruption is essential, for in one sense a crime syndicate is peculiarly vulnerable to honest law enforcement. Its activities continue over a long period of time; its places of business and at least its lower-level operatives have to be known to its customer; it has to keep open complicated lines of communication, supply, and distribution. It would be seriously hampered if it could not ensure that the police or the courts would stay out of its way.

In all these cases, organized crime flourishes because it is compatible with the American ethos of personal profit, because a substantial number of private citizens, businesspersons, professionals, and government officials place personal gain ahead of responsibility for the general welfare. In pursuing its own profits, organized crime is simply playing the same game, imbued with the very American value of making money.

EXPLANATIONS OF CRIME (SOCIOLOGICAL THEORIES)

Although partial explanations of the causes of crime have been advanced by researchers from many disciplines, no comprehensive theory has yet been developed which can account for the wide range of crimes and criminals in today's society. Explanations which seem workable for urban gang crime may not apply so well to suburban delinquency or to burglary by an individual. Other approaches, which focus on criminal and delinquent individuals, may fail completely to explain gangs and delinquent subcultures. An adequate, systematic, comprehensive explanation of the causes of crime and delinquency is a prerequisite for a meaningful program of control and prevention. In this section we will examine four

[57] Stuart L. Hills, "Combatting organized crime in America." *Federal Probation*, March 1968, p. 25.
[58] Ralph F. Salerno, "Organized crime and criminal justice." *Federal Probation*, June 11, 1969, pp. 11–17.

major sociological approaches and evaluate them in light of recent research. (A fifth approach, control theory, is described in Chapter 5.)

This approach was first introduced by Sutherland in 1939, as *differential association*. Despite its age, and with some later modifications, differential association seems to explain the widest range of criminal facts. It may be considered a "genetic" or "historical" explanation, because it deals with the processes operative during the early experiences of the criminal, as differentiated from "mechanistic" or "situational" explanations, which are based on the processes operating at the moment the crime is committed.

GROUP-SUPPORTED CRIME

Criminal behavior, according to this orientation, is the result of a learning process, the principal part of which takes place within small, intimate groups—family, friends, neighborhood peer groups, and so on. This learning includes both the techniques of committing crimes and, more important, the specific direction of motives and drives. This direction is formed as the individual learns favorable and unfavorable definitions of the legal codes; that is, in some parts of society the individual is surrounded by those who define the legal codes as rules to be followed, while in other parts of society the individual may associate only with those who define the laws as hindrances to be avoided or overcome.

The basic principle of differential association, succinctly stated by Sutherland, is that "a person becomes delinquent because of the excess of definitions favorable to violation of law over definitions unfavorable to violation of law." [59] People internalize the values of the surrounding culture, and when their environment includes frequent contact with criminal elements and relative isolation from noncriminal elements, they are apt to become delinquent or criminal. The boy whose most admired model is another member of the gang or a successful neighborhood pimp, for example, will seek to emulate this model and will receive encouragement and approval from his peers when he does so successfully.

While the child is usually in contact with both criminal and noncriminal patterns, these associations vary in frequency, duration, priority, and intensity. The concepts of *frequency* and *duration* are self-explanatory. *Priority* refers to the fact that attitudes learned early in life, whether lawful or criminal, tend to persist in later life, although this tendency has not been fully demonstrated. *Intensity* is a rather imprecise concept referring to the prestige of, and emotional ties with, the source of the criminal or anticriminal patterns.

Since Sutherland last modified his theory in 1947, it has been further adapted by other researchers. Burgess and Akers, for example, have reformulated the approach in terms of reinforcement learning. They have translated Sutherland's principle, quoted earlier, to read as follows: "Criminal behavior is a function of norms which are discriminative for criminal behavior, the learning of which takes place when such behavior is more highly reinforced than noncriminal behavior." [60] Burgess and

[59] Edwin H. Sutherland and Donald R. Cressey, *Principles of Criminology*. Philadelphia: Lippincott, 1966.
[60] Robert L. Burgess and Ronald L. Akers, "A differential association-reinforcement theory of criminal behavior." *Social Problems* 14 (Fall 1966):128–147.

Akers feel that this restatement has partially rectified their principal dissatisfaction with Sutherland's approach, which was the great difficulty of empirically demonstrating its validity.

Despite recent modifications, Sutherland's work has been the basis for many suggestions of practical steps that could be taken to reduce the incidence of crime. As summarized by Malcolm Klein in the *Encyclopedia of Social Work,* these range from group treatment of offenders in certain circumstances, reward systems, and prosocial role-playing to specific neighborhood programs such as the Chicago Area Project (to be discussed later in this chapter).[61]

ANOMIE APPROACH

This orientation, also known as the *goals and opportunities* approach, is held by many modern scholars, notably Robert K. Merton. Merton takes as his starting point the fact that a society has both approved goals and norms and approved ways of attaining them. When some members of the society accept the goals or norms but have insufficient access to the approved means of attaining them, their adherence to the approved standards of conduct is likely to be weakened, and they may try to reach the goals or norms by other, socially unacceptable, means.[62] In other words, criminal behavior occurs when socially sanctioned means are not available for the realization of highly desired goals or norms.

The disparity between goals or norms and means, or *anomie,* often varies with nationality, ethnic background, class, religion, and other social characteristics. In some nations emphasis is placed on adherence to behavioral norms—as in Japan where even gigantic antigovernment student demonstrations are conducted according to an informal but rigid code—and in such a case the degree of anomie may be fairly low. In other nations, relatively more emphasis is placed on the attainment of goals and less on achieving them through socially sanctioned norms. Merton maintains that the United States is one such society, and our status as the industrialized nation with the highest crime rate bears him out. Identifying anomie as a basic characteristic of American society, Merton lists several kinds of adaptations common in America. One of these, *innovation,* "refers to the rejection of institutional practices but the retention of cultural goals. This would seem to characterize a substantial part of the deviant behavior which has been accorded the greatest share of research attention—namely . . . 'crime' and 'delinquency.' "[63] In particular, it would seem to characterize the behavior of lower-class juvenile gang members who have adopted socially approved goals but abandoned socially approved methods of attaining them.

This kind of rejection occurs widely in groups in which the greatest "disjuncture" between goals, norms, and opportunities exists. In this country, it is most often found among those who have the most difficulty obtaining a good education or training for well-paid jobs, and particularly in lower socioeconomic groups of blacks, Indians, and Spanish-speaking

[61] Malcolm Klein, "Crime and delinquency." In Robert Morris, ed., *Encyclopedia of Social Work.* New York: National Association of Social Workers, 1971, p. 168.
[62] Robert K. Merton, *Social Theory and Social Structure.* New York: Free Press, 1968, p. 232.
[63] Merton, p. 230.

peoples. An important point, however, is that higher crime rates among such groups are not axiomatic, but may be expected only when the goals people internalize are those set for them by a society which at the same time erects barriers to their attainment through socially sanctioned means. If different goals were set for different socioeconomic classes, as under the caste systems of some other countries, presumably there would not be this connection of anomie with the poor. In Merton's words:

It is when a system of cultural values extols, virtually above all else, certain *common* success-goals *for the population at large* while the social structure rigorously restricts or completely closes access to approved modes of reaching these goals *for a considerable part of the same population,* that deviant behavior ensues on a large scale.

Since the first formulation of the anomie approach, subsequent research seems to have provided at least some support for its basic premise, although there are types of crime and delinquency which it fails to explain adequately—namely such crimes as vandalism or assault when they do not result in monetary gain.

This omission is related to the question most frequently raised about Merton's work: Is the goal of financial success and material possessions held by the lower socioeconomic classes, or is this only a middle-class goal, with the lower classes holding different values and aspirations? A study by Wan Sang Han in Atlanta, Georgia, involving white Protestant high school seniors, seems to support Merton's theory in general, although not conclusively. The students were asked how much more schooling they would *wish* to have in a society with equal opportunity for all, and how much they *expected* to receive in view of their actual situations, including their own abilities and their parents' financial resources. The answers to the question involving their wishes supported Merton, but the answers regarding the students' expectations favored those who maintain that different classes have different goals.[64]

Many sociologists have in fact come to believe that people in the lower classes tend to hold two sets of beliefs simultaneously. That is, they share the norms and values of the larger society, but are forced to develop standards and expectations of their own so they can deal realistically with their deprived environment. (This idea is discussed more fully in Chapter 6, "Affluence and Poverty.") Thus, for example, people in the lower class share with the more affluent the view that crime is bad. It is not surprising, therefore, that other studies have supported Merton's view that anomie, rather than poverty itself, is a major cause of crime and delinquency.[65]

DELINQUENT SUBCULTURES

After a ten-year period of relative calm, a resurgence in the activities of youth street gangs has recently been reported. The gangs have become more noticeably active in six of the nation's largest cities—New York, Chicago, Los Angeles, Philadelphia, Detroit, and San Francisco. In each

[64] Wan Sang Han, "Two conflicting themes: Common values versus class differential values." *American Sociological Review* 34 (October 1969):679–690.
[65] See, for example, Marcia Guttentag, "The relationship of unemployment to crime and delinquency." *Journal of Social Issues* (January 1968): 105–115.

of these cities, from 4,000 to 15,000 persons on the 10- to 30-age group are members of such gangs. The increase in the use of handguns by gang members and their habit of randomly choosing victims have rendered these gangs potentially more dangerous than those of the past.[66]

Among the sociologists who explored the origin and character of delinquent groups was Albert K. Cohen in *Delinquent Boys*.[67] Cohen views the formation of delinquent gangs as a problem-solving step taken by the boys involved to alleviate the difficulties they face at the bottom of the status ladder. Gang members are typically children from working-class homes who find themselves measured, as Cohen puts it, with a "middle-class measuring rod" by those who control access to success in the society at large, including teachers, businesspersons, police, religious leaders, and public bureaucrats. Untrained in such "middle-class virtues" as ambition, the ability to defer the gratification of immediate desires for the sake of long-term goals, self-discipline, and academic skills, and hence poorly prepared to compete in a middle-class world, they form subcultures whose status criteria they can meet.

The gang subculture may offer a special status to a young person who does not have the opportunity to meet the success standards of middle-class society.
Newsweek/
Robert R. McElroy

[66] "Street gangs turn from 'rumbles' to wanton crime." *U.S. News and World Report,* July 7, 1975, pp. 15–18.
[67] Albert K. Cohen, *Delinquent Boys.* New York: Free Press, 1971.

This delinquent subculture, which Cohen characterizes as non-utilitarian, malicious, and negativistic,

takes its norms from the larger culture, but turns them upside down. The delinquents consider something right, by the standards of their subculture, precisely *because* it is wrong by the norms of the larger culture.

It is this assertion of Cohen's which has drawn the most fire from his critics. Lerman, for example, tested adherence and non-adherence to social values in a group of 555 New York City boys and girls. Although he agreed with Cohen on the versatility of the subculture and the ambivalence of ghetto youngsters toward school and work, he found the non-utilitarian aspects of delinquency which Cohen emphasized only in the younger age ranges.[68]

Five years after *Delinquent Boys* appeared, another major work on delinquent subcultures was published by Richard Cloward and Lloyd Ohlin.[69] As with Cohen, Cloward and Ohlin draw on the work of Sutherland and of Merton, but differ with Cohen by proposing three different kinds of delinquent subcultures. The three subcultures—criminalistic, conflict, and retreatist—are based on the notion that delinquents perceive a lack of opportunity for attaining "success," measured in terms of working-class perceptions of "success." The criminalistic subculture is based on organized, predatory theft, and is most often associated with adult organized crime, into whose ranks delinquents may move as they become older and more adept. The conflict subculture is organized around battles with rival gangs, and is likely to arise when the youngsters involved have few if any contacts with the criminal world. The retreatist subculture is composed of those who have failed in normal society, are not able to compete in the theft subculture, or are cowardly or inept fighters. Those in this subculture might retreat from the dominant culture and the active subcultures through such devices as the use of narcotics.

Cloward and Ohlin differ from Cohen not only in proposing the three different subcultures, but also in maintaining that the boys who join delinquent gangs are those who have not only been unable to compete in the larger society, but who have also seen the cause of their failure as lying in the social order itself, rather than in any deficiency of their own. Once they have fixed the blame on society and communicated to each other the extent of their alienation, the creation of some sort of delinquent subculture—in this case, a gang—becomes likely. The authors maintain that the more socially disorganized the ghetto wherein this process occurs, the more likely it is that the subculture established will be of the conflict and retreatist types. Therefore, they see the decline of the old, ethnically organized ghettos and the increase in unstable social patterns in today's ghettos as leading to an increase in the violent gang subculture and a decrease in the theft-oriented subculture associated with organized crime.

Cloward and Ohlin have been criticized more frequently than Cohen, and often more vigorously. Bordua charges that they have ignored the

[68] Paul Lerman, "Individual values, peer values, and subculture delinquency." *American Sociological Review* 33 (April 1968):219–236.
[69] Richard A. Cloward and Lloyd E. Ohlin, *Delinquency and Opportunity: A Theory of Delinquent Gangs.* New York: Free Press, 1960.

life history of the boys and their families. He also maintains that "the system" is less to blame than the boys themselves, who have progressively cut off opportunities and destroyed their own abilities.[70] Bordua seems to be saying that delinquents, not working-class boys in general, have eliminated their own opportunities. Bordua also maintains that the theory of delinquent subcultures might work for blacks but not for whites, whom he sees as more or less equal regardless of class. However, he fails to substantiate his claim that cut-off opportunities are an effect rather than a cause of delinquency.

In addition to these shortcomings in Cloward and Ohlin's theory, Short and Strodtbeck have found that outside of the very largest urban ghettos, delinquent subcultures tend to be somewhat more versatile. A single gang may be engaged in all three kinds of delinquent behavior at different times.[71]

Some sociologists do not believe that delinquent subcultures are formed only in frustrated reaction to the dominant culture. Instead, they see delinquency as generated by the lower-class culture itself. A study by Walter Miller,[72] for example, which was based on his long experience with street gangs, identifies *trouble, toughness, smartness, excitement, fate,* and *autonomy* as the six "focal concerns" of lower-class culture which often lead to the violation of middle-class social and legal norms. *Trouble* is important to the individual's status in the community, whether it is seen as something to be kept out of or something to be gotten into. Usually there is less worry over legal or moral questions than over possible complications resulting from the involvement of police, welfare investigators, and other agents of society. *Toughness* is the typical emphasis on masculinity, physical strength, and the ability to "take it," coupled with a rejection of art, literature, and anything else considered "feminine." This is partly a reaction to female-dominated households and the lack of male role figures to emulate, both at home and in school. *Smartness,* in the street sense of the term, denotes the ability to outwit, dupe, or "con" someone, rather than intellectual ability. A successful pimp, for example, would be considered "smarter" than a bank clerk. To relieve the crushing boredom of ghetto life, residents of lower-class communities often appear to seek out situations of danger or *excitement,* as in gambling or in high-speed joyrides in automobiles. *Fate* is an important concern because lower-class citizens frequently feel that the important events in life are beyond the individual's control. They will often resort to semimagical resources such as "readers and advisors" on spiritual matters as a means to change their luck. Finally, *autonomy* is of major concern to this group, who are apt on the one hand to express strong resentment of any external controls or exercise of coercive authority over their

LOWER-CLASS CULTURE AND DELINQUENCY

[70] David J. Bordua, "Delinquent subcultures: Sociological interpretations of gang delinquency." *Annals of the American Academy of Political and Social Science* 338 (November 1961):134.
[71] James F. Short, Jr., and Fred L. Strodtbeck, *Group Process and Gang Delinquency.* Chicago: University of Chicago Press, 1965.
[72] Walter B. Miller, "Lower class culture as a generating milieu of gang delinquency." *Journal of Social Issues* 14 (1958):5–19.

behavior, yet on the other hand frequently seem to seek out restrictive environments, perhaps even by obtaining commitment to mental hospitals or to prisons.

After his analysis of the lower-class community, Miller turns to the specific values and attributes of lower-class adolescent street gangs. He notes several attributes common to almost all gangs: the prevalence of single-sex gangs, due to the difficulties and conflicts arising from double-sex interaction over a prolonged period of time; the psychological and educational stability, often lacking in the home, which is available to the individual through the gang; and the aid provided by gang membership in establishing and maintaining sex-role identity. Miller also points out that since the primary concerns of gang members are status and "belonging," the individual will commit gang-sanctioned illegal behavior rather than risk exclusion from the gang. In other words, gangs oriented toward these values will automatically violate middle-class legal norms against fighting, gambling, and disturbing the peace.

Miller's analysis has been criticized on the grounds that not all lower-class groups, all of which supposedly share the same focal concerns, are delinquent. And we have already suggested, the assumption that a widespread "lower-class culture" exists, untainted by middle-class values, has been called into question.

SOCIAL CONTROL

Given the alarming extent of both conventional and occupational crime, a discussion of efforts which have been made in the direction of the social control of crime is particularly significant. These efforts can be classified under four headings: retribution-deterrence, rehabilitation, prevention, and criminal and juvenile justice reforms. This last category includes efforts to control occupational, white-collar, and organized crime.

Retribution and deterrence—to "pay back" guilty persons for their deeds and to dissuade them and others from repeating them—have historically been the primary objects in society's handling of lawbreakers. It is only relatively recently that the idea of actively rehabilitating offenders—providing them with the ability and the motivation to build for themselves a law-abiding and socially approved way of life—has taken hold on any large scale; however, the greatest part of our correctional system is still oriented toward the older approach. We no longer exact retribution from the offender in the ancient "eye for an eye, tooth for a tooth" formula, which demanded that slanderers have their tongues torn out, thieves have their hands amputated, and murderers be killed, but the retributive orientation of our prison philosophy becomes abundantly clear when public outcry demands longer sentences for particularly heinous or infamous crimes such as murders or political assassinations. Their punishment arises from the fear and rage experienced by the members of society who identify with the victim of the crime.

RETRIBUTION-DETERRENCE

The punishments meted out to murderers, forgers, and others serve, or are supposed to serve, several purposes. According to Toby, in addition to the more frequently discussed roles of preventing further crime and rehabilitating the offender, punishment serves to sustain the morale of those who conform to societal rules. That is, those who identify the offender as one who willfully violates the law demand his or her punishment partly to reinforce their own ambivalent feelings about conformity. They feel that if they must sacrifice to obey the law, someone who does not should not be allowed to "get away with it." Others, seeing criminals as people who are not evil but sick and who commit their criminal acts because of an organic or psychological disorder, do not feel the desire for punishment but instead call for the "treatment" of offenders to correct the disorders which cause them to become criminals. Even this, however, may conceal a retributive bias.[73]

Some writers, such as James Q. Wilson, have suggested that there is a need within society for the firm moral authority that is secured by attaching a stigma to crime and the consequent punishment. While Wilson grants that prisoners should be able to "pay their debts" without being deprived of their civil rights after release from prison and suffering the continued indignities of parole supervision and permanent unemployment, he reaffirms the moral value of stigmatizing crime and the person who commits it:

To destigmatize crime would be to lift from it the weight of moral judgment and to make crime simply a particular occupation or avocation which society has chosen to reward less (or perhaps more) than other pursuits. If there is no stigma attached to an activity, then society has no business making it a crime.[74]

The deterrent value of punishment is also stressed. This approach has been described by Robert Martinson:

The goal is deterrence—individual and general deterrence—and the hardliners assert that punishment is the appropriate means to this goal. They demand that the threat [of punishment] contained in every penal statute be carried out promptly, so that everyone will be assured that it is a credible threat: to legally convict and then punish an offender will "deter" him from further offending; it will also "deter" potential offenders from committing crime.[75]

Actually, however, there is little proof that punishment is necessarily an effective preventive measure against crime. People are also kept from the commission of crime and other antisocial acts by their successful integration into society, although undoubtedly some people would not hesitate to engage in criminal acts if they were sure that there would be no retribution.

The argument for punishment as a deterrent is most often heard in the case of capital punishment, since execution can hardly be called either humane or rehabilitative. Even in this case, however, there is

---

[73] Jackson Toby, "Is punishment necessary?" In Harry Gold and Frank Scarpitti, eds., *Combatting Social Problems.* New York: Holt, Rinehart and Winston, 1967, pp. 307–315.
[74] James Q. Wilson, *Thinking About Crime.* New York: Basic Books, 1975, p. 71.
[75] Robert Martinson, "Planning for public safety." *New Republic,* April 29, 1972, pp. 21–23.

little evidence that demonstrates a relationship between murder rates and the use of capital punishment. Sellin, for example, has concluded that "the presence of the death penalty—in law or practice—does not influence homicide death rates." [76] Akman, in a survey of Canadian penal institutions, found no empirical justification for the argument that the policy of commuting death sentences to life imprisonment would result in additional safety hazards for prison staff and inmates.[77] Reckless has also found no evidence for the deterrent effect of capital punishment.[78]

REHABILITATION

The relatively recent development, during the last century and a half, of the idea of rehabilitating offenders rests on the concept of crime as a social aberration, and the offender as a social misfit whose aberrant behavior can be modified to conform to the social norm, or "cured." Unfortunately, there are as yet no definitive research theories specifying the form of rehabilitation which will be most effective with a particular kind of offender. The question which Robison and Smith asked in their study of the California penal system: "Will the clients act differently if we lock them up, or keep them locked up longer, or do something with them inside, or watch them more closely afterward, or cut them loose officially?" seems so far to have yielded a negative answer. Yet there is no conclusive evidence that certain alternatives, such as prison counseling programs or outright discharge, are more effective in reducing recidivism rates than other more punitive alternatives.[79] (See Figures 4-3 and 4-4.) All that can be said is that some of the rehabilitation experiments undertaken to date have met with more success than others. Some of the programs have treated the offender in the society at large, while others have attempted to work within the present institutional system of correction.

One example of the latter, institutional projects, is worthy of mention. In California, the PICO (Pilot Intensive Counseling Organization) Project was established under the California Youth Authority to assess the effect of individual interview therapy on older delinquents. The young offenders were first divided into groups which were amenable and non-amenable to treatment, and each of these two groups was then divided into a treatment group and a control group. The amenables were those who, in the judgment of an examining group at the time of admission, were "bright, verbal, and anxious," and evidenced an "awareness of problems," "insight," a "desire to change," and "acceptance of treatment." All of the delinquents in the study underwent the ordinary treatment in the California correctional system for minors, except that the treated youths received in addition one or two weekly individual counseling sessions with psychiatrists or clinical psychologists and in some cases group therapy as well. The results indicated that the treated amenable

[76] Thorsten Sellin, "Homicides in retentionist and abolitionist states." In Thorsten Sellin, ed., *Capital Punishment*. New York: Harper & Row, 1967, pp. 135–138.
[77] Dogan D. Akman, "Homicide and assaults in Canadian prisons." In Sellin, *Capital Punishment,* pp. 161–168.
[78] Walter C. Reckless, "Use of the death penalty." *Crime and Delinquency* 17 (January 1971):67–80.
[79] James Robison and Gerald Smith, "The effectiveness of correctional programs." *Crime and Delinquency* 17 (January 1971):67–80.

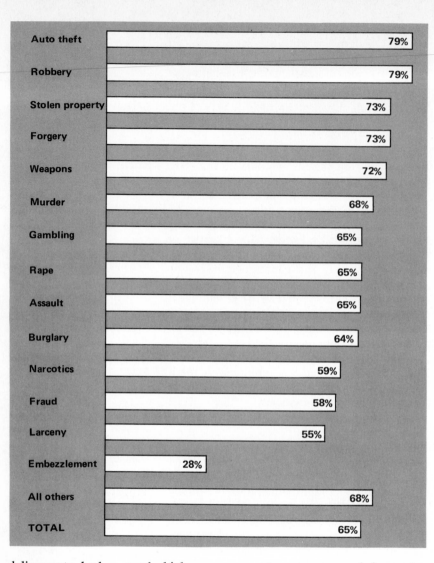

FIGURE 4-3
Percentage of Repeaters, by Type of Crime, for Persons Arrested 1970–1974

Source: U.S. Department of Justice, *Uniform Crime Reports.* Washington, D.C.: U.S. Government Printing Office, 1975, p. 49.

delinquents had a much higher success rate, as measured by early favorable discharges and continued freedom from institutional control. The two control groups, amenable and non-amenable, had almost identical rates of return to custody; the treated non-amenables, surprisingly, had the highest return rate of all. The success achieved with the amenables is encouraging, but the failure with the treated non-amenables suggests the difficulty in establishing effective rehabilitative treatment for all delinquents. Adams, reporting on the project, points out that the problem could lie either with giving the wrong treatment to non-amenables or with giving them too little treatment.[80]

[80] Stuart Adams, "Interaction between individual interview therapy and treatment amenability in older youth authority wards." In *Inquiries Concerning Kinds of Treatments for Kinds of Delinquents.* Sacramento: California Board of Corrections, 1961, pp. 27–44.

A major hindrance to rehabilitative efforts in an institutional setting lies in the very nature of our current prison system, which removes offenders from practically all contact with the general society and its norms, and instead subjects them to almost continual contact with individuals who have committed crimes ranging from murder to petty larceny, homosexual rape to fraud. Within prison walls offenders are punished by a deprivation of liberty, autonomy, heterosexual contacts, goods and services, and the security which is normally obtained from participation in ordinary social institutions.[81] According to McCorkle and Korn these deprivations, and especially the last, drive prisoners into a special social order within the prison. Adherence to this social order, which may be necessary for both mental and physical well-being, further separates inmates' goals and drives from those held by the society at large, and makes it more difficult for them to relate to whatever retraining or rehabilitative measures are available from the institutional staff. The apparently inevitable conflict between custodial and therapeutic members of the institution's staff, with the former regarding the latter as enemies of discipline and the latter regarding the former as obstacles to treatment, further aggravates the problem.[82]

Rehabilitative treatment of prisoners in our existing penal system is further complicated by the fact that individual attention and treatment cannot be provided without the loss of at least some institutional control. If a therapist were to give some special treatment to individuals who were particularly hard to handle, even if the treatment were central to the therapy the prisoners required, the other prisoners would see this special

---

[81] Toby, pp. 307–315.
[82] Lloyd W. McCorkle and Richard Korn, "Resocialization within walls." *Annals of the American Academy of Political and Social Sciences* 293 (May 1954):88–89.

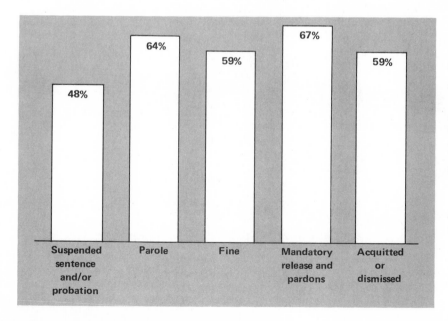

FIGURE 4-4
Percentage of Persons Rearrested Within Three Years, by Type of Release in 1972

Source: U.S. Department of Justice, *Uniform Crime Reports.* Washington, D.C.: U.S. Government Printing Office, 1975, p. 52.

Dehumanizing prison
conditions, typified by
this cage-like corridor,
make rehabilitation
difficult.
Bill Powers/Nancy Palmer

treatment as a direct result of the specially treated prisoners' deviant behavior and might well imitate them.[83]

More frequently than individual therapy, the "rehabilitation" which prisoners receive consists of work training. Unfortunately, the work most of them perform in prison is generally of a menial and unsatisfying nature, such as kitchen helper and janitor. As reported by Glaser, such work is related to the type of job obtained by convicts on their release in only 25 percent of the cases. The reasons are various: most prisons have difficulty providing enough work to occupy all of their inmates; available incentives, such as slightly better pay and work conditions, are inadequate to lure prisoners into types of work which will be most beneficial to them on their release; and the records maintained by prison officials on their work programs are poor. Glaser did find, however, that although the percentages were low, those who performed work in prison which was beneficial to them after their release had lower rates of recidivism.[84]

The difficulty of rehabilitating an offender within prison has led to varied attempts to reform the offender within, or partially within, the general society. This concept seems beneficial in several ways. Treating offenders without exposing them totally to the deficiencies apparent in the current prison system not only spares them the antisocial effects of prolonged exposure to a criminal society, but reduces the cost of custodial facilities and personnel. This makes treatment resources more available to those who seem to offer the best chance for rehabilitation, that is, those who are most amenable. Perhaps the oldest and most widely used system of this kind is the work-release program, under which prisoners are allowed to leave the institution for a certain period each day in order to work at productive jobs outside. Although this type of program is in use throughout the world and has been known in the United States since it was first authorized in Wisconsin in 1913, it has only become widely used since the mid-1950s. Today at least 24 states have authorized some form of work-release program, and the federal government in 1965 authorized such a program for federal prisoners.

Although the idea of releasing convicted felons to the general population, even for limited periods of time, has met with expected opposition, in general the programs seem to have worked well. In addition to removing convicts from the criminal society within the prison, work-release programs reimburse the state, through the prisoners' wages, for some of the costs of maintaining them, and also allow the prisoners to support their dependents, thus helping to keep them off the welfare rolls.[85] Further, the work-release program serves as a practical step in the process of reintegrating the offender into society, since many of those who successfully complete the program retain their jobs after their release.[86]

[83] Donald Cressey, "Limitations of treatment." In N. Johnston et al., eds., The Sociology of Punishment and Correction. 2nd ed. New York: Wiley, 1970, pp. 501–508.

[84] Daniel Glaser, The Effectiveness of a Prison and Parole System. Indianapolis: Bobbs-Merrill, 1964, pp. 10–11, 250–259.

[85] Serapio R. Zalba, "Work-release—A two-pronged effort." Crime and Delinquency 13 (October 1967):506–612.

[86] Stanley E. Grupp, "Work release and the misdemeanant." In Gold and Scarpitti, pp. 332–341.

In prisons, work programs have not forsaken the tradition of the "rock pile." Inmates are ushered out in groups to perform manual labor of little rehabilitative value.
Danny Lyon/Magnum

The program is not applicable to all prisoners, especially those considered incorrigible, and is less successful in some areas than in others. Johnson has noted the difficulty encountered by state agencies in finding jobs for work releases. There is also the problem of finding suitable housing for those involved, since prisons are typically located in rural areas, far from the heavily populated areas where jobs can be more easily provided.[87]

Even more innovative programs have been utilized in an attempt to rehabilitate younger delinquents. This is to be expected, since our society is less likely to consider minors fully responsible for their actions, and more likely to feel that they can still be saved from becoming lifetime criminals. In contrast to the California rehabilitation experiment described earlier, many of these programs were predicated on the concept of keeping the young offenders out of the conventional reformatory system, which resembles an adult prison system in many ways. One such program, described by Henderson, involved allowing delinquent girls to live at home but requiring them to attend special classes during the day at the San Mateo County (California) Juvenile Hall. The classes emphasized individual instruction in subjects needed for graduation from the local high school, combined with group discussions of common problems with the other girls in the program. The program involved weekly visits with the girl's probation officer and required close and reliable family supervision. From the commencement of the program in 1965, the county's rate of commitment of girls to institutions and foster homes was cut by about 25 percent. This reversed an almost 20 percent

[87] Elmer H. Johnson, "Report on an innovation—State work-release programs." *Crime and Delinquency* 16 (October 1970):417–426.

annual increase over the previous six years. This high rate of success, for which the program was largely responsible, has led the county to make plans for expanding the program to include a larger number of girls and boys.[88]

A problem with rehabilitation as it is currently practiced is that no single approach offers a guaranteed road to success. Although several programs have been notably effective in dealing with particular situations, universal criteria have not been developed. Programs which succeed in one area or with a particular kind of offender fail when moved to another part of the country or when applied to a different kind of offender. Bailey analyzed 100 studies of correctional procedures and found that "evidence supporting the efficacy of correctional treatment is slight, inconsistent, and of questionable reliability." [89] He felt this might be so for several reasons. Rehabilitative treatments may be ineffectual either inherently or due to the ambivalence of the "crime and punishment" setting within which it occurs. It may be that some forms of rehabilitation are effective for certain criminals under certain conditions, but that we have not yet adequately defined the conditions or identified the criminals. Many of the reformative attempts currently in vogue may fail because they are based on incorrect theories of the causes of delinquency and criminality. Whatever the reason, there is as yet no conclusive demonstration of the validity of various rehabilitative practices.

A final problem with prison rehabilitation programs is that they have tended to make release contingent on participation in the programs. Inmates are thus forced into behavior modification procedures, individual and group therapy sessions, and vocational training whether they like it or not, and many find themselves having to act "rehabilitated" in order to qualify for parole. Those who refuse must usually serve longer terms and endure worse living conditions. A new program developed by the Just Community of Niantic, Connecticut, has made rehabilitation voluntary, and an inmate's participation does not necessarily shorten his or her term.[90]

PREVENTION

The concept of preventing crime and delinquency before they occur is an attractive one, but, as with rehabilitation, difficult to implement. Other than the deterrent effect of harsh punishment and repressive control measures, crime prevention is customarily defined in three different ways: as the sum total of all influences and activities which contribute to the development of a nondeviant personality in children; as the attempt to deal with specific conditions within the person's environment which are believed to lead to crime and delinquency; and as those specific services provided to individuals or groups which are designed to prevent further crime and delinquency. Prevention programs under the first definition include measures designed to improve the social environment of the children concerned, encompassing such things as improved housing for

---

[88] Susan Henderson, "Day care for juvenile delinquents." *Judicature,* June–July 1969.

[89] Walter C. Bailey, "Correctional outcome: An evaluation of 100 reports." *Journal of Criminal Law, Criminology, and Police Science* 57 (June 1966):153–160.

[90] "The crime wave," p. 22.

ghetto dwellers, equal job opportunities, and other attempts to improve the quality of life of those in the lower socioeconomic classes. Although programs with these aims do exist, and one of their goals may be the reduction of crime and delinquency in the target area, they are seldom undertaken with this goal uppermost. In addition, studies of youths involved in antipoverty programs have not as yet found any positive correlation between such participation and a reduction in delinquency rates.[91]

The second definition covers programs and attempts based on Sutherland's theory of differential association, and includes efforts to reduce the exposure of children to the antisocial and/or illegal activities of those around them, to improve the child's family life, and to create a viable and conforming social structure within the community itself. Several projects of this sort have been attempted, and some, such as the famous Chicago Area Project which we will be examining shortly, have been notable successes.

Programs which attempt to work within the third definition—prevention of further delinquency and crime—are still in the majority, however. They include such established programs as parole, probation, training schools, and other institutions, as well as freer, more experimental programs.[92] The difficulty of comparing the efforts under this and the other two definitions of delinquency prevention is apparent, since each deals with quite different sets of circumstances.

The Chicago Area Project, for example, was established in the mid-1930s in the decaying urban area of Chicago, where the weakening social structure of the large immigrant population was no longer able to control the children of the area. The project set out to develop youth welfare programs, using local youths for manpower, that would be viable and permanent additions to the community after the project leaders had left. It was reasoned—correctly, as it turned out—that the local youth, who were then involved with a large network of gangs, would have better success than outside workers in establishing recreation programs (including extensive summer camping), community improvement campaigns, and programs devoted to reaching and assisting delinquent youngsters and even some adults returning to the community after release from prison. The project not only showed the feasibility of using untrained local youths to establish effective youth welfare programs, but it also indicated, despite a difficulty of establishing empirical data, a possible decrease in the delinquency rate.[93] However, most similar projects that have since been attempted have had negligible impact on delinquency rates, for reasons that remain unclear.[94]

[91] Gerald D. Robin, "Anti-poverty programs and delinquency." *Journal of Criminal Law, Criminology, and Police Science* 60 (1969):331.

[92] John M. Martin, "Three approaches to delinquency prevention: A critique." In Gold and Scarpitti, pp. 351–352.

[93] Solomon Kobrin, "The Chicago Area Project—A 25-year assessment." *Annals of the American Academy of Political and Social Sciences* 322 (March 1959): 20–29.

[94] Walter B. Miller, "The impact of a 'total-community' delinquency control project." *Social Problems* 10 (Fall 1962):169–191.

Delinquency prevention projects aimed at specific individuals rather than groups have also shown discouraging results. These studies typically contrast two groups of similar individuals, one of which receives intensive and extensive counseling from psychologists, guidance counselors, and social workers, while the other remains uncounseled, serving as a control. Powers and Witmer found, in a very detailed study of two groups of 325 "problem boys" who were considered to be "predelinquents," that the counseling the treatment group received was no more effective than the normal forces active in the community in preventing delinquent acts. They did find, however, that the control boys committed slightly more serious offenses than the treatment boys, although the difference was not statistically significant. There seems to be an indication, though, that the control group may have a higher rate of recidivism as they grow older.[95]

Meyer, Borgatta, and Jones found similar results with a group of girls entering a vocational high school over a four-year period in New York City. Measured by a wide range of criteria, both inside and outside the school system, the treatment girls, who were extensively counseled by a private, nonsectarian, voluntary social agency, failed to score significantly lower than the control group in undesirable and antisocial behavior. The conductors of the survey were able to take some comfort from the fact that the differences between the two groups, although too small to be statistically significant, did favor the girls who had received counseling services.[96]

These cases make clear the enormous difficulty of drawing any conclusions about the effectiveness of preventive measures. Although they seem to fail at least as often as they succeed, the difficulty may be more with the specific kind of counseling services offered than with the idea of prevention itself. Also, even in those studies where delinquency prevention seems to be a failure, there are some signs that it may have some beneficial effect, even if not of the magnitude desired. What must be recognized here is that most of the programs described are of an experimental nature and have not been attempted on a large-scale basis. Further research and more governmental funding for programs of this sort are two of the main needs in this field.

There is little doubt that the problems of our criminal justice system have reached crisis proportions. Many critics have pointed out that criminal justice is too often based on political considerations and that the judicial system itself is overly complicated and burdened with too many laws and too wide a diversity of procedural methods. The result is that the administration of justice to conventional, juvenile, occupational, and organized criminals alike is unfair and inconsistent.

CRIMINAL AND JUVENILE JUSTICE REFORMS

Conventional Crimes. The fact that of the 10 million violent and property crimes committed in the United States in 1974 only 21 percent were

[95] Edwin Powers and Helen Witmer, *An Experiment in the Prevention of Delinquency.* New York: Columbia University Press, 1951, pp. vii–xi, 320–338.
[96] Henry J. Meyer, Edgar F. Borgatta, and Wyatt C. Jones, "An experiment in prevention through social work intervention." In Edwin Thoman, ed., *Behavior Sciences for Social Workers.* New York: Free Press, 1967, pp. 363–383, 470–471.

"cleared" by arrests and only 5 percent ended in convictions makes crime an attractive proposition for many.[97] Part of the reason for this state of affairs is that through the process of plea bargaining—whereby the offender agrees to plead guilty to a lesser charge and release the courts from the responsibility of having to conduct a time-consuming jury trial— the majority of persons convicted for what are regarded as serious crimes receive shortened sentences. It has been estimated, however, that if the plea bargaining process were cut back to even 80 percent of the serious crimes, the number of trials would double and put an enormous strain on the court system.

A further problem with the current administration of justice is that up to now, sentencing has been a very haphazard process that has often resulted in prisoners "serving wildly different sentences for the same offense. Sentencing is too often a projection of the value system of the judge." [98] A study of the sentencing of draft evaders revealed that the length of term seemed to depend on in what part of the country the trial took place. In Oregon, for example, 33 violators were convicted and 18 put on probation; in Texas 16 were convicted and none received probation. None of the Oregon violators' sentences exceeded three years, but almost all the Texas violators were given the maximum sentence of five years.[99]

The disparity of sentencing may also be due in large part to the social class of the defendant. Jack Newfield cites a 1973 case in which the director of a nursing home corporation was found to have swindled $200 million out of the company's shareholders, making $14 million in profits for himself. For this he could have received at least a five-year prison sentence, but instead received a one-year sentence and was eligible for probation after four months. In a contrasting case the next day, a judge sentenced an 18-year-old Puerto Rican youth to five years in prison for stealing a car worth no more than $100, although the youth had not used a gun or committed any violent acts.[100] The current wide disparity in sentencing practices obviously undermines every citizen's sense of justice, as Willard Gaylin suggests:

When serious criminals go unpunished, when minor offenses are excessively punished, when a chosen group receives lesser punishment or a despised group more punishment, it threatens all of us in that society, even the law-abiders. It corrodes the basic structural prop of equity that supports our sense of justice. An excessive disparity in sentencing threatens that kind of breakdown.[101]

Juvenile Justice and Public Order Reforms. Compounding the criminal justice problem and greatly overloading the court calendars are the thou-

---

[97] "A high price tag that everybody pays." *U.S. News and World Report,* December 16, 1974, p. 31.
[98] "The crime wave," p. 18.
[99] Willard Gaylin, *Partial Justice.* New York: Knopf, 1974, pp. 6–7.
[100] Jack Newfield, *Cruel and Unusual Justice.* New York: Holt, Rinehart and Winston, 1964, p. xiii.
[101] Gaylin, p. 5.

sands of cases involving juvenile offenders and public order offenders. Many criminologists and legal authorities agree that there are far too many laws in force in most state codes that cover not just behavior that is illegal only for children—the so-called "juvenile status" crimes—but also nonviolent adult "victimless crimes," such as marijuana possession, adultery, homosexuality, prostitution, and drunkenness. Status and public order offenders constitute 40 percent of the case load in both juvenile and adult courts; there are so many status offenders appearing before juvenile court judges that they cannot devote proper attention to serious, violent offenders. Edwin M. Schur has therefore advocated a thorough reform of the concept of juvenile justice that would include a greater toleration for a broader range of behavior and would make only specific antisocial acts criminal; for these last there would be "uniformly applied punishment not disguised as treatment." [102]

Occupational Offenses. There are many facets to the legal reforms necessary to curb occupational crime. One of them focuses on increasing the penalties for occupational crime in order to create a more effective deterrent. Frequently today, a company worth hundreds of millions of dollars faces a fine of only $50,000 and its executive only $5,000 upon conviction for fraud or price-fixing.[103] This makes it easy for large corporations to view possible penalties as an acceptable risk. One way to increase fines, of course, is simply to raise the dollar amount of the allowable penalty for each crime. Another is to make penalties a fixed percentage of a company's profits.[104]

Some critics have felt that an extremely effective deterrent is to increase the likelihood of jail terms for occupational offenders. In the past, individuals convicted of occupational crime have rarely gone to jail. For example, only forty executives have been jailed for antitrust violations in the last eighty-five years.[105] Yet these criminals have much to lose by going to jail, in terms of status and community respect. The threat of prison, even for a short term, might be at least as effective a deterrent as increased fines.

There are other ways of increasing the penalties for occupational crime. A regulatory agency such as the Federal Trade Commission could require a company convicted of fraudulent advertising to use a certain proportion of its advertising budget in the next few years to inform consumers that previous claims were misleading. This type of remedy is particularly applicable in cases of consumer fraud, since its deterrent value depends on the company's fear of unfavorable consumer response.

Another aspect of legal reform involves changing laws to make them less easy or tempting to break. For example, complicated tax laws, which offer a variety of alternatives and loopholes, may be an invitation to cheating. Streamlining the laws might discourage cheating, as well as

---

[102] Edwin M. Schur, *Radical Nonintervention: Rethinking the Delinquency Problem.* Englewood Cliffs, N.J.: Prentice-Hall, 1973, p. 23.
[103] "More punch for antitrust—moves you can expect." *U.S. News and World Report,* November 25, 1974, pp. 47–48.
[104] "White collar crime: Huge economic and moral drain," p. 1049.
[105] "More punch for antitrust," pp. 47–48.

make it easier to detect when it does occur.[106] The law could also be reformed to make accomplices to occupational crimes, as well as principals, vulnerable to court action, so that for each such crime, many more individuals in a company would face punishment.

Stronger enforcement, obviously, must go hand in hand with legal reform in order for the latter to be meaningful. This means more money and more manpower for enforcement agencies. For example, to detect more income tax cheating means that more auditors must be hired by the IRS. To detect cases of collusion between corporations, the federal antitrust unit must have more investigators, with the expertise and time to gather evidence for a successful court case.

Similarly, once a case against occupational offenders has been won in court, the judge must be willing to invoke the penalties which the law allows. If the law provides for a jail term, the judge must not hesitate to send the convicted person to jail merely because he or she looks respectable, and a prison sentence seems inappropriate for a "respectable person."

These two approaches—legal reform, particularly greater penalties, and tougher enforcement—could probably be quite effective deterrents to occupational crime. More than most other types of crime, occupational crime is very much a matter of calculation and advance planning, of weighing gains against possible costs. Increasing the costs, as well as the risk of detection, might well lead occupational criminals to the rational decision that honesty is more profitable.

Another approach focuses on public education—making people realize the prevalence and the costs of occupational crime. As has already been pointed out, publicizing the names of firms convicted of such crime can be an effective tool. Public education can also lead to legal reform and tougher enforcement.

Finally, perhaps the most active effort against occupational crime at present is being conducted on the consumer front. Consumer advocates have two approaches to right the unjust balance in knowledge and power between consumers and industry. One is to make consumers less gullible and more sophisticated—for example, by teaching them to compare prices or to read contracts closely—so that they can do as well as possible under existing circumstances. The second is to increase the role of government, both local and national, in protecting the consumer. The oldest government function in this area has been that of setting standards for certain products. For example, the government has long set sanitary standards for meat wholesalers in order to protect the consumer, since it is clear that no individual consumer has the power to make sure that the meat he or she buys has been prepared in a sanitary way. Consumer advocates would like to expand these laws—particularly in the area of requiring safety features for products—and strengthen their enforcement.

Again, government can require that consumers be given true information about the products they buy—the real weight content of a package, the ingredients and nutritional value of a food product, the effective interest charges on a loan or an installment purchase. Unit pricing and the truth-in-lending law are recent attempts to gain some of these ends.

[106] Schur, *Our Criminal Society,* p. 190.

The creation of a federal "consumer advocate" agency could also do much to decrease abuses (such as false advertising) by industry as a whole, and to ensure that consumers will pay fair prices for safe products.

Combating Organized Crime. Organized crime is pervasive and costly. Authorities agree that, to date, efforts at combating it have been woefully inadequate. Only about 500 full-time employees at all levels of government, and minuscule financial and personnel resources, have been committed to fighting it.[107] One reason for the paucity of resources has been apparent public indifference to the problem. Most people do not worry about organized crime as much as they worry about the possibility of having their handbags snatched or their homes burglarized. They fail to realize that one reason for such crimes may be that drug users need money to buy drugs—and that one reason they are drug users in the first place is that the syndicate imported heroin, supplied it to the pushers, and encouraged them to create more and more customers. Because of public indifference to organized crime, there is usually little pressure on police departments to devote more people and money to the problem.

There are other reasons why it is particularly hard to fight organized crime. A major one is the difficulty of getting proof of syndicate activities that is acceptable in court. Witnesses rarely come forward—because they fear retaliation, or because they themselves are too deeply implicated. In any case, since top personnel are so well insulated from others in the syndicate, witnesses rarely possess valuable information about them and their plans. Documentary evidence is equally hard to obtain, since the transactions of syndicated crime are rarely written down. In some instances, corruption hinders effective prosecution of organized crime. In a ten-year study of the New York State Court's disposition of individual Mafia heroin dealers, the Joint Legislative Committee on Crime discovered that 47.7 percent of the cases were acquitted or dismissed.[108]

Beyond this, the basic approach of law-enforcement agencies and the courts has been short-term, focused on prosecuting in a well-publicized way particular individuals. Yet the crucial fact about organized crime is that, by definition, it is an organization, and therefore can endure regardless of the fate of individuals. In any case, again because of the insulation and protection of top members, the police are rarely able to arrest the most important leaders of syndicated crime.

It would seem that a different approach and more effective strategies are needed. Smith and Salerno, for example,[109] suggest that the need is for strategies which will weaken the organization as such, whether or not they result in putting individuals in jail. They propose five types of strategies:—to *subvert* the organization by breeding or aggravating internal dissension; to *alienate* current or prospective members by making membership unattractive; to *disrupt* activities, reducing profit and increasing costs; to *block* activities by alerting and educating the public; and to *penetrate* the organization by infiltration or purchase of information,

---

[107] *Challenge of Crime*, p. 197.
[108] Newfield, pp. xii–xiii.
[109] Dwight C. Smith and Ralph F. Salerno, "The use of strategies in organized crime control." *Journal of Criminal Law, Criminology, and Police Science* 61 (March 1970):101–111.

thereby gaining means to subvert, alienate, and disrupt. For all this to be done effectively, certain things are essential, particularly an adequate intelligence system. Syndicate activities must be studied, patterns of action and communication learned, probable future moves anticipated; and law-enforcement agencies must somehow coordinate their efforts in this direction and share the resulting information. At present three or four different agencies may be investigating the same person without each other's knowledge, resulting in waste of resources, duplication of effort, and sometimes active interference with each other's work.

The President's Commission on Law Enforcement and the Administration of Justice has also made a number of suggestions for dealing with organized crime.[110] The basic one, of course, is more money and more manpower, to carry out the work of gathering evidence and prosecuting criminals. This means establishing special units to fight syndicated crime in every state and every locality where it is necessary. Equally basic is coordination of local, state, and federal efforts. This would have the effect of increasing manpower for any one investigation and would improve efficiency. An important aspect would be the centralizing and computerizing of all data about syndicated crime collected by different enforcement agencies, so that any agency would have access to information from any source.

Other suggestions focus on methods of obtaining better, tighter proof. These include special investigative bodies set up to bypass local prosecutors or investigators who may appear incompetent or corrupt; broad statutes for witness immunity; adequate protection of witnesses, perhaps through the creation of federally administered residential facilities; and more workable rules for proving perjury. Clarification of the nature and permissible limits of electronic surveillance—wiretapping and bugging—is also urged.

Still another approach is to legalize gambling, prostitution, narcotics—all the currently illegal activities which provide syndicated crime with its initial income. If individuals could obtain such commodities legally, so the reasoning goes, sources of supply would multiply, the price would drop, "protection" would no longer be needed, and the syndicate would lose its monopoly and its profits. In regard to gambling, this is being tried: lotteries and offtrack betting corporations have been established in a few states. Whether they have in fact had a substantial effect on the syndicates is not yet clear.

Political corruption has been made more risky by the requirement that candidates disclose the sources of their campaign funds. However, syndicate figures commonly use superficially legitimate channels to funnel money to candidates they support, and it remains to be seen if politics on at least the federal level can be made corruption-free.

Finally, it has been suggested that people in business could do more themselves to prevent syndicates from infiltrating legitimate businesses. In particular, they could be more alert to the signs of syndicated crime—such as merchandise offered at lower-than-wholesale prices—and then be more ready to report it, either to the police or to special business committees which would be set up for that purpose.[111]

110 *Challenge of Crime,* pp. 200–209.
111 Grutzner, pp. 45–58.

PROSPECTS

Many have already suggested that the problems of our criminal justice system have reached crisis proportions. A House subcommittee stated that the federal government's crime program set up under the Omnibus Crime Control Safe Streets Act of 1968 was characterized by "inefficiency, waste, maladministration, and in some cases, corruption." This program, under which nearly $1.5 billion had been sent to the states to improve law enforcement, was described by the subcommittee as having had "no visible impact on the incidence of crime in the United States." [112]

Nonetheless, efforts are being made. There have been attempts to increase minority representation on police forces, to train police in techniques for handling some of the newer law-enforcement problems with a minimum of violence or coercion, and generally to improve relationships between the police and the communities they serve.

The recent outbreak of prison disturbances across the nation points to some of the problems that exist within our corrections agencies. Some criminologists have urged a de-emphasis of the role of prisons and a shift to use of halfway houses, graduated release and furlough programs, and expanded educational and vocational opportunity; yet, so far, very little has changed. The National Council on Crime and Delinquency has found that 80 percent of correctional expenditures go toward the operation of institutions, and only 20 percent to such community-based services as juvenile aftercare, parole, and probation.[113] Considering that work-release, as described earlier, seems to be among the most effective approaches to rehabilitation of the adult criminal, it is unfortunate that more funds are not allocated to such programs. The recent movement among prisoners themselves to organize and demand some recognition of their human and constitutional rights, even behind bars, together with public pressure, could produce some progress in this regard; but as yet the prospect remains fairly bleak.

Because of the concern about crime many criminologists, legislators, and officials at all levels of government are also advocating harsher and more specific penalties for every kind of crime. In addition, they are studying criminal justice reforms that will increase the chances of offenders getting caught. Congress passed a new law in 1975 to reduce recidivism by requiring speedy trials and by strengthening the supervision of those out on bail. Although $3 billion has been spent since 1967 on the "war on crime," more than half of it has gone to police forces for innovations and modernizing; authorities generally agree that much more money will have to be spent on prisons and courts. Congress is considering a law to create fifty-one more federal judgeships, since the case loads have doubled in the last ten years while the number of judgeships has increased only 25 percent. This in turn will necessitate more prosecutors, public defenders, clerks, and courtrooms.[114]

Crowded court calendars, backlogs of cases, and long delays in trials are responsible for the fact that although the number of serious crimes—

---

[112] "Crime program held inefficient." *New York Times,* April 11, 1972.

[113] *Goals and Recommendations.* National Council on Crime and Delinquency, 44 E. 23rd St., New York, N.Y. 10010.

[114] "The crime wave," pp. 19–20.

according to official statistics, at least—has quadrupled since 1960, only recently has there been an increase in the number of offenders who are jailed. Many repeat offenders do not go to jail, and it is clear that the current forms of rehabilitation have not decreased the crime rate, nor have they made released inmates any less committed to crime as a way of life. Wilson cites studies which estimate that the present rate of serious crime could be reduced by one-third if all serious offenders were jailed for a minimum of three years.[115] Though this point of view emphasizes punishment at the expense of remedying conditions that breed crime, it has gained many adherents. Prisons have begun to emphasize punishment instead of rehabilitation; and the head of the Federal Bureau of Prisons announced recently that future prison policies would concentrate on confining and isolating criminals as a way of reducing the crime rate. Authorities also see the obvious need to eliminate the disparity in sentences and make them the same for similar crimes, while also making them "more punitive, surer, more swiftly imposed, and more definite in length." [116] This will result in higher prison populations, necessitating the building of new prisons. Also, rehabilitation programs may be offered on a strictly voluntary basis so that they have no bearing on when a prisoner is released. Thus parole boards, which base their decision to parole prisoners on the somewhat arbitrary standard of how well they have rehabilitated, may find their functions reduced or eliminated.

A number of reforms are also being proposed for the juvenile justice system. In order to decriminalize status offenses, a national commission has recommended that sentences for juvenile offenders be based solely on the seriousness of the crime, and that juvenile court proceedings be opened to the public in order to make judges more accountable and to end disparity in juvenile sentences. Serious and violent juvenile cases would first be heard in juvenile courts and then tried in adult courts, which could then sentence murderers to longer prison terms than most of them currently receive.[117] The great harm done by mixing, in the same institution, status offenders with delinquents who commit serious crimes is beginning to be realized. For example, the President's Commission on Law Enforcement and the Administration of Justice proposed a radical plan similar to those adopted in some European countries: status offenders would be taken out of the juvenile justice system entirely and instead handled either by a Youth Services Bureau that would operate in neighborhoods or by the family and child welfare system.[118] The federal government has since undertaken some large-scale measures to counteract the juvenile problem. Congress allocated $384 million in 1974 under the Juvenile Delinquency Prevention Act, which established an Office of Juvenile Justice and Delinquency Prevention, created a National Advisory Committee on Juvenile Problems, and dispensed federal grants for youth programs. The act also requires that the federal Law Enforcement Assistance Administration develop programs to keep juvenile status offenders out of prison.

[115] "Lock 'em up," p. 69.

[116] "Big change in prisons: Punish—not reform." *U.S. News and World Report,* August 25, 1975, pp. 21–22.

[117] Marcia Chambers, "Radical changes urged in dealing with youth crime." *New York Times,* November 30, 1975, p. 58.

[118] Lerman, "Delinquents without crime," pp. 258–259.

It is clear that as long as the public remains indifferent to occupational crime, and does not quite believe in the reality or menace of organized crime, it will remain difficult to combat these crimes effectively. Another important point is that while both organized and occupational crime affect everyone, the poor in particular bear the brunt. Consumer frauds have a vicious impact on the poor, and syndicated crime milks the ghettos. In both cases the criminals are relatively strong and influential, while the victims are the weak—the reverse of the situation for other crimes, where the criminals often lack influence as compared to their victims. This suggests why the latter crimes have received the greatest attention from law-enforcement agencies. Occupational criminals are often leading citizens, with influence on what laws are passed and how they are enforced. Organized crime buys its influence with payoffs and force. Consumer advocates are aware of the fundamental power relationship when they insist that consumers must be organized, with their own lobbyists and spokespeople.

In light of the Watergate scandals and the exposure of widespread corporate bribery practices in recent years, Congress is now considering some of the following proposals: bringing misdemeanor charges against government and business officials who in failing to properly supervise their organizations allow criminal practices to go on; granting protection from any retaliation to informers who bring cases of illegal activities to the attention of authorities; suspending from interstate trade any organization that repeatedly fails to modify its illegal practices; making prison terms a certainty for offenses such as price-fixing and tax evasion; and fining corporations up to $500,000 for antitrust violations.[119] It remains to be seen how many of these proposals—if any—will be instituted.

In conclusion, we should remember that crime and delinquency are complex social problems. Situations of such complexity are not amenable to simple or total solutions. Certainly alleviation of the conditions of poverty, deprivation, hopelessness, and anomie would do much to reduce crime, but it is unlikely that conventional and occupational crime will be eliminated completely. One can only hope that further research and experimentation will lead to the development of successful approaches to the growing problems of crime and delinquency.

SUMMARY

The official crime statistics in the United States, which is based only on crimes known to the police, reveals only part of the true incidence of illegal activity, since much crime, particularly "white-collar" crime, goes unreported. Nevertheless, there has been a dramatic increase in the crime rate and the public has reacted with increased demands for stricter law enforcement.

Although crime in the legal sense is simply any act for which the state can apply sanctions, it can also be seen as the product of conflicting class interests and police ideology. People without influence are often put at a great disadvantage in their confrontations with the law.

Nine types of crime and criminals have been identified according to how large a role crime plays in an individual's life and the degree to which individuals define themselves as criminals. *Violent personal crime* includes such acts as robbery in which physical injury is inflicted or implied. These acts are often unpremeditated and, except in the case of murder and assault, generally

[119] "Losing battle." *U.S. News and World Report,* p. 40.

occur between strangers. *Occasional property crime* includes such acts as vandalism and shoplifting. Offenders can easily justify their actions and generally do not regard themselves as criminals. *Occupational (white-collar) crime* takes in a wide range of activities such as embezzlement, fraud, and business-government crime. It is committed by people who accept it as normal and who think of themselves as respectable citizens. Most such crime is never detected. *Political crime* includes such acts as treason and civil disobedience, which are perceived as threats to the state. Violators see themselves as acting idealistically. *Public order crimes* include such activities as drunkenness and prostitution. These are usually "victimless crimes"; offenders rarely see themselves as criminals, though they may be driven into a criminal role by society's attitude toward them. *Conventional crime* includes acts such as theft that are often committed by young adults. Offenders generally see crime as a way of life, though many give up their criminal careers as they grow older. *Organized crime* controls a large network of gambling operations, loan-sharking, and narcotics rings: it exists largely because of the public demand for the services it provides and because of corruption. *Professional crime* involves illegal acts committed by those with highly developed criminal careers. Offenders are rarely caught and are likely to continue their careers to a relatively late age. *Juvenile delinquency* is crime committed by young offenders. Though juveniles commit a large percentage of violent crimes, the bulk of juvenile crimes are status offenses that would not be illegal if they were committed by adults.

There are many explanations for the present high crime rates, such as the personal freedom, rapid technological change, and cultural heterogeneity within our society. Some observers emphasize demographic and economic factors such as the large number of crime-prone and disadvantaged youth. Still others point to family and community disorganization, physical abuse of children, and media violence to account for the high level of violent crime. Both occupational and organized crime flourish because of our cultural beliefs, such as individualism, laissez-faire government policies, and materialism.

The four major sociological explanations of crime are: (1) the *differential association theory*, which views criminal behavior as the result of a learning process and the internalization of criminal values; (2) the *anomie theory*, in which society holds out the goal of material success to all its members, but denies access and approved means of reaching it to large groups; (3) the *delinquent subcultures theory*, which suggests that those unable to compete in the larger society form their own groups that provide reachable goals and norms; and (4) the *lower-class culture theory*, which views specific lower-class values and codes of behavior as responsible for delinquency and crime.

Society's efforts to control crime can also be classified into four areas: *retribution-deterrence*, which has been the prevailing philosophy in handling criminals, is based on the principles of retribution and of providing an object lesson to others who may be tempted to commit similar crimes; *rehabilitation*, under which criminals are viewed as either victims of society or as sick people who must be led to conform to society's values or cured of their sickness; *preventive measures*, which are designed to either improve the general social environment of predelinquent children or to focus on specific crime-producing conditions; and *criminal and juvenile justice reforms* that would reduce sentencing disparities, decriminalize certain victimless crimes and juvenile status offenses, increase penalties for occupational crime, redouble efforts to combat organized crime, and make our law-enforcement system more efficient.

Albini, Joseph L. *The American Mafia: Genesis of a Legend*. Englewood Cliffs, N.J.: Prentice-Hall, 1971.

The Challenge of Crime in a Free Society: A Report by the President's Commission on Law Enforcement and the Administration of Justice. Washington, D.C.: U.S. Government Printing Office, 1967.

Chambliss, William. *Criminal Law in Action*. Santa Barbara, Calif.: Hamilton, 1975.

Clark, Ramsey. *Crime in America*. New York: Simon & Schuster, 1970.

Clinard, Marshall B., and Quinney, Richard. *Criminal Behavior System: A Typology*. New York: Holt, Rinehart and Winston, 1967.

Cloward, Richard A., and Ohlin, Lloyd E. *Delinquency and Opportunity: A Theory of Delinquent Gangs*. New York: Free Press, 1967.

Cohen, Albert. *Delinquent Boys*. New York: Free Press, 1971.

Cressey, Donald R. *Theft of the Nation: The Structure of Organized Crime in America*. New York: Harper & Row, 1969.

———. *Other People's Money: A Study in the Social Psychology of Embezzlement*. Reprint of 1953 ed. Montclair, N.J.: Patterson Smith, 1973.

Empey, LaMar T., and Lubeck, Stephen G. *Explaining Delinquency*. Lexington, Mass.: Heath Lexington Books, 1971.

Gardiner, John A. *The Politics of Corruption: Organized Crime in an American City*. New York: Russell Sage Foundation, 1970.

Gaylin, Willard. *Partial Justice*. New York: Knopf, 1974.

Gibbens, T. C. N., and Ahrenfeldt, R. *Cultural Factors in Delinquency*. Philadelphia: Lippincott, 1966.

Hartjen, Clayton A. *Crime and Criminalization*. New York: Praeger, 1974.

Hunt, Morton. *The Mugging*. New York: Atheneum, 1972.

King, Rufus. *Gambling and Organized Crime*. Washington, D.C.: Public Affairs Press, 1969.

Maas, Peter. *The Valachi Papers*. New York: Putnam, 1968.

Matza, David. *Delinquency and Drift*. New York: Wiley, 1964.

Newfield, Jack. *Cruel and Unusual Justice*. New York: Holt, Rinehart and Winston, 1974.

Quinney, Richard. *The Social Reality of Crime*. Boston: Little, Brown, 1970.

Reckless, Walter C. *The Crime Problem*. 5th ed. Englewood Cliffs, N.J.: Prentice-Hall, 1973.

Reiss, Albert J., Jr. *The Police and the Public*. 2nd ed. New Haven, Conn.: Yale University Press, 1973.

Safa, Helen Icken, and Levitas, Gloria. *Social Problems in Corporate America*. New York: Harper & Row, 1975.

Schur, Edwin M. *Radical Nonintervention: Rethinking the Delinquency Problem*. Englewood Cliffs, N.J.: Prentice-Hall, 1973.

Sutherland, Edwin H. *White Collar Crime*. New York: Holt, Rinehart and Winston, 1961.

Talese, Gay. *Honor Thy Father*. New York: World, 1972.

Tyler, Gus, ed. *Organized Crime in America: A Book of Readings*. Ann Arbor: University of Michigan Press, 1962.

5

VIOLENCE

- There are as many homicides every year in Philadelphia (population 2 million) as in all of Great Britain (population 54 million).
- Estimates of the number of privately owned firearms in the United States range from 90 million to 200 million—almost one firearm for every man, woman, and child in the country.
- By the age of 15 the average child will have witnessed over 13,000 killings on television.
- The cost of military activities to the United States from 1789 to the present has been estimated at well over $2 trillion—56 percent of all federal money spent since 1789.
- Between 1820 and 1945, 59 million human beings were killed in wars, murders, quarrels, and skirmishes.
- About 21,000 Americans (one every 26 minutes) are murdered each year, and over 55,000 women (one every 10 minutes) are raped.

In the view of many Americans, violence is a critical contemporary social problem. We have already noted, in the chapter on crime and criminals, that crime ranks high among the problems considered particularly important at the present time. Various surveys have indicated that the fear of a violent encounter—of being mugged, raped, or murdered—deters many citizens from leaving their homes after dark. Kidnappings, terrorist bombings, political assassinations, and the threat of nuclear annihilation all serve to bring home to us how pervasive violence is in our culture. The stability of our institutions and, indeed, the fate of the nation itself may depend upon present and future efforts to reduce the level and types of violence in this nation and in the world.

Much of the violence in human history has not, until recently, been recognized as such. This is particularly true in violence associated with the rise or expansion of a political party or social movement; for, since violence is generally defined as wrong, most groups will reflexively seek a way to forget, justify, or explain away their use of it in the past. As Graham and Gurr note, "Probably all nations are given to a kind of historical amnesia or selective recollection that masks unpleasant traumas of the past." [1] In this respect, America is probably no worse, and no better, than most nations. Thus, while most extralegal violence,

---

[1] Hugh Davis Graham and Ted Robert Gurr, eds., *The History of Violence in America: A Report to the National Commission on the Causes and Prevention of Violence.* New York: Bantam, 1969, p. 792.

such as murder, rape, or gangland activities, has elicited general public condemnation, other forms of violence, often linked with the historical development of the nation, have been accepted or even praised. In this category would be found the violence involved in most of the wars in which the nation has been engaged, whether for expansion or for self-defense. Likewise, in troubled times and on the frontiers, vigilante activities have often been approved by the local community as the only available means of maintaining order. In general, violence by constituted authority, or on behalf of the state, is less likely to be condemned by the majority of persons than violence by private citizens or in defiance of authority. Probably the two most famous recent examples of this were the public reaction to the confrontation between the Ohio National Guard and student demonstrators and bystanders at Kent State University in May 1970 and the Attica uprising in upstate New York in September 1971. Although the guardsmen at Kent State fired indiscriminately, and in response to minimal provocation, and although 4 students were killed and 10 wounded in this episode, the general public response was in favor of the action of the Guard and the public authorities. Similarly, although the quelling of the Attica rebellion resulted in the death of 11 guard hostages and 32 convicts—almost all shot by state police when they stormed the prison—no police officer has ever been indicted.

It is only in recent years, in the wake of a growing number of political assassinations, civil disorders, violent protests and demonstrations, and rising crime statistics, that a greater effort has been made to study the causes and effects of violence in American society. Such study was long overdue, for despite the relative stability of its institutions, the United States has evidenced a greater degree of violent behavior than other nations of comparable development. For example, in one study of civil strife in 114 nations and colonies, the United States ranked first among 17 Western democracies and twenty-fourth in the overall sample in the magnitude of strife.[2] And this record does not include recent statistics of individual crimes, which indicate that violent crimes in our society have gone up more than 200 percent since 1960. According to official statistics, which grossly underreport crime, over 21,000 Americans are murdered, over 55,000 raped, close to 500,000 seriously assaulted, and close to 500,000 robbed annually. Whereas in the past such crimes occurred almost exclusively in cities, today crime rates are increasing most rapidly in the suburbs.[3] Few, if any, areas in the nation remain unaffected by the problem of violence.

The significance of the problem of violence and the need to find means to control and prevent it are apparent. Before we can control violence, however, we must better understand its nature and origins. Therefore, we shall look briefly at the historical background of violence in America, and then survey some of the principal definitions and proposed explanations of violent behavior, before considering possible solutions to it as a social problem.

[2] T. R. Gurr, "A comparative study of civil strife." In Graham and Gurr, pp. 572–632.
[3] Federal Bureau of Investigation (FBI), *Uniform Crime Reports.* Washington, D.C.: U.S. Department of Justice, November 19, 1975, p. 10.

The "myth of peaceful progress" [4] in American history, appealing though it may be to our more idealistic inclinations, cannot survive the light of careful scrutiny. The dark shadow of violence has colored many of the highly celebrated events and movements in American history. Howard Zinn [5] has written that the failure to recognize the role of violence in American social progress and to acknowledge how much our behavior toward other nationalities and races has been characterized by overt violence has resulted in a "double standard" in the American attitude toward violence:

There is, on the one hand, a national tendency to absolutize the value of social change at the expense of human life when the violence required for this change is directed at other nations or other races; and on the other hand a tendency to absolutize the value of peace at the expense of social change *within* the national framework.

The United States was born in a violent struggle to end British rule. Independence came only after seven years of warfare, with 25,000 soldiers of the Continental Army dying in the process. The revolutionary struggle thus embedded in our national ideology the belief that violence is permissible in the service of a good cause. As Richard Maxwell Brown writes, "The meanest and most squalid sort of violence was from the very beginning to the very last put to the service of Revolutionary ideals and objectives." [6]

Violence played an important role in the development of the American nation. Both before and after the Revolution, it was freely used against the Indians, who stood in the way of the white settlers' expansion across the continent. Often, Indian lives seem to have been valued little more than those of beasts; on occasion, governments offered bounties for Indian scalps. In Zinn's words, the expulsion and extermination of the Indians represent "the shadowed underside of the most cherished events in American history." [7] Furthermore, the latter part of the nineteenth century was pervaded by the violence of the Civil War and the events leading up to and stemming from it, making this one of the most violent eras in the nation's history. Again, as in the Revolution, violence was sanctified in the name of a moral cause. The development of the frontier was punctuated by lawlessness and bloodshed, and the agrarian and labor movements both had many violent episodes. Thus, throughout our history, "the patriot, the humanitarian, the nationalist, the pioneer, the landholder, the farmer, and the laborer (and the capitalist) have used violence as the means to a higher end." [8]

The effect of this violent history and the ambivalent American attitude toward it must be taken into account when we are considering present-day

[4] Jerome H. Skolnick, *The Politics of Protest*. New York: Simon & Schuster, 1969, p. 9.
[5] Howard Zinn, "Violence and social change in American history." In Thomas Rose, ed., *Violence in America*. New York: Random House, 1969.
[6] Richard Maxwell Brown, "Historical patterns of violence in Amercia." In Graham and Gurr, p. 63.
[7] Zinn, p. 71.
[8] Brown, pp. 64, 75.

Over 200 Sioux men, women, and children were senselessly attacked and massacred at Wounded Knee, South Dakota in 1890. More than 100 Indians were buried in the mass grave shown here.

Library of Congress

manifestations of violence. We need to recognize the prominent role which violence has played in the development of the nation in order to understand its contemporary manifestations.

THE CONCEPTS OF VIOLENCE

The word "violence" has a generally negative connotation. It has been defined as "behavior designed to inflict physical injury to people or damage to property." [9] It may be viewed as legitimate or illegitimate, depending on who uses it, the purpose for which it is used, and the framework of the viewer. Some limited uses of violence, particularly in athletics, are so well integrated into the social structure that they are not usually perceived as violent, but are selectively perceived as healthy and even character-building activities.

Also not usually thought of as violence is what Galtung calls "structural violence"—that is, "the dominance of one group over the other,

[9] Graham and Gurr, p. xxx.

with subsequent exploitative practices." [10] In such a situation, the threat of or potential for violence is usually sufficient to keep the dominated group "in its place," but the effect on social relationships and development is very much the same as that of overt violence. We shall not discuss this aspect of violence at length, but it should be noted that the recognition, by a dominated group, of the structural violence which has been used against it may be a significant factor in the genesis of overt group violence such as civil disorders and rebellion.

Jerome Skolnick [11] has pointed out that violence "is an ambiguous term whose meaning is established through political processes." What a society classifies as violent is apt to depend in considerable part on "who provides the definition and who has superior resources for disseminating and enforcing his definitions." War provides a classic example of this. In a war, the acts of one's own side are generally defended as honorable, while the other side is described as the aggressor and its violent acts are viewed as atrocities. Similarly, within a single nation, accusations of violent behavior are exchanged between the political authorities and their relatively powerless adversaries:

Within a given society, political regimes often exaggerate the violence of those challenging established institutions. The term "violence" is frequently employed to discredit forms of behavior considered improper, reprehensible, or threatening by specific groups which, in turn, may mask their own violent response with the rhetoric of order or progress.

A number of writers have attempted to justify the use of violence by a colonized people against the colonial authorities, or by the "have-nots" against the "haves." Anticolonial and revolutionary art are characterized by the impassioned defense of violence when the violence is used by those rebelling against established institutions. Frantz Fanon, the African psychiatrist whose experiences in the Algerian war made him a revolutionary, speaks of violence as a "cleansing force" [12] which frees the spirit of the native and restores his or her self-esteem; it unifies the people and teaches them to assert themselves against any future attempt at tyranny, even by their own leaders. Herbert Marcuse writes of the revolutionary potential of those who have been divorced from the participatory processes of advanced industrialized nations, "the substratum of the outcasts and outsiders, the exploited and persecuted of other races and other colors, the unemployed and the unemployable." [13]

There are, then, many dimensions and facets to be considered in discussing the concept of violence. A useful distinction which could be made here is that between violence exercised on behalf of or under the protection of the state, or institutional violence, and the non-institutional violence engaged in by those acting in opposition to established authority. While violence in both these categories may be either constructive or

[10] Johan Galtung, "Peace thinking." In Albert Lepawsky, Edward H. Buehrig, and Harold D. Lasswell, eds., *The Search for World Order*. Englewood Cliffs, N.J.: Prentice-Hall (ACC), 1971, p. 124.
[11] Skolnick, p. 4.
[12] Frantz Fanon, *The Wretched of the Earth*. New York: Grove Press, 1968, p. 94.
[13] Herbert Marcuse, *One-Dimensional Man*. Boston: Beacon Press, 1964, p. 256.

destructive, institutional violence is usually presumed to be legitimate until proven otherwise, while those engaging in non-institutional violence are subject to reprimand and punishment. Thus, for example, while wars or violent police actions are usually considered legitimate because they are conducted under the aegis of the state, violent protests and demonstrations, revolutionary activity, civil disorders, and violent criminal activity do not enjoy similar official sanction. Although this situation is in part a matter of the difference in power between the "ins" and the "outs," it is based also on the traditional idea that the state may, and even must, do some things which an individual citizen may not do, in order to fulfill its responsibility for protecting the general welfare. It is when the state is seen as using its privilege of violence for ends contrary to the general welfare that the right of non-institutional violence—sabotage, terrorism, rebellion, revolution— is likely to be asserted.

Violence has obvious limitations as an instrument of social progress, the most evident being that its exercise entails the physical injury of other people. And although some advocates of revolution seem to develop almost a mystique of violence—for example, Jean-Paul Sartre's "violence, like Achilles' lance, can heal the wounds that it has inflicted" [14]— one of the principal problems facing leaders of violent groups, be they revolutionaries or military generals, is to stop the process of violence once it has achieved its desired purposes. For when people have used violence to gain some common end, they are apt to continue to use violence to gain more particular ends, or even, sometimes, almost as an end in itself. Since war began, soldiers have been looting conquered towns; and more than one united revolution has ended in brutal factional strife.

EXPLANATIONS FOR VIOLENCE

Why do people behave violently? Is it simply the way they are made? Sometimes it almost seems so.

THE BIOLOGICAL VIEWPOINT

"No person living today can question the statement that man, *Homo sapiens,* self-proclaimed to represent the pinnacle of evolution, is the most dangerous living species." [15] According to Boelkins and Heiser, in the period between 1820 and 1945, humans killed 59 million of their kind in wars, murders, quarrels, and skirmishes. This amounts to a person killing a fellow human being every 68 seconds for 126 years. There is no indication that this rate has declined in recent years. Therefore, since violence is such a common occurrence among people, some scientists have argued that humanity's aggressive tendencies have an inherent or instinctual basis.

According to this view, it is only through the development of social organization that people's violent inclinations can be kept under control.

[14] Jean-Paul Sartre, Preface to Fanon, p. 30.
[15] R. Charles Boelkins and John F. Heiser, "Biological bases of aggression." In David N. Daniels, Marshall Gilula, and Frank Ochberg, eds., *Violence and the Struggle for Existence.* Boston: Little, Brown, 1970, p. 15.

Freud's death wish, Lorenz's conception of aggression as a survival-enhancing instinct,[16] and Ardrey's territorial imperative are all based on a form of this argument:

Man is a predator whose natural instinct is to kill with a weapon. The sudden addition of the enlarged brain to the equipment of an armed, already successful, predatory animal created not only the human being but also the human predicament.[17]

Lord of the Flies, William Golding's disturbing novel of degeneration and violence among boys on a desert island, is one of many fictional presentations of the same idea.

Others say that aggression is natural, but that violence is not. Boelkins and Heiser argue that "aggression is a basic behavioral response that has multiple determinants whose precise effects vary with the sex, the age, and the species of the organism." Aggressive behavior on the part of people and animals serves an adaptive purpose, while violence is "a short-term coping mechanism that enables adjustment but which in the long run will prove maladaptive to both the individual and the species."[18] Since, in the nature of things, there can be no culture-free environment in which to test for the presence or absence of a human instinct of violence, we will probably never know the answer for certain. So far, at least, such evidence as we have does not seem to support the hypothesis of instinctive violent or destructive urges.

Other have argued that violence toward others and toward society is a form of aggression resulting from individual frustration. An unfulfilled need produces the frustration, and the frustration is vented in aggression. The strength of the impulses, needs, or wishes obstructed determines the amount of frustration, and the degree of aggression is based upon the amount of frustration. Prejudice, lack of affection, and poverty are suggested as some of the common causes of frustration.[19] This frustration-aggression hypothesis has been described as "the easiest and by far the most popular explanation of social violence—whether political turmoil, the hot summers of riot and disorder, or robberies and juvenile delinquency."[20] The main problems with it are that it fails to explain why frustration leads to aggression in some instances and not in others, and that it can be defined so broadly as to include just about any conceivable situation.

Related to the frustration-aggression model is the control theory, according to which the ability of an individual to restrain or control impulsive behavior correlates with the existence of close relationships between the individual and significant other persons. In this view, people whose relationships with others are inadequate or unsatisfactory may resort to

**FRUSTRATION-
AGGRESSION AND
CONTROL THEORIES**

[16] Konrad Lorenz, *On Aggression.* New York: Bantam, 1967, p. 235.

[17] Robert Ardrey, *The Territorial Imperative.* New York: Atheneum, 1967, p. 332.

[18] Boelkins and Heiser, p. 48.

[19] See, for example, John Dollard *et al., Frustration and Aggression.* New Haven: Yale University Press, 1939.

[20] Leonard Berkowitz, "The study of urban violence." In James C. Davies, ed., *When Men Revolt and Why.* New York: Free Press, 1971, p. 182.

violence when their attempts to relate to others in their fashion are frustrated. One study, for example, shows a lack of close relationships in a substantial proportion of teenage boys from different backgrounds who had a history of physically aggressive behavior.[21] The fact that violence is significantly more prevalent among those who are ex-convicts, alcoholics, and others who are in various ways out of the mainstream of society and estranged from family and friends, is also considered to be evidence in favor of the control thesis. Murderers, in this view, are likely to be "egocentric, impulsive, rebellious, or sadistic persons who cannot control their emotions."[22]

Of course, not all persons who fit this description become murderers, nor do all murderers fit this description. One study suggested that there were actually two discernible personality types prevalent among murderers. One type was "undercontrolled"—persons who were unable to restrain aggressive impulses, who had "never developed internal taboos against lashing out when provoked, and had few inhibitions about satisfying their acquisitive or sexual desires aggressively." The second type was the exact opposite—overcontrolled individuals who inhibited their aggressive impulses almost completely and for whom "even socially acceptable outlets for aggression, such as swearing or pounding on a table, were off-limits." Such individuals are said to hold back their anger or hostility to the breaking point, until they suddenly and unpredictably lash out in violence.[23]

It is difficult to demonstrate how valid the control thesis is, since most murders and many other violent crimes are spontaneous and unplanned, and their causes are not always clear. The lack of close relationships could simply be one factor among many that lead individuals to violent behavior. However, the control thesis does suggest one clue to why violent crimes are increasing. In the past, there were a variety of social factors—such as generally accepted moral standards, church membership, a highly favorable view of family life, and more intimate, smaller communities—that aided in the development of controlled personalities. The breakdown of traditional authorities may have led more people to feel isolated and thus made them more likely to see violence as an acceptable form of behavior.

SUBCULTURE OF VIOLENCE

It is also suggested—and this is the position of many sociologists—that violence is a learned behavior, acquired through the process of socialization. According to this view, since members of a society learn the norms of that society and behave in ways which the society defines as socially desirable, aggressive or violent actions are most likely to occur in a culture or subculture in which violence is accepted or encouraged. Members of such a subculture conform to group norms and peer pressure. This learned violent behavior can then be used in the pursuit of specific goals —"aggression by children and adolescents to secure attention, by adults to express dominance strivings, by groups in competition for scarce

[21] Travis Hirschi, *Causes of Delinquency*. Berkeley: University of California Press, 1969.
[22] Donald T. Lunde, "Our murder boom." *Psychology Today,* July 1975, p. 39.
[23] Study by Ed Magargee. In Lunde, p. 39.

values, by military personnel in the service of national policy." [24] The learning approach assumes that there will be more violence if violent behavior is presented as being a model to be emulated than if the society vigorously and uniformly deplores violent conduct.

Originally devised as an explanation of juvenile gang behavior, subcultural theory in recent years has also been seen as the key to violence in general. In this model, members of violent subgroups have a low provocation threshold, perceiving threats to their integrity in situations that would not be so perceived by members of the dominant society. Normative behavior in such groups requires spontaneous combative response to provocation.[25] There are even those who claim that all American males share to some extent in a subculture of violence. The relatively low rate of commission of violent acts by women is offered in evidence. Bianchi, for example, sees professional football as a metaphor for America's "physical brutality, profit-maximizing commercialism, . . . authoritarian-military mentality and sexism." He notes that school and family cohere in forming "male children into competitors and achievers." [26]

If violence is a consequence of social learning, frustration is not a necessary prerequisite for its occurrence. Rather, violent habits are acquired through imitation, or as a result of the rewarding of destructive behavior. It has been shown, for instance, that parents who are physically aggressive and punitive tend to have physically aggressive offspring. Other laboratory studies have indicated that children who observe adults displaying physical aggression will in their later play activities be more aggressive

[24] Ted Robert Gurr, *Why Men Rebel.* Princeton, N.J.: Princeton University Press, 1970, p. 32.

[25] Marvin E. Wolfgang and Franco Ferracuti, *The Subculture of Violence.* London: Tavistock, 1967.

[26] Eugene C. Bianchi, "The superbowl culture of male violence." *Christian Century,* September 18, 1974, pp. 842–845.

Violence in a sport like hockey is accepted and even encouraged as an important part of the game. Would less violence occur in sports—and in society as a whole—if violent behavior were not rewarded but deplored?
Roberto Borea

than children not exposed in this manner. On the basis of this and other research, Ilfeld concludes that

physical punishment by parents does not inhibit violence and most likely encourages it. It both frustrates the child and gives him a model to imitate and learn from. The learning of violence through modeling applies to more than just parental behavior. It is also relevant to examples set by the mass media, one's peers or other reference groups, and local and national leaders.[27]

The theory of the subculture of violence seemed to support the stereotype that most violent crimes were committed by young male members of nonwhite minorities who are outside the dominant culture. However, recent studies point up some fallacies. For example, one study found that men of various socioeconomic levels held essentially the same values, with no significant adherence to violence-prone values among any class or group. Another study comparing prisoners convicted of violent and nonviolent crimes also found no significant differences in the values held by individuals of both groups. And an analysis of data collected for the President's Commission on the Causes and Prevention of Violence in 1968 found a low rate of approval of interpersonal violence among all social and class subgroups. On the basis of these and other studies, Erlanger concludes that

although the subculture of violence thesis has received a certain measure of acceptance in the field, a wide variety of evidence suggests that it is questionable. . . . More of available evidence is inconsistent with the thesis than consistent with it.[28]

MEDIA INFLUENCE

One of the most important questions in the debate over the learning explanation is the role of the mass media in communicating or fostering violent attitudes. The pervasiveness of violence in the media is quite disturbing. A *Christian Science Monitor* survey of television programming conducted six weeks after the assassination of Robert Kennedy found 84 killings in 85.5 hours of prime time evening and Saturday morning programming. The bloodiest evening hours were between 7:30 and 9:00, when the networks estimated that 26.7 million children between the ages of 2 and 17 were watching television.[29] Other studies have revealed similar conditions. According to one estimate, an average American child will view over 13,000 television killings by the age of 15. So-called action-adventure programs in prime time have increased threefold in the last twenty years. Such shows are so prevalent because they are less expensive to produce and therefore more profitable, and because violence is an effective plot device for solving complications and gaining viewer attention.[30] It has also been shown that two-thirds of leading characters are

[27] Fredric Ilfeld, "Environmental theories of violence." In Daniels, Gilula, and Ochberg, p. 81.
[28] Howard S. Erlanger, "The empirical status of the subculture of violence thesis." *Social Problems* 22 (December 1974):282–283.
[29] Alberta E. Siegel, "Violence in the mass media." In Daniels, Gilula, and Ochberg, p. 226.
[30] "Drop that gun, Captain Video." *Newsweek,* March 10, 1975, pp. 81–82.

involved in violence; and that there is twice as much violence in entertainment programs in the United States than in the United Kingdom.[31]

Since television became ubiquitous about a quarter-century ago, its impact on young viewers has been the subject of a substantial body of research. Bogart, among others, believes that the "overwhelming weight of evidence from this research supports the thesis that exposure to filmed or televised violence tends to lead young children to a state of heightened excitability and to an increase in subsequent displays of aggression." [32] The Task Force on Mass Media and Violence of the National Commission on the Causes and Prevention of Violence expressed its concern that "exposure to mass media portrayals of violence over a long period of time socializes audiences into the norms, attitudes, and values for violence contained in those portrayals." [33] The task force concluded that audiences which have learned violent behavior from the mass media are likely to perform violent acts in situations where they expect to be rewarded for such behavior, where they do not observe disapproval of the portrayed violence from a fellow viewer, or where they encounter a situation similar to that portrayed.

Another study suggests that the effects of television are more subtle. Hartnagel and his associates [34] found that

TV violence influences behavior in an indirect fashion, through its impact on learned values and attitudes or through a more general impression that is communicated about the nature of social reality. Values and attitudes or perceptions of the world may be substantially affected by television programming which may, in turn, influence behavior.

This view suggests that young viewers may become calloused by overexposure to such programming and that, while they may not become violent themselves, they tolerate violence in others more readily. In Hartnagel's words,

Violent television content may also generate the attitude that violent means for resolving disputes are acceptable, or at least effective; and this attitude may, under appropriate conditions, find expression in the actual use of violent behavior. Exposure to TV violence may also create the impression that the world is a violent place and that the individual should be prepared to confront violence under certain circumstances. In these various ways, then, exposure to TV violence may have important indirect effects upon actual employment of violent behavior.

The influence of mass media, particularly television, in the reporting

---

[31] Leo Bogart, "Warning: The Surgeon General has determined that TV violence is moderately dangerous to your child's mental health." *Public Opinion Quarterly,* Winter 1972–1973, pp. 491–521.

[32] Bogart, p. 489.

[33] *Mass Media and Violence: A Report to the National Commission on the Causes and Prevention of Violence.* Washington, D.C.: U.S. Government Printing Office, 1969, p. 376.

[34] Timothy F. Hartnagel, James J. Teevan, Jr., and Jennie M. McIntyre, "Television violence and violent behavior." *Social Forces,* vol. 54, no. 2 (December 1975): 341–351.

of protests, demonstrations, civil disorders, and other forms of potentially violent activity is another important issue. There are two questions here: Do the media distort the facts by stressing the violent aspects of news events; and does the presence of media reporters at such events tend to increase the possibility that violence will occur? Both charges have been made, and both appear likely in some instances. But distortion and provocation are difficult qualities to measure, and the matter is far from settled. Lang and Lang suggest that although the general practices of the media, "both contribute to the appearance of increased frequency and accelerate the cycle of protest," the presence of television and other news media in specific situations of potential violence "probably acts more as a *deterrent of violence* at such events than as an instigator." [35] On the other hand, there is some fear that the extensive publicity given to "dramatic acts of deviant behavior," such as bomb scares, airplane hijackings, prison riots, and political assassinations, may result in a kind of "contagion phenomenon," [36] inspiring large numbers of new attempts at similar behavior. The rash of kidnappings, hijackings, and assassination attempts in recent years has been attributed in part to such media contagion.

It is an oversimplification, of course, to assume that any portrayal of violence will always transmit to spectators a desire to act out what they have just seen.[37] Both the context of the stimulus and the state of mind of the viewer must be taken into account. The wish to imitate what is seen on the TV or movie screen is likely to depend largely on the manner of presentation, although we still lack hard evidence as to what the relevant variables are. Similarly, the emotional condition of viewers will predispose them to react to what they see in certain ways. Scenes of a prison riot are likely to evoke quite different reactions from a high school dropout who feels oppressed and trapped by "the system," and from an ambitious and successful young executive.

In sum, then, although violence is certainly to some extent a consequence of social learning, we do not yet know enough about how people react to cultural symbols to say categorically that a violent culture breeds violence. The learning explanation assumes that people act more violently when they are involved in a culture that permits or encourages violence. However, it is perhaps just as plausible to reason that where people are more violent, their cultural norms will reflect this fact. Thus, the causal relationship might more accurately be described as reciprocal.

DOMESTIC VIOLENCE

For the purposes of this chapter, we shall deal with criminal violence and civil disturbances as the most critical manifestations of domestic violence. After investigating the possibilities of social action to prevent or control

---

[35] Gladys Engel Lang and Kurt Lang, "Some pertinent questions on collective violence and the news media." *Journal of Social Issues* 28 (1972):108–109.
[36] Brown, p. 59.
[37] Lawrence Alloway, *Violent America: The Movies, 1946–1964.* New York: Museum of Modern Art, 1971, p. 66.

these varieties of violent behavior, we shall discuss international conflict, or war.

Violent crime may not be the most common type of crime, but it is certainly the most frightening. Those who have had the experience of returning to their home after it has been burglarized often report a sense of revulsion at the thought of strangers' hands rifling through bureau drawers and handling prized possessions, the intrusion itself being seen as defiling even beyond the sense of loss of property. But the defilement of one's own body, one's most private possession, in a violent attack, is a far more terrifying prospect, because more than any other crime it threatens our lives and our personal integrity, and demonstrates that our destinies may not be in our own hands.

In fact, in relation to other kinds of crime, violent crime is the least prevalent. According to the Federal Bureau of Investigation's *Uniform Crime Reports,* the violent crimes of murder, robbery, aggravated assault, and forcible rape make up only about 10 percent of crimes reported; all the rest are crimes against property.[38] Further, nonviolent crimes are in general far more profitable than violent ones. The so-called white-collar crimes—tax evasion, price-fixing, embezzlement, swindling, fraud—involve billions of dollars annually. One particular corporate price-fixing conspiracy yielded more money each year it continued than all of the hundreds of thousands of burglaries, larcenies, and thefts in the nation during those same years.[39] (See Chapter 4.)

As has already been pointed out, crime statistics must be interpreted with great caution. Because of changes in police practices and better recording procedures, many crimes which previously would have gone unrecorded are now reflected in the official figures. Even allowing for this, it is still apparent that violent crime is increasing rapidly, although not as quickly as crime in general.[40] (See Table 5-1.) If we consider the forms of violent crime, we shall see some interesting similarities and differences in the patterns of their occurrence.

Criminal Homicide. Criminal homicide takes two forms. *Murder* can be defined as "the unlawfull killing of a human being with malice aforethought." Malice aforethought requires a "guilty mind" but not necessarily premeditation and planning.[41] *Manslaughter* is unlawful homicide without malice aforethought. In practice, the distinction between manslaughter and murder is often a very fine one. Someone may attack another person without intending to kill, but death may be the accidental outcome. Depending on the circumstances, one case might be judged to be murder, another manslaughter. Often the deciding factor is the degree of provocation the victim offered his or her assailant.

Paradoxically, most murderers do not have criminal records. There are, of course, those who use actual or threatened violence in the form

[38] *Uniform Crime Reports,* p. 11.
[39] Ramsey Clark, *Crime in America.* New York: Simon & Schuster, 1970, p. 38.
[40] *Uniform Crime Reports,* p. 55.
[41] Marshall B. Clinard and Richard Quinney, *Criminal Behavior Systems: A Typology.* New York: Holt, Rinehart and Winston, 1967, p. 21.

	Violent Crimes	Homicide	Forcible Rape	Robbery	Aggravated Assault
Total number	*969,820*	**20,600**	**55,210**	**441,290**	**452,720**
Rate (per 100,000 inhabitants)	*458.8*	9.7	26.1	208.8	214.2
Percent change since 1960	+ *186.8*	+ 127.4	+ 222.4	+ 310.2	+ 195.6

Source: U.S. Department of Justice, *Uniform Crime Reports,* November 17, 1975, p. 55.

TABLE 5-1
Index of Violent
Crime, 1974

of both assault and homicide as tools in criminal careers, but these cases are exceptions; professional criminals as a rule try to keep violence to a "necessary" minimum, and in particular to avoid killing because of the "heat" it will bring on them from the law. Most murderers do not see themselves as real criminals and, until the murder, neither does society.[42] Murderers do not conform to any stereotype of a criminal "type," and murder is not the final step on a ladder of criminal behavior.

There are, however, certain social and geographical patterns. To begin with, the murder rate is related to the degree of urbanization of a country, with murders occurring most often in cities. In the United States, for example, homicide is more likely to take place in large cities—but not all that much more likely. The murder rate for large metropolitan areas is about 11 per 100,000 population, compared to a rate of 6 per 100,000 in smaller cities; but the murder rate in rural areas is a surprisingly high 8 per 100,000.[43] (See Table 5-2.) Furthermore, the incidence of murder is unevenly distributed throughout large cities; as Lunde points out, "Most city neighborhoods are just as safe as the suburbs." [44] There are regional differences as well. For instance, murder is more likely to occur in the South, even though this is one of the more rural parts of the country. This seems to be due to the maintenance in this region of a culture in which personal violence and the use of weapons are more acceptable than in the North.

Most murderers are men, who are socialized to be more violent and to use guns for recreation or for military purposes, and guns are the most likely cause of fatal injuries. But both the number and proportion of women killers are increasing. In 1950 fewer than 20 percent of all murderers were women, but by 1975 about 25 percent of fatal injuries were inflicted by women. More than half of all murderers are under 35, and the average age is close to 20. Their victims are young, too, most likely under 30.[45] Victims are also likely to be members of minorities: the rate of homicide victimization for blacks and other minorities is about 9 times the total national rate. (In actual numbers, about half of all murder

[42] Clinard and Quinney, p. 22.
[43] *Uniform Crime Reports,* p. 11.
[44] Lunde, p. 38.
[45] Lunde, p. 38.

victims are members of minorities.) [46] More than 90 percent of the time, killer and victim are of the same race, and Lunde observes that "in the few instances where racial lines are crossed, it's more often whites murdering blacks than the reverse."

More significant than the demographic status of murders and their victims is the relationship between them. Several studies have indicated that this relationship is generally close, often one of family or intimate friendship. Usually the precipitating event is a quarrel: one study in Philadelphia found that approximately one-third of 588 murders resulted from general quarrels, while family and domestic altercations accounted for 14 percent, jealousy 12 percent, disagreements over money 11 percent, and robbery only 7 percent. In 59 percent of all homicides, the victims were close friends and relatives. In only one out of every eight murders was the victim a stranger.[47]

Other studies have found that one-fourth of all murderers are close relatives of their victims, and half of these are husbands or wives killing their spouses. Lunde reports that

more than 40 percent of murder victims are killed in residences. . . . More women die in their own bedrooms than anywhere else. One in every five murder victims is a woman who has been killed there by her spouse or lover. Husbands are most vulnerable in the kitchen; that's where wives are apt to pick up knives to finish family arguments.

The other half of murders involving close relatives include parents killing children, children killing parents, or other close relatives killing each other. These victims usually die in the living room from gunshot wounds. Another six percent of murders [are] between more distant relatives.[48]

[46] U.S. Bureau of the Census, *Statistical Abstract of the United States.* Washington, D.C.: U.S. Government Printing Office, 1974, p. 150.
[47] Marvin Wolfgang, *Patterns in Criminal Homicide.* Philadelphia: University of Pennsylvania Press, 1958, p. 191.
[48] Lunde, pp. 35–36.

Even though almost 30 percent of homicides today are committed during the course of a crime (the rate was 10 percent twenty years ago), these killings, too, are usually unpremeditated—a thief surprised by a night watchman, a bank robber confronted by an armed guard, and so on. By far the majority of murders occur in the heat of the moment during a quarrel between two people who know each other well. Murderer and victim both may have been drinking, perhaps together, prior to the fatal event: half of all homicides are alcohol-related. (See Chapter 3.)

The mentally ill commit murder at the same rate as the rest of the population, as Lunde points out, but multiple murderers, such as the Manson "family," are almost always psychotic, being either paranoids or sexual sadists.[49] The former may hear voices "commanding" them to kill, believe they are superhuman or "chosen" for a "special mission," and/or kill to avert imagined persecution by "others." Sadists may torture before killing and/or mutilate their victims afterward. Unlike most murderers, these psychotic killers are not likely to be personally acquainted with their victims, who are often representative of a type or class—rich, "establishment" women. Assassins may sometimes act out of strictly political motivation and as part of a group conspiracy with roots in a more or less realistic appraisal of a national cause or political situation. In the United States, however, assassinations, with very few exceptions, have not been in response to realistic situations but have been committed or attempted by emotionally disturbed or highly irrational individuals.[50]

Assault and Robbery. From a sociological point of view, murder and assault are similar kinds of crime. Assault is an attempt to injure or kill someone. Murder is therefore a form of aggravated assault, the main difference being that the victim dies. Often it is a question of chance whether an extreme case of assault becomes murder or not. It may depend on the weapon used or on the speed with which the injured person receives medical attention.

Since murder and assault are similar kinds of crime, most of the observations made above concerning murder also apply to assault. A person who commits assault is, perhaps, somewhat more likely to have a criminal record than one who commits murder, but in general neither is very likely to have such a record.[51]

Robbery may be defined as the taking of another person's property by the threat of violence, or intimidation. (A robbery in which violence was actually used is recorded as an assault.) It accounts by itself for nearly 40 percent of all reported crimes of violence. Unlike murder or assault, robbery usually occurs between strangers; it is also the one major violent crime with a high interracial and interclass rate. For example, in one survey undertaken by the National Commission on the Causes and Prevention of Violence, it was found that blacks robbed whites in 45 percent of the robberies surveyed. Robbery is obviously a criminal attempt to obtain money or other property, and whites are more likely than blacks to be perceived as affluent. It is also likely that blacks will be overrepresented

[49] Lunde, p. 39.
[50] See, for example, "The politics of terror." *Time,* March 4, 1974, pp. 11–15; and "The girl who almost killed Ford." *Time,* September 15, 1975, p. 17.
[51] Clinard and Quinney, p. 22.

in official crime statistics. (See Chapter 4, "Crime and Criminals"; Chapter 6, "Affluence and Poverty"; and Chapter 7, "Prejudice and Discrimination.") Nevertheless, a substantial proportion of robberies occur within the same race: the commission found that 38 percent of robberies involved black offenders and victims.[52] Blacks were also twice as likely to be robbed as whites.

Rape. Forcible rape is the act of having unlawful sexual intercourse with a woman against her will. This should be distinguished from statutory rape, which is sexual intercourse with a female who is under a certain age—usually 16 or 18 years, depending on the state. Most arrests for rape are in fact for statutory, and not forcible, rape.

Forcible rape accounts for about one-seventeenth of the total number of violent crimes.[53] However, probably about 80 percent of rapes go unreported because the victim usually wishes to avoid the humiliation of having to describe the event in detail both to the police and later in open court. (The recorded figures for other violent crimes, especially assault, are also lower than the actual figures. However, the number of unreported rapes is probably much greater than the number of other violent crimes that go unreported.)

In contrast to the murderer and the assaulter, the rapist is likely to have a record of prior arrests for criminal offenses. However, for the majority of convicted rapists, the forcible rape was their first sex offense, and only a relatively small proportion of rapists have a history of sex offenses.[54] Like other perpetrators of violent crimes, rapists tend to live in areas of cities with high rates of crime and violence. Also, as in robbery, the victim of a rape is less likely than the murder or assault victim to know her assailant: slightly over half of rape cases occur between strangers.[55] An overwhelming majority of rapists attack women of their own race. For example, a study of reported rapes in Philadelphia in 1972 found that only 16 percent of rapes involved black men raping white women.[56]

In the 1970s efforts of the women's liberation movement brought increasing public and research attention to the subject of rape, its perpetrators, and its victims. One result was an increase in the number of women reporting this crime. The 55,000 rapes reported in 1974 represented an increase of about 80 percent over 1968.[57] The rate of conviction on rape charges, however, is lower than for any other violent crime. Traditionally, police and lawyers have shown hostility to the plaintiff, assuming she had provoked the act or cooperated to some degree. Legal evidence requirements—eyewitnesses, bruises or torn clothing, medical evidence of penetration—are often so unrealistic as to make conviction virtually impossible. Equally unrealistic are the harsh penalties for rape,

[52] *Violent Crime: The Report of the National Commission on the Causes and Prevention of Violence.* New York: Braziller, 1969, p. 43.
[53] *Uniform Crime Reports,* p. 11.
[54] Clinard and Quinney, p. 23.
[55] *Violent Crime,* p. 44; and James Selkin, "Rape." *Psychology Today,* January 1975, p. 72.
[56] "Revolt against rape." *Time,* July 22, 1974, p. 85.
[57] *Uniform Crime Reports,* p. 55.

204 CHAPTER FIVE

in some cases life imprisonment or even death; juries are reluctant to convict if such extreme punishments are mandatory. Sometimes, the lesser charge of assault is settled on (distorting the reported crime rates somewhat more). More often, the defendant is acquitted for lack of evidence. But pressure from women's groups and sympathetic legal organizations in several states has resulted in the repeal of laws requiring unrealistic evidence or sentences. In some states, too, new laws have been passed in accord with guidelines stated by the National Organization for Women; these specifically include the principle that a rape victim's activities with men other than the accused are irrelevant.[58]

The discussion of rape in the media has served to cause many researchers, police departments, and women's groups to investigate how rape may best be prevented. One study suggests that in addition to elementary safety precautions such as not walking alone at night, "a woman's best strategy is to resist, to refuse to allow her attacker to intimidate her"—by running away, screaming, or hitting.[59] This holds true, according to this study, in all situations except where there is an obvious threat of physical danger from a weapon or the attack occurs in the home (and resistance will merely incite the rapist), both of which rarely occur. One other result of renewed interest in the subject of rape has been an increased concern for the rape victim. Many hospitals now offer round-the-clock counseling to rape victims presenting themselves at emergency rooms; police departments are setting up special rape units staffed by female officers; and in a number of cities women's organizations have established rape crisis and prevention centers and telephone hot lines.

The United States is the leader among modern, stable nations in the reported rate of murder, assault, robbery, and rape, although crime in general and violence both are increasing in most countries of Western Europe as well. The fear of violent crime has directly affected the lives of many citizens.

One-third of American householders keep guns in the hope that they will provide protection against intruders. In some urban neighborhoods, nearly one-third of the residents wish to move because of high rates of crime. . . . Bus drivers in many cities do not carry change, cab drivers in some areas are in scarce supply, and some merchants are closing their businesses.[60]

Clearly, unless this trend is reversed, the quality of American life may soon be changed dramatically. And if it is to be reversed, we need to do more than strengthen our police forces. Violent crime cannot be understood or controlled unless we examine the social conditions which serve as a breeding ground for crime—a fact which the civil disturbances during the last decade forced on our attention.

CIVIL DISTURBANCES

The civil disturbances of the 1960s were a serious manifestation of dissatisfaction with the social, economic, and political conditions with which black Americans were faced. Although it is probably not true that

[58] "Revolt against rape," p. 85.
[59] Selkin, p. 71.
[60] *Violent Crime*, p. 34.

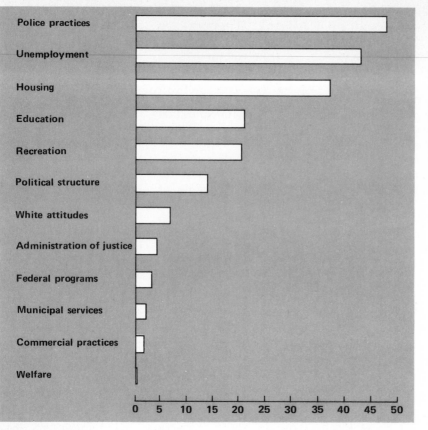

FIGURE 5-1
Relative Importance of
Grievance Categories
Underlying Civil
Disturbances

*Source: Report of the
National Advisory
Commission on Civil
Disorders.* New York:
Bantam, 1968, p. 150.

most black citizens in the United States were completely alienated from the dominant culture, or that most of those who participated in the civil disturbances possessed a clearly articulated radical ideology, it is nevertheless certain that the disturbances signaled a major change in emphasis, from nonviolent protest to a more militant mood, in the black communities.[61]

The National Advisory Commission on Civil Disorders, in investigating the origins of the disturbances, found that violence "was generated out of an increasingly disturbed social atmosphere, in which typically a series of tension-heightened incidents over a period of weeks or months became linked in the minds of many in the Negro community with a reservoir of underlying grievances." The final incident preceding the violence was often of a minor or trivial nature. "Prior" incidents, which served to increase the tension, were police actions, in almost half of the 24 cases studied; and police actions prompted "final" incidents before the occurrence of violence in exactly half the cases.[62] (See Figure 5-1.)

[61] H. L. Nieburg, *Political Violence.* New York: St. Martin's Press, 1969, p. 148.
[62] *Report of the National Advisory Commission on Civil Disorders.* New York: Bantam, 1968, p. 6.

According to various surveys, the rioters consisted of a substantial minority of the blacks in the area: a Newark survey by the commission found that 45 percent of black males between the ages of 14 and 35 residing in the disorder area identified themselves as rioters. The rioters received considerable support from their nonrioting neighbors,[63] and did not differ from nonrioters in absolute income, degree of unemployment, or length of stay in the ghetto. They were also better integrated into the community than nonrioters.[64] Geschwender suggests, in fact, that "within cities there is a positive association between high black income and riot frequency and intensity." It was generally *after* a disturbance had begun that the most deprived segments of the community participated, because they had least to lose.[65] The disturbances, therefore, cannot be dismissed as the work of a few militant hoodlums. Nor can the violent activities of the rioters, once they began, be explained by the absence of restraint characteristics of a "mob" psychology, for, in fact, there was a kind of restraint, as shown by the lack of direct personal violence and the consistency of the rioters in choosing their targets.[66]

In attempting to understand the causes of the civil disturbances and the motivations of the rioters, we must address ourselves to the "reservoir

The civil disturbances of the 1960s were usually touched off by small incidents in crowded, depressed neighborhoods. Other forms of violent protest may involve groups who feel powerless within society and who are trying to dramatize their point of view.
Howard Harrison/ Nancy Palmer

[63] Robert M. Fogelson, "Violence and grievances: Reflections on the 1960's riots." *Journal of Social Issues* 26 (Winter 1970):143.
[64] Vernon L. Allen, "Toward understanding riots: Some perspectives." *Journal of Social Issues* 26 (Winter 1970):8.
[65] James A. Geschwender, "Review." *Contemporary Sociology* (March 1975):159.
[66] Fogelson, p. 144.

of underlying grievances" mentioned by the commission. These have been outlined by Ralph Conant:

Ghetto residents in U.S. cities use middle-class white suburban living standards as a comparative point, and they feel acutely deprived, not so much of goods and services associated with the standard of suburban living, but of access to the jobs and salaries which put the desired goods and services within reach. The areas of relative deprivation for black Americans are political and social as well as economic. Blacks are not adequately represented in governing councils at the local or national levels, and they are excluded from social opportunities.[67]

The relative economic deprivation of blacks during the period when the disturbances took place is highlighted by the fact that black unemployment was three times higher than white unemployment, and black median income was little more than half that of whites. (See Chapter 7 for a full discussion of this topic.) However, in a sense, the disturbances were also a demand for a piece of the political action. Since the nonviolent protest methods of the civil rights movement had failed to gain for blacks any significant share in the government under which they lived, they resorted to violent protest. In the opinion of Feagin and Hahn, for example, ghetto disturbances are

an attempted reclamation of political authority over ghetto areas and a type of political recall, not necessarily of specific public officeholders, but of the entire political apparatus that had failed to grant a reasonable share of the political pie to ghetto residents. Collective political violence may well represent the ultimate act of popular sovereignty.

In their view, black militancy is supplemental to nonviolent and legal efforts, and may be a necessary step in the development of new methods for achieving political objectives. Out of the disturbances came leaders who voiced the black power philosophy and spurred community awareness of the need for action. Thus the self-image of blacks was enhanced in the course of the disturbances.[68]

Geschwender, on the other hand, suggests that the earlier nonviolent and other civil rights actions contributed significantly to the development of a positive black self-image; he notes that the concept of black power originated earlier in the 1960s during a civil rights march in Mississippi, and that many black leaders who later "came to be viewed as militant advocates of black power got their 'baptism of fire' in the civil rights movement." [69] It seems likely, however, that the movement toward greater black political participation and community control during the late 1960s and early 1970s was at least to some extent an outgrowth of inner city protests and disturbances.

[67] Ralph Conant, *The Prospects for Revolution*. New York: Harper & Row, 1971, p. 25.
[68] Joe R. Feagin and Harlan Hahn, *Ghetto Revolts: The Politics of Violence in American Cities*. New York: Macmillan, 1973.
[69] Geschwender, p. 159.

SOCIAL ACTION AND DOMESTIC VIOLENCE

Although we are unlikely ever to achieve a society completely free from strife, there are several general steps which might help to reduce the level of internal violence. Most of these measures would come under one of two headings.

Gun Control. In recent years there has been an increasing demand for stricter supervision, probably by federal legislation, of the purchase and sale of firearms, particularly the cheap handguns, or "Saturday night specials," which are so easily obtainable in many sections of the country. The 1972 assassination attempt on Governor George Wallace of Alabama and the two 1975 attempts on President Ford brought the issue of gun control into sharp public focus once again.

Opponents of gun control legislation, represented primarily by the National Rifle Association, constitute one of the most powerful interest groups in the nation. They argue that it is the constitutional right of Americans to bear arms in order to protect themselves and their families from danger, and that therefore gun control is unconstitutional. In the face of this and similar arguments, however, it must be noted that the statistics on violence by means of guns are appalling. In 1974, 95 of the 132 local, state, and federal police officers slain on duty were killed by handguns.[70] About 68 percent of all homicides in the nation were committed through the use of firearms; 54 percent of homicides involved handguns (see Figure 5-2). About 25 percent of all cases of assault were committed with the use of a firearm.[71] Overall, about 300,000 crimes involve the use of a gun. The United States leads every other Western nation in the number of homicides by guns, both in absolute terms and in terms of the rate per 100,000 population. The United States also leads

[70] "Big new drive for gun controls." *U.S. News and World Report*, February 10, 1975, p. 25.
[71] *Uniform Crime Reports*, pp. 15, 20.

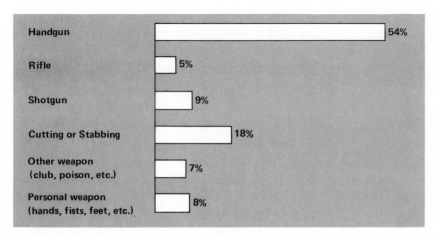

FIGURE 5-2
Homicide, by Type of Weapon Used

Note: Due to rounding, figures do not add up to 100 percent.

Source: U.S. Department of Justice, *Uniform Crime Reports*. Washington, D.C.: U.S. Government Printing Office, November 17, 1975, p. 17.

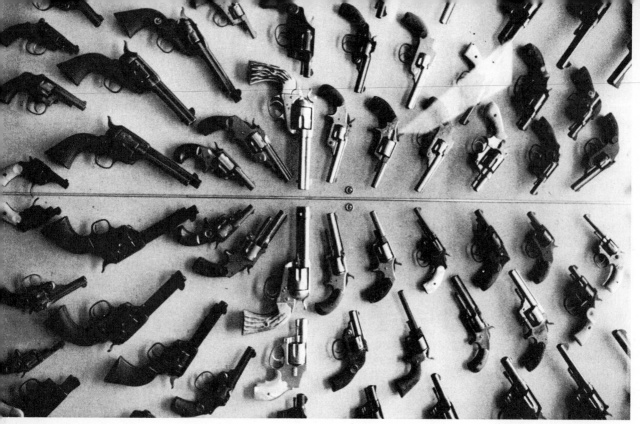

in the rates of both suicide by gun and accident by gun. Although these rates are lower today than in the 1920s and 1930s, they have been increasing steadily throughout the last twenty years.[72]

Opponents of gun control claim that anyone who has decided to kill someone will do so whether or not he or she has a gun. The person can stab, strangle, poison, or batter someone to death. Gun control would therefore make little difference. Though this argument sounds logical, it ignores the fact that guns are about five times more likely to kill the victim than are knives, the next most commonly used murder weapon. In one study it was found that for every 100 reported knife attacks, an average of 2.4 victims died, while for every 100 gun attacks, an average of 12.2 victims died.[73] And since, as we have noted, most murders and assaults are spontaneously committed in passion rather than planned in cold blood, it follows that the easy availability of guns is likely to increase the death rate in criminal assaults. In most cases, murders are the result of three factors: impulse, the lethality of the weapon, and the availability of the weapon. Strict gun control would eliminate or at least reduce the latter two.

In recent years, polls have shown that more than 70 percent of

The easy availability of lethal weapons may be one factor in the increase of violent crime. Here, a display of handguns such as the police confiscate in large numbers every year.
Donald McCullin/Magnum

[72] Christian Gillin and Frank Ochberg, "Firearms control and violence." In Daniels, Gilula, and Ochberg, pp. 241–242.
[73] Gillin and Ochberg, pp. 249–250.

Americans would approve of gun control legislation, but their will is being frustrated by the National Rifle Association, whose members can churn out as many as 500,000 letters on request.[74] The vast damage caused by guns is directly traceable to the fact that at least 40 million handguns and from 90 million to 200 million guns of all types are owned by Americans, and that up to 2.5 million more are manufactured for domestic sale each year. Following the 1968 Federal Gun-Control Act, which in part was intended to restrict the import of inexpensive handguns, the level of imports dropped. However, because of a loophole permitting the assembly of guns in this country from imported parts, there was little if any effective lessening of gun availability. Proponents of gun control argue that a strong federal law applying uniformly to all parts of the country is needed, and cite countries such as Japan and England which have such regulations and have very low gun-murder rates.[75]

Two studies have shed some light on the characteristics of gun owners and the effectiveness of gun control laws in the United States. Wright and Marston found that weapons ownership was highest in rural areas, dropping as city size increased. Nevertheless, "about a third of all residents in cities of 250,000 and larger own at least one gun, and 15 percent own a pistol." Wright and Marston also found that, contrary to popular belief, by far the highest proportion of gun owners are upper-status Protestants. Working-class white ethnics, who are commonly supposed to be arming themselves against blacks, are in fact among the least likely to own a gun. Moreover, about three-fifths of gun owners were found to be *in favor of* some gun control legislation.[76]

Murray, in a study on the effects of gun control laws throughout the United States on the rate of violence, found that such laws were ineffective. They did not lower rates of violence or even lower rates of gun ownership.[77] This suggests that gun control laws will have to be made much more stringent, and enforced much more rigidly—as they are in other countries—in order to reduce the rate and severity of violent crime.

Media Violence. Deemphasizing violence in the media is another suggested step toward reducing violence in society. Granted that we cannot prove a causal relationship between the two, "the weight of social science stands in opposition to the conclusion that mass media portrayals of violence have no effect upon individuals, groups, and society." [78] Goranson, in fact, concluded that the "burden of proof was not upon the critics to prove that violence was harmful, but upon the broadcasters to demonstrate that it was not." [79] In 1972, the Surgeon General's Study of Television and Social Behavior was concerned with how children are

---

[74] "Gun crazy." *The Nation,* March 1, 1975, pp. 228–229.
[75] "Big new drive," p. 25; and James D. Wright and Linda L. Marston, "The ownership of the means of destruction: Weapons in the United States." *Social Problems* (October 1975):93.
[76] Wright and Marston, pp. 93–107.
[77] Douglas R. Murray, "Handguns, gun control laws, and firearm violence." *Social Problems* (October 1975):81–93.
[78] *Mass Media and Violence,* p. 375.
[79] Richard E. Goranson, in Bogart, p. 495.

affected by televised violence, and commissioned more than forty new research projects to examine the issue. Although controversy surrounded the committee membership, its findings, and research (because of the large number of industry representatives on the panel), the Surgeon General, Jesse L. Steinfeld, stated that

it is clear to me that the causal relationship between televised violence and antisocial behavior is sufficient to warrant appropriate and immediate remedial action. The data on social phenomena such as television and violence and/or aggressive behavior will never be clear enough for all social scientists to agree on the formulation of a succinct statement of causality. But there comes a time when the data are sufficient to justify action. That time has come.[80]

Either by legislation or by voluntary regulation within the industry, it should be possible to reduce the incidence of killings and the reliance on shoot-and-slug formulas, especially in movie and television programming. The problem here is that the media have not, so far, been notably imaginative about devising ways to present more constructive approaches to social relations. One small step has been the "family hour," in which the first hour of prime time—from 8 P.M. to 9 P.M.—is devoted to programming considered suitable for family viewing, with the more violent shows being relegated to later hours, when they are accompanied by warnings that their content might be disturbing to some members of the audience. Clearly, however, much remains to be done to substantially reduce the level of violence on television and in the other media.

SOCIAL REFORMS

Any attempt to deal with crime and violence without recognizing the basic social conditions underlying them is foredoomed to failure. We have already noted the high correlation of crime with conditions of poverty and social deprivation. Former Attorney General Ramsey Clark has summed up the situation well:

In every major city in the United States you will find that two-thirds of the arrests take place among about two percent of the population. Where is that area in every city? Well, it's in the same place where infant mortality is four times higher than in the city as a whole; where the death rate is 25 percent higher; where life expectancy is ten years shorter; where common communicable diseases with the potential of physical and mental damage are six and eight and ten times more frequent; where alcoholism and drug addiction are prevalent to a degree far transcending that of the rest of the city; where education is poorest—the oldest school buildings, the most crowded and turbulent schoolrooms, the fewest certified teachers, the highest rate of dropouts, where the average formal schooling is four to six years less for the city as a whole.[81]

The official reaction to the rise in violence in this country has been a basically dualistic approach of reform and control, presumably on the quite reasonable theory that the needed reforms will inevitably take

[80] In Bogart, p. 521.
[81] Clark, p. 11.

time, and that in the meantime violence must not be allowed to disrupt society entirely. The danger in this dualism is that too much emphasis may be placed on the immediate need for control, to the neglect of reform. Skolnick has pointed out some of the resulting problems:

We may suggest as a general rule that a society which must contemplate massive expenditures for social control is one which, virtually by definition, has not grappled with the necessity of massive social reform. There are various possible levels of social reform, ranging from merely token and symbolic amelioration of fundamental problems to significant changes in the allocation of resources—including political power. We feel that contemporary efforts at reform remain largely at the first level. Precisely because society leaves untouched the basic problems, the cycle of hostility spirals: there is protest, violence, and increased commitment to social control. As we spiral in this direction, the "need" for massive social control outstrips the capacity of democratic institutions to maintain both social order and democratic values.[82]

In effect, Skolnick is saying that society can afford to spend only so much; if it chooses to spend most of that amount on control, it will not be able to spend enough on reform. And the chronic shortage of funds which has hampered many reform programs would seem to bear him out.

Nonetheless, some things are being done. Many of them we touch on in other chapters. Community mental health centers in some states are providing substantial help to people in need. Drug and alcohol rehabilitation programs are multiplying; educational and job-training assistance are becoming more common, and more job areas are gradually being opened up to minorities, though unemployment still remains much higher among minorities than among whites (see Chapter 7); efforts are being made to improve police-community relations, and to recruit minority members into police forces; a variety of black groups have been formed in a number of cities—such as Chicago, Philadelphia, and New Orleans—to fight crime in inner city areas [83]; and some residential facilities have been created for teenagers with troubled home lives who might turn to violent behavior.

But when people who cannot get funds for a day-care center which will free welfare mothers to work see the police force expanded and equipped with new weaponry, or watch while the government allocates huge sums for military expenditures, or see corporate officials involved in multi-million dollar crimes receive a fine as punishment while a poor teenager who shoplifts a coat gets sentenced to 6 years' imprisonment, they may understandably feel that society still has its priorities wrong. One of the most interesting recent developments is the organization of poor people and other groups to press, through the political process, for a reordering of those priorities. This may have a significant effect on what is done, and how it is done, to eliminate the causes of violence in our society in the coming decades.

[82] Skolnick, p. 9.
[83] Charlayne Hunter, "Blacks organizing in cities to combat crimes by blacks." *New York Times,* February 22, 1976, p. 1.

WAR

The immediate harm done by war is obvious: it kills people. It also costs an enormous amount of money, and it absorbs the time and energy of a great many other people. It disrupts the normal functioning of economies, causes the destruction of homes, institutions, and societies, and impedes the building of anything new to replace or improve the old. More subtly, it discourages thinking about the real causes and solutions of intersocietal problems; it is apparently easier—or more direct—to try to destroy one's opponents, than it is to learn the art of listening to and living with them.

At least, people in general seem to find it easier, for despite its disadvantages, war has long been a disconcertingly popular method of settling international disputes:

In the history of man peace is the punctuation to war. Of the last 3,421 years only 268 have been free from war. In the period between 1820 and 1949 over three hundred wars were fought causing between 1.5 and 3.0 percent of all deaths, and perhaps 10 percent if one includes indirect effects like subsequent disease and famine. Although other species fight among themselves, this amazing and nearly ubiquitous predilection to mass intergroup killing must be included among man's unique characteristics.[84]

The objects of war have varied—conquest of territory, acquisition of wealth, destruction of a threat, propagation of a religious or political faith. Correspondingly, the types of war have varied as well. In some periods, war was usually limited to the achievement of some specific objective, and there was normally no intention of destroying one's opponent. War was one more instrument of policy, a means of gaining concessions. In the classic phrase of the nineteenth-century Prussian army officer, von Clausewitz, "War is nothing but a continuation of political intercourse, with an admixture of other means." [85] Nowadays we have a less restricted concept; after two world wars, war has become "a struggle in which each contender tries to annihilate the other." [86] (Actually, the period since World War II has seen a number of what were in effect limited wars; but with our modern set of mind, they were fought with the rhetoric and the methods designed for unlimited war, and were probably rendered more horrible thereby. "War as policy" at least had the advantage of encouraging a reasonable economy of means.) Even wars of limited severity and duration carry with them the implicit threat that they might lead to worldwide nuclear destruction.

Insofar as war was recognized as an evil, earlier attempts to explain it were often based on political or moral arguments. Sociological explanations are relatively recent, and we shall examine some of them, along with some related ideas.

[84] David N. Daniels and Marshall F. Gilula, "Violence and the struggle for existence." In Daniels, Gilula, and Ochberg, p. 428.
[85] In Bert V. A. Röling, "The limited significance of the prohibition of war." In Lepawsky, Buehrig, and Lasswell, p. 233.
[86] Che Guevara, *Guerilla Warfare.* New York: Random House, 1968, p. 7.

In line with the concept, which we cited earlier, that violence is a part of humanity's inherent behavior pattern, some theorists have argued that it is in human nature to make war. But others, such as Raymond Aron, have pointed out that war is an organized social behavior, not a blind reaction to a stimulus, and have held that natural aggressiveness is therefore insufficient to explain it:

> The human animal is aggressive, but does not fight by instinct, and while war is an expression, it is not a *necessary* expression of human combativity. War has been its constant expression in the course of the historical phase, starting from the moment when societies were organized and armed. It is contrary to the nature of man that the danger of violence be definitely dispelled: in every collectivity, misfits will violate the laws and attack persons. It is contrary to the nature of individuals and groups that the conflicts between individuals and groups disappear. But it is not proved that these conflicts must be manifested in the phenomenon of war, as we have known it for thousands of years, with organized combatants, utilizing increasingly destructive weapons.[87]

If this is so, why does "the phenomenon of war" occur? Daniels and Gilula list some of the suggested causes:

> contiguity, overcrowding, habituation, social learning, obedience to authority, predation, psychological defenses (for example, rationalization, blaming, denial, displacement, and counterphobic tendencies), identification with (becoming like) the aggressor, the host of fears associated with the human condition, territoriality and power (population spacing, control of resources, group dominance), the formation of extensive expectations that cannot be fulfilled, intolerable frustration, . . . greed, revenge, ideology (truth, religion —especially Christianity and Islam—politics, nationalism), failure of

[87] Raymond Aron, *Peace and War: A Theory of International Relations.* New York: Praeger, 1970, pp. 365–366.

Most sociologists believe that violence is not innate in human beings, but is something that is learned.
Charles Gatewood

alliances and other destruction-prohibiting rituals, and the mere presence of a war-making institution.[88]

Many of these hypotheses can be subsumed under some form of economic argument—that is, that wars are fought essentially for profit. This argument is best known in its socialist form, according to which a capitalist economic system inevitably leads to war, for capitalist governments act in the interests of small groups of wealthy monopolists, and the interests of these are bound sooner or later to clash. When they do, the governments resort to violence, and war results.

Granted that this seems an overly simplistic explanation, best suited perhaps to the world of nineteenth-century Europe in which it was conceived, it nevertheless appears reasonable to assume that someone expects to profit from any war which is begun as a matter of choice. Powerful elements in any nation, capitalist or otherwise, often expect to gain profit, territory, or more power when another nation is attacked. Whether this would be equally true of the unlimited type of war is less certain.

Finsterbusch and Greisman, for example, argue that in the twentieth century war has become unprofitable. Using a cost-benefit analysis of twenty-six wars since 1900 (excluding civil strife, such as the Biafran and Vietnamese conflicts), they conclude that "for the initiator, at the very least, modern interstate wars are generally unprofitable," and have usually been accompanied by the loss of territory and high casualties. Improved technology and the higher costs of that technology, the unlimited nature of modern warfare, the modernizing of underdeveloped areas, and the diminished number of empires are responsible for this new situation. They suggest that, following World War II, "empires disintegrated in the face of independence movements and efforts to subjugate additional foreign territories have been rare, . . . many colonies have become independent, and almost no territory has been gained militarily." Furthermore, "because of the vastly improved technology of devastation and the practice of total warfare . . . wars no longer gain booty, spoils, or tribute; and they infrequently gain economic concessions." [89]

The economic argument for the origin of war has been adapted to explain wars of colonial peoples against their rulers, or of underdeveloped against developed countries. Wars of this kind presuppose two conditions: first, the poorer group have a strong desire to attain a prosperity similar to that of the wealthier group; second, the poorer group perceive oppression by the wealthier group as the cause of their own deprivation. Certainly this explanation appears plausible for many of the anticolonial conflicts of recent years; and the similarity to some explanations of civil disturbances is evident.

Another explanation of the origin of war is the notion that "the mere presence of a war-making institution" tends to promote conflict. Proponents of this view believe that the huge resources of people and money connected with military and militarily oriented interests in the major world powers have resulted in the creation of what former President

[88] Daniels and Gilula, p. 428.
[89] Kurt Finsterbusch and H. C. Greisman, "The unprofitability of warfare in the twentieth century." *Social Problems*, vol. 22, no. 3 (February 1975):450–460.

Eisenhower called a "military-industrial complex" whose very existence tends to make for pressures toward war. These pressures are of several kinds. Economically, the interests of vast numbers of people are tied up with military production—when a company loses a defense contract, workers lose jobs, and communities lose revenue and business. (See Chapter 6.) Psychologically and politically, in order to justify heavy military expenditure, it is necessary to be able to point to a threat of war—there must be enemies, who must be seen as likely to attack if they find a weak point. Hence a climate of international hostility is maintained, though we need not assume deliberate warmongering. Finally, the presence of large quantities of weapons and munitions itself increases the danger that they will be used, just as in the case of domestic crimes, where the easy availability of guns increases the possibility of homicide.

Analysis of the arms race between the United States and the U.S.S.R., especially during the Cold War years following World War II, illustrates most of these points. That contest has exhibited

a characteristic pattern of action and reaction, or, in most cases, over-reaction. This implies that Soviet military activities are determined almost exclusively by those of the United States, and *vice versa*. The tendency to over-react arises because there is no precise answer to the question of how much [military capability] is enough, and where national security is concerned, uncertainty typically leads to a preference for too much rather than too little.

More recently, because of advanced technology and the many years required for the development of new weapons and delivery systems,

participants in the "technological arms race"—primarily the United States and the Soviet Union—focus their attention not on which weapons the other side has already produced or is ready to produce, but on possible future developments in the opponent's weaponry, and then undertake programs designed to produce weapons to offset these anticipated developments. . . . The process is only exacerbated by the fact that technological advances make it possible to consider protection against increasingly remote contingencies.

The fallacy in this procedure is, of course, that the other side is following exactly the same pattern.[90]

The idea that war is inherent in humanity, the argument that it results from economic factors or relative deprivation, and the idea that war-making institutions naturally promote international conflict all have elements of validity as explanations for the origins of war. But, as with the suggested explanations of domestic violence, they are in themselves insufficient. Until we understand better why war occurs in some situations and not in others, our efforts to prevent it will be hindered.

PREVENTION OF WAR

The limitation of war has been one of the major purposes of international organizations; the United Nations was established, in June 1945, in order to "save succeeding generations from the scourge of war." [91] The

[90] Stockholm International Peace Research Institute, *World Armaments and Disarmaments, SIPRI Yearbook 1974*. Cambridge, Mass.: M.I.T. Press, 1974, pp. 125, 127–128.
[91] Preamble to the United Nations Charter. See *Charter of the United Nations Together with the Statute of the International Court of Justice*. Washington, D.C.: Department of State Publications, 2353, Conference Series 74.

United Nations has proved to be an important factor in the settlement of a few minor conflicts between nations, but its record in the peaceful handling of major international disputes is disappointing. Here the lack of meaningful sanctions and of an effective machinery of enforcement has served to erode the impact of international legal standards, with "justice" often being a question of superior military strength and commitment. However, until the nations are prepared to accept a more powerful organization, the United Nations must be assigned a key role in future attempts to control or prevent international conflict.

Another approach to the prevention of war is disarmament. The international arms race is enormously expensive: world expenditures for armaments stand at approximately $207 billion annually. This sum represents about 6.5 percent of total monetary output, and triple the quantity of the world's resources allocated for military purposes before 1948.[92] In fiscal 1977 the United States defense budget was $106 billion, an increase of $16 billion over that of fiscal 1975. From 1946 through 1974, the nation spent almost as much—over $1.3 trillion—on national security as for all nonmilitary goods and services—$1.6 trillion—since 1789. In the fifteen years from 1960 to 1974, "the United States alone accounted for between 36 and 42 percent of the world's total military expenditures."[93] In addition, the attitudes of competitive hostility and distrust generated by the arms race have resulted in a diminution of the very feelings of safety and security that strong programs of national defense are designed to produce. The danger is greater because the expanding nuclear potential of many nations has increased humanity's war-making capacity to a point well beyond that demonstrated by the bombings of Hiroshima and Nagasaki, making possible virtually instantaneous massive destruction:

Nuclear weapons can do it quickly. That makes a difference. When the
Crusaders breached the walls of Jerusalem they sacked the city while the mood
was on them. They burned things that they might, with time to reflect,
have carried away instead and raped women that, with time to think about it,
they might have married instead. To compress catastrophic war within the
span of time that a man can stay awake drastically changes the possibility of
central control and restraint, the motivations of people in change, and
the capacity to think and reflect while war is in progress. It is imaginable that
we might destroy 200,000,000 Russians in a war of the present, though not
80,000,000 Japanese in a war of the past. It is not only imaginable, it is
imagined. It is imaginable because it could be done "in a moment, in the
twinkling of an eye, at the last trumpet."[94]

It would seem that such dismal prospects would have prompted a serious and concerted effort toward international disarmament. But here, as elsewhere, good intentions have been hampered by national jealousy and procedural wrangling, as well as the legitimate concern of govern-

[92] Stockholm International Peace Research Institute, p. 123.
[93] Allan L. Damon, "Defense spending." *American Heritage,* February 1975, pp. 81, 90; and Peter J. Ognibene, "The defense budget: Pentagon prosperity." *New Republic,* February 22, 1975, pp. 10–11.
[94] Thomas C. Schelling, *Arms and Influence.* New Haven, Conn.: Yale University Press, 1966, p. 20.

ments for national security. There has, however, been some progress. The Partial Nuclear Test Ban Treaty of 1963, signed by the United States and the Soviet Union, prohibited the testing of nuclear weapons in the atmosphere, although both nations continued to conduct underground tests. There has also been an agreement to limit the use of nuclear weapons in outer space; and a 1972 treaty limiting antiballistic missile sites in the United States and Russia received overwhelming approval from the Senate. Future discussions, such as the ongoing Strategic Arms Limitations Talks (SALT), offer hope that further positive developments may be forthcoming.

Various studies have suggested that war may well be a learned rather than an ingrained pattern of behavior. Although we are not certain exactly why people go to war, we do have knowledge of tribes that are completely peaceful, and have seen that a once-warlike people, such as the Scandinavians, can become peaceful. The ultimate requirement here is an eradication of the belief that people can solve their problems by going to war, or that their fellow humans are the real enemies:

Ironically there is no paucity of either naturally occurring or man-made enemies to fight. Pestilence, famine, war, overpopulation and its products, pollution and destruction of natural resources are all very real enemies of man. At an ever-accelerating rate these real enemies encircle mankind. Since they select no particular nation, they might yet unite our species in a common effort. The struggle for existence that lies ahead is with these enemies, not one another.[95]

PROSPECTS

The history of humankind has been violent, and our studies of crime, civil disorders, and war provide little indication that the development of effective means of reducing or controlling our violent inclinations is at hand. It is an important step, however, that the vital nature and magnitude of the problem are now being recognized. Much further research is needed, particularly in the area of the origins of violence, in the development of peaceful means of settling disputes, and in the encouragement of alternatives to violent behavior, such as negotiation and nonviolent protest. Efforts should be made to reduce the frustrations caused by relative deprivation, and to provide more adequate mechanisms for the expression of social and political grievances. Also, societal condemnation of violent behavior should be uniform, and not based on a double standard condoning some forms of violence while denouncing others.[96]

In the words of one author, "It is untrue that violence settles nothing. It would be closer to the mark to assert that violence has settled all historical issues so far, and most of them in the wrong way." [97] The most immediate consequence of violence is usually not change but further violence, and it is this escalation process that must be reversed if people are ever to live at peace with themselves and their fellow human beings.

95 Daniels and Gilula, p. 431.
96 Alan J. Rosenthal and Frederic W. Ilfeld, Jr., "Summary of recommendations." In Daniels, Gilula, and Ochberg, pp. 392–394.
97 Irving L. Horowitz, "The struggle is the message." In Irving L. Horowitz, ed., *The Troubled Conscience.* Palo Alto, Calif.: James E. Freel and Associates, 1971, p. 35.

The incidence of violence in the United States has increased considerably over the past few decades, and concern over violence has become widespread. However, America has had a history of violence, from the Revolutionary War, through the extermination of the Indians and the Civil War, to the costly conflicts in the twentieth century. Violence may be viewed as legitimate or illegitimate, depending on who uses it and the purpose for which it is used.

Among explanations for violence are (1) people are innately aggressive; (2) individual frustration leads to aggression; (3) the lack of development of internal controls leads to violence (*control theory*); (4) norms of a subcultural group with a low provocation threshold make violence acceptable (*subcultural theory*); and (5) external influences, such as media presentation of violence, inspire additional violence. It is likely that all of these factors are responsible to some extent, and equally likely that no one explanation will suffice for all instances.

Crimes of violence against a person are the most frightening of all crimes, although they are the least frequent of crimes. Homicides are somewhat more likely to be urban than non-urban crimes; most murderers are men, although the number and proportion of women killers are increasing. Murderers are likely to be related to or acquainted with their victims, and to be of the same race as their victims. Most murders are not premeditated, but take place during quarrels.

Murder and assault are similar crimes, and often it is a matter of chance whether a case of assault becomes murder instead. Unlike murder and assault, robbery usually occurs between strangers. Although there is a high interracial component to robbery, blacks are twice as likely to be robbed as whites.

Rape is the least reported of violent crimes, because women traditionally have been intimidated in various ways when they do report that they have been raped. Rapists are least often convicted of all violent criminals, because traditional evidentiary requirements are unrealistic and penalties excessively harsh. Activism from the women's liberation movement is encouraging women to resist and report rapes, and is stimulating legal changes to make conviction more likely.

Civil disturbances were a serious manifestation of dissatisfaction with the social, economic, and political conditions with which many black Americans are faced. A frequent result of these actions was that necessary communications between the black community and civil authorities was initiated and community awareness among blacks was enhanced.

The proliferation of firearms in this country has had a direct impact on the number of murders, since firearms are more likely to be used in the heat of a quarrel and are more likely than any other weapon to cause death. Thus the reduction of domestic violence would require the passage and stringent enforcement of gun control legislation. Reducing the level of violence in the media would also be desirable, since there is substantial evidence that media violence causes antisocial behavior. Finally, social reforms to correct the deprived conditions that breed violence are essential.

War seems ubiquitous in human history; but in the twentieth century the nature of war has changed. Instead of limited wars there are unlimited ones, with virtually astronomic casualty figures. Suggested causes for the origin of war include the desire for profit, territory, or power, and the possibility that the very existence of a war-making capacity promotes conflict. Advanced technologies produce ever more sophisticated weapons and delivery systems, and international competition, especially the arms race between the United States and the Soviet Union, perpetuates itself. International agreements so far have been only tentative, although the waste of resources on armaments and the potential horrors of a nuclear war are apparent to all.

BIBLIOGRAPHY

Arendt, Hannah. *On Violence.* New York: Harcourt Brace Jovanovich, 1970.

Aron, Raymond. *Peace and War: A Theory of International Relations.* New York: Praeger, 1970.

Berkowitz, Leonard. *Aggression: A Social Psychological Analysis.* New York: McGraw-Hill, 1962.

Campbell, James S., Sahid, Joseph R., and Stang, David P. *Law and Order Reconsidered: Report of the Task Force on Law and Law Enforcement to the National Commission on the Causes and Prevention of Violence.* New York: Bantam, 1970.

Cohen, Norman E., ed. *The Los Angeles Riots: A Socio-Psychological Study.* New York: Praeger, 1970.

Coser, Lewis A. *Continuities in the Study of Social Conflict.* New York: Free Press, 1967.

Daniels, David N., Gilula, Marshall, and Ochberg, Frank, eds. *Violence and the Struggle for Existence.* Boston: Little, Brown, 1970.

Davies, Jame C. *When Men Revolt and Why.* New York: Free Press, 1971.

Endleman, Shalom, ed. *Violence in the Streets.* Chicago: Quadrangle, 1968.

Etzioni, Amitai, and Wenglinsky, Martin, eds. *War and Its Prevention.* New York: Harper & Row, 1970.

Fogelson, Robert M. *Violence as Protest: A Study of Riots and Ghettos.* Garden City, N.Y.: Doubleday, 1971.

Graham, Hugh D., and Gurr, Ted R., eds. *The History of Violence in America: A Report to the National Commission on the Causes and Prevention of Violence.* New York: Bantam, 1969.

Graham, Hugh D., *et al. Violence: The Crisis in American Confidence.* Baltimore: Johns Hopkins, 1972.

Grimshaw, Allan, ed. *Racial Violence in the United States.* Chicago: Aldine, 1969.

Gurr, Ted R. *Why Men Rebel.* Princeton, N.J.: Princeton University Press, 1970.

Gurr, Ted R., *et al. Anger, Violence and Politics: Theories and Research.* Englewood Cliffs, N.J.: Prentice-Hall, 1972.

Kennett, Lee, and LaVerne, James. *The Gun in America.* Westport, Conn.: Greenwood, 1975.

Kerner, Otto, *et al. Report of the National Advisory Commission on Civil Disorder.* New York: Bantam, 1968.

Lorenz, Konrad. *On Aggression.* New York: Bantam, 1967.

Marx, G. *Protest and Prejudice: A Study of Belief in the Black Community.* New York: Harper & Row, 1967.

Surgeon General's Scientific Advisory Committee on Television and Social Behavior. *Television and Growing Up: The Impact of Televised Violence.* Washington, D.C.: U.S. Government Printing Office, 1972.

6

AFFLUENCE
AND POVERTY

- Less than 10 percent of American families earn incomes of over $25,000 a year.
- In a recent year, almost 250 people with annual incomes of over $200,000—including five people with annual incomes of over $1 million—paid no taxes.
- The wealthiest 1 percent in our society own 51 percent of all corporate stock.
- Over 5,000 former Pentagon officials are employed in defense industries.
- Over 24 million people—12 percent of the nation's population—are below the government-defined poverty level.
- 31 percent of blacks and 22 percent of Spanish origin are below the poverty line, compared with 8.5 percent of whites.
- Only about 1 percent of those on welfare are unemployed males.

At home and abroad, America is thought of as a wealthy nation. This image is fostered by the media, by commercial advertising, and by politicians of every persuasion who proudly proclaim that "this is the richest country in the world." Most of us, as we contemplate our industrial output, agricultural abundance, and personal possessions—even in this time of economic difficulty—concur. And there is, indeed, objective evidence for this image: the American per capita income of $6,640 is third only to Sweden's $6,720 and Switzerland's $6,650; the American median annual income of $12,840 and gross national product of $900 billion are the highest in the world.

Unfortunately, these figures represent a misleading picture of the nature of our affluence. The fact is that in our society enormous amounts of money are concentrated in the hands of a relatively small number of people. Most Americans can either barely make ends meet or are in fact living in dire poverty. For example, almost 15 percent of America's 55 million families receive annual incomes of *below* $5,000 (see Figure 6-1). Another 24 percent earn between $5,000 and $10,000 annually, and about 26 percent earn between $10,000 and $15,000. Only 9 percent of American families receive yearly incomes of $25,000 or more.[1] This

[1] U.S. Bureau of the Census, "Consumer income." *Current Population Reports*, Series P-60, no. 97. Washington, D.C.: U. S. Government Printing Office, 1975.

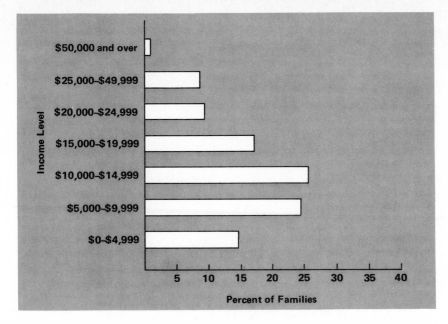

FIGURE 6-1
Percent Distrbution
of Families by Annual
Income Level

Note: Total number of
families is 55,053,000.

Source: U.S. Bureau of
the Census, "Consumer In-
come." *Current Population
Reports,* Series P-60, no.
97. Washington, D.C.: U.S.
Government Printing Office,
1975, p. 1.

income distribution pattern has not changed significantly since the Depression,[2] when President Franklin Roosevelt saw "one third of our
nation ill-housed, ill-clad, ill-nourished." [3]

In American society, middle-class values and standards are predominant, and the image of equality is widely accepted as the norm. But this
image ignores both the handful of extremely rich Americans and the tens
of millions of others who share only minimally in the national affluence.
In this chapter we describe this income discrepancy in greater detail and
indicate how our economic structure contributes to it. In addition, we
suggest ways in which gross inequality and poverty can be reduced.

THE AFFLUENT FEW

Those very few who, either through inheritance or personal effort, have
acquired great fortunes are able to live in a manner hardly comprehensible to those of lesser means. Consider Lundberg's description of the
residential pattern of the Rockefeller family:

A prime example . . . is the Rockefeller estate, *Kykuit,* of 4,180 acres. . . .
Such land in the region sells at $5 to $10 thousand per acre and higher. . . .
The place has many scores of buildings, for the maintenance and the housing
of a large staff, and includes a $1 million playhouse (at cost many years ago)
that holds bowling alleys, tennis courts, swimming pool and squash court.

[2] Lester C. Thurow and Robert Lucas, "The American distribution of income: A
structural problem." In Lee Rainwater, ed., *Social Problems and Public Policy:
Inequality and Justice.* Chicago: Aldine, 1974, p. 77.
[3] Franklin D. Roosevelt's Second Inaugural Address.

The Rockefeller brothers also have New York City residences. John III and his wife share a large duplex apartment on the upper East Side and in 1950 built a house for guests near fashionable Beekman Place. Nelson and his family occupy a triplex penthouse on Millionaire's Row of Fifth Avenue facing Central Park. . . .

Nelson owns a large ranch in the highlands of Venezuela on which he sojourns at intervals. Laurance has a plantation in Hawaii and Winthrop has a palatial working plantation in Arkansas.

When Rockefeller I died the *New York Times* (May 24, 1937) said the single granite house had cost $2 million to build, while the estate took $500,000 a year at Depression prices to maintain. The entire affair required a staff then of 350. Standard equipment throughout are elevators, air conditioning and just about anything in the way of appurtenances, comforts and conveniences one cares to name. The domicile of no potentate is any better equipped.[4]

Today there are about 155 American families worth $100 million, and 66 worth between that and $500 million.[5] These are the super-rich, and they can afford to live super-luxuriously. One such family flies flowers daily to its Florida mansion from its own New Jersey greenhouses. Another lives for part of the year in a 115-room mansion equipped with three secretaries, three chefs (one each for meats, pastries, and candy), and numerous others who are available to wait on them or their guests in three shifts around the clock.[6] A Christmas catalogue from a Houston department store typically offers the super-rich such gifts as ten private swimming lessons from Olympic champion Mark Spitz, at a cost of $115,000.[7] Olympic Tower, on New York's Fifth Avenue, has its own indoor block-long park, three-story waterfall, two floors of shops, and a private wine cellar and health club, among other amenities. A nine-room duplex with wood-burning fireplace and circular staircase, its own private elevator and sauna, costs $650,000 and a monthly maintenance of $946. Somewhat more modest is the one-bedroom suite sold for $122,000. Only 8 percent of the building's 230 apartments were financed; the remaining 92 percent were simply bought by check.[8]

The super-rich are super-consumers, and super-polluters as well. The 6 percent of the world's population that live in the United States consume about 34 percent of the world's energy, 29 percent of its steel, and 17 percent of its cut timber. Because of their disproportionately greater purchasing power, the super-rich undoubtedly account for an equivalently disproportionate consumption of these and other resources—and of the pollution that inevitably results from their production and utilization.

Affluence of the kind described above is not necessarily wrong in itself. Ease, pleasure, and beauty in life are indeed worthy and desirable goals. So much affluence, however, is far from being essential; the cost of only

[4] Ferdinand Lundberg, *The Rich and the Super-Rich*. New York: Bantam, 1968, pp. 849–851.
[5] Arthur Lewis, "The new rich of the seventies." *Fortune,* September 1973, p. 170.
[6] Ruth West, "The care and feeding of the very rich." *McCall's,* August 1969, p. 56.
[7] "Mail order Magi." *Time,* November 15, 1974, p. 99.
[8] Associated Press Dispatch.

one of the items previously mentioned would have fed, clothed, housed, and educated several poor families for an entire year. It is when super-affluence exists alongside the real, not to mention relative, deprivation suffered by a much larger group at the other end of the socioeconomic spectrum that it becomes excessive. Furthermore, as we shall see, the wealth of the super-affluent gives them undue influence in American society and, in addition, often has the effect of perpetuating the inequality that already exists.

THE RICH GET RICHER . . .

The federal income tax rate in the United States is a graduated one, ranging from zero percent for individuals making below about $5,000 annually to 70 percent for those making over $100,000 a year. This higher tax rate for upper income levels is justified largely for three reasons: the well-to-do get more out of the economic system, and thus can afford to pay more taxes; they have a greater investment in the economic system, and thus should pay more to keep it working; and, finally, redistributing at least some income from the rich to the poor is fair and just in a democratic society. Unfortunately, in actual practice the affluent do not pay their fair share of taxes. To them, the American system is an old and trusted friend: they are legally able to get more out of the economic system than they put in.

Skillful use of many provisions of the tax laws can entirely wipe out the nominally very high taxes owed by those in the upper income brackets. A 1976 Internal Revenue Service report, for example, found that there were many rich people who paid little or nothing to the government. Almost 250 people with annual incomes of over $200,000 paid no taxes at all. Included in this group were five people with annual incomes of over 1 million.[9] The fact is that although the tax rate for the highest tax bracket is 70 percent, individuals in this bracket pay, on the average, only about 42 percent of their income in taxes.[10]

Tax evasion? Not at all—at least not such as to draw any unwelcome attention from the Internal Revenue Service. It is simply that United States tax laws favor the rich, and an individual in the upper income brackets has many quite legal ways to shave his taxes. Best known of these is the capital gains tax, in which profits from the sale of investments are taxed at only one-half their true value. But there are any number of loopholes—fast depreciation on buildings and machinery, deductible expenses on farms and citrus groves, tax-free interest on state and municipal bonds, and deductions for gifts to charitable institutions (which may often be family foundations). In addition, the super-affluent can make tax-free investments that are not available to the less wealthy. State bonds, for example, are often sold in denominations of $1 million; income from them does not even have to be reported on tax returns.

It is true that the middle and upper-middle classes take advantage, whenever possible, of the same loopholes; but the benefit to the very rich is very much greater. For example, a $100 deduction reduces by about $70 the taxes of someone in the highest tax bracket, but only by about $14 the taxes of someone in the lowest bracket. If we look at the

[9] *New York Times,* May 6, 1976, p. 19.
[10] *U.S. News & World Report,* June 3, 1974, p. 49.

country as a whole, these differences become even more apparent. In 1974, for instance, the wealthiest 1.2 percent of all taxpayers received nearly one-fourth of the $58 billion in deductions, credits, and other tax-reducing advantages taken by all taxpayers, according to the Treasury Department. Another study found that in one year the country's 6 million poorest families received only about $90 million in tax credits; about 24 times that amount—over *$2 billion*—went to the richest 3,000 families, the super-affluent making over $1 million annually.[11] The graduated income tax is supposed to be a great equalizer; but the result of all the special provisions added over the years is increased inequality.

Federal income taxes have changed little over the years, while such levies as payroll and sales taxes have increased substantially. These levies are regressive, in that they disproportionately burden lower- and middle-income earners. For example, someone who earns $3,000 a year and who pays $60 in sales tax is being taxed at an effective rate of 2 percent for purchases alone; the same $60 sales tax represents a tax rate of .06 percent to someone with a $100,000 income. Furthermore, the effects of inflation and unemployment fall hardest on poorer families. As a consequence, upper-income people are actually paying proportionately less into the nation's coffers than they did 20 years ago, while lower- and middle-income people are now paying more.[12] To compound the inequality, the lower-bracket person's income, since it is almost certainly entirely derived from wages, has *already* been subject to withholding taxes, while the wealthier person's income is at least partially tax-exempt, since it is in all likelihood derived from a variety of sources, many of which are less highly taxed. As Upton and Lyons point out:

> The reality of the American capitalist system is that tax legislation, whatever its progressive intent or the country's need for revenue, is designed to protect and encourage private investment. Thus earned income (wages and salaries) which most families depend on, is subject to much higher effective tax rates than property income (dividends, interest, rent, etc.).[13]

At any time, available capital and assets are finite, and the fact that some people have more, means that other people will, inevitably, have less. It has been estimated that if the nation's wealth were evenly distributed, every adult would have a net worth of about $25,000. In fact, the super-rich 4.4 percent of the population have an average net worth of more than $200,000, while close to half the population have an average net worth of about $3,000 (see Table 6-1).[14]

What are the sources of this great wealth? A recent study found that

. . . AT THE EXPENSE OF THE POOR

[11] Brookings Institution study, in Philip M. Stern, "Uncle Sam's welfare program—for the rich." *New York Times Magazine,* April 16, 1972.

[12] Cambridge Institute Study of 1972, cited in John D. Rockefeller III, *The Second American Revolution.* New York: Harper & Row, 1973, p. 81.

[13] Letitia Upton and Nancy Lyons, *Basic Facts: Distribution of Personal Income and Wealth in the United States* (pamphlet). Cambridge, Mass.: The Cambridge Institute, 1972, p. 4.

[14] "The super-rich." *The Progressive,* August 1974, p. 41.

Position	Percent Total Income
Poorest fifth	5.5
Second fifth	11.9
Middle fifth	17.5
Fourth fifth	24.0
Highest fifth	41.1
Wealthiest 5 percent	15.5

Source: "Consumer income." *Current Population Reports*, Series P–60, No. 97, p. 43.

TABLE 6-1
Percentage of Total Income Received by Each Fifth and Top Five Percent of Families

1 percent of families and individuals with the largest incomes own *51 percent* of all corporate stock. The wealthiest 10 percent own 74 percent of all corporate stock.[15] The super-rich 4.4 percent possess not only an estimated 36 percent of the nation's entire wealth, but also 27 percent of all privately owned real estate, 40 percent of all noncorporate business assets, about 75 percent of all federal, state, and local bonds, and almost all corporate bonds and notes.[16] In contrast, the poorest 20 percent of Americans have about 5 percent of total national income and almost no assets.[17]

We have already mentioned that these proportions have remained essentially unchanged for many years. Whatever measure or standard is used, the implications are the same: the rich own more, earn more, and use more—much, much more—and they have been doing so for a long time. We shall see that this is largely because the competition for resources is unfairly and heavily weighted in favor of the already rich.

THE NATURE OF AFFLUENCE

Today wealth has largely accumulated in the hands of descendants of wealthy families. While there are still "self-made" individuals, opportunities for achieving wealth in this area of scarce resources are limited. The new fortunes are fewer, and of lesser magnitude, than the "old money." It takes many years, plus favorable conditions, to build a large fortune. For example, only a substantial amount of capital will produce an adequate return on investments. Barring a rare and unexpected windfall—building a very much better mousetrap, winning a state lottery, or writing a best seller—the lower- to middle-income person is not likely to have substantial sums available for really profitable investment. Thus the people who make money generally start out by having—that is, inheriting—money. Large fortunes accumulated with the aid of the

THE PERPETUATION OF WEALTH

[15] Marshall E. Blume, Jean Crockett, and Irwin Friend, "Stockownership in the United States: Characteristics and trends." *Survey of Current Business*. U.S. Department of Commerce, November 1974, p. 17.
[16] "The super-rich."
[17] See Thurow and Lucas.

For the well-off and the wealthy, the American economic system is a friend, and expensive consumption is the normal way of life.
Ken Heyman

income tax laws (which, as we have seen, protect capital in preference to salaried income) can be given, more or less undiminished, to one's children, aided by loopholes in the inheritance tax laws.

A quarter-century ago, it was noted that thirteen families, including the Du Ponts, Mellons, and Rockefellers, owned more than 8 percent of the stock of the 200 largest nonfinancial (i.e., nonbanking, non-insurance, non-investment) corporations. Half of the large shareholdings in those 200 corporations were directly owned; the rest were in the form of trusts, estates, and family holding companies. One family, or a few families, effectively controlled the voting stock in about 40 percent of these corporations, while these corporations in turn controlled half the remaining corporations. Thus, only 30 percent of the 200 largest nonfinancial corporations were not controlled by a small group. A more recent study suggests that this situation has not changed markedly. Lundberg states that one individual or a single family was in control of approximately 150 of the 500 biggest companies, while each of the other 350 companies was controlled by a small number of owners. The vast majority of these controlling assets were either inherited or purchased with funds obtained through inheritance. As Lundberg wryly notes, "The only dropouts from the upper strata of ownership have been produced by ending of a family line." [18]

Just how is an individual or family able to control a corporation even if it has a small portion of the stock? What is the impact of this type of control? The fact is that corporations are controlled by their investors—the stockholders—and those investors who own the largest blocks of stock have the most power in the corporation. Thus a person who owns only 5 percent of the corporation's stock but is the largest stockholder is, in effect, in control of the corporation; his or her real power is equal to the corporation's total value. A large corporation has a great influence on society—through the advertising it purchases in the media, through the institutions and foundations it supports, through its control of prices of the goods or services it offers, and so on. By and large, the power of the individuals who control the major corporations is not directed toward redistributing income fairly but toward increasing their own and their corporation's profits. (We will be discussing corporations in greater detail in the next major section of this chapter.)

Inequality is perpetuated and exacerbated, then, by several factors: the role of inheritance taxes in concentrating wealth in the hands of the already wealthy; the fact that investments, which can be a major source of income, generally require large sums of money to be profitable; the existence of tax laws that favor both investors and the rich (who are generally the same people); and the fact that rich people, as major investors, control corporations through which they exert enormous political and economic power.

WHO ARE THE AFFLUENT?

According to a census bureau study, fewer than 0.4 percent of all households are worth $500,000 or more. Of these, only 39 percent have no inherited assets.[19] One out of every thousand Americans, or 210,000 people, are millionaires.[20] As previously mentioned, about 153 men and women are worth $100 million or more. Hunt (oil), Mellon (banking), Du Pont (chemicals), Rockefeller (oil and banking), and Ford (automobiles) are among the family names (and "occupations") appearing more than once in the $200-million-and-up section of the list.

This pattern of family-oriented financial control was made possible only with the collaboration of the laws governing how fortunes are transmitted to the next generation. Inheritance taxes diminish somewhat the wealth passed on by the merely well-to-do, but through such devices as trusts and family foundations, the super-rich are able to keep and hand down large fortunes relatively intact. Thus the economic standing of children is likely to duplicate that of their parents; earning ability depends directly on inherited access to capital for investment.

The Wealthiest Class. It has been said that the rich are the least studied and least understood class in the United States.[21] Most rich people prefer

[18] Lundberg, pp. 211, 213, 292.
[19] Board of Governors, Federal Reserve System, *Survey of Financial Characteristics of Consumers.* Washington, D.C.: August 1966.
[20] *U.S. News & World Report,* February 25, 1974.
[21] See, for example, "Secrets of the very rich." *Newsweek,* October 7, 1974, p. 78.

to remain inaccessible, and are well able to hire various aides who deal with public responsibilities and guard their employer's privacy. An extreme case in point was Howard Hughes, who was ranked in the *Fortune* list as one of the nation's two billionaires (J. Paul Getty, another noted recluse, was the other), and who spent many millions of dollars on lawyers, private detectives, and guards in order to maintain total privacy.[22]

The wealthy are most likely to marry others of the same class. Such intermarriage occurs naturally, since they socialize together in exclusive neighborhoods and private clubs. One of the places they meet their peers is in private boarding schools, concentrated in the Northeast, especially New England. There is at least one exclusive private club in every major city, especially in the East, from Houston to Boston and from New York to Chicago. Other factors maintaining the exclusivity of the very rich are their interlocking social and business connections, and their similar religious background—usually Protestant. Jews and Catholics are less likely to be accepted in the schools, clubs, neighborhoods, and board rooms of the wealthiest people. For example, Jews comprise 3 percent of the population of the United States and 8 percent of its college-educated population, but less than .5% of the total executive personnel in leading American industrial companies.[23]

Corporation Executives. In 1975, the highest paid corporate officer in the United States was the chairman of the Rapid-American conglomerate, with an astonishing salary of $916,000 (a figure that does *not* include extras such as stock options). His weekly salary alone was greater than the annual salary of over 70 percent of our population. Other top executives also received more than adequate remunerations, though not only in outright wages. The chairman of ITT, for example, received a salary of over $400,000; an additional $360,000 in bonuses, director's fees, and deferred compensation raised his yearly earnings to over $700,000. In fact, the average annual earnings of the nation's thirty top corporate officers was over $500,000.[24]

Corporation executives often receive, in addition to very generous salaries, numerous perquisites or fringe benefits—profit-sharing plans and stock options, expense account dining and travel, hotels or the use of an apartment maintained by the company, taxis or transportation in a company car or airplane, life insurance, medical plans, and more. Most of these benefits are especially designed to provide additional, tax-exempt or tax-reduced compensation for key corporate officers. The expense accounts even of lower-echelon executives can easily add the equivalent of several hundred dollars a month, in lunches, cocktails, dinners, and taxis—tax-free to the executives as well as to their corporations. Over the years, only negligible changes have been made in the tax laws governing expense accounts; these chiefly require more thorough documentation of expenses. Though it may be inconvenient to jot down every tip and taxi fare, the benefits are still clearly worth it.

[22] James R. Phelan, "Howard Hughes, beyond the law." *New York Times Magazine,* September 14, 1975, p. 14.
[23] Lundberg, p. 363.
[24] *Business Week,* May 10, 1976.

AFFLUENCE AND CORPORATISM

It should be clear from the foregoing description of the affluent that wealth is concentrated in large corporations. We have already mentioned that the 1 percent of families with $50,000 or more in annual income own 51 percent of corporate stock. Similarly, corporate wealth is concentrated in a small number of very large companies. In one year, sales of the 500 largest industrial organizations amounted to $229.08 billion, nearly 42 percent of the gross national product; the 100 largest corporations accounted for 65 percent of that.[25] Approximately half of all (non-agricultural) manufacturing assets in the nation belong to about 150 corporations, while 500 own two-thirds of all assets. "But," as Berle puts it, "in terms of power, without regard to asset positions, not only do 500 corporations control two-thirds of the nonfarm economy but . . . a still smaller group has the ultimate decision-making power." [26]

Our capital gains tax laws and other laws that encourage investment by taxing its income at a lower rate have led to this situation. It is even possible for major corporations to pay no federal income taxes whatsoever; a congressional committee recently found that ten of the largest corporations paid no taxes, even though they had profits totalling $1 billion. Another twenty companies, with combined profits of 5.3 billion, paid federal income taxes at effective rates of from 1 to 10 percent.

Even when a company pays its full share of taxes (at a rate of 45 percent), the corporation itself really does not lose any of its profits. It is the consumer who ultimately pays all taxes—state or federal, property or income—for corporations, in the form of higher prices for whatever goods and services the corporation produces or supplies. Companies consider corporate taxes as just another business expense, and prices are raised to compensate for it. In effect, the consumer pays more, through multiple taxation, while the corporation and its wealthy minority of stockholders pay least.

THE CORPORATION-POLITICIAN CONNECTION

Adam Smith, a Scottish philosopher-economist in the 1700s, held that capitalism was self-perpetuating and, over a period of time, self-correcting, if governments did not intervene in the natural economic process. He protested against government policies that were advantageous to monopolies, and advocated what he called "natural liberty." But modern corporations have enormous economic and political power, wielded through campaign contributions and lobbyists. Corporate interests often conflict with the public good, and even with the will of the majority. "What's good for General Motors is good for America," stated an industrialist about to become a Cabinet member.[27] "The business of America is business," opined a laconic president.[28] Contributing to corporate advancement is clearly official policy.

[25] Lundberg, p. 296.

[26] A. A. Berle, "Economic power and the free society." In Andrew Hacker, ed., *The Corporation Take Over*. New York: Harper & Row, 1964, pp. 101–102.

[27] Charles E. Wilson, president of General Motors and nominated as secretary of defense, testifying before a Senate subcommittee, January 22, 1953.

[28] President Calvin Coolidge, Speech, January 17, 1925.

And contributing to politicians is corporate policy. Campaigning requires money, large sums of it, in this age of advertising, television, and public relations packaging. Money speaks with a loud and effective voice, especially when presented to those who might be in positions to legislate or make decisions favorable to corporate interests. Campaign contributions have often been illegal, as was demonstrated amid the welter of irregularities comprising the Watergate affair (and in previous campaigns as well), or merely injudicious. Large contributions by wealthy individuals, legal until the law limited such gifts, also significantly furthered corporate interests.[29]

Corporate interests are also advanced by high-priced lawyers and/or lobbyists whose business it is to convince legislators to act positively in regard to the concerns of their clients. The middle and lower classes have few advocates to speak for them in high places and to change corporate policies that affect the quality of their lives. Among them, Ralph Nader is a self-appointed consumer advocate; Common Cause is a grass-roots lobbying effort—and funding for both is scanty and comes mainly from small individual contributions.

While these tendencies have existed for more than a century, and are perhaps inevitable in an advanced industrial economy, the effects have become particularly obvious and onerous in the 1960s and 1970s. As Lundberg puts it,

First, the present concentration of wealth confers self-arrogated and defaulted political policy-making power at home and abroad in a grossly disproportionate degree on a small and not especially qualified mainly hereditary group; secondly, this group allocates vast economic resources in narrow, self-serving directions, both at home and abroad, rather than in socially and humanly needed public directions. . . . It can, and does, frustrate the government in various proceedings that have full public endorsement. . . . It can and does establish connections all over the world that covertly involve American power in all sorts of ways unknown, until some last-minute denouement, even to Congress and the President.[30]

Adam Smith and other classical economists believed that consumer demand would influence the output of manufacturers/producers—the "law of supply and demand"—and we tend to define the advantages of our capitalist system in terms such as "free enterprise" and "competition." But, in reality, huge corporations (which function on the same scale as many states or nations) and whole industries are themselves able to manipulate demand. Interlocking directorates (members of the board of directors of one company also serving on the board of another company), industry-wide agreements, and joint lobbying put effective decision-making power in the hands of a very limited number of individuals, who control the marketplace in ways that are anti–free enterprise. Through advertising or planned obsolescence, corporations are able to create a demand for unnecessary or unsafe products—a new-model automobile every year, cigarettes which are dangerous to health, and so on. Through industry-wide price-fixing agreements, cooperating corporations are able to maintain inflated prices, such as those charged for name-

[29] See Phelan.
[30] Lundberg, p. 29.

brand drugs. In addition, lobbyists maintained by the corporations hinder legislation that would encourage the production of cheaper and safer products. Corporations use these and other means to exert their influence, inflate costs to the consumer, keep some vital goods beyond the reach of the poor, and add enormously to corporate profits.

Since the end of World War II, the Pentagon has spent over $1 trillion on military preparedness and activities.[31] At any one time, there are at least 100,000 subcontractors working for the Defense Department, which confirms about 22,000 private contracts every year. In one recent year, production under these contracts cost $36 billion and involved 3 million employees.[32]

THE CORPORATE-MILITARY CONNECTION

The Pentagon is not, however, a particularly cost-efficient company: it is extraordinarily wasteful of time, people, money, and material. Cochran notes that

according to a 1972 Congressional analysis, since 1955 more than $4 billion was spent on twenty-eight systems that were junked before deployment, and some $19 billion on fifteen other systems abandoned after they had been deployed. A total of $40 billion was spent on thirteen major aircraft and missile programs but less than 40 percent of these yielded an acceptable electronic performance.[33]

As far as the military and its contracted corporations are concerned, the consequences of mismanagement and cost overruns on such a grand scale are minimal. The Pentagon pays the bills, increases its appropriations requests, and the Congress by and large acquiesces. More than a few contractors and subcontractors have been saved from bankruptcy—at a cost of $86 million from 1958 to 1973. Most recently a single company, the Lockheed Corporation, was rescued by an additional $250 million federal guarantee of its bank loans.[34] (Ironically, it was later revealed that Lockheed spent $22 million in bribes overseas.) The poor, in the meantime, remain unclothed, unfed, and unhoused.

Military Personnel in Private Industry. There is an intimate association between defense contractors and the Pentagon. Retired officers, who tend to leave the services at relatively early ages, are often hired by defense corporations. In the three years from 1972 to 1974, over 2,000 such recent retirees were hired by defense corporations. In some cases, the officer's advocacy of the interests of these corporations while still in the military led directly to the new job opportunity. In all cases, these officers were expected to use their government contacts to increase corporate military sales. It has been estimated that more than 5,000 former Pentagon officials are now employed in defense industries.[35]

[31] Milton Mankoff and Linda Majka, "Economic sources of American militarism." *Society,* May–June 1975, pp. 69–72.
[32] Richard F. Kaufman, *The War Profiteers.* New York: Bobbs-Merrill, 1970.
[33] Bert Cochran, "Is it the policy or the system?" *The Nation,* March 8, 1975, p. 279.
[34] See Kaufman; and Cochran.
[35] Michael D. Edwards, "Golden threads to the Pentagon." *The Nation,* March 15, 1975, pp. 306–308.

Contract Costs. Nearly 70 percent of the Pentagon's contracted purchases for $10,000 or more in one recent year—a total of $21.8 billion—went to the 100 biggest contractors, 68 of which were on the "Fortune 500" list of the nation's largest industrial corporations. Twenty-one of those 100 contractors were among *Fortune*'s top 25.[36] Small businesses, like poor people, get less—in this case, less than 20 percent of Defense Department contracts.[37]

Defense contracts are extremely lucrative, and account for almost all of the business of several corporations, including Lockheed Aircraft, United Aircraft, and General Dynamics. This last company, which specializes in aerospace production, had over $2 billion in Pentagon contracts in one year. Not all of this largess was attributable to the Vietnam War: in the five peacetime years from 1958 to 1963, the defense contract revenues of several corporations doubled.

Nor does inflation completely account for these increases. From 1945 to 1968, the Wholesale Price Index rose by 90 percent, while the cost of a machine gun went from $74 in 1946 to $579 in 1969—a jump of 700 percent. Other hardware costs reflect similar super-inflated increases. As Kaufman points out,

the higher prices are supposed to pay for higher-quality weapons, but they never seem to decline in quantity. The outstanding case is the aircraft carrier. We have had roughly fifteen attack carriers since World War II (when they cost $55 million apiece). Now they are being replaced by nuclear carriers at an enormous cost ($500 to $600 million) because, according to the Navy, the increased effectiveness is worth the price; yet the Navy still wants fifteen.[38]

Mankoff and Majka note that the "continued replacement of self-destructing arms, as well as the 'need' to improve existing weapons, assures a steady flow of business as long as war or the threat of it are ever-present." [39] In this way, maintaining an aggressive national posture inevitably becomes corporate, as well as Pentagon, policy.

Approximately 30 cents of every tax dollar is spent on and for military purposes. In 1976, about $90 billion was expended for national defense, and millions more went for other defense and/or military-related purposes (international affairs, space technology, veterans' benefits, and others). This excessive investment in expensive military hardware is a drain on resources that could otherwise be used to provide social services. Why, then, is not such a desirable transfer of resources taking place? More than a decade and a half ago, a retiring president, most of whose adult life had been spent in the military, warned "against the acquisition of unwarranted influence, whether sought or unsought, by the military-industrial complex. . . . The potential for the disastrous rise of misplaced power exists and will persist." [40] The "misplaced power" resides,

[36] See Mankoff and Majka.
[37] See Kaufman.
[38] See Kaufman.
[39] Mankoff and Majka, p. 70.
[40] Dwight D. Eisenhower, Farewell Address, January 17, 1961.

as we have seen, at the uppermost levels of corporate organization, maintained by the vested interests of the super-affluent.

THE SIGNIFICANCE OF AFFLUENCE AND POVERTY

The affluent live longer and better, can afford the best medical care in the world, the finest education, the very best materials and workmanship in all their possessions. Less publicly, by purchasing the usually un-acknowledged services of politicians, police officers, and other public officials to forward or defend their interests, they can buy social justice and influence government policy. This capacity for both conspicuous and inconspicuous consumption gives the extremely wealthy a potential power grossly out of proportion to their numbers in American society.

For the poor, on the other hand, the converse is true. America's poor seldom die of starvation, and they generally have more than the indigent in other, less developed nations. But they lead lives of serious deprivation by comparison not only with the wealthy, but with generally accepted middle-class standards. Poverty, as Bagdikian has pointed out,

is measured by the standards of a man's own community. If most of America is well-fed, the man who can't find three meals a day for his family is poor. If most of America has modern weather-proof housing, the man whose home is leaky and has no piped water is poor. If most of America has enough medical care to stay alive until age seventy, the man who can't afford to live beyond age fifty-five is poor.[41]

This relative deprivation has a profound effect on the style and quality of the lives of the poor. It extends beyond mere distribution of income, and includes inequality in education, health care, police protection, job opportunity, legal justice, housing, and many other areas (some of which are discussed in other chapters). The poor are more frequently subject to mental illness than are other Americans. They require more medical treatment and are subject to longer and more serious illnesses. Their children are more likely to die than are those of the more affluent, and their life expectancy is shorter than the national average. They are more likely to become criminals or juvenile delin-quents. Also, the poor contribute more than their share of illegitimacy, alcoholism, divorce, and violence to American society.

Not only do the poor have less money than the more affluent, but the money they have buys less. The poor must often purchase necessities as soon as they have cash—for example, with the arrival of their welfare checks; they cannot "shop around" for sales or bargains and are often victimized by shopkeepers who raise their prices on the day when the welfare checks are delivered. They seldom have enough money at one time to save by buying in bulk. When they buy on credit, the poor are subject to higher interest rates than others because they must take longer to pay and are considered poorer credit risks. Inflationary price rises affect the poor first, and more severely. The cost of essential consumer

[41] Ben Bagdikian, *In the Midst of Plenty*. New York: New American Library, p. 8.

Though America can be considered to be an affluent society, its affluence is not distributed equally. The contrast between the rich and the poor is often startling and severe.

goods, ranging from rice and sugar to toilet paper and soap, increases substantially, but the wages of the lowest paid or marginally employed persons, and various government income assistance stipends, rise slowly if at all.

Further, the poor cannot begin to approach the level of consumption portrayed as adequate by business and the advertising industry. The harmful effects of affluence-oriented advertising on the poor have been described by Herman Miller:

Far from being a symptom of affluence, the ownership of the automobile or the television set may be a cause of poverty because it is purchased in lieu of a good diet, medical care, education, or other goods that would yield a much greater return in terms of increasing productivity.[42]

These inequalities are a reflection of the ambivalent American attitude toward poverty: "On the one hand, we believe achievement is related primarily to self-reliance and self-help; on the other hand, we have been forced to concede that failure cannot always be laid at the door of the individual." [43] Those who, for one reason or another, must turn to public assistance are often pictured as lazy, lacking in character, or cheats. Their private lives are open to public view, and the procession of social workers and welfare investigators to their homes denies them their basic right of privacy. The poor who are on welfare cannot spend the money they receive as they see fit, but are treated "like children who have to account to parents for the wise use of their pocket money. . . . The very granting of relief, the very assignment of the person to the category of the poor, is forthcoming only at the price of a degradation of the person so assigned." [44]

The problems of the poor are further compounded by the attitudes of those whose economic position is not much better than their own. Recent statistics indicate that an income of about $12,000 is necessary for a decent living standard for a family of four. Almost half the families in America, including many white-collar as well as blue-collar workers, have incomes below this level, though above the level of poverty. This group has been the source of the greatest opposition to social welfare programs for the poor. Faced with an increasing tax burden, the rising cost of living, and a feeling that they have been overlooked by a government preoccupied with the less fortunate, people of the lower-middle class tend to view the poor in very negative terms.[45]

It is said that "money talks," and in America the voice of the rich is, if not always loud and clear, usually quite effective. Despite their numbers, the poor have remained largely silent, their lives constricted by their lack of means. The questions of how the poor are viewed by the more affluent, how they look at themselves, and how they might escape

[42] Herman Miller, "The dimensions of poverty." In Ben B. Seligman, ed., *Poverty as a Public Issue*. New York: Free Press, 1965, p. 27.
[43] Paul Jacobs, "America's schizophrenic view of the poor." In David Boroff, ed., *The State of the Nation*. Englewood Cliffs, N.J.: Prentice-Hall, 1965.
[44] Lewis A. Coser, "The sociology of poverty." *Social Problems* 13 (Fall 1965): 145, 146.
[45] Robert E. Lane, *Ideology: Why the American Common Man Believes What He Does*. Glencoe, Ill.: Free Press, 1962.

their predicament touch on the fundamental nature and purpose of the American system. It is hoped that these questions will be somewhat clarified by the information in the rest of this chapter.

THE NATURE OF POVERTY

Poverty is a deceptively simple term to define: For most people, poverty means not having enough money to buy the things considered necessary and desirable. Various more formal definitions have, however, been offered. Galbraith stresses the sense of degradation felt by the poor, and concludes that "people are poverty stricken when their income, even if adequate for survival, falls markedly behind that of the community." [46] Another study regards "minimum levels not only of income, assets, and basic services, but also of self-respect and opportunities for social mobility and participation in many forms of decision-making" [47] as important. Poverty, thus, may mean a condition of near starvation, bare subsistence (the minimum necessary to maintain life), or it may mean any standard of living measurably beneath the national average. To deal more effectively with poverty as a social problem, a generally agreed-upon, scientifically based, and more specific definition is needed.

Many experts have tried to determine a minimum income level, or poverty line, below which a family or individual could be officially termed poor. President Johnson's Council of Economic Advisers considered only cash income in its evaluations of what determines poverty. Others, such as the U.S. Bureau of the Census, excluded capital gains but included all other money income.

Miller and Roby [48] noted that these formulas entirely ignore several important areas, even excluding capital gains. Among them are non-income compensation or fringe benefits: free lunches, stock options, company-financed vacations, medical services, cars, subsidized education, and deferred compensation plans. Many more of these kinds of benefits are available to those at higher money-income levels, which tends to increase the contrast between the effective incomes of some groups of workers and the poor.

Unfortunately, to take account of all these factors would require figures which are unavailable, and therefore monetary income is used as the measure of poverty. Two basic approaches have been used: the fixed income line and the relative income line.

THE FIXED INCOME APPROACH

Earlier attempts to establish a dividing line between poverty and non-poverty were usually couched in terms of a specific cash income. Keyserling, for example, suggested a level of $4,000 for a family of four, which at that time qualified 23 percent of the population as poor. In addition, he regarded those with an income of between $4,000 and $6,000 as

[46] John Kenneth Galbraith, *The Affluent Society*. Boston: Houghton Mifflin, 1958, p. 323.

[47] S. M. Miller, Martin Rein, Pamela Roby, and Bertram M. Gross, "Poverty, inequality, and conflict." *Annals of the American Academy of Political and Social Science* (September 1967):18–52.

[48] Miller, Rein, Roby, and Gross, pp. 52–118.

"deprived." On this basis, the poor and the deprived together constituted 46 percent of the population.[49]

Oscar Ornati suggested distinguishing among various degrees of poverty: minimum subsistence, minimum adequacy, and minimum comfort. The income levels for these, for a family of four, he set at $2,500, $3,500, and $5,500, respectively.[50] A similar attempt was made by Herman Miller who, however, suggested that local welfare standards be used, so that poverty would be relative to the specific area or to local expectations.[51]

Because of the subjective manner in which poverty levels were being formulated, Mollie Orshansky of the Social Security Administration attempted to develop a more rigorous standard. She pointed out that the only acceptable measure of adequacy for the essentials of living is food. Standard criteria for acceptable nutrition have been established by the National Research Council, and the Department of Agriculture regularly prepares cost estimates on average food prices to achieve this nutritional minimum. Concluding that an average family spends one-third of its total income on food, Orshansky multiplied the food budget by 3 to arrive at a poverty income level. This standard placed a total of 34 million persons, or between 15 and 20 percent of the population, in an income position insufficient for simple nutritional needs.[52]

With 1963 as the base year, annual adjustments were made to take into consideration the cost of the items in the economy food budget. Because of growing differences between the rise in cost of the economy food budget and the greater rise of the overall cost of living, in 1969 the Social Security Administration definition was amended to reflect changes in the Consumer Price Index (CPI). Thus, in 1974 the poverty line, adjusted to reflect inflation and based on the CPI, was $5,038 for a nonfarm family of four. (Farm families are assigned a lower figure because it is assumed they supply some of their own food.) According to Bureau of Census figures for that year, 24.3 million people—1.3 million more than the previous year—or 12 percent of the nation's population, were poor.

THE RELATIVE INCOME APPROACH

A prime defect of the fixed income approach is that it ignores the phenomenon of relative poverty, the comparative deprivation of one category of people when measured against another. Fuchs therefore proposed that any family be classified as poor if its income were less than half of the median family income.[53] The poverty line in 1974, by this definition, was $6,420, which meant that about 20 percent of the population would be considered as poor.

[49] Leon Keyserling et al., *Poverty and Deprivation in the United States.* Conference on Economic Progress. Washington, D.C.: U.S. Government Printing Office, 1962, pp. 19ff.

[50] Oscar Ornati, *Poverty Amid Affluence.* New York: Twentieth Century Fund, 1966, p. 13.

[51] Herman P. Miller, *Rich Man, Poor Man.* New York: Crowell, 1964, p. 81.

[52] Mollie Orshansky, "Consumption, work and poverty." In Seligman, *Poverty as a Public Issue,* p. 62.

[53] Victor Fuchs, "Toward a theory of poverty." *The Concept of Poverty.* Task Force on Economic Growth and Opportunity. Washington, D.C.: U.S. Chamber of Commerce, 1956.

Contrary to the Orshansky formula or any arbitrary income standard, the use of such a relative standard implied that poverty could not be eliminated as long as income distribution remained unequal. And, in fact, the number of poor in America has tended to remain stable when measured by the Fuchs formula, while it has decreased measurably by the absolute standard of fixed income.

Fuchs recognized the shortcomings of his proposal. He admitted that using one-half rather than another fraction of median income as the measure of poverty was somewhat arbitrary. However, he contended that this liability was compensated for by the fact that his standard was politically neutral and not subject to manipulation by special interest groups. Further, he believed that it could keep pace with changing contemporary standards, whereas fixed minimum budgets are soon out of date; and that it constituted a first step toward a national policy with regard to income distribution.

No universally accepted definition of poverty has yet been formulated. Interested groups have utilized the most convenient or appropriate formula, usually either the "official" fixed income definition or one of the other types we have discussed.

WHO ARE THE POOR?

THE ELDERLY POOR

Sometimes referred to as the "poorest of the poor," the elderly account for about 15 percent of all poor people. While the median income for those between 18 and 64 is over $12,000, the median income for the elderly is slightly over $5,000.[54] Thus more than one-half of all elderly householders are either poor or bordering on poverty. Some relevant statistics concerning the elderly poor are:

1. Over 3 million elderly persons (16 percent of the aged) and their dependents are officially classified as poor. About 60 percent of the aged poor are women.[55]
2. About one-fifth of all poor families—close to a million families—are 65 years of age or older.
3. Twenty-three percent of the elderly earn less than $3,000 a year. An additional 42 percent earn between $3,000 and $7,000 annually.[56]
4. Close to 8 percent of the aged poor families, and over 10 percent of unrelated aged individuals, require welfare to support themselves.[57]

The lack of employment is a special problem for the elderly. Only about 15 percent of persons 65 years of age or older are presently work-

[54] U.S. Bureau of the Census, "Social and economic characteristics of the older population." *Current Population Reports,* Series P-23, no. 57. Washington, D.C.: U.S. Government Printing Office, 1975.
[55] U.S. Bureau of the Census, "Characteristics of the low-income population." *Current Population Reports,* Series P-60, no. 98. Washington, D.C.: U.S. Government Printing Office, 1975.
[56] *The Myth and Reality of Aging in America.* The National Council on Aging, Washington, D.C., 1975.
[57] "Characteristics of the low-income population," p. 7.

ing, and compulsory retirement rules thrust many out of the labor force unwillingly while they are still capable of productive work. Because employment is not considered a solution to the poverty problem for this group, few programs are offered to assist them in finding work. Many who have been accustomed to working all their lives wish to continue doing so, but are prevented by ill health and discrimination against older workers. They are thus compelled to live on Social Security, savings, pensions, and other means, the total of which is often insufficient for an adequate standard of living. In particular, although Social Security retirement benefits make up the greatest source of income for elderly persons, only a little over one-half of the elderly receive these payments, and a large number of this group receive only the minimum benefit provided. Widows are particularly vulnerable, since they receive less than the full amount of the husband's benefits. (We will be discussing these and other problems of the aged in Chapter 9.)

POVERTY AND FAMILY STRUCTURE

At the present time, over 45 percent of all poor families are headed by women. This segment of the poor is of especially vital concern because it is growing rapidly and because of the number of children in these families who are exposed to the circumstances of poverty (see Figure 6-2):

1. Among poor white families, the proportion of female-headed families increased from 21 to 37 percent in the period between 1970 and 1973.
2. Among poor black families, the proportion of female-headed families increased from 33 to 69 percent during the same period.
3. Fifty-five percent of all poor children live in female-headed households.
4. Thirty-five percent of female-headed households live in poverty, compared to only 5.5 percent of male-headed households that live in poverty.[58]

Primarily because of the need to care for their children, female heads of families are severely restricted as to employment. Child care is either unavailable or expensive, and typically the jobs available pay too little to make the effort worthwhile. Consequently, over 60 percent of female heads of households do not even seek employment.[59] In addition, as Cox notes, "Less than 10 percent of all U.S. female family heads, and only about 25 percent of those [women] who are employed at all, hold a full-time, year-round job." [60] (As we shall discuss further in Chapter 8, there are many hurdles standing in the way of equal employment for women of every class.)

Thus, for many female family heads, public assistance is literally necessary for survival. Some women require this help up until the time

[58] "Characteristics of the low-income population," pp. 4, 5, 95, 97; see also *The Poor in 1970*, Office of Economic Opportunity, Washington, D.C.: U.S. Government Printing Office, 1970.
[59] *Manpower Report of the President*. Washington, D.C.: U.S. Government Printing Office, 1975.
[60] Steven R. Cox, "Why eradicating urban poverty requires a long-term multi-program 'war.'" *American Journal of Economics and Sociology* 34 (1975):249–265.

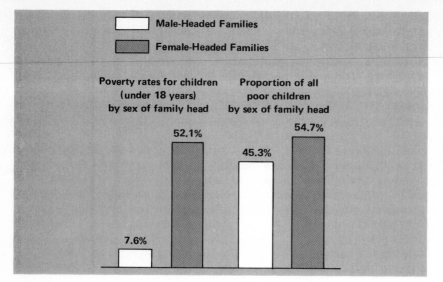

FIGURE 6-2
Childhood Poverty as
Related to the Sex
of Family Head

Source: U.S. Bureau of
the Census, "Consumer In-
come." *Current Population
Reports,* Series P-60, no.
98. Washington, D.C.: U.S.
Government Printing Office,
1975, p. 3.

their children are old enough to attend school. Others, lacking skills or education, are forced to depend on relief as a way of life. Although a large number of welfare mothers would like to work, however, the lack of facilities for job training and child care confronts them with a twofold obstacle.

In addition to the large number of female-headed households, the number of children living in poverty is an important factor to consider in relation to poverty and family structure. Some 9.5 million children live in poverty. This represents 14 percent of all children in America. The contrast between these children of poverty and other youth has been pointed out by Seligman:

Little progress has been made in more than three decades—and this is a long time. Caloric and nutritive deficiencies in their diet are serious enough to make poor children doze off in school, look fatigued, or suck their thumbs; it is difficult to pay attention when one is hungry. Poor children receive . . . less medical attention than those from more prosperous families; they are hospitalized less often and stay longer when they are admitted; and most poor children never get to see a dentist. And it is clear that poor children are much less likely to receive psychiatric attention for emotional disturbances than those from upper-income groups. The consequence is a tendency to equate emotional upset with a lack of intelligence, and this works to weaken the educational opportunities of poor kids.[61]

A program designed to assist both of these categories is Aid to Families with Dependent Children (AFDC), but the payments are so low that most families receiving aid still live in poverty and in fact fall further behind an acceptable standard of living each year. Three-fourths of the mothers in AFDC families are not high school graduates, and have few

[61] Ben B. Seligman, *Permanent Poverty.* Chicago: Quadrangle, 1968, p. 88.

work skills and little experience; even if employed, they would not be able to earn enough to lift them out of the poverty grouping.[62]

It should be noted that whites make up the largest group among welfare families. Proportionally, however, blacks and other racial minorities are overrepresented among the poor. For example, 31 percent of the black population and 22 percent of the population that are of Spanish origin have incomes below the established poverty level, compared with only about 8.5 percent of the white population.[63] Furthermore, according to one study,[64] black families own less than 1 percent of the equity in American farms and business enterprises.

Overall, the median income of whites is almost twice that of blacks. Only 17 percent of all black family heads, and a little over 40 percent of all employed blacks, work at full-time, year-round jobs. Several factors are considered responsible for the lower earning power of blacks and other minority workers. They are likely to be less well educated, for example—the high school dropout rate for blacks is about 44 percent, as opposed to 25 percent for whites. Among blacks, only 3 percent have attended college, and 83 percent have not graduated from high school.[65] Racial discrimination still closes employment opportunities to minorities. Even among college graduates, blacks earn only 80 percent as much as whites; and blacks and whites do not receive equal pay for similar work requiring the same experience and education. The higher percentage of female-headed families among blacks is another factor, which we have already considered.

The discrimination to which blacks, Chicanos, Puerto Ricans, and other minorities are subject in matters of housing, education, and health care both exacerbates the effects and increases the likelihood of lower income. In housing, minority members are often forced to choose from a smaller supply, pay higher rents, and live in dilapidated or deteriorating dwellings. In education, the quality of predominantly minority schools is often inferior to that of predominantly white schools. Concerning health care:

There may be public facilities for poor Negroes in the cities, but they serve to humiliate rather than heal. . . . Clinics may be downtown, in neighborhoods inaccessible to a poor mother. If she is working . . . a trip means lost wages. There are long embarrassing waiting periods to see several clinic bureaucrats before she gets to see the doctor, who most likely has never looked at her before nor will see her after that visit. The medical records are likely to have been mislaid, without which no diagnosis will be made or treatment prescribed. The poor are easily discouraged and then labeled as "careless" about their health or unwilling to "cooperate." [66]

[62] *Growing Up Poor*. U.S. Department of HEW, Office of Research, Demonstrations, and Training. Washington, D.C.: U.S. Government Printing Office, 1969, p. 20.
[63] "Characteristics of the low-income population," p. 2.
[64] Henry S. Terrel, in "The wealth accumulation of white and black families." Printed as part of the Proceedings of the American Economic Association, May 1971.
[65] Cox, pp. 255–256.
[66] Seligman, *Permanent Poverty*, pp. 48–49.

POVERTY AND MINORITIES

In these and other areas, the disparity between black and white opportunity and treatment is both evident and disturbing. (See Chapter 7 for a more comprehensive discussion of these problems.)

Although urban poverty is probably best known today, almost half of all poor people live in rural areas or metropolitan suburbs. This is true despite the fact that only 29 percent of the total American population live in rural areas. Rural poverty is not as visible as urban poverty. Separated from the mainstream of urban life, it has remained largely hidden on farms, on reservations, in open country, and in small towns and villages.

Unemployment is far above the national average in rural areas, particularly in Appalachia, the Ozarks, and certain Great Lakes regions. Jobs are scarce and most work is seasonal. The technological revolution in agriculture and other occupations has left poorly educated, unskilled rural workers without means of support.

The majority of rural poor are white, but a very high percentage of Southern blacks, Indians, and Mexican-Americans live in poverty. The general situation has been described by the President's Commission on Rural Poverty:

Hunger, even among children, does exist among the rural poor, as a group of physicians discovered recently in a visit to the rural South. They found Negro children not getting enough food to sustain life, and so disease-ridden as to be beyond cure. Malnutrition is even more widespread. The evidence appears in bad diets and in diseases which often are a product of bad diets.

Disease and premature death are startingly high among the rural poor. Infant mortality, for instance, is far higher among rural poor than among the least privileged group in urban areas. Chronic diseases also are common among both young and old. And medical and dental care is conspicuously absent.[67]

Further, the commission found the quality of education to be so inferior that 3 million rural adults are classified as illiterate. It also found that one in every thirteen rural houses is unfit for habitation.

The rural poor are the migratory workers, following the harvest, living in tar paper shacks, with few possessions and less hope. They are the Indians on reservations, leading lives of destitution and regimentation, their decisions made for them by faraway bureaucrats, their children sent to federal boarding schools. They are out-of-work coal miners. They are the small farmers and farm workers who cannot compete with modern, automated production techniques. Attempting to escape poverty, many of the rural poor migrate to urban areas, where they too often discover that the problems of the countryside are only magnified in the big cities, and that their shacks have been replaced by tenements and slums.

In the cities, the lack of money is aggravated by higher living costs, overcrowded and inadequate housing, bad nutrition, insufficient medical care, unsanitary health conditions, and the other major problems which beset both the recently arrived and the entrenched urban poor. The hoped-for jobs prove unobtainable. Much of the demand for unskilled

[67] President's Advisory Commission on Rural Poverty, "The people left behind." *Employment Service Review* (April 1968):17–19, p. 18.

Migrant farm workers such as these generally live in poverty, because their work is seasonal and their wages are extremely low. Often children must work as well, in order for the family to maintain itself on even a subsistence level.
Steve Shapiro/Black Star

labor has evaporated in the wake of expanding technology. As more and more businesses move to the suburbs, transportation to work becomes either unavailable or too expensive for the poor. More often than not, rural immigrants join their urban fellows on the welfare rolls.

Poverty also varies according to region. In the United States, the greatest geographical concentration of the poor is in the South; about 45 percent of all poor families, or 10 million poor persons, live in the Southern states.[68] Because the South is the most rural area of the country,

[68] "Characteristics of the low-income population."

it possesses the most prominent rural problems—low educational achievement, seasonal employment, low salaries, and few opportunities for unskilled workers—and these account in large part for the region's high percentage of poor people.

As the foregoing factors indicate, some people appear to be more vulnerable to poverty than others. As Michael Harrington puts it, the poor made the simple mistake of

being born to the wrong parents, in the wrong section of the country, in the wrong industry, or in the wrong racial or ethnic group. Once that mistake has been made, they could have been paragons of will and morality, but most of them would never even have had a chance to get out of the other America.[69]

CONCOMITANTS OF POVERTY

"Poverty," said George Bernard Shaw, "does not produce unhappiness; it produces degradation." Most Americans take for granted a decent standard of living—especially in regard to access to good health care, decent education and housing, and fair treatment under the law. We will examine the inequalities of treatment accorded to the poor in each of these areas, and the resulting degradation in the quality of their lives.

Compared with the rest of us, the poor are less healthy by almost every measure of health (see Table 6-2). For example, mortality rates for poor infants are almost double those of the affluent, and poor women are four times as likely to die in childbirth.[70] They are also more than five times as likely to give birth in a municipal hospital or on the ward of a voluntary hospital.[71] Ill-housed, ill-fed, and ill-clothed, the poor can expect to be ill more often with acute and chronic disorders—and to receive less adequate treatment for them. The poor visit doctors relatively infrequently, compared to the more affluent, and are admitted to the hospital less often; but when they need hospitalization, it is more likely to be for several times a year and for longer periods. Until recently they were less likely to have insurance for hospitalizations or surgery and consequently less likely to have elective surgery.[72] Little wonder that the life span of the poor is up to six years shorter, on the average, than the life span of the more affluent.

Discrimination against the poor is not limited to physical ailments.

HEALTH CARE

[69] Michael Harrington, *The Other America: Poverty in the United States.* Baltimore: Penguin, 1963, p. 21.
[70] Robert L. Eichhorn and Edward G. Ludwig, "Poverty and health." In Hanna H. Meissner, ed., *Poverty in the Affluent Society.* New York: Harper & Row, 1973, p. 173.
[71] Frederick S. Jaffe, "Family planning and poverty." In Meissner, ed., p. 195.
[72] Eichhorn and Ludwig, pp. 174, 175, 177; see also *Social Indicators 1973,* Office of Management and Budget, Washington, D.C.: U.S. Government Printing Office, 1973, p. 41.

Age	Family Income					
	Under $3,000	$3,000–$4,999	$5,000–$6,999	$7,000–$9,999	$10,000–$14,999	$15,000 and over
Under 17 years	2.6	2.0	1.4	1.5	1.2	1.1
17 to 44 years	10.8	7.9	5.4	4.2	3.7	3.1
45 to 64 years	43.7	25.1	18.7	14.3	10.1	7.1
65 years and over	45.7	41.0	32.9	34.8	29.7	30.5

Source: Executive Office of the President, *Social Indicators, 1973*. Washington, D.C.: U.S. Government Printing Office, 1973, p. 38.

TABLE 6-2
Percentage of Persons Limited in Major Activity because of Chronic Conditions, by Age and Family Income

There is a greater proportion of diagnosed psychosis among the poor, and they are more likely than the middle class to be institutionalized and receive shock treatment or chemotherapy—temporary relief of symptoms —in place of psychotherapy. Even if they go to clinics for psychiatric treatment, elements of the system itself—long waiting periods, selection of "motivated" patients, endless paper work, lack of empathy due to cultural differences on the part of the therapists—combine to remove the poor from individualized treatment.[73]

Not only do the poor have unequal access to health services, and receive less adequate treatment, but there is evidence that they often view sickness and health differently from those who are better off. The poor are less likely to identify symptoms for a variety of physical and mental illnesses, causing significant delay in seeking treatment. When they do get to a doctor, treatment may be cursory because the physician, aware of financial distress, is less likely to prescribe extensive diagnosis, hospitalization, or surgery, and even less likely to suggest that the patient stay away from work until completely recovered.[74]

Since the inception of Medicare and Medicaid in 1965, the poor have had somewhat better access to various medical resources.[75] But there are problems with almost all insurance programs: coverage is often inadequate, beginning only after a specified "deductible" expense level has been reached; and many people are not aware of what their insurance covers. The poor, accustomed to have their medical needs attended to in a clinical situation, continue to go there even though Medicaid would cover private health services.[76] And clinical attention, by a team or changing cast of practitioners, is inevitably less individual and less thorough than private care. Many doctors will not treat Medicaid patients; others have treated them so "thoroughly" that they have abused the program at an outrageous cost.

[73] William Ryan, *Blaming the Victim*. New York: Random House, 1971, pp. 145, 158.
[74] Eichhorn and Ludwig, pp. 178–180.
[75] Gregory L. Weiss and Robert L. Eichhorn, "Medical care programs for the poor." In Meissner, ed., pp. 271–272.
[76] Emil Berkanovic and Leo G. Reeder, "Ethnic, economic, and social psychological factors in the source of medical care." *Social Problems* 21 (1973):246, 249.

Other federal programs have established health care centers in impoverished communities. But these are still not adequate to solve the health care problems of the poor. Because most such programs allocate federal funds to match those provided by a state, county, or city, the frequent result is that these programs are underfunded precisely where they are the most needed: those localities with high proportions of poor residents are hard pressed to be able to afford these as well as all other necessary services.[77] Furthermore, each program and agency has different requirements, deadlines, and purposes, resulting in a mass of regulations, red tape, traveling about, and interminable waiting periods before services are obtained.[78] Finally, these programs do little to solve the large health problems of the poor, who are victims of malnutrition, air pollution, poor education, higher rates of venereal and other diseases, inadequate housing, inadequate sanitation, inadequate rodent control, and even inadequate clothing, as well as less satisfactory medical treatment.[79] (See Chapter 2.)

When it comes to education, the poor get less than the nonpoor in every respect. Their children are in school for fewer years, have only about a 50-50 chance of graduating from high school, and are much less likely than the children of the better-off to go on to college. They are likely to be taught in overcrowded classrooms, and to receive little if any individual attention. Also, inner city schools often have a disproportionate number of inexperienced teachers.[80] Most teachers, even if experienced, are of middle-class origin, have had little or no training in working with disadvantaged children, and bring to their jobs preconceived and pejorative notions that such children will read, speak, test, and behave poorly, and that their parents and home life do not encourage academic achievement. It is not surprising, then, that these expectations are converted into self-fulfilling prophecy: One study showed that in the early grades, there was virtually no difference in reading performance between white and black children, but that differences appeared, increasing significantly and dramatically, from the fifth grade on, after four or five years of schooling.[81] For reasons such as these, one prominent black educator has charged that "American public schools have become significant instruments in the blocking of economic mobility and in the intensification of class distinctions." [82]

Perhaps the ultimate tragedy of the inferior education the poor receive is that it perpetuates the cycle of poverty. In general, the less educated in our society receive less income and status and have greater difficulty in improving their economic condition. What is worse, children of parents with less than a high school education generally do not do as well in

EDUCATION

---

[77] Eichhorn and Ludwig, p. 176.

[78] Weiss and Eichhorn, p. 277.

[79] Pete Isaacson, "Poverty and health." *The New Republic,* December 14, 1974, pp. 15–17.

[80] Paul Lauter and Florence Howe, *The Conspiracy of the Young.* New York: New American Library, 1970.

[81] Coleman Report. In Ryan, p. 44.

[82] Kenneth Clark, in Lauter and Howe.

TABLE 6-3
Households Living in
Substandard Units,
by Income

Family Income	Number (thousands)	Percent
Total households	4,740	7.4
Less than $2,000	1,491	23.8
$2,000 to $2,999	656	15.8
$3,000 to $3,999	514	12.5
$4,000 to $4,999	419	12.3
$5,000 to $5,999	363	9.1
$6,000 to $6,999	299	7.1
$7,000 to $9,999	559	4.5
$10,000 to $11,999	308	2.1
$15,000 and over	101	0.9

Source: *Social Indicators, 1973,* p. 208.

school as children whose parents completed high school. Thus the cycle in which poverty and education are inextricably linked is perpetuated from generation to generation.

HOUSING

The poor are more likely than those better off to live in substandard housing—overcrowded, vermin-infested, in need of major repairs, lacking basic plumbing facilities, and inadequately heated. In the United States, almost 75 percent of substandard housing is occupied by the poor. Some 3 million families with incomes under $5,000 occupy such housing (see Table 6-3), more than half of which is in rural areas.[83]

The poor also live in cities, however, and particularly in "urban ghettoes" or the "inner city." Poor people in the city have been described as "block dwellers," unable to command automobile and other forms of transportation to get about and utilize the city's resources.[84] The urban poor, and especially the black and Hispanic urban poor, are isolated and segregated economically as well as racially.

Racial segregation increases as middle- and upper-income families move out of the city, and the mainly white lower-income families who can afford to move into the newly vacated residences. Along with losing their more prosperous citizens, cities lose businesses, and consequently their tax base, leaving their poor residents with fewer employment opportunities and with less adequate services from increasingly hard-pressed city governments. Such suburban zoning requirements as minimum lot size are designed to attract newcomers who will add more to tax rolls than they require in services. Restrictions on multiple-dwelling structures have the same purpose. The effect is to prevent low-income housing from being erected in such communities, and to keep low-income and minority families in the central city. As Ryan points out, tax credits available to homeowners amount to a substantial government subsidy to the nonpoor, and hasten the exodus of the middle and upper classes from the city.[85]

[83] *Social Indicators 1973.*
[84] Alvin L. Schoor, "Housing policies and poverty." In Meissner, ed., pp. 151–152.
[85] Ryan, pp. 182–183.

Rehabilitation of existing structures has been advocated as one solution to the housing problem, through which the poor "block dweller" need not be uprooted from familiar surroundings. But the cost of rehabilitating antiquated structures in deteriorating neighborhoods is too high, and the potential return on investment is too low, to appeal to private builders. Because poor families cannot afford rentals or purchase prices that would be profitable to owners and builders, there is a serious problem of how to encourage private industry to provide low-income housing. In fact, costs have risen to such an extent in the last decade that not even middle-income metropolitan area housing is an attractive investment. Each year, there is an additional deficit of hundreds of thousands of housing units for the poor.

Urban renewal, another solution that was attempted, is the rehabilitation of a neighborhood by razing and replacing dilapidated structures. But under such programs the displaced poor, and especially poor blacks, have simply been moved from one slum to another.[86] In one study of urban renewal in 26 cities where little or no relocation assistance was provided, 70 percent of displaced families entered substandard housing in the same neighborhood; in 15 cities that provided relocation aid, about a third of the families nevertheless ended up in substandard housing.[87] Another survey found that from 1949 through fiscal 1967, as many as 383,000 existing housing units were demolished—to be replaced by only 107,000 new and 75,000 rehabilitated housing units. This was a net loss of about one-half. Furthermore, although blacks constituted less than a third of the population in the cities being studied, 60 percent of the families displaced by urban renewal were black.[88] (It is small wonder that urban renewal has often been referred to as "Negro removal.") Whatever the intent of these programs, the result has been the same: the poor have been left to dwell in the very worst housing.

JUSTICE

By definition, justice should be even-handed—but in practice it is not. As we have described in Chapter 4, poor people are more likely than members of the middle and upper classes to be arrested, indicted, convicted, imprisoned, and given longer sentences for the same offense. Conversely, they are less likely to receive probation, parole, or suspended sentences. Also, poor adolescents are more likely than their more affluent counterparts to be labeled as juvenile delinquents. Well-to-do youngsters who commit crimes are likely to be sent to a psychiatrist and left in their parents' custody; poor youngsters, on the other hand, are likely to be sent to a correctional institution.[89]

The crimes poor people are likely to commit, because of their position in society—property theft and assault—tend to be those most disapproved of by the middle and upper classes, who make the laws. These personal crimes tend also to be the most visible and widely publicized.

[86] Joseph Epstein, "The row over urban renewal." *Harper's*, 1965.
[87] Schoor, p. 154.
[88] U.S. Department of HEW, *Toward a Social Report*. Washington, D.C.: U.S. Government Printing Office, 1969; see also Morton J. Schusshein, "Housing in perspective." *The Public Interest*, Spring 1970, pp. 27–34.
[89] See Ryan.

The middle and upper classes tend to commit so-called "white-collar" crimes—embezzlement, price-fixing, tax evasion, bribery, and so on. Though crimes such as these involve much more money than street or property thefts, and may even pose a greater threat to our social institutions, they tend not to be regarded as serious by our criminal justice system. Furthermore, white-collar crimes rarely become visible.

Even if arrested, prosperous citizens are more likely than poor citizens to be able to post bail, be aware of their rights, be skillfully defended, and receive a brief sentence. But the indigent defendant, unable to post bond, may be retained in jail for as long as several months. One plan to reduce the number of those held without bail was the Manhattan Bail Project, under which defendants considered good risks were paroled on their own recognizance. However, the rigid and unrealistic criteria used to determine who were good risks eliminated the most impoverished from consideration.[90]

Under the law, every accused person has the right to be represented by counsel. In some cities, counties, and states, public defenders are provided. But there are many large cities and thirty-four states without defender services, and in federal courts there are neither paid defenders nor funds to compensate court-appointed counsel, who serve voluntarily. Where public defenders and court-appointed lawyers are provided, they are usually not the most skillful, nor have they financial resources or time for extended investigation.[91]

Inadequate defense, then, is another of several reasons why the poor are more likely to be convicted and, if so, to receive more severe sentences than those who are better off. And those who have been arrested and convicted are likely to be sentenced to a jail that is overcrowded, where only a very small proportion of inmates can be given the kind of help that could truly rehabilitate them. Released, they are stigmatized, unlikely to be able to get and hold a job. They often return to impoverished urban ghettoes where the hopelessness of improving conditions in the community increases their chances of becoming involved once again with the inequities of the judicial system.

EXPLANATIONS OF POVERTY

Explanations of the causes and nature of poverty are plentiful. Two approaches have predominated: the cultural and the situational. The proponents of the first hold that a "culture of poverty" arises after periods of extended economic deprivation. To achieve goals within this depressed state, new norms, values, and aspirations are developed. These eventually become independent of the situations which gave rise to them, so that eliminating the problem does not eliminate the behavior developed to deal with it. The result is a self-sustaining system of values and behavior which is handed down from generation to generation.

[90] Junius L. Allison, "Poverty and the administration of justice in the criminal courts." In Meissner, ed., p. 167.
[91] Allison, in Meissner, pp. 169–171.

The situational approach interprets the behavior of the poor as an adaptation to their environment. Patterns of behavior develop as a response to problems associated with low income and the accompanying economic and social deprivation. The poor are forced to forego middle-class values and aspirations because these do not apply to their circumstances. Children react similarly because they must make the same adjustments to these problems as their parents did.

Oscar Lewis is one of the chief proponents of the cultural explanation.[92] His view, based on studies in several ethnic cultures, is that poverty is a subculture of society, transcending regional differences and showing "remarkable cross-national similarities in family structure, interpersonal relations, time orientation, value systems, and spending patterns." According to Lewis, the roots of this culture form in societies where certain conditions exist, such as:

THE CULTURAL EXPLANATION

1. a cash economy, wage labor, and production for profit;
2. a persistently high rate of unemployment and underemployment for unskilled labor, and low wages for those employed;
3. the failure to provide social, political, and economic organization, either on a voluntary basis or by government imposition for the low-income population;
4. the existence in the dominant class of a set of values that stresses the accumulation of wealth and property, and that explains low economic status as a result of personal inadequacy or inferiority.[93]

The culture of poverty is thus an "adaptation and a reaction of the poor to their marginal position in a class-stratified, highly individuated capitalistic society." Through this need to cope, the poor develop a "design for living" or a set of solutions to their problems, which tends to be passed down from generation to generation.

With regard to the relationship between this poverty subculture and society as a whole, Lewis holds that a "crucial characteristic" of the subculture is "the lack of effective participation and integration of the poor in the major institutions of the larger society." The poor pawn their goods, borrow from local moneylenders, use secondhand clothing and household items, do not join labor unions or political parties, make little use of banks, hospitals, or museums, hate the police, mistrust politicians, and have a low level of literacy and education. Thus deprived of leverage in the larger society, the poor have a low potential for protest.

Within the poor community itself, Lewis cites as typical "poor housing conditions, crowding, gregariousness, but above all a minimum of organization beyond the level of the nuclear family." This low level of organization contrasts sharply with the highly organized character of middle-class society. However, when a slum population is stable and ethnically homogeneous, there may be a certain sense of local community, often similar to that of a village. Even without this, there may be a sense of territoriality, a setting-off of slum neighborhoods from the city without.

[92] Oscar Lewis, *The Study of Slum Cultures—Backgrounds for La Vida*. New York: Random House, 1968.
[93] Oscar Lewis, *La Vida: A Puerto Rican Family in the Culture of Poverty—San Juan and New York*. New York: Random House, 1966.

The family in the poverty subculture is often female-centered and rather authoritarian. There is an absence of sheltering and protection in childhood, with a general lack of privacy and an early sexual initiation. Competition among siblings for limited goods and maternal affection tends to counteract a strong verbal emphasis on family solidarity.

Individuals in this culture are apt to have strong feelings of marginality, helplessness, dependence, and inferiority; they frequently have a weak ego structure, a lack of impulse control, and a strong present-time orientation which makes it difficult for them to plan or save for the future. A sense of resignation and fatalism is common.

These characteristics, Lewis holds, tend to develop in any poverty culture, and are found in both rural and urban locations throughout the world. They enable the poor to cope with the special strains of their condition, but at the same time prevent their escape from that condition. The only way the poor can eliminate the culture of poverty, according to Lewis, is to strive for organizational unity. Only by achieving solidarity within a larger group can they transcend their psychological and social traits.

Charles A. Valentine is one of the main critics of the Lewis explanation.[94] In his view, many of the "class-distinctive traits" do not indicate cultural patterns at all. Instead, Valentine contends, "many of these features seem more likely externally imposed conditions or unavoidable matters of situational expediency, rather than cultural creations internal to the subsociety in question."

THE SITUATIONAL APPROACH

Valentine divides Lewis's list of poverty-culture traits into three categories. The first of these he calls "gross indicators or correlates of poverty": unemployment, underemployment, unskilled work, low-status jobs, meager wages, crowded and deteriorated housing, and lack of education. Valentine regards these as "conditions or symptoms" of poverty, rather than as ingrained patterns of social response:

Lack of work, lack of income, and the rest pose conditions to which the poor must adapt through whatever sociocultural resources they control. That is, these conditions are phenomena of the environment in which the lower class lives, determined not so much by behaviors and values of the poor as by the structure of the total social system.

"Behavioral patterns and relationships," the second category of traits, include lack of sheltered childhood, authoritarianism, and lack of community organization. Rather than a "distinctive subcultural pattern," Valentine sees these traits as indicating a definite lack of a patterned existence, and concludes that it is uncertain whether they are "sanctioned and perpetuated by subcultural values and beliefs that are communicated through socialization" or whether they stem from "motivations that are consistent with the value orientations common to the total culture but capable of only distorted or incomplete expression within the limits of a poverty environment."

"Values and attitudes," Valentine's third set of traits, include hostility toward institutions of the dominant society, negative feelings about one's

[94] Charles A. Valentine, *Culture and Poverty: Critique and Counterproposals.* Chicago: University of Chicago Press, 1968, pp. 114–120.

place in society, and low levels of expectation and aspiration. With regard to these, Valentine writes: "All these orientations are so strikingly consistent with objective situational facts that it seems hardly necessary to interpret them as ingrained subcultural values. Indeed, for modern Western people these would seem to be almost the inevitable emotional responses to the actual conditions of poverty."

Valentine concludes that Lewis's list of traits does not add up to a separate subsystem of values for the poor. He outlines his own point of view with regard to the relationship between poverty, culture, and society in the following model, which takes a markedly activist view of how poverty and its associated cultural manifestations can be altered:

Heterogeneous Subsociety with Variable, Adaptive Subcultures

a. The lower-class poor possess some distinct subcultural patterns, *even though they also subscribe to norms of the middle class* or the total system in some of the same areas of life and are quite nondistinctive in other areas; there is variation in each of these dimensions from one ethnic group to another.

b. The distinctive patterns of the poverty subcultures, like those of earlier subsocieties, include not only pathogenic traits *but also healthy and positive aspects,* elements of creative adaptation to conditions of deprivation.

c. The structural position and subcultural patterns of the poor stem from historical and contemporary sources that vary from one ethnic or regional group to another but generally involve a *multicausal combination of factors.* . . .

d. *Innovation serving the interests of the lower class to an optimal degree will therefore require more or less simultaneous, mutually reinforcing changes in three areas:* increases in the resources actually available to the poor; alterations of the total social structure; and changes in some subcultural patterns.

e. The most likely source for these changes is one or more *social movements for cultural revitalization,* drawing original strength necessarily from the poor, but succeeding only if the whole society is affected directly or indirectly.[95]

Herbert J. Gans is critical of both the cultural and the situational approaches.[96] He finds the situational explanation, the idea that people respond to the situations and opportunities available to them and alter their behavior accordingly, too simplistic. He rejects the implication that people are "automatons," all reacting in the same manner to a common stimulus. On the contrary, he stresses the heterogeneous character of the poor:

Some have been poor for generations, others are poor only periodically; some are downwardly mobile; others are upwardly mobile. Many share middle-class values, others embrace working-class values; some have become so used to the defense mechanisms they have learned for coping with

THE CULTURAL-SITUATIONAL APPROACH

[95] Valentine, pp. 142–144.
[96] Herbert J. Gans, *People and Plans: Essays on Urban Problems and Solutions.* New York: Basic Books, 1968, pp. 321–346.

deprivation that they have difficulty in adapting to new opportunities; and some are beset by physical and emotional illness, poverty having created pathologies that now block the ability to adapt to nonpathological situations.

Gans also rejects the cultural approach, with its implication that people react to change in terms of prior behavior patterns and values and accept only those changes which comply with their culture. He criticizes the idea that culture is "holistic," that no element in it can be changed unless the entire culture is altered.

Gans's position is that people's behavior results from a combination of cultural and situational influences:

Behavior results initially from the adaptation to the existential situation. Much of that behavior is no more than a situational response that exists only because of the situation and changes with a change in the situation. Other behavior patterns become behavioral norms that are internalized and are then held with varying degrees of intensity and persistence. If they persist with a change in situation, they may then be considered patterns of behavioral culture, and such norms may become causes of behavior. Other norms can encourage change. In addition, adaptation to a situation is affected by aspirations, which also exist in various degrees of intensity and persistence, and form an aspirational culture. Culture, then, is that mix of behavioral norms and aspirations that causes behavior, maintains present behavior, or encourages future behavior, independently of situational incentives and restraints.

Gans maintains that the ultimate solution to poverty lies in the discovery of what restraints poor people are subject to in reacting to new opportunities, and how the poor can be encouraged to adapt to these new opportunities even when they conflict with their present cultural values. He believes that we must examine the kinds of change needed in our economic system, status order, and power structure, and in the norms and aspirations of the affluent majority which permit a poor underclass to exist.

Lee Rainwater, one of the outstanding sociologists working in the area of poverty, offers another explanation.[97] While he acknowledges the existence of a lower-class pattern of behavior and belief, he characterizes it differently from other theorists. According to Rainwater, conventional society has somehow managed to impose its norms on the lower class despite the fact that the members of this class cannot achieve these norms. Lower-class culture therefore contains some elements unique to its group and shares others with the larger culture. Thus the distinctive lower-class subculture has only "limited functional autonomy."

Rainwater describes three different concepts of lower-class culture. The first is that "the lower class are basically ordinary Americans who happen to be caught in an unfavorable situation for achieving their common American desires." If provided with the means, such as job training and education, lower-class citizens would be able to escape poverty and

THE ADAPTATION APPROACH

[97] Lee Rainwater, "The problem of lower-class culture and poverty-war strategy." In Daniel P. Moynihan, ed., *On Understanding Poverty*. New York: Basic Books, 1969, pp. 229–259.

become a part of regular society. Rainwater rejects this view, on the grounds that "lower-class adaptations to the actual situation of deprivation exist and interfere with the means program by making them unattractive, meaningless or distrusted."

Another concept of lower-class culture is that it possesses "distinctive . . . subcultural values, techniques for coping with the world and personality characteristics that go along with these." This implies that cultural and personality change are intrinsic to any solution to the poverty problem. Such a solution might be achieved by interrupting the intergenerational transmission of lower-class culture. However, if culture is an adaption to one's situation and if each generation is forced to adapt similarly to the same circumstances, then change will occur only when there is a change in situation.

Rainwater argues that policy should be based on a third concept, that "lower-class culture is an adaptation not to an absolute deprivation of living below some minimum standard, but to the relative deprivation of being so far removed from the average American standard that the lower-class individual cannot feel himself part of his society." Rather than "opportunity" or "culture change" strategies, Rainwater advocates "resource equalization strategy"; that is, supplying the poor with resources sufficient to eliminate this relative deprivation and to ensure that "there is no class of people below the 'average man' in terms of prestige, income or other advantages."

THE VALUE-STRETCH CONCEPT

Proponents of the culture of poverty explanation attribute to the poor a value system characterized by a lack of desire to participate in the institutions of the larger society, and acceptance of behavior considered antisocial by the more favored classes. Critics argue that the behavioral differences between the classes are not values but coping mechanisms by which the poor adjust to the realities preventing them from conforming to more socially desirable behavior. Hyman Rodman [98] agrees that all classes share the general values of society, but claims that the lower class has an additional set of values representing realistic levels of attainment. He does not hold that the lower class rejects majority values, or that they simply desire less; rather, he holds that for the lower class two sets of values exist simultaneously, in a hierarchy in which the more desirable, those values shared with the overall society, are in fact the least attainable. He therefore argues that the lower class has a wider range of values than the other classes, and he calls this the "lower class value stretch." He describes how this double-value system works:

Lower-class persons . . . do not maintain a strong commitment to middle class values that they cannot attain, and they do not continue to respond to others in a rewarding or punishing way simply on the basis of whether these others are living up to the middle class values. A change takes place. They come to tolerate and eventually to evaluate favorably certain deviations from the middle-class values. In this way they need not be continually frustrated by their failure to live up to unattainable values. The resultant is a stretched value system.

[98] Hyman Rodman, "The lower class value stretch." *Social Forces* 42 (December 1963):205–215.

Della Fave [99] introduces the terms *preference,* the ideal of preferred value; *expectation,* the level that a person expects to be able to achieve; and *tolerance,* the least a person will accept or settle for. He notes that the value-stretch mechanism is set in motion when the *reconciliation gap* between preference and expectation becomes too great. "The values of the poor do resemble those of the middle class, but only in terms of . . . preference. [They] differ most . . . in terms of expectation and tolerance." As a result of realistic adaptation to reality, say both Rodman and Della Fave, the poor expect less and are satisfied with less.

EMPLOYMENT, UNEMPLOYMENT, AND WELFARE

As we noted earlier, there is a notion among many people that the poor are largely to blame for their poverty. The general argument is as follows: "The poor class consists of unemployed people who are responsible for their condition because they will not work. If they could be persuaded to accept the value of working for a living, or if they were forced to take jobs, poverty could then be eliminated. What we have now is a group of 'freeloaders' who are getting by on welfare." The inaccuracy of this argument becomes evident when one examines the data relating to poverty, work, and welfare.

A study based on the latest available census data [100] reveals some interesting facts about the poor and unemployment. According to these figures, the composition of the poor is as follows:

WORK AND THE POOR

Children under age 14	32.8%
Elderly, 65 and over	14.6
Ill and disabled, 14–64	5.5
In school, 14–64	8.0
Total	60.9%

This means that over 60 percent of the poor are essentially unable to seek or to hold employment because of their age, state of health, or educational commitments. Of the remaining 39.1 percent:

Did not work, age 14–64	13.2%
Worked, age 14–64	25.9

Therefore, only about 13 percent of the poor could have been employed but were not. A breakdown of this group by sex is even more revealing:

Male unemployed	1.0%
Female unemployed	12.0

[99] L. Richard Della Fave, "The culture of poverty revisited: A strategy for research." *Social Problems* 21 (1974):609–621.
[100] "Characteristics of the low-income population." Figures are approximations.

Of the high proportion of women in this group, the vast majority are involuntarily out of the labor force by virtue of having small children to care for. This leaves only a tiny proportion of poor who might have secured employment but did not. This total does not compare unfavorably with the over 10 percent of the nonpoor who did not work or go to school and were not ill, aged, or disabled.

If so great a percentage of the poor are employed, what accounts for their continued poverty? Low-paying jobs and underemployment are primarily responsible. For example, almost 25 percent of the employed poor work full-time, yet still receive an income below the poverty line. The highly publicized and lucrative contracts obtained by labor unions in certain industries have obscured the plight of many other workers.[101] In addition, certain industries and groups of workers are not covered by minimum wage laws.

Of the poor who work, about three-fourths are employed in less than full-time, year-round positions. Many, particularly the unskilled, suffer because of seasonal layoffs, bankruptcies, and automation and cutbacks in certain industries. Economic recessions and depressions also contribute to unemployment. By the end of 1976, for example, the official unemployment rate was about 8 percent (involving well over 7 million people) —and official statistics generally account for only two-thirds of those actually unemployed. (See Chapter 12.) Even official statistics, however, indicate that unemployment hits some groups harder than others. The black unemployment rate of 13.5 percent, for instance, is twice the white unemployment rate. And one study has shown that each 1 percent increase in national unemployment means a 4 percent increase in unemployment among low-income groups.[102]

Of the portion of the unemployed poor who do not seek employment, most will not because they are convinced that they will not find any work. Among the possible reasons for this attitude are the belief that employers will consider them too old or too young; lack of skills, education, training, or experience; racial discrimination; language difficulties; and inadequate pay.

THE POOR ON WELFARE

As was pointed out earlier, the welfare poor have been the victims of a number of misconceptions. Among the most common are:

1. Welfare families are loaded with kids—and have more children just to get more money.
2. Most welfare families are black.
3. Why work, when you can live it up on welfare?
4. Give them more money and they'll spend it on drink and big cars.
5. Most welfare children are illegitimate.
6. Once on welfare, always on welfare.
7. Welfare people are cheats.
8. Welfare's just a dole, a money handout.
9. The welfare rolls are full of able-bodied loafers.[103]

[101] Gus Tyler, "Marginal industries, low wages, and higher risks." *Dissent,* Summer 1961.
[102] "Inflation and inequality." *New York Times,* October 13, 1975, p. 39.
[103] *Welfare Myths vs. Facts* (pamphlet), U.S. Department of Health, Education, and Welfare. Washington, D.C.: U.S. Government Printing Office, 1972.

The facts, however, contradict these widely held misconceptions about the welfare poor. In corresponding order, HEW found that:

1. Over half—54.2 percent—of welfare families have either one or two children. The usual payment for an additional child is $35 a month, an amount insufficient to cover the cost of rearing another child.

2. Whites comprise the largest racial group among welfare families, with 48.3 percent of the total. Blacks represent 43.3 percent. American Indians, Orientals, and other racial minorities make up the remaining 8.4 percent.

3. Payments for basic needs to a welfare family of four with no other income vary from a low of $197 per month in Mississippi to a high of $463 per month in Alaska. Welfare payments in all but three states, excluding payments for special needs, are below the established poverty level.

4. Most welfare families say that if they received any extra money, it would be used for essentials. Among welfare mothers, almost half would spend the money on extra food.

5. Of the more than 7 million children in welfare families, 68.8 percent are legitimate. Only in recent years has the government made family planning services available to welfare families.

6. Half the families on welfare have been receiving assistance for 20 months or less, and two-thirds for less than 3 years.

7. Only about 5.6 percent of welfare families are found to be ineligible, and less than one-half of 1 percent of welfare cases are referred for prosecution for fraud. Most errors involve honest mistakes by state and local welfare agencies or by recipients. (Conversely, studies have found that in many areas over half of those eligible for welfare do not receive it.[104])

8. Most welfare families are provided with other social services in addition to financial aid. Among these are health care advice and referrals (including Medicaid), counseling on financial and home management, employment counseling, and services to improve housing conditions and to enable children to continue in school.

9. Less than 1 percent of welfare recipients are able-bodied unemployed males. These men are required by law to sign up for work or work training in order to remain eligible for benefits. The largest group of working-age adults on welfare are 2.5 million mothers, most of them heads of families.[105]

But perhaps most pernicious of all is the myth that the poor do not share the "work ethic" of the middle class—that the poor are "lazy" or "shiftless" and would much rather be on welfare than work. Many studies have shown that the poor share strongly the work ethic of our society and in fact often feel unhappy about the fact that they are on welfare. As Goodwin notes, there are "no differences between poor and unpoor when it comes to life goals and wanting to work"; the differences are that the poor lack confidence in their ability to succeed and accept

---

[104] In Patrick Moran and Patricia Lee Austin, "The social bases of the welfare stigma." *Social Problems* 21 (1974):648.
[105] Moran and Austin; see also Subcommittee on Fiscal Policy, Joint Economic Committee, Congress of the United States, *Income Security for Americans.* Washington, D.C.: U.S. Government Printing Office, 1974.

welfare as a necessity due to chronic un- or underemployment.[106] Despite all evidence, these "welfare myths" are still widely accepted in America and have constituted a major obstacle to attempts to improve the present welfare system.

SOCIAL ACTION

The need for government to intervene in the basic economic life of Americans first became apparent in the 1930s with the unemployment and financial distress of the Great Depression. Since that time, many new types of economic programs have been developed, and more were proposed. Yet, despite programs designed to ensure adequate income or to supply the means to achieve this goal, poverty continues, and, as we saw earlier, at about the same rate as forty years ago. Before examining some of the new proposals which sociologists and economists have advanced to alleviate or eradicate poverty, it would be useful to review the programs currently in existence.

Current government programs can be divided into four basic categories: human resource development, social insurance, cash income support programs, and programs providing income-in-kind. Human resource development programs are geared toward increasing the employability of the poor by raising their educational and skill levels; they include both formal educational programs in classroom settings and on-the-job training programs. One of these is the Job Corps, a residential program which provides remedial education, training in job skills, and guidance and counseling to persons between the ages of 14 and 21. Another is the Neighborhood Youth Corps, which provides part-time work for youths in school during the school year and in the summer, consisting largely of work around the school. There is also an out-of-school program for high school dropouts, with work generally in hospitals, parks, and other public institutions.

Social insurance programs are intended to provide compensation for loss of income, regardless of income level or need. Through unemployment insurance, for example, cash benefits are paid to insured workers who are involuntarily unemployed for short periods. Workmen's compensation programs provide wage replacements to insured workers who suffer occupational injuries. Veterans' compensation plans issue benefits to disabled veterans to compensate for their loss of earning potential. Social Security payments to the elderly also fall within this category.

Cash income support programs are provided for unemployable persons, those not covered by any form of social insurance, and those with special needs. There are direct subsidies to families and individuals, such as the various kinds of public assistance, or "welfare"—aid to the blind, old-age assistance, aid to families with dependent children (AFDC), and aid to the permanently and totally disabled. These are specifically aimed at the poor. Veterans' pensions also fall within the area of cash income support programs.

[106] Leonard Goodwin, *Do the Poor Want Work?* Washington, D.C.: The Brookings Institution, 1972; see also Charles Davidson and Charles M. Goetz, "Are the poor different?" *Social Problems* 22 (1974):229; and Moran and Austin.

Income-in-kind programs provide goods and services for the poor in such areas as food, housing, and medical care. These include public housing programs and urban renewal; health programs such as Medicare and Medicaid (see Chapter 2); and food programs, such as the commodity distribution program, which distributes surplus farm products to poor households, and the food stamp program, which in effect provides discounts on food purchases.

Although the major economic and social disruptions of the Depression are today only a memory, the less drastic but nonetheless real economic problems of the 1970s—inflation, stagnating productive output, and high rates of unemployment in all sectors of the economy—are still very much with us. Government programs, some of which have been expanded to deal with current problems, have proved insufficient to free the poor from their poverty. In general, these programs fail to deal directly with the problem, do not help all of those in need, and do not aid in restoring dignity and incentive to the poor. A more equal distribution of wealth would seem to be the basic necessity, and several plans have been proposed for achieving this. They can be divided into two general types: plans for employment and economic growth, and income maintenance programs.

EMPLOYMENT AND ECONOMIC GROWTH

The mid-1970s were a period of generally high unemployment in America. During these years, the nation's productive capacity outran private and public consumption of goods, as lack of income resulted in a curtailment of spending. Presumably, if spending could be increased, it would stimulate greater business activity and a consequent job increase. A number of suggestions for accomplishing this goal were offered, all of them requiring governmental participation: stimulating the private sector, extending economic legislation, and providing public employment.

Stimulating the Private Economy. Tax cuts have been proposed, and periodically attempted, as a means of putting more money into the hands of the public. Presumably, this would bring about an increase in public spending; and if, at the same time, the level of government spending were maintained, the expected result would be more production, more jobs, and more income. An adjunct proposal was for tax cuts for corporations; by allowing corporations to keep a larger portion of their profits, it was hoped to encourage industrial expansion and investment, again resulting in more jobs, more consumer income, and more spending.

Lowering interest rates was also considered. Expanding the supply of credit might encourage industry to borrow in order to build, expand, modernize, or develop, and thus increase production. This would then lead to increased employment.

Garth L. Mangum has suggested still another method by which the government might stimulate employment for low-income groups.[107] He suggests that reluctance to hire less qualified workers be counteracted by reimbursing employers for a portion of the workers' salaries. Such a government subsidy of the unskilled worker would reduce what Mangum calls the "worker's competitive disadvantage," the gap between his or her

[107] Garth L. Mangum, "Guaranteeing employment opportunities." In Robert Theobald, ed., *Social Policies for America in the Seventies: Nine Divergent Views.* Garden City, N.Y.: Doubleday, 1969, pp. 47–50.

potential earnings on the open market and his or her desired income. This money would be considered a reimbursement to employers for training costs.

Extending Economic Legislation. Over 1 million persons are employed in occupations not regulated by the minimum wage law. If this coverage were expanded to include a greater number of workers, such as some agricultural workers and laborers, a significant increase in income, and therefore in purchasing power, would be gained by a portion of the population presently unable to secure subsistence wages.

New jobs might also be created as a result of the trend toward a shorter work week, especially if this were combined with an increase in the rate of overtime compensation. This would make it less costly for employers to hire additional employees than for them to extend the hours of their present work force.

Government as Employer. In addition to manipulating the private sector to create employment situations, the government itself might serve as the "employer of last resort," providing permanent employment in new or expanded social services or temporary jobs in major projects of shorter duration. This proposal has several advantages. It would reduce the number of people on welfare; it would provide training and experience which would ultimately qualify its participants for private employment; and it might offer a psychological incentive, by giving people the chance to earn a living rather than rely indefinitely on public assistance.

Government programs such as welfare, Social Security, and old-age assistance are intended to provide a redistribution of income to the poor. However, as we have already indicated, these programs are marred by inadequacies and injustices. It has been charged that some of these programs are a response to threats of civic disorder, and that others restrict aid so that unskilled workers are virtually required to take extremely low-paying jobs.[108] Further, the various income maintenance programs are a patchwork of requirements, standards, and benefits that differ from state to state, and, due to their diversity, they often work at cross-purposes to each other and to the results they ostensibly aim to achieve. In addition, the details of these programs are spelled out in so many regulations and directives that many potential recipients are unaware of their rights or are hindered from claiming them by red tape and bureaucratic attitudes. In some maintenance programs, benefits are reduced as outside income increases. Because many of the needy qualify for benefits under more than one program—food stamps and AFDC, for example—they may receive more in benefits than they could earn at work (especially since earnings would be subject to taxes and work expenses). Finally, the AFDC program, which has the largest share of state and federal welfare budgets, actually encourages the breaking-up of families, because families can get a higher income with the husband absent than if he is at home and working in a low-paying job.

INCOME MAINTENANCE PROGRAMS

[108] Frances Fox Piven and Richard A. Cloward, *Regulating the Poor: The Functions of Public Welfare.* New York: Pantheon, 1971.

Robert A. Levine has suggested ways in which an income maintenance program might correct the deficiencies of the present system:

1. It should from the very beginning provide a decent level of support for all recipients in all parts of the country.

2. Need alone, rather than "deservedness," should be the requirement for eligibility. Such need should be defined simply in terms of income of the family unit in need and should be based on a simple affidavit of family income. Enforcement would be by simple spot-check, as it is in the federal income tax system, rather than by detailed, dehumanizing investigation.

3. In order to preserve the incentive to work and get off the welfare rolls, the recipients should be allowed to retain a large portion of income maintenance payments as their earnings increase, up to some break-even level.

4. In order to preserve the incentive for a family to stay together, payments should be made on the same basis to intact families as to broken families. They should be made to families with employed as well as unemployed male heads.

5. The income maintenance system should be uncoupled from the services provided by social workers. Family receipt of such services should be voluntary and should not be a condition of eligibility for income maintenance.

6. The application of the system as well as its basic rules should be national and not determined by states or localities.[109]

Although many recommendations for reform have been made along these lines, one specific proposal has received widespread support. This is the negative income tax. While the mechanics of its implementation have not yet been resolved, its merits make it worthy of discussion here.

The negative income tax involves the use of the income tax system as a method of equalizing the distribution of income. Families earning less than a designated minimum would receive payments, or "negative taxes," to bring their incomes up to the minimum level. Families at the minimum level would receive no benefits, and families earning more than the minimum would be taxed, as is now the case. Thus the surplus of the more fortunate would be redistributed to compensate the poor.

To maintain the incentive to work under this plan, negative tax payments would not be decreased as fast as earned income rose. That is, if a worker's annual income increased by $1,000, his or her negative tax payment might be cut by, say, $500. Thus the worker would still have a total income of $500 more than if he or she had not worked.

The negative income tax plan has several important advantages. It would give support to the needy in the most useful form of dollar income, and would guarantee a respectable level of support to all people. Since it would apply to all needy persons, it might allow consolidation of the various specialized programs now in existence. It would shift a greater portion of the costs of the system to the federal government. Also, it would provide an incentive for workers to increase their earnings.

[109] Robert A. Levine, *The Poor Ye Need Not Have With You: Lessons from the War on Poverty.* Cambridge, Mass.: M.I.T. Press, 1970, pp. 201–202.

The plan has its opponents, however. It has been criticized as not providing for temporal or regional variations in the cost of living, and for not allowing for the special needs of certain families. Nevertheless, it is one attractive alternative to current programs.

PROSPECTS

It is clear that eradicating poverty in our society would involve not only income supports for the poor but a moderate restructuring of our economic system to achieve greater equality in income distribution. In Lee Rainwater's words, "Many of the social problems associated with poverty would not be more than moderately reduced" [110] if the poor were simply raised to a minimum acceptable standard of living. The poor must also be given the means by which to break out of the self-perpetuating cycle of poverty. A national health insurance program to assure adequate health care delivery to the less affluent, a public housing program that provides adequate living quarters for those who need them, a system of education that allows people to fulfill their capabilities, a job training program that teaches useful skills, an end to discrimination in housing and justice—these are the programs which, in addition to income support, would help to alleviate the poverty in our society.

Unfortunately, the condition of the poor is likely to remain the same, at least for the immediate future, since there is no indication that funds for the necessary programs are about to be provided. The lower and middle classes are already overtaxed; and the affluent are unlikely to give up their advantages willingly. Tax loopholes will not be closed, corporate power will not be lessened, and military spending will not be reduced so long as those in power reflect the interests of those who are wealthy. As Bartlett stated,

The greater the concentration of wealth held by any agent, the greater the political power. Gigantic corporations not only possess excessive control over their markets, but they also possess excessive control over government decisions. The same applies to extremely wealthy individuals. . . . In either the political or the market operations of a society . . . the wishes of the agents with the greatest wealth will carry the greatest weight. It is not a new "conspiracy" that makes it so. It is merely the action of self-interested rational men. [111]

How, then, is economic reform to be effected? Ultimately, the poor must organize themselves into a potent political force. Traditionally, this has been difficult for them to do: feeling that they have little stake in the system, the poor have generally taken a small part in politics. In addition, conflicts, particularly along racial lines, have divided them, weakening their political impact. The creation of the National Welfare Rights Organization (NWRO) in the late 1960s was therefore a necessary step

[110] Lee Rainwater, "Poverty in the United States." *Social Problems and Public Policy,* p. 74; see also Herbert Gans, "More equality: Income and taxes." *Society,* January–February 1974, pp. 62–69.
[111] Randall Bartlett, *Economic Foundations of Political Power.* New York: Macmillan, 1973, p. 156.

in the right direction. This organization has effectively lobbied to improve the poor's access to public aid. However, further organizational efforts must be made by the poor if they are to become effective on a larger scale. As Gunnar Myrdal put it, "No privileged class in history has ever climbed down from its privileges and opened its monopolies out of good will. I believe very much in idealism. But it plays its role only when there is pressure from below." [112]

In the absence of a rethinking of national goals and a greater commitment to domestic rather than military spending, progress in equalizing income in our society will be slow and incremental, partially determined by the ability of the poor themselves to organize and make their demands heard. The poor, then, are likely to remain with us for a while, expected to be content with little more than crumbs from the abundant national table. They continue to serve as living reminders of the gap between the rhetoric and reality of the American experience.

Though equality and affluence are believed by many Americans to be integral parts of our society, the fact is that poverty and gross inequities in income distribution are widespread. Affluence does exist in America, but it has been concentrated in the hands of relatively few, often at the expense of those less fortunate.

SUMMARY

Affluence—and inequality—have been maintained by tax laws that permit large fortunes to be passed down from one generation to the next and that subject earned income to much higher effective tax rates than investment income. In addition, the control of many corporations by rich investors gives those investors economic and political power far out of proportion to their actual number.

As great personal wealth is concentrated in the hands of a few individuals, so great corporate wealth is concentrated in a few large corporations. The power of these corporations is further concentrated in the hands of a few major stockholders. The enormous funds available to those who control corporations enable them to further their own interests by making campaign contributions to politicians, hiring lawyers and lobbyists to influence legislation, purchasing huge amounts of advertising, and engaging in price-fixing and other anti–free enterprise activities.

Mismanagement and cost overruns by the Pentagon, and by the companies contracted to it, are often subsidized at the expense of the taxpayer. The intimate connection between the Pentagon and major corporations is indicated by the fact that more than 5,000 former Pentagon officials work in defense industries and that defense contracts account for a large share of corporate business. The large-scale investment in weapons systems—encouraged by vested corporate and military interests—diverts needed resources from social services.

The poor are deprived not only by the standards of the affluent but by middle-class standards. They pay a larger portion of their limited income for essentials and are further subjected to the social stigma of poverty. Experts differ as to the definition of poverty: some use the *fixed income approach*, which sets a fixed annual income as the poverty line; others use the *relative*

[112] Interview appearing in *Boston Globe,* May 26, 1968.

income approach, which measures poverty as a fraction of median income to take into account the relative deprivation of the poor.

Some factors associated with poverty are advanced age, female-headed households, membership in a minority group, and rural residence. Compared to the more fortunate, the poor die earlier, and are more likely to be ill and receive inadequate treatment. The education they receive is often of inferior quality, which has the effect of perpetuating the cycle of poverty. They are more likely to live in substandard housing; in urban areas, they are likely to be segregated economically and socially. The poor are also more likely to be arrested, poorly defended, convicted, and given long sentences for the same crime than the more affluent.

Several explanations of poverty have been offered. The *cultural explanation,* proposed by Oscar Lewis, suggests that people create a subculture of their own as an adaptation to poverty. This subculture enables the poor to cope but also limits their effectiveness in the larger culture. It is passed on to the next generation, perpetuating the poverty cycle. Charles Valentine disagrees with this and instead offers the *situational approach:* the traits Lewis observed are not all creations of a subculture but, rather, often represent behavioral responses to existing conditions. If the poor had more money available, their behavior would change. Herbert Gans combines these two approaches, suggesting that poor people cannot be easily categorized and that their behavior results from both cultural and situational influences. Lee Rainwater believes that the lives of the poor are even more complex than Gans suggested; not only do the poor have a particular subculture and situation, but they also have absorbed some of the beliefs of the larger culture. Thus they do not feel deprived in isolation but relative to the rest of society. The *value-stretch concept* articulated by Rodman and Della Fave is an extension of this idea. It suggests that the poor have two sets of values simultaneously— those of the larger society, which are preferred, if unattainable, values, and those values they realistically expect to achieve.

There exist common misconceptions about the poor. For example, the poor are assumed to be unwilling to work; in fact, only a tiny percentage of the employable poor do not work. There are also many misconceptions regarding the poor on welfare. For example, it is believed that the welfare poor are mostly black; in fact, the largest proportion of welfare recipients is white.

Current government antipoverty programs fall into one of four categories: human resource development, social insurance, cash income support, and providing income-in-kind. Other suggestions to increase the government role include stimulating the private economy (through tax cuts, for example), extending economic legislation (by expanding the minimum wage law), and having the government serve as the "employer of last resort." Present maintenance programs can be improved by increasing benefits to a decent level, eliminating red tape and unnecessary requirements, allowing benefits to continue up to a certain point even if earnings increase, and eliminating state or local control over benefits. A *negative income tax,* which would use the income tax system to equalize the distribution of income, has also been proposed. It is unlikely that these proposals will be acted upon unless the poor organize into a political force that the affluent in power will have to acknowledge.

Ferman, Louis A., Kornbluh, Joyce L., and Haber, Alan, eds. *Poverty in America*. Ann Arbor: University of Michigan Press, 1969.

Ficker, Victor, and Graves, Herbert S. *Deprivation in America*. Beverly Hills, Calif.: Glencoe Press, 1971.

Goodwin, Leonard. *Do the Poor Want Work?* Washington, D.C.: The Brookings Institution, 1972.

Green, Christopher. *Negative Taxes and the Poverty Problem*. Washington, D.C.: The Brookings Institution, 1967.

Hacker, Andrew. *The Corporation Take Over*. New York: Harper & Row, 1964.

Harrington, Michael. *The Other America: Poverty in the United States*. New York: Macmillan, 1970.

Kaufman, Richard F. *The War Profiteers*. New York: Bobbs-Merrill, 1970.

Kosa, John, Antonovsky, Aaron, and Zola, Irving. *Poverty and Health: A Sociological Analysis*. Cambridge, Mass.: Harvard University Press, 1969.

Levitan, Sar A. *Programs in Aid of the Poor in the 1970s*. Rev. ed. Baltimore: Johns Hopkins Press, 1973.

Lundberg, Ferdinand. *The Rich and the Super-Rich*. New York: Bantam, 1968.

Meissner, Hanna H., ed. *Poverty in the Affluent Society*. New York: Harper & Row, 1973.

Miller, S. M., and Roby, Pamela A. *The Future of Inequality*. New York: Basic Books, 1970.

Moynihan, Daniel P. *On Understanding Poverty: Perspectives from the Social Sciences*. New York: Basic Books, 1969.

National Institute of Child Health and Human Development, Department of Health, Education and Welfare. *Perspectives on Human Deprivation, Biological, Psychological and Sociological*. Washington, D.C.: U.S. Government Printing Office, 1968.

Pilisuk, Marc, ed. *Poor Americans: How the White Poor Live*. 2nd ed. Chicago: Aldine, 1973.

Pivan, Francis, and Cloward, Richard. *Regulating the Poor: The Functions of Public Welfare*. New York: Pantheon, 1971.

Poverty Amid Plenty: The American Paradox. Report of the President's Commission on Income Maintenance Programs. Washington, D.C.: U.S. Government Printing Office, 1970.

Rainwater, Lee, ed. *Social Problems and Public Policy: Inequality and Justice*. Chicago: Aldine, 1974.

Ryan, William. *Blaming the Victim*. New York: Random House, 1971.

Stein, Bruno. *On Relief: The Economics of Poverty and Public Welfare*. New York: Basic Books, 1971.

Theobald, Robert, ed. *Social Policies for America in the Seventies: Nine Divergent Views*. Garden City, N.Y.: Doubleday, 1969.

Will, Robert E., and Vatter, Harold G., eds. *Poverty in Affluence*. 2nd ed. New York: Harcourt Brace Jovanovich, 1970.

7

PREJUDICE AND DISCRIMINATION

- The median income for blacks and persons of Spanish origin is about two-thirds that of whites.
- Over 23 percent of persons of Spanish origin, and about 33 percent of all blacks, are below the poverty line.
- About 82 percent of whites have completed high school, compared with about 65 percent of blacks and 52 percent of persons of Spanish origin.
- Unemployment among blacks is twice that of whites; unemployment among Spanish-speaking persons is a third higher than that of whites.
- Less than 1 percent of elected officials in this country are black.

Social inequality is almost as old as humankind. Indeed, much of recorded history is an account of the constantly shifting power relations among different peoples as some groups have sought first to achieve dominance over others and then to maintain it.

Nor is inequality peculiar to any geographical area. Within the last four decades we have seen dramatic evidence of it in many parts of the world: the repression of blacks by whites in South Africa; the repression, which finally led to a successful revolt, of the Bengalis of East Pakistan (now Sri Lanka) by the ruling groups of West Pakistan (now simply Pakistan); discrimination against Catholics in Northern Ireland and against the Jews in the Soviet Union; and many more.

The United States, too, has a long history of social inequality. But, in our case, such inequality creates a special problem, for it directly contradicts the fundamental principles on which the nation's existence is said to be based. Belief in the essential equality of people has always been at the core of the American self-concept. Our national anthem describes our country as the land of the free; we have praised it as the refuge of the world's masses yearning to be free. But many of us resist the fact that the reality falls, as realities always do, considerably short of the ideal.

The first black slaves were brought to what is now the United States early in the colonial period, and by the time of independence they numbered about three-quarters of a million. In the meantime, the original inhabitants of the continent, the American Indians, were being progressively dispossessed of their homes and livelihood as the white settlers pushed westward. And as the Industrial Revolution gathered momentum in the nineteenth century, wave after wave of immigrants arrived, to find themselves assigned to the meanest labor and the poorest conditions of life. The earlier arrivals fought their way upward in a bitterly competitive society, and the descendants of those who had come earliest defended their position at the top:

We are a nation of immigrants, but one in which the original dominant immigrant group, the so-called Anglo-Saxons, effectively preempted the crucial levers of economic and political power in government, commerce, and the professions. This elite group has tenaciously resisted the upward strivings of successive "ethnic" immigrant waves. . . . The Anglo-Americans have used their access to the levers of power to maintain their dominance, using legal force surrounded by an aura of legitimacy for such ends as economic exploitation; the restriction of immigration by a national-origin quota system which clearly branded later immigrants as culturally undesirable; the confinement of the original Indian [inhabitants] largely to barren reservations; and the restriction of blacks to a degraded caste.[1]

Achieving the promise of American equality has been natural for those whose ancestors were Protestant English; somewhat less easy if they were Protestant non-English, or Catholics, or Jews; very difficult if they were Japanese or Chinese; and almost impossible if they were Puerto Rican, Mexican, American Indian, or African.

This discrepancy between the ideal and the reality of American social opportunity was the subject of a classic study in the late 1930s and early 1940s by the Swedish economist and social scientist Gunnar Myrdal. Myrdal focused on black Americans, whose position as a "poor and suppressed minority" in the land of freedom and opportunity seemed to him to create for their white counterparts what he called the "American dilemma." The dilemma was specifically a white person's problem because, as Myrdal put it, "practically all the economic, social, and political power is held by whites."

Myrdal saw reason to hope that white Americans would eventually resolve the problem on the side of the American Creed. He believed that after a long period in which not much had happened, fundamental changes were taking place which would lead to full and real equality for black Americans.[2]

While the constitutional bases for black equality were laid in the 1860s and 1870s in the Thirteenth, Fourteenth, and Fifteenth Amendments, it was not until the mid-twentieth century that the rights asserted by these amendments began to be effectively claimed. Starting with Supreme Court decisions which affected specific small areas of life, black Americans began to work their way toward equality. The major legal breakthrough came in 1954, in the historic *Brown* v. *Board of Education*

---

[1] Hugh Davis Graham and Ted Robert Gurr, *Violence in America: Historical and Comparative Perspectives*. A Report to the National Commission on the Causes and Prevention of Violence. Washington, D.C.: U.S. Government Printing Office, 1969, vol. 2, p. 625.

[2] Gunnar Myrdal, *The American Dilemma*. New York: Harper & Row, 1962.

decision that "separate educational facilities are inherently unequal." [3] The Supreme Court later applied this "separate cannot be equal" doctrine to a wide range of public facilities.

The Civil Rights Act of 1964 was another important step. Unlike the Civil Rights Acts of 1957 and 1960, the 1964 act provided, among other things, means to fight discrimination in employment and public accommodations, and ways to deny federal money to local governmental units which allowed discrimination. There followed a comprehensive Voting Rights Act in 1965, and a federal prohibition against housing discrimination in the Civil Rights Act of 1968. Subsequent "affirmative action" orders by President Johnson aided the enforcement of these new laws; he also set up new programs, such as the Head Start program (discussed later), to counter the effects of discrimination.

But still the discrepancy remained between the legal equality of black Americans and their factual inequality. And the impatience of at least some black Americans was turning to anger. In August 1964, for example, a riot erupted in Watts, a black section of Los Angeles. Before the wave of violent protest which began in Watts subsided, it had struck almost every major urban center in the country. In 1967, following particularly destructive riots in Newark and Detroit, President Johnson appointed a National Advisory Commission on Civil Disorders to investigate the origins of the disturbances and to recommend ways to forestall or control them in the future. The commission's findings suggested that there had been very little practical advance since the work of Myrdal. Describing the basic causes of the disorders, the commission said:

The first is surely the continuing exclusion of great numbers of Negroes from the benefits of economic progress through discrimination in employment and education, and their enforced confinement in segregated housing and schools. The corrosive and degrading effects of this condition and the attitudes that underlie it are the source of the deepest bitterness and at the center of the problem of racial disorder.[4]

The commission's basic conclusion was that "our nation is moving toward two societies, one black, one white—separate and unequal." [5]

The situation of other minorities—American Indians, Chicanos (Mexican-Americans), Puerto Ricans, Asians, some white ethnic groups, and others—while less intensively studied, is similar. One form of discrimination to which these groups are particularly vulnerable is harassment at, or exclusion from, the voting booth, due to their frequently inadequate command of the English language. The 1975 extension of the Voting Rights Act attempted to alleviate this particular inequity. This bill required that cities with sizable "language minority" populations hold bilingual elections; it also permanently banned literacy tests as a voting prerequisite.[6]

[3] 347 U.S. 483 (1954).
[4] *Report of the National Advisory Commission on Civil Disorders.* Washington, D.C.: U.S. Government Printing Office, 1968, p. 203.
[5] *Report of the National Advisory Commission,* p. 1.
[6] " '75 Voting Act—Help for those who don't read English.' " *U.S. News & World Report,* August 11, 1975, p. 28.

Despite such legal advances in the status of blacks and other minorities, inequality and oppression remain facts of American life that are increasingly difficult to hide. But before we can describe these inequities, and suggest measures to correct them, we must first understand how inequality comes about.

THE MEANING OF "MINORITY"

Categories of people that receive treatment less than equal to that accorded other categories in the same society have come to be referred to as minorities. But what is a minority? How does a minority situation come about? Why are some categories of people singled out for unequal treatment?

Wagley and Harris suggest five characteristics of a minority:

1. Minorities are subordinate segments of a complex society.
2. Minorities have special physical or cultural traits which are seen as undesirable by the dominant segments of the society.
3. Minorities have a group self-awareness brought about by the special traits they share and the special disabilities these traits cause them to suffer.
4. Membership in a minority is transmitted by a rule of descent—one is born into a minority—and this rule of descent is capable of imposing the minority status on future generations, even if by then the special physical or cultural traits of the minority have disappeared.
5. Members of a minority, whether by choice or by necessity, tend to practice endogamy—that is, to marry within the group.[7]

The characteristics singled out by Wagley and Harris seem to fit best the racial or ethnic minority, especially one that is just beginning the process of assimilation, or that has not yet begun it. As assimilation proceeds, some of the minority characteristics will become weaker—group self-awareness may wane, marriage out of the group may increase, distinctive cultural traits may be abandoned. That is, there is no sharp break between totally dominant and totally minority groups, but, rather, what might be called a "continuum of minorityness." In the course of the past century or so of United States history, various immigrant groups have moved along this continuum, edging progressively closer to equality and shedding some or all of their distinctive minority characteristics more or less simultaneously. It should be pointed out, however, that the physical distinctiveness of racial minorities has made them less amenable to the process of assimilation than white immigrant groups, who are defined largely by cultural, rather than physical, traits. Thus racial minorities have tended to remain minorities for longer periods of time.

Wagley and Harris's definition is somewhat less accurate for nonracial and non-ethnic minorities. The aged, for example, constitute a minority both in absolute numbers and in regard to the treatment they receive from society, yet they are not born into a minority, nor do they neces-

[7] Charles Wagley and Marvin Harris, *Minorities in the New World*. New York: Columbia University Press, 1958, p. 10.

sarily marry within the group. Women do not marry within the group, nor is membership in the homosexual minority passed on from one generation to the next. Nevertheless, such minorities do share in the major characteristics—subordinate status, special traits, and, increasingly, a group self-awareness.

Subordinate status would seem to be the principal defining characteristic of a minority. In almost any society, the desire for some goods, tangible or intangible, exceeds the supply, and groups within the society are likely to enter into competition for these goods, and for the power to obtain or control them. The group or groups which succeed in attaining the greater share of this power become dominant over the other groups, controlling their access to the desired goods and often, ultimately, to other goods—social, economic, political, and personal—as well. The dominant group need not constitute a numerical majority; it must merely be able to prevent effective challenge to its power by the subordinate group.

Once established, however, the dominant-subordinate relationship is not thereby fixed for all time. Either by the efforts of the subordinate group itself, or as a result of changing legal or economic conditions which erode the power base of the dominant group, power relationships can be altered. We can see in our own society that women are now less subordinated than they were even a few years ago. Most of the former colonial areas in Africa, Asia, and elsewhere are now independent nations, and some formerly less influential nations, such as Japan, are now world powers. And in a few counties in Mississippi, where blacks outnumber whites by a considerable margin, extensive voter registration has enabled the once-subordinate blacks to become politically dominant.

Dominance can also vary with place. Before the Italian, Polish, Japanese, or Chinese immigrants to America left their native lands, they were members of the dominant ethnic group. When they arrived here, they became members of a subordinate ethnic group. On the other hand, the first emigrants from England to Plymouth and Massachusetts Bay left a subordinate status, as members of a persecuted nonconformist religious group, to become the dominant group in the new colonial society. And today the Soviet Jew who emigrates to Israel moves likewise from subordinate- to dominant-group status.

Except in the case of such geographical migrations, however, it is usually very difficult for members of a subordinate group to attain a share of dominance, for the dominant group naturally wants to protect its privileged position. Among the principal weapons which it uses to do so are prejudice and discrimination.

PREJUDICE AND DISCRIMINATION DEFINED

Discrimination is "the differential treatment of individuals considered to belong to a particular social group." [8] To treat a member of a subordinate group as less than equal to oneself is to discriminate against

[8] Robin M. Williams, Jr., *The Reduction of Intergroup Tensions.* New York: Social Science Research Council, 1947, p. 39.

that person. Members of the dominant group tend to use one standard of behavior when interacting among themselves and a different, less than equal, standard when interacting with any member of the subordinate group.

Discrimination is overt behavior. But to justify and explain their behavior to themselves, people tend to adopt new values and beliefs or to adapt old ones. In addition, people in general tend to be ethnocentric— to see the behavioral patterns and belief structures of their own groups as desirable and natural and those of other groups as less natural and less desirable. These two tendencies usually result in prejudice against the subordinate group—"an emotional, rigid attitude (a predisposition to respond to a certain stimulus in a certain way) toward a group of people." [9]

But while prejudices are attitudes, not all attitudes are prejudices. Both share the element of *pre*judgment—the human tendency to decide in advance how to think about a situation or an event. But what distinguishes a prejudice from other attitudes is that a prejudice carries with it such a strong emotional investment that it is not likely to be changed. Prejudiced persons tend to be so committed to their prejudgment about a category of people that even if they are presented with evidence showing that prejudgment to be wrong, they will maintain it, and probably even defend it strongly, denouncing the contrary evidence. For whatever reason, they will not or cannot adapt to the facts.

According to Gordon Allport, "Prejudgments become prejudices only if they are not reversible when exposed to new knowledge." He goes on to define prejudice directed against a category of people as

an antipathy based upon a faulty and inflexible generalization. It may be felt or expressed. It may be directed toward a group as a whole, or toward an individual because he is a member of that group.[10]

It should be pointed out, however, that prejudice need not always be an antipathy. One may well be prejudiced in favor of a person or group of people, with a similar disregard for the objective evidence.

Thus prejudice is based on one's attitude; it is a tendency to think about people in a categorical, predetermined way. Discrimination, on the other hand, is behavioral: the overt less-than-equal treatment of people because they are members of a subordinate group. Prejudice and discrimination are closely related, and both are often present in the same interaction.

Merton outlines four possible relationships between prejudice and discrimination: unprejudiced and nondiscriminatory, unprejudiced and discriminatory, prejudiced and nondiscriminatory, and prejudiced and discriminatory.[11] While people who are completely free of prejudice and completely nondiscriminatory, as well as people who are the opposite—

[9] George E. Simpson and J. M. Yinger, *Racial and Cultural Minorities: An Analysis of Prejudice and Discrimination*. New York: Harper & Row, 1965, pp. 10, 82.

[10] Gordon Allport, *The Nature of Prejudice*. New York: Doubleday, 1958, pp. 9, 10.

[11] Robert K. Merton, "Discrimination and the American Creed." In R. M. MacIver, ed., *Discrimination and National Welfare*. New York: Harper & Row, 1949, pp. 99– 126.

pure bigots—do exist, most people fall somewhere between these two extremes. It is possible to be prejudiced against a particular group, but not discriminate against it; it is also possible to discriminate against a particular group, but not be prejudiced against it.

For example, the builders of a new, expensive cooperative apartment house may not be personally prejudiced against Jews, but they may refuse to sell an apartment to a Jewish family—that is, they may discriminate against them—out of fear, founded or unfounded, that the presence of a Jewish family would make it more difficult to sell the remaining apartments.

Or the reverse may occur: in a corporation working under government contract, and thus subject to federal Equal Employment Opportunity regulations, the employment director may be very prejudiced personally against both blacks and women, but may hire a black woman as a management trainee—that is, not discriminate against her—in order to comply with the law.

However, suppose the builders were confronted with a different minority, a black rather than a Jewish family attempting to buy one of their apartments. They might very well discriminate out of personal prejudice as well as out of concern for profits. And suppose the employment director were in a different situation—his or her own exclusive community. He or she might lead the fight to keep black families from buying houses and integrating the community. This points up two facts: that, at least to some extent, prejudice and discrimination depend on which minorities and what situations are involved. In addition, it is very difficult to keep personal prejudice from leading, sooner or later, to some form of discrimination, particularly if a significant number of people share the same prejudice.

PREJUDICE AND DISCRIMINATION: SOURCES

We have said that prejudice and discrimination are weapons used by the dominant group to maintain its dominance. It would be a mistake, though, to see them as always, or even usually, conscious weapons. Unless and until the subordinate group mounts a serious challenge to the power of its rulers, prejudice and discrimination are apt to seem very much a part of the natural order of things. Their origins are many and complex, and it is necessary to consider both the felt needs of individual persons and the structural organization of society in order to account for them. To blame them wholly on warped individual psychology, or wholly on oppressive social structures, as has sometimes been done, is to oversimplify the situation. Each of these approaches has its value, and they complement one another.

Frustration-Aggression. Most human beings at one time or another feel frustrated. They want something, but because of some reasons or events or other people, they cannot get what they want. This can lead to feelings of anger and aggression, which they may deal with in any of a number of ways. The most obvious way would be to strike back at the source of the

PSYCHOLOGICAL NEEDS

frustration. But often this is impossible, either because the source of frustration is unknown, or because people are subjectively unable to recognize the source, or, finally, because they are in such a position, usually a dependent one, that they cannot risk striking back. Whatever the reason, the results are the same. They are unable to vent their anger and aggression on the real source of their frustration.

What happens instead, in many cases, is that the aggression is directed at a safer and more convenient target, usually one which is somewhat similar to the real source of frustration. That is, the aggression is displaced onto a *scapegoat*. When the scapegoat is not limited to one particular person, but is extended to include all similar people, this may result in a more or less settled prejudice.

For example, suppose that a middle-aged man, who has been working for twenty years at the same job, is told one day by his young supervisor that the job may soon be eliminated by automation. The man is understandably angry, and frightened. But were he to vent his aggression on the supervisor, he knows he would then almost certainly be out of a job. Later that night he is telling his woes to his friends at the local bar, when a long-haired young man comes in for a beer. Our man accuses the youth, and "all you lazy kids," of being good for nothing and ruining the country, and only the intervention of the bartender prevents him from beating up the young man.

It is fairly clear that this man has displaced his aggression toward his supervisor onto the "kids." Rather than deal with the supervisor and the whole range of factors which led to the prospect of his job being eliminated, he finds it much easier and more comprehensible to blame the problems of the country on all young people. (Further discussion of frustration-aggression theory can be found in Chapter 5.)

Projection. Another source of prejudice and discrimination is projection. Many people have traits which they perceive as undesirable. They have an understandable wish to rid themselves of these traits, but they cannot always do it directly—either because they find the effort too difficult or because they are unable really to admit to themselves that they possess the traits. In this case, they may relieve themselves by attributing the unwanted traits to someone else, often to some other group in society. This makes it possible for them to reject and condemn the traits without rejecting and condemning themselves, for now it is the other person or group who is guilty of them. Since the emotional pressures leading to projection can be very intense, it is difficult to undercut it by rational argument.

An often-cited example of projection is the view which, particularly in the past, whites held of black sexuality. Many whites saw blacks as inordinately sexual, as being totally promiscuous and unfettered in their sexual relations, and there was much concern about protecting white women from sexual attack by black men. Historically, however, it was in fact the white men who enjoyed virtually free rein sexually with black women, particularly during the time of slavery. At the time, however, white society regarded overt sexuality as an unacceptable behavior, and it is quite likely that white men felt some guilt or anxiety about their sexual desires and adventures. So, to get rid of that guilt, the white men projected their own lust and sexuality onto the black men—a much easier course than admitting the discrepancy between their own behavior and their values.

While the emotional needs of insecure individuals account for some prejudice and discrimination, they do not explain why certain groups become and remain objects of prejudice and discrimination. To understand this, we need to look at some larger social processes.

Competition and Exploitation. As we noted earlier, the demand for more than the available supply of certain goods gives rise in many societies to a competitive struggle for possession, which usually results in dominance for one group and subordination for the rest.[12] However, even if the initial objects of competition are economic goods, it is ultimately a struggle for power and hence a political process. Once this political dominance is established, it is likely to be reinforced by the more specifically economic process of exploitation, wherein the dominant group makes use of the labor of the subordinate group for a less than equitable return. Slavery and serfdom are the most obvious forms of such exploitation, but nominally "free" workers may also be exploited, and frequently are—for example, migrant farm workers, sweatshop factory laborers, and unorganized clerical and service workers.

Economic exploitation is one form of discrimination practiced by the dominant against the subordinate group. Other forms of discrimination also develop. Some of these are practical—members of the subordinate group may be legally prevented from owning property or voting, or they may be extralegally terrorized into submission, as often happened to striking workers in the early days of the labor movement. Some are symbolic, as when a black person is refused service in a restaurant. All are aimed, consciously and unconsciously, at keeping the subordinate people "in their place," and hence the dominant people in theirs.

Since, however, the members of the dominant group cannot help but be aware that they are treating the members of the subordinate group in a less-than-equal fashion, they need to justify this behavior to themselves. Here a typical human tendency to rationalize one's own behavior is aided by the ethnocentric tendency to see one's own group as right and worthy and other groups as therefore wrong and unworthy.

Members of the dominant group tend to tell themselves that it is right and proper for them to have more—that they are smarter, cleverer, racially superior. They come to believe that they deserve what they have. The subordinate group, as they see it, is lazy, stupid, heathen, biologically inferior, or otherwise unworthy, and therefore deserves less (or perhaps needs less).

Thus those groups in a society who are different from the dominant group, who have less power, and who are economically useful to the dominant group tend to become the targets of prejudice and discrimination.

[12] For a fuller discussion, see Donald L. Noel, "A theory of the origin of ethnic stratification." *Social Problems* 16 (Fall 1968):157–172; and Simpson and Yinger, pp. 81–82.

Social Norms. A social norm, in essence, is a social standard which specifies what kind of behavior is correct and appropriate in a given situation. It is relevant to our discussion because, while it does not tell us why prejudice and discrimination occur in the first place, it does help to explain how and why they are perpetuated.

Social norms are learned, in a process which begins almost at birth. It does not take small children long to learn what kind of behavior brings the approval of their parents and what kind is apt to be rebuked. The same learning takes place as they encounter other authority figures. Gradually children learn to incorporate into their own behavior and value structure the accepted ways of society. They receive approval from parents, from other adults, and later from peers, when they behave in socially acceptable ways; they experience disapproval when they do not.

Through this process, most children are socialized to the prevailing norms of the society into which they were born. If the society is prejudiced against certain minorities and engages in discriminatory behavior, the children will generally learn those prejudices and behaviors and will think them correct and natural. The original reasons for prejudice and discrimination may have long since disappeared, but the prejudice and discrimination themselves remain as part of the deeply embedded folk-ways and mores of the society, in the cultural heritage passed on from generation to generation. In this way prejudice and discrimination take on an existence of their own quite apart from their origins.

The normal human tendency to social conformity is also likely to support prejudice and discrimination. Even if some members of a dominant group are ambivalent toward the subordinate group and personally feel no special prejudice, nevertheless, if most people around them are prejudiced and engage in discriminatory behavior, the ambivalent people will usually go along. It is simpler for them to conform to the group norms than to make a fuss and perhaps attract hostility to themselves.

Stereotyping. Still another source of prejudice and discrimination is stereotyping, the attributing of a fixed and usually unfavorable or inaccurate conception to a category of people. Whereas social norms are concerned primarily with behavior and only indirectly with attitudes, stereotyping is basically a matter of attitude, affecting, and affected by, discriminatory behavior.

Usually a stereotype contains some truth, but it is exaggerated, distorted, or taken out of context in some fashion or other. Stereotyping has much to do with the way all human beings normally think. We tend to perceive and understand things in categories, for if we had to treat each new bit of information as separate and unrelated to anything we already knew, we would soon suffer from a serious mental overload.

Naturally, we apply this same process of thinking to people. We build up mental pictures of minorities, pictures made from overgeneralized and highly selected impressions and bits of information, and we use these pictures to define all members of a minority without regard for their individual differences. Thus we come to assume that all Indians are drunks, all blacks are lazy, all Puerto Ricans are short, all Italians are gangsters, all Jews are shrewd, all Englishmen are reserved, all Swedes are blond, all Frenchmen are lovers, all long-haired young people are drug addicts, all old people are senile, all women want to be mothers. Almost none of these generalizations will hold up to even perfunctory analysis. Yet many people habitually use such notions when thinking about minorities and other groups.

INSTITUTIONALIZED DISCRIMINATION

If discrimination is a socially learned behavior of dominant group members, designed to support and justify their continued dominance, it is reasonable to expect that such discrimination will be, often unwittingly, built into the very structure and form of society. To members of a society socialized to accept and believe that members of certain minorities "just are" to be treated as inferiors, it would be perfectly natural to formulate public policy and build public institutions which would discriminate against those minorities.

To some extent this is exactly what has happened in the United States. If many blacks, Chicanos, American Indians, Puerto Ricans, women, old people, and members of other minorities do not have the "equal protection of the laws" in their dealings with public institutions and public policy, it is not necessarily because of the conscious prejudice of public officials. More fundamentally this discrimination is the unconscious result of the structure and functioning of public institutions and policies themselves. It is almost as if the discrimination were part of the very definition of the society.

As an example, white people living near Indian reservations often see the Indians as lazy and incompetent, unable to exercise any initiative or do anything to improve their often deplorable condition of life. What such white people fail to realize is the degree to which apparent Indian incompetence is a result of the way in which the Indians are governed by white society. As Thomas points out in discussing the Sioux of the Pine Ridge reservation in South Dakota:

The Sioux tribal government is, in effect, without power. Most of the day to day decisions about Sioux life, about roads, schools, relief, are made by Bureau [of Indian Affairs] personnel. . . . Further, what decisions the tribal council makes are subject to approval by the Secretary of the Interior. . . . The Bureau of Indian Affairs is *the* economic and political force in Pine Ridge reservation. . . . Bureau personnel attend most public meetings and usually call them to get the Sioux to agree to some program or other, *and* direct them as well. . . . Tribal projects are supervised by Bureau officials. . . . The Pine Ridge reservation is, as are most American Indian reservations, an example of a very complete colonial system.[13]

In short, the Indians have been made incompetent to handle their own affairs by an administrative structure which has denied them any opportunity to learn new ways of doing so while at the same time rendering old tribal ways useless and ineffective.

[13] Robert K. Thomas, "Powerless politics." *New University Thought* 4 (Winter 1966–1967):44–53.

The field of health care provides another example. From conception to old age, minorities suffer from poor nutrition, lack of disease prevention, and inadequate medical treatment. Studies show that blacks and other minority groups suffer shorter life expectancy, greater infant and maternal mortality, and two to five times more instances of death from infectious, preventable diseases than white Americans. (See Chapters 2 and 6 for fuller discussions of this topic.) Does this mean that the dominant whites have deliberately chosen to keep minorities sick and undernourished as a form of oppression? No. It means that American health care systems, housing codes, and social welfare arrangements are structured to the advantage of the white middle and upper classes simply or mainly because it did not occur to the lawmakers that such a structure was not in the best interests of all concerned. Whether they are to be blamed for their ignorance is another question, and one with which we cannot deal properly here.

It would be difficult in this section to discuss all categories of institutional discrimination against all minorities. We will, therefore, focus on four major categories: education, employment, housing, and social justice. And we will limit our examples to four minorities: blacks, Chicanos, American Indians, and Puerto Ricans. But the patterns we will describe apply in general to other categories as well, such as health care and consumer issues, and to other minorities, including the aged and women (see Chapters 8 and 9).

EDUCATION

In the United States today probably no one issue generates more emotion than that of education, particularly, the question of whether black, Puerto Rican, Chicano, and American Indian children shall attend the same schools as white children. The question is sometimes put in terms of busing to achieve racial balance, of quality education for all, and of public tax support for private schools. Families have been known to move once, then again, and sometimes again in order to put their children into better and better public education systems. Parents in the inner cities, primarily minority parents, are demanding greater local community control over city schools. Increasingly, political campaigns are being waged on the issues of education.

American parents take their public school systems very seriously. One reason undoubtedly is that in this country education has generally been seen as the way to social and economic advancement. And it is almost an article of faith in America that children should get more education than their parents and achieve higher social and economic status.

We have long assumed that higher education leads to a higher income. Whether or not this is true (and new data have begun to call it into question), there is no doubt that among those presently working, the more highly educated typically receive substantially higher salaries.[14] However, the evidence further suggests that even better than a sheepskin (diploma) is a white skin, for blacks and other minorities at all levels of education earn less than their white counterparts.

Minorities also have less chance of finishing high school or attending

14 *The Condition of Education.* National Center for Education Statistics, U.S. Department of HEW, Washington, D.C., 1975.

college than do whites. In 1974, as many as 63.4 percent of all whites 25 years of age or older had completed four years of high school or more, while only 40.7 percent of the blacks and 36.6 percent of the Puerto Ricans and Chicanos in the same age group had gone this far.[15]

By the same token, blacks are about twice as likely as whites to be high school dropouts. In 1974, 28 percent of blacks age 20 to 24 had not completed high school, as compared with 15 percent of the whites of this age. And while blacks represent 11 percent of the total United States population, they comprised only 7 percent of the total college enrollment. And this figure represents a tremendous numerical increase during the past several years. Of all college-age blacks (18 to 24 years) only 18 percent were in college, compared to 25 percent of whites of that age group. Black students were most likely to be attending public four-year colleges, while their white counterparts were equally likely to be enrolled in public or private four-year colleges. And as a result of the even greater inequities of the past, only 8 percent of all black adults are college graduates, compared to 21 percent of all white adults.[16]

Insofar as it is built-in factors of society which cause minorities to be less well prepared for schooling at any given level, less able to pay the "hidden" costs of "free" education such as books, supplies, transportation, shoes, clothing, and class trips, and less likely to finish, minorities are the objects of institutional discrimination in American education. But they are also the objects of another kind of discrimination: the manner in which they are portrayed in textbooks used in American schools.

Of late there has been increasing recognition of the existence and seriousness of this form of discrimination. Paraphrasing a report prepared by the Indian Historical Society after evaluating forty-three textbooks on American history used in the fourth, fifth, and eighth grades in California, Jeannette Henry asks:

What is the effect upon the student, when he learns from his textbooks that one race, and one alone, is the most, the best, the greatest; when he learns that Indians were mere parts of the landscape and wilderness which had to be cleared out, to make way for the great "movement" of white population across the land; and when he learns that Indians were killed and forcibly removed from their ancient homelands to make way for adventurers (usually called "pioneering goldminers"), for land grabbers (usually called "settlers"), and for illegal squatters on Indian-owned land (usually called "frontiersmen")? What is the effect upon the young Indian child himself, who is also a student in the school system, when he is told that Columbus discovered America, that Coronado "brought civilization" to the Indian people, and that the Spanish missionaries provided havens of refuge for the Indians? Is it reasonable to assume that the student, of whatever race, will not discover at some time in his life that Indians discovered America thousands of years before Columbus set out upon his voyage; that Coronado brought death and destruction to the native peoples; and that the Spanish missionaries, in all too many cases, forcibly dragged Indians to the missions? [17]

[15] "Educational attainment in the United States: March 1973 and 1974." *Current Population Reports*, Series P-20, No. 274, December 1974, Table 3, pp. 47–52.
[16] "The social and economic status of the black population in the United States." *Current Population Reports*, Series P-23, no. 5, July 1975, pp. 3–4, 96, 98.
[17] Jeannette Henry, *The Indian Historian* 1 (December 1967):22.

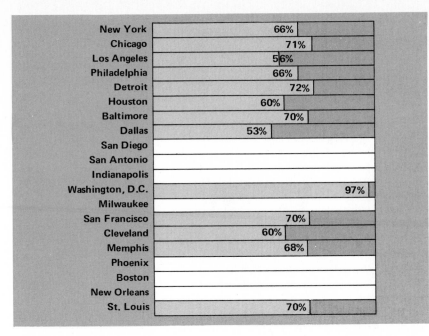

FIGURE 7-1
Major City School
Systems with Minority
Enrollment over 50
Percent

Note: Listed are 20 largest
U.S. cities; only 7 have less
than 50 percent minority
school enrollment.

Source: New York Times,
December 21, 1975, p. 3.

Discrimination and Busing. The most prominent issue with respect to minority education is, and has been for more than two decades, that of school desegregation. Desegregation has been a long time in coming. In 1972, eighteen years after the Supreme Court decision which disallowed the "separate but equal" doctrine, and seventeen years after the 1955 decision which mandated integration "with all deliberate speed," nearly a third of minority group students attended public schools with 80 percent or more minority enrollment; some 60 percent attended schools with 50 percent or more minority enrollment; and only 39.6 percent of minority students attended public schools with less than 50 percent minority enrollment.[18] (See Figure 7-1.) The school populations of thirty-five major cities were 75 percent or more black.[19]

De jure segregation—segregation required by law, once standard in the Southern states—is now a thing of the past, but *de facto* segregation, a result of housing patterns, economic patterns, gerrymandered school districts, and sometimes intimidation, is harder to eradicate. The principal remedy suggested thus far is busing—the transportation of pupils from their local schools to other schools in order to achieve a reasonable racial balance in all the schools within a particular area. Predictably, busing has become one of the most emotional political issues of our day.

The basic argument for busing is a two-step one:

1. Minority children, or perhaps all children, will receive a better education in racially balanced than in racially segregated schools.
2. Busing is an effective way to achieve racial balance.

---

[18] *The Condition of Education,* p. 70.
[19] "Busing: Why tide is turning." *U.S. News & World Report,* August 11, 1975, pp. 24–26.

Irate white parents are yelling at black children who have been bused from their neighborhoods to the predominantly white school. The black parents are watching as their children are escorted into school under police guard.
Bettye Lane/Nancy Palmer

Unfortunately, both steps of the argument have turned out in practice to be somewhat weaker than they were originally thought. Attendance at racially balanced schools has been accompanied by some increase in minority achievement, but not, overall, a great deal; and a good many school districts which have undertaken extensive busing programs to create integrated schools have found that their schools remain about as segregated as before, if not more so. Because American parents usually regard their children's education as particularly important, and because white parents fear that integration will lower standards in the schools, they may be inclined to move out of heavily integrated districts, to send their children to private schools, or to protest vehemently against busing, even though they may not be notably prejudiced or inclined to discriminate in other respects.

The case of Washington, D.C., is commonly cited in this regard: after busing was instituted, so many white residents moved to the suburbs that in 1970 the school system was 94 percent black.[20] As William Raspberry, a *Washington Post* columnist, commented early that year, "We find ourselves busing children from all-black neighborhoods all the way across town to schools that are rapidly becoming all-black." [21] Other cities have had similar experiences. In Inglewood, California, for example, combined minorities constituted 38 percent of the public school

[20] *U.S. News & World Report,* March 9, 1970, p. 30.
[21] *Washington Post,* February 20, 1970.

Bettye Lane/Nancy Palmer

enrollment when court-ordered busing was put into effect in 1970; by 1975, minority enrollment was up to 80 percent, and the busing order was rescinded by the same judge who had ordered it in the first place.

Coleman in 1966 implied that integration, by exposing minority students to the higher achievements of the middle-class majority, would improve the performance of the former without diminishing that of the latter.[22] Nine years later Coleman was to conclude otherwise: "Desegregation through the courts probably will have served in the long run to separate whites and blacks more severely than before."[23] Recognizing the complexities involved in the phenomenon of "white flight," Coleman adds that "it's not entirely lower-class blacks that middle-class whites are fleeing. They are fleeing a school system that they see as too large, as unmanageable, as unresponsive, to find a smaller, more responsive system."[24] In this regard, it has been pointed out that busing children over long distances costs money which might otherwise be used in ways more directly related to instruction, and that it tends to weaken local control

[22] James S. Coleman *et al., Equality of Educational Opportunity.* Washington, D.C.: U.S. Government Printing Office, 1966, pp. 3–7.
[23] In *U.S. News & World Report,* August 11, 1975, p. 25. The data upon which Coleman based his conclusion has since been questioned. See the April 1976 issue of *Harvard Educational Review.*
[24] In Maurice deG. Ford, "School integration and bussing: Courts, bussing and white flight." *The Nation,* July 5, 1975, p. 13.

and interest in the schools. It is difficult for parents to take an active part in school affairs when the school is not easily accessible.

Busing may also provoke racial tensions within a community, especially when community cooperation is not sought prior to a busing program. Lower-class urban whites, who do not have the means to move to the suburbs, often view attempts to integrate their neighborhood schools as threats to their way of life. For example, in 1975 a federal judge ordered the exchange of some 24,000 students between the black and southern sections of Boston, in order to counter the segregating effects of gerrymandered school districts. However, the better-quality middle-class suburban schools were not involved in the busing program (for reasons we will discuss later). In effect, blacks were being bused to city schools that were inadequate and overcrowded to begin with. The Irish and Polish of South Boston saw themselves as oppressed ethnic minorities and felt that their community, power, and cultural identities were being threatened.[25] Their opposition to busing was harsh, and it was many months before the school system achieved a semblance of order.

As previously suggested, there is also a great deal of controversy about whether or not school integration, even if achieved, will result in better education. Coleman found that the most important predictors of children's success in school were their backgrounds and social environments; schools were of relatively little importance in affecting achievement.[26] In a more recent study, Sar Levitan, William Johnston, and Robert Taggart found that "there is no proof that integration, increased outlays per pupil, more relevant curricula, or any changes have had, or will have, a rapid and significant impact"[27] on improving the school performance of black slum children. On the other hand, a statewide study of Michigan's school system suggested that there was a positive relationship between school services and student achievement.[28] And another study of ten communities across the United States by the U.S. Commission on Civil Rights found large improvements in the quality of education in all these communities as a result of school desegregation.[29] Despite the efforts of a host of experts, then, the evidence thus far is inconclusive about the effects of desegregation on academic achievement.

It should be noted, however, that improving educational quality is *not* the only purpose of desegregating schools. Many observers see desegregation as a way for whites and minority group members to learn to get along with each other on a personal basis. According to this viewpoint, stereotyping and racism are much less likely to occur when people of different groups get to know each other as individuals. As Cohen points out, desegregation "seems a necessary step toward equality because it is

[25] John Buell and Tom deLuca, "On busing." *Progressive,* April 1975, pp. 26–27.

[26] See Coleman.

[27] In Juan Cameron, "Black America: Still waiting for full membership." *Fortune,* April 1975, p. 172.

[28] James W. Guthrie *et al., Schools and Inequality.* Cambridge, Mass.: M.I.T. Press, 1971.

[29] U.S. Commission on Civil Rights, *School Desegregation in Ten Communities.* Washington, D.C.: U.S. Government Printing Office, 1973. The communities included Pontiac, Michigan, Pasadena, California, and Las Vegas, Nevada.

an obvious way to break down racist ideas and institutional arrangements." [30] Others say that it is difficult to accurately test the educational progress of students who are bused when busing and desegregation are accompanied by disruption, hostility, or violence. In Ford's words,

Very few civil rights leaders are surprised that test scores do not substantially improve, or racial attitudes markedly change, during an initial period of desegregation. . . . Indeed, given the level of violence and tension in [newly desegregated] schools, it would be a miracle if test scores did not go down and stereotyped attitudes did not become more fixed in these initial stages. The hope is not so much for the present. . . . The hope is that . . . when the present turmoil has subsided, black and white . . . children . . . will begin to go to school together in peace and begin to learn to love and respect each other and to appreciate each other's diverse talents and contributions.[31]

There is considerable evidence that busing *can* be an effective method of desegregating schools in certain situations. For example, school officials in a few smaller communities were able to ease fears about the effects of busing by calling a series of parents' meetings before the school term began. Black and white parents discussed and planned the busing program together, and racial hostilities were prevented. In the ten communities studied by the U.S. Civil Rights Commission, the busing program worked because funds were provided to upgrade the educational quality of all the schools involved.[32] School officials in some other communities (such as Goldsboro, North Carolina) created highly desirable special programs in black schools that white children could not obtain unless they were bused.[33] In other areas, compromise busing plans were developed to prevent white flight. For example, in Louisville, Kentucky, children attend their neighborhood schools two days a week and are bused to integrated schools in another county the other three days.[34] In cases such as these, desegregation was accompanied by a marked increase in educational quality for black children.

Perhaps the best way to make busing effective would be to bus children between town or city schools and much higher quality suburban schools. Not only would disadvantaged minority children obtain the best possible education, but white flight would no longer be possible. However, in 1974 the Supreme Court ruled in a case involving Detroit that while the Constitution required desegregation within a city, it did not require it between city schools and suburban schools, which are usually in another county.[35] (In fact, where city and suburban schools are combined in one county system—such as Charlotte, North Carolina, and Nashville, Tennessee—well-to-do whites could not leave the school system and busing has been successful.)[36] Despite some successful busing programs,

[30] David K. Cohen, "Segregation, desegregation, and Brown: A twenty-year retrospective." *Society,* November–December 1975, p. 37.
[31] See Ford.
[32] *School Desegregation in Ten Communities.*
[33] *New York Times,* December 21, 1975, p. 3.
[34] See Ford.
[35] Cohen, p. 34.
[36] *U.S. News & World Report,* August 11, 1975, p. 26.

most communities have either instituted busing programs in ways that provoke racial antagonisms—such as occurred in Boston—or have been forced to give up busing because a sufficient number of white students were no longer available within the community.[37]

Clearly the question of busing is a complex one, and all the evidence is not yet in. In common justice, and in conformity with the meaning of the Constitution, the nation is bound to do all it can to provide equality of educational opportunity—not only in law but in fact—for all children. The question is, how? Interestingly enough, most Americans still seem to believe that integration is a necessary and desirable part of the solution. A 1975 Harris survey found 56 percent of adults in favor and 35 percent opposed to desegregation of public schools. These percentages did not vary significantly in any region of the country. On the question of busing, however, opinions were sharply reversed: 20 percent favored busing and 74 percent were opposed to it.[38] A recent Gallup poll found that even among blacks, only 40 percent were in favor of busing, and 47 percent were opposed.[39] How, then, are we to achieve equality of educational opportunity for all children? And if by integration, how are we to manage this without compulsory busing? One possible approach is through the desegregation of housing.

HOUSING

Housing segregation, the separation and isolation of minorities into areas, cities, neighborhoods, blocks, and even individual buildings, has become increasingly solidified during the last several decades. The major demarcation is between the whites in the suburbs and the blacks and other minorities in the inner cities.

A look at some recent census findings will indicate the growth of white out-migration from cities to surrounding suburbs. In the decade of the sixties, the white population of the central cities in the Northeast went from 14.9 million to 13.5 million, a decline of 10 percent. During the same period, the white population of the suburban areas of these same cities increased from 17.6 million to 20.2 million, an increase of 15 percent.[40]

While whites were moving to the suburbs, blacks were moving to the cities at an even faster rate. During this decade, New York City experienced a net migration increase of 38.2 percent in black population. Other cities with black populations of 50,000 or more experienced similar gains. Dallas, Los Angeles, Boston, and Detroit showed net increases of over 20 percent; only Birmingham, Alabama, had a decline in black population due to out-migration.[41] Though this rate of white migration to the suburbs and black migration to the cities had declined by the mid-1970s, a segregated pattern of housing had become firmly established.

[37] Sandra Stencel, "Educational equality." *Editorial Research Reports,* August 24, 1973, p. 659.

[38] Louis Harris, *The Harris Survey.* New York: Chicago Tribune N.Y. News Syndicate, October 2, 1975, p. 1.

[39] *New York Times,* December 21, 1975.

[40] "Trends in social and economic conditions: Population change by region for central cities and suburban rings." *Current Population Reports,* Series P-23, no. 33, September 3, 1970.

[41] "Negro population in selected places and selected counties," *1970 Census of the Population.* Washington, D.C.: U.S. Government Printing Office, June 1971.

Within cities, minorities are segregated into specific, usually less affluent neighborhoods. A *New York Times* analysis of the 1970 census figures showed that more than two-thirds of New York City's 2,159 census tracts were either 90 percent white or 90 percent black. There remain, according to the *Times,* a few integrated neighborhoods in the city, but the trend is clearly toward expansion of minority-dominated areas. This usually also means the expansion of poverty and the spread of "urban blight." Dr. Abraham C. Burstein of New York's Human Resources Administration estimated that over 80 percent of the black population of New York live in the city's twenty-six officially designated poverty areas.[42] More recent statistics indicate that blacks make up only 5 percent of the nation's suburban population; three-fourths of all blacks live in urban areas and 60 percent live in the central cities.[43]

Most of today's housing crisis dates from the period after World War II, when the nation's population began to grow rapidly, accompanied by widespread migration to the cities. At that time the government, primarily by means of the mortgage programs of the Federal Housing Administration and the Veterans Administration, joined with private builders to encourage private development of the suburbs as a way to solve the housing crisis.[44] This seemed a reasonable approach, in view of the American free-enterprise tradition, and in terms of number of dwelling units provided, it worked spectacularly well. Unfortunately, the free-enterprise market created housing for those who could pay, and many minority people could not pay. For those who could, the FHA and VA guidelines for mortgage guarantees, designed to maintain the stability of neighborhoods and to encourage home ownership by young families with reasonably dependable earning prospects, presented obstacles and discouragement.[45] According to one study:

From 1935 to 1950—a period in which about 15 million new dwellings were constructed—the power of the national government was explicitly used to prevent integrated housing. Federal policies were based on the premise that economic and social stability could best be achieved through keeping neighborhood populations as homogeneous as possible. Thus, the *Underwriting Manual* of the Federal Housing Administration . . . warned that "if a neighborhood is to retain stability, it is necessary that properties shall continue to be occupied by the same social and racial group." It advised appraisers to lower their valuation of properties in mixed neighborhoods, "often to the point of rejection." FHA actually drove out of business some developers who insisted upon open policies.[46]

It was not until 1962, when President Kennedy signed a limited anti-discrimination executive order, that the federal government housing program became in any way integrationist. And although it would be inaccurate to cite federal housing policy as the only cause of housing

---

42 *New York Times,* March 6, 1972, pp. 1, 22.
43 "Social and economic status of black population," p. 1; and Cameron, pp. 168–169.
44 See, for example, Bertram Weissbourd, *Segregation, Subsidies and Megalopolis.* Santa Barbara, Calif.: Center for the Study of Democratic Institutions, 1964.
45 Eunice Grier and George Grier, " Equality and beyond: Housing segregation in the Great Society." *Daedalus* 95 (Winter 1966):77–87.
46 Grier and Grier, p. 82.

discrimination—other factors such as the refusal of some whites to sell their houses to blacks, the suburban zoning patterns which tended to keep out poorer families, and the ties within minority communities themselves all played a part—it must be said that the officially sanctioned practices and policies of the federal housing agencies from the mid-1930s until 1962 are the major reasons American housing is segregated as it is today. It has also been pointed out that although since 1965 federal law has prohibited discrimination in the rental, sale, or financing of suburban housing, this law has remained largely unenforced.[47]

What housing is available to minorities is often overpriced, primarily as a result of "blockbusting." In this too common practice, real estate agents use warnings of minority "invasion" and of lowered property values to frighten white homeowners into selling their houses at reduced prices to the agent, who then resells them at inflated prices to members of minority groups. Today, blacks occupy about one-tenth of all housing units in the country; but more than twice as many black households as white households lack some or all plumbing facilities.[48] (For a further discussion of housing and poverty, see Chapter 6.)

Statistics, of course, do not tell the whole story. Robert Burnette in *The Tortured Americans* describes the housing problems of another American minority:

Until 1961 Indians were excluded from plans for public housing projects. They lived, as many still do, in tarpaper shacks, rickety log houses, ragged tents, abandoned automobile bodies, and hillside caves. When public housing did become available to the Indians, the inevitable corruption that attaches itself like a leech to such projects made a mockery of the program's intentions.

Burnette reports how things went for his tribe, the Rosebud Sioux, after the inception of a federal housing program in 1967:

By the end of 1969 the program was a complete failure—except to those who made criminal profits from the construction of the homes. Today there are 375 cheap, defective houses made of ⅜-inch plywood on the reservation. Ceilings are caving in, roofs leak, walls are crooked, and floor joists show through the tiles. Over three hundred of the houses do not have back or frontsteps. Over a fourth of the houses are uncompleted; they have no toilets, no plumbing or bathtubs, no cupboards or cabinets or sinks.[49]

Carmichael and Hamilton sum up what "the housing problem" means in minority lives, and suggest why it is going to get worse rather than better unless positive action is taken:

In America we judge by American standards, and by this yardstick we find that the black man lives in incredibly inadequate housing, shabby shelters that are dangerous to mental and physical health and to life itself. It has been estimated that twenty million black people put fifteen billion dollars into rents, mortgage payments and housing expenses every year. But because his

This American Indian woman lives on the reservation in a shanty made of dirt and wood.
Chie Nishio/Nancy Palmer

[47] See Cameron.
[48] "Social and economic status of black population," p. 134.
[49] Robert Burnette, *The Tortured Americans*. Englewood Cliffs, N.J.: Prentice-Hall, 1971, pp. 22, 145–146.

choice is largely limited to the ghettos, and because the black population is increasing at a [high] rate . . . , the shelter shortage for the black person is not only acute and perennial, but getting increasingly tighter. Black people are automatically forced to pay top dollar for whatever they get, even a 6 x 6 cold water flat.[50]

Furthermore, as Cameron points out,

blacks who aspire to be homeowners have also been hit by a cruel economic trend; just as their incomes began rising rapidly, the cost of housing shot up rapidly too.

To make matters worse, industry has followed the move of middle-income whites to the suburbs. Effectively barred from living near the relocated businesses, blacks have found themselves shot out of jobs.[51]

One feature of the growing political awareness of American minorities has been a demand for effective action on the housing front. Most of the government-sponsored low-income housing programs of the past have run aground on corruption (see Chapter 4), poor planning, or community resistance. Somehow, in the next few years, the nation must find a way to provide decent housing for all its people.

[50] Stokely S. Carmichael and Charles V. Hamilton, *Black Power: The Politics of Liberation in America.* New York: Random House, 1968, p. 237.
[51] Cameron, p. 169.

A Puerto Rican family living in a tenement apartment in a large city. The rents for such apartments are often exorbitantly high.
Joel Gordon

The idea of work as the way to better oneself is deeply ingrained in the American ethos. Although probably no longer as pervasive as it once was, the American work ethic still holds that if you really want a job, you can find one, and if you work hard, you will make money. The corollary to this is the notion that if you are wealthy, you deserve your wealth because you worked for it, and if you are poor, it is because you are lazy.

Thus one hears the argument that if only blacks and Puerto Ricans and Indians would make the effort to find jobs and stick to them, they could improve their lot. Unfortunately, discrimination—institutionalized and other—is no less prevalent in employment than it is in education and housing.

In some ways, discrimination in employment is a direct result of discrimination in education. We have already noted the relationship between income level and education level, and the fact that minorities tend to receive less education than whites. Since today the chances of finding even an entry-level job without a high school diploma are slim, this lack of education means that many minority persons will spend their lives underemployed or unemployed. This in turn means a low income, resulting in inferior housing, probably in a segregated neighborhood, with the likelihood of a poor education for the next generation, and so on—a cycle of discrimination built into the system.

Is there any escape from this cycle? What of those jobs which inherently do not require much formal education, which one learns mostly through apprenticeship—the kind of jobs represented by many labor unions?

Historically, labor unions, especially at the higher levels, have been in the forefront of civil rights battles, but union locals have often resisted minority demands for membership. Gould points out a basic conflict between the rhetoric of union leadership and established union policies and practices. Unions, like other institutions, are resistant to internal change or economic sacrifice for the purpose of accommodating the demands of minority workers.[52] There are only so many jobs to go around, and those who have them want to keep them.

This means that union-sponsored job-training programs are for the most part closed to minority workers. Progress in opening apprenticeship and training programs has been slow and, as the national economic and general employment picture has worsened in recent years, has been marked by growing bitterness and resistance. The New York City Commission on Human Rights reported that "a pattern of exclusion exists in a substantial portion of the building construction industry, effectively barring non-whites from participation in this area."[53] With the exception of the carpenters' and electricians' unions, trade unions in New York have fought every attempt to open their programs to nonwhites. One local went so far as to reject the results of court-ordered competitive tests

[52] William B. Gould, "Discrimination and the unions." In Jeremy Larner and Irving Howe, eds., *Poverty: Views from the Left.* New York: William Morrow, 1968, pp. 168–183.
[53] In Julius Jacobson, "Union conservatism: A barrier to racial equality." In Julius Jacobson, ed., *The Negro and the American Labor Movement.* Garden City, N.Y.: Doubleday, 1968.

Mexican-American grape pickers such as these are usually forced to work at well below the minimum wage. Note the somewhat ironic label on the grape boxes.
George Ballis/Black Star

when twenty-nine of the top sixty scores were achieved by blacks, claiming that to score so high, the blacks must have cheated.[54]

Nationwide, there has been some improvement in this situation, so that by 1975 blacks comprised a third of all new members in trade unions and 12 percent of total union membership. In some unions, notably those of steel and auto workers and state and municipal employees, blacks accounted for a third of the membership.[55] However, these newly unionized black workers are among the first to be laid off (because of the union seniority system) during a recession.

The overall employment picture is not bright. Current statistics indicate that minority members hold a disproportionate number of the lower-level, lower-paying jobs. Even when they do secure better jobs, they are frequently paid less than white workers in comparable jobs. Latest figures from the Census Bureau show that blacks and people of Spanish origin are more likely than whites to be service workers and laborers and less likely to be salespeople and white-collar workers; while 6.8 percent

[54] See Jacobson.
[55] Cameron, pp. 162–165.

of the white labor force work as salespeople, only 1.9 percent of the blacks and 3.9 percent of the Spanish-origin labor force have such jobs. Even among blue-collar workers, where minorities are heavily represented, the lowest-level jobs are two to three times as likely to be held by blacks or Puerto Ricans or Chicanos as by whites. Of course, there has been some improvement in this situation over the years. In 1964 there were fewer than one out of five blacks in white-collar occupations; ten years later approximately one in three blacks had white-collar jobs. However, this is in marked contrast to the fact that whites still hold half of all of these positions.[56] Furthermore, the unskilled worker faces not only low wages but also the prospect of job elimination as a result of technological change.

Sharp differences still exist between the average income of black and white workers. In 1951 the median income of black workers was about 57 percent of that for white workers. Today the gap is not much narrower. For example, in 1974 the median income for whites was estimated to be $13,400; for blacks, it was $7,800 [57] and for families headed by a person of Spanish origin it was $9,600.[58] About 35 percent of black families earned more than $10,000 a year; but about a third of all black families (8 million people) were below the poverty level, a figure that had remained constant for some half-dozen years.[59] (See Figure 7-2.) Unemployment among minorities is also much worse than among whites (see Figure 7-3). By the end of 1974 the unemployment rate for whites was 6.4 percent, for blacks 12.5 percent, and for Spanish-speaking workers, 8.2 percent. For more than two decades the unemployment ratio of blacks to whites has been approximately 2 to 1, except for a temporary narrowing of the gap in 1970–1971.[60] For teenagers the gap is even greater: in 1975, the unemployment rate for black teenagers was 39.8 percent, compared to 18 percent for their white peers.[61]

The employment plight of blacks and other minorities is well summed up by Fein:

What is recession for the white (say, an unemployment rate of 6 percent) is prosperity for the non-white. . . . Therefore, perhaps it is appropriate to say that whites fluctuate between prosperity and recession but Negroes fluctuate between depression and great depression.[62]

The final area we will examine in our attempt to highlight the pervasive nature of institutionalized discrimination is the realm of justice. Two basic assumptions in American law have always been, first, that justice

SOCIAL JUSTICE

[56] *Manpower Report of the President.* Washington, D.C.: U.S. Government Printing Office, April 1975, pp. 34–35.

[57] "Social and economic status of black population," pp. 1, 2.

[58] "Persons of Spanish origin in the United States: March 1975." *Current Population Reports,* Series P-20, August 1975, pp. 2, 7.

[59] Cameron, p. 162.

[60] *Manpower Report of the President,* pp. 33–35.

[61] "Social and economic status of black population," p. 2.

[62] Rashi Fein, "An economic and social profile of the Negro American." In Talcott Parsons and Kenneth B. Clark, eds., *The Negro American.* Boston: Beacon Press, 1966, pp. 114–115.

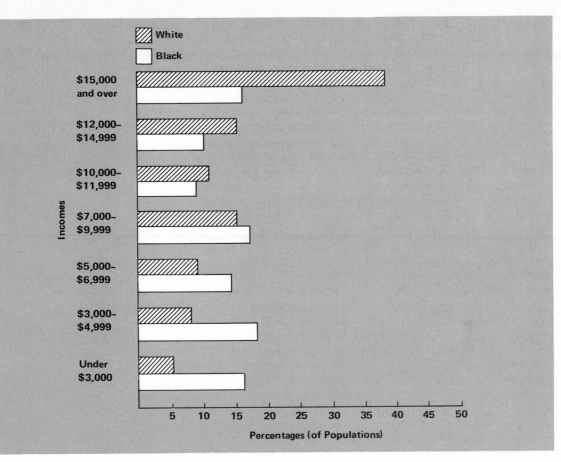

White
Black

$15,000 and over

$12,000–$14,999

$10,000–$11,999

$7,000–$9,999

$5,000–$6,999

$3,000–$4,999

Under $3,000

Incomes

5 10 15 20 25 30 35 40 45 50

Percentages (of Populations)

FIGURE 7-2
Black and White
Family Incomes

Source: U.S. Department of Commerce, Bureau of the Census. *Statistical Abstract of the United States.* Washington, D.C.: U.S. Government Printing Office.

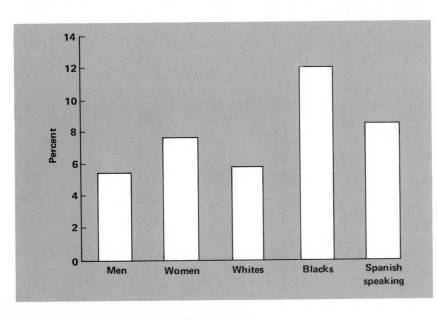

14

12

10

8

6

4

2

0

Percent

Men   Women   Whites   Blacks   Spanish speaking

FIGURE 7-3
Unemployment Among
Various Labor Force
Groups

Source: Manpower Report of the President. Washington, D.C.: U.S. Government Printing Office, 1975, p. 33.

is blind—that racial, ethnic, economic, or social considerations should have no influence in findings of guilt or innocence under law—and, second, that people accused of a crime are to be considered innocent until proven guilty in a court of law. The question is, do these assumptions apply equally to minorities and to whites?

As noted in Chapter 4, minorities are overrepresented in official arrest records, and it seems probable that a minority individual is, in general, more likely than a white individual to be arrested and charged with a crime, whether or not he is guilty. Following arrest, there is the bail system to cope with. And it is here that the American social justice system is perhaps inherently discriminatory against minorities. To begin with, bail is a question of money: those who have money can usually secure release following their arrest, to await trial in freedom, subject to the limitations of the bail agreement. Second, the long wait in many jurisdictions (particularly in large cities) between arrest and trial creates a particular hardship for those who cannot make bail. They must remain in jail until trial, often for months, sometimes for more than a year. This borders on punishment before conviction, and certainly runs counter to the American legal precept of presumed innocence.

One of the few systematic studies of the entire bail system, the Manhattan Bail Project, found that abuses of the bail system were responsible for even more inequality than this. The theoretical objectives of bail are to prevent punishment before conviction and to ensure the attendance at trial of the accused. However, most judges use bail punitively—they set excessively high bail simply to make it more likely that defendants will be detained. Unfortunately, defendants who cannot raise bail and who therefore spend time in jail are less likely to receive favorable dispositions of their cases.[63] As Wice points out, "Numerous studies clearly show that detained defendants are far more likely to be found guilty and receive more severe sentences than those released prior to trial. Limited visiting hours, locations remote from the counsel's office, inadequate conference facilities, and censored mail all serve to impede an effective lawyer-client relationship." [64]

In effect, then, under the current bail system, minority defendants are often presumed guilty because they are poor. Subsequent studies have since confirmed the widespread misuse of the bail system. For example, the United States Commission on Civil Rights found similar practices with regard to Chicanos in the Southwest:

The system of bail in the Southwest frequently is used more severely against Mexican-Americans than against Anglos as a form of discrimination. In certain cases, Mexican-American defendants are faced with excessively high bail. Defendants in other cases are held without any opportunity to put up bail or are purposely confused by local officials about the bail hearing so that they unknowingly forfeit their bail. In one area local farmers put up

Declan Haun/Black Star

---

[63] Charles E. Ares, Anne Rankin, and Herbert Sturz, "The Manhattan Bail Project." *New York University Law Review* 38 (1963):67–92.
[64] Paul Bernard Wice, *Bail and Its Reform: A National Survey*. Washington, D.C.: U.S. Government Printing Office, 1973, p. 23.

bail or pay fines for migrant workers and make them work off the amount in a situation resembling peonage or involuntary servitude.[65]

In his survey, Wice found a nationwide problem of bail being used punitively. The most significant factor affecting the amount of bail set was the seriousness of the crime charged, despite evidence that this is not directly related to whether or not the defendant will appear for trial. The criterion least frequently considered by judges was, paradoxically, the one with the greatest influence on defendants' ability to post bond—namely, their financial status.[66]

From this evidence it is easy to see why more minority defendants are convicted than are acquitted. Even those who can make bail can rarely afford a costly defense, and those who are detained have little opportunity to prepare a defense at all. It also follows that a disproportionate number are on probation, and have their mobility and employment opportunities limited by criminal records.

This inequality in the administration of justice extends even to the sentencing process itself. Though blacks constitute about 11 percent of the population, they comprise 42 percent of the jail population; whites are much more likely to be released on their own recognizance or given suspended sentences. In prison, black sentences tend to be longer than white sentences, particularly for serious offenses (see Table 7-1). In a recent year, for example, the average prison sentence for murder or kidnapping was *ten times* longer for blacks than for whites (for those sentences not being appealed). Fully half of all those sentenced to death were black.[67]

Such discrimination was not in the original intention of American justice, though the perversion of that justice by the forces of the law has sometimes been deliberate. The fact that various organizations concerned with constitutional law and civil liberties are becoming increasingly alert to the existence and the dangers of discriminatory justice gives hope that some abuses will eventually be eliminated. But given what seems to be a common human propensity to take advantage of the weak, we can assume that social justice can never be trusted to take care of itself. Here, if anywhere, eternal vigilance is in truth the price of liberty.

SOME CONSEQUENCES OF PREJUDICE AND DISCRIMINATION

The harmful effects of prejudice and discrimination are not limited to minorities. The lives of members of the dominant group are nearly always stunted by the artificial barriers and warped perceptions which such

[65] *Mexican Americans and the Administration of Justice in the Southwest.* A Report of the United States Commission on Civil Rights. Washington, D.C.: U.S. Government Printing Office, 1970, p. 52.
[66] Wice, pp. 4–5, 13–14.
[67] "Social and economic status of black population," pp. 6, 162, 170–171.

TABLE 7-1
Length of Sentences
for Selected Crimes,
by Race

Appeal Status and Type of Crime		Median Number of Months Sentenced	
		Black	White
NOT ON APPEAL			
Murder or kidnapping		66.1	5.8
Rape		10.7	5.9
Robbery		52.9	11.5
Burglary		10.5	10.8
Assault:	Aggravated	13.3	11.1
	Simple	6.0	2.6
Larceny:	Grand	10.0	10.2
	Petty	2.9	2.8
Auto theft		5.6	4.7
Drugs:	Sale	9.3	5.0
	Possession or use	11.2	5.4
ON APPEAL			
Murder or kidnapping		598.9	439.7
Rape		498.9	598.9
Robbery		236.1	166.8
Burglary		37.4	86.8

Source: "The social and economic status of the black population in the United States." Current Population Reports, Series P–23, No. 54, July 1975, p. 174.

social divisions entail. Here, however, we will consider principally the effects on the subordinate group, for these are usually more demonstrably serious.

What happens to people who must live in an environment of institutionalized discrimination and its accompanying prejudice? There are, of course, effects on the individual personalities of minority members. And both individuals and groups develop protective reactions against this prejudice and discrimination.

First, let us consider the effects of discrimination on individual personalities. In his ground-breaking work, *Children of Crisis,* psychologist Robert Coles documents some of the personality effects among the first black children to attend desegregated schools in the South. These children were subjected to blatant discrimination and bitter prejudice, including outright mob action against them and their parents. Over a period of months, Coles observed the children and particularly the way they perceived their world and themselves as expressed in drawings. His account of the drawings of one black girl, Ruby, during this time is particularly fascinating. For months she would never use brown or black except to indicate the ground. However, she distinguished between white and black people.

She drew white people larger and more lifelike. Negroes were smaller, their bodies less intact. A white girl we both knew to be her own size appeared several times taller. While Ruby's own face lacked an eye in one drawing, an ear in another, the white girl never lacked any features. Moreover, Ruby drew the white girl's hands and legs carefully, always making sure that they had the proper number of fingers and toes. Not so with her own limbs, or those of any other Negro children she chose (or was asked) to picture. A thumb or forefinger might be missing, or a whole set of toes. The arms were shorter, even absent or truncated.

At the same time Jimmy, a white classmate of Ruby's, always depicted blacks as somehow related to animals or at least extremely dirty and dangerous. Over the course of about two years of contact with Ruby and other black children in his desegregated school in New Orleans, Jimmy grew less fearful of blacks, and the change was reflected in his drawings. Coles concludes that children of each race were conditioned to fear and distrust members of the other race, but that with continuing friendly contact these prejudices were broken down and that the children eventually helped to change the parents' attitudes as well.[68]

Kenneth Clark describes the destructive effect of discrimination as he perceived it in some black adults:

Human beings who are forced to live under ghetto conditions and whose daily experience tells them that almost nowhere in society are they respected and granted the ordinary dignity and courtesy accorded to others will, as a matter of course, begin to doubt their own worth. Since every human being depends upon his cumulative experiences with others for clues as to how he should view and value himself, children who are consistently rejected understandably begin to question and doubt whether they, their family, and their group really deserve no more respect from the larger society than they receive. These doubts become the seeds of pernicious self- and group-hatred, the Negro's complex and debilitating prejudice against himself. . . . Negroes have come to believe in their own inferiority.[69]

Black separatism is one reaction to the discrimination and prejudice of the dominant white. In his autobiography, Malcolm X claimed that integration is a way out of the ghetto existence only for the very few "white-minded" middle-class blacks who are "more anti-black than even the white man is," not for the masses of black people who actually prefer associating with their own kind. The hope he had for them leads elsewhere:

The American black man should be focusing his every effort toward building his *own* businesses, and decent homes for himself. As other ethnic groups have done, let the black people, wherever possible, patronize their own kind, hire their own kind, and start in those ways to build up the black race's ability to do for itself. That's the only way the American black man is ever going to get respect. One thing the white man never can give the black man is self-respect! The black man never can become independent and recognized as a human being who is truly equal with other human beings until he has what they have, and until he is doing for himself what others are doing for themselves.[70]

[68] Robert Coles, *Children of Crisis*. New York: Dell, 1968, pp. 47, 53, 60.
[69] Kenneth B. Clark, *Dark Ghetto*. New York: Harper & Row, 1965.
[70] Malcolm X and Alex Haley, ed., *The Autobiography of Malcolm X*. New York: Grove Press, 1964, pp. 173, 177.

The Indian occupation of Wounded Knee and the efforts of Cesar Chavez to organize Chicano migrant farm workers are indications that minority groups are no longer willing to tolerate prejudice and discrimination against them.
Michael Abramson/ Black Star

Marcus Garvey, in the 1920s, espoused another, more extreme form of separatism. His plan was to seize control of Africa from European colonial powers and build a free United Black Africa. This was to be achieved by repatriation of New World blacks and the cooperation of like-minded Africans. Garvey did not believe the race problem in America would work itself out:

There is not one instance where a slave race living in the same country (within the same bounds as the race that enslaved them and being in numbers less than the race of the masters) has ever yet ruled and governed the masters. It has never been so in history, and it will never be so in the future.[71]

But the most common reaction against inequality during the last decades has been public protest. Following the success of the Montgomery bus boycott of 1955–1956 (when blacks avoided riding buses until discriminatory seating rules were eliminated), a broad social movement for desegregation emerged. Initially under the leadership of Dr. Martin Luther King, Jr., protests were directed against laws which were enforced unequally, or which created a statutory inequality—that is, against obstructions maintained to deny minorities rights and privileges enjoyed by other Americans.

[71] Amy Jacques Garvey, ed., *Philosophy and Opinions of Marcus Garvey*. New York: Atheneum, 1970, p. 57.

In the 1960s, however, as perceptible progress slowed, and resistance and backlash increased with growing economic pressures and political uncertainty, minority protest sometimes took more violent forms. Feelings of anger, frustration, and rage provoked riots in many cities throughout the United States. Often, the last straw that led to a riot was the arrest of blacks by white policemen.[72] The police served as visible symbols of the attitude of the entire white majority: white power, white discrimination, white repression. It is no wonder, then, that in situations where blacks felt themselves to be the victims of bitter discrimination, the police often sparked a violent response. At no time, however, did a majority of blacks approve of the violent protests that took place, whether or not they felt that these helped the black cause.[73] In fact, by the mid-1970s race riots had ceased to be the dominant form of protest by blacks. The recession during this period saw whites as well as blacks suffering from high unemployment rates and inflation (though not, as we have seen, in the same proportions), and expectations of progress were reduced. Furthermore, the end of the Vietnam War and the draft caused a general decline in protest movements, which may have affected blacks as well. There may also have been a sense that riots had reached the limit of

[72] *Report of the National Advisory Commission,* p. 206.
[73] Peter Godman, *Report from Black America.* New York: Simon & Schuster, 1970, pp. 229–270.

their effectiveness in changing the condition of blacks, and that more deliberate, organized efforts had become necessary. There is also the possibility, as Piven and Cloward have theorized, that welfare rolls were increased in response to the riots and that this had the effect of mollifying blacks.[74] (See also Chapter 5, "Violence.")

In any event, blacks apparently still felt that institutions were not responsive to their needs and problems. Whereas in 1963, the federal government was seen as a positive force by 83 percent of blacks, by 1972 black confidence in government was down to a low of 16 percent. (This paralleled a similar but not as dramatic trend among whites.) Along with reduced confidence was a sense that much still remained to be done: for example, 79 percent of blacks favored an increase of federal assistance to the poor.[75] Another survey found that four out of ten blacks hold the view that the American system is no longer viable and that radical alternatives to end discrimination are necessary.[76] Though the majority of American blacks still hope for peaceful change, they share with their more radical brothers and sisters the sense that discrimination is still rampant in our society and that it will require major efforts on a legal, political, and economic front to completely eliminate it.

Recent years have also seen a growing activism on the part of Chicanos and American Indians. Cesar Chavez, the head of the United Farm Worker's Union, led strikes and instigated nationwide boycotts of grapes and lettuce to improve conditions for his migrant Chicano workers. American Indians protested against their economic and social powerlessness in places such as Wounded Knee, South Dakota, Phoenix, Arizona, and Alcatraz prison in California. These skirmishes were less visible because they usually took place in isolated or sparsely settled areas and were comparatively nonviolent. But the growth of "red power" movements and new efforts to organize Chicano workers clearly heralded a reawakened American Indian and Chicano consciousness.

SOCIAL ACTION

With the rise in consciousness of blacks and other minorities and the demands of minorities for a more equal share in the benefits of the American way of life, various programs have been instituted to alleviate the effects of prejudice and discrimination on the minorities of this country. In this section we will examine some of these programs in terms of their approaches, goals, and effectiveness.

[74] Frances Fox Piven and Richard A. Cloward, *Regulating the Poor: The Functions of Public Welfare.* New York: Random House, 1971. For further discussion of this thesis see Michael Betz, "Riots and welfare: Are they related?" *Social Problems,* vol. 21, no. 3 (1974); "Correspondence." *Social Problems,* vol. 22, no. 2 (1974); and William A. Muraskin's review in *Contemporary Sociology* (November 1975).
[75] Louis Harris, *The Harris Poll.* New York: Chicago Tribune N.Y. News Syndicate, November 22, 1972.
[76] "Black Americans, 1963–1973." *Editorial Research Reports,* August 15, 1973, p. 624.

With the inception of the "War on Poverty" in 1964, there was a major shift of emphasis in national manpower policy. In the past, the principal concern had been with manpower as an economic resource to the nation, and particularly with the scientific and technical manpower needed to support the expansion of technology. Now the focus was changed to center more on the worker—on helping those who had difficulty finding employment because of inadequate training and/or a lack of available jobs. The concurrent economic recession has made this an especially difficult task, since evidently no amount of training can guarantee a job if no employer is hiring. Consequently, there has been considerable pressure on the government to provide jobs—to act as the "employer of last resort"—as well as to train workers. (See Chapter 6 for a discussion of government employment programs.)

(See Chapter 6 for a discussion of government employment programs.)

The training effort itself has been hampered by a lack of coordination among the various programs. There is no federal manpower policy as such. Programs have been established under the Manpower Training and Development Act, the Vocational Education Act of 1963, the Vocational Rehabilitation Program, manpower components of the Economic Opportunity Act, and the Comprehensive Employment Training Act of 1973. Each of these legislative efforts was drafted to meet a current crisis, without much thought to its relation to the others. They are also underfunded and simply too small in scale for the size of the problem. For example, the average enrollment at any given time in all training programs for the disadvantaged is under 300,000; yet in a recent year 1.3 million people were unemployed for fifteen weeks or longer, and the total number of jobless was over 6 million.[77] The fifteen-week unemployment figure alone is thus more than four times the average number of trainees.

The manpower programs that began in the late 1960s did, however, make some positive contributions. In addition to those persons who received job training and consequently secured higher-paying jobs, many more upgraded their skills in other ways. Some participated in counseling programs and academic study, and thus were better able to hold onto their jobs; and others qualified for high school equivalency diplomas, which improved their chances of finding employment. Motivation, for example, is an important factor if job training is to be effective, and actual on-the-job experience is often necessary for those unaccustomed to the discipline of job-holding.

Thus there are two major problems involving these manpower programs that remain to be solved. First, a way must be found to relate the training programs to the marketplace, so that, after training, there will be a reasonable likelihood of obtaining an actual, paying job. At the present time only about 62 percent of enrollees in these programs find employment.[78] Second, the underfinancing of these programs must be ended. Only a massively expanded manpower training program could begin to deal in a significant way with the lack of job training among minority groups.

MANPOWER TRAINING PROGRAMS

Head Start is a blanket term covering most federally funded preschool intervention programs aimed at preparing disadvantaged youngsters for

HEAD START

[77] *Manpower Report of the President,* pp. 29, 82, 114.
[78] *Manpower Report of the President,* p. 115.

school. They were at one time the most popular programs among parents, administrators, and activists, although their principles and effectiveness have since been attacked from both the left and the right.

At its inception and during its early operation, Head Start performed a number of roles. It was a showcase program whose immediate effects became political capital to its supporters. Early research found improvements of 8 to 10 points in the IQs of 480 children in a summer Head Start program in Baltimore in 1965.[79] These immediate measurable gains in cognitive achievement heralded an enormous expansion of Head Start operations and a push for year-long programs throughout the country. From small beginnings, Head Start mushroomed to a program costing several hundred million dollars annually, serving over a half-million children, and supported by everyone from Congress to parents, but especially by educators and their lobbyists.

The initial goals of Head Start and its early popularity obscured some basic flaws. For one thing, while the concept of early intervention was popular among child development researchers, and while their research did in fact suggest that there is a real potential for intellectual improvement through early childhood training, there remain to this day few unchallenged guidelines as to exactly what is to be taught, how, when, and by whom.[80]

As with most massive social action programs, Head Start eventually went through a period of severe internal and external criticism. It has been criticized primarily on two grounds: first, that it has not done its job, and, second, that it has done the wrong job.

Most speakers for the first viewpoint feel that the early gains in cognitive achievement by Head Start participants were deceptive. Results of an evaluative study by the Westinghouse Learning Corporation and Ohio University indicated that gains in cognitive skill disappeared by the third grade, and that disadvantaged students who had not participated in Head Start performed at equivalent levels.[81] These results were the main reason federal funding for Head Start was eventually reduced.

Other critics argued that Head Start intervened too late and for too short a period to be effective. According to this view, the most important period for a child's emotional, social, and intellectual development is the first three years of life, when the child begins to acquire language and learn to manipulate the surrounding world. Parents, not teachers, are therefore the most important educators of the child, and for intervention to be effective, it must begin during infancy in the child's own home. One experimental program in Brookline, Massachusetts, is attempting to test the effectiveness of this very early intervention approach by supplementing the parents' role with trained teacher-counselors who visit each young child regularly.[82]

[79] Sar A. Levitan, "Head Start: It is never too early to fight poverty." *Federal Programs for the Development of Human Resources.* Washington, D.C.: Joint Economic Committee, Subcommittee on Economic Progress, 1968, pp. 425–428.

[80] Walter Williams and John W. Evans, "The politics of evaluation: The case of Head Start." *Annals of the American Academy of Political and Social Science* 385 (September 1969):122.

[81] See Williams and Evans.

[82] Maya Pines, "Head Head Start." *New York Times Magazine,* October 26, 1975, p. 14.

Defenders of Head Start argue that cost-effectiveness analysis is inappropriate in this type of program, suggesting that many of the gains do not show up on IQ tests. They point to improvement in motivation and psychological adjustments among Head Start students and suggest that these students have pulled the non–Head Start disadvantaged up to their level rather than regressing themselves.[83]

Radical critics of childhood intervention policy suggest that the whole thrust of the program is wrong. Stephen and Joan Baratz question the logic of intervention and its theory, which they say equates difference with inferiority. In fact, they believe, the inability of many minority children to learn in the standard educational environment may be a consequence not of their fundamental unpreparedness for learning, but of the school's unwillingness to teach them on the basis of the often considerable linguistic and cognitive skills they have already acquired in their own culture. Rather than destroy the disadvantaged preschoolers' culture, by eradicating their natural linguistic and logical methods, they recommend teaching the white middle-class majority's social *modus operandi* only in addition to the minority's ways. To brand children as incompetent in the school system and at the same time strip away the skills they have developed in order to survive in their subculture is a double punishment.[84]

Ray Rist expands on this criticism, suggesting that Head Start programs are based on the assumption that "what poor children needed was an initial boost of socialization to acquaint them with the values, behaviors, and ideas of non-poor middle-class Anglo conformity so that they would . . . pull themselves out of poverty." According to Rist, this approach ignores the institutional, economic, and social barriers minority groups face even after they leave school. It also ignores the fact that "each minority and ethnic culture has within it valuable and positive attributes that could be of contribution to the fabric of American society." What is needed, Rist believes, are educational settings "where those values and cultural forms valued by the minority group would be retained, but also where minority-group members would be equipped to partake of the dominant culture as they desire." All such programs are bound to fail, however, as long as prejudice and discrimination continue to exist in the rest of society.[85]

Some good, then, may have come from early childhood intervention and enrichment programs, but even at best they are not a panacea. The educational deficiencies of disadvantaged minorities, like all poverty-related problems, are not susceptible to simple, one-shot solutions. However, since the chances are that education will, for the most part, continue to be carried on in terms derived from the majority culture, it will be necessary to provide minority children with a fair chance to learn those terms—not as better than theirs, but simply as more useful in the particular situation. On the other hand, for the benefit of *all* students,

[83] "How head a Head Start?" *New Republic,* April 25, 1969, pp. 8–9.
[84] Stephen S. Baratz and Joan C. Baratz, "Early childhood intervention: The social science base of institutional racism." *Harvard Educational Review* 40 (Winter 1970):29–50.
[85] Ray C. Rist, "Race, policy, and schooling." *Society* (November–December 1975):59–63.

the cultural values and insights of the minority groups must be allowed into our school systems, as they are beginning to be in the form of black studies and women's studies programs at various levels; and all of the other forms of discrimination which we have discussed—in housing, unemployment, health care, legal justice, and the rest—must be corrected if minority children are to be as free to learn and to grow as their white classmates.

PROSPECTS

We have seen that the effects of prejudice and discrimination are harmful both to individuals and to the society as a whole, and we have considered some of the effects which are becoming evident today and some of the efforts being made, both by government agencies and by minorities themselves, to improve the situation. Some things are better today than they were a few years ago, and it is unlikely that America's minority groups will ever again accept uncomplainingly the subordinate status to which they were long condemned. What is not yet certain is whether improvement can continue to the point of real practical equality.

It is clear that designing effective busing programs will depend on changes in white attitudes toward minority groups or, at the very least, changes in the laws that now keep high-quality suburban schools off limits to inner city students. It is unlikely, however, that such changes will take place in the immediate future. For this reason, recent new efforts have been launched to improve the quality of minority group education without busing. In particular, cases have been filed to have the courts declare as unconstitutional inequities in school financing. (These inequities may be caused by the fact that city schools are poorly financed from public funds while suburban schools are well-financed from property taxes or by the fact that property values differ from one area to another.) However, in related cases the Supreme Court has shown itself reluctant to reform school funding practices; it therefore remains to be seen how true educational quality for all students can be achieved.

Attacks on exclusionary zoning ordinances that put the cost of suburban housing out of the reach of the poor, including minority group members, have been hampered by a Supreme Court decision that nonresidents of a community have no right to contest its zoning regulations. A recent decision by the U.S. Court of Appeals in New York did give nonresidents the right to challenge federal Housing and Urban Development grants to a community with discriminatory zoning practices. If this decision is upheld, communities who wish to qualify for federal funds will have to modify their zoning rules.[86] However, the decision leaves unaffected those communities that do not wish to receive grants. A more hopeful development was the Supreme Court's 1976 decision that the Department of Housing and Urban Development would have to provide low-cost housing for minorities in white suburbs if its public funding

[86] "Another crack in the suburban zoning wall." *Business Week,* July 21, 1975, p. 11.

programs contributed to segregation within the city. It is likely, however, that most suburbs will remain off limits to those who desperately need decent low-income housing, and that public funds will have to be used to supply or subsidize adequate housing in poorer communities.

Large-scale improvement of minority group employment opportunities will depend, of course, on improvements in education, expansion of manpower training programs, the ending of discriminatory wage and hiring practices, and a renewed dedication to a full-employment economy. In the meantime, the "last hired, first fired" policies of many companies must be ended if minority groups are to hold onto the gains they have made in the past fifteen years. A recent district court decision addressed this very situation when it held that a company must keep three separate seniority lists—for white males, women, and minority group members—so that layoffs would not change the proportions of these groups in the work force.[87]

Equality of justice ultimately depends on the eradication of conditions that breed crime and of prejudices that lead to overrepresentation of minority groups in arrest rates. Much can be done in the meantime, however, to reduce the discriminatory effects of the criminal justice system itself. For example, bail reform projects in many towns and cities have ensured pretrial release of those defendants who are good risks but who are otherwise likely to be detained because they cannot raise high bail. The method they generally used was to set a moderate bail, notify the defendants repeatedly of their scheduled court appearances, and supervise them casually throughout the pretrial period. Wice found that these programs were significantly more effective in assuring appearance at trial than traditional bail practices.[88] Inequities in sentencing can be reduced by limiting the judge's role in the setting of penalties. For example, mandatory minimum and maximum penalties can be established for each crime, thus reducing the effects of a judge's personal prejudices in sentencing.

SUMMARY

Social inequality has a long history in the United States, but contradicts the the egalitarian principles on which the nation was established. All minorities, ethnic as well as racial, have been subordinate to the dominant White Anglo-Saxon Protestant majority culture, but in particular blacks, Hispanics, and American Indians have been and continue to be exploited. The constitutional bases for equality were buttressed by U.S. Supreme Court decisions, several Civil Rights acts, and various other acts and presidential orders. But realities have not caught up with principles or laws.

Minority groups have been defined as categories of people that receive treatment less equal to that accorded other categories. The principal characteristic of a minority group is its subordinate status. The principal weapons the dominant group uses to maintain the status of the subordinate group are prejudice—irreversible prejudgment—and discrimination—overtly unequal treatment.

[87] "Affirmative action and layoffs." *Monthly Labor Review,* February 1975, pp. 77–78.
[88] See Wice.

Psychologically, prejudice and discrimination can result from feelings of frustration that lead to scapegoating, and from projection. Sociologically, they can result from the competition of groups for economic goods, which can lead to political dominance of one group and the exploitation of the other. Eventually prejudicial attitudes become stereotypes and discriminatory practices become social norms.

Institutional discrimination exists in many areas, particularly education, housing, employment, and social justice. The effort to compensate for the effects of educational discrimination through busing has run into opposition. There is doubt as to whether or not integration has lead to gains in learning or achievement, but considerable agreement that the turmoil that usually accompanies it can be detrimental to learning. Movements for reform of school financing to more nearly equalize per pupil expenditures and to improve education where the children are instead of busing them are gaining adherents.

Housing segregation has resulted in the clustering of minorities in substandard dwellings, usually in inner cities. Discrimination in employment results in minorities having lower-paying jobs and higher rates of unemployment. Arrest, bail, and sentencing practices also are more likely to fall with discriminatory harshness upon minority groups. Some reforms and improvements are beginning to be felt in these and related areas, including affirmative action plans in hiring and job training; early intervention in education; challenges of federal grants to communities with discriminatory zoning laws; and bail reform projects.

Prejudice and discrimination have resulted in feelings of personal and group inferiority; in movements for separatism; in general hostility toward members of the dominant culture; and, in the mid-1960s, in civil disturbances. However, the majority of blacks have been shown to be still hopeful of peaceful change, although younger people are less patient. And the majority of whites favor integration, although they strongly disapprove of such measures as busing to achieve it. The effects of discrimination may yet be eliminated if the majority is willing to share its privileges, if the working classes of all races can cooperate for mutual benefit, and if all Americans seriously consider the implications of their belief that all persons are created equal and implement that belief.

BIBLIOGRAPHY

Addison, Gayle. *The Black Situation*. New York: Horizon Press, 1970.

Bahr, Howard M., Chadwick, Bruce A., and Day, Robert C. *Native Americans Today: Sociological Perspectives*. New York: Harper & Row, 1972.

Banton, Michael, and Harwood, Jonathan. *The Race Concept*. New York: Praeger, 1975.

Blauner, Robert. *Racial Oppression in America*. New York: Harper & Row, 1972.

Clark, Kenneth B. *Dark Ghetto*. New York: Harper & Row, 1965.

Fantini, Mario D., and Weinstein, Gerald. *The Disadvantaged—Challenge to Education*. New York: Harper & Row, 1968.

Goldstein, Sidney, and Goldscheider, Calvin. *Jewish Americans: Three Generations in a Jewish Community*. Englewood Cliffs, N.J.: Prentice-Hall, 1968.

Greeley, Andrew M. *Ethnicity in the United States*. New York: Wiley, 1974.

Greenspan, C. L., and Hirsh, L. M. *All Those Voices: The Minority Experience.* New York: Macmillan, 1971.

Howard, John R., ed. *Awakening Minorities: American Indians, Mexican Americans, and Puerto Ricans.* Chicago: Aldine, 1970.

Kitano, Harry H. *Race Relations.* Englewood Cliffs, N.J.: Prentice-Hall, 1974.

Liebow, Elliot. *Tally's Corner.* Boston: Little, Brown, 1967.

Moore, Joan W., and Cuellar, Alfredo. *Mexican Americans.* Englewood Cliffs, N.J.: Prentice-Hall, 1970.

Pettigrew, Thomas. *Racially Separate or Together?* New York: McGraw-Hill, 1971.

Pinkney, Alphonso. *Black Americans.* 2nd ed. Englewood Cliffs, N.J.: Prentice-Hall, 1975.

Rainwater, Lee. *Behind Ghetto Walls: Black Families in a Federal Slum.* Chicago: Aldine, 1970.

Simpson, George E., and Yunger, J. M. *Racial and Cultural Minorities: An Analysis of Prejudice and Discrimination.* 4th ed. New York: Harper & Row, 1972.

Sung, Betty L. *Mountain of Gold: The Story of the Chinese in America.* New York: Macmillan, 1967.

Yetman, Norman R., and Steele, C. H., eds. *Majority and Minority: The Dynamics of Racial and Ethnic Relations.* 2nd ed. Boston: Allyn and Bacon, 1975.

8

SEX ROLES
AND INEQUALITY

- The proportion of women of working age in the labor force has increased by one-third since 1950, to about 45 percent; however, women's median annual earnings as a percentage of men's has declined since 1950, from about 65 to 57 percent.
- Women are concentrated in service occupations, making up, for example, 99 percent of the nation's secretaries but less than 1 percent of the nation's engineers.
- Thirty-three percent of families headed by a woman are below the poverty line, compared to 6 percent of families headed by a man.
- Surveys of school textbooks consistently find that females are underrepresented; when females do appear, they are generally pictured in passive or dependent roles.
- Women who do not conform to traditional stereotypes of femininity, and men who do not conform to traditional stereotypes of masculinity, are more likely than other men and women to be labeled as mentally ill.

"You've come a long way, baby" is the advertising slogan for a brand of cigarettes that seeks to project an image of the independent but glamorous woman. "The woman who smokes our cigarettes," the ad seems to say, "is professional but sexy." In many ways, this combination of traits symbolizes both the progress of women in our society and the long road to equality that still stretches ahead of them. On the one hand, many career opportunities that were once closed to women are now open to them, and more women than before can aspire to positions of independence and prestige. On the other hand, many barriers still stand in the way of women's advancement, not the least of which is the widespread notion that an important—and perhaps central—part of a woman's role is to try to be sexually appealing.

Over the past several decades women have made some notable gains. In 1940, less than 17 percent of women in the labor force were married. Today over 40 percent of women in the labor force are married.[1] The proportion of women in law, medical, and engineering schools, though

[1] See U.S. Department of Labor, *Manpower Report of the President*. Washington, D.C. U.S. Government Printing Office, 1975; and U.S. Bureau of the Census, *Statistical Abstracts of the United States 1975*. Washington, D.C.: U.S. Government Printing Office, 1975, p. 346.

still low, is rising steadily.[2] Even in such traditionally male fields as business and the military, women are being represented in increasing numbers. (At the same time, more men are entering such traditionally female occupations as nursing, librarianship, and elementary-school teaching.) The attitudes of the American public toward women's advancement have also undergone a marked change: whereas in 1970 a Harris poll indicated that only 42 percent of Americans approved of "efforts to strengthen and change women's status in society," a Harris poll in 1975 indicated that 63 percent of Americans approved such efforts, including more than half of American men.[3]

Despite some gains achieved by women, however, sharp disparities still exist in the treatment accorded men and women in our society. And, in fact, in some ways women are actually worse off than they were before. Whereas in 1956 women's full-time, year-round median wages were 63 percent of men's, in 1974 they were only 57 percent.[4] Women are still shunted into traditional "women's work": over 40 percent of the women in the labor force are in such service positions as secretaries, receptionists, telephone operators, and clerks. Women today account for a lesser percentage of college faculties than 100 years ago, and a smaller proportion of graduate students than in 1930.[5] Notwithstanding the progress made in many areas, women today still make up only 5 percent of elected officials in the United States, only 10 percent of the nation's physicians, and only 7 percent of the nation's lawyers and judges.[6] Even where women are in the same professions or occupations as men, their salaries are lower. Statutes that discriminate against women (discussed later) are still "on the books"; subtle but persistent discrimination in employment and salaries is still widespread. In the meantime, efforts to have the Equal Rights Amendment—which would help combat these inequities—added to the Constitution remain stalled.

Clearly, the position of women in our society—and, as we shall see, in many other contemporary societies—is a subordinate one. Women are still kept from full and equal participation in society. (Conversely, men are being kept from less stressful, rigid, and aggressive roles and occupations. As we shall see, both women *and* men are adversely affected by sexual inequality.) In this chapter we will explain how and why such disparities between men and women have come to exist; we will also examine these disparities in greater detail, and suggest ways in which they can be reduced or eliminated.

ORIGINS OF TRADITIONAL SEX ROLES

In Chapter 7 we suggested that prejudice—a predisposition to regard a certain group in a certain way—often becomes the justification for discriminatory behavior. That is, if we believe that a certain group is

[2] J. B. Parrish, "Women in professional training." *Monthly Labor Review,* May 1974, pp. 40–43.
[3] "Women of the year." *Time,* January 5, 1976, pp. 6–16.
[4] "The American woman." *U.S. News & World Report,* December 8, 1975, p. 57.
[5] Warren Farrell, *The Liberated Man.* New York: Random House, 1975, p. 150.
[6] "Women of the year," p. 8; "The American woman," p. 57.

"inferior" or "different," we can easily defend our treating that group as less than equal. We also suggested that an important source of prejudice and discrimination is the norms of a society. If an entire society is prejudiced against a certain group and behaves in a discriminatory manner toward it, such prejudice and discrimination will be accepted by most members of that society as natural and right.

Until relatively recently in our history, it was a widely accepted norm that the only desirable role for a woman is that of wife, mother, and housekeeper and that a woman should revolve her entire life around these roles. Betty Friedan was among the first contemporary feminists to identify and criticize this traditional view of women, and she labeled it the "feminine mystique":

The feminine mystique says that the highest value and the only commitment for women is the fulfillment of their own femininity. It says that the great mistake of Western culture, through most of its history, has been the under-valuation of this femininity. It says this femininity is so mysterious and intuitive and close to the creation and origin of life that man-made science may never be able to understand it. But however special and different, it is in no way inferior to the nature of man; it may even in certain respects be superior. The mistake, says the mystique, the root of women's troubles in the past, is that women envied men, women tried to be like men, instead of accepting their own nature, which can find fulfillment only in sexual passivity, male domination, and nurturing maternal love. . . . The new mystique makes the housewife-mothers, who never had a chance to be anything else, the model for all women . . . a pattern by which all women must now live or deny their femininity.[7]

So pervasive was this view, and so internalized by men and women, that Friedan called the dissatisfaction of the women she studied with their traditional roles "the problem that has no name."

Many of us now think of the traditional role of women as being some-what outdated or at least as representing one of many roles that women today can adopt. At the time Friedan wrote her book, however, and to a large extent even today, such a view was the basis for widespread prejudice and discrimination against women. Women were considered too delicate to do "man's work," and so were legally denied many career and job opportunities; women were considered "different" from men, and so were treated differently by our social institutions—including, as we shall see, our government and our legal system. The way we socialize our children and educate them in our schools—in fact, the entire range of the norms and values of our society—in some measure has reflected and continues to reflect the different standards of behavior we have for men and women. Nevertheless, few people questioned whether these different standards were justified. As John Stuart Mill wrote,

Everything which is usual appears natural. The subjugation of women to men being a universal custom, any departure from it quite naturally appears unnatural.[8]

In part, the traditional view of women sees women as sex objects, useless except for their appearance and sexuality. The model shown here at a boat show is being used as little more than a decorative fixture for the boat.
Wide World Photos

[7] Betty Friedan, *The Feminine Mystique*. New York: Dell, 1963, p. 43.
[8] John Stuart Mill, "The subjugation of women." In *Three Essays by John Stuart Mill*. London: World's Classic Series, 1966, p. 441.

This double standard of behavior is not unique to our own society. In many contemporary Latin American and Moslem countries, for example, the status of women is a far more subordinate one than in our own. Comparatively few women in these societies have the sexual freedom that men have or have careers outside the home. And though, ostensibly, women in Communist countries have greater equality with men—most of the doctors in the Soviet Union, for example, are women— in fact disparities exist in these countries as well. Women still do most of the housework; and they are underrepresented in political parties, which are those countries' most powerful groups.[9]

The seeming dominance of men in many societies—reinforced by the generally unquestioned prejudice that women were somehow best suited for home and family life—has caused many researchers to ask, Why does such prejudice and male dominance exist? What factors gave rise to the different standards of behavior for men and women that continue to exist today? We hope to suggest some answers to these questions in the discussion that follows.

Hunting and gathering societies provide us with a unique opportunity to study the development of *sex roles*—that is, the specific interests and behaviors that society assigns to each sex. Not only were such societies the probable antecedents of our own, but they have also existed throughout the entire course of human history. Studying such societies today can suggest to us how sex roles developed in the past. And, in fact, studies of hunting and gathering societies suggest that they have, to some extent, contributed to the development of traditional sex roles.

Perhaps the most fundamental purpose of hunting and gathering societies is to obtain an adequate amount of food. In most such societies, the people who obtain food are perceived to have the most important roles to play.[10] Because of the conditions of life in these societies, it was and is much more likely that hunters and food-gatherers would be men. Few people in primitive conditions survived to adulthood, and birth control methods were virtually unknown. As such, women had as many children as they could, and were pregnant a great deal of the time. Even when they were not pregnant, they were likely to be nursing their infants —often for as long as three years.[11] Pregnant or taking care of infants, women were generally restricted to staying close to home. Men, with fewer child-raising responsibilities and somewhat greater strength and stamina, were therefore more likely to work in the fields or hunt for animals away from home. (Readers should keep in mind that this is something of an oversimplification—hunting and gathering societies vary and have varied enormously.)

This division of labor by sex was soon generalized to include a wide variety of activities not directly connected to a reproductive or a food-

THE REQUIREMENTS OF HUNTING AND GATHERING SOCIETIES

[9] See Robert R. Bell, *Marriage and Family Interaction.* 4th ed. Homewood, Ill.: Dorsey Press, 1975, pp. 368–369.

[10] Gerhard Lenski, *Human Societies.* New York: McGraw-Hill, 1970, p. 180.

[11] Clellan S. Ford, "Some primitive societies." In Georgene H. Seward and Robert C. Williamson, eds., *Sex Roles in Changing Society.* New York: Random House, 1970, p. 31.

gathering role. Women, because they generally remained close to home, tended to become involved with domestic activities—cooking, weaving, and the like. Men tended to be involved in what were considered to be higher-status tasks as weapon-making or boat-building.[12] Eventually it became convenient to socialize men and women into the different tasks they would have to perform:

> One of the major reasons for sex differences . . . is that sex role assignment is the means whereby we justify not having to train each child in *every* type of activity. If society classifies all newborns into categories based on the probability that members of each category will engage in a specific set of adult behaviors, . . . then it is economical and to society's advantage to do so.[13]

Not only were men and women trained to do different things, but they were also socialized to behave differently. In most (though by no means all) societies, men were brought up to be more aggressive, because they would have to fight wars and do more physical work; women were generally brought up to be more passive and dependent, because they would usually be involved mainly in childbearing and domestic activities and could rely on men for food and protection.

Though the tasks and personalities defined as masculine and feminine varied from society to society, no society failed to distinguish between the genders. Men and women were raised to do different things, and the things men did were generally considered to be more important. Men and women socialized into their culture in turn raised their own children in accordance with their society's expectations. In this way, the different sex roles were perpetuated from generation to generation.

According to Susan Brownmiller,[14] another fundamental cause of women's subjugation by men is related to the size and strength differences between men and women. Because men have tended to be bigger and stronger than women, they have, throughout history, been able to force women into a subordinate role. Brownmiller does not assert that men always exercised their greater physical power; rather, she suggests that the threat of physical harm and, more specifically, the threat of rape, were an implicit part of the relationship between men and women. And it led to the development of social institutions that kept women dependent and subordinate.

According to Brownmiller, the threat of rape was very real in most human cultures because, unlike animals, humans can be sexually active all the time and do not depend on the female's periodic readiness. Given the fact that men were stronger than women, men could act on their sexual desires whether or not women agreed to participate with them—in

THE THREAT AND USE OF FORCE BY MEN

[12] Roy G. D'Andrade, "Sex differences and cultural institutions." In Eleanor E. Maccoby, ed., *The Development of Sex Differences*. Stanford: University of California Press, 1966.
[13] B. G. Rosenberg and Brian Sutton-Smith, *Sex and Identity*. New York: Holt, Rinehart and Winston, 1972, p. 70.
[14] Susan Brownmiller, *Against Our Will: Men, Women, and Rape*. New York: Simon & Schuster, 1975.

effect, men could rape. In order to keep from being raped, women were forced to rely on men for their own protection. As a consequence, they became dependent:

Female fear of an open season of rape, and not a natural inclination towards monogamy, motherhood, or love, was probably the single causative factor in the original subjugation of woman by man, the most important key to her historical dependence, her domestication by protective mating. . . . But the price of woman's protection by some men against others was steep. Disappointed and disillusioned by the inherent female incapacity to protect, she became estranged in a very real sense from other females, a problem that haunts the social organization to this very day. And those who did assume the historic burden of her protection—later formalized as husband, brother, clan—extracted more than a pound of flesh. They reduced her status to that of chattel. The historic price of women's protection by man against man was the imposition of chastity and monogamy. A crime committed against her body became a crime against the male estate.[15]

The concept of woman as male property was eventually codified in religious and civil law. For example, among the ancient Hebrews a woman who was raped would, under certain circumstances, be sold at a lower price to whoever would buy her. Under English law through the twelfth century, a rapist would receive no punishment if his victim would agree to marry him. Her property would then become his. To this day, many men believe they have the right to beat their wives and are shocked to discover that they do not have this right.[16]

Sigmund Freud's theories on sexual development in humans did much to bring the subject of sexuality into the open at the turn of the twentieth century and had a liberating effect on our sexual attitudes (see Chapter 11). However, his psychoanalytical theories on women served to affirm conventional Victorian views on the differences between men and women and had the effect of justifying women's subordinate status. Judd Marmor has outlined the main features of Freud's theories on women:

THE FREUDIAN THEORY OF ANATOMICAL DESTINY

1. *Anatomy is fate.* The basic nature of woman is determined by her anatomy; most importantly by her discovery that she does not possess a penis.
2. *Penis envy.* All female children naturally envy males for having penises, and the desire for a penis is a universal fact of normal feminine psychology. . . .
3. *Masochism and passivity.* These are outgrowths of normal feminine developments and are natural and essential components of healthy femininity.
4. *Faulty superego development.* Due to the fact that the feminine castration complex (precipitated by the little girl's discovery that she has no penis) pushed the little girl *away* from her mother *into* an Oedipal attachment for her father, the little girl has greater difficulty than the boy in resolving the Oedipal complex. Consequently, she tends to develop a defective superego. . . . The result in women, according to Freud, is an

---

[15] Brownmiller, pp. 16–17.
[16] See, for example, Susan K. Steinmetz and Murray A. Straus, *Violence in the Family.* New York: Dodd, 1974.

inadequate sense of justice, a predisposition to envy [and] weaker social interests.[17]

Freud's view of women as being formed by their physiology, as having no sexuality of their own, as desiring to be subservient, and as being envious and unjust very much reflected the ideas of the Victorian era in which he lived. However, because of Freud's stature these views achieved some prominence and continue to affect people's attitudes to this day. For example, it has been shown that women who do not conform to traditional stereotypes of femininity are more likely than other women to be labeled as mentally ill (see Chapter 2).

Other psychologists have since faulted Freud's view as ignoring the cultural influences—some of which we have already described—on the personalities of men and women. For example, as Clara Thompson has written,

It has been shown that cultural factors can explain the tendency of women to feel inferior about their sex and their consequent tendency to envy men; that this state of affairs may well lead women to blame all their difficulties on the fact of their sex. Thus they may use the position of cultural underprivilege as the rationalization of all feelings of inferiority.[18]

In this sense, "penis envy" was not a basic biological force in women but rather a symbol of their subordination to men. Similarly, passivity is not something unique to women but reflects how women in our society have been socialized to behave.

THE RISE OF FEMINISM

Considering the powerful social and cultural influences that kept women subordinate, it seems surprising that any variation from traditional sex roles ever occurred. In fact, depending on the time and place, sex roles in even the most rigid societies sometimes departed from the prevailing norm. Historically, individual women have always been able to transcend the limitations imposed on them by their culture; and in certain circumstances—such as when the survival of a society was threatened—women have sometimes been given equality with men. For example, pioneer women settlers in the western United States generally were on equal footing with men, despite the fact that they had been socialized into traditional sex roles; the hardships that people then faced made adherence to rigid sex roles counterproductive. (Women as well as men were needed to work the fields, stand watch, and so on.) Later, when communities became more established, traditional sex roles were reasserted.

[17] Judd Marmor, "Changing patterns of femininity." In Arlene S. Skolnick and Jerome H. Skolnick, *Family in Transition*. Boston: Little, Brown, 1971, pp. 214–215.
[18] Clara Thompson, " 'Penis envy' in women." In Jean B. Miller, ed., *Psychoanalysis and Women*. New York: Penguin, 1973, p. 52.

The widespread dissatisfaction with traditional sex roles that is being manifested today, however, is not a temporary phenomenon. Instead, it is the culmination of a historical process that began in the early part of the nineteenth century. In the section below, we describe the important elements in this process.

The Industrial Revolution that took place in the early part of the nineteenth century had a number of important effects on family structure. The dominant family form in agrarian societies was the extended family—parents, children, and other relatives being together or in close proximity. (See Table 8-1.) It was best suited for agrarian society because it provided the workers who were needed in the fields. As society became more industrialized, however, the smaller nuclear family—parents and children being apart from other kin—became more prevalent. This form of the family was better suited to industrial societies. Instead of working their own piece of property, people had to be able to move where jobs were located, and a smaller family was more mobile. In addition, a large family was no longer economically useful—in fact, it was a hindrance. The family was supported by one or two wage-earners, whose earnings would be insufficient for an extended family.[19] (See Chapter 10.)

This change in the form of the family also affected male and female sex roles. The agrarian extended family had reinforced traditional sex roles: men were needed to work in the fields, and women did the house-

INDUSTRIALIZATION

[19] See W. J. Goode, *The Family.* Englewood Cliffs, N.J.: Prentice-Hall, 1964.

TABLE 8-1
Family Changes Deriving from the Urban-Industrial Revolution

	Then	Now
Family size	Many children, high infant mortality. Many relationships to maintain.	Few children, low infant mortality. Fewer relationships to maintain.
Authority	Husband-father authority supreme.	Husband-father authority declining in relation to wife and also children.
Work	Closely related to total family activity; a division of labor involving all family members, the results visible to all.	Husband-father works outside home. Wife-mother often does so too. Housekeeping less integrated into a family division of labor. Children have little or no "work."
Child rearing	Father and mother fairly equal in child-rearing responsibilities. Child rearing covered most of parents' lives.	Mother plays greater role than father. Child rearing over sooner, leaving many women "jobless."
Role consensus	High consensus; roles clearly and compatibly defined.	Low consensus; roles often ambiguous or conflicting.
Role compatibility over family life cycle	High compatibility over family life cycle.	Lower compatibility, especially in empty nest stage of family, after children leave.
Durability of nuclear family	High durability (low divorce rate).	Low durability (high divorce rate).

Source: Alan P. Bates and Joseph Julian, *Sociology: Understanding Social Behavior.* Boston: Houghton Mifflin, 1975, p. 332. ©by Houghton Mifflin Company. Reprinted by permission.

work. In addition, the presence of so many other family members tended to keep family life conventional. In the modern nuclear family, there was no valid economic reason to have the women do the housework, and the influence of other relatives was lessened. Moreover, because of the fragmented nature of family life in industrial society, social pressures to conform to conventional norms were less effective.

The movement from farms to factories also affected sex roles in other ways. For example, because industrialization meant that machines could do a great deal of the work that once required male strength, traditional sex roles were no longer as meaningful—women as well as men could work. This meant that women could occupy jobs and achieve a certain measure of independence from men. In addition, because husband and wife had to rely almost completely on each other for fulfillment of their needs, the power of women within the family tended to increase.[20]

In our own society, women's subordination was dealt a serious blow during the Depression and during World War II. Many men could not support their families during the Depression, and so their wives were forced to work.[21] And during the war, most men were in the military while women took over many traditionally male jobs. The reimposition of traditional sex roles that was attempted after World War II (and that Friedan labeled the "feminine mystique") can be seen as an attempt by men returning from the war to reduce competition for jobs.[22] However, the tendencies toward sexual equality continued to make themselves felt.

One result of industrialization that has had a particularly strong effect on sex roles is related to fertility patterns. The advances in medicine that typically accompany industrialization tend to reduce infant mortality rates. This is another reason why women need to spend less of their time having babies—the babies they do have are much more likely to survive. In addition, the development of convenient birth control devices gives women much greater control over their reproductive lives, and tends to reduce the birthrate still further. The net result is that women have much more free time available and are able to participate in the labor force.

THE FEMINIST MOVEMENT

The 1960s was not the first decade to generate a brand of American feminism that examined and proposed reform of almost every aspect of our society. The drive for sexual equality actually began in the early 1800s. Although American feminism is commonly equated with the suffrage movement, the right-to-vote campaign was really the culmination of a multi-issued struggle for women's rights.[23]

Early women's advocates, such as Emma Willard, campaigned for expanded educational opportunities for women during the 1820s. How-

[20] William J. Goode, "Industrialization and family structure." In Norman W. Bell and Ezra F. Vogel, *A Modern Introduction to the Family.* Rev. ed. New York: Free Press, 1968, p. 118.
[21] Georgene H. Seward, "Sex roles, ancient to modern." In Seward and Williamson, p. 121.
[22] Marmor, p. 212.
[23] This discussion is based on Judith Hole and Ellen Levine, *Rebirth of Feminism.* New York: Quadrangle, 1971, pp. 1–14.

ever, during the 1830s the explosive issue of the abolition of slavery became a paramount concern of women. Many women saw similarities between their own condition in society and that of the slaves; by working for the abolition of slavery, they felt they could begin to achieve equality for themselves. In fact, women activists who struggled for abolition along with men quickly learned that men did not consider them political equals. Women abolitionists who led active public lives were bitterly denounced for their "unconventional" behavior. As such, women abolitionists tended to organize apart from men and emphasized women's rights as well as an end to black slavery.

The most famous early gathering of American feminists and women abolitionists took place at Seneca Falls, New York, in 1848. The Seneca Falls Convention called for suffrage, reform of custody and divorce laws, and endorsed the right of women to control their lives and their property. It spawned women's rights conventions in every major American city before the Civil War. The Civil War itself had a major impact on the women's movement; feminists were urged to hold their own claims in abeyance and fight for emancipation of the slaves, only to be confronted at the close of the war with a version of the Fourteenth Amendment that extended the constitutional guarantee of equal protection under law to males only.

These setbacks fueled the suffrage campaign but produced a split in the women's movement. The radicals, led by Susan B. Anthony and Elizabeth Cady Stanton, used the right to vote as a focus for a host of other issues involving women's rights, while the conservatives, led by Lucy Stone, ignored the broader issues in an effort to keep the movement "respectable." By 1890, the conservatives had temporarily won control of the major organizations.

The next major development was the rise of second-generation feminists after the turn of the century. The new leaders made only limited gains until they were spurred into action by the fiery Alice Paul, a militant radical who used mass demonstrations, hunger strikes, and parades to draw attention to the need for a federal suffrage amendment. Although many more moderate feminists disagree with Paul's methods, most agreed that she was largely responsible for the eventual ratification of the Nineteenth Amendment in 1920, which gave women the right to vote. Since the movement had come to focus entirely around suffrage, most activists equated universal suffrage with complete sexual equality, and American feminism fell into a dormancy that was to last forty years.

Jo Freeman [24] has analyzed the contemporary Women's Liberation Movement, and sees it as originating from two distinct branches. The older "reform" group was led by the National Organization of Women (NOW), which was formed in 1966. The decision to form NOW was influenced by a series of federal and state commissions on the status of women that had documented women's unequal status; by the publication of Betty Friedan's book *The Feminine Mystique,* which criticized the traditional roles women were expected to play; and by the passage of

[24] Jo Freeman, "Origins of the Women's Liberation Movement." In Joan Huber, ed., *Changing Women in a Changing Society.* Chicago: University of Chicago Press, 1973, pp. 30–49.

the 1964 Civil Rights Act, which prohibited discrimination on the basis of sex. Federal officials made it clear they were unwilling to enforce this provision of the act, and NOW was formed specifically to fight for women's civil rights.

NOW attracted older women already skilled in manipulating the traditional political machinery. These women shared a basic faith in the underlying social structure and sought to bring it more in line with the historic American ideals of egalitarianism and democracy. They concentrated on the legal and economic issues affecting women.

By contrast, the younger or "radical" group got its start in small, anti-hierarchical projects at the grass-roots level; usually organized around one or more anti-Establishment issues—particularly the protests against the Vietnam War. The radicals perceive the push for women's rights as one facet of a broader effort to completely revamp government, culture, and society. Despite their ambitious visions, they avoid leadership and organization as elitist and antithetical to creative struggle. They lack the broad consensus and ability to sustain concerted mass efforts on any issue. They also place priority on self-transformation and development as an important precondition of meaningful political change. According to Freeman, the "radical" branch has been the most fertile source of ideological innovations, experimental publications and institutions, and feminist ideology, but has failed to implement its ideas. The "reform" group, on the other hand, has shown less creativity but more skill at using the prevailing political structure to make women's influence felt.

THE NEED FOR EQUALITY

One additional factor that has contributed enormously to contemporary dissatisfaction with traditional sex roles has been the growth of knowledge about the origins of male-female differences and about sex roles in other societies. Whereas it was once supposed—by Freud, for example—that behavioral differences between men and women were innate, today we know that these differences are largely learned by individuals as they are socialized into their culture. (See also Chapter 11.) And though it was once believed that there were universal standards of "masculine" or "feminine" behavior, in fact other societies have standards far different than our own.

In the 1950s, for example, sex researcher Money and his colleagues found that the best predictor of a person's sex role was not his or her physiological sex but the sex he or she had been assigned at birth. Specifically, male children who had been raised as females, or female children who had been raised as males, identified as members of the other sex even after their physical sex became known to them.[25] For reasons such as this, many researchers use the term *gender identity* to refer to a person's sexual self-image and to distinguish it from physiological gender.[26]

Several studies have been done that show how boys and girls in our society are socialized into their traditional sex roles. Serbin and O'Leary,

[25] John Money et al., "An examination of some basic sexual concepts: The evidence of human hermaphroditism." *Bulletin of the Johns Hopkins Hospital* 97 (1955): 301–319.
[26] Clarice S. Stoll, ed., *Sexism: Scientific Debates.* Reading, Mass.: Addison-Wesley, 1973, p. 7.

for example, found that nursery-school teachers responded much more to a boy's behavior than to a girl's, tending to reinforce aggression among boys and passivity among girls. (Interestingly enough, the teachers were unaware that they were doing this.) [27] Hartley found that small boys were taught that they should not be "sissies" and that girls were weak and unimportant.[28] When women are not socialized into a conventional pattern—as fewer and fewer women today are—their behaviors begin to resemble those of men. For example, Winick found that today's women are far stronger and more athletic than their counterparts of thirty years ago and that they are meeting male standards of physical performance. This suggests that even a woman's "weakness" is to a large extent a reflection of traditional social expectation.[29]

The effect of cultural conditioning on sex differences can also be seen by examining sex roles in other societies. Margaret Mead studied three primitive tribes in New Guinea and found that the behaviors considered normal for men and women varied enormously from tribe to tribe. Among the Arapesh, for example, both men and women were gentle and nonaggressive by our standards, and violence was rare. On the other hand, both men and women of the Mundagumor tended to be ruthless and violent. In these tribes there did not appear to be a sharp distinction made between male and female attitudes, as there is in our own society. Among the third tribe Mead studied, the Tchambuli, there was in fact a complete reversal of the stereotypic "masculine" and "feminine" roles of our own culture: Tchambuli men were dependent and emotional, while Tchambuli women tended to be dominant and impersonal. Mead concluded that any infant could easily be socialized into any of the three tribes, and that "we no longer have any basis for regarding . . . behavior as sex linked." [30]

Even among more modern societies, there is considerable variation in the kinds of attitudes and behaviors considered appropriate for each sex. Stoll notes that it is quite common in the Middle East for men to be emotional and for women to be stolid and practical—the reverse of traditional roles in our society.[31] In Sweden, 75 percent of crane operators are women.[32] Swedish schools have compulsory coeducation in such subjects as sewing and child care; divorced women without children receive no alimony.[33] In the Soviet Union, women make up over half the civilian labor force and over 70 percent of that nation's doctors.[34] In France, however, women have traditionally been kept in an extremely

[27] Lisa A. Serbin and K. Daniel O'Leary, "How nursery schools teach girls to shut up." *Psychology Today,* December 1975, p. 57.
[28] Ruth E. Hartley, "Sex role pressures and the socialization of the male child." In Joseph H. Pleck and Jack Sawyer, eds., *Men and Masculinity*. Englewood Cliffs, N.J.: Prentice-Hall, 1974, pp. 7–13.
[29] In Stoll, p. 107.
[30] Margaret Mead, "Sex and temperament in three primitive societies." In Skolnick and Skolnick, pp. 44–50.
[31] Stoll, p. 9.
[32] Farrell, p. 158.
[33] Bell, p. 369.
[34] Cynthia F. Epstein and William J. Goode, eds., *The Other Half*. Englewood Cliffs, N.J.: Prentice-Hall, 1971, p. 2; and Carolyn C. Perrucci and Dena B. Targ, eds., *Marriage and the Family*. New York: McKay, 1974, p. 25.

Though sex discrimination exists on a wide scale in many communist countries, more occupations have been open to women in these countries than in our own society. Soviet pilot Marina Popovich, shown here, holds several world flight records.
Tass/Sovfoto

subordinate position. Until 1965, for example, wives could not work outside the home without the consent of their husbands.[35]

The constitutions of many socialist and Communist countries expressly forbid discrimination on the basis of sex. For this reason, countries such as Sweden and the Soviet Union have somewhat greater equality between the sexes than many other Western nations, particularly because most types of work are open to women. It should be noted, however, that even in socialist countries sexual discrimination is still rampant. For example, Hilda Scott found that women in Eastern Europe were paid less than men and tended to occupy the bottom rung of jobs (as they tend to do in the United States). Doctors, who are mostly women, get paid less than workers in heavy industry; medicine is apparently considered an offshoot

[35] Catherine B. Silver, "Salon, foyer, bureau: Women and the professions in France." In Huber, pp. 74, 85.

of a woman's traditional caring function rather than a distinguished profession. In general, Scott found that the attitude that a woman's natural role was to be a mother and a man's natural role was to be dominant was still widespread in socialist countries.[36]

Nevertheless, it seems clear that there is considerable variation in the the types of behaviors considered appropriate for men and women, and that to a large extent these behaviors reflect the values of a particular society more than any innate or natural qualities. While the values of our own society have, until recently, reinforced traditional sex roles, it is becoming increasingly apparent that these values conflict with what is perhaps our society's highest value: freedom. As Williams points out,

the American conception of freedom is clearly that . . . of the protection of particular liberties and the tolerance of disagreement rather than the homogenization of private groups and individuals into an omnipotent general will. . . . So long as American society safeguards the right of the individual to a wide range of moral autonomy in decision making, so long as the representative character structure of the culture retains a conscience that is more than simple group conformity—so long will freedom be a major value.[37]

Owen suggests that traditional sex roles limit human freedom because they prevent women and men from fulfilling their full potential. Men in our society, for example, frequently feel that they must deny the satisfactions they feel as husbands or fathers in order to single-mindedly pursue their careers; women feel they must make their roles as wives and mothers paramount and deny those abilities they have in other areas. Moreover, the career choices women and men make frequently reflect cultural expectations rather than their inner needs and desires. To Owen, the breaking down of traditional sex roles will open up the possibility of freedom to many women and men—people will be free to do what is best for them.[38] As one observer put it,

The present models of neither men nor women furnish adequate opportunities for human development. That one half of the human race should be dominant and the other half submissive is incompatible with a notion of freedom. Freedom requires that there not be dominance and submission, but that all individuals be free to determine their own lives.[39]

THE NATURE OF SEXISM

Sexism is the counterpart of racism and agism, which are discussed in Chapters 7 and 9, respectively. It may be defined as the "entire range of attitudes, beliefs, practices, policies, laws, and behaviors discriminating

[36] Hilda Scott, *Does Socialism Liberate Women?* Boston: Beacon Press, 1974.
[37] Robin H. Williams, Jr., *American Society*. 3rd ed. New York: Knopf, 1970, pp. 482–483.
[38] George C. Owen, "Sexual equality and human freedom." In Robert Theobald, ed., *Dialogue on Women*. Indianapolis: Bobbs-Merrill, 1967, pp. 88–94.
[39] Jack Sawyer quoted in Perrucci and Targ, p. 9.

against women (or against men) on the basis of their gender."[40] In this section we will describe some of the attitudes and practices that are a part of the sexism in our society.

As we stated in Chapter 7, a source of prejudice and discrimination is stereotyping, which we defined as the attributing of a fixed and usually unfavorable and inaccurate conception to a category of people. Stereotypes often make it easier to justify unequal treatment of the stereotyped person or group.

STEREOTYPING

We have already mentioned the popular, traditional stereotypes about women—that women are naturally passive, domestic, mindless, envious, and so on. It was this catalogue of stereotypes that Friedan lumped together and labeled the "feminine mystique." However, as Fasteau points out,[41] there is a "masculine mystique" as well—a set of stereotypes about men that limits their ability to function fully and effectively. The masculine stereotype is that all men are tough, unemotional, and dominant; and however unrealistic and inaccurate this stereotype is, many men (and women) believe it. Many men avoid performing traditionally female tasks (such as washing dishes or working as a secretary) for fear that through such performance their masculinity will somehow be threatened. And undoubtedly many men who would prefer the role of homemaker nevertheless feel compelled to seek careers in business or sports because they have been socialized to believe that domestic work is not masculine.[42] Not only does the masculine stereotype limit the freedom men have to engage in any activity or occupation they desire, it also limits their personal relationships. Many men feel that they cannot discuss their feelings with other men, for fear they will be ridiculed. Instead, they may tend to be extremely competitive (or, collectively, even violent) toward other men. They also feel compelled to try to dominate women, instead of relating to them as equals. (See also Chapter 4 for a discussion of the effects of male socialization on crime patterns.)

One of the unfortunate effects of stereotypes is that even people who are victimized by them tend to believe that they are true. Thus women to a measurable extent share attitudes that are prejudicial to women; this causes them to undervalue the work of other women and sets up psychological barriers to their own achievement. Goldberg, for example, found that women valued professional work that they thought was done by a man more highly than they valued the same work if they thought it was done by a woman. This held true even if the professional field was traditionally reserved for women (such as nursing).[43] Horner found that many women were motivated to avoid success, fearing that the more ambitious and successful they became, the less feminine they would be. Thus, in certain competitive situations, many women became anxious

[40] Constantina Safilios-Rothschild, *Women and Social Policy*. Englewood Cliffs, N.J.: Prentice-Hall, 1974, p. 1.
[41] Marc F. Fasteau, *The Male Machine*. New York: McGraw-Hill, 1974.
[42] See Robert E. Gould, "Measuring masculinity by the size of a paycheck." In Pleck and Sawyer, p. 96; and Sandra L. Bem, "Fluffy women and chesty men." *Psychology Today,* September 1975.
[43] Philip Goldberg, "Are women prejudiced against women?" In Constantina Safilios-Rothschild, ed., *Toward a Sociology of Women*. New York: Wiley, 1972.

about the prospect of doing well and performed poorly when compared to their performance in noncompetitive situations. Horner suggests that the stereotype that women need to be wives and mothers is preventing many able women from achieving their full potential.[44]

It is probably the stereotypic notions that men have about women, however, that most stand in the way of women's achieving equality with men, since men still hold most positions of authority in our society. One survey of 1,500 managers (almost all male) found that in making personnel decisions, managers unconsciously relied on traditional stereotypes about men and women. Thus managers were much more supportive of men than of women, assuming that men would give their careers top priority while women would give their family responsibilities top priority. Managers tried harder to retain male employees than female employees, and in general favored the advancement of men more than of women. After analyzing these data, the authors of the survey concluded:

When the results are extrapolated to the entire population of American managers, even a small bias against women could represent a great many unintentional discriminatory acts, which potentially affect thousands of career women. The end result of these various forms of bias might be great personal damage for individuals and costly underutilization of human resources.[45]

JOB OPPORTUNITIES AND SALARIES

Women are overwhelmingly concentrated in the lower-status jobs at the low end of the pay scale, making up, for example, 85 percent of all file clerks, 96 percent of all typists, and 99 percent of all secretaries. (See Table 8-2.) Conversely, men make up over 80 percent of all white-collar administrators, over 95 percent of all blue-collar supervisors, and an even higher percentage of corporate directors. Women, who receive almost the same amount of education in the United States as men, comprise close to 45 percent of college enrollments.[46] Yet, after graduation, men get the better jobs and the higher incomes. Though about the same proportion of women and men are professional or technical workers, women are concentrated in lower-paying fields such as nursing or teaching, while men are in such higher-paying fields as law and medicine.[47]

This kind of sex differentiation—the distinctions made in the types of jobs men and women are permitted to perform—helps account for the fact that women's median annual salary is little more than half that of men ($12,150 for men vs. $6,960 for women).[48] (See Table 8-3.) This salary differential becomes apparent as soon as people enter the labor

[44] Matina S. Horner, "Femininity and successful achievement: A basic inconsistency." In Judith M. Bardwick *et al.,* eds., *Feminine Personality and Conflict.* Belmont, Calif.: Brooks/Cole, 1970.
[45] Benson Rosen and Thomas H. Jerdee, "Sex stereotyping in the executive suite." *Harvard Business Review,* March–April 1974, pp. 45–58.
[46] See "Educational attainment in the United States." *Current Population Reports,* Series P-20, no. 274, December 1974.
[47] *Manpower Report of the President;* and *U.S. News & World Report,* January 14, 1974, p. 69, and May 27, 1974, p. 41. See also Valerie K. Oppenheimer, "Demographic influences on female employment and the status of women." *American Journal of Sociology* (January 1973):961–964.
[48] "Money income in 1974." *Current Population Reports,* Series P-60, no. 101, January 1976, p. 2.

	Number of Women Workers	Proportion of Jobs Held by Women		Number of Women Workers	Proportion of Jobs Held by Women
Secretaries	2,922,000	99%	Food-service workers	2,277,000	70%
Receptionists	423,000	97	Retail clerks	1,600,000	69
Typists	980,000	96	Social workers	195,000	55
Child-care workers	341,000	96	Office managers	132,000	42
Nurses, dietitians	879,000	96	Real-estate agents	128,000	37
Hairdressers, cosmetologists	354,000	91	Cleaning-service workers	680,000	33
Bank tellers	252,000	88	Restaurant workers	160,000	32
Bookkeepers	1,393,000	88	Writers, artists, entertainers	284,000	32
Cashiers	864,000	87	College teachers	130,000	28
Health-service workers	1,310,000	87	Accountants	155,000	22
File clerks	231,000	85	Bank, financial officers	81,000	19
Librarians	125,000	83	Sales managers	90,000	16
Counter clerks (nonfood)	243,000	74	Physicians and dentists	58,000	9
Office-machine operators	480,000	71	Science technicians	75,000	9
			Police officers, fire fighters	65,000	5–6
School teachers	1,988,000	70	Lawyers	12,000	4
			Engineers	9,000	Less than 1
Health technicians	220,000	70	Construction crafts workers	20,000	Less than 1

Source: Reprinted from *U.S. News & World Report,* January 14, 1974, p. 69. © 1974 U.S. News & World Report, Inc.

TABLE 8-2
The Jobs That Women Hold

Major Occupational Group	Median Income	Percent of Men's Income
Professional and technical workers	$8,796	68%
Nonfarm managers and administrators	7,306	53
Clerical workers	6,039	63
Sales workers	4,575	40
Operatives, including transportation	5,021	58
Service workers (except private household)	4,606	59
Private household	2,365	fnt.
Nonfarm laborers	4,755	63

[1] Percent not shown where median income of men is based on fewer than 75,000 individuals.

Source: U.S. Department of Labor, *Manpower Report of the President.* Washington, D.C.: U.S. Government Printing Office, 1975, p. 63.

TABLE 8-3
Median Incomes of Full-Time Women Workers by Occupation

market. Among recent college graduates, for example, 15 percent of men but only 3 percent of women earn more than $10,000 a year.[49] Even when their jobs are the same, men and women earn vastly disparate salaries. For instance, on the average, female salespersons earn 40 percent of what male salespersons earn; female professionals earn about 65 percent of what their male counterparts earn.[50] Women are also more likely than men to be laid off, because it is assumed men need jobs more than women, who are assumed to have family responsibilities.[51] Unfortunately, it is those women who are at the low end of the wage scale who suffer the effects of wage and job discrimination the most: 33 percent of families headed by a woman are below the poverty line, compared with 6 percent of those headed by a man.[52]

Wage and job discrimination are illegal according to the Equal Pay Act of 1963 and the Civil Rights Act of 1964, yet they continue to exist. Each year, for example, the Equal Employment Opportunity Commission receives about 20,000 charges of sex discrimination.[53] One way such discrimination works was demonstrated by Levinson in a study of job inquiries.[54] Levinson and his co-researchers selected several classified advertisements in newspapers and defined the jobs advertised as "male" or "female," depending on their present sex composition. Male researchers inquired by telephone about the traditionally female jobs (such as secretary) and female researchers inquired about traditionally male jobs (such as auto mechanic). Afterward, this procedure was reversed, and researchers of each sex called to inquire about jobs considered appropriate for them. Levinson found that in 35 percent of all cases there was clear-cut sex discrimination. Male inquirers for a secretarial job, for example, were told the job was filled, while subsequent female callers were encouraged to apply. Sometimes the discrimination was more blunt: for example, women callers were told directly that "we don't hire girls as fuel attendants." Frequently, men inquirers for "sex-inappropriate" jobs were encouraged to apply for higher-level managerial positions, while women callers were told to apply for lower-level jobs.

Clearly, sex-typing of jobs is a major part of sex discrimination. However, Fuchs, in a study of wage differentials by sex, concludes that sex discrimination is much more broadly based and

can be explained by the different roles assigned to men and women. Role differentiation, which begins in the cradle, affects the choice of occupation,

[49] Anne M. Young, "Labor market experience of recent college graduates." *Monthly Labor Review,* October 1974, pp. 33–40.

[50] *U.S. News & World Report,* May 27, 1974, p. 41.

[51] See "Employment and unemployment during 1975." *Monthly Labor Review,* February 1976, pp. 11–20.

[52] "Characteristics of the population below the poverty level." *Current Population Reports,* P-60, no. 102, January 1976, p. 2.

[53] Citizens' Advisory Council on the Status of Women, *Women in 1975.* Washington, D.C.: U.S. Government Printing Office, 1976.

[54] Richard M. Levinson, "Sex discrimination and employment practices: An experiment with unconventional job inquiries." *Social Problems,* vol. 22, no. 4 (April 1975):533–543.

labor force attachment, location of work, hours of work, and other variables that influence earnings.[55]

Fuchs concludes that a change in "role discrimination" is necessary before wage and job discrimination can be reduced.

Many of our current laws and statutes discriminate against women and reinforce prejudice against them. (See Chapter 5 for a discussion of discriminatory rape laws.) Some states, for example, still require that women be given longer sentences than men for the same crime, on the assumption that female criminals require more rehabilitation. (Conversely, many states treat women offenders more leniently than men, on the assumption that women require the state's protection—a type of reverse discrimination.) In Alabama, women were excluded from jury duty until a federal court ruled in 1966 that this was unconstitutional.[56] However, the Supreme Court has upheld the right of states to keep women from being automatically selected for jury duty—in many states women must volunteer for jury duty or else they are not called, while men are selected automatically. The justification for this was stated in the Supreme Court decision, which clearly expresses a stereotypic view of a woman's role:

> Despite the enlightened emancipation of women from the restrictions and protections of bygone years, and their entry into many parts of community life formerly considered to be reserved to men, woman is still regarded as the center of home and family life. We cannot say that it is constitutionally impermissible for a State, acting in pursuit of the general welfare, to conclude that a woman should be relieved from the civic duty of jury service unless she herself determines that such service is consistent with her own special responsibilities.[57]

Schulder points out other examples of legal discrimination of women.[58] For instance, a 1966 Supreme Court decision upheld a Texas law which stated that a married woman could not enter into a binding contract on her own. In most states, it is illegal to be a prostitute but not illegal to frequent one; thus, prostitutes are routinely arrested while their customers remain free. In New York, where prostitutes and their customers are considered to be in equal violation of the law, male customers are still rarely prosecuted. Also, some states quasi-officially permit the "passion shooting" by a husband of a wife caught in an infidelity; the reverse, as Schulder puts it, "is known as homicide."

It is the economic discrimination legally directed at women, however, that has perhaps most reinforced their subordinate status. A wide variety of laws and statutes are based on the idea that males are the breadwinners of a family and that women are dependents. This concept

LEGAL, CIVIL, AND ECONOMIC RIGHTS

[55] Victor R. Fuchs, "Differences in hourly earnings between men and women." *Monthly Labor Review,* May 1971, pp. 9–15.
[56] Hole and Levine, pp. 59–60.
[57] *Hoyt v. Florida,* 368 U.S. 57 (1961).
[58] Diane B. Schulder, "Does the law oppress women?" In Robin Morgan, *Sisterhood Is Powerful.* New York: Random House, 1970.

results in the fact that the work women (and men) do in the home—and even the work women do outside the home—is consistently undervalued. Thus, for example, a woman automatically gets Social Security benefits if her husband dies, because her dependence on his wages is assumed. For a man to collect benefits if his wife dies, however, he must prove that he was financially dependent on her. (Even then, his benefits were lower than a widow's would be—until 1975, when the Supreme Court ruled that benefits must be equal.) While this provision of the Social Security Act discriminates against men, it also perpetuates the antiquated idea that women are not wage-earners.[59] The Supreme Court at the end of 1975 also revoked another long-standing statute that discriminated against women, when it ruled that pregnant women could receive unemployment benefits during the last three months of pregnancy. Up until that time statutes in many states assumed that unemployed women in the final stage of pregnancy were unable to work and therefore were not entitled to unemployment benefits.

Homemakers, who are still mostly women, suffer the greatest form of legal economic discrimination. Although it has been estimated that the work homemakers perform is worth up to $6,500 annually (depending on the number of children in their care),[60] no federal, state, or insurance agency takes the economic value of a homemaker into account. Thus, for example, homemakers cannot obtain private disability insurance, even though their spouses would have to hire help if they were disabled. Disability-insurance policies are written for those who earn wages— even though the work homemakers perform represents a clear economic contribution. In fact, at present, homemakers cannot be enrolled in the Social Security system in order to qualify for disability benefits, even if they pay the required taxes.

The undervaluation of the work of homemakers—the services performed by them are not even included in the gross national product— results in a number of other inequities. For example, homemakers do not receive full tax credit for the expenses of running a home, even though businesspersons can write off everything from telephone bills to lunches as business expenses. They are also ineligible for workmen's compensation. Perhaps most important, the monetary undervaluation of the work of homemakers results in the undervaluation of the homemaker *role*. Lekachman suggests, in fact, that redefining the household as an economic unit is a prerequisite for sexual equality. If this is done, he suggests,

running an efficient home enterprise will confer respectability on the woman *or* the man who freely chooses this occupational alternative. Both sexes will be encouraged to make rational comparisons between home and outside employment. In many marriages it will make excellent economic and emotional sense for husbands to run homes and wives to forage in the outside world, particularly when female marriage partners can earn substantially more. . . . Liberalization of household-expense deductions

[59] Women's Rights Project, *Social Security and Sex Discrimination*. New York: American Civil Liberties Union, July 17, 1974.
[60] "Economic value of a housewife." *Research and Statistics Note,* U.S. Department of Health, Education, and Welfare, August 28, 1975.

will facilitate, as a third choice, outside employment for husband and wife and engagement of child- and home-management specialists—male or female.[61]

SEXISM, SOCIAL CLASS, AND RACE

The position of women of different social classes and races in our society can be succinctly described with a baseball metaphor: if you are a female, that's one strike against you; if you are a poor female or a nonwhite female, that's two strikes against you; if you are a poor, nonwhite female, you have struck out.

Although unemployment rates are higher for women than for men (approximately 8 percent vs. 6 percent), it is the condition of women who work that best exemplifies the sexism in our society. Despite the ever-rising proportion of women in the labor force and the increasing educational level of women, nearly two-thirds of full-time, year-round female workers earn less than $7,000 a year. This contrasts sharply with the fact that more than three-fourths of full-time, year-round male workers earn *more* than $7,000 a year. This large disparity in earnings between men and women has persisted, and even increased, over the past two decades, even when hours of work and level of education are equalized.[62] (See Chapter 6 for further information on women and poverty, and Chapter 9 for information on elderly women.)

We have already mentioned that one-third of families headed by a woman are below the poverty line. Women as a group are restricted in their employment opportunities, but women with children are even more restricted than their childless counterparts. In practical terms, the presence of children in the house limits the kinds of jobs female heads of families can have, because they cannot travel far from home or work the longer hours that higher-paying jobs typically require. (See Figure 8-1.) Moreover, because day-care centers are generally unavailable, few mothers can work. Those who do work must use part of their meager salaries to pay someone to stay with their children while they are at work. Because only low-status, low-paying jobs are available to these women, and because of the lack of child-care facilities, over 60 percent of female heads of households do not even seek employment. Unfortunately, the proportion of female heads of families has approximately doubled since 1970 and is continuing to increase. The problem of poverty among this group is therefore a constantly growing one.[63]

Female members of minorities tend to suffer double discrimination: on the bases of sex and of race. Thus nonwhite females have even higher rates of unemployment than their white sisters, and are also even more likely to be working in blue-collar jobs. Unemployment among Spanish-

[61] Robert Lekachman, "On economic equality." *Signs—Journal of Women in Culture and Society,* vol. 1, no. 1 (Autumn 1975):100.

[62] *Manpower Report of the President.*

[63] "Characteristics of the low-income population." *Current Population Reports,* Series P-60, no. 98. Washington, D.C.: U.S. Government Printing Office, 1975.

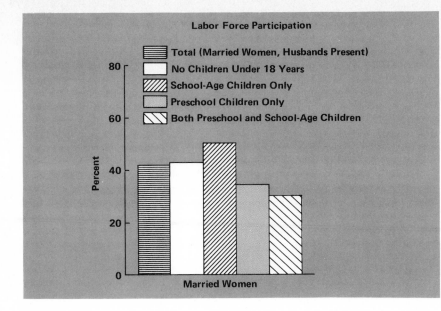

FIGURE 8-1
The Effect of Preschool
Children in the Home
on Labor Force Par-
ticipation Rates

Source: U.S. Department
of Labor, *Manpower Report
of the President.* Washington, D.C.: U.S. Government
Printing Office, 1975, p. 58.

speaking women, for example, is about 10 percent, a higher rate than
among white women; and only 6 percent of Spanish-speaking women are
in professional jobs, compared to 16 percent of all employed women.[64]
In addition to job and wage discrimination, however, nonwhite women
also suffer a number of additional stresses and strains caused by the
difficult roles they must play and the stereotypes that exist about them.
Some of these stresses are detailed below.

According to available statistics, the black woman suffers the most
from race and sex discrimination. Though a larger proportion of black
women than white women work, black women are even more concentrated in the low-status jobs at the low end of the pay scale. For example,
more than three-fourths of working black women are in service jobs;
nearly half work in occupations (such as domestics) not covered by the
federal minimum wage. The average black woman's wage is lower than
the average salary of a white man, of a black man, and of a white woman
—even for the same work.[65]

BLACK WOMEN

To Blakey, the economic discrimination against black women is, however, only one facet of the double discrimination they suffer. As he put it,

It should not be necessary to cite the . . . lack of child care for working
women, the failure to receive equal pay for equal work, the raping of black
women by white and black men, the increasing number of forced sterilizations
of black women, and the miserable treatment black women receive in prison

[64] "Spanish-U.S. women assayed by census." *New York Times,* May 2, 1976.
[65] See Virginia E. Pendergass *et al.,* "Sex discrimination counseling." *American
Psychologist* (January 1976):44.

in order to make the point that however bad a black man has had it, black women have it worse.[66]

Beal echoes this point of view, suggesting that black women have been among the most exploited groups in our society. She cites the fact that unions with membership made up predominantly of nonwhite women (such as the International Ladies Garment Workers Union) usually have white males as their leaders, and suggests that these men have generally been insensitive to the needs of their union members. Beal also points out that in several states black women on welfare have been pressured to undergo sterilization procedures in order to continue to qualify for welfare benefits.[67]

Other researchers have explored the stereotypes that exist about black (and other nonwhite) women and the special psychological stresses to which black women are subjected. For example, black women have traditionally been believed to be more sexually promiscuous than white women; and, as we suggested in Chapter 7, this myth is one reason white men have exploited black women sexually, particularly during the time of slavery. The myth persists to this day, however: it is a popular stereotype that black women on welfare have many more children than white women on welfare, when the fact is that they have approximately the same number (see Chapters 6 and 7).

The special pressures that black women experience include the fact that black men have tended to adopt the prejudicial attitudes toward women in our society. Thus black women are not only denied equality in the larger society but are frequently kept in a subordinate position by black men. Also, as Pendergass and her colleagues have described, black men may try to dominate their wives in order to compensate for their frustration in dealing with a society that discriminates against them.[68]

PUERTORRIQUEÑAS

Some of the problems Puerto Rican women face in our society are faced by Puerto Ricans in general: a lack of experience with the English language, different cultural background and customs, and a lack of preparedness for the racial inequality of our society. (Puerto Rico is a racially mixed society in which members of different groups are generally treated as equals.) Like other minorities, Puerto Ricans suffer from discrimination in housing, education, employment, and wages that keeps them in a severely deprived condition.

Here again, however, Puerto Rican women are in many ways even more deprived than their male counterparts. The median income of Puerto Rican women is about half that of Puerto Rican men (which, in turn, is only about two-thirds of the white median income). And unemployment among Puerto Rican women is twice as high as among Puerto Rican men. Like other minorities, Puerto Rican women, even more than Puerto Rican men, are concentrated in the lower-paying occupations.

It is Puerto Rican women who are heads of families who suffer from

[66] William A. Blakey, "Everybody makes the revolution." *Civil Rights Digest,* vol. 6, no. 3 (Spring 1974):19.
[67] Frances M. Beal, "Double jeopardy: To be black and female." In Morgan, pp. 340–353.
[68] Pendergass *et al.,* p. 44.

discrimination the most. Because Puerto Rican children have special language and cultural needs, the shortage of child-care facilities prevents Puerto Rican women from seeking employment. Only about 13 percent of female heads of Puerto Rican families are able to work full time; an astonishing 60 percent of Puerto Rican families headed by a woman live below the poverty line.[69]

Like black women, Puerto Rican women in the United States suffer from a number of popular stereotypes about them: for example, they are seen as docile, pampered, and inordinately sexual. However, it is the prejudice they face as women—both in their own culture and in the larger American society—that has, in addition to the prejudice they face as Puerto Ricans, most prevented their advancement. As King put it,

The Puerto Rican woman in the United States is caught between two forces. On the one hand, she is entrapped between the bleak economic and political powerlessness affecting the Puerto Rican population in general. On the other hand, she suffers from the socialization of sex roles which causes her to have guilt feelings about the fulfillment of her potential and its expression in a society which looks down . . . at her and her people.[70]

Like many black women, however, Puerto Rican women have been generally reluctant to affiliate themselves with the women's movement, because they stereotypically perceive it as being anti-male or anti-family.

NATIVE WOMEN

We have many fewer stereotypes for native, or American Indian, women than for native men. Most of the native women who lived and died on this continent passed silently through our history, with hardly a heroine or a colorful epithet to confer some distinction upon them. There are a few exceptions; the names of Sacajawea, Pocahontas, and Malinche stand out, but primarily as the women who were responsible for encouraging contact with white settlers or for sacrificing themselves for them. One derogatory stereotype is that of the stolid "squaw," an Algonquin word that originally meant "woman" but later degenerated into "drudge." [71]

Despite the militant stands taken at Alcatraz and Wounded Knee, native people are still a barely visible minority (see Chapter 7). And native women are totally invisible. The facts available about the condition of American Indians largely refer to Indians as a people because few statistical agencies bother to keep separate records for each sex. What statistics are available indicate that native peoples are a marginal group economically, being extremely dependent on federal funds for basic survival. The average length of education for Indians under federal supervision is about five years of school. Only one out of thirty graduates from college, compared to a national figure of one out of three. Winter unemployment rates reach 90 percent on some reservations. The birth and infant mortality rates are high; life expectancy is low. In fact, the health level of the American Indian was once described by President Johnson as "the lowest of any major population group in the United States." [72] The

[69] Lourdes M. King, "Puertorriqueñas in the United States." *Civil Rights Digest,* pp. 20–27.
[70] King, p. 25.
[71] Shirley Witt, "Native women today: Sexism and the Indian woman." *Civil Rights Digest,* p. 29.
[72] In Witt, p. 34.

Bureau of Indian Affairs (BIA), which is the federal agency responsible for native Americans, has few native men (and fewer native women) in mid-level or top-level administrative positions. Even in states in which Indians comprise a majority of BIA employees, a disproportionate number are in lower-level jobs.

The education of native Americans is also a BIA responsibility, and it is in this area where discrimination against Indian women is most visible. In Indian boarding schools, girls may study only domestic or secretarial work, while boys study such things as farmwork or crafts. Unfortunately, Indian women can rarely use even the domestic skills they have learned:

> Reservation life . . . cannot support the picture of the average American homemaker. The starched and relatively expensive advertised clothes are out of place and unobtainable. The polished floors and picture windows are so removed from the hogan or log cabin as to become unreal. The many convenient appliances are too expensive and would not run without electricity. The clean and smiling children require more water than the Navajo family can afford the time to haul. Parent Teacher Association meetings, of which she may have read, are the product of tax-supported schools with the parent in the ultimate role of employer. On the reservation the government-appointed teacher is viewed more as an authority figure than a public servant.[73]

Trapped by their education in low-level service jobs and by the condition of their race in extremely deprived circumstances, native women are among the greatest victims of racial and sex discrimination.

CHICANA WOMEN

The Chicana, or Mexican-American woman, has traditionally been closely identified with family life. She has been bound by customs which stress her importance as a wife and mother and the need to obey her husband. This has created, as Nieto put it, a double dilemma for the Chicana:

> On the one hand, she struggles to maintain her identity as a Chicana. On the other hand, her demands for equity as a woman involve fundamental cultural change. . . . Many Chicanas support the women's movement as it relates to equity and pay opportunities, for instance. Yet for some . . . the closer the movement comes to their personal lives, the more difficult it becomes to tear themselves away from the kinds of roles they have filled.[74]

According to Nieto, the Chicana's task to achieve equality is made more difficult by the fact that she is often competing with Chicano males (rather than whites) for the same, low-level job. Trapped by racial discrimination at the lower strata of society, she is often unable to compete with men even at this low level because of her culture's norms about the role she should play.

[73] In Witt, p. 31.
[74] Consuelo Nieto, "The Chicana and women's rights movement." *Civil Rights Digest*, p. 36.

Asian-American women are subjected to a number of different stereo-types and stresses. Most Asian cultures have stressed the subordinate role of women, and Western culture has vulgarized this to the point of portraying Asian women as pliant, eager to please, and exotically sensual. On the other hand, many Asian-American women come from upwardly mobile families who place heavy emphasis on education and assimilation into the predominant culture. Thus, while Asian-Americans do suffer from a racism based on appearance, like blacks, most of them have not grown up in dead-end slums with little hope for future advancement. For this reason many Asian-American women have identified with the Women's Liberation Movement and have formed groups to press for sexual, as well as racial, equality.[75]

SOURCES OF SEXISM

We have described some of the causes of women's subordination from a historical point of view and have indicated some of the major inequities women face in our society and in other countries. In this section we will discuss in some detail the processes by which institutions in our society perpetrate, reinforce, and perpetuate sexism.

Socialization refers to the process by which individuals develop into social beings. Chafetz has suggested that

through the socialization process humans came to more or less internalize the roles, norms, and values appropriate to the culture and subculture within which they function. Cultural definitions become personal definitions of propriety, normality, and worthiness.[76]

Most socialization takes place during interaction with other people, that is, how other people react to what we do will eventually influence how we will behave. We are also socialized through popular culture—the films we see and the books we read, for example. Socialization may be consciously imposed—for instance, compulsory education—or it may be as subtle and unconscious as the nuances we take for granted in our language.

A primary agent of socialization in our culture is the family—specifically parents. And a number of studies have been done to determine how parents socialize their children into traditional sex roles. However, the broad and traditional outlines of how parents raise their children to be men and women in our society do not need to be clarified by researchers, for they are self-evident. Long before their child is born, parents are deciding how they will treat it if it is a boy or a girl—what name the child will have and whether the nursery will be painted blue or pink, for example. Later, when the child is born, the socialization process takes a number of obvious forms: little boys will be given toy

[75] See *Asian Women*. Berkeley: University of California, Dwinelle Hall, 1971.
[76] Janet S. Chafetz, *Masculine, Feminine, or Human?: An Overview of the Sociology of Sex Roles*. Itasca, Ill.: Peacock, 1974, p. 69.

trucks, while little girls will be given dolls; boys are encouraged to play ball, while girls are told to play house.

It is the more subtle forms of socialization that have interested researchers. Lewis, for example, found that parental influences cause differences in the behavior of boys and girls within the first two years of their lives:

> From the earliest age, girl infants are looked at and talked to more than boy infants. For the first six months or so, boy infants have more physical contact than girl infants, but by the time boys are six months old, this reverses and girls get more physical contact and more nontouching contact. . . . The motive appears to be cultural; mothers believe that boys should be more independent than girls and that they should be encouraged to explore and master their world.[77]

Lewis theorizes that this tendency of mothers to talk more to their daughters accounts in part for the greater linguistic skills that women demonstrate. The lack of physical contact experienced by boys after the age of six months, suggests Lewis, may account for the fact that they tend to be more independent as adults—and also more restricted in their expression of feeling.

Lynn suggests that one cause of male-female differences is the fact that, traditionally, children have been raised by their mothers while the father was at work, absent from the home. The effect on little girls who are raised in this way, Lynn theorizes, is that they can easily identify with their mothers, who are always there; however, they will tend to regard the absent father—and by extension, males in general—as more powerful and prestigious. Boys, on the other hand, will have few male models available with which to identify. As such, their concepts of maleness will be based on an unrealistic cultural definition of masculinity, rather than on human models. They will have to learn what is expected of them from their peers and from whatever guidance they can derive from the media. Lynn suggests that the more critical identity problem with which boys are confronted accounts both for their greater problem-solving ability in adulthood and their constant anxiety about their masculinity.[78]

EDUCATION

Education represents a more formal type of socialization. Considering the amount of time children are in school, the socialization they receive there inevitably has an effect on how they behave. Several studies have indicated that by and large schools reinforce traditional sex-role stereo-types and socialize children into traditional sex roles.

One study by Maye and McMillan [79] found that some female elementary-school teachers—who are disproportionately represented in elementary schools—shared traditional prejudices about women. One in four of those studied believed women functioned best as wives and mothers and

[77] Michael Lewis, "There's no unisex in the nursery." *Psychology Today,* May 1972, p. 56.
[78] David B. Lynn, *Parental and Sex Role Identification: A Theoretical Formulation.* Berkeley: McCutchan, 1969.
[79] In Chafetz, pp. 86–90.

that women were less reliable workers than men. It is likely that such attitudes cause teachers to set different standards of behavior for boys and girls. Howe, for example, found that boys were permitted to be far more active and boisterous in the classroom.[80]

Even if teachers are informed and well intentioned, other parts of the educational system still stymie attempts to eradicate sexist training. For one thing, many school texts perpetuate stereotypes, myths, and half truths. In a survey of elementary-school readers,[81] researchers found that boy stories predominated (in a 5:2 ratio), that boys outnumbered girls in illustrations, and that there were more stories about smart boys who exercised initiative and achieved their goals than there were about girls. The same stereotypes were found in a study of prize-winning preschool texts:[82] females were underrepresented; they were pictured as passive and dependent, and were seen as playing traditional domestic roles. Boys were pictured as being much more decisive and adventurous. It is little wonder that by the age of 4 the relative advantages of each sex role are recognized by children: fully half of girls prefer the male role, while only a fourth of boys prefer the female role.[83]

The separate treatment generally accorded boys and girls in school serves to further segregate the sexes and reinforces traditional roles. Boys and girls are generally lined up separately, for example, and in many schools are given different courses—girls take typing, while boys take shop. It is the sex segregation that occurs during career counseling that is most insidious, however, for it locks individuals into lifetime careers on the basis of sex rather than ability. Too often, counselors advocate only traditional female occupations to young women who are qualified and eager to enter so-called male preserves. A young girl who is a good math student may be told to go into teaching, while a young boy with equal skills may be told to go into engineering. As Chafetz described it,

Counselors defend such practices on the basis of what youngsters may "realistically" expect to face in the future: marriage, child care, and a lack of opportunity in a number of career fields for females, and the need to support a family at the highest income and status levels possible for males. "Realism" however, has always been an excuse for maintaining the status quo, and it is no different in the case of sex role stereotypes. If, for instance, females do not prepare to enter previously masculine fields, such fields will remain male-dominated, allowing another generation of counselors to assure girls that females can't work in them. In addition, it is questionable whether counselors' notions of "reality" in fact keep pace with reality. There is undoubtedly a lag between expanding opportunities and changing sex role definitions on the one hand, and counselors' awareness of these phenomena on the other.[84]

[80] Florence Howe, "Sexual stereotypes start early." *Saturday Review,* October 16, 1971, p. 81.
[81] In Chafetz, p. 83.
[82] Lenore Weitzman *et al.,* "Sex role socialization in picture books for preschool children." *American Journal of Sociology* (May 1972):1125–1150.
[83] Farrell, p. 36.
[84] Chafetz, p. 88.

The traditional view of women is that a woman's primary role is that **FAMILY** of homemaker. However, women who adopt this view of themselves and who accept their traditional role do not always find that they thereby achieve equal status even within the home. The very role of homemaker, as it is presently designed and regarded, often seems to perpetuate a woman's subordinate status, limit her freedom, and leave her feeling unfulfilled. As Bell put it,

It has been observed that women are often caught up in a vicious circle because of their economic dependance on their husbands and their lack of contact with the work world; and their being tied down to the house restricts, to a great extent, the kind of decisions over which they can claim expertise and, ultimately, control.[85]

Even in many nontraditional marriages in which there is a great degree of equality between husband and wife, the husband often has a more privileged position. One study of husband and wife psychologists,[86] for example, found that even when both members of a couple are professionals, the woman often is forced into a somewhat subordinate position. It is assumed that the man's career is more important or more likely to be successful than the woman's career. Though the woman is more productive than a nonprofessional woman, she tends to be less productive than her husband, assuming a more supportive role and handling more than her share of domestic chores. The net result is that wives in professional pairs are less likely than their husbands to be satisfied with their careers.

Many studies of different types of marriages tend to confirm the fact that husbands are generally more satisfied with marriage than their wives and that wives make more concessions in their marriages. Among unhappy marriages, wives tend to feel more frustrated than their husbands: women go for marriage counseling more than men and initiate most divorce proceedings. Even among happy marriages, however, women report higher rates of dissatisfaction and depression than men, and women must make most of the adjustments to make the marriage work. In Jessie Bernard's words,

Because women have to put so many more eggs in the one basket of marriage they have more of a stake in its stability. Because their happiness is more dependent on marriage than men's they have to pay more for it.[87]

The psychological consequences of overidentifying with a woman's domestic role was described by Pauline Bart in her study of depression in middle-aged women. Bart found that, contrary to popular opinion, women did not become depressed in middle age because of hormonal changes caused by menopause but rather because they found themselves left without any important function. She found that the lowest rates of

[85] Bell, pp. 370–371.
[86] Rebecca B. Bryson et al., "The professional pair." *American Psychologist* (January 1976):10–17.
[87] Jessie Bernard, "The paradox of the happy marriage." In Vivian Gornick and Barbara K. Moran, eds., *Woman in Sexist Society*. New York: Basic Books, 1974, p. 149.

depression occurred among middle-aged working women, who had their jobs to keep them occupied and give them satisfaction. Higher rates of depression were found among housewives whose children had grown up and left home; the housewife had fewer people dependent on her domestic role, and her sense of identity suffered. Bart found the highest depression rates among housewives who had overinvolved or overprotective relationships with their children. For these women, the departure of their children from the household represented the negation of a central role in their lives and led to a considerable loss of self-esteem.[88]

Rossi has pointed out that the development of technological tools to do human work has eliminated many of the tasks the traditional homemaker used to have—laundry is done largely by machine instead of by hand, cooking takes less time because of ovens and "instant foods," and so on. The resulting time savings have not resulted in more free time for home-makers; instead, the other aspects of the traditional role—particularly motherhood—have, until recently, assumed greater importance. Women have been expected to devote full time to the task of rearing children; motherhood has become a "full-time occupation." [89]

This overemphasis of the importance of motherhood inevitably causes guilt feelings in women who are unfulfilled by the mother role and undoubtedly contributes to the depression described by Bart. Moreover, the emphasis on motherhood devalued the importance of the father's role in a child's upbringing. Farrell cites several studies that indicate that problems in a relationship with the father were more significant than problems in a relationship with the mother in producing delinquent or maladjusted children.[90] Nevertheless, the myth that a woman is best suited for the task of raising a child persists, preventing many women from exercising their capabilities outside the home and preventing many men from exercising their capabilities inside the home. The result is a sex differentiation that keeps women in a subordinate role and prevents members of both sexes from sharing in their family and work responsibilities.

PSYCHIATRIC MEDICINE

We have already described Freud's theories on women and suggested how they tend to reinforce the traditional view of a woman's role. As we shall see, many of Freud's theories, along with other traditional male attitudes, have over time become institutionalized in the fields of psychology and psychiatry. Because these disciplines, more than any others, define thoughts and behaviors as normal and adjusted or abnormal, unhealthy, and maladjusted, the exercise of prejudicial attitudes toward women within these fields has had extremely harmful effects.

There can be little doubt that psychologists and psychiatrists—who are predominantly male—have stereotypic notions about women. Bruno Bettelheim once said that "as much as women want to be good scientists

[88] Pauline B. Bart, "Depression in middle-aged women." In Gornick and Moran, pp. 163–186.
[89] Alice Rossi, "Equality between the sexes: An immodest proposal." *Daedalus*, Spring 1964.
[90] Farrell, p. 117.

and engineers, they want first and foremost to be womanly companions of men and to be mothers." Erik Erikson wrote that a woman has "an 'inner space' destined to bear the offspring of chosen men, and with it, a biological, psychological, and ethical commitment to take care of human infancy." [91] A major survey of women psychologists who had been in psychotherapy found that therapists tended to foster traditional sex roles and were biased in their evaluations of their women patients. Some of the biases found in the survey include:

1. "The therapist lacks awareness and sensitivity to the woman client's career, work, and role diversity."
2. "The female client's attitude toward childbearing and child rearing is viewed as a necessary index of her emotional maturity."
3. "The therapist defers to the husband's needs in the conduct of the wife's treatment."
4. "The therapist . . . fosters concepts of women as passive and dependent."
5. "Therapist has a double standard for male and female sexual activities." [92]

As we discussed in Chapter 2, mental health clinicians have different standards of mental health for men and women: they believe that healthy *women* are passive and dependent, while at the same time they believe that healthy *adults* are active and independent.[93] The net effect of this bias is to reinforce traditional roles in women patients and to identify those women who do not fit the traditional mold as maladjusted or ill. Bell put it more generally:

The psychiatric influence has been such that any problem is seen as individually based rather than socially determined. As a result, many women who have felt miserable and unhappy as housewives have defined themselves at fault or inadequate rather than recognizing that in many cases they are victims of social situations that cause their problems.[94]

LANGUAGE AND THE MEDIA

One of the dominant features of our society is the explosive growth of the communications industry over the past two decades. The number of books published increases every year and people are spending increasing amounts of time watching television. The way these and other media treat sex roles is therefore likely to have a considerable impact on people's attitudes and behaviors.

Language in the media (and in textbooks) often reinforces traditional sex-role stereotype by its overreliance on male terms and its tendency to describe men and women in terms of outmoded clichés. Typical

---

[91] Bettelheim and Erikson quoted in Naomi Weisstein, "Psychology constructs the female." In Gornick and Moran, pp. 364–365.
[92] "Report of the task force on sex bias and sex-role stereotyping in psychotherapeutic practice." *American Psychologist* (December 1975):1169–1175.
[93] Phyllis Chesler, *Women and Madness.* New York: Avon, 1972, p. 68. See also Mary B. Parlee, "Psychology." *Signs—Journal of Women in Culture and Society,* pp. 119–138.
[94] Bell, p. 377.

stereotypic phrases might be "the future of man" instead of "the future of humanity"; "Bill and his attractive wife" instead of "handsome Bill and attractive Joan" or "Bill and Joan"; and "scatterbrained female," "clumsy male," and so on. The use of male pronouns when neutral subjects are referred to also implies that women are excluded from active life: for example, "the typical doctor enjoys *his* leisure time" instead of "doctors typically enjoy *their* leisure time."

While sexism in language is generally subtle and unconscious, in advertising it is often blatant. One analysis of commercials shown during children's programs showed that almost all narrators were male, more females than males were involved in domestic activities, ten times as many boys as girls were physically active, and every child shown as economically dependent was a girl.[95] Researchers who analyzed the roles portrayed by women in print advertisements found that

the advertisements presented the following cliches about women's roles: (1) a woman's place is in the home, (2) women do not make important decisions or do important things, (3) women are dependent and need men's protection, and (4) men regard women primarily as sexual objects; they are not interested in women as people.[96]

Far fewer women than men were portrayed as working, despite the fact that almost half of all women do work. No women were shown in executive positions; instead, they tended to play largely decorative roles in these advertisements. Finally, the vast majority of the buying decisions were shown to be made by men, particularly those involving major purchases, such as buying a car. In addition, as Lucy Komisar suggests, the woman in advertisements seems to be totally preoccupied with her domestic role or with attracting a man.[97] Such stereotypes tend to negate the changes that are already occurring in our society. Furthermore, they serve to reinforce traditional sex roles and make it difficult for men and women to see broader possibilities in their roles and their relationships.

Women attend church more frequently than men
· pray more often than men
· hold firmer beliefs than men
· cooperate more in church programs than men
Yet organized religion is dominated by men.[98]

ORGANIZED RELIGION

In their theological doctrine and in their religious hierarchies, churches and synagogues tend to reinforce women's subordinate role. Organized religion has, historically, served to reinforce many secular traditions and norms. As such, it has tended toward the traditional view that men are

[95] Chafetz, pp. 82–83.
[96] Ahmed Belkaoui and Janice M. Belkaoui, "A comparative analysis of the roles played by women in print advertisements: 1958, 1970, 1972." *Journal of Marketing Research* 13 (May 1976):168.
[97] Lucy Komisar, "The image of woman in advertising." In Gornick and Moran, p. 306.
[98] Joseph H. Fichter, in Virginia K. Mills, "The status of women in American churches." *Church and Society,* September–October 1972, p. 50.

primary and women are secondary, and that a woman's most important role is procreative. In Judaism, women are required to obey fewer religious precepts than men because less is expected of them. Devout male Jews recite a prayer each morning thanking God for not making them a woman. The Catholic Church still assumes overall authority over a woman's sexual behavior, forbidding birth control devices because they prevent reproduction. In all churches, God is still referred to as "He"; and women are barred from performing the most sacred rituals or attaining the highest administrative posts. The consequences of this are summed up well by Daly:

As long as qualified persons are excluded from any ministry by reason of their sex alone, it cannot be said that there is genuine equality of men and women in the church. . . . By this exclusion the church is saying that the sexual differentiation is—for one sex—a crippling defect which no personal qualities of intelligence, character, or leadership can overcome. In fact, by this policy it is effectively teaching that women are not fully human and conditioning people to accept this as unchangeable fact.[99]

The federal government has a long history of discrimination against women.[100] An official study by the Women's Bureau (a congressionally created federal agency) in 1919 found that women were barred from applying to 60 percent of all civil service positions, notably those involving scientific or other professional work. Women were considered in a separate employment category than men, and had limitations placed on their salaries. The professionals in the Women's Bureau, for example, were limited by an act of Congress to receiving half the salaries males received for doing the same work in other federal agencies.

GOVERNMENT

During World War II, the pattern of official discrimination continued. Despite the shortage of men to fill government positions, women were kept from most administrative and professional positions. The situation, if anything, was worse in the armed forces. For example, although the Army had a severe shortage of medical personnel, it refused to commission women doctors. Only an act of Congress in 1943 forced the Army to change its hiring policies. In the domestic labor force, as was previously mentioned, women were of necessity permitted to enter fields that had been closed to them. But although the National War Labor Board insisted on a uniform pay scale for both sexes, it permitted a number of loopholes which in effect discriminated against women: for example, the equal pay provisions did not apply to traditionally female jobs, and industries were permitted to assign different job titles for men and women, even when the same work was involved.

While discrimination against women has had less overt support by the government in recent years, patterns of discrimination still exist at the federal level. The 1964 Civil Rights Act, which prohibited discrimination on the basis of (among other things) sex, specifically excluded federal,

[99] Mary Daly, "Women and the Catholic Church." In Morgan, p. 134.
[100] The following discussion is based on William H. Chafe, *The American Woman: Her Changing Social, Economic, and Political Roles, 1920–1970.* New York: Oxford University Press, 1972.

state, and local governments from its provisions. One result is that women who work for the government are overwhelmingly concentrated in lower-level clerical or service-type jobs, while administrative posts are largely held by men. Federal policy toward day-care funding has also had the effect of discriminating against women. One New York survey found that seven out of eight mothers who utilized day-care centers would not be able to earn a living wage without them. Nevertheless, federal funding for day-care centers has been low, and in recent years these funds have been cut back; in 1976, for example, President Ford vetoed a bill that would have provided funds for the improvement of day-care centers already in existence.

We have already mentioned some of the laws that discriminate against women, such as those relating to jury duty. These laws, however, represent a small part of an entire legal structure that is based on the idea that men are the wage-earners in the family, while women are the home-makers.

THE LEGAL SYSTEM

Hole and Levine have outlined many of the legal barriers to sexual equality.[101] For example, many state labor laws passed during the late nineteenth and early twentieth centuries set work standards that were designed to protect all workers—the maximum hours that people were required to work, the maximum weights that they were required to lift, and so on. The Supreme Court found, however, that such labor restrictions were unconstitutional as far as men were concerned, because they violated constitutional liberties. Women, on the other hand, could still be required to obey these restrictions. In its 1908 decision, which upheld a state law limiting the hours women factory employees could work, the Court stated:

History discloses the fact that woman has always been dependent on man. He has established his control at the outset by superior physical strength, and this control in various forms, with diminishing intensity, has continued to the present. . . . Differentiated by these matters from the other sex, she is properly placed in a class by herself, and legislation designed for her protection may be sustained, even when like legislation is not necessary for men, and could not be sustained.[102]

This decision in effect legalized and perpetuated those state laws that differentiated between men and women. As late as 1965, the Equal Employment Opportunity Commission (EEOC), which was empowered to enforce the 1964 Civil Rights Act, stated that state laws designed to "protect" women were not discriminatory.

The problem of legal differentiation between men and women exists in areas beside that of employment. Some state educational institutions are permitted to exclude women, either from their student bodies or their faculties. Many technical high schools admit only boys; other high schools prohibit pregnant or married girls from attending, but permit unmarried fathers or married boys to attend.

Hole and Levine also note that in most states, statutes applicable to

[101] Hole and Levine, pp. 18–67.
[102] In Hole and Levine, p. 32.

married adults are dominated by the common-law tradition that recognized the husband as head of the family and guardian of his wife. As soon as she was married, therefore, a woman's legal identity became subordinate to that of her husband. Most states still require a woman to adopt her husband's name and place of residence. The family's property is usually in the husband's name, and thus the wife has no legal property rights. Women who are single or widowed often have difficulty obtaining credit, because it is assumed that they have no earning potential. Some states also required a married woman's husband's consent to an abortion before it is performed. This requirement was declared unconstitutional by the Supreme Court only in July 1976.

Men also suffer from inequities in family law. Husbands in most states are legally obligated to support their wives, regardless of the wives' financial status. Alimony is usually awarded automatically to wives, only rarely to husbands, even if the wife can support herself (see Chapter 10). A father in a child-custody battle bears a heavy burden of proof that he is a more fit parent than the child's mother; child custody is routinely given by the courts to the mother and only in cases where the mother is demonstrably negligent will the father's claim be seriously considered.

SOCIAL ACTION

Suggestions for reducing and eventually eliminating sexism in our society generally focus on two broad areas: changes in the socialization process and changes in the legal system. Altering the socialization process is necessary, because it is through socialization that norms and values are transmitted from one generation to the next. If children are to learn that men and women are equal, and that no attitude, aptitude, behavior, or role is limited to one sex alone, then parents, schools, and the media will have to change the substance of what they are now conveying to children. Changes in the legal system are necessary, because at present many laws codify traditional attitudes about sex roles and permit discrimination on the basis of sex to occur.

Perhaps the major obstacle to women's equality has been the "motherhood cult"—the idea that women are most fulfilled as mothers and that children, particularly young children, require a mother's constant attention if they are to grow up to be healthy and adjusted.

CHANGES IN CHILD-REARING PRACTICES

It seems evident that young children do need loving, consistent care and attention, and the chance to build up a relationship with one or two regularly present adults. However, there is no evidence that these adults must be female. In fact, as we have already suggested, the absence of male figures can have detrimental effects on the growing child. By the age of 3 or 4, children no longer seem to need the one-to-one relationship so constantly; rather, they need to be able to explore, to test their surroundings and themselves, in an atmosphere of security. This relative independence tends to increase as children grow, and while they continue to need adults to whom they can go for guidance, comfort, and role models, it is not evident that they need them to be constantly available.

One of the first steps, then, that will have to be taken toward achieving sexual equality is to have fathers share equally in the process of child raising (and homemaking in general). This does not mean that all fathers or all mothers will have to do exactly half the work raising children (or keeping house) involves. Rather, it means that it must become accepted within our society that men have as much to contribute to family life as women, and that members of each family are free to decide among themselves how best to allocate family responsibilities. It is obvious, however, that unless a sufficient number of women are freed from their family and household tasks, women will be unable to compete with men on an equal footing. Conversely, unless the status of the homemaker role is raised and more men participate in it, many men who would be enriched by the homemaker role will be forced by social pressure to pursue outside careers.

Aside from officially recognizing the economic contribution made by homemakers, as we discussed earlier, there are a number of other steps that need to be taken to make it easier for men and women to share domestic tasks. For example, many companies already permit maternity leaves for their women employees who wish time off to take care of their children. What is needed is for *parental* leaves to become institutionalized, so that men or women who want to take some time to raise a child will be free to do so without losing their jobs. Such a system is already in existence in Sweden, where parents are given a six-month leave upon the birth of their child; the six months can be divided equally between father and mother.[103]

Another idea is to upgrade the importance of part-time work, particularly by institutionalizing many of the benefits full-time work now has —fringe benefits, possibility of collecting unemployment insurance if fired, the possibility of seniority, and so on. In this way men and women will be freer to share the responsibilities of both supporting the family and taking care of the home and the children. Finally, men and women must decide on an individual basis to assign household tasks equitably. Sharing such tasks will not only give many women more time for self-fulfillment; it will also enable men and women to begin to relate to each other as equals and help prevent children from developing stereotypic notions about the role of each sex.

In many instances, however, even such reforms will not go far enough. For those men and women who do not wish to or cannot afford to stop working for an extended period of time, and, most important, for those women who are heads of families, provision for child day care must be made. At the present time, there are over 6 million children with working mothers, yet there are well under a million places for them in day-care centers all over the country.[104] This means that many children of working mothers are without any care at all. Furthermore, many more mothers who would work if they could find proper day care remain unemployed.

There is some controversy over institutional day care for young children. It is well known, for example, that babies and children in large,

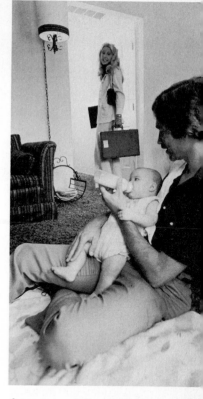

As our society moves toward greater sexual equality, women and men will find greater flexibility in the roles they are permitted to play.
Bruce Roberts/Photo Researchers

[103] Safilios-Rothschild, *Women and Social Policy*, p. 21.
[104] Elinor C. Guggenheimer, "The battle for day care." *Nation*, May 7, 1973, p. 596.

Well-run day-care programs will free many homemakers to seek employment. In addition, such programs will make positive contributions to children's development.
Guy Gillette/Photo Researchers

impersonal residential institutions are often noticeably retarded in many aspects of their growth. It has also been noted that communally raised children, such as those of the Israeli kibbutz, while they usually grow up to be well-adjusted adults, tend to be somewhat lacking in qualities of imagination and ambition (see Chapter 10). However, there can be little doubt that a well-staffed (say, a five-to-one ratio of children to teachers), well-organized day-care center can offer children opportunities and stimuli for exploration and discovery that may be considerably greater than they get at home. Since the physical plant would be set up for children, most of the "don't touch" and "be careful" admonitions that might be necessary at home would be eliminated. Well-trained teachers would be alert to budding interests and abilities and would know how to encourage them; and there would be more space and a greater variety of play equipment than in most private homes.

It is obvious, however, that changes in the way children in our society are socialized must, ultimately, occur on an individual, day-to-day level, and not only in our social institutions, if real sexual equality is ever to occur. Parents and teachers must learn to relate to each child as an individual rather than as a member of a sex. For example, children should have a wide range of toys available (not just dolls for girls and trucks for boys) so that they can determine for themselves which ones interest them. They should also be taught at an early age that any occupation is open to them. Only if children are permitted to develop their own capacities can they become free of stereotypes that might otherwise hinder them.

As with changes in child-rearing practices, changes in educational practices will involve the numerous social interactions that pupils and teachers have on a daily basis. Teachers and school administrators must become more sensitive to their own stereotypes about boys and girls (or men and

CHANGES IN THE EDUCATIONAL PROCESS

women) and begin to treat students of both sexes equally—for example, by paying equal attention to male and female students and by not assigning tasks according to traditional sex-role stereotypes.

Rossi has suggested that one way to help break down the idea that only women take care of children (while men "work") is to attract more male teachers in the lower grades.[105] There is also a clear need for an end to hiring discrimination at the school administrative level, which at present is predominantly male. Not only would qualified women be able to obtain jobs previously closed to them, but students would see that women as well as men can attain top positions. Changes in the standard curriculum and in vocational guidance would also be required to prevent traditional occupational and role stereotypes from arising. Boys and girls should be free (or required) to participate in both cooking and shop classes, for example, and both sexes should participate in whatever sports activities are available. Along similar lines, students should be able to determine for themselves in what field or occupation they are interested. Teachers or guidance counselors should help students make these choices based on the students' abilities, not their gender.

Some major publishers are beginning to become more sensitive to sexism in textbooks, and have issued guidelines to their editors on how to avoid it. Most books published today, however, still reflect traditional sex-role stereotypes: boys are still shown in active roles in illustrations, while girls are shown in passive subordinate roles; and male pronouns (such as "he" or "him") still predominate in the language of the text. What is needed is a greater effort on the part of publishers to show females and males in a variety of occupations and roles—women and men working in the professions, for example, as well as men and women performing domestic tasks.

CHANGES IN THE LEGAL SYSTEM

Title VII of the Civil Rights Act of 1964 forbids discrimination on the basis of sex. However, as we have seen, wage and job discrimination against women continue on a wide scale. Red tape that interferes with filing discrimination complaints; the backlog of cases that already exist; less than total enthusiasm on the part of the EEOC to enforce this provision of the act; and loopholes in the act, such as those exempting local, state, and federal governments, have all hindered the effective operation of this act. Similarly, the Equal Pay Act of 1963 (as amended by the Education Amendments of 1972), which prohibits discrimination in salaries, has not solved the problem of wage discrimination. Such discrimination is difficult to prove—even in those relatively few instances when a woman is angry enough to sue—and the act does not cover hiring and promotion policies.

The Equal Rights Amendment (ERA) was passed by Congress in 1972; if ratified by thirty-four states it will become the Twenty-Seventh Amendment to the Constitution. (As this book goes to press, the amendment remains five states short of ratification.) ERA is designed to fill loopholes in previous anti–sex-discrimination acts and to forbid sex discrimination in the private sector as well as at every level of government. Its provisions are:

[105] See Rossi.

Section 1. Equality of rights under the law should not be denied or abridged by the United States or by any State on account of sex.
Section 2. The Congress shall have the power to enforce by appropriate legislation the provisions of this article.
Section 3. The amendment shall take effect two years after the date of ratification.

Passage of this amendment will make it far more difficult for discrimination to occur: state educational institutions will no longer be able to deny women admission; criminal laws for men and women will become uniform; companies will find it harder to keep jobs sex-typed (particularly if the enforcement aspect of the admendment is made severe); more men will be able to retain custody of their children in divorce cases—the entire range of institutions and laws that serve to differentiate women and men will be affected. While large institutions are already required (by a federal Executive Order) to have affirmative action programs, with quotas and timetables to increase women's representation, ERA will inevitably require all institutions to have such programs. Over a period of time, if ERA is ratified, the wholesale sex discrimination that exists at present should be markedly reduced. It should be noted, however, that laws directly related to physiological differences between men and women—such as those requiring maternity benefits or separate toilet facilities for men and women—will *not* be affected by ERA.

There are several other aspects of the legal system, not covered by the antidiscrimination measures we have discussed, that nevertheless impede women's equality. For example, tax laws need to be changed to permit larger tax deductions for day care; in this way many more parents could afford to work. State laws that keep many women from obtaining abortions also need to be eliminated. Some states, for instance, require that abortions be performed in a more costly hospital rather than in a physician's office; this requirement in effect restricts the number of women, particularly poor women, who can receive abortions. In addition, many health insurance plans do not cover the expense of an abortion; thus for many poor women the cost of an abortion is prohibitive.

PROSPECTS

Although temporary setbacks may occur, it is unlikely that the progress women have already made toward achieving equality will be significantly hindered in the near future. And there are many indications that progress will continue to be made. Only a decade ago, for example, less than 6 percent of women entering college planned careers in traditional male fields such as business, medicine, law, or engineering; today approximately 17 percent of women in their first year of college plan to enter such fields.[106] Several companies have begun "management awareness programs" to make managers more sensitive to their attitudes toward hiring and promoting women employees.[107] And some church branches

[106] *New York Times,* January 25, 1976, p. 8.
[107] Farrell, p. 141.

(such as the American Lutheran Church) have begun to ordain women clergy for the first time.

Under pressure from concerned women and men, antidiscrimination laws already in existence are being somewhat more stringently enforced, and new laws to increase sexual equality are constantly being proposed. In a landmark 1973 settlement, for example, AT&T was forced to pay $15 million in back pay to its female employees, because it had been giving its female employees less pay than men for the same work (a violation of the Equal Pay Act). The Equal Credit Opportunity Act, signed into law at the end of 1974, makes it unlawful for any creditor to discriminate against anyone on the basis of sex or marital status. And new legislation introduced into the House of Representatives would provide Social Security coverage for homemakers as if they were self-employed workers, thereby allowing disabled homemakers to collect disability benefits and making widows or widowers eligible for survivor's benefits to help pay for substitute homemaker services.

Demographic changes that are continuing also make it more likely that pressures toward women's equality will increase. Childless marriages, for example, are becoming more widespread, freeing women and men for full-time employment. More and more people are postponing marriage and childbearing, at least until their education is finished and their careers are under way. As the number of educated women continues to grow, dissatisfaction with lower-status and lower-paying jobs will also increase, forcing employers to make changes in their hiring and promotion policies. Finally, the growing availability of birth control devices, and increases in the life span, make it likely that women will spend less time raising children and more time in the labor force.

What would some of the probable effects of sexual equality be? One obvious answer is that society's supply of talent in every segment of the work force would increase. More men would participate in traditional female fields, such as elementary-school teaching, and more women would participate in such traditional male fields as science or engineering. The opening up of these fields to both sexes would be likely to increase the number of people participating in them; thus the talent and creativity available in our society would grow. Breaking down the occupational barriers that now separate women and men would also help women and men to relate to each other as equals. Also, because fewer men would be providing sole support for their families, there would be more flexibility in working life: men and women will be freer to leave their jobs if they are unhappy in them, and in general there will be a greater sharing of economic and homemaking responsibilities. This will reduce the pressures that exist today for men to "succeed" and for women to remain "dependent." The most important result of true sexual equality, then, may be simply that people will be free to be themselves.

SUMMARY

Though women in our society have made much progress in recent years, they still have a long way to go before they achieve equality. Progress has been hampered by the prejudicial attitude that women are best suited for the role of wife, mother, and housekeeper and that men should be dominant.

Sex roles—the specific interests and behaviors society assigns to each sex—developed out of the differentiation of tasks that took place in hunting and gathering societies. An added factor, according to Brownmiller, was that women were forced to rely on men for their own protection. Finally, Freud's view that women were naturally passive helped perpetuate a double standard of behavior for women and men.

Contemporary dissatisfaction with traditional sex roles arose out of industrialization, which caused women to spend less time in child rearing and made it possible for more women to work and be independent. The feminist movement, which began to operate in an organized fashion as early as the 1820s, also helped to change discrimination laws and to free men and women of the traditional view of themselves.

Studies of the wide variety of sex roles in other societies suggest that differences in sex roles between men and women are not innate but are learned by individuals as they are socialized into their culture. In our own society, traditional sex roles are being increasingly seen as limits to individual freedom.

Sexism is the range of attitudes and behaviors that discriminate against women and men. Inaccurate and unrealistic stereotypes about men and women are a part of sexism: many of those who are victimized by these stereotypes believe them, limiting their own freedom of action; more important, these stereotypes are used by those in authority to justify discriminatory behavior. Thus, for example, jobs and wages have become sex-typed: women have been concentrated in lower-status, lower-paying jobs, and receive lower wages even when they perform the same work as men. The legal system also codifies traditional stereotypes about the kinds of things men and women do.

Black women, Puertorriqueñas, native women, Chicanas, and Asian women typically suffer double discrimination—on the basis of sex and of race. Even more than their male counterparts, they are concentrated in the lower strata of society.

Socialization is a primary source of sexism. Parents begin to reinforce traditionally masculine behavior in boys and feminine behavior in girls as soon as their children are born. Schoolteachers, guidance counselors, and textbooks also differentiate between boys and girls along stereotypic lines. Traditional family roles also perpetuate sexism, because they require that women give up more of their freedom than men. Psychiatry perpetuates sexism, because it tries to force women into traditional patterns of behavior. Language and the media reinforce sexism, because they take male dominance and female subordination for granted. Finally, organized religion, government, and the legal system make it difficult to end sexism, because they give legitimacy to traditional views of women and men.

Suggestions for eliminating sexism in our society involve changing the socialization process and the legal system. Despite occasional setbacks, such changes are likely to take place as more women become educated and enter the labor force and as more women and men come to understand the benefits that sexual equality would bring.

Bell, Robert R. *Marriage and Family Interaction*. 4th ed. Homewood, Ill.: Dorsey Press, 1975.

Brownmiller, Susan. *Against Our Will: Men, Women, and Rape*. New York: Simon & Schuster, 1975.

BIBLIOGRAPHY

Chafetz, Janet S. *Masculine, Feminine, or Human?: An Overview of the Sociology of Sex Roles*. Itasca, Ill.: Peacock, 1974.

Chesler, Phyllis. *Women and Madness*. New York: Avon, 1972.

Epstein, Cynthia F., and Goode, William J., eds. *The Other Half*. Englewood Cliffs, N.J.: Prentice-Hall, 1971.

Farrell, Warren. *The Liberated Man*. New York: Random House, 1975.

Fasteau, Marc F. *The Male Machine*. New York: McGraw-Hill, 1974.

Friedan, Betty. *The Feminine Mystique*. New York: Dell, 1963.

Gornick, Vivian, and Moran, Barbara K., eds. *Woman in Sexist Society*. New York: Basic Books, 1974.

Hole, Judith, and Levine, Ellen. *Rebirth of Feminism*. New York: Quadrangle, 1971.

Huber, Joan, ed. *Changing Women in a Changing Society*. Chicago: University of Chicago Press, 1966.

Maccoby, Eleanor E., ed. *The Development of Sex Differences*. Stanford: University of California Press, 1966.

Miller, Jean B. *Psychoanalysis and Women*. New York: Penguin, 1973.

Perrucci, Carolyn C., and Targ, Dena B., eds. *Marriage and the Family*. New York: McKay, 1974.

Pleck, Joseph H., and Sawyer, Jack, eds. *Men and Masculinity*. Englewood Cliffs, N.J.: Prentice-Hall, 1974.

Rossi, Alice S., ed. *The Feminist Papers*. New York: Bantam, 1974.

Safilios-Rothschild, Constantina. *Women and Social Policy*. Englewood Cliffs, N.J.: Prentice-Hall, 1974.

————, ed. *Toward a Sociology of Women*. New York: Wiley, 1972.

Seward, Georgene H., and Williamson, Robert C., eds. *Sex Roles in Changing Society*. New York: Random House, 1970.

Skolnick, Arlene S., and Skolnick, Jerome H. *Family in Transition*. Boston: Little, Brown, 1971.

9

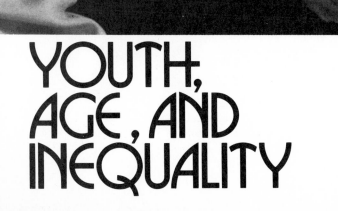

YOUTH, AGE, AND INEQUALITY

- About 93 percent of persons of high school age and 43 percent of 18- and 19-year-olds are enrolled in schools.
- Of men and women age 16 to 19 in the labor force, over 16 percent are unemployed.
- Only about one-fifth of 18- to 20-year-olds and just over one-fourth of 21- to 24-year-olds vote in a non-presidential election.
- Half the elderly are over 73 years of age. There are 1 million people over 85 and 100,000 over age 100.
- The elderly are the fastest-growing age group in the nation, and their rate of growth is accelerating.
- At age 65, half of all women are widows; at age 75, two-thirds are widows.
- About 40 percent of single older citizens have total assets of less than $1,000.
- About half the elderly live on less than $90 a week.
- Nearly 60 percent of the elderly are women.

Aging is a universal and natural process. It is something that begins with our very first breath and continues inevitably until our last. Most of us, however, don't think of aging as an ongoing process; we think of it as something that will suddenly happen to us in the distant future, toward the end of our lives. In fact, the very term "aging" has come to have a stigma attached to it, and we assign it only to the elderly. We use more euphemistic terms, like "growing" or "developing," to describe young people who are growing older.

In almost all societies, age is one of the major characteristics (along with others such as sex, race, and kinship) upon which groupings and role assignments are based. How old people are plays a large part in determining how they feel about themselves, with whom they identify, and what society expects of them. As Eisenstadt puts it,

Every human being passes through various ages, and at each one he attains and uses different biological and intellectual capacities. . . . This gradual unfolding of power and capacity is not entirely a universal, biologically conditioned, inescapable fact. . . . Their cultural definition varies from society to society. In all societies, age serves as a basis for defining the cultural and social characteristics of human beings, for the formation of some of their

natural relations and common activities, and for the differential allocation
of social roles.[1]

More poetically, Shakespeare makes a similar point in *As You Like It:*

All the world's a stage,
And all the men and women merely players;
They have their exits and their entrances;
And one man in his time plays many parts. . . .

The fact is, however, that in our society both the young and the aged
play "roleless roles," with little or no specified function. The young are
given minimal time on stage, and are only allowed to play minimal parts.
Past the age of indulgence that is childhood, but not yet admitted to fully
adult roles, youth are legitimately accepted only as students, athletes,
consumers, and soldiers. The elderly, in turn, are asked to relegate themselves to bit parts and to make early exits. They are retired, voluntarily
or not, from their productive roles in the labor market until they become,
in Neugarten's words, "removed from active participation in other areas
of society and are thus relatively isolated and ignored."[2] In this chapter
we will discuss some attitudes toward the young and old and describe
the social problems with which these age groups are confronted.

WHO ARE THE YOUNG AND ELDERLY?

WHO ARE THE
YOUNG?

For our purposes we will define as young those people who range in age
from 14 to 24 years. The estimated population of this group is 43.8
million, approximately 21 percent of the nation's total population.[3]
Today's young people were born during the so-called baby boom—the
period from 1950 to 1963 when the United States experienced the highest birthrate in its history.

Culturally, youth is almost always defined as a transitional phase
from childhood to adulthood.[4] In primitive or traditional societies, this
transitional phase is often invested with a great deal of meaning: young
people are given special training or roles to prepare them for the responsibilities of adulthood. Elaborate rites may mark the occasion when a
young person achieves adulthood. However, in modern societies, particularly in our own, young people are categorized as adolescents; and,
as Friedenberg argues,

adolescence is not an *intermediate* stage between childhood and adulthood
but a status in most respects inferior to both; a position the postpubescent
young are compelled to assume in order to expose them most completely to

[1] S. N. Eisenstadt, "Archetypal patterns of youth." In Erik H. Erikson, ed., *Youth:
Change and Challenge.* New York: Basic Books, 1963.
[2] Bernice L. Neugarten, "The aged in American society." In Howard S. Becker,
ed., *Social Problems: A Modern Approach.* New York: Wiley, 1966.
[3] "Characteristics of American youth." *Current Population Reports,* Series P-23,
no. 51, April 1975.
[4] Eisenstadt, p. 17.

the effects of socialization and reduce their freedom to struggle against it effectively. Adolescents command less respect, arouse more hostility and mistrust, and are obliged to face difficult situations with less social support and greater risk to themselves than either children or adults.[5]

The stage of adolescence has been prolonged in recent years by what Parsons and Platt call the development of the "studentry"—the period when young people undergo extended socialization in the school system.[6] This phase provides young people with values and skills, but postpones still further their participation in adult life. Thus young people who in earlier times would have been considered adults by their late teens are today still characterized as adolescents when in their twenties.

The origins of the concept of adolescence (or "teenagerdom") are many and complex. Perhaps the most important factor was the rise of the nuclear family as the dominant family form in industrial societies. In preindustrial cultures, the extended family—parents and children living together with other relatives—was more common. This type of family was well suited to agrarian societies, because everyone could help to plan and gather crops (see Chapter 10). Thus children and young people were considered different from adults only in that they were physically unable to do as much work. They still contributed to the family or society, however, and so were not considered solely as dependents. In industrial societies such as ours, extended families are no longer the norm because they are not economically useful: families are no longer producers, they are consumers. Socially, the main purpose of the modern nuclear family is to raise children until they are ready to start families of their own. Thus children and young people are considered dependents until they are fully socialized and ready to assume adult responsibilities.[7]

There are other factors that affect the characterization of young people as adolescents. In this century improved public health, large-scale immigration, and increased urbanization and industrialization have resulted in increased competition for jobs. As a result, the period of dependency of youth has been extended—for example, by unnecessarily increasing educational requirements for jobs—so that young people would be absorbed as late as possible into the labor market (see Table 9-1). In addition, Friedenberg argues, "adolescent status is defined as it is precisely to afford society an optimal opportunity to arrest more human potential than it can accept in its members." [8] For a society that values achievement, self-control, and the acquisition of wealth, the humane concerns and spontaneity of young people are likely to be perceived as undesirable weaknesses. Thus the labeling of young people as "adolescents" or "teenagers" not only serves an important economic function

According to Friedenberg, our society finds it difficult to deal with the idealism of youth, and so young people are accorded subordinate status.
Howard Harrison/ Nancy Palmer

[5] Edgar Friedenberg, "Adolescence as a social problem." In Becker, p. 43.
[6] Talcott Parsons and Gerald M. Platt, "Higher education and changing socialization." In Matilda W. Riley *et al.*, *Aging and Society: A Sociology of Age Stratification.* New York: Russell Sage Foundation, 1972.
[7] See, for example, Shulamith Firestone, *The Dialectic of Sex.* New York: Bantam, 1971.
[8] Friedenberg, "Adolescence as a social problem," p. 47.

Income	Male		Female	
	14–19 Years	20–24 Years	14–19 Years	20–24 Years
Number of persons (in thousands)	691	3,671	436	2,477
Under $1,000	7.5%	2.0%	7.9%	2.1%
$1,000 to $1,999	6.1	2.7	8.8	2.6
$2,000 to $2,999	10.1	2.8	10.9	5.8
$3,000 to $3,999	15.1	4.5	25.3	10.5
$4,000 to $4,999	14.0	8.1	19.7	19.1
$5,000 to $5,999	13.9	11.1	12.8	18.5
$6,000 to $6,999	12.5	13.1	7.4	15.9
$7,000 and over	20.7	55.6	7.2	25.4
Median income	$4,786	$7,472	$3,880	$5,530

Source: "Characteristics of American youth." Current Population Reports, Series P–23, No. 51, 1975, p. 24.

TABLE 9-1
Annual Income of Year-Round Full-Time Workers 14 to 24 Years Old, by Age and Sex

but also allows adult society to regard the ideas and concerns of the young as inferior to its own.

WHO ARE THE ELDERLY?

There are about 21,127,000 Americans over 65, around 10 percent of the total population.[9] The age of 65 as a demarcation point for the elderly was institutionalized by the Social Security Act of 1935, which arbitrarily selected 65 as the age of retirement. However, as Blau points out, this conventional conception is based on a life span that existed more than seventy years ago and does not correspond to the situation today.[10] The average life expectancy in 1900 was 47 years, and those over 65 comprised only 4 percent of the population. Today, there are many more old people, and they are much more visible and likely to be healthier than their counterparts of previous generations. In fact, the physical and emotional capabilities of the elderly are now more dependent on the health and adjustment of the elderly throughout life than on any chronological age.[11] For this reason, many observers are beginning to distinguish between the "young-old," who are between 55 and 75 and increasingly likely to be healthy and active, and the "old-old," who are over 75 and likely to need supportive social services.[12]

Neugarten has pointed out that "many of the current stereotypes of

[9] U.S. Bureau of the Census, "Social and economic characteristics of the older population." Current Population Reports, Series P-23, no. 57, 1975.

[10] Zena Smith Blau, Old Age in a Changing Society. New York: Watts, 1973, p. 191.

[11] Robert N. Butler, Why Survive? Being Old in America. New York: Harper & Row, 1975.

[12] See, for example, Bernice L. Neugarten, "The future and the young-old." Gerontologist (February 1975):4–9.

the aged are based on the needy rather than on the typical aged."[13] Most of the elderly are healthy—which is why, after all, they have survived to old age—though they may be afflicted with certain chronic disorders. Over 80 percent of those over 65 are able to move about freely; only 5 percent are institutionalized.[14] Most old people are either living with someone else or are in at least occasional contact with other members of their families.

Nevertheless, as we shall see, the problems of isolation and poverty are more prevalent among the elderly than among any other age group. The evolution of the modern family has affected the old as well as the young. Old people are no longer considered productive members of society, and so they too have become stereotyped, as crippled, senile, or useless dependents. Moreover, the rapid social change that takes place in modern industrial societies has eliminated one of the traditional functions of the elderly as a source of useful wisdom of the past. The ideas of the old are felt to have little value in a world that seems to change every generation.

Social attitudes toward the elderly also have an economic base, since the scarcity of employment opportunities makes it desirable for adult society to impose retirement upon the elderly. This mandatory retirement policy is then justified through the widespread use of stereotyped notions about the aged. Finally, the aged are isolated because they are constant reminders of mortality. The notions of aging and death are particularly hard to face in a society that is so present-oriented and that emphasizes productivity. Thus, terms like "Senior Citizen" or "Golden Ager" become euphemisms that try to disguise the fact that the elderly are considered unnecessary and unwanted.

SIMILARITIES BETWEEN THE YOUNG AND THE ELDERLY

Most of those who are elderly now came of age during the 1920s, a period similar in many ways to the 1960s, which were formative years for most of today's young people. Both decades were, to begin with, characterized by larger populations of young people than the decades that preceded them, by increased educational opportunity, and by liberalized social attitudes. Women achieved increased freedom of movement and occupational opportunity in both eras—for example, in the twenties women got the vote and in the sixties the Women's Liberation Movement developed as an important political force. In both decades birthrates began downward trends due to improved contraceptive techniques, the diaphragm in the earlier decade and the pill in the latter. In both decades too there was increasing materialism, leisure, urbanization, and disaffection with government. In contrast, the formative years for today's adults were the Depression and war-scarred years of the 1930s and 1940s.

More important than the similarities of the decades in which the young and old came of age, however, are the similar treatment they receive today at the hands of adults and from our economic system. Both are kept from full participation in adult activities and are discriminated against in many ways. In Ditlea's words,

The young and the old are equally oppressed and alienated by a prejudiced

[13] Neugarten, "The aged in American society," p. 170.
[14] Butler, *Why Survive?*, p. 17.

Joel Gordon

society. Both groups account for the highest suicide rates in the country. Both are the first to be fired and the last to be hired. Both are segregated and patronized by institutions and government agencies.[15]

And the anxiety of the young, as Simone de Beauvoir points out, "as they enter upon social life matches the anguish of the old as they are excluded from it." [16]

Others note additional similarities. For Friedenberg, "Both the aged and the young in our culture are socially and economically marginal. Both . . . are treated as helpless objects who require costly and profitable services to help them do what they are usually not allowed to do for themselves, or what they have lost the courage or initiative to try." [17] Kalish elaborates on this theme, suggesting that in our age-segregated society, both young and old are adjacent to the category that controls the country, and both are viewed stereotypically by members of that category. Both are seen as taking out of the system rather than putting in, are constantly reminded of their nonproductive roles in society, are seen as existing upon a type of charity offered by the working-age

[15] Steve Ditlea, "A new kind of odd couple." *Mademoiselle,* August 1973, p. 72.
[16] Simone de Beauvoir, *The Coming of Age.* New York: Warner, 1973, p. 807.
[17] Friedenberg, "Adolescence as a social problem," p. 36.

category, and are thought of as having perhaps too much leisure time by a society that still has a fairly strong work ethic. Both are viewed as inadequately educated. The aged lack formal education (because for most of them it was not available more than a half a century ago, and because the content of education has changed dramatically since that time); the young are seen to be in need of formal education and life experience. Both groups are poor, and therefore vulnerable and weak. Both are suspicious of the educational process (and the highly educated), though for different reasons—the young because it represents the "establishment" and may be dehumanizing or irrelevant, the elderly because it tends to negate their life experience. Neither group is considered entitled to sexual relationships, although both need physical affection. Finally, both young and old people become alienated when they see that society has no place for them.

The similarities between the youth and the aged may be abundant, but there is one crucial difference that should be mentioned. In the young lies the community's investment for the future; thus young people are seen as deserving of support. On the other hand, help for the elderly is viewed, at best, as compensation for past services, and most often as a form of charity, because the elderly are no longer needed.[18]

AGISM: PREJUDICE AND DISCRIMINATION AGAINST THE YOUNG AND THE OLD

Agism, a counterpart of sexism and racism, can be defined as any set of beliefs and practices dictating that age differences between people are inherently related to significant attributes and that such differences are a legitimate basis of invidious distinction between socially defined age categories, such as youth and the elderly. In this section we will describe the extent to which agism against the young and old exists in our society.

THE MINORITY POSITION OF YOUNG PEOPLE

Friedenberg has compared society's attitude toward young people to its attitude toward early immigrants who were of low economic status. Like these immigrants, young people are seen "as childish and irresponsible, warmhearted and lovable, but uncontrolled and unstable." Both groups are seen as having unusual capacities for violence and lust. Furthermore, like the immigrant, the adolescent must "abandon whatever mode of life has become natural to him and consent to his own socialization."[19]

In some respects, however, the young persons are penalized even more than immigrants; they experience legal restrictions unlike those imposed on any racial or minority group. In the words of a Presidential Panel on Youth,

Young people are compelled to attend school, excluded from any gainful employment, denied the right to drive automobiles, prohibited from buying

---

[18] Richard M. Kalish, "The old and the new as generation gap allies." *Gerontologist*, no. 9 (1969):83–89.
[19] Friedenberg, "Adolescence as a social problem," pp. 50–51.

alcoholic beverages, firearms, and cigarettes, barred from the most interesting movies, and deprived of countless pleasures and liberties available to adults.[20]

Of course, the young soon outgrow their youth and achieve legal adulthood. But the very concept of legal "coming of age" is an artificial construct that has little to do with the qualifications young people have—qualifications that could, after all, be measured or tested in certain situations. Instead, the legal age of adulthood represents the time society is finally prepared to grant equality to those it has kept in a subordinate position.[21]

We have already suggested that the subordination of youth as a special class serves an important function in that it reduces the economic competition for adults. In 1930, some 2 million young people under the age of 18 were employed; one-third of these were under 16. The onset of the Depression, in which growing numbers of adults became unemployed, caused one member of the National Child Labor Committee to declare in 1933:

It is now generally accepted that the exploitation of children, indefensible on humanitarian grounds, has become a genuine economic menace; . . . children should be in school and adults should have whatever worthwhile jobs there are.[22]

The child labor laws and trade-union restrictions passed during this period were meant to protect children and young people from hazardous occupations. However, "hazardous" has traditionally been loosely defined, and the net effect has been to keep young people from being gainfully employed even where there is no danger to them. Moreover, teenagers became unable to acquire the experience that is a prerequisite for well-paying jobs.

Similarly, compulsory school attendance laws were ostensibly designed to ensure a proper education for all citizens. In fact, the retention of the young within the educational system has become the primary method of postponing economic competition and of inculcating the young with the values of adult society. The laws, after all, do not call for mandatory school attendance until competence has been achieved; instead, they compel attendance until a certain age is reached.[23] In addition, as Friedenberg points out:

The educational codes of several states provide for considerably more restraint than even the compulsory attendance provisions provide. . . . It becomes the basis for indoctrination with the values of a petty, clerical social subclass. Regulations on dress, speech, and conduct in school are justified as being necessary because school is supposed to be businesslike. . . . This leaves the young with the alternative of becoming little-league businessmen or

[20] *Youth: Transition to Adulthood.* Report of the Panel on Youth of the President's Science Advisory Committee. Chicago: University of Chicago Press, 1974, p. 29.
[21] Edgar A. Friedenberg, "The generation gap." *Annuals of the American Academy of Political and Social Sciences* 382 (1969):32–42.
[22] In *Youth: Transition to Adulthood,* p. 35.
[23] Friedenberg, "Adolescence as a social problem," p. 55.

juvenile delinquents, for refusal to obey school regulations leads to charges of delinquency.[24]

Attempts are made periodically by adults to justify mandatory education laws and to encourage furthering one's education in college on the grounds that the better jobs are available to the better educated. In fact, as many observers have pointed out, the economic value of even a college diploma has declined considerably in recent years, largely for two reasons: the wage increases unionized workers have received and the job shortages in many liberal arts fields. Also, many of the educational requirements for employment are not really job-related. Instead, they exist to still further reduce competition for jobs.[25]

The legal and economic discrimination suffered by the young is compounded by the social discrimination to which they are subjected. Young people are not only denied adult roles, they are also denied adult relationships. For example, physical maturation is occurring at an earlier age than even a generation ago, but young people are denied legitimized sexual relations until they become economically self-sufficient. In practical terms, this may mean a decade after puberty. Young people are also kept apart from adult role models whose example would ease the transition to adulthood. This age segregation is self-perpetuating: deprived of association with adults, the young then turn to each other for companionship. The result is a lack of trust and understanding between the generations.

As we pointed out in Chapter 6, the median income of the elderly is just over $5,000 annually. This figure is lower than the median income for any other racial or minority group for which statistics are available, and in fact means that more than half our elderly are living in or close to poverty. Nearly 12 percent of the elderly (and 25 percent of elderly blacks) reside in substandard housing, a proportion 50 percent higher than for the rest of the population.[26] Only 15 percent of those over 65 are presently employed even part-time. Compounding this physical deprivation are social and psychological circumstances that make the lives of the elderly even more difficult. The extended family has indeed become far less common than in the past: three-fourths of widowed men and women over age 65 live alone, as do more than one-fourth of all the elderly.[27] And while the suicide rate for elderly women has shown some decline in recent years, the suicide rate for older men is still the highest for all groups in the United States.[28] In Robert Butler's words,

THE AGED AS A MINORITY

For many elderly Americans old age is a tragedy, a period of quiet despair, deprivation, desolation and muted rage. . . . We have shaped a society which is extremely harsh to live in when one is old. The tragedy of old age is not the fact that each of us must grow old and die, but that the process of doing so has been made unnecessarily and at times excruciatingly painful,

24 Friedenberg, "The generation gap," pp. 37–38.
25 Friedenberg, "The generation gap," pp. 72–73.
26 Sylvia Porter, syndicated column, May 2, 1975.
27 "Social and economic characteristics," pp. 1, 26.
28 *U.S. News and World Report,* July 1, 1974, p. 47.

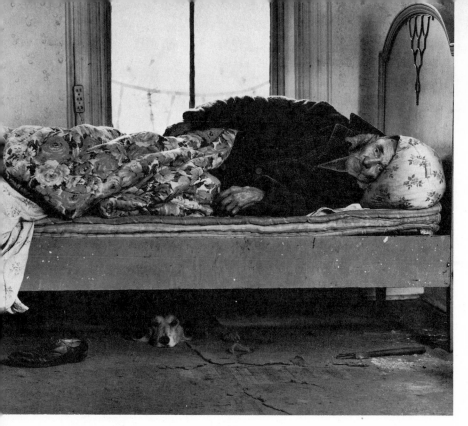

Too many of the elderly
live isolated in board-
ing rooms, with no
access to food,
medical care, and
other essentials of life.
Bruce Davidson/Magnum

humiliating, debilitating and isolating through insensitivity, ignorance and poverty. The potentials for satisfactions and even triumphs in late life are real and vastly underexplored [but] for the most part the elderly struggle to exist in an inhospitable world.[29]

Perhaps the greatest factor affecting the condition of the aged in our society is the existence of compulsory retirement regulations. These discriminate against the aged, because they arbitrarily select an age at which people can be legally removed from the labor force—whether or not they are still qualified to work. This, of course, causes the income of the elderly to be suddenly and substantially reduced. Perhaps more important, however, it also denies the elderly a productive role in our society, and removes from them a major source of their status and self-esteem.

Zena Blau [30] has analyzed the condition of the aged in terms of what she calls *role exit,* defined as the cessation of any stable pattern of interaction and shared activities between two or more persons. When role exit occurs, it results in feelings of extreme depression and uncertainty, unless other roles are found or restitution is made of the lost role. For the young, for example, graduation is a form of role exit; appropriate role restitution would be finding a job. In general, role exit may come about in four ways:

[29] Butler, *Why Survive?*
[30] See Blau.

1. Through an act of nature—the death of a spouse, for example
2. Through voluntary action, such as when a person leaves a group
3. Through involuntary action, such as being left by one's partner
4. Through expulsion by the group or larger collectivity—for example, forced retirement

Blau compares and analyzes the two major role exits of old age—retirement and widowhood—in light of their different effects on individuals. She concludes that mandatory retirement is more detrimental to the "associational life, morale, and self-concept" of older people than even the death of a spouse. To Blau, forced retirement is a deliberate act of expulsion by the group, analogous to excommunication or dishonorable discharge, except that the retiree has done nothing but reach a certain age. What is worse is that society fails to offer meaningful role restitution to the elderly to replace the social roles it has taken away from them. For the aged, then, the entire social and economic system results in large-scale discrimination, similar to that against other minorities—except that the discrimination toward minorities is practiced covertly, while mandatory retirement has, in Blau's words, "official and public sanction."

Blau indicates that the role exit of retirement adversely affects men more than women because, in the present generation of the elderly, women were never in the labor force in significant numbers. As female employment continues to rise, however, and work occupies a more prominent part of the lives of women, it can be expected that retirement will be at least as traumatic for coming generations of older women as it is for older men at present. Even today's elderly women do not escape the problems of role exit, however. Most of them have experienced a series of role exits, beginning in late middle age with the "empty nest" syndrome, as their children left home and their role as mother was more or less abruptly terminated. In addition, a wife's adjustment at the time of a husband's retirement is usually a difficult one. Finally, women are also aware of society's attitude toward the elderly, and their awareness of aging may make them depressed as well.

Additional Job Discrimination. We have already suggested that the economic impact of retirement is usually severe: paychecks and savings disappear, pension plans—which fewer than half of all Americans have—prove inadequate, and Social Security payments barely keep one above the poverty level. Moreover, coverage by company health plans is lost precisely at the time when health costs are likely to increase. Forced retirement at age 65 is not, however, the only form of job discrimination to which the elderly can be subjected. For example, mandatory retirement ages are becoming lower than 65 in many areas and industries, and it has been predicted that by the year 2000 the age of retirement will be 55 [31]—a time when most people have several potentially active decades ahead of them. Moreover, involuntary "retirement" is being used increasingly by cost-conscious companies to dismiss higher-salaried older workers so that lower-salaried younger workers can be hired instead.

Older workers also encounter job discrimination when they try to seek new employment. The 1967 Age Discrimination in Employment

[31] *New York Times,* December 21, 1975, Section 4, p. 14.

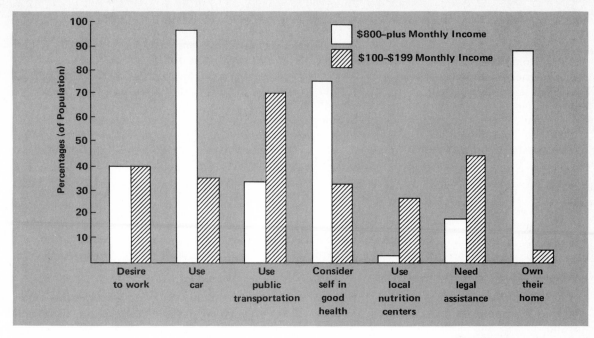

Percentages (of Population)

□ $800–plus Monthly Income
▨ $100–$199 Monthly Income

Desire to work · Use car · Use public transportation · Consider self in good health · Use local nutrition centers · Need legal assistance · Own their home

Act, which was designed to protect workers between the ages of 40 and 65, has still not succeeded in eradicating agism. Blatant discriminatory advertising, such as "applicants must be under 30," has become rare, but many ads still call for applicants with "1 to 3 years' experience"—effectively eliminating qualified older workers. Other older workers find that they are rejected as "overqualified" when they apply for a job. For reasons such as these, older workers who are jobless remain unemployed far longer than their younger counterparts.

Additional Problems in Housing. As previously mentioned, a substantial minority of the elderly live in substandard housing—housing that has inadequate plumbing or is structurally unsafe. An even larger number of the elderly occupy poor housing—a tiny bedroom in a rooming house, a tenement in an urban ghetto, a decaying or isolated house in a rural area or deserted town. City-sponsored housing for the elderly has never existed in adequate numbers to meet the demand, and today the situation is even worse. Construction of new housing has all but ceased, as building costs have increased enormously and the financial condition of cities has deteriorated.

Because their income is limited, the elderly pay a higher proportion of their income for rent or real estate taxes. Often, allocations for necessities such as food, clothing, medical care, and transportation are cut back so that house payments can be made. Also, because they so often live in poorer areas, where crime rates are high, and because they are so physically vulnerable, the aged often fear going out into their own neighborhoods. They remain in their homes or apartments in virtual isolation; only a fortunate few can depend on friends or neighbors for shopping and other essentials. (See Figure 9-1.)

FIGURE 9-1
Income Level and Self-Sufficiency Among the Aged

Source: Retirement Living Magazine, June 1975, p. 13.

Distorted Images and Stereotypes of the Aged. In Chapter 7 we described how stereotyping makes it easier for prejudice and discrimination to take place. Attributing certain characteristics to groups of people prevents us from seeing people as individuals and justifies our negative attitudes and behaviors toward them. This is as true for stereotyping of the aged as it is for stereotyping of racial or other minority groups. Seeing older people as senile, old-fashioned, sexually incapacitated, and unhealthy makes their frequently deprived condition easier to ignore.

Just how widespread are distorted images of the aged? One comprehensive study found that only a small minority of the public saw older people as "bright and alert," "open-minded," or "very good at getting things done," while the majority of older people saw themselves in this way (see Table 9-2). In general, people under 65 saw old age in much harsher terms than older people did.[32]

Other studies have found that age-related stereotypes are reinforced by the media, particularly television. A content analysis of television drama showed that the elderly are seldom presented. When they do appear they are invariably shown as having problems, in contrast to competent adult men and attractive adult women. Television commercials in which the elderly appear are generally for laxatives or denture cleaners. The young, too, are stereotyped on television: both age groups are shown as having more than the average share of difficulties and relying on adults to help solve them.[33]

The harmfulness of such stereotypes does not only lie in the fact that they make the old easier to ignore. Old people may soon come to see themselves as a burden on the rest of society, rather than as active participants in it. On a personal level, they may withhold advice or affection for fear it will be ignored or ridiculed. (The phrase "dirty old man" is a good indication of how sexuality in old age is seen as inappropriate in our society.) Younger people, in turn, might develop a fear of growing older. This will not only make it difficult for them to accept their own inevitable aging; it will also cause them to neglect necessary planning for their later years, and prevent them from enjoying their old age.[34]

The Social Security system was never designed to be the main source of income for the elderly. Instead, it was intended to be a form of insurance against a sudden drop in income due to the retirement, disability, or death of a wage-earning spouse. However, only about a third of married couples and a sixth of single individuals who are receiving Social Security benefits also derive income from pensions.[35] The fact that most old people are retired (as a result of mandatory retirement laws), coupled with the fact that most people do not have pensions, investments, or savings sufficient

SOCIAL SECURITY: A SPECIAL FORM OF AGISM

---

[32] *The Myth and Reality of Aging in America.* Washington, D.C.: The National Council on the Aging, 1975.

[33] Herbert C. Northcott, "Too young, too old—Age in the world of television." *Gerontologist* (April 1975):184–186.

[34] *The Myth and Reality of Aging,* pp. 38–39.

[35] Barbara Koeppel, "The big Social Security rip-off." *Progressive,* August 1975, p. 14.

	Self-Image of Public 65 and over	Total Public's Image of "Most People over 65"	Net Difference
Very friendly and warm	72%	74%	+ 2%
Very wise from experience	69	64	− 5
Very bright and alert	68	29	−39
Very open-minded and adaptable	63	21	−42
Very good at getting things done	55	35	−20
Very physically active	48	41	− 7
Very sexually active	11	5	− 6

Source: *The Myth and Reality of Aging in America.* A study for the National Council on the Aging, Inc. by Louis Harris and Associates, Inc. Washington, D.C.: The National Council on the Aging, 1975, p. 53.

TABLE 9-2
Self-Image of Public Age 65 and over Compared with Total Public's Image of "Most People over 65"

to support them in their old age, has made Social Security a major source of income for the elderly. Thus the inequities—described below—that are built into the Social Security system add enormously to the burdens of the aged.

Perhaps the greatest flaw in the Social Security system is the fact that its benefits are too small. Just prior to 1972, when benefits were increased, the average annual payment to individuals was $2,256; couples received average annual benefits of $3,744.[36] (These are full benefits, payable at age 65; persons may receive 80 percent of benefits if they retire at 62.) The 1972 Social Security amendments permitted benefits to rise to a *maximum* payment per individual worker of about $3,500 a year in 1975. Subsequent benefit increases have been tied to increases in the cost of living—in effect maintaining the same low level of payments indefinitely.[37] For this reason, close to 80 percent of retirees must live on less than half their preretirement annual incomes. Some 16 percent of the elderly who receive Social Security benefits are still below the poverty line.[38]

Social Security is financed by fixed wage and payroll taxes on the first $16,500 of income each year. Income over this amount is not subject to the Social Security tax. This means that poorer workers pay a higher proportion of their income in tax than wealthier employees. Social Security benefits, however, depend on the amount of tax paid, not on its percentage of total income. Thus workers who were poorest before retiring will remain poorest after retiring, because they will receive lower benefits.

Those who wish to supplement their Social Security by continuing to work find that they are confronted with the heaviest tax burden of any age or income group. Until age 72, a person cannot earn more than $230 a month without incurring a reduction in Social Security benefits. For

[36] Koeppel, p. 13.
[37] Robinson Hollister, "Social mythology and reform: Income maintenance for the aged." *Annals of the American Academy of Political and Social Sciences* (September 1974):28.
[38] Koeppel, p. 14.

every dollar earned in excess of that, 50 cents in Social Security is deducted—in effect, a 50 percent tax rate. Moreover, the earned income is fully liable for both income and Social Security taxes. Thus individuals over 65 who work are not only deprived of a pension they have already paid for, but they must continue paying for this benefit even though they are not permitted to receive it. The inequity is compounded by the fact that nonwage income—such as capital gains or interest on savings— may be earned in any amount without affecting Social Security benefits. The well-to-do, who are most likely to have nonwage income, can therefore receive their Social Security in full. Only salaried workers, who are likely to need their Social Security payments the most, are penalized.[39]

Another part of the Social Security system results in inequality for retired women. Under Old Age and Survivors Insurance, at age 65 a woman is entitled to personal benefits equal to half the benefits her husband receives, whether or not she has ever worked. If she has worked, she can either receive benefits on her own account—because she has paid Social Security taxes—or receive benefits through her husband. She cannot do both. Since most husbands work longer and for higher salaries than their wives, most wives can collect more by drawing benefits off their husbands' accounts. As a result, there is usually no difference in the amount that nonworking and working women receive. Thus the working woman often collects none of the money she has paid in Social Security taxes.

SOME CONSEQUENCES OF AGISM

We have seen that prejudice and discrimination against the young and old exist in our society. As a result, the young and old are prevented from making full use of their capabilities, much like some racial or other minority groups. In this section we discuss some outcomes of agism, particularly its effect on the social and psychological condition of youth and the elderly.

FOR THE YOUNG

We have already suggested that adult society tries to arrest the development of human potential in young people. As noted, one way it does this is to retain young people in school, where education often takes a second place to discipline. The young are literally and figuratively told to "keep in line" in order to make them more acceptable to adults. Actual preparation for the adult world is, however, rare. In the words of a Presidential Panel on Youth, schools

do not provide extensive opportunity for managing one's affairs, they seldom encourage intense concentration on a single activity, and they are inappropriate settings for nearly all objectives involving responsibilities that affect others.[40]

[39] Robert C. Alberts, "Catch 65." *New York Times Magazine,* August 11, 1974, p. 11ff.
[40] *Youth: Transition to Adulthood,* p. 146.

More generally, sociologist S. N. Eisenstadt has stated that

owing to the long period of preparation and the relative segregation of the
children's world from that of the adults, the main values of the society are
necessarily presented to the child and adolescent in a highly selective way,
with a strong idealistic emphasis. The relative unreality of these values as
presented to the children—which at the same time are not given full ritual
and symbolic expression—creates among the adolescents a great potential
uncertainty and ambivalence toward the adult world.[41]

This gap between young people and adults has grown in recent years, as
educational requirements for jobs have been increased and prolonged
schooling has become necessary. It should be noted that those who are
unable or unwilling to stay in school and "drop out" do not thereby
achieve the status of adults. More often than not, they find that society
has no appropriate social and economic roles for them.

   In primitive or traditional societies, there is usually a natural progres-
sion from one life stage to the next. Though young people may be considered to be in a special age category, they are still regarded as an
integral part of society. Modern societies, however, provide few institutions or roles that allow the young to meaningfully express their interests or values within the context of the larger culture. Thus it becomes
difficult for young people to discover who they are or to find constructive
outlets for their energies. Forced—by exclusion from adult life—into
peer groups, the young must try to compensate for their marginal status,

[41] See Eisenstadt.

often attempting to create a separate culture of their own. The famous rallying cry of the 1960s—"Never trust anyone over 30"—was one such attempt to clearly differentiate between the values of young people and those of adults. However, such efforts to create a "youth culture" are generally unsuccessful, because most young people share the values of adults. In addition, young people are so powerless that they are not able to form an effective culture of their own. In Friedenberg's words:

There is no genuine "adolescent society" or "peer culture." . . . People who have no home or economic roots of their own, and who are constantly controlled and bombarded by a dominant social group into which they themselves know they must ultimately be absorbed, do not develop a culture of society. The most they do is devise, like prisoners, customs, insignia, and an etiquette with which to maintain a little freedom and privacy.[42]

FOR THE ELDERLY

More than half of all American workers are employed by organizations having a mandatory retirement age of 65. The psychological and economic harm caused by such retirement regulations have been noted. For now, it is sufficient to say that it is illogical—and untrue—to suppose that a person's abilities decline precipitously the moment he or she reaches 65. Most of the elderly are physically and mentally able to work full-time; and, in fact, many individuals, from artists to writers to scientists to Supreme Court Justices, have done their best work in their old age.[43]

Anthropologist Margaret Mead—who is over 75—has observed that, "when I advocate some unpopular point of view, my age is used as a target and some fanatic is likely to denounce me as senile."[44] The stereotyping of old people as "fuddy-duddies" is completely inappropriate to today's vigorous elderly. It persists only as a weapon to be used against them. Butler has detailed the effect of such stereotypes:

All too many old people have been brainwashed and pacified into believing they are powerless. Part of this results from their acceptance of the culture's stereotyping of them as helpless. They have been patronized and infantilized. They are treated like children and insulted by labels referring to old age as "second childhood." The physical diseases and chronic health problems which beset so many encourage their acquiescence to this attitude. They are intimidated by crime, dangerous living conditions, and inaccessible transportation. They are often treated discourteously in public and even at home. Frequently they have been pacified by drugs. Medical personnel in and out of institutions over-medicate them, quieting their body movements and their emotional reactions. They have been subdued into apathy and depression by the crushing social circumstances of old age, which add unnecessary burdens to their daily lives and waste their vitality. Token service programs and other half-measures deceive them into thinking their problems are being attended to.

[42] Friedenberg, "Adolescence as a social problem," pp. 57–58.
[43] "New outlook for the aged." *Time,* July 2, 1975, p. 47; and *The Myth and Reality of Aging,* pp. 55, 91, 101.
[44] Margaret Mead, *Blackberry Winter.* New York: Simon & Schuster, 1972.

	Under $3,000	$3,000–$6,999	$7,000–$14,999	$15,000 and over	White	Black	Total
Looked forward to stopping work	33%	52%	59%	47%	50%	42%	48%
Did not look forward to stopping work	61	43	33	49	45	50	45
Not sure	6	5	8	4	5	8	6

Source: *The Myth and Reality of Aging in America.* A study for the National Council on the Aging, Inc. by Louis Harris and Associates, Inc. Washington, D.C.: The National Council on the Aging, 1975, p. 217.

TABLE 9-3
Attitudes Toward Retirement (of Public Age 65 and over Who Are "Retired" or "Unemployed")

The sense of powerlessness has truly terrible consequences. Many of the old hate themselves and their age group, seeing nothing useful or interesting in late life. They may resist identifying with their age peers. The strongest and most fortunate can avoid some of the impact of stereotypes by denying that they are old and maintaining their distance from the economically disadvantaged. The result of this is the fragmentation of the elderly into isolated groupings.[45]

The policies in our society that affect people on the basis of supposed group characteristics, rather than deal with them as individuals, are by any definition discriminatory. It should be added that those hardest hit by the stereotypes and inequities of agism are those elderly who have faced discrimination all their lives. Blacks, for example, are more likely than other groups to be forced into retirement against their will.[46] (See Table 9-3.) Elderly women and members of all minority groups are forced to live on lower incomes in old age because of restricted job opportunities during their younger years.

The failure of society to make room for all its members leads to isolation of and conflict between the generations. Young people in today's society are better educated and more mobile than their elders. They are able to move away from their communities for better jobs elsewhere, "leaving their parents behind geographically and socially," as Cowgill put it. This separation of the generations

FOR BOTH THE YOUNG AND OLD

most assuredly reduces the frequency and intimacy of contact; it militates against immediate availability of help in times of crisis; . . . the older generation is deprived of much of its earlier socializing role and is incapable of sharing the experiences and problems of the younger generation. The generation gap becomes a nearly unbridgeable chasm.[47]

[45] Robert N. Butler, "Pacification and the politics of aging." *International Journal of Aging and Human Development,* vol. 5, no. 4 (1974):394–395.
[46] *The Myth and Reality of Aging,* p. 87.
[47] Donald O. Cowgill, "Aging and modernization." In J. F. Gubrium, ed., *Late Life.* Springfield, Ill.: Charles C Thomas, 1974, pp. 131, 133, 136.

If the demands of the job market cause the young and old to grow apart, the life experiences of the different generations in a rapidly changing society can separate them even further. Mead speaks of older people as being "immigrants through time,"[48] adjusting to new social orders several times as the world changes about them. In a similar vein, Mannheim refers to the coexistence of different generations with different values as the "non-contemporaneity of the contemporaneous."[49] One result of the gulf between the generations is that the young are ready to take over power before their elders are ready to concede it, while older people are reluctant to give up their power because they see no adequate roles in the future to replace it. At the same time, young workers with great financial responsibilities may resent having to contribute money for Social Security and pensions for older workers and retirees, whom they perceive as being at a stage in life when they have fewer financial burdens.[50] Such resentment may increase as the median age of the population rises, and fewer young people are supporting growing numbers of the elderly.

This situation could be prevented if the forces of agism in our society were reduced—if, for example, more people of advanced age were permitted to work, and more young people were allowed to participate in society, so that they would feel a sense of identification with those older than themselves. The Gray Panthers, an activist organization, is attempting to forge a working coalition of young and old to help improve conditions for both groups. One leader of this movement has stated, "The old and the young live outside the mainstream of society. Agism . . . deprives both groups of power and influence."[51] Becoming aware of their mutual stake in reducing agism can begin to bring both age groups closer together.

SOCIAL POLICY AND PROSPECTS

As the most recently recognized form of discrimination in our society, agism is just beginning to be grappled with on an individual and policy level. In this section, we will detail some of the efforts that have been made to reduce age-related inequality, and indicate where progress must still be made.

FOR THE YOUNG

A major change in the status of the young over the past decade was the 26th Amendment in 1971, which lowered the legal voting age in federal elections from 21 to 18. In its wake forty-one states also lowered the legal age, so that in most places young adults 18 years and older at least enjoy a measure of legal and medical rights. (Unfortunately, many of the young

[48] Margaret Mead, *Culture and Commitment.* Garden City, N.Y.: Natural History Press, 1970.
[49] K. Mannheim, "The problems of generations." In P. Kescskemeti, ed., *Essays on the Sociology of Knowledge.* London: Routledge and Kegan Paul, 1953.
[50] Blau, see Chapters 1 and 3.
[51] In Ditlea, p. 72.

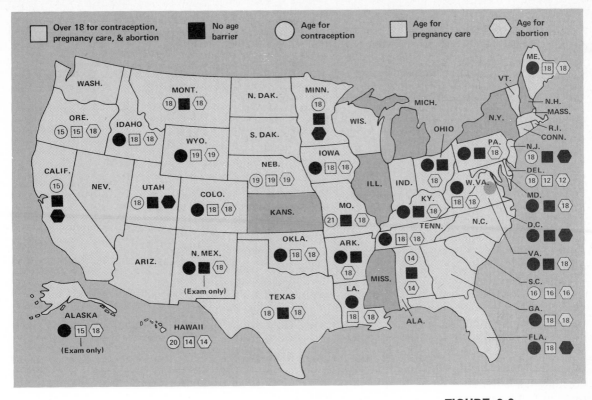

Legend:
- Over 18 for contraception, pregnancy care, & abortion
- No age barrier
- Age for contraception
- Age for pregnancy care
- Age for abortion

FIGURE 9-2
Ages of Consent

Source: "Kids, Sex and Doctors." *Time,* November 25, 1974, pp. 91–93.

are alienated from our political institutions, and a relatively small number vote in any election.) But for younger teenagers the picture is spotty. Civil liberties organizations are attempting to gain for them the right to sex-related medical services—contraception, abortion, and treatment for venereal disease—without parental notification. Fewer than half the states recognize the right of those under 18 to purchase and use contraceptives, and fewer than a third permitted abortions for this age group without parental consent (see Figure 9-2). In a July 1976 decision, however, the Supreme Court limited the right of states to require parental consent for abortion for "mature" individuals under 18. And the right to treatment for venereal disease without parental knowledge is by now accepted almost everywhere in the United States.

Positive measures to make schooling truly more relevant are being discussed seriously in some areas. For example, one study urged that education planners consult with industry leaders and revise high school and post-secondary training according to projected employment opportunities.[52] Policies regarding mandatory school attendance are also being questioned. A new law in California, for instance, permits students age 16 or 17 to leave school if they have their parents' permission and can pass a proficiency exam. The National Commission on the Reform of

[52] "Schools urged to focus on private jobs." *New York Times,* January 15, 1976, p. 31.

Secondary Education has recommended that students be required to attend school only until the age of 14, since physical maturity is occurring earlier and young people should not be denied access to jobs. Others propose that schoolwork be combined with work in the community so that young people will be exposed to the real world at an earlier age and have a greater opportunity to discover their interests.[53] Many of these reforms are only in the discussion stage, however, and whether they will be effected remains uncertain.

In other areas the legal status of young people has undergone measurable improvement, particularly as a result of the student protests of the 1960s. Regulations on such matters as dress, residence, speech, and access to school records and letters of recommendation have been loosened considerably in most colleges and in some high schools. Most high schools, however, still have strict regulations governing student appearance and behavior. Some of these regulations, such as administrative supervision of student newspapers, are being challenged in the courts. Real improvement in these areas will probably occur only when public attitudes toward youth change—when there is widespread agreement that schools should perform an educative, and not a custodial, function. Finally, the Supreme Court has also affirmed the right of students to free speech within the schools and the right of minors to due process and equal protection in the juvenile court system (see Chapter 4).

Job discrimination against young people can be expected to diminish somewhat as the number of young people declines over the next several years, and adult fears of job competition are reduced. In the meantime, the National Committee on the Employment of Youth has recommended that child labor laws be more selectively applied, so that those who find schools too constricting, or who seek the responsibilities of a job, can be permitted to work in nonhazardous occupations.[54] It should be noted that the employment problems of certain segments of young people, particularly school dropouts and minority group members, will require greater changes in social attitudes and institutions before they are eliminated. These young people suffer several kinds of discrimination simultaneously —against their age, their race, their education, and their background— and only massive improvement in the entire social system will help them achieve equality (see Chapters 6 and 7).

FOR THE ELDERLY

According to present estimates, between now and the year 2000 there will be a 40 percent increase in the number of the elderly, to over 30 million persons. This means that the elderly may soon comprise about one-eighth of the total population.[55] In addition, improvements in health technology and delivery of health services should result in an increase in the number of productive years available to the elderly. These trends, coupled with a widespread and growing concern for personal fulfillment among all age categories, should considerably increase the social, political, and economic influence of the aged.

[53] "New look at the 'quitting age.'" *New York Times,* Section 4, January 18, 1976, p. 18.
[54] *Youth: Transition to Adulthood,* p. 44.
[55] "Social and economic characteristics," p. 2.

There are indications that this increase in influence has already begun to occur. Neugarten has suggested that

> with increased numbers of retired persons living on fixed incomes, and with the host of other economic and social changes that lead to increasing visibility of the aged as a group, a social movement is being created in which consciousness of age is the dominant feature.[56]

Realizing that the aged suffer inequalities that can only be remedied by concerted political action, a number of organizations devoted to the elderly have emerged in the last decade or so. The American Association of Retired Persons is a lobbying and service group that informs its constituents of relevant issues and coordinates political activities, such as letter-writing campaigns to influence legislation and policy. The AARP, with over 2,000 local chapters and more than 8 million members age 55 and over, offers community activities, educational materials, special medical, automobile, and health insurance policies, and an employment agency specializing in part-time or temporary jobs for the officially retired. The National Council on the Aging and the National Caucus on the Black Aged combine lobbying efforts with the dissemination of relevant information to their members. The Gray Panthers combine activism and consciousness-raising for the elderly, and are pioneering practical efforts to get the young and the aged involved in cooperative projects.

One recent trend that may reduce the differences in educational attainment between the generations, and thus help to close the "generation gap," is the increase in adult and continuing education programs. Blau, among others, notes that older people who return to college or graduate school are far less alienated from the young. In addition, going to school can provide the elderly with a meaningful role after retirement, and allow them to renew their interests and capabilities. This trend toward continuing education is likely to continue or even expand in the foreseeable future. However, as Blau has stated, it

> needs to be supported and implemented in various ways: through the mass media, through labor unions and voluntary associations, through community and governmental subsidies to build and staff community colleges, and through subsidies to existing educational institutions for additional space and staff.[57]

At present, the aged have not yet achieved the political impact that can be theirs. Butler has pointed out that the voting record of older people is better than that of most other age categories. An extremely high percentage are registered, and a relatively large proportion of these turn out to vote in elections.[58] However, the elderly do not vote as a bloc, but vote according to their individual political viewpoints. Nor has the historical trend in the United States for political leaders to be older (the average age of the signers of the Declaration of Independence was under 40 years) resulted in improved conditions for the elderly. American politicians over 55 are generally healthy as well as employed, and they

Jill Krementz

Anthropologist Margaret Mead, who was over 75 in 1976, was still active as a writer and lecturer; pianist Arthur Rubinstein, who was over 90, still gave public concerts. Though stereotyped notions about the aged have lost whatever validity they may have had, many people still hold them.

Marion Bernstein

[56] Neugarten, "The aged in American society," p. 193.
[57] Blau, p. 198.
[58] Butler, *Why Survive?*

have not manifested any particular concern for the aged. It can be expected, however, that as more of the elderly become aware of their mutual interests, attain a better education, and achieve greater vigor and health, they will grow more insistent about solving their problems and become a more potent political force.[59]

Programs and Problems. Kalish offers a few reasons why the elderly should become more relevant to society: they provide a link with the past in our here-and-now, anti-tradition society; and they offer, as grand-parents, a sense of family continuity and time perspective, as well as affection without discipline. He notes that grandparents often lead to "children's first contact with the decay and dying aspects of humanity," helping them to "recognize the reality of death and change." [60] These are, however, passive notions. They depend on how the younger generation views the elderly, and ignore how society can make use of a rich resource in the aged. Blau has stated that the difficulty an old person has

to continue "to be," instead of being consigned to the status of a "has been" is the problem that policy-makers, social scientists, and organized groups of senior citizens have yet to address.[61]

Only sporadic efforts have been made in our society to provide older people with socially useful functions. This contrasts markedly with a country such as Japan, which is an advanced industrial society that has preserved meaningful roles for the aged. The Japanese maintain high status for their older citizens by promoting respect for the aged and integrating them with other generations in extended families and in the labor force. Most of the elderly continue to live with their children and perform important functions in the household. The majority of Japanese men continue to work after 65, and participate in community clubs and activities.[62] Certain Scandinavian countries, which do not have the mixing of generations that is characteristic of Japan, are nevertheless far advanced in providing necessary services for the aged. Home help services, low-cost loans for housing, rent subsidies, national health and pension programs, and special educational programs for the aged are some examples of what is made available.[63] In the United States, little effort is made to improve the status of the elderly or integrate them into society. Those programs that exist attempt to deal with the effects of isolation of the aged, such as ill health or poverty, rather than with root causes. And, as we shall see, these programs are often administered in a halfhearted or ineffective manner.

Pension reform, for example, has been a persistent issue in the United States for many years. In the past, employees would pay a part of their salaries into a pension fund, only to lose all their money and protection

[59] Neugarten, "The aged in American society," pp. 193–195; and Neugarten, "The future and the young-old," pp. 7–8.

[60] Kalish, p. 89.

[61] Blau, p. 114.

[62] Erdman Palmore, "The status and integration of the aged in Japanese society." *Journal of Gerontology,* vol. 30, no. 2 (1975):199–208.

[63] "The Scandinavian experience." *Aging* (April 1975):10–12.

if they left their jobs before retirement or their companies went out of business. The Employee Retirement Security Act of 1974 was designed to deal with this problem. It set minimum funding standards for private pension plans, and offered termination insurance to protect employees if their companies ended the plans for any reason. By 1976, just before the bill was to go into effect, over 5,000 pension plans had been terminated, and up to 160,000 workers had been left without coverage. The companies involved said the plans were too expensive to operate.[64] Unfortunately, these and other workers have no legal recourse to recover funds they have lost, and their income upon retirement will have to come largely from Social Security.

One government program that has great potential for dealing with poverty among the aged is called Supplemental Security Income. This measure, started in 1974, is administered by the Social Security system but funded from general tax revenues. It provides for a minimum income floor for the aged, blind, and disabled, supplementing Social Security benefits if these are below the minimum. While this program is a step in the right direction, it suffers from several key drawbacks: it replaces federal and some state aid programs, so that, for example, the aged who participate can no longer receive food stamps; funds are insufficient for maintaining an adequate standard of living; and less than $100 a month can be earned before benefits are reduced.[65] Expansion of this program and elimination of its inequities could do much to begin to reduce the economic plight of the elderly.

A particularly appalling example of poorly run programs for the aged involves the nursing home industry, which receives about $3.5 billion in federal, state, and private funds a year. Of the 23,000 nursing homes in the nation, a small number, usually managed by churches and other charitable groups, provide acceptable care. However, these can accommodate only a relatively small number of patients. The majority of the ailing aged are in privately run homes where, with few exceptions, financial exploitation and patient neglect, if not abuse, are prevalent. These "homes" are inadequately staffed, largely with untrained personnel who are paid low wages and who are indifferent to the needs of their patients. Conditions in these nursing homes include minimal expenditures for food, furnishings, services and medical care, constant sedation of patients, and impersonal, hasty physicians' visits. Paradoxically, nursing home exploitation increased with the influx of Medicare and Medicaid funds that were intended to aid the indigent and elderly ill. Real estate and other speculators moved into the nursing home field and charged the government enormous amounts of money for their patients while making few, if any, improvements in patient care.[66]

Small-scale projects and programs, usually on neighborhood or community levels, have had some success, and may point the way for utilizing the energies and abilities of older people. For example, persons may visit or telephone to maintain communication with the shut-in or handicapped elderly, or provide other services to the needy aged. In "adopt-a-grand-

[64] *New York Times,* January 1, 1976.
[65] Hollister, pp. 29–32, 34.
[66] "Exploiting the aged." *Time,* June 3, 1974.

parent" programs, retirees can provide companionship or tutoring to institutionalized or below-grade-level children. "Luncheon clubs" and senior citizens social centers provide hot meals and companionship for the lonely, who frequently simply will not bother to shop and cook adequate meals for themselves. There are also agencies that provide employment opportunities. The availability of counseling and referral services at such centers is important, so that appropriate intervention may be available when problems arise.[67] It should be noted that the existence of such senior citizen centers depends on the organizational and political efforts of senior citizens within each community.

Public housing policy has become the subject of much debate in recent years. Blau, for example, advocates age-homogeneous housing as a way of solidifying the aged as a group and expanding their social activities and friendships. Asserting that "age-heterogeneous housing is an instance of 'false consciousness,' " she argues that while it may appear that age-homogeneous housing contradicts the principle of democratic equality, it has been found that "dispersing old people in the general community not only isolates them socially but also undermines their capacity to join together to become a significant political force." [68] Bultena agrees with Blau in some respects, but points out that age-concentration may be beneficial to some but deleterious to others, depending on the personality and orientation of each individual. Those who prefer an active social life and who have positive attitudes toward leisure do well in a community of their peers, but those with more conservative attitudes toward work and leisure, and who are more accustomed to some social isolation will probably be better adjusted in an age-integrated community.[69] Recent surveys indicate that most of the elderly prefer to associate with members of all age groups, and not just their peers.[70] Clearly, whatever housing policy is adopted must be flexible enough to meet the needs of a variety of individuals. It remains unclear, however, if our society is prepared to embark on any comprehensive program that will begin to solve the housing problems of the aged. Federal housing programs for the aged are already inadequate. As the number of elderly increase, the need for a massive national effort to improve housing conditions for the aged will become even more apparent.

Among all generations, attitudes toward leisure, education, careers, and life styles are becoming liberalized. For example, the new trend toward taking time off in the middle of one's education to work or travel is becoming more widespread. As three- or four-day work weeks evolve in some companies, as company-paid or union-sponsored sabbaticals or retraining programs become more available, the creative and productive uses of leisure time and the changing of jobs in mid-career will become

FOR THE ELDERLY AND THE YOUNG

[67] U.S. Department of HEW, *Let's End Isolation*. Washington, D.C.: U.S. Government Printing Office, 1971.

[68] Blau, pp. 96–98.

[69] Gordon L. Bultena, "Structural effects on the morale of the aged: A comparison of age-segregated and age-integrated communities." In Gubrium, *Late Life*, pp. 18–31.

[70] *The Myth and Reality of Aging*, p. 71.

Maggie Kuhn, founder
of the Grey Panthers.
Wide World Photos

accepted practices. Thus it will become more likely that some inter-
mingling of the generations will occur, as more people share the same
life experiences at different stages of their lives.

A number of projects to bring young and old together have already
shown some promise. For example, the Gray Panthers are building a
residence for both old and young people near the University of Pennsylvania's West Philadelphia campus, aiming to develop a sense of community between them. This effort is seen as an example that might be
followed by others.[71] In New York City, a project organized by a
neighborhood house with foundation and some federal funding involves
teenagers, some of whom are paid, some of whom are volunteers, and
some who receive academic credit. They work with the homebound
elderly, doing marketing, laundry, and light housework, communicating
in person and over a telephone "hot line." In a few colleges, young and
elderly students share dormitory facilities as well as classes, to the cultural
enrichment of both age groups. Stereotypes of young people as "radicals"
and old people as "conservatives" are quickly broken down, and young
and old people come to have respect for each other's values and experi-

[71] Ditlea, p. 74.

ences.[72] These, however, are isolated instances. Much remains to be done before we become, in Neugarten's words,

an "age-irrelevant" society, one in which arbitrary constraints based on chronological age are removed, and in which all individuals have opportunities consonant with their needs, desires, and abilities, whether they be young or old.[73]

SUMMARY

Age is one of society's bases for designating group and role assignments. Agism is any set of beliefs and practices dictating that age differences between people are inherently related to significant attributes and that such differences are a legitimate base of invidious distinctions between socially defined age categories, such as youth and the elderly.

In our own society, young people are largely regarded as irresponsible dependents, and old people are seen as useless dependents, for a number of reasons. These include: the rise of the nuclear family in industrial societies, which has eliminated traditional functions of the young and old; growing job competition, which makes it profitable for adults to keep the young and the old out of the labor market; and the values of contemporary society, which deny the humanistic concerns of the young and the inevitability of old age and death. These factors have justified prejudicial attitudes and discriminatory practices against the young and old.

Young people have been characterized as adolescents—that is, immature and unstable. They are required to attend school, even though they might prefer to work, and are denied certain jobs even though they might be capable of performing them. In school, they are victimized by regulations that have more to do with controlling them than with educating them. They are also denied relationships with adults and legitimate outlets for their sexuality.

Old people are poorer than any racial or minority category, and a large percentage of them live in substandard or poor housing. The aged are also discriminated against in jobs. More than half are required to retire, regardless of their individual desires and capabilities, by mandatory retirement regulations. Compulsory retirement has been analyzed by Blau as a form of *role exit* that is highly detrimental to the elderly, because it is a form of public expulsion without compensating role restitution. After retirement, most of the aged are forced to live in or near poverty, because Social Security benefits are inadequate to begin with and are reduced if a certain amount of income is earned.

The stereotypes of agism have certain consequences for the young and old. The segregation of the young from the world of adults causes them to mistrust that world and to try to form a separate culture of their own. The young may also come to fear the aging process. The elderly, in turn, may accept society's stereotyping of them, and come to see themselves as powerless. The result is an isolation of, and competition between, the generations.

There have been some recent changes in the status of the young—the voting age has been lowered, and regulations on appearance and behavior

---

[72] See, for example, Catherine Davis, "Fairhaven's senior freshmen." *American Education* (May 1975):6–10.
[73] Neugarten, "The future and the young-old," p. 9.

have been liberalized in most colleges. Most high schools, however, still try to impose their standards of propriety on their students, and job discrimination against the young is still widespread.

As health advances improve the quality of life for the elderly, and as their numbers increase, it may be expected that the aged will become more insistent about solving their problems. At present, a number of groups exist to further the cause of the aged. New laws, such as the Supplemental Security Income and the Employee Retirement Security Plan, have been passed to reduce poverty in old age. However, these must be improved and expanded before they can become effective, and much else needs to be done. For example, housing for the elderly is a national scandal, exemplified by the exploitation of the aged in nursing homes. Hopefully, as more people share the same experiences at different stages of their lives, stereotypes of the different age categories will begin to break down and agism in our society will be reduced. As yet, however, an "age-irrelevant" society is far from being a reality.

BIBLIOGRAPHY

Atchley, Robert C. *The Social Forces in Later Life: An Introduction to Social Gerontology.* Belmont, Calif.: Wadsworth, 1972.

————. *The Sociology of Retirement.* New York: Halsted Press, 1975.

Blau, Zena Smith. *Old Age in a Changing Society.* New York: Watts, 1973.

Butler, Robert N. *Why Survive? Being Old in America.* New York: Harper & Row, 1975.

de Beauvoir, Simone. *The Coming of Age.* New York: Warner, 1973.

Erikson, Erik H., ed. *Youth: Change and Challenge.* New York: Basic Books, 1973.

Gubrium, J. F., ed. *Late Life.* Springfield, Ill.: Charles C Thomas, 1974.

Kenniston, Kenneth. *Youth and Dissent: The Rise of a New Opposition.* New York: Harcourt Brace Jovanovich, 1971.

Manning, Peter K., and Truzzi, Marcello, eds. *Youth and Sociology.* Englewood Cliffs, N.J.: Prentice-Hall, 1972.

Mead, Margaret. *Culture and Commitment.* Garden City, N.Y.: Natural History Press, 1970.

Riley, Matilda W., *et al. Aging and Society: A Sociology of Age Stratification.* New York: Russell Sage Foundation, 1972.

Youth: Transition to Adulthood. Report of the Panel on Youth and the President's Science Advisory Committee. Chicago: University of Chicago Press, 1974.

10

COURT WAITING

FAMILY
PROBLEMS

- Over a million American children are the victims of neglect or mistreatment each year.
- Over 10 percent of births in the United States are illegitimate.
- 33 to 40 percent of U.S. marriages end in divorce.
- The average marriage in America lasts only about 7 years.
- Over 25 percent of the elderly in this country live alone or with non-relatives.

The American family is sometimes said to be on the verge of collapse. However, since similar warnings have been issued in numerous societies over hundreds of years, there is probably no need for panic. Moreover, the reported threats to family life always seem to be similar: breakdown of parental authority, strife between husbands and wives, and increasing disregard of sexual morality. It seems that virtually everywhere there is a societal ideal of what family life and organization should be, and that deviation from that ideal is considered to be a serious threat to society.

However, in a rapidly changing society such as our own, family problems may be regarded as partly the result of new social conditions. These problems need not constitute simply a breakdown; they may also be part of a general movement toward constructive reorganization of the family. Like other institutions, the family is affected by social change and seeks out new forms that are more compatible with newer societal patterns.

Also, it is important to distinguish between the problems of individual families and changes in the overall family system in a given society. Many marriages may end in divorce; many children may be raised by one parent or by other relatives; but a societal system may presume that these situations will occur and continue to regard the nuclear family as the norm. In another society, an extended family system might remain the norm despite frequent breakup into nuclear units. A social problem arises only when the pressure for change can no longer be accommodated within the limits of the existing societal structures, or when those who wish to maintain these structures fear that they cannot.

This chapter, therefore, will examine various types of problems related to family structure today and alternative family structures which may become more common as society changes.

KINSHIP UNITS

A kinship unit is a group of individuals related to one another either by bloodlines or by some convention equivalent to marriage. Within the group there is usually a division of authority, privilege, responsibility, and economic and sex roles.

Definitions of kinship may differ from one society to another, resulting in differing behavioral standards. The unit may consist of a *nuclear family* —father, mother, and their children living apart from other kin—or an *extended family*—parents, children, grandparents, aunts, uncles, and others all living together. In the latter instance, parents may retain authority over their married sons and daughters, and marriage between first or even second cousins may be forbidden; in the former case, the nuclear family unit will probably be independent, and marriage of second, if not first, cousins may be considered perfectly normal.

The nuclear family is the predominant type of family in industrial societies, whereas the extended family is more likely to be found in agrarian cultures. The emergence of industrial centers seems to favor the development of smaller family units, which are geographically and socially more mobile, although extensive ties with relatives may still exist.

The further change from a more or less classical industrial society to an increasingly affluent technological one may be expected to cause additional changes in the structure and functions of the family. Economic pressures for family stability may be reduced; more women may be able to raise their children without reliance on the children's fathers. Indeed, some sociologists believe that the transition of societies from agrarian to industrial to technological has steadily reduced the economically useful size of the family; whereas the farming family may have needed all the "hands" it could muster in order to work the land, families in industrial systems—at least where child labor is outlawed—are better able to manage in smaller sizes.

But whether extended, nuclear, or as yet undefined, all family types are characterized by an organization of roles. If the family is to function adequately, its members must perform these roles in ways compatible both with the expectations of other family members and with society's standards.

Five criteria of adequate family functioning have been suggested by Paul and Lois Glasser:

ADEQUATE FAMILY FUNCTIONING

1. "Internal role consistency among family members." In order for family members to contribute to the proper functioning of the family, they must understand what is expected of them and of other family members.
2. "Consistency of family roles and norms and actual role performance." The requirements each family member is expected to fulfill do not suddenly change, nor is there a severe change in the way family members fulfill their required roles.

3. "Compatibility of family roles and norms with societal norms." For adequate family functioning, the "internal organization of the family must be carried out in behavior acceptable to the external system or environment surrounding it." The limits of society's tolerance of nonconformity to its norms vary, as might be expected, from society to society.
4. "Meeting the psychological needs of family members." A family does not function adequately if it is unable to meet the long-run emotional and psychological needs of its members.
5. "The ability of the family group to respond to change." To maintain itself over a long period of time, the family must be able to respond to demands for change, whether these demands originate inside or outside the family unit.[1]

Failure to perform any one of these functions could lead to problems within the family. Such failure is usually involuntary, as a result of either external or internal crises.

External crises are those imposed from outside the family; for example, one parent may die. This event disrupts the role relationships, for the roles of the deceased parent, such as child care, housekeeping, or financial support, must be shifted to other persons, and adjustments must be made. Similarly, role relationships may be disrupted by wars and economic depressions. Absence of a parent during military service changes both his or her roles and those of the other parent, while unemployment of a parent who works can be psychologically unsettling to the entire family. The parent suffers a loss of self-esteem and perhaps of authority, and all members of the family are likely to be frightened and anxious over the unexpected economic insecurity.[2]

Internal crises are those imposed from within the family, such as a serious physical or mental disorder of a child or parent. Many families adjust to these problems and are able to assume the roles of the handicapped member and to accept the responsibility for helping him or her. However, the burden of caring for the handicapped member may cause a great deal of tension and strain between family members. Marital infidelity can be another source of internal crisis, particularly if one or both of the partners perceives it as a threat to the family. A major change in family role may also provoke an internal crisis: For example, the parent who suddenly decides to work, instead of taking care of the children, or the parent who stops working, may cause other family members to feel threatened or confused. Often, the very factor that keeps families functioning well—the consistency of roles and behaviors—may threaten the family's functioning when flexibility becomes more important.

These stresses, as well as other kinds of interpersonal problems, may so impair the ability of family members to fulfill their usual roles that the family may become an "empty shell," kept together not so much by feelings of warmth and attraction among the members as by outside

[1] Paul H. Glasser and Lois N. Glasser, "Adequate family functioning." In Irvin M. Cohen, ed., *Family Structure Dynamics and Therapy*. Psychiatric Research Report no. 20. Washington, D.C.: American Psychiatric Association, 1966, pp. 8–17.
[2] Robert F. Winch and Rae Lesser Blumberg, "Societal complexity and familial organization." In *Selected Studies in Marriage and the Family*. 3rd ed. New York: Holt, Rinehart and Winston, 1953, pp. 70–92.

pressures. Within the shell, members of the family feel no strong attachments for each other; they neglect mutual obligations and in general keep communication to a minimum.

Carolyn Cline has distinguished three types of empty-shell marriages.[3] The first she refers to as the conflict-habituated relationship, which is characterized by a great deal of tension and conflict. The husband and wife may quarrel frequently in private, yet appear compatible when in public. The atmosphere in such a home is rather tense and bitter.

A second type is the devitalized relationship, in which the interaction between husband and wife is devoid of any real interest or excitement. Apathy and boredom constitute the main elements of the marriage, but serious or violent arguments are rare.

The third type is the passive-congenial relationship. In this, both partners are comfortably content with their lives and have a feeling of adequacy rather than of positive happiness. There is little overt conflict, and the partners may have interests in common. However, these interests tend to be somewhat insignificant, and there is little evidence that the spouses contribute in any meaningful way to each other's real satisfactions.

In a sense, it is surprising how often these empty-shell marriages manage to continue. Habit is probably an element here, and fear of the unknown risks of change. There is also the economic factor—one spouse may doubt his or her ability to manage alone, and knows it would cost more to support oneself and/or pay alimony than to maintain a single-family household. More positively, husband and wife may feel strongly that divorce or separation would be wrong or would harm the children. There is usually a social pressure to stay together: in many places, particularly the suburbs, social life for adults more or less presupposes married couples. Also, some marriage counselors assume that their job is to preserve the marriage, even though some of their clients might be happier unmarried. Unhappiness within families is unfortunate, but it is not usually seen as a threat to society; divorce or separation, on the other hand, are often regarded as social "evils" or "problems." Many families, then, stay together even after they have ceased to function well as a family.

FAMILY HAPPINESS AND WORKING WIVES

One of the major changes that has taken place in our society over the past 15 to 20 years is the growing number of women—married and unmarried—who work. In 1960, for example, women comprised 32 percent of the labor force. An even smaller percentage of married women worked or were seeking work. Today, about 44 percent of married women are in the labor force. (Women's median salary, however, is still only about 62 percent of that earned by men[4]—a situation we discussed in greater detail in Chapter 8.) The number of married women employed outside the home is thus growing rapidly.

Recent research indicates that in many cases, far from being a hin-

[3] Carolyn Cline, "Five variations on the marriage theme: Types of marriage formation." *Bulletin on Family Development* 3 (Spring 1962):10–13.
[4] U.S. Bureau of the Census, *Statistical Abstract of the United States 1975*. Washington, D.C.: U.S. Government Printing Office, 1976.

drance to family health and happiness, the wife's job may be a help. Orden and Bradburn, in a study reported in 1970, investigated the relationship between perceived marriage happiness and the work status of the wife, and concluded that where the wife worked as a matter of choice, the marriage was as happy or happier than if she chose to remain at home; whereas if she worked out of necessity, marriage happiness suffered. The relative values of work by choice and remaining at home varied at different stages of the family life cycle: when there were preschool children, happiness was rated as higher if the wife remained at home; when the children were in grade school, work by choice seemed to make for greater happiness; after the children entered high school the two choices seemed about equal. Only where the wife worked as a matter of necessity was marriage happiness in all cases lowered.

Orden and Bradburn conclude:

Since the freedom to choose among alternative life styles is clearly an important variable in predicting happiness in marriage, efforts to extend this freedom should have positive effects on the marriage happiness of both husbands and wives. . . . If society moves toward its national goal of better educational opportunities for all its members, there should be an increase in the proportion of women who choose to enter the labor force in prestigious occupations to which they will have a real sense of commitment. We predict that this phenomenon will not be detrimental to the institution of marriage. On the contrary, there is evidence to support the contention that there might be a strengthening of the marriage relationship, both for the husband and for the wife.[5]

Children are commonly believed to bring joy to any household, and the desire to have them is certainly one of the major reasons why people get married. However, in a study of the degrees of satisfaction and emotional well-being over 2,000 people expressed at different stages of their lives, researchers have discovered that young, married, childless couples were the happiest of all groups considered. (Single people were least happy.) Once married couples began to have children, their reported happiness decreased and feelings of stress rose markedly. Some dissatisfaction was due to the financial burden and sacrifices involved in bearing and raising children; some of it was due to the fact that most young parents suddenly found that they had much less time to spend together. It was not until after the children had left home that married couples regained a state of satisfaction comparable to what they had experienced as childless newlyweds. (See Figure 10-1.)

Many young couples in this country have decided that children are not necessary for marital happiness, as evidenced by the large decline in the U.S. birthrate; and some sociologists believe that childless marriages are less stressful and more emotionally satisfying. The above survey also revealed that childless couples over 30—particularly the husbands—were the most satisfied with their lives, probably because they experience less financial anxiety than same-aged fathers. Childless wives over 30 reported

FAMILY HAPPINESS AND CHILDREN

[5] Susan R. Orden and Norman M. Bradburn, "Working wives and marriage happiness." *American Journal of Sociology* 57 (1970):392–407.

almost the same degree of satisfaction in their lives as same-aged mothers, an indication that many young wives today do not regard childbearing as necessary to a woman's role.[6]

THE BLACK FAMILY

There has been considerable interest in recent years in the distinctive character of the black family in America. It has been hypothesized that the poverty and discrimination consistently experienced here by black people may have led to special adaptations in family life, as in other aspects of ghetto living. Since family life is basic to personality development, these adaptations may be helping to perpetuate some of the conditions which contribute to poverty and discrimination. Such is the implication of the so-called Moynihan Report,[7] which identifies the problem of black poverty as being rooted in a "tangle of pathology" and the weaknesses of a matriarchal family structure characteristic of the lower-class black community. The report established the stereotype of the black family as female-headed or female-dominated, a situation which is said to emasculate the male and to lead to patterns of low education, low achievement, unemployment, crime, and poverty.

Undoubtedly, there is a high percentage of female-headed families among the black poor, as well as a high rate of illegitimacy. It should be remembered, however, that these characteristics tend to be more common at the lower socioeconomic levels of any ethnic group, so that poverty is as likely to be the cause as it is to be the effect of black family structure. It is too easily forgotten that the majority of black families, as well as

FIGURE 10-1
Low and High Feelings of Stress by Sex, Family Status, and Life Stage

Source: Angus Campbell, "The American way of mating: Marriage sí, children only maybe," *Psychology Today*, May 1975, p. 40.

[6] Angus Campbell, "The American way of mating: Marriage sí, children only maybe." *Psychology Today,* May 1975, pp. 38–43.
[7] Daniel Moynihan, *The Negro Family: The Case for National Action.* Washington, D.C.: U.S. Department of Labor, Office of Policy Planning and Research, 1965.

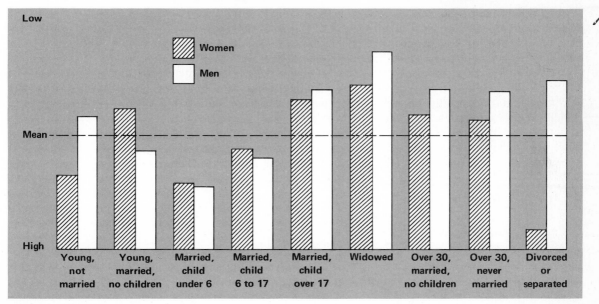

white, are stable and male-headed. As lower-class blacks move up the socioeconomic ladder into the middle class, instability decreases among them, as it does among whites.[8] It should also be remembered that, as we have noted before, statistics about deviant behavior tend to be unreliable, and to exaggerate the amount of deviance among both the black and the poor. In fact, the data and the conclusions of the Moynihan Report have been challenged by researchers in the Chicago area. Berger and Simon compared the juvenile delinquency rates, at all socioeconomic levels, in a large sample of black and white families in Illinois and concluded that there is little difference in the ways these families treat their children and that the black female-headed family is not the primary cause of antisocial behavior patterns.[9]

Nevertheless, there are certain fairly consistent differences between black and white families. Instability among lower-class black families does seem to be somewhat greater than among similar white families, and the illegitimacy rates of blacks are higher. The female-headed family is also more common among black than among white poor (see Chapter 6).

It seems quite probable that poverty and discrimination can account for most of these differences. In our culture, as in most, it is still expected that the man will be the principal breadwinner of the family, yet the black man finds this much more difficult than his white counterpart, particularly if he has had little education or job training. In some ways, the welfare system, which was set up to counteract the effects of poverty, has also contributed to the instability of the black family. Because the most common welfare grants, Aid to Families with Dependent Children (AFDC), are given only to the mother, the system encourages the father to abandon his family and so establish the woman as head of the household.[10] It has also been suggested that the welfare system encourages black men to "abandon" their families because abandonment will enable the families to receive both welfare benefits and the husband's job earnings, each of which would be inadequate as a sole source of family support. In any event, women may come to regard men as unreliable providers and see little reason to marry. Instead, they may prefer a less formal arrangement that allows them to leave or to send the men away when they choose, while retaining full rights to any children of the union.[11]

In brief, insofar as the black family is distinctive, this is probably a consequence, for the most part, of the special intensity and duration of the poverty and discrimination suffered by black Americans—conditions which we discussed in Chapters 6 and 7. In effect, the black family is not so much a social problem as it is a current sociological issue. Hence we shall not undertake a detailed study of the black family as such, but consider the evidence and possible causes of problems among families

[8] John H. Scanzoni, *The Black Family in Modern Society*. Boston: Allyn & Bacon, 1971.

[9] Alan S. Berger and William Simon, "Black families and the Moynihan Report: A research evaluation." *Social Problems* 22 (December 1974):160–61.

[10] Elliot Liebow, *Tally's Corner*. Boston: Little, Brown, 1967, p. 86.

[11] Hallowell Pope, "Unwed mothers and their sex partners." In Robert Staples, ed., *The Black Family: Essays and Studies*. Belmont, Calif.: Wadsworth, 1971, p. 365.

in general, bearing in mind that some of these may occur with particular frequency among the black poor.

PROBLEMS IN TRADITIONAL FAMILIES

The purpose of social organization, whether in society as a whole or in a small group such as the family, is collective action to achieve mutual goals. Since the most clearly necessary function of the family, as a family, is the bringing up of children, it is natural to judge the condition of a family by how well it appears to be doing this. Only recently have the emotional health and happiness of the adult members of the family come to be regarded as perhaps equal in importance to the welfare of the children; and even now, when the two appear to conflict, society usually comes down on the children's side. There is good reason for this, for children, especially young children, need care and protection if they are to survive in a world where death by starvation, exposure, disease, or physical abuse is quite possible. They also need proper education if they are to survive as assets and not as liabilities to society. Adults, having more strength, knowledge, and experience, are expected to be better able to fend for themselves and adjust to unfavorable circumstances.

In this section we shall consider a number of types of family problems prevalent today. Two of these, illegitimacy and divorce, appear to be of particular concern to society. Both seem to threaten the institution of marriage, which is considered to be a vital part of American society. (In fact, as we shall see, there is some evidence that the high expectations people in our society have of marriage contribute to the incidence of divorce.) In addition, both family problems generally result in children who are being cared for by only one parent. This is not only widely considered to be bad for the child's development; but it might result in an additional economic burden to the rest of society. A third type of problem—child abuse—has existed for ages, but has only recently come to be regarded as a serious and widespread social problem.

Child abuse is a centuries-old phenomenon. Until quite recently, the concept of "children's rights" was relatively unknown, and parents, teachers, and masters were allowed virtually total authority over the children in their care. Severe treatment of the child was often justified by "the belief that severe physical punishment was necessary either to maintain discipline, to transmit educational ideas, to please certain gods, or to expel evil spirits." [12] Today, child abuse is a serious problem in the United States. According to the results of a national study of child abuse, over 1 million children in the United States are the victims of neglect or physical mistreatment each year; one in five, or 200,000, die from causes and "circumstances associated with abuse and neglect." Douglas Besharov, director of the National Center on Child Abuse and Neglect, states:

CHILD ABUSE

[12] Samuel Radbill, "A history of child abuse and infanticide." In R. Helfer and C. Henry Kempe, eds., *The Battered Child*. 2nd ed. Chicago: University of Chicago Press, 1974.

"If you had a communicable disease that struck as great a rate of children, you'd say you had an epidemic on your hands." [13] Only in the last few years has any attempt been made to deal with the problem on a national scale. The Child Abuse Prevention and Treatment Act, or the Mondale Law, was passed by Congress in January 1974 to help states and communities organize programs for parents who abuse their children.[14] Also in 1974, the National Institute of Mental Health established a national center in Denver to study the problem more thoroughly and set up a national commission to resolve the complicated legal problems and to change federal and state laws involving child abuse.[15] Grant programs have also been funded under the new law to identify the causes of child abuse and to provide treatment through self-help programs and lay therapy.

Despite this, why has the general public been so little concerned until now? Several years ago, an authority on the subject noted:

Our ignorance regarding the problems of child abuse and child neglect is . . . not quite total, but is severe enough to be inexcusable. We do not know what the incidence nor prevalence of these conditions are. We do not know how to go about casefinding and/or identification of these conditions. We have little knowledge of how to discriminate levels of severity, and are poor at prognosticating future course, with or without available treatments, in many instances. Finally, we do not know how to "treat" either of these social conditions in the sense of bringing about enduring change in the parents involved with much consistency, and with any efficiency. Other than that, we are scientifically in an excellent position.[16]

The reasons for this passivity to the problem of child abuse are many. One is the difficulty of definition. How are we to define child abuse? And how are we to establish that abuse has actually occurred in a particular case? Is the degree of injury to the child the only criterion, or must the parent's intention be considered as well? Elizabeth Elmer reports one study of 33 hospitalized children whose injuries (multiple bone injuries over a period of time) appeared to be unequivocal evidence of abuse; yet in 11 cases, or one-third of the total, the researchers concluded after fuller investigation either that the child had not been abused, or that it was impossible to tell whether he or she had been abused or not.[17] To clarify the issue, David Gil has proposed the following conceptual definition of child abuse:

Physical abuse of children is the intentional, nonaccidental use of physical force, or intentional, nonaccidental acts of omission, on the part of a parent

---

[13] "Child abuse rate called 'epidemic,'" *New York Times,* November 30, 1975, p. 44.
[14] Celeste MacLeod, "Legacy of battering." *The Nation,* June 8, 1974, p. 719.
[15] *National Conference on Child Abuse: A Summary Report.* Rockville, Md.: National Institute of Mental Health, 1974, p. 6.
[16] Norman Polansky, "The current status on child abuse and child neglect in this country." *Report to the Joint Commission on Mental Health for Children,* February 1968.
[17] Elizabeth Elmer, "Hazards in determining child abuse." *Child Welfare* 45 (January 1966):28–33.

or other caretaker interacting with a child in his care, aimed at hurting, injuring, or destroying the child.[18]

However, as Gil himself notes, this definition is unsatisfactory because in real-life situations "it may not always be possible to differentiate between intentional and accidental behavior." In most cases the parents are the ones to testify, and a claim that the child's injury was "accidental" is hard to disprove. Although clinical advances have enabled physicians frequently to identify a specific "battered child syndrome," the problem of differentiation remains a serious one.

A second obstacle to research is a concern for the traditional rights of the parent. If parents are to be responsible for raising and training children, they need to exercise a certain degree of authority, including the right to punish. Our culture has traditionally approved of corporal punishment ("Spare the rod and spoil the child"), and has strongly defended the right of individual parents to govern their children as they think right. Ironically, one of the first court cases in which an outside agency successfully intervened to protect an abused child was the Mary Ellen case in New York City, in 1866, in which the plaintiff was the Society for the Prevention of Cruelty to Animals.[19]

The recent concern with "children's rights" has somewhat changed this picture. Child labor laws, actions of the Society for the Prevention of Cruelty to Children, and the changes in handling juvenile delinquents which have resulted from the Gault decision of the Supreme Court (see Chapter 4) have helped to reinforce these rights. However, the rights of parents and the preservation of the family unit are still regarded as of primary concern, even in those cases in which the nature of the injury would, in any other situation, warrant criminal investigation and possible prosecution. For example, in a nationwide opinion survey, two-thirds of the respondents opposed any punishment of parents who committed violent acts against their children, and over 50 percent felt that the abused child should be removed from the home only as a last resort.[20]

The belief that children are better off in their own homes is reinforced by the recognized inadequacy of facilities in many child-care institutions. When we consider that in one year in California alone some 20,000 children were found to be in need of protective services,[21] the possibly disastrous effects of a wholesale removal of such children from their homes can be imagined. Partly for this reason, there has been an increasing movement toward alternative solutions which seek to treat rather than punish parents, in an effort to eliminate the causes of abuse without breaking up the family.

Some authorities feel that the definition of child abuse should be broadened to include such things as psychological violence, malnutrition, inadequate medical care, poor education, and poverty. While these obviously result in harm to the child, they are not usually as direct an effect of family interactions as are assault or neglect by parents or other home

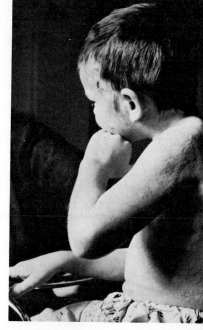

The burns on the child's body are due to the fact that he had a pot of scalding water poured over him. The child's parent also came from an abusive and neglectful family.
Nicholas de Sciose/ Photo Researchers

[18] David Gil, *Violence Against Children*. Cambridge, Mass.: Harvard University Press, 1970.
[19] Serapio R. Zalba, "Battered children." *Trans-Action* 8 (July–August 1971):60.
[20] Gil, *Violence Against Children*, pp. 92–98.
[21] Zalba, p. 59.

caretakers. Hence, and for reasons of space, we shall restrict ourselves in this chapter to the narrower definition.

Social and Cultural Factors. A number of recent studies have attempted to identify the significant social and cultural factors related to child abuse. Since the first nationwide study was undertaken only in 1965,[22] the findings of these studies must be regarded as preliminary.

According to a study by David Gil, the victims of child abuse appear to be fairly evenly distributed over all age groups and between the two sexes, although there are some changes in sex distribution during different stages of childhood and adolescence. At least half of the victims had been abused prior to the reported incident. A significant proportion of children seem to invite abuse through provocative behavior, although this plays a much smaller role in explaining attacks on children than the manner in which "American culture encourages subtle, and at times not so subtle, ways the use of 'a certain measure' of physical force in rearing children in order to modify their inherently nonsocial inclination." Of all cases of abuse, almost 90 percent were committed by the children's parents, and among these 14 percent of the mothers had themselves been victims of abuse as children.[23]

The family in which there is child abuse typically manifests one or more of the following characteristics: there is only one parent with a very low level of educational attainment and low socioeconomic status; the family is likely to have received some kind of public assistance aid within a year of the abuse incident and has four or more children in it; and the family changes its place of residence frequently and the parents are highly authoritarian.[24] While this profile matches in many ways the one usually associated with families living in poverty, we must point out that any correlation is inherently biased by the fact that "the poor and nonwhites are more likely to be reported for anything they do or fail to do." [25] There are, however, specific problems which are unique to poverty-striken families:

the poor are subject to the same psychological conditions which may cause violent behavior toward children as the nonpoor; but, in addition to this, they are subject to the special environmental stresses and strains associated with socio-economic deprivation. Moreover, they have fewer alternatives and escapes than the nonpoor for dealing with aggressive impulses toward their children.[26]

Because studies based on official statistics do tend toward an inherent bias against the poor, it is of interest to consider briefly another study,

[22] David Gil, "Child abuse—a nationwide study of child abuse and its connection with accident research." In Roger J. Meyer, ed., *Childhood Accidental Injury Symposium Proceedings.* Charlottesville, Va.: University of Virginia School of Medicine, April 1966, pp. 19–26.

[23] Gil, *Violence Against Children,* pp. 104–134.

[24] Gil, *Violence Against Children,* pp. 92–133.

[25] Gil, *Violence Against Children,* p. 138.

[26] David Gil, "Physical abuse of children: Findings and implications of a nationwide survey." *Pediatrics Supplement* 44 (November 1969):862.

this one by Steele and Pollock.[27] During a period of five and a half years the authors, both psychiatrists, studied a total of 60 families in which significant child abuse had occurred. These families were not chosen by any valid sampling technique and therefore cannot be regarded as statistically representative; they were merely those who happened to come to the authors' attention. However, they spanned a wide range of socio-economic and educational levels, and they included urban, rural, and suburban residents. The information obtained from them led the authors to conclude that conditions of poverty, alcoholism, unemployment, broken marriages, and similar social and demographic factors were less significant than previous studies had seemed to suggest. Rather, they found a typical personality pattern among abusive parents: the parent demands a high level of performance from the child, at an age when the child is clearly unable to understand what is wanted and unable to comply; and he or she expects to receive from the child a degree of comfort, reassurance, and loving response such as the child would ordinarily receive from the parent. The authors, quoting an earlier study of Morris and Gould, refer to this situation as "a reversal of the dependency role, in which parents turn to their infants and small children for nurturing and protection." When the expected performance and nurturing are not forthcoming, the parent retaliates as a small child might, with violence; but in this case, unfortunately, the violence is not by the weak against the strong, but by the strong parent against the weak and defenseless child.

It is important to note that in every case studied, Steele and Pollock found that the abusive parents had themselves been subject in childhood to similar unreasonable demands, and that in a few cases they found evidence of the same experience among the grandparents. It would seem, therefore, that child abuse could well be part of a behavior pattern transmitted down through the generations among some families, and that it might be found to correlate with other factors in family organization.

In order to break this cycle of abuse, some therapy groups have attempted to teach "parenting" techniques to mothers and fathers who themselves were abused children. The clinic workers try to supply these parents with substitute satisfactions and encourage them to call for help whenever they feel tempted to strike their children. Parents are also encouraged to seek meaningful relationships with other adults and not to invest their children's behavior with so much significance. Dr. C. Henry Kempe, who initiated the first treatment programs for parents at the Denver Child Abuse Center, found that 80 percent of the children could be returned to their parents "without risk of further injury, if their parents received intensive help during that period [when the child lived in a temporary foster home], and if there was a follow-up program after the child went home." For those parents who resist the "therapeutic approach" because of past unfortunate experiences with social workers, there is Parents Anonymous, established in 1970 and organized in ways similar to Alcoholics Anonymous. Regular meetings are held during which parents help each other to stop mistreating their children. There

___

[27] Brandt F. Steele and Carl B. Pollock, "A psychiatric study of parents who abuse infants and small children." In Helfer and Kempe, pp. 103–113.

are now 100 chapters in the United States, and many other groups have begun to use the same technique.[28]

Some recent studies attribute the growing incidence of child abuse—a more than 35 percent increase since 1972—to wider social factors, such as economic recession and the typical isolation of the nuclear family. According to Vincent Fontana, the head of New York City's Task Force on Child Abuse, the rising rate of abuse has been caused in large part by the economic frustrations of high unemployment and the deteriorating quality of life in the United States. In this view, child abuse now frequently occurs in more stable middle-class families because the recent recession has thrown so many parents out of work. Unemployed fathers, unaccustomed to spending so much time at home, suffer from a loss of self-esteem and "unfocused rage," which they take out on their children.[29]

Others see the lack of an extended family and friendly neighbors as being partially responsible for the high incidence of child abuse.

There has probably never been a country where the nuclear family is as totally responsible for child raising, or where so many people live in isolation. . . . In other time and places, parents in stress could send their children to a sister or neighbor for a while. An abused child might run to such homes for refuge, until mom or dad calmed down. Infant battering was hard to hide when the rest of the family lived close by and neighbors knew one another well.[30]

Some social workers believe that an adequate number of day-care centers for abused children could provide the kind of refuge needed, and eliminate by half the number of placements of abused children in foster homes.

In conclusion, child abuse constitutes a serious and growing national problem. Although efforts have been made to identify causes of abuse, the nature of the problem and its solution indicates the need for expanded social services and legal protection, for a wider-based attack on sources of environmental and psychological stress, and for a careful reconsideration of the value and use of physical violence in the rearing of children. Some observers, such as David Gil, advocate laws against any and all kinds of physical punishment in schools and child-care institutions; Gil believes that violence between adults is directly traceable to the violence they received as children. Fontana emphasizes this same point: "The probable future tendency of abused children is to become murderers, robbers, rapists, and perpetrators of violence in society." [31]

The anthropologist Bronislaw Malinowski has suggested that in most primitive societies there is a social dogma which states that "every family must have a father; a woman must marry before she may have children; there must be a male in every household." [32] In other words, every child born is expected to be provided with a legitimate father who will act as its

ILLEGITIMACY

[28] MacLeod, pp. 719–20.
[29] "Hard times for kids, too." *Time,* March 18, 1975, p. 88.
[30] MacLeod, pp. 720–721.
[31] In MacLeod, p. 722.
[32] Bronislaw Malinowski, *The Sexual Life of Savages in North-Western Melanesia.* New York: Halcyon House, 1941, p. 202.

protector and guardian. When the principle is violated, the violators are punished in some way.

Actually, there are societies in which marriage is not always a social prerequisite for parenthood. In parts of West Africa, for instance, a woman may bear a child out of wedlock, and no stigma will be attached either to her or to her child so long as there is reasonable certainty as to the father's identity. Here it is not sexual activity out of wedlock, but rather promiscuity, which is frowned upon.

In our society many of the social stigmas traditionally associated with premarital pregnancy and illegitimacy have been reduced, as is attested to by the fact that today, compared to a few years ago, relatively few illegitimate children are given up for adoption. Nevertheless, premarital pregnancy is still frowned upon by many, generally because it indicates that sexual behavior out of wedlock has occurred; it is considered redeemable only if the couple are willing to marry before the child is born. Society still expects children to be provided with two recognized parents in at least a minimally stable and recognized situation, and the failure (or indifference) of parents in this respect may, even today, meet with various degrees of social condemnation. One form of such condemnation is the legal classification of the child as illegitimate.

It is important to bear in mind this legal aspect when considering the social problem of illegitimacy. Granted that the one-parent family faces special problems—and especially so in a society where the nuclear family is the norm—these problems are in themselves no different whether the single parent be unmarried, widowed, or divorced. Many of the distinctive difficulties of the unwed mother and her child, at least in the United States, are a matter of legal status.

The legal consequences of illegitimacy vary greatly from country to country and, in the United States, from one state to another. In many Communist countries, there are no legal sanctions against illegitimacy. In Sweden, Norway, and Denmark, illegitimate children are given substantially the same rights as legitimate ones. However, in many countries, including the United States, the laws concerning illegitimacy are very old, and discriminate to a greater or lesser degree against the illegitimate child.

Usually, the major legal discrimination against illegitimate children involves the right to inherit the father's property. For example, the New York State Court of Appeals has upheld a state law that prevents a child from inheriting from his or her father unless paternity has been established in court within two years of the child's birth and while the father is still living.[33] Other legal discrimination factors include the ineligibility of the mother to collect various forms of welfare support for the child, and the child's not having the right to use the father's name under certain circumstances. Historically, the "bastard" was legally *filius nullius*, no one's son. Gradually legislation was enacted which obliged the parents to provide support and to relieve the public of responsibility. Since that time —the sixteenth century—there has evolved a patchwork of laws on the subject, many of which are now common in the United States.

In 1964 the United States Supreme Court struck down as unconstitutional some laws which discriminate against the illegitimate child. In

[33] "Illegitimate child barred inheritance." *New York Times,* November 30, 1975.

Levy v. *Louisiana,* the state of Louisiana had argued that greater rights should be granted to legitimate offspring than to illegitimate ones, primarily in order to safeguard the institution of marriage. But the Supreme Court decided that such discrimination was not justified, regardless of the importance of marriage, because it amounted to punishing one individual for another's behavior.[34] The Supreme Court has since further declared unconstitutional sections of the Social Security Act that prohibit illegitimate children of a disabled worker from receiving benefits if they were born after the worker became disabled. According to the Court, "Illegitimacy is a characteristic determined solely by the accident of birth, . . . is a condition beyond control of the children, and it is a status that subjects the children to stigma of inferiority and a badge of opprobrium."[35]

As a result of such decisions and others, it can be anticipated that the legal position of the child born out of wedlock will be substantially improved in the next few years. Already a number of states have discontinued the practice of noting illegitimate status on birth certificates, and at least two—Arizona and Oregon—have abolished the legal concept of illegitimacy altogether.[36] This is a hopeful development, for, granted that legal disabilities hardly constitute the whole problem, their removal makes it much more likely that we shall be able to deal effectively with that part of the problem which remains.

Statistical Trends in Illegitimacy. The total number of illegitimate births occurring annually in the United States has more than quadrupled in the past generation. In 1940 it was estimated that 89,500 children were born to unmarried women; in 1971 the figure was 416,000—more than 10 percent of all births.[37] This does not, however, mean a greater than fourfold increase in the illegitimacy rate.

A study of the relevant figures shows four distinct periods during this time. Between 1940 and 1960, the illegitimacy rate—the number of births per 1,000 unmarried women of childbearing age—more than tripled (from 7.1 to 21.8), even while the total number of such unmarried women declined. Beginning in 1960, however, the illegitimacy rate rose much more slowly, but the number of unmarried women increased sharply, as the "baby boom" children of the 1940s reached maturity and as women tended to marry somewhat later than in the 1940s and 1950s. From 1965 to 1970, the rate of illegitimate births climbed rapidly to its highest point (25.7 per 1,000). Most of the increase during this five-year period was accounted for by white teenagers, whose illegitimate birthrate rose at an annual rate of 7 percent per year, while that of nonwhite teenagers rose at a rate of only 3 percent. By 1971, however, the advent of legal abortion had dramatically reversed the rise in the illegitimacy rate. From its high point of 25.7 in 1970, the illegitimate birthrate de-

[34] Harry D. Krause, "Why bastard, wherefore base?" *Annals of the American Academy of Political and Social Sciences* 383 (May 1969):65–67.
[35] "Illegitimates as dependents." *Monthly Labor Review,* October 1974, pp. 68–69.
[36] Krause, p. 70.
[37] J. Sklar and B. Berkov, "Abortion, illegitimacy, and the American birth rate." *Science* 185 (September 13, 1974).

clined to an estimated 24.2 in 1972, a decrease of 6 percent, with women in the 20- to 24-year-age group—usually the most fertile—showing the greatest drop.

The theoretical concept that explains this drop in the illegitimacy rate is provided by Shirley Hartley, who suggests that "whenever a society or social group . . . promotes one or several of the alternatives to child-bearing out of wedlock, the levels of illegitimacy will be low." [38] In practical terms, demographers emphasize the role of legal abortion in reducing the illegitimacy rate by citing two trends. First, by the early 1970s progressively younger persons were engaging in premarital intercourse and engaging in it far more frequently than ever before. Second, young girls were under increasing social pressure "to be completely 'spontaneous in the act of love,' that is, to refrain from all contraceptive planning." [39] These trends should have made the illegitimacy rate climb drastically. That it fell instead, at a time when the number of legal abortions was increasing in the United States, leads to the conclusion that legalized abortion has reduced the number of illegitimate births in this country.

Despite the sharp 1965–1970 increase in the illegitimacy rate among white teenagers, a disproportionate number of illegitimate births are still recorded among the non-white population. In fact, the illegitimacy rate among non-whites is more than 5 times the rate among whites.[40] Differences in socioeconomic level may account for a substantial part of this, since a higher proportion of non-whites are among the poor and disadvantaged. Illegitimacy is probably more common among the poor for several reasons—welfare policies that encourage the breaking-up of families, the lack of birth control and abortion clinics among the poor, and the simple fact that the poor are less able to afford abortions. It is also probable that the poor—and therefore a disproportionate number of non-whites—are more likely to be counted in illegitimacy statistics because they are more likely to come into contact with social service agencies. Unfortunately, illegitimacy statistics do not show socioeconomic level, so this hypothesis is difficult to test.

Age is a factor about which we can be considerably more certain. Women between the ages of 15 and 24 constitute roughly 40 percent of the total population of childbearing age, yet they account for 80 percent of the illegitimate births.[41] Many women in this age group are not knowledgeable about the reproductive process and tend not to use contraceptives. The relatively young age of these women suggests one reason why illegitimacy is a serious social problem: the great majority of illegitimate children are born to girls and women who are simply not yet prepared, by education, experience, or maturity, to undertake the dual responsibility of parenthood and economic support. Unless some way can be found to overcome these disadvantages, society inevitably has to provide a good part of the family's support, usually through some form of welfare payments; and society has not shown itself notably generous about doing so.

[38] Shirley F. Hartley, *Illegitimacy*. Berkeley: University of California Press, 1975, p. 112.
[39] Sklar and Berkov, p. 910.
[40] See Sklar and Berkov.
[41] *Statistical Abstract, 1975*, pp. 31, 56.

The Problems of Illegitimacy. Recent evidence suggests a growing acceptance of illegitimacy on the part of society. For example, in her study of unwed mothers, Prudence Rains found that "the most striking feature of the girls' accounts of their first experiences in finding themselves pregnant is the extent to which they expect far more severe reactions from others than they typically experience." [42] Similarly, Catherine Briedis found that "in spite of girls' anxiety about telling their parents of illegitimate conception, moral repercussions are seldom forthcoming." [43] The relaxation of sexual mores, the widespread increase in sexual activity, and the growing independence of women have resulted in the present situation, in which more unmarried women are having and keeping their children rather than obtaining abortions or giving their children up.[44]

In fact, when we speak of the social problems of illegitimacy today, we nearly always mean primarily the problems created by the presence in society of numbers of one-parent families headed by women unable to earn an adequate living for themselves and their children. The mother who gives up her child for adoption is absorbed back into the general population and ceases to be regarded as a problem—or at least as this kind of problem; and her child, if adopted, rarely becomes one. Likewise, the mother who is able to support herself and her child, or the married woman who raises her illegitimately conceived child as a member of her legitimate family, arouses little concern.

Thus the problem of illegitimacy results from the fact that the lower-class unwed mother who decides to keep her child is likely to be ill equipped to support and care for it. Vincent, in a study of white women attended at two California maternity homes, found that those who chose to keep their children scored lower, as a group, on a personality profile than did those who released their children for adoption. Those who kept their children were slightly older than those who did not, but had less education, and came from families of lower socioeconomic status. They were more likely to have experienced broken or mother-dominated homes, and showed more negative attitudes concerning sex. These findings corroborate the opinions of many counselors and caseworkers, that "many of the unwed mothers who are most insistent on keeping their child appear the least likely, because of personality and family-life experiences, to become adequate mothers." [45]

In this sense, the social problem of illegitimacy is part of the problem of poverty, for middle- and upper-class unwed mothers who keep and raise their children are generally no less financially adequate as parents than their married counterparts. In one study of unwed mothers who kept their children, almost 42 percent reported incomes near or below the poverty line.[46] If this kind of situation is to be avoided, provision must

[42] Prudence Rains, *Becoming an Unwed Mother.* Chicago: Aldine, 1971.
[43] Catherine Briedis, "Marginal deviants: Teenage girls experience community response to premarital sex and pregnancy." *Social Problems* (April 1975):489.
[44] See Hartley.
[45] Clark E. Vincent, *Unmarried Mothers.* New York: Free Press, 1961, p. 191.
[46] Mignon Sauber and Eileen Corrigan, *The Six-Year Experience of Unwed Mothers as Parents.* New York: Community Council of Greater New York, 1970, p. 38.

be made to enable these women to complete their education and to obtain and hold adequate jobs. Counseling services must also be made available. Perhaps more important, in a preventive sense, the poor must be given greater access to birth control and abortion facilities. As it is, the unwed mother who is forced to rely on Aid to Families with Dependent Children or other forms of public assistance is almost assured thereby of poverty and social disapproval. Our policy seems to be to provide enough help to keep people from freezing or starving, but not enough to enable them to become self-sufficient.

Some European countries have far outstripped us in this respect. In Denmark, for instance:

> By law Mother's Aid centers are set up all over the country; they centralize a broad service that reaches almost all unmarried mothers. Contact is assured through a national vital statistics registry. Originally set up to provide mandatory supervision of all illegitimate children under the age of seven, the program now provides help to the unmarried family in all the areas of living in which assistance is required. Above all neither the unmarried parent nor the out-of-wedlock child is stigmatized—a factor that probably accounts in large measure for the ready acceptance of the service offered.[47]

As we have already suggested, making contraception and abortion widely available and encouraging their use will do much to reduce the problem of illegitimacy. For families with illegitimate children, adequate financial assistance, aid in all necessary aspects, and refusal to stigmatize are necessary. With these, many more of our illegitimate children and their mothers might be enabled to become accepted, contributing members of society, instead of being resented as burdens on the taxpayer.

DIVORCE

> In the first year of the reign of King Julief, two thousand married couples were separated, by the magistrate, with their own consent. The emperor was so indignant, on learning these particulars, that he abolished the privilege of divorce. In the course of the following year, the number of marriages in Agra was less than before by three thousand; the number of adulteries was greater by seven thousand; three hundred women were burned alive for poisoning their husbands; seventy-five men were burned for the murder of their wives; and the quantity of furniture broken and destroyed, in the interior of private families, amounted to the value of three million rupees. The emperor re-established the privilege of divorce.[48]

It would seem, judging by this account (reportedly once inscribed over the city gate of Agra in India), that concern over rising divorce rates is nothing new. Certainly it forms a part of almost any discussion of the moral condition of our own society today.

The usual measure of divorce is the number of divorces per year per 1,000 population. By this standard, the rate of divorces and annulments in the United States has varied considerably over the past generation

---

[47] Ruth Chaskell, "Illegitimacy—the dimensions of prevention." *Social Casework* 50 (February 1969):101.

[48] *Niles Register* 229 (June 11, 1825). In Doris Jonas Freed and Henry H. Foster, Jr., "Divorce American style." *Annals of the American Academy of Political and Social Science* 383 (May 1969):88.

TABLE 10-1
Divorce Rates,
1960–1975

Year	Number of Divorces	Rate per 1,000 population
1960	393,000	2.2
1961	414,000	2.3
1962	413,000	2.2
1963	428,000	2.3
1964	450,000	2.4
1965	479,000	2.5
1966	499,000	2.5
1967	523,000	2.6
1968	584,000	2.9
1969	639,000	3.2
1970	708,000	3.5
1971	768,000	3.7
1972	839,000	4.0
1973	913,000	4.4
1974	920,000	4.4
1975	981,000	4.6

Source: U.S. Bureau of the Census, *Statistical Abstract of the United States: 1975;* and U.S. Department of HEW, *Monthly Vital Statistics Report,* April 24, 1975.

or so (see Table 10-1). From a low of little more than 1.3 per 1,000 in the Depression years of the early 1930s, it rose to about 2.2 by 1941, and then shot up to 4.3 in the mid-1940s, with the end of World War II and the release of vast numbers of men from military service. By 1948 it had dropped again to 2.8, and it continued to decline until 1958, when it was about 1.2, approximately the 1940 rate. Since then, however, the U.S. divorce rate has more than doubled and is now the highest in the world. Starting at 2.2 in 1960, it climbed steadily to its highest point ever of 4.6 in 1975. The divorce rate rose as much between 1971 and 1975 alone as it did in the previous decade.[49]

This marked rise in the divorce rate has affected almost all segments of society. The traditional correlations between socioeconomic and educational levels and frequency of divorce are no longer as true as they once were. For example, divorce used to be much more likely among those with only a high school education than among those who had completed college, and among the poor than the middle- and upper-middle classes. But in the last few years, the divorce rate has been rising among college-educated couples and among those in the higher socioeconomic groups.[50]

Divorce rate figures tell us relatively little, beyond suggesting a rough correlation with large-scale socioeconomic happenings—for example, low divorce and drastic economic recession, high divorce and the massive

[49] *Information Please Almanac, 1975,* p. 711; *Statistical Abstract, 1975;* and U.S. Department of HEW, *Monthly Vital Statistics Report,* April 24, 1975.
[50] Paul C. Glick, "Some recent changes in American families." In U.S. Bureau of the Census, *Current Population Reports,* Series P-23, no. 52, 1975, pp. 7–8.

readjustment demanded by the end of an all-out war. A study by Ferriss of divorce rates, based on marriage cohorts—persons whose marriages took place in the same year—gives a somewhat more refined picture.[51] While it confirms the common belief that a marriage is most vulnerable in its early years—about one-third of divorces take place within the first three years of marriage and 65 percent within the first nine years—it also showed that in most cases the divorce rate for a given length of marriage remained fairly stable. There was a slight decline in the divorce rate for those marriages of six to seven years' duration and a slight increase in the rate for marriages of fifteen years' duration or more. This analysis by cohort makes it possible to see more clearly where the strains are most likely to occur. It also suggests that the causes are to be sought not only in dramatic social changes but also in continuing basic conditions which may be somewhat aggravated by the special pressures of our time.

Some Explanations for Divorce Trends. The institution of marriage is experiencing severe pressures today, and one of the results is the sharp increase in the frequency of divorce. To examine all of these pressures would be beyond the scope of this chapter, but we can point out some of the more easily recognizable ones. Most commonly cited, perhaps, is the change from the extended family to the nuclear family system. Another is the degree to which functions once performed by the family have now been assumed by outside agencies. Other factors are the relaxation of attitudes regarding divorce, the reformation of divorce laws so that divorces are more easily obtainable, and the growing number of educated women who can earn a living independently of their husbands. (The general change in role expectations, particularly among women, is fully discussed in Chapter 8.)

The change to a smaller family unit, coupled with the high mobility of many modern families, lays more complete responsibility on husband and wife for the satisfaction of one another's emotional needs. Where once there were plenty of relatives or long-term neighbors at hand, so that the marriage partners had others to go to when they needed companionship, today they must more often count on receiving it from each other.

The decrease in family size has been accompanied by a decrease in family function. Food production, education, entertainment, and other activities once centered in the home are now performed by outside agencies. As James Peterson, a sociologist and family counselor, describes it:

The family used to be rich and full in the variety of the interactions which were located in the home. These were directed by the family leader in ways which made the output of the family significant both for the maintenance of the family and the economic and cultural systems. Today the transactions within the family are minimized, while those with nonfamily systems are maximized. The family has shrunk not only in size but in the number and scope of its inner transactions. The bonds of the family shrivel as its members work and play and worship in specialized systems away from home.

[51] Abbott L. Ferriss, "An indicator of marriage dissolution by marriage cohort." *Social Forces* (March 1970):357.

At the same time, what is left for the family to provide is more difficult and perhaps even more intensely needed:

While the increased traffic with nonfamily systems occasions opportunities for intra-family conflict, this traffic also imposes on the family increased responsibility in its socialization function. Furthermore, the social system with its mobility, isolation and competitive status system involves for people such anxiety and trauma that the small contemporary family becomes more and more essential for its members in terms of emotional support and therapy. Consequently, the family, while losing previously held functions, must function with considerably more expertise and emotional expenditure on the functions that remain.[52]

That is, we are demanding more of the family, while narrowing the scope of activity and interrelationship through which that "more" can be supplied. The result is an increase of strain.

Another probable cause of family tensions is the whole complex of difficulties which arise out of cross-class marriages. Scanzoni considers some of these in detail in a study based on interviews with wives in both continuing and dissolved marriages. He found that the dissolved marriages were much more likely than the existing marriages to be between persons of significantly different occupational or educational backgrounds. Thus 43 percent of divorced women in the study came from white-collar backgrounds and had married sons of manual or skilled workers; 18 percent came from families of skilled workers and had married sons of manual workers. A further 19 percent came from backgrounds of lower class than their husbands. By contrast, the largest percentage of women in existing marriages came from the same general occupational backgrounds as their husbands. Similar figures appear for educational level. This implies that persons of different backgrounds are apt to hold different expectations of achievement and behavior in marriage, and that these differences may create significant strains between the partners.

Further differences noted by Scanzoni may or may not be class-related. Partners in the dissolved marriages were less likely to share the same friends than partners in the existing marriages; conflict was more frequent in the dissolved marriages, and (at least as the wives perceived it) the husband was more likely to be the final decision-maker, with or without his wife's counsel. In most existing marriages, decisions were made together.[53]

Somewhat surprisingly, Scanzoni did not find very much difference between the dissolved-marriage and the existing-marriage groups with regard to their attitude toward divorce. Both groups apparently tended to believe both that marriage should be permanent and that divorce might sometimes be preferable. This led him to hypothesize that most people keep both beliefs "in readiness," as it were, and employ whichever is called for by their particular situation. The rise in divorce rates, he suggests, results from the increase in need for divorce and from the

[52] James A. Peterson, "Marriage on the rocks." *The Humanist* 30 (May–June 1970):25.
[53] John Scanzoni, "A social system analysis of dissolved and existing marriages." *Journal of Marriage and the Family* 30 (August 1968):452–461.

change in overall social arrangements which puts a greater strain on marriage:

In the premodern settings prior to recent times, marriage partners came from backgrounds that were socially homogamous, and they possessed similar levels of what meager education there was to be had. Expectations regarding the production of income and resultant life-style were centered in the agricultural enterprise and were thus comparable. Friends and kin were mutually shared. For all these reasons the probability of conflicts and serious strain was lessened, and the probability of compromise was increased. . . . However, as societies modernize, . . . people marry others from widely different backgrounds; and in the marriage the probabilities of all types of polarization (economic-occupational, kin, significant-other friendships, etc.) increase markedly over what they are in a traditional setting. Consequently, the incidence of widely divergent values, norms, and behaviors also increases substantially. The rise in conflict levels is often accompanied by a corresponding decrease in effective compromise.[54]

Another study of marital stress suggests a more refined picture of the effect of class on marriage. Leonard Pearlin found that inequality in status was not in and of itself a significant cause of stress in marriage. A more important factor was the desire of a partner to improve his or her status. Those for whom status improvement was not important, or who married a partner of higher status, were relatively undisturbed by the different status of their partners. Those who wished to improve their status, however, were more likely to experience marital stress if they had married a partner of lower status. In Pearlin's words,

Status inequality by itself is of little or no consequence. The importance of such inequality to marital problems . . . depends on the meaning and value that are attached to it.[55]

Because of an increased tolerance for divorce, it can be presumed that partners who might once have resigned themselves to an unhappy marriage, or fought constantly but stayed together, may now feel more inclined to seek their freedom. Women—at least educated women—are better able than they once were to earn an adequate living, and the increasing tolerance of sexual activity outside of marriage liberates them in another aspect. The child of divorced parents is no longer so likely to suffer embarrassment, pity, or discrimination in school. And the chances for remarriage of divorced persons, at least men, appear to be fairly high.

However, there are still many problems associated with divorce, and these problems have not been reduced simply because divorce has become much more common. The process of divorce, even when it is desired by both partners, almost inevitably brings with it considerable emotional and financial burdens. These stresses fall particularly hard on women, who may have to work and care for children without adequate

[54] Scanzoni, pp. 460–461.
[55] Leonard I. Pearlin, "Status inequality and stress in marriage." *American Sociological Review* 40 (June 1975):356.

Number of Years Since Date Of Court Order	Full Conformity	Partial Conformity[1]	No Conformity
1	38%	20%	42%
2	28	20	52
3	26	14	60
4	22	11	67
5	19	14	67
6	17	12	71
7	17	12	71
8	17	8	75
9	17	8	75
10	13	8	79

[1] Partial conformity indicates that *some* money was contributed by the father during the year for the support of his children, although it was less than the court order and in some cases constituted a single payment.

Source: Adapted from Kenneth Eckhardt, "Deviance, visibility and legal action: The duty to support." *Social Problems* 15 (Spring 1968): 473.

TABLE 10-2
Rates of Conformity to, and Deviance from, Court-Ordered Child-Support Payment, in Percentages by Years Following Divorce Action

economic and psychological help from their partners.[56] Well-educated women, because of the increased job opportunities available to them, are better able to cope and in fact may voluntarily choose not to remarry. Other women have more restricted options. Most husbands, for example, do not continue supporting their families after a divorce, although they are often legally required to pay at least child support (see Table 10-2). Divorced mothers are therefore frequently forced into poverty and have to accept welfare. They are also more intensely stigmatized by divorce than their husband and are often refused credit in banks and department stores. Our society assumes that divorced people will soon remarry, and so adequate supports are not provided to single parents. In fact, because of their restricted social and economic opportunities, women are far less likely to remarry than men.[57]

Thus it is clear that divorce still creates problems, both for individuals involved in it and for society as a whole—particularly with the the recent unprecedented increase in divorce. However, many of the social and economic barriers to divorce that have been lowered undoubtedly created more severe problems in the past. It can be said, in fact, that most people have come to regard divorce as, if not always a good, at least a lesser evil in their own cases. These social and economic changes have been accompanied—sometimes with more than a little delay—by changes in divorce laws, the means by which society formally legitimizes the ending of a marriage contract.

[56] Campbell, p. 43.
[57] R. A. Brandwein, C. A. Brown, and E. M. Fox, "Women and children last: The social situation of divorced mothers and their families." *Journal of Marriage and the Family* 36 (August 1974):498, 501.

Divorce Laws. American divorce law has its roots in the ecclesiastical law of pre-Reformation England.[58] Under this law, absolute divorce was theoretically impossible, but legal separation was permitted, as was annulment if it could be shown that the marriage was invalid. These provisions, together with various informal arrangements, stretched the formal rigidity of the marriage law enough to make something equivalent to divorce available to a fair proportion of those who wished it.

A further provision, that of parliamentary divorce, was instituted during the period of the Restoration. By this means, a special statute could be obtained, decreeing divorce in a particular case. Such legislative divorce was extremely expensive, so that it was in practice available only to the very wealthy.

Ecclesiastical law was never introduced into the American colonies, but legislative divorce was, and it flourished, with considerable abuse, until constitutionally prohibited in the mid-nineteenth century. Judicial divorce—that is, the granting of divorce by the courts—developed in the eighteenth century. By the mid-nineteenth century most states allowed divorce on several grounds, the most common being adultery, physical cruelty, and desertion. New York allowed only adultery as grounds for divorce, and South Carolina permitted no divorce at all until 1949.

In the first decade of the twentieth century, it became known that divorces could easily be obtained in Nevada, and soon it became common for persons from states with strict divorce laws to migrate to Nevada, establish residence for the necessary period (at first 6 months, later reduced to 6 weeks), obtain a divorce, and return home. Such "migratory divorce" was not a new nor a peculiarly American phenomenon, and after a number of court tests in the 1940s and 1950s its validity was established, provided the granting state had jurisdiction over at least one of the parties at the time the decree was granted. This, of course, undermined the position of the states with stricter laws, and was probably one reason for the gradual addition of further grounds for divorce in most jurisdictions. New York, for instance, in its Divorce Reform Law of 1966, added abandonment, cruel and inhumane treatment, and imprisonment to its former sole grounds of adultery, and—perhaps more important—created new no-fault grounds whereby divorce became possible after a two-year separation agreement or decree.[59] A number of other states have made similar changes, and cruelty is now frequently construed to include "mental cruelty" or "mental suffering," which can almost always be alleged by the plaintiff if no more tangible grounds are available.

Nevertheless, many lawyers and others concerned with marriage and divorce are convinced that present laws need drastic reform. Their basic contention is that the very concept of "fault" in divorce proceedings is not only erroneous but harmful. Not only does it force the court to assign blame for a marital breakdown which is in reality the result of a whole complex of factors, but it makes the process of getting the divorce unnecessarily painful and damaging to everyone concerned. Intensely

---

[58] See Freed and Foster.
[59] Henry Foster, Jr., "Reforming a divorce law." *The Humanist* 30 (May–June 1970):16–17.

private and personal matters may have to be publicly discussed and even fought over, children may have to testify about their parents' behavior, and whatever bitterness and resentment are present are likely to be heightened and rendered more permanent. The consequences for the children, who are bound to be caught in the middle in such affairs, are especially bad.

Even when the divorce is uncontested—as the great majority are— the fault concept is dangerous, according to its critics. As David Cantor explains:

Because the defendant can always delay a divorce, and often defeat it, the divorce itself becomes an object of trade. . . . The defendant . . . negotiates by offering the plaintiff an uncontested hearing—for a price. The price will normally be agreement to terms of alimony, support, custody, visitation or division of joint assets which the plantiff, if not under duress, would not accept. These issues then become determined not on the basis of objective fairness, but rather on the basis of the plantiff's desperation.[60]

Cantor's proposed solution is simple but drastic—anyone who asks for a divorce should be thereby entitled to it. He or she should not have to prove anything, nor should any defense or delay be permitted. This, Cantor feels, would free the discussion of arrangements regarding money and children from undue pressure, so that there would be a chance of a reasonably fair settlement. It would also minimize the emotional damage to the parties and their children.

There is much to be said for this approach. It would amount to legal recognition of the fact that a dead marriage cannot be held together in any but the most superficial sense by court action, and of the parallel fact that the parties themselves are best qualified to know when the marriage is dead. As Goldstein and Gitter point out, "The state . . . has no way to implement a denial of divorce; it cannot force people to establish a meaningful relationship." [61]

Goldstein and Gitter's proposed divorce status differs significantly from Cantor's only in that it provides for a statutory waiting period between the initial application and the granting of divorce. The state would be responsible for ensuring a fair settlement with regard to assets and children, but it would not be permitted to inquire into the reasons behind the divorce. The decision, by either party, to divorce would itself be taken as sufficient proof of marital breakdown.

This policy—that no marriage must be *maintained* without the full and free consent of husband and wife—is but a concomitant of the state's policy that no marriage can be *established* without the full and free consent of the parties.[62]

Despite the misgivings on the part of those committed to the fault concept, or of those who fear that easy divorce will endanger marriage and the family, the trend seems to be in this direction. California was the

[60] David J. Cantor, "A matter of right." *The Humanist* 30 (May–June 1970):10.
[61] Joseph Goldstein and Max Gitter, "Divorce without blame." *The Humanist* 30 (May–June 1970):13.
[62] Goldstein and Gitter, p. 15.

first to eliminate most of the traditional grounds and replace them with one: "irreconcilable differences." Texas, while retaining the old grounds, has added the new one that divorce may be granted if the marriage has become "insupportable" to either party.[63] Since 1970 it has been possible to receive a divorce "on demand" in thirteen states; eleven more states have included a no-fault provision along with the traditional fault grounds,[64] and by 1974 almost all state legislatures were planning to do the same. However, it would be misleading to conclude that no-fault divorce laws have won the day entirely, as Glick points out:

> In states where no-fault is only one of several grounds for divorce, one spouse may threaten to charge the other "with fault" but settle for a no-fault divorce in return for a more favorable property or support settlement. For this reason, the number of no-fault divorces in those states may not indicate the true number of couples who obtained divorces without negotiations involving fault and the adversary concept.[65]

Alimony—the money one marriage partner pays for the support of the other, usually the husband to the wife—has been closely tied to the concept of fault and guilt in divorce proceedings. Until the no-fault provisions were adopted in most states, the main purpose of a divorce trial was to fix blame on one party or the other and to make the guilty party, usually the husband, pay a certain amount over and above what he would have done ordinarily; if the fault rested with the wife, she would have received less than the ordinary amount. However, now that a decree of divorce can be granted without the need to punish one or the other partner, alimony can be awarded on the more realistic basis of financial need and ability to provide. Theoretically, this means that it will no longer be unusual for a man to receive some form of alimony payment from his ex-wife, if she has the greater earning power; and that a woman with no children will not necessarily be granted alimony from her husband, or, if at all, the alimony she receives would be only temporary to give her time to become self-supporting.

However, the no-fault reforms and reduced alimony settlements have sometimes resulted in unfair treatment of women. The great increase in the number of divorces has released many women into an employment market that cannot absorb them. They have therefore been forced to seek welfare since the courts have had little power to compel so many ex-husbands to contribute to their ex-wives' support. Another injustice involves the rights to property held in common between husband and wife. Several states retain common-law property rulings that permit the holder of the title to the property to keep it. In this way, a woman may have allowed her husband to hold in his name assets belonging to both; if she divorces him, she loses any claim to this property and is not compensated for her loss by higher alimony payments.[66]

---

[63] James B. Brady, "Introduction" to a symposium on divorce law reform. *The Humanist* 30 (May–June 1970):9.

[64] Steve McDonald, "The alimony blues: Now women sing them too." *New York Times Magazine,* March 16, 1975.

[65] Glick, pp. 8–9.

[66] See McDonald.

Another tendency in divorce reform has been for the courts to urge or to require some form of family counseling and therapy. In theory this is a good practice—reconciliation may sometimes be possible if the partners are helped to gain a better understanding of themselves and their problems, and if social agencies can do something to alleviate unfavorable external conditions (such as by locating a more adequate apartment or finding a spouse a job). The danger lies in the fact that such a system requires highly competent personnel and considerable understanding and sensitivity on the part of all the officials involved. In the hands of an unimaginative bureaucracy it could become a Kafkaesque monster, forcing on people useless "help" without understanding or sympathy. Until our family courts can be better financed and better staffed than they often are, compulsory reconciliation procedures seem risky. Optional services, provided by the exceptional official or provided in the unusually favorable personal situation, could, however, be of real value.

In conclusion, it can be said that while divorce represents the failure of a social institution—marriage—to provide the intended physical, emotional, and other satisfactions to its members, it also offers freedom to the parties, once such a failure has occurred, to start over on their own or to try marriage again. Divorce will probably never be a pleasant experience, but it can be made considerably less painful and harmful than it has generally been. Divorce law reform is an important and necessary step toward that end.

FAMILY PROBLEMS OF THE AGED

The aged and the problems of aging were discussed fully in the previous chapter; here we shall consider briefly the demographic patterns of the elderly and the effects of widowhood and retirement on family life. About 11 percent of the U.S. population is 65 years of age or older.[67] By the year 2000 this figure is expected to reach almost 13 percent.[68] Problems of the aging, already serious, will be of increasing concern in the coming years. For in a society which values youth, vigor, and rapid progress, there seems to be little place for the elderly in the productive work force; and in a family system which has become small and "streamlined," the elderly have an ever-diminishing role. And since one marriage partner usually dies before the other, the elderly survivors—commonly the women—may face many years of relative solitude and loneliness, at an age when it is difficult for them to establish new relationships.

In the extended family system, grandparents and even great-grandparents lived in close contact with the rest of the family. The division of labor was not clear-cut, and old people played a significant role in raising children. Even someone too old to earn money, cook, or clean house was probably capable of, and appreciated for, keeping an eye on the young ones.

But there is no real place for the elderly in the nuclear family. For example, one study has shown that contact between the older person and the families of his or her married children tends to be strictly of the

[67] *Information Please Almanac, 1975,* pp. 706–707.
[68] George S. Rosenberg, "Implications of new models of the family for the aging population." In Herbert A. Otto, ed., *The Family in Search of a Future.* Englewood Cliffs, N.J.: Prentice-Hall (ACC), 1970, p. 171.

Have Contact With		When Last Seen				
		Within Last Day or So (including live with)	Within Last Week or Two	A Month Ago	Two to Three Months Ago	Longer than Three Months Ago
Children	81%	55%	26%	8%	3%	8%
Brothers and sisters	79	22	22	15	10	31
Parents	4	32	23	8	11	26
Grandchildren	75	46	28	10	5	11

Source: Adapted from *The Myth and Reality of Aging in America.* A study for the National Council on the Aging, Inc. by Louis Harris and Associates, Inc. Washington, D.C.: The National Council on Aging, 1975, p. 166.

TABLE 10-3
Family Contacts of Those Age 65 and over with Families

"hands off" variety, stressing above all "noninterference" of the grandparent in the way grandchildren are raised.[69] In addition, the mobility of the nuclear family makes it relatively unlikely that parents will live close to their children and grandchildren, whereas in the extended family system relatives tended to live near one another. (See Table 10-3.)

The tendency to segregate the elderly is reinforced by certain demographic patterns. For example, small villages outside urban areas tend to have the highest proportion of persons over 65 years old. In contrast, suburban districts are apt to have many small children, but rather a small number of old people. Organizations, also, have a tendency to be age-graded. Church groups and social clubs tend to have separate sections or a separate structure for the old, in much the same way as they do for youth, young couples, and so on.[70]

The difficulties of elderly people are compounded by the high probability that one spouse will die before the other. Since the wife is more likely than the husband to be the survivor, there is an increasing "surplus" of widowed older women in the population. In a recent year, for example, about 11 percent of all men between the ages of 65 and 74 were widowed, as compared with 43 percent of women of that age. Among those 75 years of age and over, 26 percent of the men had lost a spouse, whereas 70 percent of the women were widows.[71] The effects of the loss of a spouse, therefore, fall more heavily on older women. They are more likely than men to be widowed, and just for this reason they are less likely to find new husbands if they wish to remarry: after age 55, men tend to remarry at a rate about five times greater than women.[72]

Rosenberg, recognizing these difficulties, discusses a possible alternative family form for the aged:

[69] Paul H. Glasser and Lois N. Glasser, "Role reversal and conflict between aged parents and their children." *Journal of Marriage and the Family* (February 1962): 223.

[70] M. Riley, M. Johnson, and A. Foner, *Aging and Society.* New York: Russell Sage Foundation, 1972, vol. 3, p. 202.

[71] *Statistical Abstract, 1975,* p. 38.

[72] Rosenberg, pp. 172–173.

For many of the elderly, especially widows, life may consist of a furnished room and visits to the cemetery.
Laurence Cameron

Since the . . . realities severely limit the possibility of monogamous remarriage of an elderly widow . . . attention has been directed to polygynous marriage as one possible solution to the problem of the bereft female in old age. Does polygyny offer the elderly widow . . . the opportunity to re-establish meaningful conjugal relations? Can a society which institutionalizes monogamy as the sole form of marriage accommodate itself to polygynous unions among members of a particular subgroup? [73]

Whatever solutions may ultimately be found for the problems of the aged, the present tendency is to continue segregating them from the rest of the community. They are often placed in old-age or nursing homes, or they move to "retirement communities," where they interact primarily with other old people. It is not clear that this is the best and most humane way of treating the majority of the elderly. As we discussed in Chapter 9, many of them are much more active and ambitious than is commonly believed. Public policy, perhaps, should be designed to reverse current custom and reintegrate the elderly with the rest of society.

[73] Rosenberg, p. 173.

ALTERNATIVE KINSHIP UNITS

We can distinguish two basic approaches to the question of revitalizing the family. One is to assume that the traditional Western ideal of the two-partner family remains essentially right, and to seek ways of overcoming the recognized disadvantages which it faces in today's world. In this regard, it is often suggested that young men and women be offered courses in marriage and family life as early as high school to enable them to overcome their false or unrealistic ideas about married life. Sometimes proposals are made for more effective services—family counseling, day care, further increases in work opportunities for women— but sometimes more fundamental innovations in the family itself are suggested. The other approach is to consider the possibility of one or more forms of large-group relationship.

John F. Cuber has noted some of the considerations which, in his view, should govern any attempt at alternative family structures. Among them:

1. The functional requisites deriving from a two-sex species and a dependent childhood must be met.
2. There should be no serious disruption of the overall basic values of the society, such as political and religious freedoms.
3. An alternative system should be a minimally-coercive system. Individuals and pairs should be allowed wider choices than the current *de jure* system grants, should be able to exercise these choices with greater freedom of conscience, and should be obliged to observe less concealment and pretense than is usually now the case. . . .
4. Consequently, the proposed sex-marriage-family modes would be pluralistic, that is, not all married pairs, not all parent-child relationships, not all sexual conduct would be expected to be the same.[74]

Within the limits of these conditions, any number of new arrangements can be imagined. Some are already being practiced, and seem well on the way to tacit if not formal acceptance. Proposals for others have been received with varying degrees of approval by experts, "opinion leaders," and the public.

The most conventional of these arrangements is what has been called "serial monogamy" or "serial polygamy"—the cycle of repeated marriage and divorce, so that in the course of a lifetime an individual may have many marriage partners, but always one at a time. It is commonly assumed that this represents a series of failures in personal or sexual relationships, and probably in many cases it does; but this does not mean that it need always represent this. If society chose to regard such serial pairings as healthy and acceptable, it is conceivable that many people could find their personal and interpersonal experience enhanced by such a series of relationships. Or, perhaps, marriage might be regarded as a contract renewable at periodic intervals, thus giving the partners the option of ending it by simply letting it lapse, rather than having to go

THE TWO-PARTNER FAMILY

[74] John F. Cuber, "Alternate models from the perspective of sociology." In Otto, pp. 17–18.

through the more complicated proceedings of a divorce.[75] The possibility of lifelong marriage, if and when the partners wished it, would remain, and such marriages might turn out to be happier, on the average, than long-term marriages often are today. The short-term ones, meanwhile, would no longer be burdened by the need for pretense, at least to the world and perhaps to the partners themselves, that the intention is for life.

What must be found is some way of taking care of the needs of children. If husband and wife separated after, say, five years of marriage, how could it be guaranteed that the parent-child relationship could continue essentially unharmed? Legal responsibility for support could, of course, be maintained. But, under our present divorce system, one parent nearly always loses close contact with the children, and tensions and bitterness are almost always created. If it is desirable that children have a dependable relationship with both parents, this problem must be solved before short-term marriage can become fully acceptable.

Another possibility is a two-step marriage sequence, such as that proposed by Margaret Mead.[76] Under this system, two individuals could contract an "individual marriage" which would be valid for as long as they wished to continue it, but under which they would not be allowed to have children. The purpose of individual marriage would be to enable the couple to explore and develop their mutual relationship, with or without sexual activity. If they wished to end the marriage, divorce would be easy, and there would be no obligation on either party to support the other afterward.

The second step, "parental marriage," would be undertaken in order to have a family. It would be more difficult to contract, with the partners required to give evidence of their ability to provide economic support, and to undergo some sort of testing of their physical and emotional suitability for parenthood. It would have to be preceded by a period of individual marriage to ensure that the partners had had time to get to know one another and to develop a reasonably secure relationship. Divorce would be possible but would take longer than for individual marriage, and arrangements would be made to ensure economic and emotional support for the children.

This system formally separates the two stages which exist in present marriages, and makes certain that the first stage lasts long enough to lay the foundations for personal satisfaction and growth. Mead feels that, at present, young people are encouraged to become parents before they have really learned to be husbands and wives, and that the marital relationship usually suffers in consequence.

Here, too, society would be in a sense legitimizing an existing practice. It is increasingly common for young men and women to live together, often for months or years, without formal marriage. Sometimes they feel that legal marriage is actually wrong—that it is hypocritical or deadening, or simply that one's sexual life is none of the state's business—and sometimes they are just not ready to make the marriage commitment. Bloch and Blum encountered both attitudes in discussions with a number of young unmarried couples:

[75] Virginia Satir, "Marriage as a human actualizing contract." In Otto, pp. 62–66.
[76] Margaret Mead, "Marriage in two steps." *Redbook Magazine,* July 1966.

Peter and Linda, when we first met them, believed that formally marrying would destroy the spontaneous aspects of their relationship that they most treasured. . . . Most of all they wanted to avoid the hypocrisy and stereotyped impersonality that characterized so many marriages they knew of, particularly among older people. The question they were concerned with was how to treat each other as people, not as things or possessions.

One important reason some of the couples chose not to marry was that they felt too immature, too unsettled emotionally, to be ready for a permanent commitment. Living together, they felt, was giving them time to come to grips with their own ambivalent feelings.[77]

In most cases, when such couples begin to want children, they marry— thereby, as it were, progressing to Mead's second stage. Pressure to marry comes partly from without—from parents, relatives, legal considerations —but more intensely, it seems, from within. For many, marriage appears to be the natural culmination of the successful living-together relationship. As one of Bloch's informants explained:

While we were living together, marriage was what I grew to want. In all my previous relationships I wasn't very good at giving, but this time I found myself wanting to make every commitment in the book, and I suddenly realized that those commitments are called marriage.

It would seem, then, that we already have something approximating Mead's proposed arrangement. It has its disadvantages, one of which is that there is at present no way of controlling the possibility that children will be born at the living-together, or individual marriage, stage, with possible legal and psychological inconvenience resulting. Perhaps formal legitimization of the system could lessen some of these disadvantages.

All such proposals and practices are alarming to many people, who feel that the family in its traditional form constitutes the essential foundation of a stable society. Their position cannot be dismissed as merely out of date. However, we considered earlier in this chapter some of the forces which have led to important changes in the role of the family, and hence have made it doubtful whether the family of an earlier time is adequately designed to serve the present needs of its adult, as well as its juvenile, members. The fact that so many people, and not always the younger ones, are finding that, in practice, the present marriage system does not meet their needs is no guarantee that every alternative they try is a good one; but it certainly suggests strongly that the need for alternatives is real.

THE COMMUNAL FAMILY

In a sense, the modern communal movement is probably a natural outgrowth of the general interest in psychology which reached the United States some decades ago. When the psychologists, and particularly the psychoanalysts, first made us aware of the emotional malformations which handicapped our lives in varying degrees, we were told that the causes lay, for the most part, in the repression of natural impulses. Then there came a greater realization of the role of interpersonal relationships in the formation of personality. Still later we began to see that inter-

[77] Donald Bloch, with Sam Blum, "Unwed couples: Do they live happily ever after?" *Redbook Magazine,* April 1969.

personal relationships are governed in considerable part by social norms, and those norms touch our lives at every point in social institutions. Our encounter with reality is socially structured.

Once this was recognized, it was virtually inevitable that people would begin to ask, "If our personal lives are unhappy and unfulfilled, is this in some degree because society is organized in such a way as to prevent fulfillment and happiness?" That is to say, the belief that personal happiness was to be achieved by "adjusting" oneself to the social environment could no longer stand unchallenged once it was conceived that the social environment itself might be fundamentally wrong.

It will be recalled that one of the prerequisites for the existence of a social problem is a belief on the part of a significant number of people that a condition should be changed. Ethnic inequality ceased to be a mere existing condition and became a social problem when people decided that something ought to be done about it; overpopulation and ecological abuse are now social problems for the same reason. And what we may call institutionalized alienation has become a social problem because large numbers of people—mostly young, middle-class people—have decided that it is wrong and should be changed. In this lie the roots of the modern communal movement.

Actually, communalism is not itself a new phenomenon. The Essenes, a Jewish messianic sect in the centuries immediately before and after the time of Jesus, lived communally; Christian monasticism, though it began with a few isolated hermits, rapidly became almost exclusively communal; the great oriental religions have long had similar monastic communities; and, in the West, various minority sects developed some form of more or less communal life. As the influence of religion waned in the eighteenth and nineteenth centuries, secular communes made their appearance, and the history of the United States in those years is rich in sagas of Utopias established on the foundation of one or another social or economic doctrine.[78] Most of these last failed, usually because their members were unable to support themselves or because they could not resolve severe internal dissensions.

Today, it has been estimated that there are from 2,000 to 3,000 communes in the United States.[79] The modern communalists are, as a group, concerned first and foremost with human relations and personal growth. As one young woman said, referring to her involvement in civil rights work—which was in a way a kind of forerunner to communalism— "Finally it all boils down to human relationships. It has nothing to do finally with governments. It is the question of whether we—whether I shall go on living in isolation or whether there shall be a we."[80]

It is this rebellion against isolation which powers the communal rejection of many of the values and institutions of American society. In the

[78] For firsthand accounts of some of these communities, see Charles Nordhoff, *The Communistic Societies of the United States.* New York: Schocken, 1965. (Originally published in 1875.)

[79] Laurence Veysey, "Individualism busts the commune boom." *Psychology Today,* December 1974.

[80] In Ron E. Roberts, *The New Communes: Coming Together in America.* Englewood Cliffs, N.J.: Prentice-Hall, 1971, p. 4.

view of Ron E. Roberts, a student of the communal movement, there are in the thinking of communalists three main aspects to this rejection:

1. Materialism: "No society can be 'free' without proper attention to spiritual matters," and American concentration on material prosperity has consistently devalued the spiritual.
2. Sexual repression—the monogamous family: "It is no accident that social systems with a highly repressive sex code tend toward totalitarian politics. . . . Authoritarianism is caused by the sexual possessiveness of the monogamous family."
3. Corporate capitalism—technology: Capitalism, whether of the corporation or of the state, "uproots man from his community, alienates him from his labor, and in essence turns him into an object. . . . The price for enhancing one's 'standard of living' is frequently paid in damage to the human spirit." [81]

Given their intense concern for human relationships and personal growth, the communalists seek to realize their goals in certain general ways: a tendency to reject all forms of hierarchical organization (unlike some extremely hierarchical Utopias of the past); small size, to allow each member to relate meaningfully to all the rest; and a deliberate avoidance of any kind of bureaucratic structure. These features give them both strengths and weaknesses, and the communes which develop ways to to handle the weaknesses are those which are most likely to survive.

Richard Fairfield, after an extensive tour of communes in the latter part of the 1960s, classified them under six headings: religious, ideo-

[81] Roberts, pp. 5–7.

For many young people, traditional family relationships no longer seem attractive. Here members of a commune share household tasks, companionship, and recreation in their effort to develop an alternative way.
Bonnie Freer/Photo Researchers

logical, hip, group marriage, service, and youth.[82] Of these, it is the hip and group marriage types which have attracted the most publicity and, usually, the most hostility. Building on sometimes highly colored tales of these groups, the popular imagination has often seen communes as in general composed of approximately equal parts of sex, drugs, nudity, laziness, and dirt. In fact, of course, this is an unwarranted simplification. Sex and drugs have been an important element in the experience of many communalists, but in the stronger communes they are rarely used indiscriminately. Not infrequently psychedelic drugs are regarded as being, if not perhaps actually harmful, at most an aid to getting started on openness and growth, or a tool to be used within limits. Likewise, sex is expected to be a means of full-person intimacy, not a mere animal coupling. And unwillingness to work may stem from deep confusion and fear of the depersonalizing effects of work as it is often found in the "straight" world; as one leader in a fairly successful commune explained:

A lot of young people don't want to center their energy, they're afraid to, they're afraid they're going to get hung up, so they stay so scattered that they're useless. . . . Some of these people have had such rough times with their families that they think that anything that has anything to do with the system is really ugly and anything like work is a bummer.[83]

Religious communes have always had a longer life expectancy than secular ones, apparently because religious belief provides a common focus which helps to hold members together. Several of the stronger-seeming communes visited by Fairfield were of this type. For example, the Lama Foundation in New Mexico was a well-established group oriented toward a blending of Christian and Eastern spiritual principles. Members followed a fairly strict daily regiment, including religious exercises and organized work.

Hip communes, for the most part, are much more loosely structured. Several have adopted the "open land" principle—"land access to which is denied no one"—among them Morning Star Ranch and Wheeler's Ranch in California and Tolstoy Farm in the state of Washington. Others have an ideal of a limited and integrated community, but have trouble refusing would-be members. At their best they seem to be characterized by a sense of great freedom and joy; but their general lack of decision-making structures, and of any ideology which can justify asking individuals to do what the group wants if it conflicts with their "own thing" of the moment, has seriously weakened many of them. A recent study has concluded that the free wandering and migrating between hip communes has contributed to their instability: "In this milieu, what is freely chosen may be cast aside with almost equal ease. Freedom includes the right to pack up and go, even if it threatens the survival of the community. Behind the urge to keep moving lies another attribute of free choice—the desire to break off relationships at will, whenever they become too 'heavy' or demanding." [84] Hip communes are the ones most likely to be attacked by neighbors and authorities on the real or manufactured grounds that they constitute health hazards or public nuisances.

[82] Richard Fairfield, *Communes USA: A Personal Tour.* Baltimore: Penguin, 1972.
[83] In Fairfield, p. 107.
[84] Veysey, p. 77.

The group marriage is the basis of a number of communes, and is held as part of the ideal of many others. The rationale behind it is that sexual union can be an important aid to close and understanding relationships between people as whole persons, and that it should not be restricted to a single relationship in the life of each individual.

As psychologist Albert Ellis points out, group marriage has existed for a long time, usually on a small scale. It consists of a number of adults —at least two of each sex—"living together, sharing labor, goods, and services, bearing and raising their children in common, and engaging in promiscuous sex relations, so that every male in the group has intercourse, at one time or another, with every female in the group," [85] or at least has the opportunity for it. Modern group marriages seldom last more than a few years at best, and often no more than a few months, though those involving one man and two women appear to be much more stable than most other combinations.[86] The reasons for the breakup are not necessarily sexual—some members may be unwilling to perform their share of the work, or personalities may clash violently. A group marriage seems to require more, not less, work than a conventional monogamous marriage if it is to be successful, for the greater number of people involved inevitably increases the opportunities for trouble. There are more personalities and more expectations to harmonize. In addition, a sense of competition for the sexual favors of preferred mates almost always develops unless the group is very skillful at anticipating and dealing with it, and the results are invariably destructive of group harmony. Of three primarily group marriage communes visited by Fairfield, only one seemed to him to be in really healthy condition. Of the others, one was badly torn by dissension, and one was tending toward stable monogamous pairing, with some resentment on the part of members left out of the pairs. Laurence Veysey interviewed the members of Harrad West, a group marriage commune in Berkeley, and discovered several additional destabilizing tendencies, the most serious of which were a subtle expectation of failure from the outset that "infects the quality of commitment" and selfish attitudes on the part of many who used the group primarily for "their own continuing self-development" and "personal fulfillment." [87]

It is particularly difficult to judge the possible viability of group marriage as an institution, because all of the first-generation participants in such experiments have been thoroughly socialized in a monogamous society, and inevitably carry with them certain expectations about sexual life derived from that society. It is hard to determine, for example, whether sexual competitiveness and jealousy are natural concomitants of shared sex, or whether they are merely culturally instilled reactions to the violation of a monogamous norm.

Ideally, the commune, whether based on group marriage or not, possesses many of the characteristics of a cohesive family. All work and all economic rewards are the property of the group; private property does not exist or is kept to a bare minimum. Children are raised collectively and given a common education. In addition, productive work and recrea-

---

[85] Albert Ellis, "Group marriage: A possible alternative?" In Otto, p. 75.
[86] Barry L. Constantine and Joan M. Constantine, *Group Marriage*. New York: Macmillan, 1974.
[87] Veysey, p. 77.

tion are centered within the group—characteristics of the old-fashioned natural family but rarely of the modern one. The community is "a centralized, coordinating organization, often combining all of life's functions under one roof. Economic, social, political and family life may all occur within the community and be coordinated by it." [88] In a sense, there is a kind of "retribalization" of individuals who are no longer willing to live in the fragmented and isolated fashion prescribed by technological society.

The great majority of communes fail, in the sense that they do not continue as identifiable entities. However, even when they fail, they may have served useful social functions. For individual members, they may have provided an opportunity to ask some questions about life and to find some personal answers; and for society at large they may serve as a kind of social experiment or living laboratory, testing the possibility of alternative arrangements and the necessity of some of our basic cultural assumptions.[89] Even if the traditional monogamous marriage turns out in the end to be the most satisfactory arrangement, our future approach to the nature and meaning of "family" is likely to be very much affected by the hungers and the ideals which are now being manifested in the communal movement.

The Kibbutz Society. Of all recent types of command society, perhaps the most stable is the kibbutz, a type of communal farm native to Israel. The first kibbutz was founded in 1909; today there are about 80,000 Israelis living in about 200 kibbutzim.[90] The kibbutz society has impressed many sociologists with its ability to survive and reproduce itself, as well as with its approach to child rearing, which seems to minimize the development of delinquency and emotional disturbance.

In a kibbutz, all of the profits from working the land or from the light manufacturing which provides economic support benefit the entire community. Meals are eaten in a communal dining hall, and children are brought up collectively, rather than by their own parents. Couples are usually monogamous and are in effect married to one another, although many do not bother with a formal marriage service and may not be married in the eyes of the state. Usually if the couple is expecting a child they will marry so that the child will not be illegitimate.[91]

A peculiar feature of kibbutz child rearing is that boys and girls in most kibbutzim live in the same dormitories, sleep in the same rooms, and share the same bathroom facilities. The sexes are often not segregated until after the children finish school at about 17 or 18 years of age; in some cases they are segregated at the onset of puberty.

According to Bettelheim, the apparent casualness in the kibbutz with regard to sexual matters actually conceals a certain puritanism.[92] Al-

[88] Rosabeth Moss Kanter, *Commitment and Community: Communes and Utopias in Sociological Perspective.* Cambridge, Mass.: Harvard University Press, 1972, p. 2.
[89] Kanter, p. 236.
[90] Bruno Bettelheim, *Children of the Dream.* New York: Avon, 1970, p. 23.
[91] Melford Spiro, "Is the family universal?" *American Anthropologist* 56 (1954): 840–846.
[92] Bettelheim, p. 66.

though in theory there are no rules against sexual relationships among young people, in practice such conduct is frowned upon until they leave school and become adult members of the kibbutz.

Thus there is a certain dualism in kibbutz life. On the one hand, the family as we know it does not exist, and most of the functions of the nuclear family become the functions of the entire kibbutz society.[93] On the other hand, marriage exists, and children know their own parents and have a special relationship with them, despite the fact that they are not brought up by them. The kibbutz therefore preserves institutions which more radical kinds of communes do not.[94]

The egalitarian philosophy of the kibbutz has a kind of leveling effect on the children, an effect which Bettelheim has studied in some detail. Although there is little delinquency, and little severe emotional disturbance, it seems that kibbutz-bred children tend to display a "literalness, a matter-of-fact objectivity which has no place for emotions." [95] In other words, although the life does not appear to have serious adverse consequences for children—indeed in many respects kibbutz children are extremely healthy both physically and mentally—some price may be paid in the form of a loss of individuality.

It is far from clear that kibbutz experience is generalizable. It may be that a kibbutz could not survive anywhere except in Israel, because the kibbutz philosophy is a product of unique circumstances which are part of Israeli history and culture. Kibbutz life is closely linked with Israeli nationalism, and flourishes because of the dedication of its members and because most of the people in the country support the kibbutz movement.

PROSPECTS

The family, as we have seen, is a dynamic institution, changing its shape in accordance with the needs of society. Possible indications of future change are evident in the symptoms of family problems that we have explored—illegitimacy, child abuse, the high divorce rate, and the plight of the aged. Clearly the family is in a state of flux, but the form it will ultimately take remains uncertain.

One important trend that has not been discussed so far but is symptomatic of the changing status of the family is the large increase in the rate of singleness in the United States. Throughout the 1940s single people accounted for only 1 out of every 10 households; now they account for 1 in every 5. Furthermore, young men and women at what have been considered the most marriageable ages—20 to 24 years—are choosing to remain single. In 1960, 28 percent of the women and 53 percent of the men in this age group chose to remain single; by 1975, 40 percent of the women and 57 percent of the men had chosen to do so.[96] It is impossible to say whether this trend will continue indefinitely or how it will affect

[93] Spiro, pp. 503, 507.
[94] See Leslie Rabkin, "The institution of the famliy is alive and well." *Psychology Today,* February 1976, p. 66.
[95] Bettelheim, p. 297.
[96] Glick, pp. 3, 12–13.

traditional living arrangements, but it does indicate a fundamental change in basic attitudes toward marriage and the desirability of family life. It would seem that young persons of marriageable age are more interested in experimenting with other life styles and developing their own potential than in conforming to traditional marriage patterns.

The low marriage and high divorce rates of the 1970s are not necessarily signs that family life is less valued today than it was in the past. Instead, the figures may mean that people are forming more realistic attitudes about what they expect from marriage; and with the easing of divorce and alimony laws, they are not hesitating to end inviable relationships. Another factor in this trend is that women are finding more roles open to them than ever before in the employment market, are apparently enjoying their independence, and are discovering more satisfying alternatives to marriage.

The two most serious effects of family problems—the high incidence of child abuse and the appalling neglect of the aged—will hopefully be alleviated as the public's awareness of them grows. The problem of child abuse has already begun to receive the prominent attention it deserves, and its behavioral and economic causes have started to emerge. And as the median age of the population increases, more attention will undoubtedly be paid toward integrating the elderly into our society.

In the future, there may be no single family model to describe the vast majority of families in the country, as individuals build family structures which best meet their needs. However, there may be new pressures which cause new family forms to develop or which perpetuate marriage and family relationships as we now know them.

SUMMARY

Kinship units consist of individuals related to one another through bloodlines or marriage, and usually take the form of *nuclear* or *extended families*. The small nuclear family is a product of industrial society; the new technological society that is now evolving from it has made some roles and functions of the nuclear family unnecessary.

The family is subject to many kinds of internal and external pressures, which may cause tension and strain between family members and lead to various types of "empty-shell" marriages. Wives are increasingly finding outside employment, a trend that has been found to help family stability; they are having fewer children or none at all, a trend that indicates that many young wives do not regard childbearing as necessary to a woman's role. The female-headed family and its relationship to the welfare system have become a problematic issue.

The most prevalent symptoms of family problems today are child abuse, illegitimacy, divorce, and the isolation of the aged. The incidence of child abuse has risen drastically in the last few years, and several organizations are now dealing with the problem on a national scale. Until abortion was legalized, the illegitimacy rate was on its way to an all-time high; even so, illegitimacy is still a serious social problem because of the legal sanctions against illegitimate children and the economic burden they may place on society. The divorce rate is now at its highest in history, and its incidence is not confined to any particular social class; the most common reasons for divorce include the increased tension within the isolated nuclear family, the cooptation of family functions by outside agencies, the increasing independence of women, and the availability and acceptance of divorce. However, the no-fault divorce and alimony laws that have made divorce so easily available have also made divorced mothers a new deprived social group. The problems of the elderly are becoming increasingly serious as the median age of the population moves upward; the aged are often excluded from their families and segregated from the rest of society in special communities.

The alternatives to the traditional lifetime marriage between two partners might involve a more flexible series of monogamous and polygamous arrangements, contract marriages, two-step marriages, and various forms of group living. Short-term exploratory marriages would release young adults from premature commitments and permit more relaxed relationships to develop.

The commune movement arose from deep dissatisfaction with traditional life styles and a belief that human relationships require new forms in which to grow and develop. Communalists prefer small, intimate, relatively unstructured groups, of which the Israeli kibbutz has shown itself to be the most stable form so far.

BIBLIOGRAPHY

Adams, Bert N. *The Family: A Sociological Interpretation*. 2nd ed. Chicago: Rand McNally, 1975.

Bernard, Jessie. *The Future of Marriage*. New York: Bantam, 1973.

Billingsley, Andrew. *Black Families in White America*. Englewood Cliffs, N.J.: Prentice-Hall, 1968.

Constantine, Barry L., and Constantine, Joan M. *Group Marriage*. New York: Macmillan, 1974.

Cooper, David. *The Death of the Family*. New York: Pantheon, 1970.

de Beauvoir, Simone. *The Coming of Age*. New York: Putnam, 1972.

Fairfield, Richard. *Communes USA: A Personal Tour*. Baltimore: Penguin, 1972.

Goode, William J., *et al. Social Systems and Family Patterns*. New York: Bobbs-Merrill, 1971.

————. *The Contemporary American Family*. Chicago: Quadrangle, 1971.

Hartley, Shirley F. *Illegitimacy*. Berkeley: University of California Press, 1975.

Kephart, William. *The Family, Society and the Individual*. 3rd ed. Boston: Houghton Mifflin, 1972.

Lopata, Helena Z. *Widowhood in an American City*. Cambridge, Mass.: Schenkman, 1972.

Riley, Matilda, and Foner, Anne. *Aging and Society*. Vol. 3. New York: Bobbs-Merrill, 1971.

Scanzoni, John H. *The Black Family in Modern Society*. Boston: Allyn & Bacon, 1971.

Sussman, Marvin. *Sourcebook in Marriage and the Family*. 4th ed. Boston: Houghton Mifflin, 1974.

11

PROBLEMS IN HUMAN SEXUALITY

- In more than half of contemporary societies, some homosexual activity is considered acceptable under certain circumstances or for certain members of the community.
- No detectable personality differences have been found between homosexuals and heterosexuals.
- Thirty-six states now prohibit homosexual acts between consenting adults; a majority of states also prohibit heterosexual oral-genital contact.
- There are an estimated 275,000 prostitutes in the United States.
- Studies have shown that child molesters and rapists tend to have below-average exposure to pornography.
- At least three-fourths of men and women feel that schools should offer courses in sex education.

Only a decade or two ago, it would have been fairly easy to state what the commonly accepted American attitudes toward sexual behavior were: normal sex was that which tended naturally to the procreation of children within a socially legitimated family. Occasionally, premarital intercourse was held to be within the narrowly defined range of acceptable behaviors, if it led to marriage fairly quickly. Today, although sexual matters are being discussed more openly than ever before, it is much more difficult to say precisely what American attitudes toward sex are; our attitudes are much more ambiguous, ambivalent, and inconsistent. On the one hand, a considerable variety of sexual behavior is available in the media, on the streets, in schools, and, for many of us, in our bedrooms. On the other hand, many people decry our new sexual freedoms, citing them as examples of "permissiveness." Many communities oppose even basic sex education in their schools. And, in many states, laws prohibit many sex acts of a nonheterosexual or a nonmarital nature—and even some sex acts between husband and wife.

At present, then, our sexual norms are complex and often inconsistent and contradictory. Part of the reason for this is that they are in a process of change that has not yet been completed. Already, behaviors and situations that were once rare—or unmentionable—in the United States have become much more commonplace. For example, surveys taken in both 1937 and 1959 indicated that only 22 percent of respondents approved of premarital sex; in a 1973 survey comparable to Kinsey's studies, more than three-fourths of men and over half of women found premarital intercourse acceptable. This same 1973 survey also found greatly increased acceptance and practice of oral and anal sex since Kinsey's studies in 1948 and 1953.[1] And whereas sex-change operations first took place in the early 1930s, they were not widely publicized until 1952, when the revelation of Christine Jorgensen's sex-change operation met with widespread shock and disapproval. Yet recent estimates are that some 1,500 people have now undergone such operations.[2]

However, despite the seemingly radical nature of such developments, many of the traditional sexual attitudes still manifest themselves—not only in our laws, but in our behaviors as well. For example, while more of us have become permissive toward premarital, oral, and anal sex, we still prefer these and other sexual practices within the context of close and affectionate relationships. As Hunt comments,

A growing body of research literature has established the fact that much of the current premarital coitus on campuses and in the big cities takes place between males and females who live together in what are essentially trial marriages or companionate marriages with firm emotional ties, conventional standards regarding fidelity, and a definite social identity as a couple. . . . The new sexual freedom operates largely within the framework of our long-held cherished cultural values of intimacy and love.[3]

In short, we seem to be moving toward a new sexual order through reform (gradual, partial change), rather than through revolution (sudden, radical change). Our traditional values often coexist with—or at least help shape —our contemporary values.

We suggested in Chapter 1 that social change and conflict are often accompanied by social problems. The changes and conflicts in our attitudes toward human sexuality are no exceptions to this principle. For example, our growing sexual freedom has given rise to rapidly increasing rates of venereal disease. And while more teenagers than in the past are engaging in sexual intercourse, many studies have found that most such teenagers do not use or only rarely use contraceptives, and are misinformed about the time during the menstrual cycle when pregnancy is most likely to occur. Conversely, many people are still quite concerned about sexual behaviors that depart from traditional norms—such as homosexuality and prostitution—and would like to see such behaviors eliminated. We will be discussing problems in human sexuality such as these in this chapter. But before we begin, it would be helpful to review the origins of our current views on sexuality and to briefly examine attitudes toward sexuality in other cultures. In this way the problems in human sexuality in our society can be seen in perspective and be better understood.

[1] Morton Hunt, *Sexual Behavior in the 1970s.* New York: Dell, 1974, pp. 11, 21, 23.
[2] John Gagnon and Bruce Henderson, *Human Sexuality: The Age of Ambiguity.* Boston: Little, Brown, 1975, p. 4.
[3] Hunt, pp. 153–154.

ORIGINS OF TODAY'S ATTITUDES

What is defined as acceptable or non-acceptable sexual behavior varies from culture to culture, and varies within the same culture or society during different periods. A major part of our own sexual legacy comes from our Puritan and Victorian forebears, who elaborated on certain aspects of Judeo-Christian tradition.[4]

The Old Testament, and traditional Judaism, approved of coitus only within the context of marriage and only for begetting children; it also condemned masturbation, homosexuality, and various other sexual practices. However, Jewish tradition validated sex—within permitted boundaries—as pleasurable. Early Christianity took a more ascetic view and, following St. Augustine, regarded sex as degrading or evil. Sexuality was seen as the irrational part of human nature that had to be controlled; it existed only for the purpose of procreation. In practice, such attitudes prevailed only infrequently over the next 1,000 years. Sexual behavior among all classes and even among the religious hierarchy often strayed from the stated standards of the Judeo-Christian tradition.

After the Reformation that began in the sixteenth century, some sects at first took a more practical view of sexuality—for example, the requirement of celibacy was eliminated for the Protestant clergy. Eventually, however, Protestant sexual codes became strict and repressive. The importance of hard work and austerity was emphasized, and self- (and sexual) denial was considered a virtue. Puritanism, which was for a while the dominant Protestant sect in England, also emphasized rigid adherence to religious law and a life of asceticism. The Puritan tradition eventually became extremely influential in the United States, because the Puritans were among the first to colonize America in the seventeenth century.

The sexual codes of the Western world's major religious, already firmly entrenched, were further reinforced by the rise of capitalism during the eighteenth century:

When capitalism came along, sex got bound up in the economic ethic—prudence instead of profligacy, privatization instead of public display, savings instead of expenditures. The Puritan-dominated sex ethic became that of penny-pinching Adam Smith. . . . The moral values of the new middle classes, with their belief in hard work, delayed gratification, and avoidance of pleasure, including the sexual, were to triumph during the Victorian age, not only in England but in most of Western Europe.[5]

Such influences, of course, were felt not only in Western Europe but in the United States as well. And, in fact, the Victorian moral system, which grew out of the religious and economic values we have described, was the most direct antecedent of our traditional sexual code. Victorian values stressed the importance of self-control; "giving in" to one's sexual desires was seen as a weakness. Perhaps more important, in terms of our

[4] Gagnon and Henderson, pp. 15–17.
[5] Gagnon and Henderson, p. 16.

own culture, the Victorians had strong ideas about the proper status and behavior of women:

The good woman was virginal before marriage—undamaged property—had many children, and exhibited no pleasure in sexuality. The bad woman willingly "gave it away," wasted her sexual capital, and lost the opportunity to marry.[6]

The sexual activities of men, on the other hand, were tolerated, so long as they took place not with "respectable" women but with servants or prostitutes. This denial of female sexuality, and the setting of different standards of behavior for men and women, formed the basis of the "double standard" that characterized American society and that to some extent still exists today.

Whatever attitudes people have taken toward sexual behavior, they have rarely been able to ignore it. The art of primitive peoples abounded with phallic symbols and other sexual imagery; and at the very height of the Victorian era, there was a brisk trade in erotic drawings and novels. We know today that sexuality plays an important—possibly even a central—role in the human experience. It was perhaps inevitable that people's preoccupation with the subject would eventually lead to the formal study of it. And as we shall see, such formal studies of human sexuality in the late nineteenth and twentieth centuries contributed to the liberalization of our sexual behavior.

FORMAL STUDY OF HUMAN SEXUAL CONDUCT

The first major student of human sexuality in modern times was Sigmund Freud. The insistent intrusion of sexual material in the recollections of his patients led Freud in the 1890s to postulate that the sex drive was a fundamental part of human life, and that it was present at birth or perhaps even in the developing fetus. Such a view was courageous and innovative, since at that time sexuality was considered an abnormal part of human nature. It was believed to make its appearance only when procreation became possible, in adolescence. The new idea that sexuality was a critical part of human development provoked much shock and outrage at the time; but eventually Freud's ideas were to have a liberating effect on Western society. Not only did sexual feelings become more acceptable, but the entire subject of sexuality was taken "out of the closet" and legitimized as the object of research. (Some of Freud's ideas, however, are considered antiquated today—particularly those on female sexuality. See Chapter 8.)

More practical researchers in Freud's time (such as Havelock Ellis) and beyond were concerned more with dispelling ignorance about sexual matters than with proposing new theories of sexuality. Alfred C. Kinsey, an American zoologist, began in the late 1930s to systematically study sexual practices in the United States. His *Sexual Behavior in the Human Male,* published in 1947, reported on interviews with 5,300 white American men. It provided documentary evidence that our national sexual behavior did not conform to our stated moral values. Some 83 percent of Kinsey's subjects had experienced premarital intercourse, half of those who were married had committed adultery, nearly all (92

---

[6] Gagnon and Henderson, p. 16.

percent) had masturbated to orgasm, and one-third had had at least one homosexual experience since puberty, mostly early in adolescence. Five years later *Sexual Behavior in the Human Female* was published, detailing interviews with 5,940 white American women. This volume showed that, while the old double standard was still alive and well, women were not as asexual as both men and women liked to think. More than half of all women interviewed had had premarital intercourse, and one-fourth of those who were married had had extramarital intercourse. Such statistics on female sexuality were particularly shocking during a time when women were expected to be "ladies." But all of Kinsey's material on masturbation, premarital intercourse, adultery, and homosexuality was disturbing and controversial. Kinsey's data were widely disseminated in the press, and for the first time, people in the United States were confronted with the fact that their sexual practices differed widely from their sexual norms. One probable effect was that many people became freer in their sexual behavior—or at least felt less guilty about it—secure in the knowledge that they were joining sizable numbers of their fellow citizens.

In the late 1950s a pair of American researchers, Dr. William H. Masters and Virginia Johnson, began to investigate the physiology of sex. Their findings have influenced the present climate of sexual and sex-role change. Freud had asserted that vaginal orgasm was the superior form of female response. By means of ingenious laboratory equipment and procedures, Masters and Johnson found that there is no physiological difference between a clitoral orgasm and a vaginal orgasm. With the publication of this finding (among others) in *Human Sexual Response* (1966) they enhanced the sex lives of those women who had previously believed themselves inadequate because their bodies did not live up to the Freudian ideal. With the additional, verified facts that some women are able to enjoy numerous orgasms in succession, and that both men and women are capable of enjoying sexual activity into advanced old age, sexual expectations for both sexes were transformed. Turning their attention next to the great amount of human unhappiness caused by various forms and degrees of sexual incompatibility or dysfunction, Masters and Johnson went on to research and publish *Human Sexual Inadequacy* (1970), and to establish a sex treatment center for couples having severe adjustment problems. Sex treatment clinics (not all of them legitimate) have proliferated in the 1970s. So have "do-it-yourself" books such as *The Sensuous Woman* and *The Sensuous Man,* with advice based on Masters and Johnson (such as that women should masturbate to discover their own orgasmic capacity) combined with more romanticized recommendations.

From a Puritan-Victorian ethic in which an educated woman at the turn of the century could believe that it was "more wholesome to sleep alone and avoid the temptation of too frequent intercourse," [7] we have come to believe that everyone has a right to the full enjoyment of sex. But while to many observers it seemed that there were notable changes in the national sex life since Kinsey, no one had measured the distance

[7] "A sex poll (1892–1920)." *Time,* October 1, 1973, p. 63.

we have traveled. That gap was closed in 1973, when Morton Hunt undertook an extensive national survey on sexual practices. Hunt found what many had suspected, that today premarital sex begins at an earlier age and is more frequent than in Kinsey's era. Over half of the college men interviewed had had intercourse before they were 17. About three-fourths of single women under 25 in Hunt's sample, compared with only one-third in Kinsey's, had had intercourse. Some 80 percent of young married women (ages 18 to 24) were not virgins at marriage, a significant increase from just over half of all wives, as reported by Kinsey. Hunt also found that the practice of oral sex is increasing, especially among the young. (Contrary to expectations, he also found that homosexuality has not become more prevalent since Kinsey's time.)

It would seem, then, that much has changed since Freud first proposed his revolutionary theories in human sexuality 80 years ago. And we need not rely solely on Kinsey's and Hunt's studies to tell us how much has changed: street clothes have become more varied, colorful, and revealing; bathings suits have become flimsier; sex is discussed fully and frankly on television; and films in legitimate theaters depict in full detail a great variety of sex acts. But, as we have already suggested, the change has not yet been completed. There is still a great deal of ignorance about sexual matters, as our high rates of illegitimacy and venereal disease indicate. Many of our sex laws reflect the religious attitudes that are still prevalent in our society. The Supreme Court struggles—on an almost annual basis—with defining pornography. (Its 1975 decision states that a work must meet "community standards" of decency—which at best leaves the issue unresolved.) And in a 1976 decision, the Supreme Court upheld the right of states to make homosexual acts (and, by implication, all acts of sodomy) between consenting adults illegal. Clearly, despite the general liberalization of our sexual practices, many of us still perceive certain aspects of our sexual behavior as social problems.

THE VARIETIES OF HUMAN SEXUALITY

One way to get a perspective on sexual norms in our society is to consider the fact that virtually every conceivable sexual activity and orientation have, at some time and place, to some degree, by at least some people, been socially acceptable. Premarital sex, sex only for the purpose of procreation, homosexuality, lifelong celibacy, adultery, monogamy, polygamy (more than one wife), polyandry (more than one husband)—each has been a behavior standard of some human community. Not even incest, which is the most widely proscribed sexual relationship, has been universally tabooed: it was institutionalized among royal families in some ancient cultures as a way to maintain the purity of the royal line. And in 1976 a government committee in Sweden recommended that all laws prohibiting incest be dropped, on the assumption that the social and genetic harm of incest had been exaggerated.[8]

Perhaps the most outstanding characteristic of human sexuality, then,

[8] *New York Times,* Section 4, March 7, 1976, p. 7.

is that its manifestations are extraordinarily varied. And the kinds of sexual behavior defined as appropriate or inappropriate vary from place to place and from time to time. For example, only a small minority (the United States among them) of the 190 contemporary societies studied by Ford and Beach prohibit sexual expression in children. The Trobriand Islanders encourage premarital sex as an important preparation for marriage; among the Ila-speaking peoples of Africa, boys and girls are permitted to play man and wife even before puberty;[9] and the Lepcha people of Asia believe that girls need sexual intercourse in order to mature.[10] Conversely, in many South American and Moslem societies, premarital chastity is highly regarded, particularly among women. A woman who is not a virgin upon marriage is likely to be shamed and ostracized.

Sexual attitudes in the United States have been shaped not only by the religious and economic influences described earlier, but also by a frontier tradition that places great emphasis on conformity to a masculine ideal. As a result, male homosexuals have been among the most harassed and despised people in our society. However, in most other societies—past and present—homosexuals have at least been tolerated and sometimes even respected. Male and female homosexuality was an accepted part of life in ancient Greece. Today, among some peoples in Africa and New Guinea, anal intercourse is a normal part of a young boy's life. Female as well as male homosexual practices are encouraged in northern Sumatra, where adolescents of each sex live in peer group residences until they are ready for marriage. During this period, all youngsters learn homosexual techniques from older adolescents of the same sex.[11] Interestingly enough, where homosexuality is considered a normal part of adolescent development, the transition to a heterosexual relationship in marriage is apparently not impeded.

Given the great variety of human sexual expression, there seems little doubt that human sexual behavior is learned. Being born male does not automatically produce the stereotypic "red-blooded American he-man," interested only in sports and women; being born female does not automatically produce a docile Moslem woman, comfortable with wearing a veil on her face. The attitudes of others, the acceptable role models available, rituals, schools, and eventually society as a whole all influence the kinds of sexual behaviors that one will find acceptable. Males and females in every society must *learn* what "turns them on"—the psychosexual stimuli to which they respond have far more to do with cultural expectations than with their biological sex. (See also Chapter 8.) As Gagnon and Henderson comment,

We assemble our sexuality beginning with gender identity, and we build upon that the activities that we come to think of as fitting to ourselves. Our belief in what is correct and proper results more from our social class,

[9] Clellan S. Ford and Frank A. Beach, *Patterns of Sexual Behavior*. New York: Harper & Row, 1951.
[10] Gagnon and Henderson, p. 14.
[11] Gagnon and Henderson, p. 11.

religion, style of family life, and concepts of masculinity and femininity than from the specifically sexual things that we learn.[12]

CLASSIFYING PROBLEMS IN HUMAN SEXUALITY

We have seen that sexual practices in other cultures have differed markedly from our own, and that our own sexual norms have evolved from our unique religious, economic, and cultural experiences. It will be helpful to keep these facts in mind as we consider the sexual practices that are regarded in our society as social problems.

DEFINING SEXUAL SOCIAL PROBLEMS

As we stated in Chapter 1, social problems are acts which depart from a norm or value to such an extent and in such a way that a significant number of people or a number of significant people feel that something should be done about them. The difficulty with applying this definition to sexual acts is that it is hard to say which norms are really operative or enforced. Even in Kinsey's time, there was a great difference between the purported norms of our society and people's actual behavior. Today, it has become even more difficult to define sexual variance or sex-related social problems. Many sexual behaviors that were once considered reprehensible are now believed by most people to be fairly, or even completely, acceptable. Not long ago, for example, cunnilingus and fellatio were considered wrong or immoral acts; today, the vast majority of young people have engaged in these acts. Until recently, masturbation was considered sinful, harmful to society, and unhealthy; today it is widely assumed that masturbation is not only normal but beneficial for the individual's sexual development.

Nevertheless, as we have already suggested, there are still some sex-related acts or conditions that are widely regarded as so variant as to be social problems: illegitimacy (discussed in Chapter 10), homosexuality, prostitution, and pornography are seen by many people as problems society should do something about. As have other writers, we have (in the previous edition of this book) used the term "deviance"—sexual behavior that does not conform to norms—in referring to such problems. But we now avoid this term whenever possible, because it implies a value judgment that there is a normal and therefore proper form of sexual expression, and also because it has acquired the same stigma as such terms as "degenerate," "perverted," or "sick." We prefer instead to refer to those sex-related acts or conditions which are perceived as social problems as sexual variance or more directly as sex-related social problems.

SEX CRIMES

One way to try to determine precisely what sexual matters are considered variant or social problems is to look at the legal system. Presumably, acts or conditions that depart extensively from social norms or values

[12] Gagnon and Henderson, p. 30.

will be declared illegal. Most sex laws in the United States take into account four elements in a sexual relationship: the degree of consent—banning forcible rape, for example; the nature of the object—restricting legitimate sex objects to human beings of the opposite sex, of a certain age, of an acceptable distance in kinship, and to the spouse; the nature of the sexual act—restricting behavior to certain practices in heterosexual intercourse; and the setting in which the behavior occurs—generally prohibiting public sexual activity.[13]

There are, however, many difficulties with using such laws to help define sex-related social problems. For one thing, according to the studies we have mentioned, substantial portions of the adolescent and adult population of this country are already violating these laws. Thus, some of these laws do not seem to be directly related to people's real sexual attitudes and behavior. In addition, many of these laws date back to the very beginning of United States history, when sexual norms were far different from what they are today. For example, the prohibitions against adultery which are on the books in almost all states date back to the seventeenth-century Puritans of Massachusetts Bay Colony, who made adultery a crime punishable by death. Other laws seem even more antiquated. As Katchadourian and Lunde point out, "Almost all sexual activity that may occur between husband and wife, with the exception of kissing, caressing, and vaginal intercourse, is defined as criminal in every state of the union." [14] It is not clear how such laws are related to contemporary sexual attitudes; they therefore seem to be of limited usefulness in helping determine what sex-related matters are social problems.

One final reason sex laws are unreliable indicators of sexual norms is that they vary from state to state. In Texas, for instance, two unmarried adults who have intercourse can be fined $500; in Rhode Island the penalty for the same behavior is $10, and in Arizona this behavior constitutes a felony with a potential sentence of up to three years' imprisonment. In many states, married women who engage in extramarital sex with single men would probably be charged with adultery, but married men who do the same with single women are more likely to be charged with fornication, which usually carries a lesser penalty and in some states is not a crime. Still other inequities show up in the standards used in different jurisdictions. Los Angeles, for example, which has the highest rate of forcible rape in the nation, defines almost any approach of a man to a woman who is a stranger for purposes of "sexual gratification" as rape.[15]

In short, because the laws are so inequitable and variable, because they proscribe even some forms of private behavior between consenting adults, and because differing standards are used in defining the same offense, the legal definitions of sexual social problems are unreliable as an analytical tool for sociological purposes.

[13] See Marshall B. Clinard, *Sociology of Deviant Behavior*. 4th ed. New York: Holt, Rinehart and Winston, 1974.

[14] Herant Katchadourian and Donald T. Lunde, *Fundamentals of Human Sexuality*. 2nd ed. New York: Holt, Rinehart and Winston, 1975.

[15] Duncan Chappell *et al.*, "Forcible rape: A comparative study of offenses known to the police in Boston and Los Angeles." In James M. Henslin, ed., *Studies in the Sociology of Sex*. Englewood Cliffs, N.J.: Prentice-Hall, 1971, p. 181.

A more useful classification of sex-related social problems is offered by Gagnon and Simon, who distinguish between three categories of sexual variance or problems. We will use our own labels for the three categories.

Tolerated Sex Variance. This category includes such acts as heterosexual oral-genital contact, masturbation, and premarital intercourse. These acts "are generally disapproved, but . . . either serve a socially useful purpose and/or occur so often among a population with such low social visibility that only a small number are ever actually sanctioned for engaging in [them]." [16] Such acts are minor problems at worst; they are behaviors that arouse little special interest or social pressure for their regulation. It is likely that as our society becomes more tolerant, these behaviors will become socially acceptable and in no way be regarded as social problems.

Asocial Sex Variance. This category includes incest, child molestation, rape, exhibitionism, and voyeurism. These acts are usually committed by one individual or, at most (as in gang rape), a small number of persons. While there are social influences on the incidence of such acts, on an individual basis these acts must be understood primarily within a psychological or social-psychological viewpoint (see Chapter 1). Persons who engage in these behaviors do not have a social structure that recruits, socializes, and provides social support for the behaviors. Major forms of asocial sex variance—incest, rape, and child molestation—elicit widespread, strong disapproval even among other lawbreakers.

Incest—sexual relations between persons so closely related that they are by law or custom forbidden to marry—is nearly universally prohibited. According to Weinberg,

Were incest tolerated and prevalent, each family would splinter off in a quasi-autonomous isolation which would disrupt the large society into disconnected social fragments and would result in a basic loss of societal cohesion. [17]

Weinberg found that where father-daughter incest occurs, the family is likely to be characterized by paternal dominance, with the father intimidating and controlling the other family members. When sibling incest occurs, the parents are not dominant and do not "restrain the siblings from mutual sex-play." In cases of mother-son incest, the family is characterized by maternal dominance, with the father either absent or extremely subservient. In any case, Weinberg found, incest confuses family roles and creates rivalries within the family. It also creates personal conflict within the involved child or children and disturbs even those family members who may be only subliminally aware of what is occurring.

Hunt, in his survey, found that incest in the United States occurs rarely. According to Hunt, however, if the definition of incest is broadened to include noncoital acts such as petting and sexual acts between

[16] John H. Gagnon and William Simon, *Sexual Deviance*. New York: Harper & Row, 1967, p. 8.
[17] S. Kirkson Weinberg, *Incest Behavior*. New York: Citadel Press, 1955.

relatives outside the nuclear family, then the incidence of incest is high. Hunt found that 14 percent of males and over 9 percent of females had had incestuous contacts with relatives (usually cousins). Well over half of these contacts, however, involved relatively isolated cases of petting between children or adolescents. Hunt also suggests that the common belief that incest occurs more frequently among families of low socio-economic status is erroneous. He found that incestuous acts were more common among higher socioeconomic levels. He attributes the higher reported rates of incest among lower socioeconomic groups to the fact that

the poor, the ignorant and the incompetent come to official attention, while people of higher socioeconomic status are either able to keep their incestuous acts hidden or, if discovered, to keep the discovery from becoming part of the official record.[18]

Child molestation in most societies, including our own, is deplored and feared, and results in humiliation and loss of status for the participating adult. Contrary to popular belief, heterosexual child molestation is far more common than homosexual child molestation. Nor is the child molester the stereotypical "dirty old man." The average age of the male heterosexual offenders studied by Gebhard and his colleagues [19] was 35; only one-sixth were over 50.

In the cases studied by Gebhard and his colleagues, most young girls who were molested knew their molesters. In Gebhard's words,

Contrary to general opinion and to parental fears, it seems that the immature female is more vulnerable to friends and acquaintances than to mythical strangers lurking in concealment.

Approximately 31 percent of the child molesters were married, almost as many were widowed or divorced; 40 percent had never married. In about 30 percent of the cases, alcohol was involved. These men were not physically dangerous, however; they did not use force, and seldom attempted coitus. They were, psychologically, apparently "unable to defer the gratification of their impulses." [20] (The role of alcohol in these cases is apparently to release inhibitions that otherwise would stand in the way of a person's accosting a child—see Chapter 3.)

Forcible rape—coercive heterosexual coitus with a woman of legal age—is the most common form of sexual aggression and assault, with about 60,000 cases reported annually and, according to various estimates, perhaps three and a half times as many unreported cases occurring. Our concern here is with some of the psychosocial factors involved in the commission of rape. (See Chapters 4 and 5 for a discussion of rape as violent crime, and Chapter 8 for further analysis of rape as a reflection of traditional male-female sex roles.)

Many studies have found that rapists are young and unmarried; some studies also suggest that a disproportionate number of convicted rapists

[18] Hunt, pp. 341, 343, 347.

[19] Paul H. Gebhard et al., "Child molestation." In Edward Sagarin and Donald E. J. MacNamara, eds., Problems of Sex Behavior. New York: Crowell, 1968.

[20] Gebhard et al., pp. 245, 247, 258.

are physically handicapped in some way.[21] Ostensibly, then, sexual deprivation is a key causative factor in rape. However, most analysts believe that the desire for sexual gratification is at most a secondary motive for rape. In this view, rape is an act of aggression or sadism in which a person engages in order to bolster a weak self-image and to feel powerful and omnipotent.[22]

Whether or not a person chooses rape as the means for such ego-bolstering seems to be related to his culture's views of sexuality and to its attitudes toward men and women. There are some societies in which rape does not exist. Among the Arapesh of New Guinea, for example, the masculine role is so non-aggressive and peaceful that rape is incomprehensible to them. Conversely, some societies have an incidence of rape that is higher even than that in the United States. For example, the Gussi tribe in Kenya has a rape rate at least five times higher than the United States. Men and women of the Gussi tribe traditionally regard each other as competitors, and women typically resist intercourse even with their husbands.[23]

In the United States, there are two opposing theories of the relationship of rape rates to the social climate. The first, suggested by Merton's theory of anomie (see Chapter 4), is that where heterosexual contact is valued, but where access to such contacts are restricted, the rape rate will be higher. According to this hypothesis, then, the more sexually permissive a society, the lower will be its rape rate. The alternate hypothesis holds that the forcible rape rate is higher when a relatively permissive sex ethic prevails. In this view, as Chappell and his colleagues put it,

A rejected male in a nonpermissive setting is more able to sustain his self-image by allegating that it is the setting itself that is responsible for any sexual setback he suffers. Women are too inhibited, church rules are too oppressive, parents too strict, or laws too stringent—any of these conditions may be used to "explain" an inability to achieve a desired sexual goal. In the permissive setting, the rejected male becomes more hard-pressed to reinterpret his rejection. We would argue that forcible rape represents a response arising out of the chaos of a beleaguered self-image.[24]

Chappell and his colleagues believe that even in a permissive society, there will still be many rejected men and many men who are inhibited from attaining sexual gratification in the usual ways. In their comparison study of rape rates in Los Angeles and Boston, they confirmed their hypothesis: rape rates were significantly higher in Los Angeles, a notably permissive city, than in Boston, which is traditionally nonpermissive.

Minor forms of a social sex variance are exhibitionism, the deliberate exposure of one's sex organs, and voyeurism, watching persons who are undressing or undressed or performing a sexual act. "Flashers" and "peeping Toms" may be somewhat annoying, but perhaps because they are not as threatening as the other forms in this category these behaviors have not received much analysis.

[21] See Chappell et al., p. 172.
[22] See Manfred S. Guttemacher, *Sex Offenses.* New York: Norton, 1951.
[23] Chappell et al., pp. 174–175.
[24] Chappell et al., pp. 175–176.

Structural Sex Variance. Behavior in this category is fairly well organized, participated in by substantial numbers of people, and involves several different roles and supportive social structures. Although supported and engaged in by large numbers of people, these behaviors do run counter to prevailing norms and legal statutes. Thus these acts lend themselves readily to sociological analysis. Three examples of structural sexual variance that we shall examine in some detail are homosexuality, prostitution, and pornography.

HOMOSEXUALITY

Homosexuality is a sexual preference for members of one's own sex. Some individuals are exclusively homosexual, others are predominantly heterosexual but under special circumstances, such as imprisonment, may engage in homosexual behavior, while still others have both homosexual and heterosexual experiences. Both males and females may be homosexuals; female homosexuals are usually referred to as lesbians. To date, a great deal more research has been done on male homosexuality than on lesbianism.

Homosexuality has alternately been regarded by society as a sin or as caused by some form of physical or mental disturbance. Not so long ago in American society it was generally considered so shameful and indecent that it could not be spoken of openly. As with other areas of sexuality, society has become more tolerant of open discussion of homosexuality in recent years. However, a great many misconceptions about it still prevail. A Harris poll found that 63 percent of Americans viewed homosexuals as "harmful to American life." [25]

It is difficult to determine with any accuracy the number of homosexuals in the United States. In the past, most estimates were based on Kinsey's studies. Kinsey found that about 4 percent of white males, and 2 percent of white females, are exclusively homosexual. He estimated that 37 percent of American males have some homosexual experience to the point of orgasm between adolescence and old age, and that 10 percent of American males have long periods of more or less exclusive homosexuality. However, because Kinsey had to make special efforts to locate and interview homosexuals, most experts believe that Kinsey's statistics are overestimates. Hunt found that if his own figures on those who considered themselves predominantly or exclusively homosexual were combined with those who considered themselves "equally heterosexual and homosexual," a little over 2 percent of males and 1 percent of females—half the proportions noted by Kinsey—could be classified as homosexual.[26]

Hunt himself believes that even these statistics are unreliable, because homosexuals are essentially inaccessible to conventional sampling techniques. One problem, of course, is that many homosexuals are secretive about their sexual preference, and may never come to the attention of

---

[25] Robert R. Bell, *Social Deviance*. Homewood, Ill.: Dorsey Press, 1971, p. 282.
[26] Hunt, pp. 309–310.

any statistics-gathering agency. For example, even though homosexuals are supposed to be barred from the armed forces—and efforts are made to find them prior to enlistment—studies have found that many homosexuals succeed in completing military service without being discovered.[27]

One of the most common misconceptions about homosexuals is that they are an easily identifiable group. The common stereotype of a male homosexual is of a person who is obviously effeminate in manner, dress, and speech, and who is likely to work in the creative arts. In reality, there is a wide divergence among homosexuals, and they can be found in any occupation, including such stereotypically "masculine" activities as sports. It has been estimated that only about 10 percent of all homosexuals are easily identifiable, conforming in appearance or manner to the stereotype. And many of these may do so only for a brief period, when they have first publicly acknowledged their homosexuality and feel compelled to act it out for a while.[28] Nor do homosexuals share any evident pattern of personality characteristics. Evelyn Hooker administered three common clinical projective tests to both homosexuals and heterosexuals. Experts who examined the results of the tests found that they did not distinguish reliably between homosexuals and heterosexuals.[29] Other psychologists administered similar tests to lesbians and heterosexuals, and also could find no personality differences between the two groups.[30]

The one thing which homosexuals have in common is their sexual preference and the social and psychological strains which this preference imposes in a society which powerfully disapproves of it. The ways in which they satisfy their desires and cope with the attendant problems vary—to some extent along socioeconomic lines.

One important distinction between homosexuals is how willing they are to "come out" and publicly proclaim their homosexuality. Some are completely open about it. These may be individuals with relatively low-status and/or low-visibility jobs, which they are in no danger of losing because of their homosexuality; they may work in fields where homosexuality is frequently taken for granted, such as the theater; or they may be the young who have not yet made family and career commitments, and who believe that their sexual needs are more important than jobs and social position. These may be the ones who have made the most definite commitment to the homosexual life. More than others, their social lives may revolve almost completely around their homosexuality—they are usually the ones, for example, who frequent "gay" bars. Others may come out for idealistic reasons—to confirm their identity publicly, to live truthfully, and in a small number of well-publicized cases, to change public opinion or challenge legal proscriptions. On the other

[27] Bell, p. 281.

[28] William Simon and John H. Gagnon, "Homosexuality: The formulation of a sociological perspective." *Journal of Health and Social Behavior* 8 (September 1967):177–185.

[29] See Evelyn Hooker, "The adjustment of the male overt homosexual." *Journal of Projective Technique* 21 (1957):18–31; and Evelyn Hooker, "Male homosexuality and the Rorschach." *Journal of Projective Techniques* 22 (1958):33–54.

[30] "Lesbians' life adjustments—same as straights." *Psychology Today,* December 1975.

hand, many overt homosexuals lead quite conventional stable lives, lives that are simply like homosexual counterparts to conventional heterosexual patterns. They have steady jobs, and a regular social life, which may center around groups of homosexual friends; they generally avoid public settings like bars.

Many homosexuals remain covert because they may be employed in positions, such as teaching, the ministry, or other professions, where discovery of their homosexuality would mean instant dismissal. Some may have married, for reasons of convenience or status, and may have children. These ties to the conventional life will influence where they go for homosexual contacts. These individuals are less likely to go to gay bars, where it is more difficult to remain anonymous. Instead, they are likely to frequent public toilets, known by homosexuals as "tearooms," or Turkish baths, where sexual encounters are strictly impersonal. Some men may stop at these places for a few minutes on the way home from work. They may not admit even to themselves that these encounters are homosexual, since they may make a distinction between whether they take an active or passive role in the exchange. It is likely that their wives are totally unaware of the situation.[31]

Some married homosexuals may pretend to enjoy intercourse with their wives. A few may be genuinely bisexual, enjoying the sex act with either male or female partners. But most are more comfortable in homosexual relationships, and have married for domestic stability, companionship, and respectability. In Belgium, Ross[32] studied several married couples where one of the partners was homosexual (including one lesbian wife). He found that all of the homosexuals had been aware, to varying extents, of their homosexual orientation before marriage, but most had had little actual experience with either sex before that time. Several had married at least in part as a vain attempt to end their sexual attraction to members of the same sex. Almost all of the wives were from relatively conservative if not puritanical backgrounds and in almost every case were ignorant of the partner's homosexuality at the time of marriage, and had remained so for long if not indefinite periods. Of those who did learn of it, very few were accepting. These marriages were characterized by infrequent sexual relations and a lack of sexual satisfaction for both partners, producing frustration, bitterness, and a sense of victimization in the heterosexual partner. However, almost all of the couples had decided against separation or divorce. Ross theorized that the desire to conform to social norms and sheer inertia—at least on the part of the wives, who seemed to have limited role opportunities outside marriage—were responsible for these couples' remaining together.

Some male homosexuals have many sexual partners over the course of a lifetime. Many, however, desire and seek stable relationships with one other male, and many are able to achieve this. A study by Paul Gebhard showed that 81 percent of his subjects achieved a deep emotional relationship with at least one other male for a relatively long

[31] Maurice Leznoff and William A. Westley, "The homosexual community." *Social Problems* 3 (April 1956):257–263.
[32] H. Laurence Ross, "Odd couples: Homosexuals in heterosexual marriages." *Sexual Behavior*, vol. 2, no. 7 (July 1972):42–49.

period of time.[33] Interestingly enough, these relationships often parallel some traditions and symbols of heterosexual marriages. Homosexuals may exchange rings, celebrate wedding anniversaries, and dream of raising a child. However, contrary to popular belief, it appears that roles within homosexual marriages are not clearly dichotomized into "masculine" and "feminine," or dominant and submissive.[34]

A special category of homosexuality is the situational—that is, homosexual activity which takes place in circumstances where heterosexual contact is virtually impossible. A great deal of such behavior occurs in prisons, some of it best characterized as rape.[35] According to Gagnon and Simon, however, homosexual rape in prisons is rare; it is most likely to occur in those institutions where custodial discipline is lax or where there is a transient population with different types of lawbreakers grouped together. Gagnon and Simon also found that homosexual behavior in prisons was not universal: only 30 to 45 percent of imprisoned men have homosexual contacts, generally because they need meaningful emotional relationships or because sexual prowess is an important part of their self-image.[36]

Homosexuality also tends to be relatively frequent in sex-segregated schools, mental hospitals, and military installations, when students, inmates, or military personnel are substantially cut off from contact with members of the opposite sex. Probably the majority of people who take part in homosexual acts in such settings do not continue them once they return to the outside world, but for some the pattern may become permanent.

Another form of situational, transitory homosexuality is practiced by certain lower-class delinquent youths, who engage in a limited form of homosexual prostitution with an adult male fellator. Reiss[37] found that many boys from the lowest socioeconomic stratum in large cities are taught this behavior and are encouraged in it by a delinquent peer group or gang, whose older members know how to locate potential clients. These encounters occur at places well known in the community, such as street corners, parks, public toilets, or certain movie houses. Not all lower-class boys will accept such relationships. There are several prerequisites for those who do: the boy must be a member of a group which accepts and encourages this behavior; the group must indoctrinate him into its practices; he enters such relationships strictly as a way to make money and never for the purpose of sexual gratification ("easy money," as one boy put it). Certain specific expectations govern the transaction

[33] Paul H. Gebhard et al., Sex Offenders. New York: Harper & Row, 1965, p. 347.
[34] Evelyn Hooker, "The homosexual community." In James O. Palmer and Michael J. Goldstein, eds., Perspectives in Psychopathology: Readings in Abnormal Psychology. New York: Oxford University Press, 1966.
[35] See, for example, Alan J. Davis, "Sexual assaults in the Philadelphia prison system." Trans-Action 6 (December 1968).
[36] John H. Gagnon and William Simon, Sexual Conduct. Chicago: Aldine, 1973, pp. 244–250.
[37] Albert J. Reiss, Jr., "The social integration of queers and peers." In Howard S. Becker, ed., The Other Side: Perspectives on Deviance. New York: Free Press, 1964, pp. 181–210.

itself: only oral-genital fellatio, with the adult client being the fellator, and no other sexual act, is permitted; the client must pay for the service; and no close or ongoing relationship should develop. The boy and/or his peer group will resort to violence if the adult does not conform to the established customs for such transactions. If the boy's behavior is within this pattern, he will not be defined by the peer group as a homosexual, and therefore he will not so define himself. Because they do not view themselves either as prostitutes or homosexuals, this is a transitory role for most boys involved in such transactions, and "simply another one of the activities which characterizes a rather versatile pattern of deviating acts," according to Reiss. The boys never become part of the homosexual community, and their adult clients are apparently not active members of that community either; they are likely to include secretly homosexual husbands.

In addition to the variety of behavior patterns among different individuals, the same individuals may deal with their homosexuality in different ways at different stages of their lives. The most important distinction here seems to lie in whether or not individuals recognize themselves as homosexuals, and how they react to that knowledge. Mary McIntosh [38] has noted that a major influence on how individuals deal with their homosexuality is society's attitude toward it. She suggests that homosexuality should be regarded as a social role, rather than as a condition or trait, because how it is expressed reflects social expectations. As we have already suggested, personality traits of homosexuals and heterosexuals are generally indistinguishable, and homosexuals can be found in all social strata and occupations. Yet society expects that all those who engage in any homosexual activity will share specific traits: that they will be exclusively or predominantly attracted to people of the same sex; that in personality and appearance, they will be effeminate if male and masculine if female; that all their relationships with members of the same sex will be sexually loaded; and that they will be attracted to and probably try to seduce younger people of the same sex. Such expectations inevitably influence the self-image of anyone who identifies as a homosexual, leading these individuals perhaps to assume that they should adopt some of these behaviors to conform to the homosexual "role" as defined by their society.

The phenomenon of "coming out"—defined by Simon and Gagnon as "that point in time when there is self-recognition by the individual of his identity as a homosexual and the first major exploration of the homosexual community" [39]—has been the subject of an important study by Barry Dank.[40] Dank found that most people did not make this identification for some time after they first became aware of homosexual desires in themselves. The average interval was six years, but it might be considerably longer. Usually this lag occurs because society has provided

[38] Mary McIntosh, "The homosexual role." *Social Problems,* vol. 16, no. 2 (Fall 1968):182–192.
[39] See Simon and Gagnon, "Homosexuality."
[40] Barry M. Dank, "Coming out in the gay world." *Psychiatry* 34 (March 1971): 180–197.

individuals with no conceptual meaning for the term "homosexual" which they can relate to themselves. As one of Dank's subjects said:

I really didn't know what a homosexual was. In the back of my mind, my definition of a homosexual or queer was someone who wore girls' clothes and women's shoes, 'cause my brother said this was so, and I knew I wasn't.

Or:

I had always thought of them as dirty old men that preyed on 10-, 11-, 12-year-old kids.

Consequently, these persons may carry on homosexual relationships for years while defending themselves by various mental expedients, and usually with some degree of self-rejection, from calling themselves homosexuals.

Generally it is through contact with admitted homosexuals that coming out finally takes place. Gay bars, tearooms, YMCAs, and such one-sex environments as prisons, mental hospitals, the military, and some schools, are frequent settings for this experience. Occasionally, a person comes out as a result of reading, rather than through interpersonal contact, but this is the exception. In either case, the significant fact is that individuals encounter a concept of the homosexual with which they can identify, unlike the highly negative concept usually instilled in them by "straight" society. For nearly all homosexuals, this discovery comes as a great relief, as one of Dank's subjects described:

I knew that there were homosexuals, queers and what not; I had read some books, and I was resigned to the fact that I was a foul, dirty person, but I wasn't actually calling myself a homosexual yet. . . . The time I really caught myself coming out is the time I walked into this bar and saw a whole crowd of groovy, groovy guys. And I said to myself, there was the realization, that not all gay men are dirty old men or idiots, silly queens, but there are some just normal-looking and acting people, as far as I could see. I saw gay society and I said, "Wow, I'm home."

In some ways, the most troubled homosexuals are those whom Dank calls the "closet queens"—the persons with homosexual desires and perhaps homosexual activities, who never make the contacts which will enable them to accept themselves as homosexuals.

In view of the increasingly free circulation of non-negative information about homosexuality, and of the increasing visibility of the homosexual community, Dank hypothesized that a larger number of homosexuals than in the past will be enabled to identify themselves as homosexuals, and to do so at an earlier age. This may make it easier for homosexuality to be regarded as a way of life rather than as a crime or a mental illness, and may in turn make possible greater integration of homosexuals into the general society.

People have always wondered what causes someone to be a homosexual, but so far no one has come up with definite answers. Some authorities have posited that it is biologically determined, and studies have been done with identical twins that suggest there may be a genetic, or inherited hormonal, determinant. Schlegel, for example, found that in 95 percent of his identical twin pairs, both subjects were homosexuals, while among fraternal twins the figure was only 5 percent.[41] However, the biological studies have in general been inconclusive, and the twin studies are confused by environmental factors. To date, there is no strong evidence that homosexuality is biologically determined—although, according to Evelyn Hooker, a large proportion of homosexuals themselves believe that this is the case.[42]

More important than biological factors, probably, is the social environment in which an individual grows up. As we have suggested, the crucial thing about human sexual behavior is that it is learned. Human beings may or may not have a basic need for sex, but the manner in which it is expressed is shaped by learning experiences. Psychiatrists and psychologists, however, have not been particularly successful in identifying the early experiences which result in homosexuality. Certain pathological situations do seem to appear with significant frequency in the case histories of homosexuals: the family drama often includes a dominant or seductive mother, and a weak, detached, or overly critical father, factors which prevent the male child from identifying with the masculine role. Yet no clear explanation has yet been brought forward as to why homosexuality develops only in some, and not in all, children reared under these conditions, and in fact many researchers question the entire notion that homosexuality is caused by a pathological family situation. While some personality problems appear to many observers to be shared by many homosexuals, it is arguable, and homosexuals themselves often make this point, that many of these are due mainly to excessive societal pressures on them to conform to arbitrary norms. That is, it is society's stigmatizing of homosexuals which causes them to develop certain traits sometimes identified with homosexuality; these traits are not the cause of their becoming homosexuals.[43]

Psychology has had little success in changing the sexual orientation or life style of homosexuals, and in December 1973 the American Psychiatric Association voted to remove homosexuality from the list of mental disorders in its diagnostic manual. Few homosexuals desire to become heterosexual, and in fact few sought counseling from traditional therapists, since the professional bias tended to view the problem as a mental illness affecting sexual behavior. Many psychologists now emphasize helping troubled homosexuals to accept themselves and their life style with minimal conflict, instead of attempting to "cure" them.

The particular concern of the sociologist is not so much with the psychology of the homosexual as it is with homosexuality as a life style or career, to be studied like any other life style. In this study, the question of original causes is only one element. The social forces which influence the development of the homosexual life style at all its stages are equally important, as is the reciprocal influence of the homosexual presence on

[41] W. S. Schlegel, "Die konstitutionsbiologischen Grundlagen der Homosexualitat." *Zeitschrift für menschliche Verebung. Konstitutionslehre* 36 (1962):341–346. See also F. J. Kallmann, "Twin and sibling study of overt male homosexuality." *American Journal of Human Genetics* 4 (1952):136–146.
[42] See Hooker, "The homosexual community."
[43] See M. T. Saghir *et al.,* "Homosexuality: III. Psychiatric disorders and disability in the male homosexual." *American Journal of Psychiatry* 126:1079–1086.

society in general. To learn something about these influences, we shall look more closely at some aspects of the homosexual subculture.

Like many other groups, homosexuals have certain subcultural features, in that they share significant activities, and possess group norms and a special argot.

SUBCULTURAL
ASPECTS OF
HOMOSEXUALITY

The homosexual subculture exists in most large cities in the United States. In these cities, certain neighborhoods, streets, or buildings have large homosexual populations. According to Hooker, "Although homosexuals as a total group do not have a bounded territorial base, they are, nevertheless, not randomly distributed throughout the city, nor are the facilities or institutions which provide needed services and function as focal gathering places." [44] These facilities include certain parks, public restrooms, steam or bath houses, gyms, and, perhaps most important, the gay bar.

One segment of the homosexual subculture frequents the public restroom or "tearoom" in which impersonal sex is readily available. Humphreys [45] believes that the accessibility, invisibility, variety, and impersonality of the tearooms make sexual encounters there particularly attractive to covert male homosexuals. These places are in locations accessible to men before and after work and during the lunch hour, while other places for casual sex, such as bars and baths, [46] are usually open only at night and may be in distant neighborhoods; further, they would require more time spent in socializing, and could not be as readily fitted into a work-and-commuting schedule. In addition, public restrooms provide individuals with an alibi should they be found there; there is a constantly changing population, providing a variety of potential sexual partners; and sex without relationship or emotional involvement is appealing to the man who is maintaining a heterosexual life style.

The gay bar provides a much more significant gathering place for the homosexual community. Once clandestine establishments, gay bars are no longer likely to be targets of police harassment; they have proliferated throughout the country, and now number about 4,000. [47] Because the homosexual seeking new contacts will often patronize several bars in a single evening, the bars are conveniently clustered in certain areas. This may influence residential patterns, or it may be a response to such patterns. The bars, and what they tell about the neighborhood, are especially useful to homosexuals who have just arrived in a new city; they make it easy and relatively safe for them to find new friends and partners. One of the most significant functions of the gay bar, however, is that it provides a setting for coming out, for socializing new members into the subculture. Many individuals come out in gay bars, because that is where they are able to observe and meet homosexuals with whom they can identify.

[44] See Hooker, "The homosexual community."
[45] Laud Humphreys, *Tearoom Trade: Impersonal Sex in Public Places.* Chicago: Aldine, 1975.
[46] See Martin S. Weinberg and Colin J. Williams, "Gay baths and the social organization of impersonal sex." *Social Problems,* vol. 23, no. 2 (December 1975): 124–136.
[47] "Gays on the march." *Time,* September 8, 1975, p. 33.

The homosexual subculture is becoming increasingly politicized. Homosexual organizations probe politicians' stances on homosexual rights and participate in mass "gay pride" demonstrations which reject the notion that homosexuality is an illness or an aberration, and demand an end to discrimination against gay people.
Howard Petrick/Nancy Palmer Photo Agency

Furthermore, the subculture provides homosexuals with a language they can use to communicate with and recognize one another. A homosexual who is "cruising," or looking for a sexual partner, can tell by fairly standardized behavioral gestures which of the men he meets are interested in a pickup, and even what kind of sexual activity they are willing to engage in. Since the danger of detection and arrest is never far from the homosexual in a public place, knowledge of such in-group language is important to him if he wishes to make any contacts at all.[48]

One of the most important functions of the homosexual subculture is to provide its members with a way of understanding and accepting their sexual orientation. This function is performed not only by the gay bar and similar meeting places, but also by some homosexual organizations, which, particularly in recent years, are becoming increasingly vocal. Among the best known of these groups are the Mattachine Society, founded in the early 1950s, and the newer National Gay Task Force. These groups work to abolish laws which discriminate against homosexuals, and to persuade homosexuals themselves and society in general that there is nothing shameful or harmful about being homosexual.

LESBIANISM

It is even harder to obtain accurate estimates of the number of lesbians in the United States than it is of the number of male homosexuals. For many reasons, lesbians are less conspicuous. They are generally less publicly active and have fewer sex partners than male homosexuals—less likely to cruise or to frequent bars—and hence less likely to be picked up by the police. And while some male homosexuals can be

[48] Bell, p. 274.

identified by their appearance as homosexuals, very few lesbians would strike an observer as in any way different from heterosexual females.

In addition, social custom makes it easier to conceal female than male homosexuality. A woman who is unmarried or who does not go out with men is usually assumed to be simply uninterested in, or afraid of, sex, rather than suspected of lesbianism. Also, it is considered more acceptable for two women to share an apartment, or kiss or touch in public, than it is for men.

Finally, the laws against homosexuality are usually concerned primarily with male actions. As Bell points out, the legal controls over sexual behavior have generally been developed by men, and men have rarely seen female homosexuality as a serious threat.[49] This, plus the aforementioned tendency of lesbians to be less publicly active than their male counterparts, has usually kept the police from paying very much attention to them, so that they seldom appear in arrest records and official statistics.

It is generally assumed that the total number of lesbians is lower than that of male homosexuals, but for the reasons given above it is hard to be sure. Kinsey estimated that about 2 percent of American women were exclusively homosexual, while in Hunt's survey 2 percent of single women and "an insignificant fraction of 1 percent" of married women were predominantly or exclusively homosexual. Hunt also found, however, that 9 percent of married women and 15 percent of single women reported at least one homosexual experience.[50]

While female homosexuals are not all alike any more than male homosexuals are, there are some general differences between the ways in which male and female homosexuals manage their homosexuality. Many of these differences appear to arise from the differing socialization of males and females in general. Homosexuals, as much as heterosexuals, are affected by society's expectations about the kind of behavior that is appropriate to each sex. Well before a girl begins to experience homosexual tendencies, she is absorbing society's assumptions about how females should act—for example, that they should be less aggressive and that sex is permissible only as part of a lasting emotional relationship.

Further, sexual experience, of whatever sort, usually begins later for females than for males. A boy is likely to have sexual experience to the point of orgasm—usually by masturbation—relatively early in adolescence, while the corresponding experience for a girl is likely to come late in adolescence or early in adulthood. (At least this has been so in the past—today the pattern may be changing.) Thus it is likely that a girl learns to think in terms of emotional attachment and permanent love relationship before she develops any strong commitment to sexuality; and when that commitment appears, whether heterosexual or homosexual, it is fitted into the total "love" context. For boys, with their earlier experience, sex is apt to remain much more an independent and autonomous drive, possibly but not necessarily linked with love. Thus, for most of the lesbians studied by Gagnon and Simon, the first actual

[49] Bell, p. 288.
[50] Hunt, pp. 311–312.

sexual experience came at a late stage of an intense emotional involve-ment.[51]

These developmental and socialization differences underlie many of the subsequent behavioral differences between male and female homo-sexuals. The lesser sexual activity of the lesbian, for example, has simply paralleled the behavior of women in general in our society. Lesbians typically, though not always, come out at a later age than male homo-sexuals. When a lesbian does come out, she usually looks for one partner and remains with her as long as the relationship is a satisfying one. When she is between partners, she is less likely than the male to look for "one-night stands" as a means of satisfying purely sexual needs. As a result, she is less likely to frequent the gay bars and other gathering places which are so important to the male homosexual.

A lesbian subculture does exist, particularly in large cities, but its function differs somewhat from that of the male homosexual subculture. For women, the gay bar is less a source of pickups and more specifically a means of socialization into the homosexual community. The subculture may also serve a disinhibiting function, overcoming some of the sexual-repression training of childhood, and teaching the woman how to express her sexuality more freely and directly. But probably its major contribu-tion is as a locus of companionship, a setting in which the lesbian can relax and be open with friends from whom she need not conceal what she is.[52]

Just as the stereotype of the male homosexual includes effeminacy, so that of the lesbian includes masculinity. Actually, it appears that "male" and "female" roles are seldom sharply defined in lesbian rela-tionships. There are masculine, or so-called "butch," lesbians, but they seem to be the exception. Like her male counterpart, the lesbian who has newly come out may feel a need to act out her variant role for a time by adopting distinctive behavior, in order to redefine her identity. How-ever, in the case of the lesbian, there may be another and quite different reason for the adoption of some masculine characteristics: as an unmar-ried, self-dependent woman she frequently has to shoulder the kind of responsibilities which in many families or households would fall to the male. It is largely because these are socially defined as male functions that a woman appears masculine in exercising them.

A special category of female homosexuality is that found in prisons. Rose Giallombardo, in her study of social organization in a women's prison,[53] found that the prisoners engaged widely in homosexual activity, although most of them maintained that it was legitimate to do so only because heterosexual contacts were unavailable. The lesbian—who ac-tually preferred homosexual relationships—was looked down on and regarded as sick. Perhaps because of this basic commitment to hetero-sexuality, the masculine-feminine roles were much more sharply defined in prison relationships than in outside relationships. Both in the homo-sexual "marriage" and in the more casual, exploitative relationships, one

---

[51] Gagnon and Simon, *Sexual Conduct,* pp. 176–216.
[52] For a fuller discussion of the lesbian subculture, see Bell, p. 294.
[53] Rose Giallombardo, "Social roles in a prison for women." *Social Problems* 13 (Winter 1966):266–288.

partner consistently assumed the male role. Such partners, known as "stud broads" or "daddies," were regarded as fulfilling a difficult function, and were accorded considerable prestige in inmate society. Homosexuality was so widespread, and regarded as so natural an adjustment to prison circumstances, that the "square" who abstained from it was pitied and even ostracized, or strongly pressured to conform. She was less likely than the male prisoner, however, to be forced into homosexuality by violent assault.

Gagnon and Simon found that women in prison tended to form family-like groupings. They attributed this tendency to the need of these women to give some order and security to their lives. They concluded that

a minor part of the overt female homosexual contacts may arise from deprivation of sexuality, but the primary source is the lack of emotionally satisfying relationships with members of the opposite sex and the desire to create the basis for a community of relationships that are stable and predictable.[54]

Like the free lesbian, the female homosexual in prison seems to be adapting a traditionally feminine socialization pattern to unusual conditions. As a rule she returns to heterosexual activity once she is free to do so.

Research on lesbianism has been especially scant, and much of what is known about it is based on data from a limited number of subjects, plus what might be called at best "educated speculation." As with most varieties of sexual behavior, further study is much needed.

SOCIAL CONTROL

In recent years there has been a growing debate over how homosexuals should be dealt with. To date, through its laws, various employment policies, and informally, society has taken a repressive approach. In most of the United States, homosexual behavior is illegal, both in public and in private. In some states, penalties range from ten years in jail to life imprisonment. As yet, only Colorado, Connecticut, Delaware, Hawaii, Illinois, North Dakota, Arkansas, Ohio, Oregon, California, New Mexico, Maine, and Washington do not restrict private sexual acts between consenting adults. Obviously, laws against homosexual behavior are difficult to enforce in cases of private encounters between two consenting individuals, for in such cases no complaint will be lodged. In general, homosexuals who are arrested are those who have been cruising or soliciting in public places.

Today, particularly as homophile organizations become more militant and politically oriented, restrictive laws are coming under attack as violating constitutional rights and attempting to legislate private morality. The justification usually given by those who support restrictive laws is that they are necessary to protect young boys from seduction, and that legalizing homosexual behavior will encourage more people to express any homosexual tendencies they would otherwise suppress. Against this must be set the loss to society when homosexuals are legally or informally banned because of their sexual preference from pursuing certain

[54] Gagnon and Simon, *Sexual Conduct*, p. 254.

careers, and the cost of the personal suffering imposed on them and their families by society's moral rejection.

In 1957, in England, the Wolfenden Committee released a report on homosexuality which urged that homosexual behavior in private between consenting adults be legalized. The committee found that

the law itself probably makes little difference to the amount of homosexuality which actually occurs; whatever the law may be, there will always be strong social forces opposed to homosexual behavior. . . . There is no valid reason for supposing that any considerable number of conversions would follow the change in law.[55]

The committee also found that there is no evidence that homosexuals who start with adult partners will at any stage of their life attempt to seduce young boys. In 1967, the British Parliament adopted a law incorporating the recommendations of the Wolfenden Committee.

In the United States, legal restrictions against homosexuals have not been lessened, except in the few states just mentioned; in fact, in recent years some states have increased the penalties for homosexual behavior. Georgia recently broadened its sodomy law to include lesbian sexual relationships.[56] And the March 1976 decision of the United States Supreme Court, declining to hear arguments on a lower court ruling, in effect held that states may prosecute and imprison people committing private homosexual acts even when both parties are consenting adults. While the Supreme Court action did not require states to reinstate sodomy prohibitions or to enact them, it was seen as reducing pressure on states to repeal such laws, and as slowing the movement for homosexual rights in employment, housing, and other areas.

Many experts, however, urge liberalization. In its 1969 report, the National Institute of Mental Health's Task Force on Homosexuality recommended that homosexual behavior between consenting adults be legalized. As did the Wolfenden Committee, the task force found that these laws do not have their intended effect of preventing homosexual behavior, and that instead they may contribute to the mental health problems of many homosexuals. The task force also recommended that the employment policies of some government agencies, in which homosexuality is a ground for barring from hiring or for instant dismissal, be changed. The usual justification for these policies is that a homosexual in a high position is subject to blackmail and is thus a security risk. The task force noted that this would not be the case if the laws against homosexuality were changed, and that these regulations also have the effect of causing mental stress in homosexuals and blocking their hopes for careers.

Some careers, noticeably medicine, law, teaching, and the military, have been virtually out of the question for acknowledged homosexuals, though medical and law schools are beginning to accept homosexual applicants. According to Williams and Weinberg, 2,000 to 3,000 persons

[55] *Report of the Committee on Homosexual Offenses and Prostitution* (The Wolfenden Report), par. 58, 1957. The American edition of this report is published by Stein and Day, New York.
[56] *Time,* September 8, 1975, p. 35.

discovered to be homosexuals or to participate in homosexual acts are separated from the armed forces annually, usually with an "undesirable" discharge, which does not entitle them to certain benefits and may deter subsequent employers or otherwise handicap their civilian lives.[57] Homosexuals often have difficulty obtaining insurance, because they may be considered insurance risks; they also can be evicted from privately owned housing, and are usually unable to obtain security clearances in either government or industry, for fear of blackmail.

Some recent court decisions have upheld the rights of homosexual teachers, and a few school boards, including those of the District of Columbia and San Francisco, prohibit discrimination against homosexuals in hiring. Some corporations have also announced an antidiscrimination hiring policy, and in July the Federal Civil Service Commission reversed its previous position that homosexuals were unfit for public service.

Nowhere is homosexuality itself a crime; only certain acts, usually referred to as sodomy and including both oral-genital and anal-genital contact, are defined as crimes, and these laws have been used primarily against male homosexuals. In August 1973 the American Bar Association called for repeal of all state laws defining any form of private noncommercial sex between consenting adults as criminal.[58] Fisher notes that very few nations, Russia and China among them, join the United States in punishing homosexual acts, and that numerous Western nations, including Italy, Mexico, Switzerland, Great Britain, and Canada, do not include private homosexual acts between consenting adults in their penal codes.[59]

PROSTITUTION

Prostitution can be defined as sexual intercourse on a promiscuous and mercenary basis, with no emotional attachment. Prostitutes sell sexual favors, to those who will pay, as a way of making a living. Most prostitutes are females, catering to male clients; there is also a smaller number of male homosexual prostitutes.[60]

Prostitution has existed in almost every society since the dawn of history—it is sometimes referred to as "the oldest profession"—but its place and the prevailing attitudes toward it have varied. In early societies it often served religious functions; groups of prostitutes might be attached to the temples, and respectable women might "serve the god" in this way during some part of their lives. Occasionally secularized prostitution has been legitimized—with a certain amount of reluctance—as it is today, for example, in some parts of Nevada. The usual rationale for

[57] Colin J. Williams and Martin S. Weinberg, *Homosexuals and the Military: A Study of Less Than Honorable Discharge.* New York: Harper & Row, 1971.

[58] Sandra Stencel, "Homosexual legal rights." *Editorial Research Reports,* no. 10 (March 8, 1974):181–200.

[59] Peter Fisher, *The Gay Mystique: The Myth and Reality of Male Homosexuals.* Briarcliff Manor, N.Y.: Stein and Day, 1972, p. 128.

[60] See, for example, David J. Pittman. "The male house of prostitution." *Trans-Action* 8 (March–April 1971):21–27.

Shown here is a legal house of prostitution in Nevada. Certain areas of Nevada are the only places in the United States where prostitution has been legalized.
Marvin Newman/Woodfin Camp & Associates

this has been that there are going to be prostitutes, and men are going to patronize them, so it is better to have the practice out in the open where some supervision can be exercised. More often, especially in the past century or so, prostitution has been banned—with greater or lesser efforts at enforcement of the ban—and the prostitute has been regarded as a "fallen woman," degraded and disreputable. Late Victorian ideals of womanhood were particularly conducive to this view, for when "nice" women were expected to regard sex as a disagreeable duty, the woman who knew too much about it, practiced it often, and even prepared to enjoy it was necessarily suspect, debased, and unwomanly. Today the prostitute is still looked down on, but less for her sexual proficiency and more for her exploitative, loveless use of it.

It is difficult to estimate the number of prostitutes in the United States today, particularly because many of them have part-time or full-time legitimate jobs which serve to conceal their activities as prostitutes.

Clinard has estimated that there are about 275,000 women in America today whose full-time occupation is prostitution.[61]

Prostitutes do not constitute a homogeneous category. There are several fairly well defined professional levels among them, with typical differences in education, fees, methods of attracting customers, and types of customers served. Fees for services vary not only according to the "class" of the prostitute, but also according to the community or neighborhood, and such other factors as inflation.

The aristocrat among prostitutes is the *call girl*. She is the best educated, best dressed and most attractive, and may often do part-time work as a model or actress. Call girls never solicit; all their clients come through personal references and arrangements are usually made by telephone. Call girls are usually paid $50 for an evening, but may receive $100 or more, and the evening may include dinner at an expensive restaurant. Their clients, predictably, come from the upper-middle and upper classes. The call girl considers herself totally distinct from other prostitutes, and in fact will not use the word prostitute to refer to herself at all.

Hustlers are similar to call girls in that they are attractive and place great value on the status symbols, such as good clothes, which separate them from other types of prostitutes. Unlike call girls, however, hustlers solicit directly, working from night clubs and bars, and they are paid less, getting about $25 for "turning a trick," or performing sexual intercourse. Unlike call girls, they may have several clients per night.

A *house girl* works in a brothel, or house of prostitution; she is in the position of employee to the madam who runs the house. She must accept any client whom the madam assigns to her, and is allowed to keep half of the $20 or more fee for each trick.

Somewhat looked down upon by all other prostitutes is the *streetwalker*. She solicits customers wherever she can find them, and charges about $20 a trick. In small towns, under highly competitive conditions, or if she is desperate, a girl may charge less.

Prostitutes at these various levels have little to do with each other; they work in different places and attract different clients. The only movement between the groups, generally, is downward; when a call girl begins to lose her attractiveness and is less in demand, she may be forced to solicit directly, while hustlers and house girls may eventually be reduced to walking the streets.

A recent mode in prostitution is the massage parlor, which in recent years has become a national phenomenon. In these business establishments a man can pay to be stimulated to ejaculation, a procedure known as a "local." More extensive services are also available. Velarde and Warlick[62] studied owners, masseuses, and customers in a suburban West Coast community. Fees ranged from $10 to $15 for an hour's massage, although the plusher places charged more. In addition, there was usually an extra fee or tip to the girl; the more services she performed, the higher was the extra fee. Virtually all of the girls were young and unskilled, and had taken this job as a means of earning money. They had

[61] See Clinard.
[62] Albert J. Velarde and Mark Warlick, "Massage parlors: The sensuality business." *Society,* vol. 11, no. 1 (November–December 1973):63–74.

to become licensed masseuses first, and were instructed by the owners in the local solicitation laws, which make it illegal for the girl to solicit. The girl had to become expert in getting the customer to solicit her services and in detecting undercover policemen.

Velarde and Warlick found few typical characteristics among masseuses. Many, however, had a low opinion of other masseuses and rationalized extensively to avoid defining themselves as prostitutes. Most were either married or had boyfriends, and apparently none were lesbians. There was a high rate of employee turnover due to conflicts with the owners, as the girls went to other parlors in search of a better, less exploitative, boss. Most customers were white males over 35, middle-class businessmen. A second category consisted of transients such as traveling salesmen, men new to the area, or younger married men who were having marital problems. A third category consisted of men who were physically or mentally unattractive, men with deformities, or men seeking debasing treatment along with sex.

Sociologists have raised the question of what function or functions does prostitution perform. This inquiry really has two facets: first, why prostitution as an institution has persisted, which encompasses the question of why men frequent prostitutes; and, second, why individual women become prostitutes.

REASONS FOR PROSTITUTION

Prostitution as Socially Functional. The classic study of the causes of prostitution as an institution was done by Kingsley Davis in 1937. He related prostitution to several fundamental aspects of human physical nature and of society. First, unlike most female animals, which have well-defined periods of fertility that correspond to sexual responsiveness, human females can be sexually receptive at all times. Second, a relatively long period of time is required to bring up and socialize human young. Given these facts, it is imperative for society to find a way to control the sex drive and to make it compatible with the nurture of children. Otherwise, society could not perpetuate itself. As Davis puts it, "Erotic gratification is made dependent on, and subservient to, certain cooperative performances inherently necessary to societal continuity." [63]

Most human societies accomplish this control of the sex drive primarily through the device of the family unit, making sexual gratification permissible chiefly within the family, in which the young are brought up. Sexual expression which contributes to the family's existence or cohesion is approved and recommended; in proportion with its failure to do so, it is disapproved. This suggests why commercial prostitution has been so universally condemned, for prostitution implies that sexual gratification can be for pleasure alone, unrelated to socially functional ends. Sex that is purely mercenary and impersonal is a challenge to the foundation of the family, on which society depends; thus society condemns prostitution.

The very features of prostitution which are contrary to the stated values and norms of society and make it universally condemned, how-

[63] Kingsley Davis, "The sociology of prostitution." *American Sociology Review* (October 1937):746.

ever—its mercenary and impersonal nature—also, paradoxically, make it functional. Many individuals feel unable to satisfy their sexual needs within the family structure. Not only do unmarried men and widowers have no legally recognized outlet in this framework, but some married men want more (or more varied) sexual satisfaction than their wives want to or can supply. Others, such as members of the armed forces, or salesmen whose work entails much traveling, may be absent from their families for extended periods of time. Such men may be unable or unwilling, because of possible complications, to set up a permanent liaison with any one woman, and the brief, impersonal, non-obligating relationship with a prostitute fulfills their immediate needs. There are those, too, who feel a desire for unconventional forms of sexual activity —sadomasochistic practices, for example—which they hesitate to reveal to their wives or friends, or who suffer from physical deformities which, rightly or wrongly, lead them to suppose that the only kind of sex they can get is that which they can pay for. For such men, anonymity is highly valuable. A prostitute is quickly available, she is knowledgeable enough to provide a variety of sexual satisfactions, and when the business is done, she can be paid off and forgotten. Emotional complications and possible pregnancy are her concern, not the customer's. Even in a society which unofficially countenances more or less permanent extramarital affairs, as ours does, the prostitute seems to fulfill a common need.

Therefore, prostitution has endured. According to Davis, the only society in which it could conceivably disappear would be one of complete sexual permissiveness. Such a society is highly unlikely, however, because total sexual freedom could spell the demise of the family, making it virtually impossible to bring up the young. Prostitution is therefore less of a threat to a society than the conditions which would eliminate it. In any case, Davis points out that even a totally permissive society could not eliminate prostitution unless all desires were complementary. Since there will always be an unequal distribution of attractiveness and desirability, some people will always desire others who do not return their interest. The ones less favored would be driven to try to purchase the sexual favors of others.

Davis, then, concludes that prostitution will never entirely disappear. Its rate, however—that is, the extent to which it exists—varies according to the particular sexual norms of a society at any given time. In a relatively permissive society, when people can find sexual gratification fairly easily, prostitution will be less prevalent than in a more strictly regulated atmosphere—and, in fact, in our own society, which has become more permissive, young people frequent prostitutes far less frequently than young people have in the past.[64] But because no society can ever be totally sexually permissive, and because desires will never be completely complementary, prostitution will continue to occur.

Why Women Become Prostitutes. Society looks with disfavor on prostitution and considers it an unacceptable and degrading occupation. Why, then, do women become prostitutes? It is usually assumed that because of society's disapproval, to ask why an individual becomes a prostitute is

[64] Hunt, p. 144.

a different type of question than to ask, for example, why a woman becomes a journalist. Robert Bell has questioned this assumption, suggesting that the answers to the two questions may not be so different, and that more attention should be given to some of the answers which prostitutes themselves give when asked why they go into their line of work. If good pay, association with glamorous people, and the chance to marry a client are acceptable reasons for becoming an administrator, why should they not be so for becoming a prostitute? And Kingsley Davis has suggested that perhaps the truly puzzling question is why more women do not become prostitutes. He asks why so many women stick with tedious jobs as secretaries or maids or waitresses, when they could make more money in less time as prostitutes. Evidently society's norms against prostitution work very strongly for most women.

Some studies approach the question psychologically. Such studies really consider two things—the unique life history and psyche of an individual, to see what factors might predispose her to become a prostitute; and the psychological defenses or mechanisms which she develops after becoming a prostitute to maintain an acceptable self-image in the face of society's disapproval.

One study which touches on both these questions is that of Jackman, O'Toole, and Geis.[65] Fifteen prostitutes, all streetwalkers, were interviewed, and certain common background characteristics were identified. In general, the women were alienated from their parents and had usually had a total break with their fathers, toward whom they expressed hostility. Before becoming prostitutes, they had felt themselves to be isolated in an urban society, without real friends. Similar findings are reported by Nanette Davis, in another study of streetwalkers. Most of her subjects had felt since early childhood that they were considered "bad" or "slow" or "troublemakers" or "different" by their families and teachers.[66] Davis concluded that this early negative informal labeling contributed to the later emergence of an identity as a prostitute.

As to how an individual woman manages to maintain her self-respect once she becomes a prostitute, Jackman and his co-workers found that one mechanism commonly adopted was to claim that prostitutes are no more immoral than anyone else, but are simply less hypocritical. As evidence, the girls can point to their customers, often respected men cheating on their wives. They also say that society only pretends to scorn prostitutes, whereas in reality it needs them and depends on them. Another common defense is to exaggerate other values, such as the financial rewards of prostitution.

Not all of Jackman's subjects adopted the same defense. The prostitutes had different "reference group orientations"—that is, different groups with whom they identified and whose standards they adopted. The first of these reference groups was what the authors called the "criminal world contraculture"—pimps, other prostitutes, racketeers, and

<hr/>

[65] Norman R. Jackman, Richard O'Toole, and Gilbert Geis, "The self-image of the prostitute." *The Sociological Quarterly* 4 (April 1963):150–161.
[66] Nanette J. Davis, "The prostitute: Developing a deviant identity." In James M. Henslin, ed., *Studies in the Sociology of Sex.* Englewood Cliffs, N.J.: Prentice-Hall (ACC), 1971.

hustlers. By identifying with this group, a prostitute could share its contempt for the rest of society as hopelessly square, hypocritical, and dead, and could place supreme value on money, flashy possessions, and a swinging nightlife.

Other prostitutes manifested a "dual world" reference group orientation; they separated their work from the rest of their lives, did not associate much with other prostitutes, professed solid middle-class values, identified strongly with their families, and were eager to be considered good mothers. Unlike prostitutes oriented toward the criminal world contraculture, who often said they enjoyed sex, those in the second group dissociated themselves from the sexual acts in which they engaged, and showed a strong unwillingness to discuss sex at all.

Still other prostitutes fell into neither group and were categorized as "alienated." They were apathetic, identified with no one, and were often heavy drinkers. In effect, this group was the least successful in maintaining a satisfactory self-image; they did not resolve the problem at all.

A more directly sociological approach has focused on the types of structures, particularly informal ones, which exist to direct a girl into prostitution. They deal more with the "how" than with the "why" of becoming a prostitute.

Nanette Davis, in the study of streetwalkers previously referred to, interviewed 30 prostitutes in correctional institutions and found a typical three-stage pattern by which her subjects had progressed from casual promiscuity through a transitional phase to full-fledged prostitution. Her findings led her to conclude that the crucial influences in this process are those which lead an individual to identify herself as someone who has departed from the values and norms of society and to organize her behavior accordingly.

The first stage in the process, a period of gradual drift from promiscuity to the first act of prostitution, might take a number of years, but typically began at an early age. Of Davis's subjects, 19 had had intercourse by age 13. The mean age for the first act of prostitution was 17.3 years, but the earliest age was 14. In the three cases in which sexual intercourse did not occur until age 17 or 18, the families were very strict, with strong control and a rigid attitude toward sex, so that sexuality became an avenue of rebellion for the girls. But most of the girls' families were highly permissive, exercising little or no supervision, and peer group norms favored early sexuality, so that both the opportunity and encouragement for promiscuity were present.

During adolescence and even earlier, most of the girls were already considered "bad," "different," "troublemakers," "slow," and otherwise unsatisfactory by parents, teachers, and others. In most cases their family life was unstable, and more than half had spent part of their childhood in foster homes or otherwise separated from the nuclear family. Twenty-three were sentenced to correctional institutions during adolescence, for truancy, sex delinquency, or other causes, where they became acquainted with more experienced inmates who made prostitution seem prestigious. Since the girls were usually confused about their identity at this point, they were glad to learn a new and attractive role.

The girls who were not institutionalized generally experienced peer group pressures toward prostitution—"everyone was doing it." Some of the girls were encouraged by pimps who provided clients and a kind of secure relationship which the girls badly needed; this was the precipitating factor in their choice of prostitution as a career. And those from overly strict families reacted by doing what their suspicious parents apparently expected they would do.

During the second stage, which Davis calls "transitional deviance," the girl was learning the skills of prostitution, engaging in prostitution on an occasional basis, but not yet thinking of herself as "a prostitute." She usually retained some commitments to the straight world—a job, marriage, nonprostitute friends—and rationalized her behavior by various expedients. Economic motivation now became primary, together in some cases with loneliness and/or entrapment by the pimp. Eventually this stage culminated in some situation, such as arrest, which forced the girl to perceive herself unequivocally as a prostitute.

The final stage is that of professionalization. Labeled by society as a prostitute, perceiving herself as such, the girl makes sex her vocation and shapes her whole life around it. Most of Davis's subjects claimed that they would not want to go back to the "square" life, though some maintained that prostitution was only transitional, a road to another career, such as modeling or dancing. Only a few actually succeeded in retaining some tokens of middle-class respectability, such as maintaining a home with children, and these few had to keep their "respectable" and "unrespectable" lives and associates strictly separated.

It would appear, then, that the low-status prostitute typically drifts into her profession through a combination of circumstances, facilitating social structures, and the internalization of social labeling. Rarely has she set out deliberately, with free choice, to become a prostitute.

The case of the higher-status prostitute may be somewhat different. James Bryan has studied how call girls, who make their contacts through personal reference, primarily by telephone, and who are usually better educated and have wealthier clients, are recruited.[67] He found that most call girls get their start as the result of a personal contact with someone else in the field. A girl who wishes to become a call girl may approach a known call girl directly, or she may get to become one as a result of her association with a pimp. Usually, she does not go out on her own right away: most girls go through a period of training or apprenticeship, usually lasting two to three months. The training may be given by the pimp, or by an experienced call girl, in which case the trainee usually lives in the other girl's apartment. During this time, she is taught a certain philosophy toward her work, including the attitudes she should take toward prostitution and toward her customers. For example, she is taught that males are exploitative and that therefore it is all right to exploit them in return. The imparting of such values serves to create a certain in-group solidarity among call girls and a shared contempt for the rest of the world. The training also covers practical business matters—how to converse with a client or arrange a fee. Very little is taught about direct sexual techniques. The chief function of the apprenticeship is to make it possible for the novice call girl to build up a clientele. Once she has achieved this, she moves out on her own.

[67] James H. Bryan, "Apprenticeships in prostitution." *Social Problems* 12 (Winter 1965):278–297.

Like members of other subcultures, prostitutes usually develop their own specialized knowledge, language, folklore, and network of relationships, in this case with other prostitutes, pimps, customers, and police. Becoming a prostitute means more than selling sex for money: it means becoming part of a well-defined, distinct world. Robert Bell has described some of the features of the prostitute subculture.[68]

A major part of this subculture involves the roles of those who participate in it. One important role, obviously, is that of the customer.[69] The prostitute learns to see the customer in strictly economic terms, as her source of income. This is facilitated by the attitude that the customer is basically corrupt—a belief which, as discussed earlier, prostitutes adopt as a way of maintaining their self-image.

Another subculture figure important to many prostitutes is the pimp. A pimp lives off the earnings of one or more prostitutes, serving as manager, protector, and companion/lover. According to Jennifer James, who studied 72 prostitutes and 38 pimps, virtually all streetwalkers have a pimp, who may be a husband or boyfriend, usually referred to as "my man." Although in the past pimps often acquired customers for their girls, now their responsibilities are primarily financial, and they almost never appear on the street, except occasionally to check up on their women. Although most of the prostitutes in James's sample claimed to have previously worked as waitresses, nurses' aides, or clerks, the pimps generally had not had previous job experience and appeared "totally uninterested in traditional occupations." The mean age of the pimps was 30.2 years, a few years older than their girls, whose mean age was 22.6 years. James believes this age differential reflects traditional male-female role relationships, according to which an "older male is more likely to exercise authority over a younger female." [70]

A study by two anthropologists [71] found that part of the attraction of pimping was the pimps' delight in exercising total control over women, who they felt should be completely subservient to men. This feeling might have been enhanced by the fact that many of the pimps studied were black, while many of their prostitutes were white. Another considerable attraction, of course, was the chance to make a great deal of money while doing virtually nothing. The study found that pimps put great value on material possessions, lavish parties, and expensive jewelry and clothing, and in general on living an elegant life, free from strain and drudgery.

Although pimps exploit their prostitutes, it is clear that these women derive something from the relationship which they feel they need. James found that a streetwalker's status within the subculture derived from that of her pimp—how good-looking and well dressed he was, and whether he drove a flashy, prestigious car. Without a pimp, she was an "outlaw," likely to be harassed, or threatened with assault or robbery on the street.

[68] Bell, pp. 237–247.

[69] An insightful and often amusing account of a sociologist's first visit to a brothel is provided in George Lee Stewart, "On first being a john." *Urban Life & Culture,* vol. 1, no. 3 (October 1972):255–274.

[70] Jennifer James, "Prostitute-pimp relationships." In *Medical Aspects of Human Sexuality,* November 1973, pp. 147–163.

[71] Christina Milner and Richard Milner. Their study was briefly described in *Time,* January 11, 1971.

Also, the pimp took care of business matters, paying bills, arranging bail and lawyers' fees when necessary, and so on.

Another pertinent element is the fact that a prostitute and her pimp are usually lovers. Common belief has it that the pimp simply uses a prostitute for his own pleasure, while she gets no sexual satisfaction from him. This is related to the myth that women become prostitutes because they are frigid. Probably, however, most prostitutes achieve orgasm at least as often as most wives. If prostitutes do become sexually unresponsive, it is generally an effect of their disillusionment with men, resulting from too much exposure. The same applies to the common belief that women become prostitutes because they are lesbians: the prostitutes who become homosexual generally do so as a result of their prostitution experiences which have caused them to become disillusioned with men.

In addition to sexual satisfaction, the pimp also provides his prostitutes with a sense of roots, of family, of being taken care of. It has been pointed out that the pimp-prostitute relationship is similar to a traditional husband-wife relationship, with the economic roles reversed. The prostitute makes money and the pimp provides her with a sense of security and family.

James discusses several myths about prostitutes and their pimps. For instance, it is widely believed that pimps use force to get prostitutes to work for them. In fact, they will most likely talk a woman into working, because streetwalkers will not stay with a man who abuses them. Again, with very few exceptions, pimps are not likely to seduce young girls, because the legal problems of involvement with underage females are too much trouble. It is also widely believed that pimps control women by getting them addicted to heroin. However, according to James, an addict is not of much value as a prostitute, because she will usually not want to work unless she needs a fix. Many women, however, turn to prostitution after becoming addicts, in order to pay for their drug supply. (Winick, who studied prostitutes in the New York area, disagrees; according to his research, substantial numbers of the girls in the East are narcotics addicts, and pimps are very likely to be the major source of drugs for them. He suggests that this and other differences between his and James's findings, which were based on a West Coast area study, perhaps reflect regional differences in the subculture.[72])

SOCIAL CONTROL

Currently, prostitution is illegal everywhere in the United States except in some counties in Nevada. While there does not seem to be any strong movement afoot in any of the other states to follow Nevada's example, many arguments have been offered in support of legalization. It is claimed that prostitution exists and will continue to exist regardless of the law, and that recognizing this fact will bring many benefits. For one thing, legislation would make prostitutes' income taxable. It might also eliminate or reduce the frequent connections of prostitution with crime and governmental corruption. And it would make it possible for government to enact and enforce health regulations for prostitutes, reducing the incidence of venereal disease. It has also been suggested that legalization of

---

[72] Charles Winick, commentary on James. *Medical Aspects of Human Sexuality,* p. 160.

brothels would result in the reduction of streetwalking and public solicitation, which disturb neighborhood residents.

Many advocates of legalization point out the class differential with which the laws are enforced. Unless very indiscreet, call girls and their upper-middle-class customers are seldom the targets of police action. It is the lower-class practitioners, with their lower-class customers, who bear the brunt of antisolicitation laws. It has also been pointed out that prostitution is usually a victimless crime, since the customer participates willingly and generally has few complaints.

Since most laws against prostitution and solicitation require specific evidence of an offer to exchange money for sexual services, a major means of curbing prostitution has been for plainclothes policemen to pose as customers. There have been objections that these laws are unjust in singling out only one party to the crime. This line of reasoning holds that if a prostitute commits a crime, so does her customer, who should be equally liable. Oregon (and a few other states and some cities) now has a law which states that a man can be jailed for as much as a year and fined up to $1,000 for offering to pay for sexual services. The city of Portland has female police officers pose as streetwalkers. Even so, the law isn't enforced equitably, and far fewer johns are arrested by female officers than prostitutes by male officers.[73] Entrapment of participants of either sex is protested by civil libertarians, who argue that this is a violation of the right to privacy; they also favor legalization, on the ground that sex for a fee is a private matter between consenting adults. Supporters of legalization also argue that it is harmful to the social order to have laws on the books which are regularly flouted, and that since the laws against prostitution are not effectively enforced, it would be better not to have them at all.

Still another reason why it might be worthwhile to legalize prostitution is that this would mean that prostitutes would no longer be lawbreakers. This change in status might go a long way toward reducing the tension and stress to which most prostitutes are subject at present. Legally, at least, they would no longer have to define themselves negatively, and they would no longer be constantly in fear of arrest, even though by other norms prostitution would still be regarded as a social problem.

In Nevada, legalized prostitution seems to work quite well. There are about 30 to 40 brothels in the state, with 7 to 10 girls in each. The brothels do a brisk business, bring in considerable tax revenue, and are inspected regularly by physicians. And there seems to be no greater amount of prostitution in counties in which it is legal than in those in which it is not.

PORNOGRAPHY

A third area which needs to be discussed in relation to sex-related social problems is that of pornography, which may be defined as the depiction of sexual behavior in a way intended to sexually excite the viewer.

[73] Joan Libman, "Prostitution law in Oregon may end a double standard." *Wall Street Journal,* October 18, 1974, pp. 1 ff.

Pornography has existed for centuries—the covert vendor of "feelthy pictures" is an old cartoon staple—but it has become a social problem today because of the vast increase and unprecedented openness of its distribution, and because of serious disagreement, even among responsible thinkers, as to what actually constitutes pornography, as well as to the wisdom of permitting or suppressing it.

Gagnon and Simon make the interesting point that the very words "pornography" and "obscenity" used to describe a book, a film, or an event define that thing as being sexually stimulating, and

can produce a psycho-sexual response in the labeler and his audience very similar to that produced by the pornographic object itself. The very act of labeling generates a sense of sexual anticipation and engages our fantasies about the business of pornography and the erotic character of those who produce it.

Sexual attitudes and behavior are, as we have seen, learned. Among the things we learn is that anything "pornographic" is something other than an appropriate sex object that has the capacity to arouse us. This belief in the power of pornography is related to the view of sex as innate, overwhelming, and instinctive. Pornography is held to be capable of unleashing the sexual beast in us all (especially males), and to have, as Gagnon and Simon put it, "a magical capacity to push men into overt sexual action." In their view, pornography deals not only explicitly with sex, but with illicit sex. It does not describe "conventional sexual activity that occurs within a marital relationship. The rule is: if the activity is conventional, the context is not (the relationship, the motives, etc.); if the context is conventional, the activity is not." [74] It is for its illicit emphasis that pornography arouses controversy in our society.

Any discussion of pornography is bound to touch on the question of censorship, and hence, in the United States, on the issue of First Amendment rights under the Constitution. Today, when many persons feel that there has been an increasing attempt by government to curtail the exercise of these rights, freedom of speech becomes a particularly sensitive issue. Serious arguments both for and against the suppression of pornographic material can be made. It is argued, on the one hand, that censorship is damaging to artistic and literary efforts, since past experience has shown that works of sound artistic value are apt to be judged pornographic or obscene if they contain any explicit sexual material, no matter how it is used; that the vagueness of all existing legal definitions of pornography gives too much latitude to judges or other authorities, enabling them to suppress material, in effect, merely because they themselves consider it offensive; that the reading or viewing of pornographic material is a private act, which does no harm to society and therefore cannot legitimately be prohibited by society; and that, in any event, if pornography is freely available, people of sophistication and critical judgment will soon become bored with it and turn to more worthwhile entertainment. On the other hand, the claim is made that habitual exposure to pornography is indeed harmful to individuals, particularly to

[74] John A. Gagnon and William Simon, "Pornography: Social scripts and legal dilemmas." In Gagnon and Simon, *Sexual Conduct*, pp. 260–282.

young persons, and hence to the society of which they are a part; and that when pornography becomes so widespread that those, presumably a majority, who wish to avoid it find it excessively difficult to do so, it is legitimately a matter for social control. It is this latter argument that has prompted several Supreme Court attempts to define and control pornography, culminating in the June 1976 decision that it is constitutional for municipalities to restrict the proliferation of pornographic theaters and bookstores through zoning regulations.

Unfortunately for the objectivity of these discussions, there has until recently been a serious lack of empirical research into either the effects of pornography or the extent of exposure to it. Even now, the surface has barely been scratched. However, over the past decade, some studies have been made, notably in connection with the work of the U.S. Commission on Obscenity and Pornography, reported in 1970. On the basis of these studies, the commission concluded—although not unanimously— that no social or individual harm could be shown to result from exposure to pornographic material. They therefore recommended the relaxation of most existing restrictions on such material. The sharp, and largely

Pornography has always been available to those who knew where to look for it, but today the age of discretion and the plain brown wrapper seems to have passed. New York's Times Square area, with its peepshows, adult bookshops, and explicitly erotic movies, is only the best known and perhaps the largest of the nation's pornography marketplaces.
Charles Gatewood

nonrational, rejection of these findings and recommendations, both in government and elsewhere, suggests the degree to which empirical study in this area must contend with the deeply ingrained fears of the population at large.

What, exactly, have the scientific investigations of the last decade revealed? For one thing, they have made clear that some degree of exposure to pornographic material is quite common in our society, and apparently has been so for a long time. The study of Abelson and his colleagues, done under the auspices of the Obscenity Commission, showed that, of a nationwide representative sample of 2,486 adults, 84 percent of the men and 69 percent of the women had been exposed to some kind of explicit sexual material.[75] Other studies show similar results. Younger adults and people with some college education were more likely than older adults and people with only high school education to have encountered sexual materials. Among men, geographic location made a difference—the greatest exposure was in large metropolitan areas and in the northeastern part of the country, the least in the north central states—but for women this difference did not hold.

However, the number of persons reporting extensive experience with erotic materials was relatively small. Of Abelson's subjects, only 14 percent of the men and 5 percent of the women reported having seen specific types of sexual pictures as often as five times in a two-year period. Since the design of the study made it likely that this was a somewhat low figure, the Obscenity Commission concluded that probably "somewhere around one-fifth or one-quarter of the male population in the United States has somewhat regular experience with sexual materials as explicit as intercourse," [76] and a somewhat smaller number has regular experience with depictions of oral-genital or sadomasochistic activities.

How early does this exposure begin? In Abelson's study, 74 percent of the men and 51 percent of the women had encountered explicit sexual materials before age 21, 54 and 44 percent before age 18, and 30 and 17 percent before age 15. Again, other studies tend to confirm this pattern. The replies of those questioned suggest that early exposure has been more common among younger adults than it was among those of an older generation, but the commission points out that older people often have trouble recalling the exact year when a given event in their youth took place, so that this difference may not be a reliable one.

Apparently, among both adults and teenagers, exposure to pornographic material does not usually take place directly through the "dirty book" store. Most persons reported having been shown or given their material by friends, and most viewing of such material took place as a part of social activity, not in solitude. Those who do patronize the "adult bookstores" are apt to be white, male, age 26 to 55, middle class, married, and shopping alone. The average patron of sexual movies is

[75] H. Abelson, R. Cohen, E. Heaton, and C. Suder, "Public attitudes toward erotic materials." *Technical Reports of the Commission on Obscenity and Pornography.* Vol. 6. Washington, D.C.: U.S. Government Printing Office, 1970.
[76] *The Report of the Commission on Obscenity and Pornography.* Section F: "Patterns of Exposure to Erotic Material." Washington, D.C.: U.S. Government Printing Office, 1970.

similar, save that he may be somewhat more likely to attend with companions—the literature seems to disagree on this last point.[77]

Why do people seek exposure to pornographic material? This is a question which needs further research, but some data are available. Many of the adult-movie patrons surveyed by Nawy said that viewing such movies enables them to enjoy their own (largely heterosexual) sex experiences more, and to introduce new variety into their sex lives. A lesser but still substantial number simply enjoyed the viewing for itself. Substantial numbers of Abelson's subjects said that pornographic material excited them sexually, provided entertainment and information, and in some cases helped to improve their marriage relations. These may be true effects of pornographic experience, or they may be rationalizations developed by the users in order to justify their activity to themselves; the evidence gathered so far leaves the question open.

Probably the most widespread assumption, though, and the greatest fear, about pornography is that it leads to crime, specifically to sex crimes. The former head of the FBI, J. Edgar Hoover, asserted in a 1956 statement to a congressional committee that "the circulation of periodicals containing such salacious materials plays an important part in the development of crime among youth of our country." [78] Vast numbers of people would have agreed with him then, and many probably would do so now; yet the evidence we have simply does not prove anything of the sort. In a 1971 survey of the major studies of pornography-crime correlation, Wilson pointed out that in most cases the sex-crime offenders turned out to have significantly less experience with, and later introduction to, pornographic materials in their youth than had their control normals.[79] Similar findings were reported by Goldstein and his associates in a California study of institutionalized sex-crime offenders.[80] Child molesters and rapists had significantly less exposure to pornography during adolescence than a control group of non-offenders outside the institution. Those offenders with excessive exposure to pornography had formed unorthodox sexual identities prior to such exposure. Less information is available with regard to sex crimes among juveniles, but in the period from 1960 to 1969, during which sexual materials generally became far more widely available than they had been before, the number of juvenile arrests for sex crimes decreased.[81] On the basis of these statistics, it appears that the commission was justified in its rejection of an association between pornography and criminal acts.

[77] See Abelson *et al.;* also H. Nawy, "The San Francisco erotic marketplace"; M. M. Finkelstein, "Traffic in sex-oriented materials: Part I"; and C. A. Winick, "A study of consumers of explicitly sexual materials: Some functions served by adult movies." *Technical Reports of the Commission on Obscenity and Pornography.* Vol. 6.
[78] In *Obscene and Pornographic Literature and Juvenile Delinquency.* Interim Report of the Committee on the Judiciary. 84th Congress, 2nd Session, June 28, 1956, p. 2.
[79] W. Cody Wilson, "Facts versus fears: Why should we worry about pornography?" *Annals of the American Academy of Political and Social Sciences* 397 (September 1971):105–117.
[80] Michael J. Goldstein, Harold S. Kant, and John J. Hartman, *Pornography and Sexual Deviance.* Berkeley: University of California Press, 1974.
[81] Wilson, p. 113.

Similar data are reported from Denmark, where first a liberalization (in 1967) and then the repeal (in 1969) of the obscenity statute made it possible to compare the incidence of sex crimes in a before-and-after situation. As summarized by Wilson, the Danish study showed that

the number of sex crimes decreased by 40 percent in the two years following the first liberalization of the availability of pornography as compared with the relatively stable average of the previous nine years; the number of sex crimes reported to the police decreased 30 percent further in the year in which the second liberalization of the pornography law occurred.[82]

However, the decrease was only in such "passive" crimes as voyeurism and exhibitionism; more aggressive sex crimes showed no significant diminution. While Wilson warns that this decrease may reflect, in part, a decreased inclination to report minor sex crimes to the police, he believes that it also reflects an actual reduction in the number of such crimes. In this instance, we can theorize that the stimulation provided for some individuals by pornography is, in its absence, sought in certain forms of public sexual acting-out behavior. Pornography is, therefore, a functional substitute for such behavior, and to this extent at least it may even be socially beneficial.

Thus, insofar as the case for suppression of pornography rests on the supposed relationship between pornography and crime, it can be regarded as at least tentatively disproved. But a number of thoughtful writers question whether pornography, or at least the wide and open dissemination of it, may not result in more subtle harm, which society cannot safely afford to ignore. Irving Kristol sums up the problem rather succinctly:

The question we face with regard to pornography and obscenity is whether, now that they have such strong legal protection from the Supreme Court, they can or will brutalize and debase our citizenry.[83]

It is foolish to claim that frequent exposure to pornography, and to an environment presupposing it, will have no effect on an individual's tastes and outlook. This would be equivalent to saying that no experience or encounter affects human development—that, in fact, no learning is possible. The question, then, is whether, in the case of pornography, the effect is harmful—whether what is learned is something which society has a legitimate interest in preventing. Kristol argues that pornography offers a degraded view of human beings, depriving them of their specifically human character by depicting sex not as part of a personal relationship between two people but as a mere physical act, "animal coupling . . . a public spectacle. . . ." He asserts that pornography "appeals to and provokes a kind of sexual regression," because "it is a masturbatory exercise of the imagination." For this reason it discourages the mature development of healthy adult relationships, and has an infantilizing effect on society. It was, he feels, in recognition (whether explicit or not) of this that the people of an earlier time felt justified in suppressing pornographic material: they "took care not to let themselves be governed by the more infantile and irrational parts of themselves." [84] Walter Berns,

[82] Wilson, p. 113.
[83] Irving Kristol, "Pornography, obscenity, and the case for censorship." *New York Times Magazine,* March 28, 1971, p. 24.
[84] Kristol, pp. 112–113.

writing in *The Public Interest,* makes essentially the same point from a slightly different angle. He sees a connection between shame, self-government, and democracy: "To live together requires rules and a governing of the passions, and those who are without shame will be unruly and unrulable." Those "who have carried liberty beyond any restraint" have lost the capacity for self-government, and are likely to succumb to tyranny or enforced restraints imposed by others.[85]

A number of counter-arguments are offered in favor of permitting the unhindered distribution of pornographic materials. First, as we have already indicated, the alleged negative social impact of pornography is difficult if not impossible to prove; in fact, existing evidence seems to show no clear association. The danger of censorship of ideas, however, is clear and real. Therefore, the burden of proof should be upon those who would censor pornography, to demonstrate conclusively that it does have significant negative impact to justify censorship. Second, censorship of sexually explicit materials has, in the past, led to censorship of some fine works of literature and other arts. We laugh now at the standards of public morality involved in adding fig leaves to nude Greek and Roman statues, or adding shadows to Breughel's paintings. Yet in some areas of the country even today books are routinely banned for being too sexually explicit, and sexually explicit films—whatever their merit—are still rated with an "X." Censorship directed at works of art may also lead to the censorship of unpopular ideas, and thus threaten the foundations of democracy. Many claim, with justification, that the right to produce pornography is constitutionally protected as freedom of speech. Finally, we are now in a generally more permissive and liberated climate as far as sexual matters are concerned. Part of the reason, perhaps, is the recognition that freedom from sexual inhibition is far better than repression of our sexuality, which in the past caused severe problems for many people, including guilt and difficulties in sexual adjustment.

Empirical studies have not shown, and probably cannot show, the effects of a more or less pornography-suffused, or at least very pornography-permissive, atmosphere on a whole society, or on members of a society. Yet there cannot help but be effects, and they may be very good or very bad—or they may be socially irrelevant. To deal rationally with the question requires resort to other disciplines as well as sociology, such as history and even philosophy, and in such disciplines exact knowledge is rarely possible. Evidently, then, we are likely to have to make our decision without the aid of precise scientific proof for or against the harmlessness of pornography in this wider sense, and in the absence of such proof we are not likely to reach agreement.

PROSPECTS

In recent years, society—or at least some parts of it—seems to have been taking an increasingly liberal attitude toward sexual expression. Magazines regularly publish articles on such sexual phenomena as group sex,

[85] Walter Berns, "Pornography vs. democracy: The case for censorship." *The Public Interest* (Winter 1971):3–24.

there is abundant nudity on screen and on stage, the double standard for men and women is gradually being dropped or eased, and, occasionally, respectable authorities support the idea of trial marriages for young couples. Hunt's investigations indicated to him that "the average American now holds many opinions about sex that a generation ago were rarely held by any but highly educated big-city sophisticates and bohemians."[86]

However, despite increasing permissiveness, more liberated behavior, and the availability of frank publications and X-rated movies, more than 75 percent of the adults questioned by Hunt believed that sex education should be part of school curricula. It is clear that while our knowledge has expanded, we need to know more, and to disseminate more effectively what we do know. As Hunt points out,

Almost all human societies . . . educated their young in sexual matters, including the mechanics of copulation. In some societies, parents, other elders or priestly persons have explained the sex act in words. In others, songs, drawings and sculpture have been used to explain what happens in intercourse. In still others, the young have had ample opportunity to see or overhear adults doing it. And in some, the sexual act has been publicly demonstrated during fertility rites or orgiastic celebrations. American society, however, has long been without any officially sanctioned system of teaching the young sexual skills.

His survey showed that for most people, information about sex had been learned from friends. The fathers of two-thirds of the men and of more than four-fifths of the women had never discussed sexual matters with their children before or during their children's high school years; neither had the mothers of three-quarters of the men and of nearly half of the women.

The lack of readily available and accurate information has consequences for individuals and for society. Hunt believes that "countless cases of psychosexual disability or limitation of function . . . innumerable flawed marriages and . . . an unmeasurable amount of needless human unhappiness and frustration" can be traced to "defects in the sexual education of young Americans." [87] Zelnik and Kantner, who studied sexually active teenage girls, found that ignorance and misinformation about their chances of becoming pregnant resulted in more than three-fourths of them using contraceptive methods only irregularly if at all.[88] Yet, despite the seemingly widespread approval of sex education, many communities still do not have sex-education courses in their school curricula. Those who attempt to make sex education part of a school program continue to encounter strong community opposition in many parts of the country.

What effect, if any, will current sexual attitudes have on homosexuals

[86] Hunt, p. 24.

[87] Hunt, pp. 120–131.

[88] Melvin Zelnik and John Kantner, "Sexuality, contraception, and pregnancy among young unwed females in the United States." In U.S. Commission on Population Growth and the American Future, *Demographic and Social Aspects of Population Growth.* Washington, D.C.: U.S. Government Printing Office, 1972.

and prostitutes? Again, prospects are ambiguous. In many parts of the country, it seems probable that in the near future homosexuals will gain greater acceptance. Organized homophile groups are doing a great deal, at least in major cities, to make the public aware of some of the problems of discrimination which homosexuals face. Possibly this will result in the removal of some, if not all, legal restrictions in many areas. On the other hand, as we have seen, most states continue to prohibit certain sex acts between consenting adults, and have received Supreme Court justification for so doing.

It does not seem as if the general change in sexual attitudes is having much of an effect on attitudes toward prostitutes. One effect it seems to be having is to decrease the demand for prostitutes' services, as the double standard becomes weaker and free sex becomes increasingly available. Prostitutes have been proclaimed by some women's liberationists as the only honest women, but prostitutes do not seem to relish this championship; and other than that, they have been largely ignored by social movements. For this reason, some prostitutes have formed an organization of their own (called Coyote) to fight for the decriminalization of prostitution. It is possible that as public attitudes become generally more liberal, prostitutes will suffer less from legal sanctions; widespread acceptance of prostitution, however, seems unlikely to occur in the foreseeable future.

It is clear that in only a few places have attempts been made to change sex laws (and sex education) to conform with present behavioral realities. Even as more people espouse a more permissive attitude, the national ambivalence toward sexual matters that we noted at the beginning of this chapter shows few signs of abating.

SUMMARY

Although there has been a far-reaching liberalization of sexual attitudes in the United States, traditional attitudes still influence our sex laws and behaviors. These traditional attitudes stem from Judeo-Christian tradition, which accepted sex only within the context of heterosexual marriage. In addition, the influence of capitalism, with its emphasis on delayed gratification, reinforced repressive sexual attitudes. Finally, traditional attitudes stem from the Victorians, who stressed self-control and who had a "double standard" of sexual behavior.

Formal study of human sexuality helped to liberalize our sexual attitudes, starting with Freud's theory that sexuality was an integral part of human development through Kinsey's revelations that American sexual behavior differed from its professed norms. Studies of sexual behavior in other cultures indicate that virtually every form of sexual activity has at some time and place been acceptable, suggesting that human sexual expression is, to a large degree, learned, not instinctive.

Gagnon and Simon distinguish between three categories of sex-related problems. *Tolerated sex variance* refers to acts that are disapproved but that are rarely criminally sanctioned. *Asocial sex variance* includes acts such as incest, child molestation, and rape, which are not reinforced by a social structure. *Structural variance* is problematic sexual behavior that has supportive social structures.

Homosexuality is a sexual preference for members of one's own sex. Not everyone who engages in homosexual acts identifies as a homosexual. Nor are homosexuals an easily identifiable group; they are found in every occupation and social stratum. They also differ in the ways they deal with their homosexuality. The homosexual subculture does, however, share certain activities and norms. Differences in the way male and female homosexuals manage their homosexuality reflect society's different patterns of socialization for men and women.

Prostitution is sexual intercourse on a promiscuous and mercenary basis. There are several levels among prostitutes, ranging from the call girl to the streetwalker. Prostitution continues to exist largely because it serves a socially useful function. Early self-identification as someone who varies from social norms is apparently an important influence in the background of many prostitutes.

Pornography is the depiction of sexual behavior, usually illicit, in a way intended to sexually stimulate the viewer. Although the connection between pornography and sex crimes has largely been disproved, controversy still exists about the social effects of pornography.

Despite the fact that sexual attitudes in the United States have become more liberal and restrictive sex laws in many parts of the country have been repealed, in many areas all except the most traditional sex behaviors are still prohibited.

BIBLIOGRAPHY

Altman, Dennis. *Homosexual: Oppression and Liberation*. New York: Piterbrodge and Diemstfrey, 1971.

Becker, Howard S., ed. *The Other Side*. New York: Free Press, 1964.

Bell, Robert R., and Gordon, Michael. *The Social Dimensions of Human Sexuality*. Boston: Little, Brown, 1972.

Benjamin, H., and Masters, R. *Prostitution and Morality*. New York: Julian Press, 1964.

Benson, R. *In Defense of Homosexuality: Male and Female; A Rational Evaluation of a Social Prejudice*. New York: Julian Press, 1965.

Cappon, Daniel. *Toward an Understanding of Homosexuality*. Englewood Cliffs, N.J.: Prentice-Hall, 1965.

Cory, Donald W., and LeRoy, John R. *The Homosexual and His Society: A View from Within*. New York: Citadel Press, 1963.

Gagnon, John H., and Simon, William, eds. *The Sexual Scene*. 2nd ed. Chicago: Aldine, 1973.

————. *Sexual Conduct*. Chicago: Aldine, 1973.

Goldstein, Michael J., and Kant, Harold S. *Pornography and Sexual Deviance*. Berkeley, Calif.: University of California Press, 1974.

Greenwald, Harold. *The Elegant Prostitute: A Social and Psychoanalytic Study*. New York: Walker, 1970.

————. *The Call Girl*. New York: Ballantine, 1958.

Hoffman, Martin. *The Gay World: Male Homosexuality and the Social Creation of Evil*. New York: Basic Books, 1968.

Hunt, Morton. *Sexual Behavior in the 1970's*. New York: Dell, 1974.

Johnson, Cecil. *Sex and Human Relationships*. Columbus, Ohio: Charles E. Merrill, 1970.

Karlen, Arno. *Sexuality and Homosexuality: A New View*. New York: Norton, 1971.

Ruitenbeck, Hendrick M., ed. *Homosexuality: A Changing Picture*. Atlantic Highlands, N.J.: Humanities Press, 1974.

Sagarin, Edward, and MacNamara, Donald E., eds. *Problems of Sex Behavior*. New York: Thomas Y. Crowell, 1968.

Schofield, Michael G. *Sociological Aspects of Homosexuality: A Comparative Study of Three Types of Homosexuals*. Boston: Little, Brown, 1965.

Schur, Edwin M., and Beday, Hugo A. *Victimless Crimes: Two Sides of a Controversy*. Englewood Cliffs, N.J.: Prentice-Hall, 1974.

Teal, Donn. *The Gay Militants*. New York: Stein and Day, 1971.

Williams, Colin J., and Weinberg, Martin S. *Homosexuals and the Military: A Study of Less Than Honorable Discharge*. New York: Harper & Row, 1971.

Winick, Charles. *The Lively Commerce: Prostitution in the United States*. Chicago: Quadrangle, 1971.

The Wolfenden Report: Report of the Committee on Homosexual Offenses and Prostitution. New York: Stein and Day, 1963.

12

WORK

- If given the chance to begin their working life anew, only 43 percent of white-collar workers, 24 percent of blue-collar workers, and 19 percent of unskilled workers would choose the same line of work.
- Thirty years ago, only one married woman in five was in the labor force; today the ratio is almost one out of every two.
- Since World War II, the average work week has decreased from almost 60 hours to 36.2 hours.
- Over 100 studies in the last twenty years have demonstrated that almost all workers want responsibility in their jobs as well as the feeling that the work they do has significance.

"What do you want to be when you grow up?" is a question first asked of us when we are little children. As we mature, the question becomes more pressing. By the time we graduate from high school, we are usually expected to have, at least tentatively, chosen a vocation. Thus we are introduced to the great importance of work in our society.

A division of labor exists in all societies, at least to provide food and shelter for the members. But in our society, some form of employment is also necessary in order for an individual to stay in the mainstream of life. Much is made of the fact that, ostensibly, everyone has an opportunity to work; and one of the major responsibilities of our entire educational system is to prepare people for the occupations and professions which keep society functioning. While unemployment compensation and welfare payments are made available to people who are either temporarily out of work or unable to support themselves over long periods, such compensation is designed to maintain them at a subsistence level. Prosperity (and self-respect) are only for the productive.

It would seem, therefore, that work is more than a means to provide the worker with the essentials of life and society with goods and services. In our society, great emphasis is placed on the "work ethic." That is, we share a belief in the value of work. Because work is considered useful, productive, and honorable, people feel that if they are to consider themselves worthwhile and to be so considered by others, they must work. Thus, when a representative sample of people was asked, "If by some chance you inherited enough money to live comfortably without working, do you think that you would work anyway, or not?" 80 percent said that they would prefer to keep on working.[1] Another study, limited to manual and service workers, replicated this finding. Eighty-three percent of these workers said that they would continue working even if they had enough money to stop.[2]

The importance of work in our society is also indicated by the extent to which a person's occupation determines his or her place in the social structure. In the past, class origins often determined social position, and this in turn determined the vocational choices available. Today the situation has changed somewhat. Vocational choice, which we regard as properly self-determined, largely delimits our social position. We value jobs differently, but we nearly always accord status on the basis of occupation. This is one reason why older persons, whom we might expect to be eager to retire after many active years, are often reluctant to do so; employment gives them a place in society, and permits them to participate in and contribute to community life. (See Chapter 9.)

Work has not always been held in such high regard. The early Greeks viewed work as a curse imposed on humanity by the gods.[3] With the exception of agriculture, which brought both a livelihood and independence, work was seen as essentially a brutalizer of the mind, rendering it unfit for thinking about truth or practicing virtue. As Aristotle remarks in his *Politics,* "No man can practice virtue who is living the life of a mechanic or laborer," and "We call those arts vulgar which tend to deform the body, and likewise all paid employments, for they absorb and degrade the mind." [4] While the Romans added commerce to agriculture as an acceptable employment, they generally regarded work in the same light as the Greeks: it was vulgar and demeaning.

The Hebrews' attitude toward work was somewhat ambivalent. Like the Greeks, they regarded it as drudgery; but they also believed that through it a person could atone for original sin. Herzberg has discussed this attitude toward work as the difference between an "Adam" view of human nature and an "Abraham" view.[5] Adam, expelled from the Garden of Eden, is forced to work for his daily bread. However, for Abraham, God's chosen man, work is not an act of the body so much as a means of spiritual fulfillment.

The early Christian inherited this more complex concept of work and elaborated upon it. They accepted the idea of work as a punishment for original sin, but they also believed that a person worked both to make his

[1] Nancy C. Morse and Robert S. Weiss, "The function and meaning of work." *American Sociological Review* (April 1955):191–198.
[2] Curt Tausky, "Meaning of work among blue-collar men." *Pacific Sociological Review* 12 (Spring 1969).
[3] Adriano Tilgher, "Work through the ages." In Sigmund Nosow and William H. Form, eds. *Man, Work and Society.* New York: Basic Books, 1962, pp. 11–12.
[4] Aristotle, *Politics.* Book 3, section V; Book 8, section 11 (Jowett translation).
[5] Fredrick Herzberg, *Work and the Nature of Man.* New York: World, 1966, pp. 15–16.

or her own living and to help those in need. Thus work became important to physical and spiritual well-being. But, as Tilgher notes, in itself it still had no intrinsic worth.[6]

With the advent of Protestantism, work became the acknowledged basis of society. To Martin Luther, labor was a service to God. When one worked well, whatever his or her calling, God was served in the best possible way. Luther thus endowed work with a certain religious significance, which it has retained to this day. It was Calvin's teachings, however, which transformed the religious view of work into a wellspring of modern capitalism. Calvin preached that work is the will of God, but that people should renounce the fruits of their labors and use their profits to launch new ventures, which in turn would provide more profits for investment, and so on. Humanity must discipline itself to work ceaselessly to make the Kingdom of God manifest on earth. Calvin also believed that a person should not be bound to an occupation by the chances of his or her birth. Instead, he argued, people should seek out the work which brings the greatest success to themselves and to their society. These are the roots of our modern-day ethic of work for work's sake, an ethic now stripped of its religious connotations.

Because so many people work for such a large part of their lives, it is important to try to understand the social problems related to work. In this chapter, we will discuss four of these: unemployment, automation, the need for job satisfaction, and leisure time. Each affects a significant number of people. The economic recession of the mid-1970s created a serious and growing unemployment problem in our society, for a high rate of unemployment creates both personal and social difficulties.

Increasing automation, while it may provide many benefits, presents certain kinds of problems as well. Many workers see automation principally as a threat to their job security, but the social implications of automation are in reality considerably more complex. It is widely feared that increased automation may subordinate people to the machine, resulting in more depersonalized tasks which offer the worker very little satisfaction.

The final problem to be considered, the use of leisure time, may not seem at first to be a problem at all. We would all like to have more time to ourselves. Yet the use of the increasing amount of leisure time available to most employed Americans poses special problems which could cause a change in the work ethic itself.

TRENDS

The world of work, like other important areas in our society, has been undergoing a number of significant changes. Before going into a detailed discussion of the problems stated above, we want to explore four patterns of change, or trends, which seem particularly important. These are: the increase in the number of white-collar workers; specialization; the emergence of an "employee society"; and changes in the age and sex composition of the labor force.

[6] Tilgher, pp. 13–20.

The greatest change in America's occupational structure has been the transition from an agricultural base to an industrial and distributive one, dominated by corporations and government organizations. The magnitude of the resulting change in the labor force can be gauged from a few figures. In 1900, 27 percent of the total labor force were farm workers and 18 percent were white-collar workers. In 1974, only 3.5 percent of the total labor force were farm workers, whereas 48.6 percent were white-collar workers.[7]

White-collar workers—professional, managerial, clerical, and sales personnel—now comprise the largest occupational category in the nation, having surpassed the blue-collar group in 1956. Most of the white-collar increase is attributable to growth in the professional and clerical fields. The latter has increased its proportion more than 500 percent since 1900, so that today it comprises 17.5 percent of all employed persons. Clerical personnel now vie with skilled and semiskilled workers as the largest occupational group in the labor force.

The decline in farm employment since the turn of the century has been as dramatic as the rise in white-collar employment. Farm workers—farmers, managers, and farmhands—were once the largest occupational category in the United States, and are now the smallest.

While the total proportion of blue-collar workers in the labor force has remained quite stable since about 1900, their composition has undergone some important changes. Semiskilled and skilled operatives and craftsmen have increased proportionately, while the proportion of unskilled labor has decreased.

Similarly the slight overall net gain shown by service occupations masks some important changes within that category. People employed as private household workers now comprise only 1.4 percent of the total labor force, whereas in 1900 they accounted for 5 percent of the total. Other service personnel, such as hotel workers, guards, waiters, and barbers, have increased their proportion by 200 percent. They now comprise 11.8 percent of all employed persons, as compared to 4 percent in 1900.[8]

Our discussion of the shift to a white-collar economy involved only four broad categories of employment (white-collar, blue-collar, service, and farm workers). Within these categories, of course, there are literally thousands of jobs. The *Dictionary of Occupational Titles,* published by the U.S. Department of Labor, lists 21,741 different jobs—a total which contrasts sharply with the 323 occupations recorded by the census of 1850.[9] The vast difference indicates the increasing specialization of labor and the complexity of its divisions. As Moore points out, this increase in specialization has been so great that it may now be more appropriate to speak not of the division but of the diversification of labor.[10] He noted

THE INCREASE IN WHITE-COLLAR WORKERS

SPECIALIZATION

[7] Seymour Wolfbein, *Work in American Society.* Glenview, Ill.: Scott, Foresman, 1971, 45; and *Manpower Report of the President.* Washington, D.C.: U.S. Government Printing Office, 1975, p. 35.

[8] *Manpower Report of the President,* p. 226.

[9] Wolfbein, p. 43.

[10] Wilbert E. Moore, "The attributes of an industrial order." In Nosow and Form, p. 96.

some of the unusual jobs one might choose—tea taster, water smeller, clock winder, and the like. We are all familiar with the increasing variety of specialists in the medical profession; sometimes it seems as though one could go to a different doctor for each part of the body.

Specialization has several important implications. First, lower-echelon workers who were trained only for a single, narrow job, and who lose that job, may have difficulty obtaining work for which their training qualifies them. Second, a worker in such a job often feels he or she is merely an adjunct to a machine or a process, with little chance to develop and use more than minor skills or abilities. This feeling often prompts dissatisfaction with the work. Finally, the increase in specialization has created problems of worker coordination and cooperation which present the managers of organizations with some of their greatest challenges.

It is not an uncommon experience, upon asking people what they do for a living, to be given the name of the organization for which they work. Increasingly, the modern American worker is an "employee." After 1950 the proportion of working people classified as self-employed dropped from 17 percent to approximately 8.5 percent today.[11] Small business owners and independent shopkeepers survive in small cities, suburbs, and older big-city residential districts, as do some family-owned and -managed companies. But their number diminishes every year, and each year they employ fewer members of the labor force. Self-employment is disappearing because small business owners find it increasingly difficult to compete against the large corporate establishments in industry, farming, and the professions, and because many people prefer the job security of working for a large organization to the high risks of entrepreneurship.

As self-employment and small-business opportunities dwindle, increasing numbers of people go to work for large bureaucratic organizations. A bureaucracy can be defined as a large organization with a systematic administration characterized by specialization of functions, objective qualifications for office, action according to fixed rules, and a hierarchy of authority. Max Weber, the pioneer of bureaucratic analysis, offers a slightly different, though fundamentally parallel, definition: a hierarchical arrangement of centralized authority, the slotting of people in well-defined roles with set duties, explicit rules and procedures governing both normal and emergency operations, and a formal system of rewards and punishments to assure appropriate behavior. Such bureaucratic systems are found in government, large corporations, unions, public school systems, universities, hospitals, and most other private and public institutions.

The labor force, as defined by the government, consists of all persons, 16 years of age or over, not in institutions, who worked one hour for pay during one survey week (the employed) and those who did not work during the survey week, do not have a job, and are actively seeking work (the unemployed).[12] In this total force, the most significant trend is

AN EMPLOYEE SOCIETY

AGE AND SEX COMPOSITION OF THE LABOR FORCE

[11] U.S. Bureau of the Census, *Statistical Abstract of the United States, 1975.* Washington, D.C.: U.S. Government Printing Office, 1975.
[12] R. A. Nixon, "An appreciative and critical look at official unemployment data." In Melvin Herman, Stanley Sadofsky, and Bernard Rosenberg, eds., *Work, Youth and Unemployment.* New York: Crowell, 1968, p. 31.

toward the inclusion of married women and the exclusion of older men.

Older men are being eliminated from the labor force primarily because of educational and occupational obsolescence. As we discussed in Chapter 9, employers hesitate to keep or hire older men when younger and better-trained people are available, usually at lower salaries. Middle-aged women have displaced older men in many clerical and professional jobs, and young high school and college graduates are starting to replace them in all fields. Thus, whereas 40 percent of males over age 65 were in the labor force in 1954, by 1964 only 28 percent were still in the work force;[13] by 1975 their participation declined to 22 percent. Meanwhile, increasing numbers of women aged 20 to 64 have entered the labor market, with the first great increase appearing in the 45- to 54-age group. Forty-one percent of these women participated in 1953–1954; by 1975 their rate of participation rose to almost 55 percent. The second great increase occurred between 1965 and 1975, as young women in the 20- to 34-age group joined the labor force; this younger generation of women was much better educated, many of them having had some years of college. Nevertheless, in spite of their greater education, most of them had to take jobs as secretaries, waitresses, bookkeepers, teachers, retail clerks, and typists. Although women are now being employed in greater numbers than ever before, the economic recession of the mid-1970s has caused a general decline in their employment, particularly among those who are heads of households;[14] and while many women are highly motivated to work, outside employment has not released most working married women from their household and family tasks. The married woman typically works many hours at home in addition to her outside job. (See Chapter 8.)

PROBLEM ASPECTS OF WORK

Among the work-related problems which arise in our society, the alienation of workers from their daily jobs would seem to be of major social importance. Marx and other nineteenth-century social critics attacked the assignment of people to activities which had no inner meaning for them as individuals. Factory workers, they claimed, were simply part of a productive process; losing control of both the process and the product, they became commodities. Alienation, as Marx conceived it, is a process which takes away people's capacity to express themselves in their work.[15]

In modern work situations, several elements combine to produce a sense of alienation. But the essential source is the clash between a person's self-image and the kind of person the work forces him or her to be. A person who sees himself as needing the companionship of others may feel as if an important part of himself is stifled in a job which does not give him time to be sociable with fellow workers. Another person is

[13] Susan S. Baker, "The growth and structure of the labor force." *The Conference Board Record* (October 1965):45–54.
[14] *Manpower Report of the President,* pp. 32–33, 205.
[15] Daniel Bell, *The End of Ideology.* Glencoe, Ill.: Free Press, 1960, p. 338.

apt to feel alienated if she sees herself as intelligent and yet has little opportunity to use her own judgment, or prides herself on being thorough and efficient but holds a job which stresses speed over care and quality. Other people may see themselves as independent and decisive, but find that in their jobs their bosses are constantly and closely supervising them.

A common assumption is that alienation resulting from work has serious social consequences beyond the immediate experience of the worker. Seeman has summed up this "generalization" idea of alienation:

Alienated work is troublesome because its effects generalize out of the work sphere into other areas of social life; the lack of control in work leads to a sense of low control in political and social affairs; the hostility bred in the work situation overflows into intergroup antagonism; the disagreement at work encourages loose commitment to the normative order in general.[16]

However, in a study conducted in Sweden, Seeman found that work alienation did not in fact generalize in this way. He had predicted that the correlates of work-induced alienation would be a sense of powerlessness, prejudiced attitudes toward minority groups, distrust in the larger society, and avoidance of political activity, coupled with a lack of knowledge about political affairs. But the data, based on a random sampling of 558 working men aged 20 to 79, did not support his predictions. It may be that these workers simply came to terms more easily than might be thought with the kind of work life offered by their society. They may not have felt a need to convert their work into a source of deep satisfaction, and may have been content simply to make it an acceptable part of life, usually by creating situations, however minor, of humor, sociability, competitiveness, or argument.

Studies more recent than Seeman's tend to contradict his findings. Several researchers have found that many of those in boring, monotonous jobs experience deep feelings of anger. These feelings sometimes result in severe psychological damage, causing workers to develop depressed personalities or to escape into fantasies or drugs.[17] Harold Sheppard and Neal Herrick found that alienation does result when work is unsatisfying, and that alienated workers often feel politically powerless, do not vote regularly, and favor extremist and authoritarian candidates.[18]

Nor are the symptoms of alienation necessarily confined to blue-collar workers. Alienation seems to be an inescapable result of any pyramidal, hierarchical management system that limits the individuals' autonomy and chances to use their skills. Growing numbers of white-collar workers feel estranged from their employers and the long-term interests of the companies they work for. Turnover rates for white-collar workers are high, and white-collar union membership has increased substantially over the past two decades. One study of 25,000 white-collar workers found a considerable decline in job satisfaction since 1965.[19] Management, in turn, reinforces white-collar employees' sense of powerlessness, estrange-

[16] Melvin Seeman, "On the personal consequences of alienation in work." *American Sociological Review* (April 1967):274.

[17] Report of a Special Task Force to the Secretary of Health, Education, and Welfare, *Work in America.* Cambridge, Mass.: M.I.T. Press, 1973, p. 22.

[18] Harold L. Sheppard and Neal Herrick. *Where Have All the Robots Gone?* New York: Free Press, 1972.

[19] Judson Gooding, "The fraying white collar." *Fortune,* December 1970.

ment, and insecurity by viewing them as "expendable." Unlike many blue-collar workers, white-collar workers have little job security and are often the first to be fired when a company's business goes bad. In addition, most have no union funds to tide them over if they get laid off.[20]

Work is a very important part of our culture, and until recently, to be unemployed in America was to be out of the cultural and social mainstream. The serious economic recession of the 1970s, however, has made unemployment a commonplace occurrence. It is no longer unusual to find holders of advanced college degrees lining up at state unemployment offices or taking menial jobs. (The desire to work becomes much stronger when a person's very subsistence is threatened; for this reason, millions of workers are holding fast to jobs they do not like, rather than resigning and trying to find better jobs.[21]) As will be discussed, prolonged joblessness causes serious psychological and social damage. A significant part of today's work force has been denied not only the financial benefits of a regular and sufficient income from their work efforts, but also the secondary emotional rewards that arise from a steady job: the sense of self-worth which comes from performing a job well and having others value that performance; the chance to associate with others, to discuss the events of daily life, to share discontents and satisfactions; in sum, the feeling that one is participating in society and contributing to it. The unemployed person, whether he or she is older and involuntarily retired, partially or intermittently out of work, or chronically unemployed, is denied many of these rewards. And each of these three groups constitutes a growing proportion of the population.

[20] *Work in America*, p. 40.
[21] "Staying put: What recession is doing to job hopping." *U.S. News and World Report*, April 14, 1975, pp. 65–66.

UNEMPLOYMENT

In America, being without a job means more than standing on line in unemployment offices. Unemployed persons are cut off from an important focus of social contacts and shared interests, as well as from a main source of their own self-respect.
Charles Gatewood

The Involuntarily Retired. Since 1890, the proportion of all men in the labor forces of several Western societies, including the United States has declined at an accelerating rate. The decrease is especially true for men age 65 or older. A study by C. D. Long sought reasons for the decline, but eliminated almost everything which might come quickly to mind:

No statistical evidence could be found . . . that the decline has been the immediate result of increases in real income, extension of pensions and social security, physical deterioration (compared with elderly men in earlier periods), or of changes in self-employment, the pace of industry, or the level of employment.[22]

The real reason seems to be a decline in the opportunity to work. Educational and occupational obsolescence were mentioned earlier as factors which prevent older men from obtaining and holding jobs. For example, in the Atlanta office of the Internal Revenue Service, 1,000 employees held jobs which involved processing tax returns. In 1959, the IRS decided to computerize this operation, and virtually all of the 1,000 jobs were eliminated. New jobs were created, of course—for computer programmers, console operators, and tape librarians. But the new jobs were in Martinsburg, West Virginia, where the IRS centralized most of its machines. Exactly 32 jobs were assigned to Atlanta. Even more to the point, few of the 1,000 displaced clerks could qualify for the new specialized work. Most had only a high school education and were over 45 years of age. The older people among them had no chance at all to obtain the jobs.[23]

Another aspect of the same situation is the decline in the number of "old-people jobs" compared to the number of old people. Many jobs once open to the elderly have almost disappeared; elevator operators, for instance, are a vanishing species. And even though the need for other service personnel, such as guards, doormen, and watchmen, is growing, the number of elderly people who would like such jobs is growing even faster. As opportunities decline—and as the age for retirement continues to drop—the number of persons who wish to continue to work but cannot will no doubt increase.

The Intermittently and Chronically Unemployed. In a competitive society, job insecurity is a common condition. Even in times when the national unemployment rate was low, many people who worked during the year were also unemployed for one or more periods. Part-time work is another constant factor. For some people such as semi-retired doctors or lawyers, students or homemakers with spare-time jobs, or "moonlighters" who take part-time work as a second job, part-time work is a matter of choice. For others it means denial of the opportunity to earn an adequate living.

Most serious, however, has been the recent sharp rise in intermittent

[22] C. D. Long, *The Labor Force Under Changing Income and Employment.* Princeton, N.J.: Princeton University Press, 1958.
[23] Ben B. Seligman, "Automation and the work force." In Robert Theobald, ed., *The Guaranteed Income.* Garden City, N.Y.: Doubleday, 1966.

and long-term unemployment. The national jobless rate jumped from 5.2 percent in 1974 to over 9 percent in 1975, the highest it had been since the Great Depression; by 1976 it had declined a bit, but still ranged between 7 and 8 percent. The mid-1970s recession affected not only the chronically unemployed—women, minorities, teenagers, the unskilled, and the semiskilled—but highly specialized white-collar employees such as middle-level managers and engineers, and also skilled workers in construction, manufacturing, and trade—most of them adult males and heads of households.

A very large number of the unemployed are young and/or nonwhite. During the 1960s and early 1970s, two nonwhite persons were unemployed for every unemployed white person; in the mid-1970s the nonwhite jobless rate continued its steep climb, but because of the large increase in the white jobless rate, nonwhite-to-white unemplyoment declined to a ratio of 1.7 to 1.[24] Nevertheless, the nonwhite employment rate of 13.8 percent is far above the national average,[25] and the nonwhite teenage unemployment rate of 42.6 percent is disastrously high.[26] Unfortunately, the chronically unemployed and their children rarely acquire the capacity to break out of the unemployment pattern without some state or federal help. Many of them are high school dropouts, and their low educational level equips them only for those low-skill jobs which are disappearing from the occupational structure. These young men and women may not have family obligations, but they often have the pride and sense of self we associate with youth; consequently, they are reluctant to take dead-end jobs as domestics, hotel kitchenworkers, or busboys. (See Chapters 6, 7, and 8 for fuller discussions of unemployment, poverty, and discrimination.)

The "Invisible" Unemployed and the "Discouraged" Worker. As we stated earlier, the labor force is made up of those persons, age 16 or over, not in institutions, who worked one hour for pay during the survey week (the employed) and those persons who did not work during the survey week, do not have a job, and are actively seeking work (the unemployed). By definition, all other persons over the age of 16 are not in the labor force and are therefore not included in government unemployment reports. This definition, as R. A. Nixon and others point out, results in a persistent underestimate of the size of the labor force and the volume of unemployment. For one thing, it excludes from the labor force those unemployed persons who, though able and willing to work, did not, for whatever reason, actively seek work during the survey week. A second factor is the failure of the official data to reflect adequately the underemployment of people who would like to work full-time but can find only part-time jobs. Citing several research studies directed at uncovering the magnitude of such "hidden" unemployment, Nixon concludes that "an accurate measure of currently available, unutilized manpower resources

[24] D. P. Klein, "Employment and unemployment in the first half of 1975." *Monthly Labor Review* (August 1975):11–12.

[25] Eileen Shanahan, "Jobless rate for 6 months stays 'on virtual plateau,'" *New York Times,* December 6, 1975, p. 58.

[26] U.S. Bureau of the Census, *Current Population Reports,* Series P-60, no. 98, Washington, D.C.: U.S. Government Printing Office, 1975, p. 63.

requires an increase of at least 50 percent in the official estimates." [27] Thus, if the officially derived unemployment rate is 8 percent, the actual rate, according to Nixon's estimates, is 12 percent or more.

The problem of "invisible" unemployment became more serious with the recent economic recession. The average duration of unemployment increased from a low of 9.3 weeks in 1973 [28] to more than 15 weeks in 1975, the longest in 10 years. Furthermore, a substantial number (36 percent of the unemployed, or 1.3 million people) had been jobless for up to 6 months or more; and over a million had stopped looking for work altogether because they thought it would be impossible to find. These became known as "discouraged" workers, people who were out of work not because of personal disadvantages such as being too old or too young, untrained or overeducated, but because industries and manufacturers had cut back production and had eliminated a large number of jobs. [29]

What happens to people without work? A 1960 study of 105 unemployed able-bodied men in Detroit showed that the outstanding common characteristic was extreme personal isolation. [30] Half of the men could name no close friends, half never visited neighbors, and few were members of organizations or spent any time in organized activities. These findings were in sharp contrast to the social life of an equal-sized sample of employed men. Such data tend to substantiate the thesis that work is necessary if a person is to be in any full sense "among the living." When work ties are cut, participation in community life declines and a sense of isolation grows. Thus individuals with the most tenuous work connections—the retired, the elderly, those who have been squeezed out of the labor market, and those who seldom get into it—are often isolated people in their communities and in American society.

Further studies on the emotional and social effects of long-term unemployment were conducted by D. D. Braginsky and B. M. Braginsky in 1975. [31] The Braginskys confined their research to high-status unemployed men who had been thrown out of work in the mid-1970s recession, an ever-growing class in the United States. The subjects consisted of two groups, one a control group of employed white-collar men and the other a group of 46 jobless men age 23 to 59. Almost half of the jobless men were college graduates, many had been engineers and company managers, and 80 percent had become unemployed for the first time in 20 years.

According to the study, these men undergo a "social transformation"; the trauma of unemployment causes a permanent change of attitude that persists even after they are reemployed. Sudden drop in salary and expanded free time result in low self-esteem and a high degree of alienation from the social institutions they had once trusted. Depression was common, and most of the men spent their days writing résumés and looking for work; but many of the others slept late and watched television.

[27] Nixon, pp. 35–36.

[28] *Manpower Report of the President,* p. 28.

[29] Klein, pp. 12–13.

[30] Harold L. Wilensky, "Work as a social problem." In Howard Becker, ed., *Social Problems.* New York: Wiley, 1966, p. 129.

[31] D. D. Braginsky and B. M. Braginsky, "Surplus people: Their lost faith in self and system." *Psychology Today,* August 1975, p. 70.

Most suffered from deep shame and avoided their friends. Their low self-esteem was reflected in the fact that many said they felt insignificant and obscure, that they were no more than a statistic, and that they could easily be replaced in their families. Almost all had had the demeaning experience of being treated insolently by employment office bureaucrats. Those in the study group who were able to find jobs never fully recovered the self-esteem they had had before being laid off.

Perhaps the most dangerous and disturbing effect of prolonged unemployment, however, was the loss of faith in the social order. Practically all of the unemployed men had put their trust in higher education, believing that it would guarantee permanent job security. Most felt a growing cynicism toward society, considering it "callous" and "indifferent" toward people on a personal level—an attitude that intensified even after they had found other jobs. Political beliefs were shaken and radicalized: each man was forced to question how much he was really valued, how much confidence he should have in social institutions, and how much responsibility the political system has for his present unfair treatment.

Yet another consequence of chronic unemployment was highlighted by the National Advisory Commission on Civil Disorders in 1967. Noting that grievances concerned with unemployment and underemployment were second in intensity only to complaints about police practices, the commission reported that

employment problems have drastic social impact in the ghetto. Men who are chronically unemployed or employed in the lowest status jobs are often unable or unwilling to remain with their families. The handicap imposed on children growing up without fathers in an atmosphere of poverty and deprivation is increased as mothers are forced to work to provide support.

The culture of poverty that results from unemployment and family breakup generates a system of ruthless exploitative relationships within the ghetto. . . . Children growing up under such conditions are likely participants in civil disorder.[32]

Thus it becomes clear that work plays a fundamental social role in our society. The lack of it is felt as a serious deprivation. At best, the individual without work is a lonely, second-class citizen; at worst, he or she is a hopeless reject, who may readily vent a sense of alienation and frustration in antisocial activity, perhaps in violence.

AUTOMATION

In the next few decades, automation may produce fundamental changes in the character of work in America. It will not replace workers. No matter how widely or quickly it spreads, there still will not be full automation—self-regulating, self-correcting, self-maintaining, and self-perpetuating. The popular vision of robots assembling everything society needs will not become a reality for a very long time. The most elementary production work still calls for complex coordination of hands, eyes, and body strength. In the words of one observer, "A task as apparently simple as polishing a fender to a desired glow requires exact feedback on a scale

[32] *Report of the National Advisory Commission on Civil Disorders.* New York: Bantam, 1968, pp. 13–14.

which challenges the parameters of available engineering." [33] But automation certainly will modify existing jobs, create new jobs, and require training or retraining for new skills on a greater scale than any technological advances of the past. Workers will inevitably face certain adjustment problems during this transformation.

The Areas of Automation. There have been three major developments in the computer-controlled production methods we call automation. The first consisted of linking together into a continuous process several production operations which had been performed separately. In such an integrated system—first developed for the oil refining and chemical industries, which need a high degree of control—the product moves from start to finish completely automatically.

Electronic data processing (EDP), which records, stores, and processes information, was the second development in automation. The most familiar example of this is the office computer which handles bookkeeping, accounting, billing, and countless other clerical operations. Electronic data processing permits a bank teller to take the dates and sums from a savings passbook and to give the waiting customer an instant report on his or her compounded interest. On more than half of all long-distance telephone calls, EDP eliminates the need for an operator by doing the routine work—recording the numbers of caller and receiver, checking the time and charges—while managing the information more quickly and accurately than the operator could.

The third development was that of feedback control computers, or servo-mechanisms, which compare the work actually being done with the work as it should be done, and automatically adjust the work process when necessary. A simple and familiar example is the living-room thermostat, which automatically controls the heating system of a household to maintain a specified temperature. The same principles are employed in a Great Lakes steel mill computer which keeps track of over 1,000 variables, and controls mill operations with a speed and accuracy far beyond any human ability. If the computer finds an error in a product item, it can make the necessary adjustments to correct the error on the next item in a fraction of a second.[34]

Impact on Organizational Structures. What are the effects of such technology? Thus far we have discussed the way in which automation affects workers. But Marshall Meyer, among others, points out that computer control will also alter the administrative structure of the bureaucratic organization.[35] For one thing, most automated operations require a separate data-processing staff. Such computer specialists are often somewhat different from many of the other people in a factory. They have skills which the others do not understand, and their job is not to actually

[33] Sar A. Levitan and William Johnston, *Work Is Here to Stay, Alas.* Salt Lake City, Utah: Olympus, 1973, pp. 104–105.
[34] Seligman, p. 143.
[35] Marshall W. Meyer, "Automation and bureaucratic structure." *American Journal of Sociology* (November 1968):256–264.

produce the product but to provide efficient means of producing it. Automation, therefore, creates a new kind of interdependence between the people whose work directly concerns the end product and the data-processing staff, whose work helps to accomplish the others' goal. Individuals with high status in the organization but no technical expertise must deal cooperatively with technical experts, such as programmers or systems analysts, who have no supervisory authority at all—a relationship unique to modern organizations. Such cooperation is not easy to achieve. Because of their lack of computer expertise, managers may insist on a technically unreasonable request, and may use the authority of their position to force the data-processing staff to comply with their wishes. Conversely, data-processing specialists may use the authority of their expertise to deny even a reasonable request if it is not convenient. In addition to being a problem in human relationships, such line-staff conflicts are a problem of administration in an organizational structure. Meyer speculates that as automation takes over, the interdependence between the high-status non-experts and the low-status experts will increase to such a point that organizations will have to adjust their basic structure.

Effect on Workers. When automatic processes become more widespread, as is likely to happen, they will affect every type of worker—white- and blue-collar, supervisor and manager, semiprofessional and professional— whether he or she works in a factory, a laboratory, an office, or a store. However, we still do not know precisely in what directions automation will go. Therefore, almost all current predictions about the effects of automation are educated guesses.

Studies of how automation affects workers produce contradictory findings. For example, one study showed that computerization decreased workers' job satisfaction almost to a point of leading them to quit.[36] But the same study also reports that, in the long run, workers derive pride and satisfaction from the same factors—such as the faster working pace required—that in the short run created discontent. Further, it was at first generally assumed that automation would reduce the need for supervision and permit workers to share in decision-making. Here too, however, some studies show opposite findings. Finally, it has been predicted that automation will upgrade jobs and raise the working class to what Daniel Bell [37] calls a white-collar salariat. Yet at least one study indicates that automation in fact reduces the level of necessary skill and increases the tedium of a job. Amid the conflicting opinions shown in study results, there are a few trends which suggest the probable changes facing the different strata of American workers. Many of these changes seem likely to induce problems.

For people of the working class—that is, those performing manual work and services—one trend is the shift to a different kind of work performance. Future jobs will probably require less physical ability and greater mental ability and concentration. Instead of operating one machine on a production line, the new worker may have a multiplicity of

[36] Meyer, p. 257.
[37] Daniel Bell, "Work and its discontents." In Bell, *The End of Ideology*.

tasks and responsibilities—monitoring several machines, for example, and keeping the entire system functioning smoothly.

Among office workers—clerks, salespeople, supervisors, bookkeepers—the net result of automation is likely to be a reduction in the skills which their jobs require. Since the object of automation is to replace human fallibility—with machines which control other machines, measure electronically, record, self-correct, and make decisions faster than a person can react—it would seem likely that the jobs left over for people will be those requiring only low skills. When automation reaches most offices, the heavy job concentration will probably be at the low end of the salary scale—for instance, in key-punching, which is simple, monotonous, precise, and nerve-rackingly high-speed work that is often regarded as a dead end.

It is on the higher levels that automation may change work most dramatically. New hierarchical patterns are already emerging, and certain traditional roles of top and middle management are diminishing. Ida Hoos discovered that as computers run more operations, EDP executives wield more power, and top people in other departments find their functions being undercut and their authority lessened. Even vice-presidents find themselves bypassed when the computer takes over business operations relating to procurement, production, sales, and similar functions. " 'Vice presidents in charge of,' " writes Hoos, "find their official functions atrophying; there is not much for them to be in charge of." [38]

It seems, then, that automation may exacerbate conditions which

One of the consequences of automation has been a concentration of monotonous jobs at the low end of the salary scale. Note that almost all the keypunch operators in this office are women.
Leo Choplin/Black Star

[38] Ida Russakoff Hoos, "When the computer takes over the office." *Harvard Business Review* 79 (July–August 1960):102–112.

produce job discontent. Work will probably become more demanding and precise, perhaps making it less appealing. At the same time, workers may become even more alienated from their jobs, because they will be even less involved in the actual making of a product. Also, opportunities for human interaction may decline.

Yet there is another side. Money and job security for workers will probably be greater. Because machines will run automatically, workers may have more free time available on the job. In addition, it is possible that workers will establish freer relationships with those higher up in the organizational hierarchy, because they will be working closely with planners and programmers. In any event, while we cannot know precisely how future generations of workers will react to large-scale automation, it seems safe to say that ways will be found to keep work at least tolerably satisfying.[39]

As previously stated, there are some contradictions in the research findings related to job satisfaction. Perhaps the only definitive statement possible at this point is that it is a rather complex subject to investigate. Job satisfaction seems to be related to the kind of work one does, and in particular to the degree of autonomy, the amount of prestige, and the financial rewards of the job. We have already cited two studies in which over 80 percent of the subjects said that they would continue to work even if it were not financially necessary for them to do so. This seems to indicate that most Americans derive at least some amount of satisfaction from their work. Yet, in another study, wide variations in response were encountered when people in several occupations were asked if they would go into the same kind of work again (see Table 12-1). Only 43 percent of professional and white-collar workers, 24 percent of blue-collar

JOB SATISFACTION

[39] Harold L. Wilensky, "Work as a social problem." In Howard S. Becker, ed. *Social Problems: A Modern Approach*. New York: Wiley, 1966, pp. 117–166.

TABLE 12-1
Percentages in Occupational Groups Who Would Choose Similar Work Again

Professional and Lower White-Collar Occupations		Working-Class Occupations	
Urban university professors	93%	Skilled printers	52%
Mathematicians	91	Paper workers	42
Physicists	89	Skilled autoworkers	41
Biologists	89	Skilled steelworkers	41
Chemists	86	Textile workers	31
Firm lawyers	85	Blue-collar workers, cross section	24
Lawyers	83	Unskilled steelworkers	21
Journalists (Washington correspondents)	82	Unskilled autoworkers	16
Church university professors	77		
Solo lawyers	75		
White-collar workers, cross section	43		

Source: Robert L. Kahn, "The meaning of work." In Angus Campbell and Philip E. Converse, eds., Table 5, "Proportions in Occupational Groups Who Would Choose Similar Work Again," *The Human Meaning of Social Change*. New York: Russell Sage Foundation, 1972, p. 182. © 1972 by Russell Sage Foundations, New York.

workers, and 10 percent of unskilled workers report that they would continue in the same line of work.[40]

Job Satisfaction and Dissatisfaction. Stanley Parker has identified a number of common themes in various studies of job satisfaction.[41] He reports the sources of satisfaction as:

1. creating something—perhaps the most commonly expressed feeling;
2. using skill—which is different from creating something in that it emphasizes workers' pleasure in their own ability rather than in the end product they create;
3. working wholeheartedly—which most workers genuinely enjoy provided they do not feel that they will lose financially from it;
4. using initiative and having responsibility;
5. mixing with people;
6. working with people who know their job—the satisfaction of mutual professional respect.

It might be expected that if these are sources of satisfaction, their absence would give rise to feelings of dissatisfaction. Yet, in Parker's summary, different factors were seen to account for dissatisfaction. Some workers complained of repetitive work, in which one boring task followed another, or the same task went on forever. They also disliked making only a small part of a product, or doing fragmented tasks, which made them feel like onlookers rather than participants in the work process. Dissatisfaction also was likely to arise from doing a job which made many workers superfluous. A final cause seemed to be excessively close supervision.

In one study, Herzberg and others tested the premise that job satisfaction and job dissatisfaction are not simply the opposite ends of a continuum but are, in fact, separate phenomena.[42] Over 200 engineers and accountants were asked to describe two separate events. First they were asked to tell of a time on their jobs when they felt exceptionally good. After that incident had been thoroughly explored, they were asked to discuss a time when they had felt exceptionally bad. Analysis of the responses showed that the factors which produced feelings of satisfaction were achievement, the recognition that comes with achievement, responsibility, the nature of the work itself, and advancement and growth. Factors linked to feelings of dissatisfaction were supervision, working conditions, pay, interpersonal relations, and benefits. In the case of pay and benefits, the dissatisfaction arose out of the clash between people's expectations about such factors and the actual quality of the factors. For example, employees might be disappointed with salary increases or hospital benefits which do not come up to their expectations.

---

[40] *Work in America,* p. 15; and Robert Blauner, "Work satisfaction and industrial trends in modern society." In Reinhard Bendix and S. M. Lipset, eds., *Class, Status, and Power.* New York: Free Press, 1966, p. 476.
[41] Stanley Parker, *The Future of Work and Leisure.* New York: Praeger, 1971, pp. 44–45.
[42] Frederick Herzberg, Bernard Mausner, and Barbara Snyderman, *The Motivation to Work.* New York: Wiley, 1959.

Herzberg and his co-workers concluded that the sources of satisfaction are in fact different from the sources of dissatisfaction. It appears that the factors which lead to job satisfaction relate to the job content, while the factors which lead to feelings of dissatisfaction make up the job context, the environment in which the work is being done. Several replications of the study with other occupational groupings have produced results fairly consistent with those of Herzberg and his co-workers.

Income and Satisfaction. It is becoming increasingly apparent that the chance to do meaningful work is of primary importance. Workers may even rate such a consideration as more important than the amount of money they are paid. However, in many jobs, there appears to be little chance for the workers to find such a sense of meaning. For workers who already earn enough to live adequately, additional income cannot always offset the increasingly common meaninglessness of work in our society. This applies particularly to younger workers, who are apt to be better educated and less concerned than their predecessors about such problems as job security. They particularly resent toiling at jobs they consider trivial and boring, and they feel a need to exercise control over the circumstances of their labor. In one instance, over 85 percent of the eligible workers at the newly automated automobile assembly plant in Lordstown, Ohio, turned out for a strike vote in early 1972; 97 percent voted in favor of the strike.[43] At the heart of the workers' protest was their dissatisfaction with the assembly-line process and their demand for a greater voice in decisions affecting their immediate working lives.

What Herzberg, among others, seems to be saying is that through the intrinsic nature of our work we strive to realize our potential as growing, maturing beings; through those factors extrinsic to the work itself, such as pay, we must be able to satisfy our need for the material things which sustain that process of self-development. Where such satisfaction is blocked, the results are apt to be frustration and self-conflict for the worker, and personnel problems such as strikes, high employee turnover, and industrial sabotage for the employer.

Attempts to Make Work More Satisfying. Organizations have made various efforts to enhance employee job satisfaction. Occasionally this has been done solely because it was believed to be important for people to have satisfying and rewarding work. For the most part, however, such programs have been undertaken with the hope of raising employee productivity, improving quality, or reducing various personnel and operating costs. There have been two basic approaches to improving employee job satisfaction. One, centered on "human relations," [44] focuses on the social context of work, and seeks to improve satisfaction by improving communication among levels in the organizational hierarchy and by increasing employee involvement in decision-making. In Europe, but not to any great extent in the United States as yet, blue-collar workers have begun

[43] Barbara Garson, "Luddites in Lordstown." *Harper's Magazine,* June 1972, pp. 68–73.
[44] Fritz J. Roethlisberger and William J. Dickson, *Management and the Worker.* Cambridge, Mass.: Harvard University Press, 1939.

For every creative, challenging job there are hundreds that are unimaginative, routine, and boring, like these endless repetitive chores on an automobile assembly line. Young workers are increasingly demanding that their work be reorganized to allow them a sense of involvement and achievement.
Ken Heyman

to participate in management decisions and to have greater say in company policy. For example, the French government has encouraged industries to consult their workers about closings, working conditions, assembly-line reorganization, and other plans involving expansion, production, mergers, and pensions.[45]

The other approach is to make the work itself more satisfying, through actual changes in the content and structure of the job. Designated as "job enrichment," this is intended to give workers an opportunity to achieve and grow in their work by assigning them complete jobs rather than fragmented tasks, and giving responsibility to workers as well as to managers. In such programs, workers are often allowed to develop their own methods and procedures for doing their jobs.[46] An experiment in a Swedish drill factory confirmed that allowing workers to decide on their own methods and procedures under minimum broad specifications could result in greater productivity and job satisfaction.[47] Instead of a single worker performing one specific, repetitive, simple task, teams of two to four workers were formed, each team being responsible for the assembly from start to finish of a certain number of machines. For the first few months the workers experienced heightened tension and irritability because they had to learn wholly new methods of working and cooperating: each worker was forced to learn all the steps of assembly and finishing and to take into account the working habits of others. But since all the workers shared the same goals, and since each was more familiar than before with the rationale of the production schedule and flow of material, the overall process became more flexible in that it could cope more easily

[45] "Workers on the board." *Time,* May 19, 1975, p. 57.
[46] See Robert N. Ford, *Motivation Through the Work Itself*. New York: American Management Association, 1969; and Fred K. Foulkes, *Creating More Meaningful Work*. New York: American Management Association, 1969.
[47] Lars E. Björk, "An experiment in work satisfaction." *Scientific American,* March 1975, pp. 17–23.

with rush orders and relays. Productivity rose 5 percent, and at the end of the experiment, none of the employees wanted to go back to the traditional assembly-line method.

Job Satisfaction and Life Satisfaction. Few studies have analyzed job satisfaction in relation to satisfactions in other areas of life. The study by Seeman which we cited earlier failed, as we noted, to find a correlation between alienation at work and certain anticipated social effects. On the other hand, a study by Kornhauser, which assessed the mental health of factory workers in a sample of large and medium-sized automobile factories, found that approximately half of such highly skilled workers as printers showed "good" mental health, as against about one-third of the "ordinary" semiskilled workers and an even lower proportion of the "repetitive, machine-paced" semiskilled workers.[48] Good mental health included absence of anxiety and emotional tension; trust in and acceptance of people rather than hostility toward them; sociability and friendship rather than withdrawal; self-esteem; and overall satisfaction with life. The results of this study of people with very different personalities and backgrounds suggest that if job satisfaction and life satisfaction are inseparable, the picture of the American workers as "contented" is a distorted one.

In his classic study of automobile factory workers, Ely Chinoy cited the "coming to terms" which Seeman hypothesized as the worker's "solution" to the problem of alienation:

Men cannot spend eight hours per day, forty hours each week, in activity which lacks all but instrumental meaning. They therefore try to find some significance in the work they must do. Workers may take pride, for example, in executing skillfully even the routine tasks to which they are assigned. . . . They may derive a moral satisfaction from doing "an honest day's work.". . . They may try to squeeze out some sense of personal significance by identifying themselves with the product, standardized though it may be, and with the impersonal corporation in which they are anonymous, replaceable entities.[49]

At this point it is difficult to draw conclusions from the research on job satisfaction. It does seem likely that the amount of deep dissatisfaction with work is greater than most research indicates, and that various work and career situations make a great difference in job satisfaction. But there is still much to be learned about why we like our work or don't.

MORE LEISURE TIME

The problem of what to do with free time may seem to be a false issue to the many millions of unemployed in the 1970s; for them it is a matter of filling up months of unwanted "leisure" with some form of productive activity. Their plight illustrates the difficulty of discussing leisure activity apart from work, for leisure is meaningful only when it occurs at regular intervals in a person's work cycle, and in some ways represents a reward for time spent working—which for most people means doing something

[48] Arthur Kornhauser, "Toward an assessment of the mental health of factory workers." *Human Organization* (Spring 1962):43–46.
[49] Ely Chinoy, *Automobile Workers and the American Dream*. Boston: Beacon, 1955, pp. 130–131.

not necessarily enjoyable. In spite of the recent economic slowdown, however, the majority of workers today have almost 1,200 more hours of leisure time per year than did their counterparts at the turn of the century; they also start working later and retire earlier, giving them an average of nine more years of life in which they do not work.[50]

If leisure were a sphere separate from work, new nonworking time could be taken care of by building more theaters and resorts, starting education for leisure activities in grammar schools, and offering adult classes in retirement. But leisure is related to work. Despite everything else, Americans want to work for the income that lets them buy what they feel they need and want—a house, a car, a color television set, a sailboat. For most people, the question is still not one of work *or* leisure. It is work *and* leisure.

How are people using their leisure? What is its meaning and function? Are people, caught in stultifying jobs, turning to leisure to give their lives significance and satisfaction, even challenge? Is our society, which was built on the industrial system, shifting its center from work to leisure? Are the lines between work and leisure blurring—somewhat as they were in preindustrial days—with interpersonal relations becoming more important in each? The social effect of leisure is becoming a serious concern for possibly the first time since industrialization and the Protestant ethic made work the primary business of living. In the early days of industrialization, Adam Smith envisioned factory life as so degrading that only the hours away from work could restore human qualities and values. He, and later Marx, saw the factory as completely dehumanizing. But both were viewing the new industrial life in contrast to a somewhat romanticized view of the lives of peasants and yeomen, with which they were still in touch; and both overlooked the passive and boring elements which had always existed in that pastoral world. They also missed the touches of creativity—the tricks of the trade or the imaginative employee "sabotage" —which existed in the factories of their times, and which indeed still exist. Yet it is fair to say that industrialization developed so rapidly, and forced people of a rural tradition into factories with so little preparation, that merriment was pushed to the far corners of daily life. The "fringe benefits" of both hard factory work and the Protestant ethic occurred during whatever was left of the night and on Sundays, in the taverns and churches, as well as during occasional "seasons" of unemployment and on the increasingly rare holidays.

The Use of Leisure Time. As we have said, leisure in many ways reflects work. While most workers use their leisure time in a seemingly different manner from that in which they use their working time, their approaches to work and leisure are often similar, in structure if not in content. A worker who takes a package tour of Florida or Africa is participating in an activity organized in much the same way as most offices and factories. Other workers may gravitate toward leisure activities which involve behavior similar to that of their work—thus they may gain relief from the monotony of work without making the return to work a difficult adjust-

Because work is a prime source of social contacts, people may participate in company- or business-related leisure activities along with their coworkers, as this member of a New York Stock Exchange baseball team illustrates.
Courtesy of New York Stock Exchange.
Photo by Edward C. Tapple.

[50] Juanita Kreps and Joseph Spengler, "Future options for more free time." In Fred Best, ed., *The Future of Work*. Englewood Cliffs, N.J.: Prentice-Hall, 1973, pp. 87–88.

ment.[51] Stanley Parker cites the popular game of bingo as an example of such use of leisure.[52] Bingo has several features which imitate the work experience of many people who enjoy it—concentration, limited movement patterns, supervision, and intervals for refreshments.

Another example occurs in the research of Fred Blum, who studied the specific leisure pursuits of packing-house workers.[53] Workers typically carried their work attitudes into the weekend, even though they were tired and wanted to get away from work and everything it represented. Often they chose fishing, which seems, at first sight, quite unlike their work. It was relaxing, it took them outdoors and let them "get away from it all." But, like their work, fishing did not demand much initiative or attention on their part. Most of all, noted Blum, it permitted the psychological mechanisms of "busy-ness" to continue. Thus fishing actually requires the same attitude, effort, and attention as the job from which it was superficially so different.

People whose work demands considerable involvement and responsibility are likely to blend their leisure with their work. A survey by Gerstl and Hutton indicated that 23 percent of professional engineers had hobbies related to the field of engineering.[54] As many as 73 percent have work-connected reading as one of their hobbies. Riesman observed that people often move from jobs where good performance requires them to cope with many interpersonal situations to leisure activities where interpersonal relations require them to give workmanlike performances.[55]

By contrast, people whose work involves only a few hours on the job, or whose work is unrewarding, tend to follow a leisure style like that of people with no jobs at all. Much of their leisure is spent watching television indiscriminately to pass the hours. They seem to be trying to dispel their restlessness by habitual retreats into escapist entertainment.[56] (See Figure 12-1.)

For one segment of the work force the leisure problem consists of an extraordinary lack of leisure time. People in the upper working strata may take longer holidays and retire earlier than most others, but they usually find their work absorbing, and spend many extra hours at it, week after week. Such a pattern is typical of leaders in politics, business, the military, the academic disciplines, the arts, and entertainment, as well as of millions of other individuals at less exalted levels. However, this growing minority who wish to work 55 hours or more a week generally receive incomes that compensate them for their limited leisure time.

Work-Leisure Fusion. While off-time leisure is increasing, leisure also colors life on the job. In some companies, union shop stewards spend much of their energy—once directed entirely toward resisting the abuses

[51] Irving Howe, "Notes on mass culture." *Politics* (Spring 1948).

[52] Parker, p. 73.

[53] Fred H. Blum, *Toward a Democratic Work Process.* New York: Harper, 1953, pp. 109–110.

[54] J. E. Gerstl and S. P. Hutton, *Engineers: The Anatomy of a Profession.* London: Tavistock, 1966, pp. 138–139.

[55] David Riesman, "Some observations on changes in leisure attitudes." *Antioch Review* 4 (1952):417–436.

[56] Harold L. Wilensky, "Mass society and mass culture: Interdependence or independence?" *American Sociological Review* (April 1964):173–197.

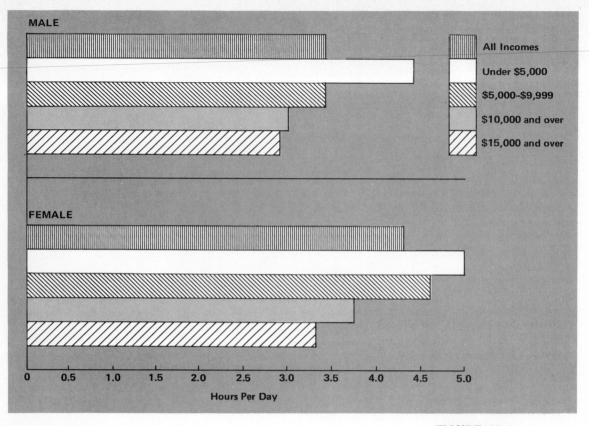

FIGURE 12-1
Television Viewing,
by Household Income
and Sex

Source: U.S. Department
of Commerce, *Social
Indicators.* Washington,
D.C.: U.S. Government
Printing Office, 1974, p. 222.

and encroachments of management—maintaining a comfortable level of sociability and gossip. In addition, management has had to design and furnish its plants and factories to accommodate employee tastes developed during their increased leisure-time activities. This is one reason why many companies have moved their factories to pleasant suburbs.

Leisure at work may include such off-time activity as the coffee break, the executive lunch "hour," and the card games enjoyed by night-shift workers. In addition, other devices to create free time through work life are appearing. For example, an increasing number of companies are allowing vacations longer than the usual two weeks, depending on the number of years worked.

The growing presence of leisure in the work-leisure situation is evident in the way in which leisure now confers status on work, where once work alone conferred status. According to Riesman and Bloomberg, workers have their own symbols of glamor—color television sets, stereo systems, sleek cars, and similar consumer hard goods.[57] In the same way, they can bring their personal status to their workplace from the world outside by indulging in such exotic or exciting activities as big-game hunting or race-car driving, by traveling extensively, or by engaging in union or local

[57] David Riesman and Warner Bloomberg, "Work and leisure: Fusion or polarity?" In Nosow and Form.

politics. Instead of the slow climb up the in-plant hierarchy, younger workers can now outrank many "senior" employees in terms of a more personal—and visible—kind of status.

Tilgher suggests, indeed, that the secular religion of work which flourished most richly in America seems now to be producing its exact opposite, a religion of recreation, pleasure, and amusement.[58] Today our society allocates a significant part of its economic resources (at least 4 percent of the national income) to pursuits that have no practical, adaptive, or "serious" value. Popular entertainers and athletes are among our most highly paid citizens. It would seem that leisure, humor, and play will always take up a great deal of human energy, whether they have to be "worked at" or not.

SOCIAL ACTION

In the preceding section we focused on four significant work-related problems: unemployment, automation, job satisfaction, and use of leisure time. Thus far, no comprehensive, systematic plans to solve any one of these problems have been made. In some instances, in fact, attempts at action have exacerbated the problem. The federal government's attempts to stop inflation, which in the mid-1970s had the side effect of increasing unemployment, are one example, Nonetheless, independent efforts are being made to alleviate various aspects of these problems. For example, one goal of the increased use of paraprofessional personnel in various fields has been the reduction of chronic unemployment. In this section we will discuss the use of paraprofessionals, as well as the movement toward a four-day work week, flexible work hours, and various projected changes in the use of leisure time.

It is not often that a single course of action presents a possible solution to a variety of social problems. However, there is a new, rapidly growing occupational category—paraprofessionals—which seems likely to help to alleviate a number of significant problems. The use of paraprofessionals, people trained in a particular field, to work alongside the professionals and take over some of their duties, helps to reduce both chronic unemployment and the perennial gap between the need for professional services and the available supply. It also helps to bridge the communication gap which frequently exists between professionals and their clients, thereby increasing the availability and improving the quality of the service. Paraprofessional training opens career opportunities to many people who would otherwise have difficulty obtaining steady work because of their limited education and skill levels. Again, by assuming some of the professional's traditional duties, the paraprofessional frees the professional to help more clients or to devote more time and attention to each client. Finally, because many paraprofessionals come from the communities in which they work, they provide a valuable social link between the professional and the client: they can talk to clients in their own language and can in turn understand them and their problems in a way in which the middle-class professional frequently cannot. Paraprofessionals

PARA- PROFESSIONALS

[58] Tilgher, pp. 22–24.

are becoming increasingly important members of the medical, teaching, and social work professions.

Medicine. It has long been demonstrated by the Army Medical Corps that a person can provide satisfactory medical care without spending eight years in college and professional school. But, until recently, such trained personnel as medics could not expect to find civilian medical jobs open to them above the level of hospital orderly. In the past few years, however, a growing number of medical schools and hospitals have begun to offer programs, generally requiring two years, to train "physicians' assistants." In addition to ex-medics, these programs are open to selected candidates whose educational records may range from grammar school dropout to a master's degree in public health. The main purpose of the programs is to create a new manpower pool to help meet the growing health care crisis in the United States, for it has become increasingly evident that the present number of trained professionals is drastically insufficient to meet the need. (See Chapter 2.)

The physician's assistant is trained to relieve doctors of a variety of time-consuming tasks—performing physical examinations, taking histories, doing diagnostic procedures and routine laboratory work, providing emergency care, making hospitals rounds, providing home and nursing-home care, and performing numerous administrative duties. Doctors are thus freed to spend more time diagnosing conditions and prescribing cures. In this way, physicians may be able to treat several people in the time they would previously have spent with a single patient.

Career opportunities for physicians' assistants should increase if doctors and patients learn to trust their capabilities, and if there is a reasonable measure of legal protection for the employing physician. With regard to the first condition, one study of 180 patients who were examined first by a paraprofessional and then by a doctor found only two cases of disagreement. As for legal protection, laws in a number of states now permit physicians to make use of paraprofessional assistants, provided their work is carried out under a physician's supervision.[59]

Teaching. The use of paraprofessionals in public schools to relieve the pressure on certified teachers has been growing rapidly in recent years.[60] Frequently referred to as teacher aides, these personnel perform a wide variety of tasks in two general categories: work involving direct contact with students, and clerical and technical tasks. The teacher aide may read to pupils, tutor individual pupils, supervise recess and study halls; or he or she may set up and run machines such as film projectors, type instructional materials, and help teachers with assorted administrative duties. In addition, the presence of teacher aides in ghetto schools often helps to reduce friction and increase communication among teachers, parents, and pupils.

There are few formal training programs for people who want to be teacher aides. However, several experimental training programs have been conducted. One such project in Washington, D.C., was designed to

[59] *Time,* November 9, 1970, p. 38.
[60] Paul C. Shank and Wayne McElroy, *The Paraprofessionals or Teacher Aides.* Midland, Mich.: Pendell, 1970.

prepare returning veterans for careers in education. Eight large city school systems and eight colleges cooperated in the project. The participants attended local colleges on a part-time basis, and were at the same time employed by the cooperating school district as assistants or aides to teachers and other school personnel. It was hoped that the veterans would provide models for ghetto youths and also be able to use the occupational skills they had developed in their military training. The program was also designed to attract more males into urban education, to expand the successful model of the Teacher Corps into the paraprofessional field, to encourage diversified staffs in urban schools, and to encourage the development of training programs using federal, state, and local resources.[61]

It is much more common to provide inservice training for teacher aides. This is generally done through on-the-job training by a teacher, administrator, or experienced teacher aide; a brief orientation program conducted by school district administrators; or a one- or two-week workshop run by personnel from outside the school district.[62]

Social Work. Professionals in the social welfare field have traditionally been defined as those persons who hold a master of social work degree, regardless of what their particular assignment is. Anyone else who provides social services has been called a paraprofessional, including workers holding a bachelor's degree. Today, however, there is an increasing use of workers with less than a college degree in the direct provision of social services. Here, as in medicine, the employment of paraprofessionals can often help to ease a chronic manpower shortage, and may make it much easier to establish and maintain contact with the community for whom the services are intended. Use of paraprofessionals also provides meaningful and productive work to many chronically unemployed persons, and places members of the community in staff positions and involves them in decision-making processes.

The jobs filled by paraprofessionals cover a broad range—psychiatric aide in a child guidance clinic, inner city neighborhood worker, welfare eligibility investigator, and more. This multiplicity of roles causes difficulty in identifying the common skills and tasks of paraprofessionals, with a resulting proliferation of job titles and training programs.

Despite these difficulties, the employment of paraprofessionals in the social work field is increasing throughout the country; and, in fact, in public welfare agencies, the use of such personnel is now required by law.[63]

THE FOUR-DAY WORK WEEK

The idea of a four-day work week has become more popular in the last few years, although at present the great majority of employees in the United States work a five- or six-day week. The shorter work week was first tried in smaller manufacturing plants, but recently service and retail

[61] Jack Marcussen and Jerry Calendine, "Pilot program for veterans in public service: Final report." In *Education Research Information Center* (January 1972): p. 92.
[62] Shank and McElroy, p. 19.
[63] Frank M. Loewenberg, "On the training of paraprofessionals and professionals for social welfare services." *Public Welfare* (Summer 1971):329–330.

industries, city governments, hospitals, and insurance companies have instituted four-day and even three-day work schedules. It is currently estimated that 650,000 full-time employees are working a four-day week and that another 190,000 are working a three-day week. If those who work a four-and-a-half-day week are included, 1.1 million employees, or 2 percent of all working people in the United States, are working less than a five-day week.[64]

One survey of 1,056 organizations, conducted by the American Management Associations, reported 143 already operating with a four-day week, 237 considering the change, 13 having discontinued the plan, and 663 not considering it at the time of the survey. There were sound economic reasons for considering such a change. Of the 143 organizations which had adopted a four-day week, 62 percent showed improved production, while only 3 percent showed reduced production; 51 percent showed higher profits, while 4 percent registered a decline; 66 percent recorded an improvement in efficiency, while 3 percent showed a drop in efficiency; and 38 percent experienced reduced labor costs, while 11 percent showed increased labor costs.[65]

It had been predicted that one result of the four-day week would be a marked reduction in absenteeism, and one early survey reported this to be so. It was believed that employees paid by the hour would be more reluctant to forgo 25 percent of their weekly earnings than the 20 percent lost for each day absent under the standard five-day week.[66] A 1974 survey found, however, that after the "novelty of the four-day week wore off," absenteeism returned to the same level as for five-day workers.[67]

Nevertheless, gains in productivity, efficiency, and profits are potent reasons for organization managements to consider the four-day work week. Indeed, in virtually every company in which the plan has been tried, it has been introduced as a result of management initiative. But the advantages are not all on the management side. For workers the most obvious immediate advantage of the four-day week is an increase in usable leisure time. For example, by working four 10-hour days, employees have a three-day weekend. Furthermore, since they come to work only four days a week, employees save 20 percent of their commuting time and expenses. Other savings include costs of restaurant lunches and child care.[68]

For the economy as a whole, the four-day work week might result in an increase in employment. Since work would be performed in a shorter length of time, more workers could be hired to fill the extra day that would be made available. The shorter work week would be particularly appropriate for recently automated industries that have eliminated many jobs and thereby aggravated the problems of long-term unemployment.

---

[64] Janice Neipert Hedges, "How many days make a work week?" *Monthly Labor Review* (April 1975):29.

[65] *U.S. News and World Report,* March 20, 1972, p. 82.

[66] Gertrude Samuels, "Thank God, it's Thursday." *New York Times Magazine,* May 16, 1971, pp. 32–33, 96–98.

[67] Hedges, "How many days make a work week," p. 33.

[68] Janice Neipert Hedges, "A look at the 4-day work-week." *Monthly Labor Review* (October 1971):34.

It has also been suggested that workers could use some of their new leisure time to train themselves in areas related to their jobs; in this way the shorter work week would be instrumental in raising the general level of education and competence of many workers.[69]

One survey studied 474 white-collar workers who had been working on the four-day system for a year, but with a different day off each week. Most employees reported an increase in job satisfaction because reduced supervision and staggered hours had forced them to expand their knowledge of other workers' jobs and increased their general sense of responsibility. They also appreciated the extra leisure time and felt that the shortened work week had helped their marriages and social lives.[70]

At least one argument against the four-day work week merits attention —the contention that the four-day week may have harmful effects on workers' health. The health and safety of workers was a major reason for the progressive shortening of the workday over a period of many years. By this logic, the extension of the workday to up to ten hours under the four-day-week plan may seem retrogressive. This may be especially true in jobs which entail great mental or emotional stress. In the white-collar survey mentioned above, two-thirds of the employees complained of fatigue at the end of a ten-hour day and hesitated to work overtime. Supervisors had trouble coordinating employees' work schedules and consequently had been able to take off only half the number of vacation days coming to them. It was also found that some kinds of work do not lend themselves to a four-day schedule, especially those involving coordinated groups of workers and those that must provide continuous customer service.[71]

For the four-day work week to be implemented on a broad scale, a number of changes would have to be made in federal and state labor laws and in negotiated union contracts. Many of the present regulations reflect concern for the effects of long days on a worker's well-being; as a result, they generally require overtime pay at premium rates for work in excess of eight hours a day, regardless of the number of hours worked per week.[72] An additional union concern is that during economic recession employers will adopt the four-day work week without increasing the length of the working day in order to reduce salaries.

The four-day work week has been somewhat slow in being accepted because of the introduction of gliding work hours, or "flexitime," which is part of the current trend among some employers to adjust the needs of the company to those of the employees. Under flexitime scheduling, employees are free to determine, within certain limits, when they will arrive at work and when they will leave, as long as they put in the normal quota of hours per week or month.[73]

FLEXIBLE WORK HOURS

[69] "The shorter work-week." *The Nation,* March 1, 1975, p. 229.
[70] Robert J. Trotter, "On-the-job satisfaction." *Science News,* December 7, 1974, p. 363.
[71] Brian Weiss, "The four-day week: The yeas and nays." *Psychology Today,* December 1974, p. 36.
[72] Hedges, "A look at the 4-day work-week," pp. 34–35.
[73] Fred Best, "Flexible work scheduling." In Best, pp. 95–96.

This system, which has been adopted extensively in Switzerland and Germany, allows workers to take care of personal business without using valuable work time, and also allows for individual differences in efficiency. It satisfies employers because workers are paid only for the actual number of hours they work, no time being lost because of lateness or "unrecorded leaves." As a result of being able to determine their own work periods, employees report that they experience less physical and emotional tension and higher morale. Flexible scheduling has also introduced a "democratizing" influence between workers and management, since supervisors traditionally have had freer schedules than workers, and workers now have a greater sense of professional responsibility for getting work done.[74]

THE USE OF LEISURE TIME

Whether or not the four-day work week and flexible work hours are widely adopted, there most likely will be an increase in leisure time in the next few years due to the present slowdown in economic growth and decreased demand for labor. And even if these factors are not present, there will still be expanded leisure time resulting from increased automation and the progressive lowering of retirement ages. The question, then, is how such time is to be used.

As leisure time has increased, there has been a proliferation of organizations and agencies, both commercial and nonprofit, devoted to planning and carrying out recreational activities. In the future we can expect more and better community planning for recreation and increased public recreation services from higher levels of government. Indeed, some researchers predict that recreation will take on the attributes and status of a profession in the near future.[75] Recreation professionals would have the task of developing and coordinating recreational activities to satisfy the needs of society and of the individual.

One requirement for the future is the development and implementation of educational changes which will prepare people for a "leisure age." Vocational preparation should not be the sole objective of education in a society in which the demands of work on people's time and energy are expected to decrease. Rather, the goal of the schools should be to provide people with the skills and capabilities required to achieve self-actualization in a non-work-oriented world.[76]

PROSPECTS

Despite the Full Employment Act of 1948, which made explicit the policy of government to work toward the reduction of unemployment, millions of persons today are without jobs, many of them for long periods of time. As we suggested in Chapters 6 and 7, government policies have, at best, resulted in only a minimal decline in the unemployment picture. Substantial new efforts must be made to reduce the discrimination which

[74] Janice Neipert Hedges, "New patterns for working time." *Monthly Labor Review* (February 1973):4–6.
[75] Norman P. Miller and Duane Robinson, *The Leisure Age: Its Challenge to Recreation.* Belmont, Calif.: Wadsworth, 1963, p. 12.
[76] William Faunce, *Problems of Industrial Society.* New York: McGraw-Hill, 1968, pp. 173–174.

prevents women and minorities from achieving job equality and to increase the number of jobs available to all.

One method the government has been particularly reluctant to use in order to reduce unemployment is to hold corporations partially accountable for the decline in available jobs. Corporations at present employ over 50 percent of the work force;[77] in view of this fact, corporations really can no longer be considered "private" institutions with all the rights, autonomy, and freedom of action of individuals. As many critics are beginning to contend, corporations will have to reevaluate their interests and priorities and accept a much larger share of public responsibility. For example, instead of building more profit- and efficiency-enhancing automated factories that throw thousands out of work, corporations should be expected, and perhaps forced by government regulation, to try to create more jobs overall to help relieve part of the unemployment problem—or at least to help keep it from increasing.[78] The government might also subsidize companies to maintain their payrolls in time of economic recession, as many European governments do.

Another area that may require some major changes in public policy is the so-called education inflation. During the 1950s and 1960s, it was assumed that people would have to be educated for a longer time, and more intensely, for the highly demanding technological jobs that were certain to evolve in the future; and at first the increase in white-collar and professional jobs made a college education seem necessary for many people. This in turn bred "credentialism," an attitude among employers who valued the number of degrees a prospective employee had more than his or her actual learning and experience. Indeed, economic studies during those years harped on the financial rewards that would accrue to those who held MAs and PhDs.[79]

However, it has been seen over the last twenty years that the great majority of jobs have demanded no increase in education. As one authority has stated:

The fact is that 80 percent of our jobs require little more than a high school diploma. Yet we are still sending 60 percent of our recent high school graduates and an increasing proportion of other age-group members to college. . . . The result is a surplus of educated workers and an unnecessary boosting of educational requirements for jobs which in reality have not become more difficult.[80]

As would be expected, most of these "overeducated" workers tend to be unhappy with their undemanding jobs. Studies show that the more education workers have, the more likely they will be to seek better jobs, and be less productive and more dissatisfied with their present ones. In one survey, over 33 percent of the employees interviewed believed they had more education than their jobs required.[81]

Any prospective solution to the overeducation problem will have to

[77] *Work in America,* pp. 21–22.
[78] Neil W. Chamberlain, *The Limits of Corporate Responsibility.* New York: Basic Books, 1973, pp. 204, 206.
[79] *Work in America,* p. 135.
[80] Best, p. 101.
[81] Levitan and Johnston, p. 74.

consider individual needs and capabilities, and eventually the traditional patterns of education and work may have to be altered. There will always be those who wish to educate themselves in universities for an occupation. But perhaps the great majority would do better by going to college only after they have had some work experience; and still others might find themselves learning all the skills they need directly from the job.[82]

We can expect these problems to become important issues of public policy if the trends we have discussed—such as high unemployment, greater automation, the need for more corporate responsibility, and over-education—continue to manifest themselves strongly. Of course, by the time we succeed in adjusting our institutions to the needs created by these developments, a whole new set of innovations will probably have begun, attended by new dislocations and opportunities.

While work provides workers with the essentials of life, and society with the goods and services it needs, it also confers a sense of self-worth and determines the individual's place in the social structure. Although work was viewed by the Greeks and Romans as a curse, the Hebrews and Christians regarded it as important to physical and spiritual well-being; Luther endowed work with religious significance, and Calvin transformed it into an end in itself.

SUMMARY

Since 1900 the occupational structure of the United States has changed from a largely agricultural base to one dominated by white-collar employment and specialized into thousands of different occupations. Large bureaucratic organizations employ the great majority of workers today, and there are many fewer self-employed persons. Older men are gradually being eliminated from the labor force, and women of all ages are beginning to participate in greater numbers.

The lack of any deep satisfaction in much routine work today has produced the social phenomenon of alienation, with its attendant psychological damage, in both blue- and white-collar employees. The severe economic recession of the 1970s and, to a lesser degree, automation have created another major social problem, that of large-scale unemployment. Automation at present seems to serve the needs of management more than workers; if adopted on a wide scale, it would involve a reduction of work skills for most workers and a realignment of authority for a few.

Job satisfaction and dissatisfaction seem to depend on separate factors. Satisfaction is related to achievement, recognition, responsibility, meaningful work, and, of course, income; dissatisfaction is caused by factors such as too close supervision, poor working conditions, low pay, isolation, and boring work.

In spite of the economic slowdown, most working people have more leisure time than ever before. Leisure time, however, is often meaningful only in relation to work; and many persons' leisure time activities share common characteristics with their work.

Many independent efforts are now being made to solve the problems of unemployment and alienation. The use of paraprofessionals, for example, has begun to reduce chronic unemployment and to close the gap between the need for and supply of professional services. Paraprofessionals are being used widely in medicine, teaching, and social work. The four-day work week has been instituted in many companies with good results: productivity and

[82] Hedges, "New patterns for working time," p. 7.

efficiency have improved, and job satisfaction and profits have increased. The acceptance of flexible work hours is another recent innovation that allows workers to determine their own working periods and has produced higher morale and improved efficiency.

Many social critics are advocating that corporations take on a larger share of responsibility for solving many work-related social problems, in view of the fact that they employ such a large part of the work force. Another shift in public policy will have to occur in order to make the educational criteria for most jobs more realistic.

BIBLIOGRAPHY

Best, Fred, ed. *The Future of Work*. Englewood Cliffs, N.J.: Prentice-Hall, 1973.

Blau, Peter, and Duncan, Otis D. *The American Occupational Structure*. New York: Wiley, 1967.

Buckingham, Walter. *Automation: Its Impact on Business and People*. New York: New American Library, 1961.

Chamberlain, Neil W. *The Limits of Corporate Responsibility*. New York: Basic Books, 1973.

Chinoy, Ely. *Automobile Workers and the American Dream*. Boston: Beacon, 1965.

Fromm, Erich. *The Sane Society*. New York: Holt, Rinehart and Winston, 1955.

Gooding, Judson. *The Job Revolution*. New York: Walker, 1972.

Herman, Melvin, Sadofsky, Stanley, and Rosenberg, Bernard, eds. *Work, Youth, and Unemployment*. New York: Crowell, 1968.

Jaques, Elliot. *Work, Creativity, and Social Justice*. New York: International Universities Press, 1970.

Levitan, Sar A., and Johnston, William B. *Work Is Here to Stay, Alas*. Salt Lake City, Utah: Olympus, 1973.

Marcson, Simon. *Automation, Alienation, and Anomie*. New York: Harper & Row, 1970.

Mills, C. Wright. *White Collar: The American Middle Classes*. New York: Oxford University Press, 1951.

Nosow, Sigmund, and Form, William H., eds. *Man, Work and Society*. New York: Basic Books, 1962.

Parker, Stanley. *The Future of Work and Leisure*. New York: Praeger, 1971.

Report of a Special Task Force to the Secretary of Health, Education, and Welfare. *Work in America*. Cambridge, Mass.: M.I.T. Press, 1973.

Sexton, P., and Sexton, B. *Blue Collars and Hard Hats: The Working Class and the Future of American Politics*. New York: Random House, 1971.

Terkel, Studs. *Working*. New York: Avon, 1972.

Udy, Stanley H., Jr. *Work in Traditional and Modern Society*. Englewood Cliffs, N.J.: Prentice-Hall, 1970.

Vroom, Victor H. *Work and Motivation*. New York: Wiley, 1964.

Whyte, William H., Jr. *The Organization Man*. Garden City, N.Y.: Doubleday, 1957.

Wolfbein, Seymour. *Work in American Society*. Glenview, Ill.: Scott, Foresman, 1971.

13

THE POPULATION CRISIS

- The world's population is increasing at the rate of 200,000 people a day.
- If the current rate of population growth continues, the population of the world will double in 35 years.
- Nine out of every ten people added to the world's population will be in the poorer, developing countries.
- By the year 2000, Asia alone will contain almost as many people as there are in the entire world today.
- From 1965 to the present, world food production has increased by about 32 percent. Because of population growth, however, per capita food production has increased only 7 percent, and this is mostly in the developed countries. In the developing countries, per capita food production has dropped *below* 1965 levels, even though total food production has increased.

In recent years animal studies have provided clear evidence of some of the harmful effects of overpopulation. Laboratory animals which are subjected to serious overcrowding become nervous, irritable, and often abnormally aggressive; natural cleanliness gives way to soiled fur and littered cages; mating may not take place or females may abandon their newborn young; even cannibalism can eventually be expected to occur, especially among rodents. Such behavior seems to result from physiological damage brought on by the stress of the crowded condition; and this damage will not be completely healed even if the animal is later returned to a normal environment.

Sometimes, too, a delicate equilibrium between population and environment can be catastrophically upset by what appears to be a minor change. For example, the addition of even one or two more fish to a fully populated aquarium may be enough to destroy the vital oxygen balance and kill off large numbers of fish. Likewise, a few extra sheep or goats on an overgrazed pasture may kill the grass and allow heavy rains to erode and destroy the land.

The harmful effects of human overpopulation are more difficult to prove. Yet it is not hard to find similarities to the animal situation. Crowded living conditions in cities or neighborhoods seem to be associated with a rise in tensions, hostilities, violence, and outright crime;

and dirty streets, dirty air, and inadequate garbage collection are almost standard.

Other, more specifically human problems are also accentuated by overpopulation. How shall we provide jobs for all those who need to work? How shall we ensure adequate housing and recreation for everyone? How shall we even maintain the services without which a complex society could not function—reliable public transportation, adequate power supply, firefighting, medical care, food and product distribution?

These are problems of industrialized and highly urbanized nations such as ours. The so-called developing nations, still largely agrarian, face critical problems of a different type: how to bring basic education and health care to growing numbers of mostly rural poor; how to initiate and carry out major economic development projects when the gains are offset—often before they can even be felt—by having to be divided among an ever larger number of people.

Even more far-reaching problems have begun to claim our attention. We are realizing that at present expanding rates of demand, the world's available supplies of oil, coal, and natural gas may be used up in a few generations, and that there may be a limit to the amount of food our planet can be expected to produce. Rapid encroachments on the shrinking wilderness have placed many species of wild animals in serious danger of becoming extinct. Chemical pollution appears to be endangering our largest lakes and possibly even the oceans; and the damages thus caused could turn out to be irreversible. (These and other environmental problems are considered more fully in Chapter 14.) Finally, nations with a large share of the world's population may eventually insist on receiving a proportionate share of its wealth, which they do not at present have, and it is not inconceivable that nuclear war might result.

For all these reasons, overpopulation cannot safely be left to itself in the hope that, if ignored, it will somehow go away. In the following sections, we shall look at some types of population statistics and their meaning, and then consider in greater detail the effects of rapid population growth in advanced and in underdeveloped countries.

SCOPE OF THE POPULATION PROBLEM

In the middle of the seventeenth century, roughly the start of what most historians call the modern era, world population stood at about half a billion people. It had taken nearly 2.5 million years—the estimated time during which humanity and its human-like ancestors have existed—to reach that level. But by 1850, only two hundred years later, another half billion people had already been added. By 1950, the count had reached 2.5 billion—a further increase of 1.5 billion in a mere hundred years.[1] In 1976, total world population was estimated at over 4 billion—an increase of 1.2 billion people in 26 years.[2] By the year 2000, accord-

[1] Philip M. Hauser, "World population growth." In P. M. Hauser, ed., *The Population Dilemma*. 2nd ed. Englewood Cliffs, N.J.: Prentice-Hall, 1970.
[2] Agency for International Development, *Annual Report*. Washington, D.C.: U.S. Government Printing Office, 1976.

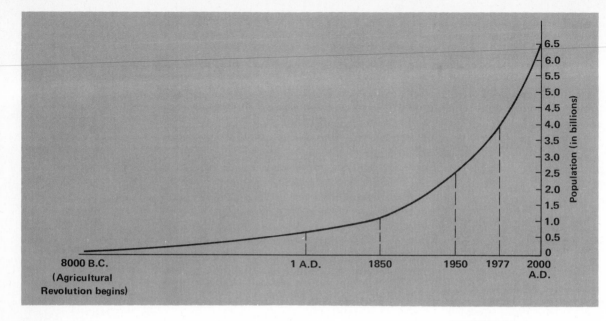

8000 B.C.
(Agricultural
Revolution begins)

1 A.D. 1850 1950 1977 2000 A.D.

Population (in billions)

FIGURE 13-1
World Population
Growth (8000 B.C.
to A.D. 2000)

Source: Adapted from
United Nations figures.

ing to United Nations' estimates, the population of the world will probably total 6.5 billion.[3] (See Figure 13-1.)

As we consider the dimensions of the population explosion, we should bear in mind this fact: the areas with the highest annual rates of population growth are also those which rank near the bottom of the scale in per capita gross national product (GNP)—that is, the individual's share of the GNP, or estimated total of a nation's income from the sale of all

[3] "The grinding arithmetic for the year 2000." *UNESCO Courier*, May 1974, p. 9.

TABLE 13-1
Probable Pattern of
Population Growth

Region	Present Population (in millions)	Estimated Population in the Year 2000 (in millions)	Percent Increase
Asia	2,300	3,757	63
Europe	478	540	13
Africa	395	834	111
Latin America	327	625	91
North America	242	296	22
Russia	255	321	26
Oceania	21	33	57
World	*4,018*	*6,406*	*59*

Note: Over 80 percent of the world's population is in the poorer, developing regions. Over 90 percent of the population increase will take place in these regions.

Source: Adapted from United Nations, *Demographic Yearbook.* New York: United Nation, 1976; and *U.S. News and World Report*, October 21, 1974, p. 54.

its products, goods, and raw materials. (See Table 13-1.) An agrarian nation usually has a relatively small GNP, for it does not produce the refined or manufactured items which normally command the highest market prices. In addition, the larger the number of people among whom a nation's income is *theoretically* divided, the smaller each one's share. (Note the emphasis on "theoretical" shares and divisions. In reality, of course, income is not divided equally among all residents of a nation.) In short, those countries where people's lives and living conditions are most in need of improvement are precisely the countries whose population is increasing so rapidly that most people are scarcely better off than they were a generation ago, despite often gigantic efforts by their own and other governments and by the United Nations.[4]

We will not discuss here the political implications of such a situation, but they do exist. Without fundamental changes in the social institutions of many underdeveloped nations, it is likely that the relentless pressures of expanding populations will contribute to an accumulation of tensions and hatreds and to the outbreak of revolutions and civil wars.[5] (See Figure 13-2.)

POPULATION GROWTH

Rapid population growth is not a new phenomenon. For at least 50 years, the rate of growth in the poorer nations has been steadily rising, whereas in the wealthier countries it has been dropping steadily for more than a century.[6]

Most of us probably think of the population boom as basically the result of a rising birthrate. The reality is more complicated and involves several factors.

Crude Birthrate. A 2 percent crude birthrate means that each year a given group of 1,000 people will produce 20 babies. This does not tell us what percentage of the population is of childbearing age, or how many people can afford children. Nor does it tell us how long those 20 babies are likely to live—particularly, whether or not they will live long enough to produce children themselves.

Fertility Rate. The fertility rate is the number of births per 1,000 women between 15 and 44 years of age. This provides a better picture of the overall birth trend and future age structure of a society than does the crude birthrate.

Death Rate. If, in a group of 1,000 people, the annual death rate is 1 percent, the total number of people will be reduced by 10. Again, this figure tells us nothing about the distribution of deaths—whether they occurred among old people or among people of childbearing age.

[4] See Paul R. Ehrlich, *The Population Bomb*. Rev. ed. New York: Ballantine Books, 1971.
[5] See Kingsley Davis, "Population policy: Will current programs succeed?" In Daniel Callahan, ed., *The American Population Debate*. Garden City, N.Y.: Doubleday, 1971, pp. 227–258.
[6] See John D. Durand, "The modern expansion of world population." *Proceedings of the American Philosophical Society* 3 (June 1967):137; and Hauser, p. 15.

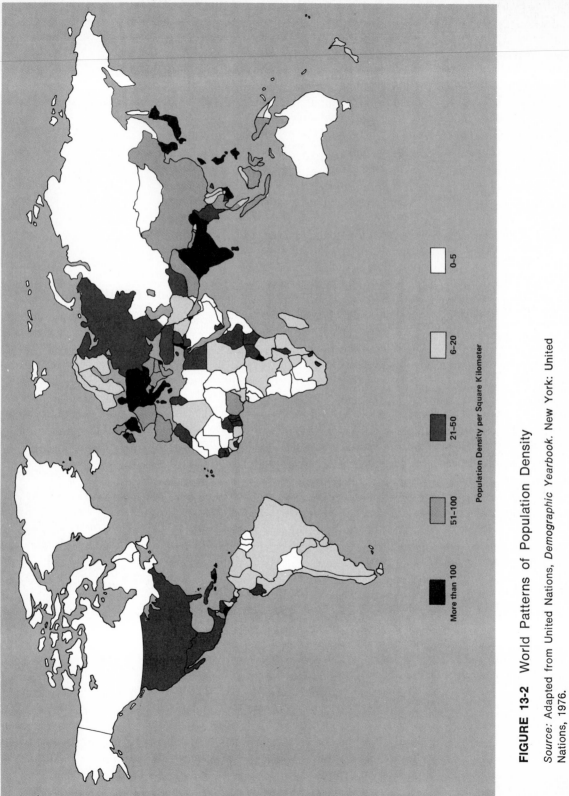

FIGURE 13-2 World Patterns of Population Density

Source: Adapted from United Nations, *Demographic Yearbook.* New York: United Nations, 1976.

Population Density per Square Kilometer

More than 100 | 51–100 | 21–50 | 6–20 | 0–5

Rate of Population Growth. The differential between the (crude) birth-rate and the death rate is called the rate of population growth. (It is also affected by migrations to and from the particular unit, a factor that can be discounted for the purposes of this discussion.) In our hypothetical 1,000-person group, in which 20 people were added by birth and 10 removed by death, the total population at the end of the year is 1,010—a rate of population growth of 1 percent. (*Zero population growth,* in the sense the term is popularly used, is not directly related to birth and death rates. It is a condition that exists when a generation produces only enough children to replace itself—that is, when an average of about two children are born to each set of parents.)

Taken as a whole, the peoples of the world are not reproducing at a rate higher than in the past. But more people are living to the age of fertility and beyond. In effect, more babies are surviving to produce babies themselves.

This change is traceable to several causes: enormous advances in sanitation, medicine, and public health; our increased ability to control excessive cold, heat, and other life-threatening aspects of our environment; and our greater power to prevent or quickly counteract the effects of famine, drought, flood, and similar natural disasters.

Thus the population crisis of our time bears out the thesis proposed in the opening chapter of this book: social problems are problems that affect large masses of people and are the unintended, unanticipated results of values and behavior patterns that have previously been regarded as useful and good.

THE EFFECTS OF POPULATION GROWTH

The social and ecological effects of overpopulation are serious wherever they occur. However, they are experienced differently by the highly industrialized, relatively affluent nations on the one hand and by the largely agrarian poorer nations on the other. For this reason it is necessary to consider the two areas separately.

Economic Growth. The more prosperous nations of the world include those of Europe and North America, plus Japan, Israel, Australia, New Zealand, and South Africa. They are well developed industrially, and their per capita GNP is high. In such countries, it is no longer unreasonable to aim at eliminating poverty altogether.

POPULATION PROBLEMS IN INDUSTRIAL COUNTRIES

It has been contended, particularly in recent years, that poverty is an inevitable by-product of Western capitalism. The implication is that socialism and communism, the other major economic systems of the modern world, tend naturally to eliminate poverty. Since neither pure capitalism nor pure communism is followed at present by any major industrialized nation, the proposition cannot be definitively tested. Most Western nations have found it necessary to introduce a considerable amount of government regulation of prices, profits, hours, and conditions of work, and of much else which bears on the creation and distribution of wealth. In the meantime, the socialist U.S.S.R. has had to make some concessions to the profit motive in order to stimulate production; and while the mass of Russian people are infinitely better off than they were in czarist days, economic inequalities and outright poverty have not, at least so far, been eliminated.

In any case, it seems increasingly evident that whatever the politico-economic system of a society, rapid population growth impedes the effort to distribute more equally even abundant material wealth. For one thing, population growth is usually more rapid among the poor. In the United States, for example, birthrates are consistently higher among the poor and among minority groups than they are among relatively well-to-do whites. (However, it is not true that the majority of the poor in the United States are nonwhites, nor that the majority of nonwhite families are poor. See Chapter 7.) "Approximately 42 percent of American families with more than 5 children are poor, whereas only 10 percent with 1 or 2 children are poor." [7] Whatever the underlying reasons for this pattern, the result is social and economic strain. For the United States, and for most other industrialized nations, a low or even zero rate of population growth appears to be economically desirable.[8] As Ansley J. Coale has pointed out:

In the short run, not only does a population with reduced fertility enjoy the benefit of dividing the national product among a smaller number of consumers; it enjoys the additional benefits of a larger national product to divide.[9]

Other important challenges in today's urban, industrialized nations—equalization of employment opportunities and of access to housing, more efficient dispensing of essential public services, and the like—are similarly more difficult to meet if population growth is not curbed. Indeed, some leading economists suggest that population control in a country such as the United States must go hand in hand with a questioning of the traditional capitalist assumption that an ever-greater labor force consuming an ever-growing national product is essential or even desirable.

Kenneth E. Boulding, for one, argues that our country operates on a "cowboy economy," an exploitative way of life which appeared perfectly legitimate when it seemed that the wide frontier spaces of America could never be filled up. Now, however, we have begun to realize that the resources of even the richest nation are limited, and that we must learn how to live within those limits. We must develop, says Boulding, a "spaceman economy," geared to efficient use and reuse of the supplies we carry aboard this "spaceship earth." [10] In such an economy, the values of unlimited production and consumption would give way to a recognition of the interdependence of all aspects of life, and to careful planning, so that all needs might be adequately met. Part of the program would necessarily be regulation of population expansion.

[7] Paul R. Ehrlich and Anne H. Ehrlich, *Population, Resources, Environment.* 2nd ed. San Francisco: Freeman, 1972, p. 322.

[8] See Stephen Enke, "Is a stationary U.S. population desirable and possible?" General Electric *Tempo,* mimeograph, 1969.

[9] Ansley J. Coale, "Population and economic development." In Hauser, p. 70.

[10] Kenneth E. Boulding, "The economics of the coming spaceship earth." In Garrett de Bell, ed., *The Environment Handbook.* New York: Ballantine Books, 1970, p. 96.

Quality of Life. Many of the problems associated with rapid population growth can be expressed in dollars and cents, or in figures on a table or a graph. But others are harder to define, and these are concerned with what has come to be called the "quality of life."

One can measure, for example, the loss to commercial lumber interests when fire destroys a great section of forest. But how can we measure the loss in recreation, in personal renewal and discovery of the world, when a wooded area rich with wildlife becomes a corporate subdivision or a shopping center? One can estimate the number of commuters delayed, and the work hours lost, in a traffic tie-up on a congested freeway. One can count the unemployed youths lined up outside a plant where an inadequate number of job openings have been announced. But what of the energy spent in rage that might have been turned to creative achievement; what of the hopelessness and resentment where there might have been joy and friendship? There was a time when such questions were held to be irrelevant, but unless we are prepared to believe that humanity's highest goal is mere physical survival, they may no longer be so.

To the extent that rapid population growth is a factor in creating or aggravating these problems—which to varying degrees are faced by all industrialized societies today—it is a serious social problem to be reckoned with. Some say it is the first problem to be reckoned with:

The crux of the matter is not whether the world can adjust to the present high rates of population growth but rather how much better the prospects for development would be if these high rates could be reduced.[11]

Hunger. As we shall see later in the chapter, there exists a heated debate among experts about whether or not the world can produce an adequate amount of food to feed its population. What is not debatable, however, is that large numbers of people are not now being adequately fed. In fact, some 50 percent of the world's population is undernourished; many millions of these die of hunger each year. An additional 15 percent of the world's population is malnourished, subsisting on a diet that is below the acceptable minimum for human beings.

Most of the world's hungry live in the nonindustrialized, agrarian countries of Asia and Africa, such as India and Ethiopia. Ironically, many agrarian nations were once exporters of food. However, their huge population growth during the past quarter-century has turned them, as a group, into food importers. These countries no longer produce enough food by themselves to feed their own populations. By United States nutritional standards, for example, India produces enough food to feed only 90 million of her 550 million people. Even accelerating food aid from other countries has not kept pace with the growth in population. At best, increasing numbers of people in the developing countries are being kept at the same inadequate level of nutrition. The worse—and more likely—prospect is that the number of people dying of starvation will increase, unless some way can be found to feed more people or reduce the rate of population growth. (See Figure 13-3.)

POPULATION PROBLEMS IN AGRARIAN COUNTRIES

[11] George C. Zaida, "Population growth and economic development." *Studies in Family Planning,* no. 42. New York: Population Council, May 1969, p. 1.

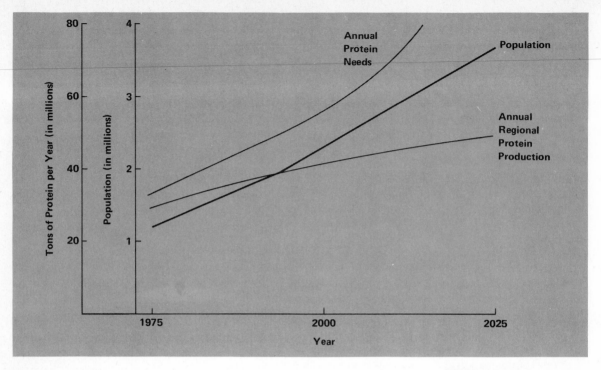

FIGURE 13-3
South Asia's Food Gap

The graph shows that as South Asia's population grows, her protein needs will increasingly surpass her food production, resulting in a protein deficit of an estimated 50 million tons by the year 2025. Even if these 50 million tons were available for export to South Asia from other countries, the transport and distribution problems involved would be massive.

Source: UNESCO Courier, July–August 1974, p. 33.

The relationship between population and food supply is brought into focus when it is realized that a little over one acre of farmland is required to produce the minimal amount of food each person requires. Unfortunately, most of the world's available land is already being cultivated. Increasing the crop yield of each acre—the purpose of the so-called green revolution—requires expensive tools and methods beyond the reach of most poor countries. The most effective fertilizers, for example, are derived from petroleum, the cost of which has gone up enormously in the past decade. The agrarian nations simply cannot afford the agricultural equipment and technology they so desperately need. As a result, most of their ever-increasing population must live with the pain of hunger on a daily basis, and suffer enormously high rates of disease and death because of malnutrition.[12]

Effects on Economic Development. To understand why the economics of underdeveloped, largely agrarian societies are affected by rapid population growth in a fashion different from that of industrialized countries, it is necessary to first explore in somewhat greater depth the concept of per capita income.

According to accepted economic thinking, to raise the economic standard of its people, a nation with a stable population must be able to invest (whether in private or in public funds) between 3 and 5 percent

[12] Shirley F. Hartley, "Our growing problem: Population." *Social Problems* 21 (Fall 1973):190–206.

of its annual income in new income-producing development. When population is growing at the rate of 3 percent a year, which is not unusual in the underdeveloped nations today, an investment of up to 20 percent of the national income is necessary before any rise in a nation's economic standard can take place. This is a rate which few poor nations can come anywhere near affording. In those which do, by considerable sacrifice, attain it, the continuing population growth spreads the resulting benefits so thin that they are apt to seem scarcely worth the struggle. It is important to realize that a population with a growth rate of 3 percent a year *doubles* in only 23 years, and it would require near-miraculous efforts on the part of a nation for its economic development to even keep pace with such population growth.

South America provides a good example. In the 1960s (prior to the worldwide recession of the 1970s), total investment of the Latin American countries in their own development amounted to 16.8 percent of their aggregate gross national product.[13] Under conditions of population stability, this would have been sufficient to bring Latin Americans a per capita increase in their incomes of at least 4 percent per year. Instead, because of excessive population growth, the rise in per capita income was barely more than 1.5 percent per year—an increase of only $15 on every $1,000.[14] In other words, the economic growth of these nations barely kept pace with their increased populations. As the Red Queen in *Alice in Wonderland* said, "Here, you see, it takes all the running you can do to keep in the same place."

Thus, whereas the industrialized nations are attempting to distribute more equitably their considerable national wealth and are foiled to a substantial degree by population growth, the underdeveloped nations are struggling simply to achieve a bare subsistence level for most of their people. In this effort, their even higher rate of population growth is an enormous handicap. To be sure, agrarian societies in our time have to contend with other serious internal problems as well—problems of education, health, language, political instability, and in many cases tribal or regional rivalries that interfere with efforts at united action. But almost all authorities agree that little progress can be anticipated on any front while populations continue to grow at the present explosive rates.

Is there any prospect that the rate of increase in the agrarian societies will actually lessen? Some population experts, on the basis of a "theory of demographic transition," [15] believe it will. According to this theory, in all societies the lowering of the death rate is eventually followed by a voluntary drop in the birthrate. Ultimately this results in a slower rate of population growth. In Europe, for instance, the death rate began to decline as early as 1650, as a result of such factors as commercial and agricultural changes, increased political stability, and the disappearance of the long-endemic Black Death. After 1850, with the effects of the Industrial Revolution and the rise of modern medicine, the decline became almost spectacular. During the first part of this period, the birthrate remained

In some crowded, underdeveloped nations, the street is the home and starvation is the lot of the poor. Here a drought victim in Niger is begging for food.
Chester Higgins /Photo Researchers

[13] *Economic Bulletin for Latin America* 11 (April 1966):8.
[14] Theodore Morgan and George W. Betz, *Economic Development: Readings in Theory and Practice.* Belmont, Calif.: Wadsworth, 1970, p. 19.
[15] For a fuller explanation of this theory, see Hauser, pp. 13–15.

high. Consequently, Europe's population increased, despite emigration to America, from about 103 million in 1650 to about 144 million in 1750, and to almost double that number by 1850.[16]

But sometime in the nineteenth century, or slightly earlier in some places, the birthrate began to fall, and continued to do so well into the twentieth century, until during the depression years of the 1930s a few European countries actually faced the possibility of overall population declines. This trend was reversed to some extent after 1940, but the birthrate remained low enough so that European growth rates today average less than 1 percent per year, as compared with an average of 2.1 percent for the world as a whole, and over 3 percent in some of the underdeveloped nations.

Proponents of the theory of demographic transition believe that in modern times the death rates in developing countries will eventually decline to the point where a drop in the birthrate will follow. This drop in the birthrate will eventually slow the population growth of poorer nations to a more desirable pace. Thus Barry Commoner advocates the massive export of funds, medical personnel, and food from the industrialized countries to the poorer countries so that the death rates in the developing nations will be lowered. Only then, he suggests, will these countries be motivated to lower their birthrate.[17]

Critics of the theory are somewhat less than reassured. For, as they point out, the industrialized West, even at its height of population expansion in the late nineteenth century, experienced a growth rate considerably lower than that of today's poor nations. A voluntary drop in birthrate which would be enough to slow down significantly the 2.4 to 3 percent annual growth rate of these poor nations is, admittedly, somewhat difficult to imagine, even if enormous food and medical supplies are sent. Moreover, poor agrarian nations have an excessively high proportion of children and young people in their populations. These will probably raise the birthrate to even higher levels. (See Figure 13-4.)

Furthermore, in order to expand its economy through industrialization, a society needs not only capital (money to be invested in new income-producing developments) but also labor (a significant proportion of its inhabitants trained and available for productive work in the new industrial facilities). Not only do these people help to produce new wealth, but by spending their increased earnings, they help to consume it, thereby increasing profits and supplying new capital to continue the cycle of expansion. (This traditional concept of constant economic expansion is applied today primarily to the underdeveloped nations; it must be modified with regard to the heavily industrialized ones.) Thus, in Brazil, the largest single group in the population is that between the ages of 5 and 9, followed by those between 1 and 4 and between 10 and 14. In Sweden, by contrast, the largest group is between 20 and 24, followed by that between 25 and 29. Clearly, the labor force in Sweden is much larger, in proportion to the total population, than in Brazil. (Actually, in Brazil, children of 14 and under probably do a great deal of work; in most

[16] Ehrlich and Ehrlich, pp. 16–17.
[17] Barry Commoner, "How poverty breeds population (and not the other way around)." *Ramparts,* August–September 1975, pp. 21 ff.

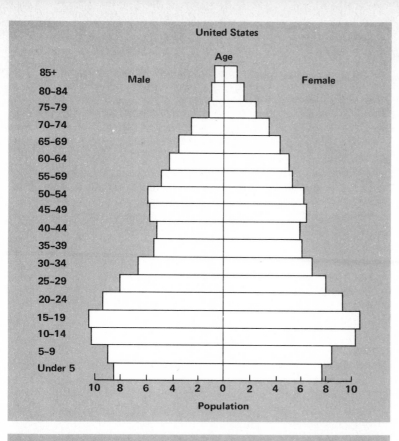

United States

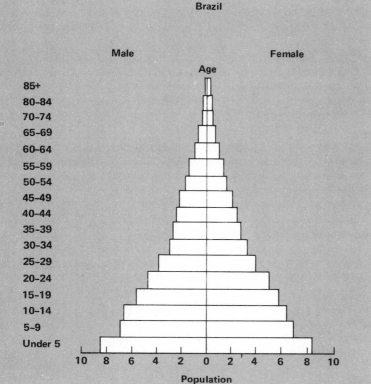

Brazil

FIGURE 13-4
Population (in Millions) by Age and Sex, Developed and Underdeveloped Countries

Because large numbers of Americans are in or moving into their reproductive years, the population of the United States will increase through the 1980s. However, if the present decline in the birthrate is maintained, U.S. population growth will eventually level off and even decline. Brazil, on the other hand, is already overpopulated and will increase its population for the foreseeable future unless stringent birth-control programs are adopted. Those persons at the low end of the age scale represent the largest proportion of Brazil's population and will eventually have more children, adding enormously to Brazil's population problem.

Source: *United Nations Demographic Yearbook, 1975.*

underdeveloped nations child labor is a major factor in the work force. However, the children tend to work in farm areas, not in industries.)

It is not only the young children in a society who are unavailable for income-producing work. Those who take care of them, whether parents, relatives, or neighbors, are also, as a rule, economically unproductive. The recent movement to establish day-care centers is an effort to deal with this situation as it manifests itself in our own society. In agrarian nations, the problems can be partially met by having the child accompany the parent to work in the fields, but such a solution is impracticable on a modern assembly line. Regardless of the child-care methods employed, a society with a high proportion of young children will have to spend more of its working hours than it can probably afford in looking after them. Furthermore, since poor nations tend to have higher fertility rates than industrialized ones, the Brazilian mother is probably bearing children more often and over a greater part of her potential childbearing span than the Swedish mother, and is therefore out of the labor market for a longer time.

Meanwhile, the breadwinners are struggling to support expanding families. In an agrarian society they are likely to be unskilled laborers who work a dawn-to-dark schedule at low-paying jobs in order to provide even bare subsistence for themselves and their dependents. Even if training for skilled, higher-paying work were available, the chances are they would not have the time or energy to take advantage of it. And if, drawn by rumors of riches, they move their families to the city, they are likely to find that the pay for them is no better, and the cost of living is far higher, than in the village they left. Either way, on the farm or in the city, they are likely to remain only marginally productive.

In addition, the adverse consequences of this production of more children than the society needs or can use carries over into the next generation. To break the cycle of poverty requires, among other things, education; but a nation, most of whose people have barely enough food to live, can seldom build many schools or pay many teachers. Most children in these societies will be offered no more than elementary education, if that; and many will enter the labor market at such an early age that they may not even have learned to read and write. Those who do manage to stay in school and acquire substantial training may well find that, with no capital available for industrial development, their country has few jobs in which they can use their knowledge; so they too will remain unproductive and poor.

Finally, as we have already suggested, these children will bear more children, in ever-increasing numbers. What will be the population pressures and the poverty then? And is there any way in which the cycle can be broken? The picture, most authorities agree, is grim. It becomes grimmer when one considers the political aspects. In the past, the great majority of human beings tended to accept poverty as their fate, as the will of God, as something unpleasant but inescapable. Now people of even the poorest nations have been exposed to the idea that economic betterment is possible, and increasingly they are demanding it as a right. Insofar as explosive population growth prevents the improvement of living conditions, it contributes to the political unrest which breeds revolutions, topples governments, and sustains bloody civil and international wars.

TABLE 13-2
The Twelve Fastest-
Growing Cities in
the World

City	Population in 1976 (in millions)	Expected Population in 1985 (in millions)	Percent Increase
1. Bandung, Indonesia	1.2	4.1	242
2. Bangkok, Thailand	2.2	7.1	223
3. Lagos, Nigeria	1.4	4.0	186
4. São Paulo, Brazil	6.0	16.8	180
5. Karachi, Pakistan	3.5	9.2	163
6. Mexico City, Mexico	7.8	17.9	129
7. Baghdad, Iraq	2.2	4.9	123
8. Bombay, India	6.0	12.1	102
9. Teheran, Iran	4.0	7.9	98
10. Lima, Peru	3.2	6.2	94
11. Bogotá, Colombia	3.3	6.4	94
12. Seoul, South Korea	5.5	10.3	87

Source: Adapted from United Nations figures.

Urbanization. In the process of building up its industry, a nation inevitably builds up its cities as well. As agricultural improvements make it possible to produce more crops with less labor, the surplus rural population migrates to the towns to find work in the new factories and mills. The more rapidly this population shift takes place, the more likely it is to give rise to substantial social problems. In the West, a rapid and explosive rural-to-urban population shift took place in the nineteenth century, during the height of the Industrial Revolution. In the United States, for example, no more than 6 percent of the population lived in urban centers in 1800. By 1850, the percentage had risen to 15; and by 1900, 40 percent of the population lived in the increasingly dense urban-industrial complexes. Today about 75 percent are concentrated in and around urban centers.[18] The trend shows no sign of stopping.

The same thing is happening in many of the developing nations today, but it is happening a great deal faster. The population of Nairobi, the capital of Kenya, is now growing at the rate of 7 percent per year. This is double the growth rate of Los Angeles in the boom decade of 1950–1960. Abidjan, the capital of the Ivory Coast, is growing by nearly 10 percent per year. Lusaka, the capital of Zambia, and Lagos, the capital of Nigeria, are each expanding at the unprecedented rate of 14 percent per year. If this rate of growth continues, Lagos, which in 1970 had a population of 1.4 million, will have 4 million by 1985—almost tripling its population in fifteen years.[19]

It is not generally realized that, of the twenty largest cities in the world—all of which have populations in excess of 3 million—more than half are in poor, developing nations (see Table 13-2): India (Bombay), Indonesia (Jakarta), Pakistan (Karachi), Brazil (São Paulo and Rio de Janeiro), Egypt (Cairo), Iran (Teheran), South Korea (Seoul), Mexico (Mexico City), and China (Shanghai, Peking, Tientsin, Mukden, and

[18] Ehrlich and Ehrlich, pp. 43–45.
[19] "Exodus to the city," *UNESCO Courier,* July–August 1974, pp. 40–41.

In poorer nations, the solution to the problem of housing an exploding population may be a disease-ridden, firetrap shantytown.
United Nations

Chunking). Only six (New York, London, Moscow, Leningrad, Tokyo, and Madrid) are in the countries we generally think of as urban and industrialized.[20]

If cities in urban, industrialized America are suffering today from overcrowding, inadequate housing and services, and all the other consequences of too-rapid population growth, it is not difficult to imagine what the situation must be like in the poor nations of Africa, South America, and Asia. There, societies have had, on the whole, far less time to cope with results of explosive industrialization. Also, their impoverished rural masses come to city life at a far lower level of education, vocational aptitude, and general readiness for the demands of the urban environment than do rural emigrants in the Western nations.

The physical congestion and environmental deterioration of some of the giant cities of the underdeveloped nations make a horrifying impression on Westerners, even those who know the ghettos of Washington or New York, or the slums of Liverpool. "Shantytowns" spring up on city

[20] *Demographic Yearbook,* United Nations, 1976.

hillsides, in public parks, on malls, in vacant lots, along rivers, even on rooftops. Like multiplying amebae they spread, housing thousands upon thousands of people in flimsily built shelters. They have inadequate sanitation facilities, or none at all. Personal hygiene and privacy are virtually unknown. Their inhabitants, illiterate and hungry, are ready prey to sickness, violence, and utter despair. The number of such squatters in the cities of Peru has been estimated to be 1 million, and growing. In Manila, the total is expected to reach 800,000 by 1980. In Ankara, Turkey, nearly half of the city's total population is said to be composed of shantytown squatters.[21] That the misery of the situation is everywhere compounded—and solutions further complicated—by too-rapid population growth in the country as a whole is only one more aspect of the painfully complex problems facing the poor and underdeveloped nations today.

ATTITUDES TOWARD POPULATION CONTROL

Given all these facts, and the conclusions we have drawn from them, it might seem that no one could realistically doubt the existence of a serious worldwide population crisis. In fact, there are those who do, including reputable scholars who cannot simply be written off as crackpots or bigots. The denials of the population crisis tend to fall into one of four main categories:

"There is no population problem as such. The problem is only how to devise means of supporting a growing population." The proponents of this view include some highly intelligent believers in the infinite power of science and technology to increase food supply indefinitely through the green revolution (the development of more nourishing and higher-yield varieties of grain and other staple food crops); tap as yet untouched reserves of water far below the earth's surface; develop hitherto undreamed-of materials to replace dwindling natural resources; harness new sources of power from beyond our planet; and find ways to halt or even reverse the damaging effects of population. As one of their spokespeople has maintained, "Natural resource scarcity and diminishing returns through time are not a curse that society must bear." [22]

In support of this contention, spokespeople point to humanity's past records of discovery and invention, and to the fact that to date all prophets of the starvation or self-destruction of *Homo sapiens* have been wrong. It should be noted, however, that there have never been as many people on the earth as there are today, nor has there ever been such a global scarcity of natural resources. Furthermore, even if a growing population could somehow be supported, the quality of life on earth—in terms of pollution and crowding, for example—would almost certainly decline.

"The population problem is really a problem of the distribution of

[21] Charles Abrams, "The uses of land in cities." *Scientific American* 213 (September 1965).
[22] Harold J. Barnett, "The myth of our vanishing resources." *Trans-Action,* June 1967.

people." Resettle or relocate people so as to break up overly dense concentrations, says this argument, and the economic, ecological, and social problems automatically become smaller, more manageable, ultimately more susceptible to solution. As Herman P. Miller says:

We have serious population problems today and they are likely to intensify in the next 15 years. These problems relate to the geographic distribution and to the values of our people rather than to their numbers and rates of growth.[23]

The resettlement or redistribution view is carried by some to its logical extreme in the argument that ultimately the solution to overpopulation will be enforced or voluntary migration to sparsely settled areas of the globe, or even to other planets and to artificial satellites.

The feasibility of this solution is questionable. Much of the remaining unsettled portion of the earth is desert, mountain, or arctic land, incapable of supporting more than a sparse population at best; and of the rest, some areas are vitally needed as wilderness. The vast Amazon basin, for example, is the world's largest reservoir of oxygen-producing vegetation. As for extraterrestrial migration, unless there is a considerable technological breakthrough, it seems unlikely to be possible for any large number of people. The largest spacecraft yet launched have carried only three in their crew, on a short journey to our own nearby moon, and at a cost of billions of dollars. To maintain the earth's population at its present level, some 200,000 people per day would have to be transported into space.

"There is a population problem, but it is not our problem. Anyway, it is not all that urgent." Many Americans take this position, according to a Gallup Poll.[24] Eighty-seven percent of those sampled conceded that population growth in America was a problem now "or would be by the year 2000." However, only 54 percent feared that it would affect the quality of their own lives, and only 41 percent considered it a major issue requiring immediate action. The majority of those who did view overpopulation as critical, urgent, and likely to affect them personally were people under 30, especially the college-educated among them.

Even experts sometimes view the population problem as essentially someone else's:

Population growth is no longer a major social problem in the United States. . . . This is a very different picture from that which presented itself only a few years ago when it looked as if the U.S. was heading into a very severe population crisis. It now appears that we have resolved it.[25]

"The population crisis is a ruse, a lie, or greatly exaggerated nonsense." There are relatively few advocates of this rather extreme position, but they command attention because of the sensitivity of the issues on which

---

[23] Herman P. Miller, "Is overpopulation really the problem?" *National Industrial Conference Board Report,* vol. 7, May 1970.

[24] Gallup Organization, Inc. News release, Research Department, Planned Parenthood-World Population, April 1971. This was the most recent Gallup Poll on this subject.

[25] Donald J. Bogue, "Population growth in the United States, 1970–2000." Paper delivered to a demographers' advisory group to the U.S. Census Bureau, April 1970.

they base their charges—notably racial bigotry, prejudice against the poor, and the desire of the powerful to retain their power. "Black genocide," for example, was the accusation made in an anti–birth control resolution passed at a Black Power Conference in Newark, New Jersey. The same charge is leveled by *Muhammad Speaks,* the official newspaper of the Black Muslim movement.[26] Many, even though certainly not all, black citizens would tend to agree: "It's just another scheme to keep black people down." Or: "Our birthrate is the only thing we have. If we keep on producing, they're going to have to either kill us or grant us full citizenship." [27]

Because of the complexity and historical importance of the views of various religions on population growth and its control, they merit special consideration. The official Roman Catholic doctrine on birth control is, of course, best known and most controversial in our society. Briefly, it states that sexual intercourse is intended by God as a means both to the growth of love between the partners and to the transmission of new life, and that if one part of this purpose is deliberately frustrated, God is disobeyed and harm is done to everyone concerned. Therefore, the use of any artificial means of preventing conception is considered sinful—a violence done to the natural order of things as established by God.

RELIGIOUS ATTITUDES

However, in spite of the Church's prohibition on the use of contraceptives of any kind, they have been increasingly adopted by otherwise devout American Catholics. (According to one study, 80 percent of Catholic couples sampled had used, or expected to use, some method of contraception.[28] In another sample, 588 of 846 white Catholic women favored the use of birth control; an additional 196 favored the "rhythm method" but rejected others.[29]) Officially, the Church has sanctioned only the rhythm method, in an apparent effort to strike a middle course. Finally, in 1968, after the controversy over permissible methods of birth control had reached monumental proportions, Pope Paul issued his encyclical, *Humanae Vitae* (On the Transmission of Human Life).[30] To the disappointment of many among the faithful, the pope reiterated the Church's ban on artificial contraception. While recognizing that "responsible parenthood" may sometimes entail the deliberate limiting of family size, he maintained that since the Church has no power to change the moral law established by God, it therefore cannot legitimize artificial methods of preventing birth, for any reason whatsoever. This decision has evidently been unacceptable in practice to many otherwise devout

[26] *Muhammad Speaks,* January 10, 1970, pp. 27–28.
[27] Mary Smith, "Birth control and the Negro woman." *Ebony,* March 1968.
[28] Pascal K. Whelpton, Arthur A. Campbell, and John E. Patterson, *Fertility and Family Planning in the United States.* Princeton, N.J.: Princeton University Press, 1966, p. 185.
[29] Charles F. Westoff and Norman B. Ryder, "Recent trends in attitudes toward fertility control and in the practice of contraception in the United States." In S. J. Behrman, Leslie Corsa, Jr., and Ronald Freedman, eds., *Fertility and Family Planning: A World View,* Ann Arbor, Mich.: University of Michigan Press, 1969, p. 401.
[30] Text of the encyclical is available from the United States Catholic Conference, 1312 Massachusetts Ave., Washington, D.C.

Roman Catholics, and has resulted in a good many conflicts of conscience among them. In fact, one 1976 study suggests that a massive decline in church attendance could be directly attributed to *Humanae Vitae*.[31]

Actually, the encyclical makes some thoughtful points about the possible harm to persons and society as a result of contraceptive practice, although it does not give clear proof of the cause and effect of this harm. For instance, it is possible that the habit of intercourse for pleasure alone, without the responsibility implied by the possibility of conception, may ultimately encourage the participants to regard one another merely as instruments of rather selfish pleasure, thus preventing any depth of personal relationship. On a broader scale, a government might plausibly claim that if contraception is permissible for individuals, it may also be imposed by the state "for the good of society," which in turn could open the door to violation of basic human rights, tyranny, and even genocide.

Certainly, it is hardly to be expected that widespread use of artificial contraceptives will affect *only* the birthrate. Unfortunately, *Humanae Vitae* failed to address itself seriously to the population question as a whole, and offered no real guidance to persons physically or psychologically unable to use the rhythm method. Consequently, it has seemed to most people to be merely a restatement of an outmoded position, and has been largely disregarded in practice.

Most of the other major religions have taken a less restrictive approach. Well before World War II, for example, many Protestant teachers had advanced the position that contraception was not an ecclesiastical concern but was a matter to be decided by the couple directly affected, in the light of conscience and in view of their particular situation. Most branches of Judaism have likewise held that contraception does not destroy the spiritual sanctity of marriage and may, in fact, enhance it by freeing the couple from the burden of unwanted children. The Eastern Orthodox Churches, while taking the official position that contraception is an evil, defer in practice to the wishes of the couple who must make the decision. Two of the three major Oriental and Near Eastern religions—Islam and Hinduism—have traditionally rejected any interference with fertility and birth. Yet the attitude and practices of adherents have changed. The Islamic heads-of-state of Iran, Jordan, Malaysia, Tunisia, and the United Arab Republic have issued a joint "Statement of Population" in which they urged adoption of family planning by Muslims.[32] Buddhism, the third large Oriental faith, regards procreation and family life as of secondary importance, so that, apparently, contraception is not an issue.[33]

POPULATION CONTROL PROGRAMS— VOLUNTARY OR COMPULSORY

It seems clear that if a prompt and substantial drop in the population growth rate of a nation is to be achieved, some kind of large-scale

[31] Father Andrew Greeley, *Catholic Schools in a Declining Church*. New York: Sheed and Ward, 1976.
[32] See W. Parker Maudin, *Muslim Attitudes to Family Planning*. New York: Population Council, 1967.
[33] Arthur McCormack, *The Population Problem*. New York: Crowell, 1970, p. 157.

program is needed. The question is, what kind of program? Most particularly, can a program of voluntary birth control suffice, or must some sort of legal compulsion be used?

Voluntary birth control is customarily thought of in terms of family planning, and organized attempts to promote it began in England at least as early as the 1820s. During the period from 1830 to about 1870, a number of books on the subject appeared both in England and in the United States. Religious, governmental, and medical opposition mounted during this time, and in 1873 the passage of the "Comstock law" outlawed the dissemination by mail of birth control information in the United States. Most of the states also passed suppressive legislation, and in 1890 the importation of birth control literature was banned. For practical purposes, any distribution of birth control information or equipment was illegal in this country until well into the twentieth century. After about 1916 physicians were permitted to prescribe birth control for health reasons, first in New York State and later elsewhere; but it was not until 1965 that the Supreme Court ruled unconstitutional a Connecticut statute forbidding the use of contraceptives, and not until the following year that the last of the "Comstock laws" was repealed (by Massachusetts).

Similar situations existed in many European countries. Yet, as we have seen, the rate of population growth in the Western world has dropped during this period; and today, with improved methods of birth control and greatly relaxed restrictions on their use, it might seem not unreasonable to hope that voluntary family planning would be sufficient to keep the world's population within bounds. Is this in fact the case?

What is Family Planning? Essentially, a voluntary family planning program is an attempt to make it possible for married couples to have the number of children they want. While in most cases this means enabling them to limit childbearing, it can also mean helping women who want children and have been unable to have them. The stress is usually placed on the good of the family—especially the health of mother and children, and the ability to provide education and other desired advantages.

Weaknesses of Family Planning. Kingsley Davis points out [34] some fundamental weaknesses of the family planning approach as a means to large-scale population control. Chief among these is its basic assumption that the number of children a couple want is the number they ought to have. In a poor country with a growth rate of 3 percent per year, the family of five or six children, which will probably be desired by the majority of couples, will be anything but desirable for the economic health of the country—or for the family's own chances of economic betterment.

A second criticism of the family planning emphasis is that by concentrating on married couples, it neglects the whole field of pregnancy among unmarried women. Certainly it is true that even in a country like the United States, in which contraceptives and contraceptive information are in general quite freely available, the number of pregnancies among unmarried women and young girls remains high. (See Chapter

[34] Davis, pp. 229–238, 247–248.

10.) A successful population control program would have to deal with this aspect of the situation.

Again, the strongly medical emphasis of the usual family planning program can limit its effectiveness for large-scale use, particularly in the underdeveloped countries where doctors and nurses are usually scarce.

Social Change and the Birthrate. There is no doubt that certain changes in overall attitudes and social structures can have considerable effect on the way in which individuals plan their lives. The women's liberation movement of the past few years has undoubtedly created (or reinforced) in many women of childbearing age a disinclination to be "just wives and mothers." As better job opportunities become available to women, as sexual relationships independent of marriage are increasingly taken for granted, as women begin to see themselves as creative and productive persons who may or may not choose to include marriage and childbearing in their personal lives, there is bound to be an effect on the birthrate. Recent surveys suggest that, already, the number of children desired by the average young married woman in the United States is less than it was a few years ago. (See Chapters 8 and 10.) And one may speculate as to whether there is a connection between the relatively low birthrate in many countries of Europe and the fact that these countries lost so many of their men during World War II that business and the professions were forced to open up to women to a much greater degree than in the less war-damaged United States.

However, Davis proposes much more drastic and deliberate social changes than these as a means of discouraging population growth. For instance, financial advantages, such as tax benefits, might be offered to the unmarried; financial disincentives, such as the loss of tax deductions or of insurance benefits, might be imposed for any child above a certain number. Other changes would seek to weaken the institution of the family rather than merely limit its size: dropping the use of family names; giving the school more control than the parents over the children; releasing grown children from any responsibility for the support of their parents. Quite possibly such moves would in fact tend to cut down on the birthrate. They would also outrage so many sensibilities that it seems unlikely that most of them could be imposed by legislative fiat, at least in the United States in the near future. Changes in attitude over a period of time might in the long run, however, make some of them acceptable.

COMPULSORY BIRTH CONTROL

In some primitive societies, sexual taboos have, sometimes inadvertently, created a more or less compulsory birth control system fairly well adapted to the particular tribal situation. Among certain African tribes, for instance, a woman may not have intercourse as long as she is nursing a child—which usually means for about two years. Modern societies are not prepared to function on this basis, however, and various proposals have been made by experts who believe that some sort of compulsion is needed if population growth is to be stopped short of global disaster.

One such possibility would be the sterilization of each woman after she had given birth to a specified number of children, or of the man after he had fathered a given number of children. Alternatively, Kenneth E. Boulding has suggested a licensing system, whereby a woman at her marriage would be issued a license entitling her to a certain number of children. She could sell or give her rights, if she did not wish to use them, to another woman who might want more than her licensed share.

If researchers succeed in developing a long-term timed-release contraceptive for implantation under the skin, this could be used to sterilize temporarily all girls at puberty and all women after childbirth; government approval would be required in order to have it removed. Or perhaps an antifertility agent (of a type not yet developed) could be added to water supplies or staple foods.

The dangers to freedom and the possibilities of abuse inherent in any program for compulsory birth control are obvious. It is hard to imagine how, except under a strong totalitarian system, such a program could be enforced. Probably the majority of people would accept it only if they were seriously convinced that nothing less could save the world from imminent catastrophe. Certainly, in the underdeveloped countries which most urgently need to curb their population growth, any government which tried to institute compulsory sterilization at present would be almost sure to bring about its own downfall in the process. For the time being, voluntary birth control seems to be the most realistic—and most desirable—road to take.

POPULATION CONTROL PROGRAMS IN THE ADVANCED NATIONS

As has already been pointed out, the birthrate in the industrialized nations had begun to drop before the institution of organized family planning programs. The organized programs have probably speeded the process in a number of ways, however, especially in the United States: they have made information and contraceptives more widely available; they have worked for repeal of laws against the use of contraceptives; and they have built up a climate of opinion favorable to birth control. In both the United States and Europe today, most couples use some form of contraceptive technique, though not always the most effective ones.

Nevertheless, even in this part of the world the birthrate remains higher than is necessary for replacement. The population of the United States and Europe is growing at the rate of just under .8 percent per year—a figure which seems small until it is realized that if the population continues to grow at its present low rate the United States and Europe will double their population in about 90 years. (At present rates, the entire world will double its population in less than 35 years.)

Some encouragement is offered by statistics showing a decline in the fertility rate among poor women, traditionally a high-fertility-rate group.[35] Though the rate is still much higher than that for women at higher income levels, it has nevertheless dropped substantially—by over 20 percent. The fact that this decline has occurred at a time when family planning programs, now federally assisted, and improved contraceptive methods are rapidly becoming available to poorer couples suggests that organized family planning may have been a significant factor.

It is still too early to fully assess the effect on population growth of the movement toward legalized abortion, though it is already clear that the availability of abortion has caused a decline in the number of illegi-

[35] Frederick S. Jaffe, "Low-income families: Fertility changes in the 1960s." *Family Planning Perspectives* 4 (January 1972):43–47.

timate births. (See Chapter 10.) No matter what method of voluntary contraception is used, a certain number of unwanted pregnancies are bound to occur, and it is safe to assume that many women who would not risk an illegal abortion will avail themselves of a legitimate one. It is also fairly safe to assume that at least some of these women would have preferred a perfectly reliable and convenient contraceptive which would have saved them from pregnancy in the first place; so perhaps legalized abortion as a method of birth control will turn out to be a temporary stopgap measure, useful principally until unwanted pregnancies no longer need to happen.

All things considered, if present trends continue, it is reasonably likely that the advanced nations will be able to hold their population growth to desirable levels by voluntary means. But these countries at present contain less than a quarter of the total world population. What about the rest of the planet?

POPULATION CONTROL IN THE DEVELOPING NATIONS

Efforts to reduce the population growth rate in the underdeveloped countries face considerably greater obstacles than in the older industrialized nations. In an agrarian society, large families are both a source of pride and an economic asset. A man's virility may be judged by his power to beget children; a woman's main purpose in life may be to bear and rear them. Children work in the fields from an early age, and when grown, they provide means of support to aging parents. Sometimes extra children are useful in a developing country in which educational opportunities are beginning to open up, since the children can work and help put the eldest through school. Later, the eldest can earn the extra income to put the next child through school, and so on down the line.[36] Such cultural patterns, in a tightly knit traditional society, are not easily changed.

In addition, many people in these parts of the world are still largely uninformed about even basic sanitation, personal hygiene, and such routine matters as keeping to a schedule. There are still back-country clinics where a doctor dares not give an outpatient a week's supply of pills, because the patient is likely to go off and swallow the whole lot at once. Medication has to be doled out one dose at a time, and taken on the spot while the attendant watches. The difficulties of using an oral contraceptive, or for that matter the rhythm method, under such conditions hardly need to be pointed out. Likewise popularizing the use of diaphragms, condoms, and other such devices is difficult in a culture that has never had experience with these forms of contraception.

The severe shortage of trained medical personnel in most underdeveloped countries also hampers the establishment of effective programs. Such contraceptive devices as the diaphragm must be individually fitted and prescribed, and the IUD, in some ways the most desirable for large-scale use, must be inserted by a doctor and should be periodically checked. As for sterilization, it requires a doctor and, for women, hospital facilities.

Despite these handicaps, a few of the poor nations have made sig-

[36] See Mahmood Mamdani, *The Myth of Population Control.* New York: Monthly Review Press, 1972.

nificant progress in curbing population growth by means of voluntary, government-supported programs. Most of these programs were begun in the 1960s (India's dates from 1952, but was slow in getting under way), and by the mid-1970s over 20 countries had official family planning programs of one sort or another. The most successful so far have been in relatively small and comparatively developed areas such as Taiwan, Hong Kong, and Singapore. In the two former, the birthrate had started to drop slightly even before the official programs were begun, but the programs appear to have accelerated the process. By the end of the 1960s the birthrate in Taiwan was down about one-third from the rate ten years earlier. Hong Kong and Singapore showed similar drops.[37] No other poor nation has come close to matching these rates of decline. Yet every one of these countries still has an overall population growth rate of more than 2 percent—sufficient to double its population in less than 35 years.

At the opposite end of the scale from these small and, for Asia, relatively prosperous countries lies the state of India, with one-third the area of the United States, two and one-half times its population, and a per capita gross national product of $110 per year as compared with over $6,000 for the United States. In 1965 India completely reorganized its family planning program. Clinics, camps, and mobile units were established, and a vigorous educational campaign was begun. Vasectomy and the IUD are the methods favored, and vasectomy clinics are often set up in such public places as railroad stations, rather than in hospitals, which are frightening places to many Indians. A small fee is paid to each man who consents to be vasectomized, and likewise to the person who persuades him. After five years of this program, it was estimated that about 12 percent of the couples of childbearing age were sterilized or were using some form of contraception.[38]

Part of the difficulty in India is the existence of several non-Western medical traditions, which have tended to oppose the program. But probably the greatest problem is the sheer size of the task—the attempt to inform and persuade some 90 million couples of childbearing age, jammed into city slums or scattered in thousands of tiny villages, heirs of a wide variety of regional cultures and languages, and many of them still so conditioned by centuries of abject poverty that they simply cannot imagine that any human effort could possibly make a difference. In addition, to a member of an ancient traditional culture, "the way it has always been" is usually very precious, even if life is hard; and proposals for change seem much more dangerous than they do to the Westerner who is accustomed to reading about a new technological miracle every other Monday. Before the birthrate can be lowered significantly, India's government will have to find some way to overcome these psychological obstacles and the opposition of the native medical systems. In the meantime, the growth of industrialization and improved agricultural production seem to be making some small headway against ancient poverty, even in the face of rapid population growth. Whether they can continue to do so until the growth rate can be brought down, only time will tell.

This Indian woman is being offered a contraceptive device as part of her country's family planning program. It is not likely she will use it, for tradition in India encourages large families.
Paolo Koch/Photo Researchers

[37] Frank W. Notestein, Dudley Kirk, and Sheldon Segal, "The problem of population control." In Hauser, p. 150.
[38] Ehrlich and Ehrlich, pp. 315–317.

China, the other giant of Asia, presents a special case, and information about it has become available only in the past decade.[39] An initial family planning movement in the 1950s was relatively ineffective and was abandoned after two or three years. In the 1960s, after the upheavals of the Cultural Revolution subsided, the effort was renewed, and appears to have had considerably more success. While precise national figures are not available, the growth rate is estimated to have dropped from 2.9 percent in 1968 to about 2.5 percent in 1969–1970; and the goal is a 1 percent rate by the end of the century. More recently, the United Nations estimated the growth rate at 1.8 percent.[40]

Birth control education has been most effective in the cities—as many as 70 percent of the women of childbearing age in Peking use some method of birth control—but in recent years a vigorous campaign has been carried to the countryside as well. In this, the extensive political organization of Chinese Communism has helped, for it provides a vast network of village-level workers who can urge family planning on the villagers as friends and fellow laborers. Stress on the personal advantages of a small family is combined with appeals for loyalty and self-abnegation on behalf of the state, and social pressure, rather than outright coercion, is applied. The recommended minimum age for marriage is 25 for women, 30 for men, and there is considerable pressure to adhere to it.

Oral contraceptives are the most commonly used, followed by intra-uterine devices (a specially shaped IUD has been developed which is less likely than others to be expelled by women doing heavy manual labor). A once-a-month pill is also being tried experimentally. All contraceptives are available free or at very low prices, and the village "barefoot doctors" provide instructions on their use. Abortions are likewise free or inexpensive, and are available on demand.

Since China's present population is in the neighborhood of 800 million, even a 1 percent increase would add about 200 million by the end of the century, in a country where available cropland is already farmed as intensively as any on earth. China thus faces a need to reduce her growth rate much more rapidly than any other nation has been able to do so far, while greatly modernizing and expanding her productive capacity. Apparently the sheer size and urgency of the task have forced the implementation of an unusually vigorous and effective program. It may be, therefore, that some of the Chinese techniques will eventually prove useful in other heavily populated areas as well, particularly those of Asian cultural tradition.

PROSPECTS

The social problems confronting the nations of the world in the wake of the global population explosion of the twentieth century are unprecedented in their complexity. The tangle of conflicting interests, of short-

[39] See *Population and Family Planning in the People's Republic of China.* Washington, D.C.: Victor-Bostrom Fund Committee and Population Crisis Committee, 1971.
[40] "The grinding arithmetic for the year 2000," p. 9.

range benefits versus long-range risks, of clashing motivations and contradictory impulses is so forbidding as to render the most cheerful optimist cautious, if not downright pessimistic, about the prospects for solution to the problem of overpopulation.

Whatever other issues the world and its individual nations attempt to solve—hunger or plenty, war or peace, environmental disruption and pollution or conservation, economic growth or stagnation, political freedom or faceless regimentation, capitalism or socialism in its various forms —it seems safe to say that unless the problems of overpopulation which complicate and aggravate them all are confronted first, or at least simultaneously, there is likely to be no satisfactory solution to any of them.

In the United States the average number of births per family is now 1.9—below the number for zero population growth. However, because the large number of people born during the "baby boom" of the late 1940s and early 1950s are now in their reproductive years, the population of the United States will actually increase until the 1980s. Only then, if present birthrates are maintained, will the population of the United States begin to level off. Until that time, the problems caused by an increasing population—crowding, loss of recreational areas, pollution—may be expected to multiply.

In other parts of the world, the picture is quite gloomy. Many developing countries with relatively successful birth control programs are experiencing a modest decline in their birthrates. However, because their birthrates have been so high, their populations continue to increase. Some other countries with rapidly expanding populations have no birth control programs at all. For example, 13 countries with close to half of Africa's population have no family planning programs. The population of some of these countries will quadruple within 50 years.[41]

What will be the consequences of such population growth? In many of the developing countries, starvation and death on a massive scale already seem imminent. However, the growing political consciousness of these countries makes it unlikely that they will willingly accept the wholesale decimation of their citizenry, particularly when people in other countries have an overabundance of food. Wars and uprisings are likely to increase as the developing nations demand their fair share of the world's resources.

Other consequences may be more subtle, but in the long run may be almost as harmful. For example, in some of the developing countries, such as India, the idea of mandatory sterilization is becoming more popular. But many of those who undergo sterilization procedures are unaware of the purpose of these operations—they are merely offered some payment for submitting to them. The idea of freedom, as it is understood in Western nations, may become obsolete in the developing countries if a policy of forced sterilization is adopted. And if population growth in these countries is not curbed voluntarily, forced sterilization may become the only available alternative.

The United States and Western Europe will be able to feed their own populations for the foreseeable future. However, they too will be affected by the population crisis and not just because their quality of life will

---

[41] *UNESCO Courier,* July–August 1974.

deteriorate or because they may be forced by other nations to share their wealth. They will be affected because the entire moral or ethical foundations upon which these countries are presumably based will be shaken as the numbers of those starving to death continue to grow. Already there are those who favor a "lifeboat ethic," which suggests that the poorer nations be permitted to starve. As one spokesperson for this point of view put it:

So long as nations multiply at different rates, survival requires that we adopt the ethic of the lifeboat. A lifeboat can hold only so many people. . . . It is literally beyond our ability to save them all. . . . International granaries and lax immigration policies must be rejected if we are to save something for our grandchildren.[42]

Such a philosophy must be rejected if Western nations are to survive in their present form; for if life in other countries is considered meaningless, it will soon be so considered in our own. It is the responsibility of the developing countries to curb their burgeoning population growth; it is the responsibility of the wealthier, developed countries to help feed the population that already exists. Whether these responsibilities will be met remains to be seen, but at present the prospects are not hopeful.

SUMMARY

The population of the world has been increasing at an enormous rate, largely because advances in medicine and technology have enabled more people to survive and reproduce.

In the industrialized nations, the consequences of this population growth have been a hampering of economic development and a reduction in the quality of life. In the developing countries, population growth, coupled with a diminishing food supply, has resulted in increased starvation and death. Also, the economic development that would enable these countries to be self-sustaining has been stifled. The nation's wealth, already inadequate, must be divided among greater numbers, and the large proportion of young children in these societies means that not enough labor is available for productive work. One added consequence of population growth has been a rapid increase in the urban population in the developing countries, as whole families leave marginal farm areas in the usually vain hope that they will find work in the cities.

There are those who maintain that a population crisis does not exist— that a growing population can be supported or overly dense populations can be broken up. Others feel the problem is not serious, or that it has been exaggerated. Such individuals ignore the fact that world resources are already strained, and that much of the world's available croplands are already being farmed. Yet most of the world's population already experiences hunger on a daily basis.

It seems clear that a large-scale birth control program is needed. Voluntary family planning programs already exist in many countries, though their effectiveness is limited by their medical emphasis and their concentration on married couples. In the developing nations, there are often cultural barriers to birth control programs, though countries such as India and China continue

[42] Garrett Hardin, in Commoner, p. 22.

their efforts to make such programs more acceptable. Although some experts advocate compulsory birth control programs, compulsion carries with it a great potential for abuse and a great threat to human freedom.

BIBLIOGRAPHY

Blake, Judith. *Population Policy for Americans: Is the Government Being Misled?* Berkeley: Institute of International Studies, University of California, 1969.

Chamberlain, Neil W. *Beyond Malthus: Population and Power.* New York: Basic Books, 1970.

Davis, Kingsley. *World Urbanization, 1950–1970.* Berkeley: Institute of International Studies, University of California, 1969.

Ehrlich, Paul R., and Ehrlich, Anne H. *Population, Resources, Environment: Issues in Human Ecology.* 2nd ed. San Francisco: Freeman, 1972.

Goldscheider, Calvin. *Population, Modernization, and Social Structure.* Boston: Little, Brown, 1971.

Hardin, Garrett James, ed. *Population, Evolution, and Birth Control: A Collage of Controversial Ideas.* 2nd ed. San Francisco: Freeman, 1969.

Hartley, Shirley F. *Population: Quantity vs. Quality.* Englewood Cliffs, N.J.: Prentice-Hall, 1972.

Heer, David M. *Society and Population.* 2nd ed. Englewood Cliffs, N.J.: Prentice-Hall, 1975.

Kammayer, Kenneth C. *Population: Sociological Perspectives.* Scranton, Pa.: Intext, 1971.

McCormack, Arthur. *The Population Problem.* New York: Crowell, 1970.

Meadows, D. H. *The Limits of Growth in a Finite World.* New York: Wiley, 1974.

Meadows, Donella H., *et al. The Limits to Growth: A Report for the Club of Rome's Project on the Predicament of Mankind.* 2nd ed. New York: Universe, 1974.

National Academy of Sciences. *Rapid Population Growth: Consequences and Policy Implications.* Baltimore: Johns Hopkins Press, 1971.

Population and the American Future: The Report of the Commission on Population Growth and the American Future. New York: New American Library, 1972.

Stanford, Quentin H. *The World's Population: Problems of Growth.* New York: Oxford University Press, 1972.

United Nations, Department of Economic and Social Affairs. *Human Fertility and National Development: A Challenge to Science and Technology.* New York: United Nations, 1971.

Westoff, Leslie A., and Westoff, Charles F. *From Now to Zero: Fertility, Contraception and Abortion in America.* Boston: Little, Brown, 1971.

14

THE ENVIRONMENTAL CRISIS

- Since 1750, 799 species of plants and animals have become extinct in the United States.
- Air and water pollution cause $23.8 billion worth of damage annually to health, property, and crops in the United States.
- In one recent year, over 2 million acres of land were urbanized, paved, or flooded.
- Some 300 million tons of human-made pollutants are added to the air every year.
- Every day each New York City resident inhales enough cancer-producing substances to equal two packs of cigarettes.
- At present rates of demand, world reserves of such vital materials as lead, silver, tungsten, and mercury will be exhausted within 40 years.

All animals depend on air, water, land, energy, and other organisms for their existence. Human beings are no exception. With the growth of our urban, industrial society, however, we have become increasingly estranged from a day-to-day awareness of our relationship to the physical environment. For most people, water is something which comes out of a tap; the air is everywhere; and if the city seems crowded, one can always move to the suburbs. But the cumulative effect of what we are doing on and to the earth seems to be bringing us to the brink of an environmental crisis: by intervening in the many natural cycles that permit the life process to continue through renewal and replenishment, we are seriously compromising the life-support capacity of our environment. An increasing number of people are making more and more demands on a world with fixed resources, and the world is beginning to show signs of having reached the limits of its ability to satisfy those demands.

The air is becoming filled with pollutants, many of which are highly toxic to human beings and other organisms. Our waterways have, in many cases, become nothing more than open, running sewers, and the discharge of our effluents is "killing" bodies of water as vast as the Great Lakes and befouling the oceans, incidentally endangering an important part of our food supply. We are creating mountains of solid waste for which we are running out of disposal sites. Although we know that there is no biologically safe level of radioactivity, we are committing ourselves to the construction of numerous nuclear power plants. And the noise levels in our cities are sufficiently high to affect our physical and emotional well-being.

Not only are we polluting what we may perhaps be unable to clean up, but we are destroying what cannot be replaced. We have already caused the extinction of several species of animals; and, in our eagerness to produce all the material goods we think we need, we are rapidly depleting the available stocks of gas, oil, coal, and other mineral resources. The question is whether we will become aware of what we are doing to the environment, and be willing to change, before we end by destroying ourselves.

There are two social ramifications to this question. First, the environmental crisis has been caused, fundamentally, by the socially organized activity of human beings. Social goals, social values, and, social norms and operations have led to the practices that have disrupted the proper, balanced processes of nature. Second, the environmental crisis in turn can be expected to affect society. The pressures of increasing scarcity—of space, of raw materials, of food, of water and clean air, of quiet—are likely to make people more dependent on one another, and at the same time tempt them to compete more bitterly with one another. Such competition will increase many of the existing social problems—poverty and all its associated ills, the difference in living standards between rich and poor nations, international jealousy, violence at all levels of society—and could easily result in wars.

Because of society's role in causing the environmental crisis, we must reorganize and redirect our social organization if we are to have any hope of really solving the crisis. And the new organization will have to take into account the fact that the human population is vastly larger than ever before in history, while the natural environment is not. This means that the changes will probably have to be very deep and basic: we will not be able to "go back" to much of any system that may have worked in the past.

To reach an understanding of why this is so, and what kinds of changes will be needed, we must examine some aspects of the environmental problem more closely.

DIMENSIONS OF THE PROBLEM

Four ecological concepts are basic to our understanding of the environmental crisis: interdependence, diversity, limits, and complexity. *Interdependence* literally means that everything is related to, and depends on, everything else; there is no beginning and no end to the "web of life." *Diversity* refers to the existence of a number of different life and life-support forms. A cardinal principle of ecology is that the greater the diversity of species, the greater the probability for survival of any given species. *Limits* are of several kinds. First, there is a finite limit to the growth of any organism. Second, there is a limit to the numbers of a given species that an environment—including other organisms—can support. Finally, there is a finite limit to the amount of materials available in the earth's ecosystem. *Complexity* refers to the intricacy of the relationships that constitute the "web." Because of this complexity, interventions in the environment frequently lead to unanticipated and undesired consequences. DDT, for example, was once repeatedly sprayed over large areas of land for the purpose of eliminating various disease-carrying or crop-destroying insects. To an impressive degree it succeeded. But DDT is a very long-lasting chemical, and its effects are not limited to insects. Much of it was washed from the farmlands and forests into rivers and oceans, where it was taken up by small organisms at the bottom of food chains. Eventually, as small creatures consumed tiny plants and larger creatures consumed smaller ones, several species of fish-eating birds accumulated so much of the poison in their bodies that their eggs had thin shells, which consistently broke before hatching. Thus the species were in grave danger of extinction, though the users of DDT never intended such a result.[1] Only federal restrictions on the use of DDT prevented the wholesale elimination of these bird species.

One of the major difficulties in dealing with the environmental crisis, then, is the number of problems involved and the complexity of their relationships. A full discussion of the nature of our environmental problems must take into account air and water pollution, land degradation, natural resource depletion, solid waste disposal, and a variety of other environmental hazards. Each of these problems and their interrelationships will be considered below. Then we will turn to an examination of our technological and social systems, to determine the origins of this complex problem.

Let us take two hypothetical people and do terrible things to them. We will put the first person into a box and seal it so it is airtight. As the person breathes, the oxygen in the box will be replaced with carbon dioxide. Eventually, there will be an imbalance that will result in this person's death.

AIR POLLUTION

The second person will also be placed in a sealed box, but in this case there is an entry tube into which we can rapidly pump a large quantity of automobile exhaust. This person will succumb well before the oxygen–carbon dioxide balance is disturbed.

These examples demonstrate certain important facts about air and our relationship to it. First, we have evolved over the millennia in an atmosphere of a given composition and quality, and our biological health is dependent on the atmosphere remaining in approximately that state. Second, just as the sealed box limited the amount of air available to the person, so too is our atmosphere limited. Third, the air can be a carrier of substances which are harmful or lethal. An excess of any such substance in a given place is what we mean by the term pollution. For, if the atmosphere is not overburdened, natural processes will cleanse it and preserve its composition. Through photosynthesis, for example, green plants combine water with the carbon dioxide we (and other

[1] See, for example, Paul R. Ehrlich and Anne H. Ehrlich, *Population, Resources, Environment*. 2nd ed. San Francisco: Freeman, 1972, pp. 208–209.

organisms) exhale, and produce oxygen and carbohydrates; this is one of the basic life cycles. But these natural processes, like other resources, have limits. They can remove only a limited quantity of harmful substances from the air; and if the pollution exceeds their capacity to remove it, the air will become progressively more dangerous to humanity.

Yet we are overtaxing the atmosphere. Although the specific nature of air pollution varies from one locality to another (as a function of geography, climate, and type and concentration of industry), we can identify some of the common primary components. These include organic compounds (hydrocarbons); oxides of carbon, nitrogen, and sulfur; lead and other metals; and particulate matter (soot, fly ash). In urban areas, it is estimated that at least 60 percent of the air pollution is caused by motor vehicles.[2] The remainder comes from the burning of fossil fuels (oil and coal) in power-generating plants, airplanes, and homes; airborne "wastes" from manufacturing processes; and municipal trash burning. In total, close to 200 million tons of pollutants are poured into the atmosphere over the United States each year.[3] (See Table 14-1.) Furthermore, certain chemical processes frequently render these pollutants more dangerous after they reach the atmosphere. In the presence of sunlight, the emission of hydrocarbons and nitrogen oxides (primarily from cars) produces the photochemical soup called "smog" that hangs over most of our cities; and various oxides combine with water vapor in the atmosphere to produce corrosive acids.

In recent years air pollution has increased to the point where it can only be classified as chronic or acute; we seem no longer to think of there being "no" pollution. New York City had a particularly acute

[2] Robert Rienow and Leona Train Rienow, *Moment in the Sun.* New York: Ballantine, 1967, p. 143.
[3] Ehrlich and Ehrlich, p. 147.

545 **THE ENVIRONMENTAL CRISIS**

Category	Carbon Monoxide	Sulfer Oxides	Hydrocarbons	Particulates	Nitrogen Oxides	Total
Transportation	77.5	1.0	14.7	1.0	11.2	105.4
Fuel combustion (stationary)	1.0	26.3	0.3	6.5	10.2	44.3
Industrial processes	11.4	5.1	5.6	13.5	0.2	35.8
Agricultural burning	1.6	—	0.3	0.3	—	2.2
Solid waste disposal	3.8	0.1	1.0	0.7	0.2	5.8
TOTAL	95.3	32.5	21.9	22.0	21.8	193.5

Source: Environmental Protection Agency.

TABLE 14-1
Major Sources of Air Pollution (in Millions of Tons Annually)

incident on Thanksgiving, 1966, when a thermal inversion (a mass of cool air flows over a hot air mass and prevents the hot air mass from rising, thus trapping the pollutants over an area) developed over the city. The numbers of those hospitalized for respiratory ailments, particularly among the very young and very old, increased sharply.[4] But New Yorkers were more fortunate than the residents of Donora, Pennsylvania, in 1948, when a similar incident trapped all the fumes from a steel mill, a sulfuric acid plant, and a zinc plant. Over 40 percent of the town's population of 14,000 became ill, and 20 people died before the four-day crisis ended. And the "Black Fog" in London, in 1952, lasted four days and resulted in the deaths of approximately 4,000 people.[5]

The effects of chronic air pollution on human health are less dramatic and direct than those of the acute situations described above, but they are of greater long-run significance for human health. Continued exposure to air pollutants and the accumulation of them in the body—essentially a slow poisoning process—result in increased incidence of such illnesses as bronchitis, emphysema, and lung cancer.[6] Air pollution also causes severe eye, nose, and throat irritations; it has been estimated that breathing the air in New York City is the equivalent of smoking two packs of cigarettes a day, with comparable consequences.[7] Poor visibility as a result of smog has also been cited as a major factor in both automobile and airplane accidents.

Air pollution has economic effects as well. Accelerated deterioration of property results in increased maintenance and cleaning costs: blighted crops mean lost income for farmers and higher food prices for the consumer; pollution-caused illnesses cut into productivity, reduce workers' earnings, and raise the cost of medical care for large numbers of people. The sulfur emitted each year from the smokestacks of factories and

[4] Gerald Leinwand, *Air and Water Pollution*. New York: Washington Square Press, 1969, p. 13.
[5] Donald E. Carr, "The disasters." In Rex R. Campbell and Jerry L. Wade eds., *Society and Environment: The Coming Collision*. Boston: Allyn and Bacon, 1972, pp. 131–132.
[6] Ehrlich and Ehrlich, pp. 147–152.
[7] Rienow and Rienow, p. 141.

power plants in the United States would be worth at least $300 million if it could be recovered.[8] In total, the dollar cost of air pollution is estimated to be $11 billion a year.[9]

Finally, air pollution may be having a dangerous long-term effect on the earth's ecosystem. For example, some studies suggest that fluoro-carbon gases, which are commonly used in spray cans and refrigerating systems, may be breaking down the earth's protective ozone layer.[10] (The ozone layer surrounds the earth at an altitude of from 8 to 30 miles above sea level; it screens out a great deal of the sun's harmful rays.) Fluorocarbon molecules, according to these studies, are not broken down in the earth's lower atmosphere, but continue to rise to a much higher altitude. Here they are broken up by high intensity radiation, and begin to chemically destroy ozone molecules. If this theory proves correct, the destruction of the ozone layer will lead to a much higher worldwide incidence of skin cancer and crop failure; there may also be changes in the world's climate. Preliminary tests that have been performed thus far suggest that fluorocarbons may, indeed, be harmful to the earth's ozone layer.[11]

Other effects of air pollution may involve harmful temperature changes. For example, the amount of carbon dioxide in the atmosphere is estimated to have increased about 25 percent during the past century and is expected—assuming we do nothing to prevent it—to increase by another 25 percent in the next 30 years (see Figure 14-1). Some scientists are concerned that such a buildup could result in what is termed a "greenhouse" effect in the atmosphere. That is, the carbon dioxide would trap heat near the earth's surface, raising the average temperature of the atmosphere. Such overheating, even by a few degrees, could lead to the melting of the polar icecaps, with calamitous results. So far, however, the danger appears to be in the opposite direction: the average world temperature has actually declined slightly since 1940, and this has given rise to the fear that suspended particulates in the air may be preventing solar energy from reaching the earth. If so, this could eventually result in a cooling sufficient to usher in another ice age.[12]

WATER POLLUTION

Water is constantly on the move, in what is known as the hydrologic cycle. It is found in the atmosphere as vapor; it condenses and falls to the earth as rain, snow, or dew; it percolates underground or runs off the surface into streams, rivers, and finally oceans; it evaporates into the atmosphere as vapor once again; and the cycle continues. While on the ground, it may be taken up into the roots of plants, and through the leaves eventually be evaporated back into the atmosphere; or it may be drunk from streams by animals or people, and be evaporated or

[8] Leinwand, pp. 24–26.
[9] C. W. Griffin, Jr., "America's airborne garbage." In Campbell and Wade, p. 145.
[10] See Philip H. Howard and Arnold Hanchett, "Chlorofluorocarbon sources of environmental contamination." *Science,* July 1975, pp. 217–219.
[11] "Spray-can scare: The latest findings." *U.S. News & World Report,* September 29, 1975, p. 62.
[12] Tom Alexander, "Some burning questions about combustion." In Campbell and Wade, pp. 137–138; and Ehrlich and Ehrlich, pp. 237–242.

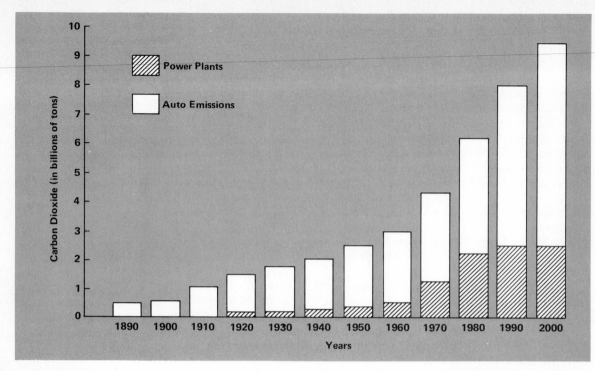

FIGURE 14-1
The Increase in
Artificially Produced
Carbon Dioxide

Source: Arthur S. Boughey,
Fundamental Ecology.
Scranton, Pa.: Intext, 1971,
p. 48. Reprinted by
permission.

excreted back into the earth or air. Or it may sink into underground reservoirs and be stored up for millions of years, perhaps under enormous pressure, until it is released back into the cycle.

It is quite possible for water to be used more than once as it passes through a single round of the hydrologic cycle, if it is sufficiently purified, between uses, by natural or artificial means. But we have been accustomed to using "new" water rather than purifying the "old," and as a result we are removing fresh water from the continent faster than it is being replaced through the cycle. The nation's daily water requirement is expected to reach 1,300 billion gallons by the end of the century, but the best estimates indicate that only 700 billion gallons can be made available.[13] Intensive reuse is thus a necessity—but for water to be reused, its quality must be maintained, and we render much of our water unfit for reuse through various kinds of pollution: raw and inadequately treated sewage, oil, synthetic organic chemicals (detergents, pesticides), inorganic chemicals and mineral substances, plant nutrients, radioactivity, and heat. Thus we face a dual crisis with respect to water: the amount available to us will be insufficient for our demands, and what is available is of steadily deteriorating quality.

Just as air has the capacity to cleanse itself if it is not overburdened, so too can rivers and lakes and oceans purify themselves naturally. But we have been discharging wastes, directly and indirectly, into our water-

[13] John Hamer, "Drinking water safety." *Editorial Research Reports,* February 15, 1974, pp. 136–137.

ways in amounts which preclude such natural purification. Existing sewage treatment facilities discharge between 20 and 30 percent of our sewage raw into whatever body of water they use for disposal.[14] The bacteria in such untreated sewage renders the water unfit for drinking, swimming, and many industrial uses. Shellfish become inedible because pollution renders them capable of causing disease in those who consume them. Finally, the use of oxygen to decompose the waste reduces the life-support capacity of the water, with a consequent decline in the number and variety of fish. As our population grows, the problem of waste disposal will become even more acute.

Current farming practices, such as the extensive use of nitrate and phosphate fertilizers, also have a serious deleterious effect on water quality. Rain and irrigation cause the runoff of large quantities of these materials into rivers and lakes. The fertilizers work in the water much as they do on the land, resulting in what are termed algae "blooms"— huge masses of algae which grow very quickly and then die. As with the decomposition of sewage, the decay of these "blooms" consumes oxygen, thus killing off fish and other animals that have high oxygen requirements. As the algae decay, they settle to the bottom of the water, along with various compounds of nitrogen and phosphorus. The bottom of Lake Erie at one point had a layer of such muck ranging from 20 to 125 feet in thickness.[15] Only intensive efforts by environmentalists to stop pollutants from being discharged into the lake and adjoining interways saved Lake Erie from total destruction.

The use of long-lasting pesticides, such as DDT, has resulted in widespread contamination of water, as was noted above. Such compounds are especially dangerous to health, because when ingested by an animal they are not excreted but accumulate in the tissues. In addition to the accumulation of DDT causing the near extinction of several species of birds, its accumulation in fish has rendered some of them inedible. Although the use of DDT has now been banned for most purposes, we and other organisms will continue to accumulate that which has already been deposited. The process of ingestion of the poison begins for many humans at birth, because of particularly high concentrations in human milk. Our knowledge of the effects on human health and longevity of ingesting and storing such poisons is still sketchy, but we shall find out as new generations of children mature. In effect, we are conducting a massive global experiment in which we and all other living things are the guinea pigs.

One reason why long-lasting poisons such as DDT and radioactive wastes pose such a serious problem is the process known as biological magnification, whereby the concentration of a given substance increases as it ascends a food chain. Thus a study of the Columbia River in the western United States revealed that while the radioactivity of the water was insignificant.

> the radioactivity of the river plankton was 2,000 times greater;
>
> the radioactivity of the fish and ducks feeding on the plankton was 15,000 and 40,000 times greater, respectively;

[14] Donald E. Carr, "The politics of pollution." In Campbell and Wade, p. 84.
[15] Ehrlich and Ehrlich, p. 231.

the radioactivity of young swallows fed on insects caught by their parents in the river was 500,000 times greater;

the radioactivity of the egg yolks of water birds was more than a million times greater.[16]

It is presumed that the radioactive isotopes are released into the river by the nuclear power plant at Hanford, Washington. People who live in areas downriver from such plants ingest and store radioactive isotopes with the water they drink and the fish and other local foods they eat. Because

[16] Richard Curtis and Elizabeth Hogan, *Perils of the Peaceful Atom*. New York: Ballantine, 1969, p. 194.

Water pollution not only makes water unfit for human use but also kills off fish life. The discharge of industrial pollutants has destroyed all the fish in this body of water.
Gilles Peress/Magnum

most radioactive substances retain their potency for many years—even centuries—the presence of these isotopes adds significantly to the normal "background" radiation naturally present in the environment. This means an increased potential for damage to human health, in terms of a higher incidence of cancer and genetic defects.

Another form of water pollution comes from heat—the so-called thermal pollution. The effluents of many factories and generating plants—especially nuclear power plants—are warmer than the rivers and lakes into which they flow, and when discharged in quantity they may raise the water temperature by as much as 10 to 30 degrees Fahrenheit. Such thermal pollution can be ecologically devastating.[17] Because most aquatic animals are cold-blooded, they are the mercy of the surrounding water temperature. If the temperature rises beyond the point of an organism's capacity for metabolic adjustment, the animal will die. Since larvae and young fish are far more susceptible to death through slight temperature variations than are mature organisms, and since rises in temperature also interfere with the spawning and migratory patterns of many organisms, thermal pollution may cause some aquatic populations to die out through reproductive failure.

Other serious and widespread forms of water pollution include:

the discharge of oil—both unintentional, through the "blowing" of offshore wells and leakage from storage facilities and ships, and intentional, through the practice of flushing out tankers at sea—with consequent destruction of marine and bird life and the despoiling of beaches;

the discharge of various industrial chemicals such as methyl mercury into rivers and oceans, where they accumulate to lethal levels in the bodies of fish through the process of biological magnification; [18]

the discharge, from food processing, textile, paper, steel, and other plants, of wastes which either are toxic themselves or combine with so much dissolved oxygen in the water as to prove indirectly fatal to fish; [19]

acid runoff from strip mining, which is destructive of life in streams and rivers.

NONRENEWABLE RESOURCES AND SOLID WASTE DISPOSAL

We have noted that both air and water have the capacity to cleanse themselves if they are not overburdened. In that sense, they can be considered to be renewable resources. Once an oil field has been pumped out, however, it is not going to fill again, and once a vein of iron ore has been mined out, the earth is not going to generate another one in its place—at least, not within the probable life span of the human race. Fossil fuels, metals, and other minerals are, therefore, nonrenewable resources: they exist only in finite quantity. The problem is that we behave as though the supply were infinite. We take resources which occur

---

[17] John R. Clark, "Heat pollution." In Campbell and Wade, p. 94.
[18] Rienow and Rienow, p. 250.
[19] Carr, "The politics of pollution," pp. 81–83.

in limited, concentrated form in nature and, via our technology, disperse them into the environment in such a way that they are neither technologically nor economically recoverable. There is no way, for instance, to reclaim the lead which is added to automobile fuel and then released, along with other exhaust products, into the air, where it disperses throughout the Northern Hemisphere as far as the Arctic icecap. Usage of this sort is doubly destructive. Not only are we running out of lead, but we are turning it into a pollutant which is ingested and stored in our bodies at a level approaching toxicity.

In order to satisfy the requirements of its standard of living, the United States, although it constitutes only 6 percent of the world's population, accounts for approximately 30 percent of the annual world consumption of industrial raw materials.[20] This has several important consequences. First, we now import many of those materials from the underdeveloped areas of the world. As these areas increase the pace of their development, they are going to restrict the export of such resources, and the competition for what is exported will increase. How then will we insure a steady supply of needed raw materials without exacerbating world tensions?

Second, as noted above, we do not really "consume" most products, despite our designation as a "consumer society." It is more accurate to say that we buy things, use them, and then throw them away, with the result that we have several hundred million tons of solid wastes to dispose of every year. These wastes include food, paper, glass, plastics, wood, abandoned cars, cans, metals, paints, dead animals, and a host of other things. Estimates of the annual cost of disposing of such wastes run as high as $3 billion.[21]

The two principal methods of solid waste disposal are landfill and incineration. Although landfills are supposed to meet certain sanitary standards, the U.S. Department of Health, Education, and Welfare found that "less than half the cities and towns in the United States with populations of more than 2,500 dispose of community refuse by approved sanitary and nuisance-free methods." [22] "Sanitary landfills" are allowed to deteriorate to the point where they become breeding grounds for rats, and improperly designed municipal incinerators are principal contributors to urban air pollution. Many cities on the sea use the ocean as their dumping ground for waste disposal. New York City's practice of hauling tons of refuse out to sea each day and dumping it has created a large area in the Atlantic Ocean in which nothing lives.

The introduction of plastics and other synthetic materials on a large scale has produced a new waste disposal problem, for whereas organic substances are eventually decomposed through bacterial action, plastics are generally totally immune to biological decomposition, and thus remain in their original state if they are buried or dumped. If burned, they become air pollutants in the form of hydrocarbons and nitrogen oxides.

Nuclear power plants too pose a special problem. For various technical reasons, the fuel in a reactor's core must be replaced periodically. This

[20] Ehrlich and Ehrlich, p. 70.
[21] Rienow and Rienow, p. 137.
[22] Sheldon A. Mix, "Solid wastes: Every day, another 800 million pounds." In Campbell and Wade, p. 184.

requires careful planning and handling, because the radioactivity of nuclear fuels increases as they are used. David Lilienthal, the first chairman of the Atomic Energy Commission, describes the problem:

These huge quantities of radioactive wastes must somehow be removed from the reactors, must—without mishap—be put into containers that will never rupture; then these vast quantities of poisonous stuff must be moved either to a burial ground or to reprocessing and concentration plants, handled again, and disposed of, by burial or otherwise, with a risk of human error at every step.[23]

The danger from such wastes is evident when we consider that absorption of less than one curie of strontium-90—a radioactive isotope—is lethal to a human being, and that by the year 2000, assuming present nuclear power plant construction plans are carried out, radioactive wastes will contain 6 billion curies of strontium-90. These wastes will have to be safely stored for up to 1,000 years before they decay to a harmless state. Even assuming that such burial sites are not disrupted by earthquakes or wars, we are saddling future generations with their perpetual custodianship.

LAND DEGRADATION

A forest is full of life: trees, grass, moss, and other plants; deer, squirrels, birds, and other animals; worms, maggots, bacteria, and other inhabitants of the soil. All of these draw their sustenance from the soil, and eventually die and are decomposed to provide sustenance for succeeding generations. The forest depends upon water for its survival and also serves as a giant storage facility for water, trapping rainfall in its spongy soil and releasing it gradually to streams and springs. Other water is taken up into plants and released into the surrounding atmosphere. Meanwhile, by photosynthesis, the foliage takes up carbon dioxide from the air and releases oxygen, thus helping to maintain the natural atmospheric balance.

Any ecosystem, such as a forest, swamp, or prairie, is a complex matrix of interrelated and interacting organisms and processes, functioning both in support of its own patterns of life and as a contributor to those of the larger regional, continental, and planetary ecosystems. Serious alteration of a local ecosystem, therefore, can affect the balance of life in a larger area. Yet, through greed and/or ignorance of ecological principles, humanity has diminished or destroyed the life-support capacity of large land areas, and we are only beginning to recognize the extent of possible consequences.

When white people first appeared in what is now the continental United States, over 40 percent of the land was forested; today, after several centuries of logging, clearing for farms, and building of towns, that figure is only slightly more than 20 percent.[24] Ehrlich and Ehrlich have described the sequence of events which follows the wholesale logging of a forest:

Numerous animals that depend on the trees for food and shelter disappear. Many of the smaller forest plants depend on the trees for shade; they and the

[23] In Curtis and Hogan, p. 175.
[24] Fairfield Osborn, *Our Plundered Planet*. New York: Pyramid, 1968, p. 145.

animals they support also disappear. With the removal of trees and plants, the soil is directly exposed to the elements, and it tends to erode faster. Loss of topsoil reduces the water-retaining capacity of an area, diminishes the supply of fresh water, causes silting of dams, and . . . flooding. . . . Deforestation . . . reduces the amount of water transferred from ground to air by the trees in the process known as "transpiration." This modifies the weather downwind of the area, usually making it more arid and subject to greater extremes of temperature.[25]

Even huge deserts can result from humanity's misuse of the environment. The Sahara was created partly by overgrazing, deforestation, and poor irrigation of land which was once capable of supporting at least some plant and animal life. And the Sahara continues to grow: today it is advancing southward at a rate of several miles a year. The same process can be seen in many parts of Asia, India, and Europe: in 1882, 9.4 percent of the earth's total land area was classified as desert or wasteland; by 1952, 23.3 percent was so classified. And in America in 1934, a "vast transcontinental windstorm" blotted out the sun from the Rocky Mountains to the Atlantic Coast, announcing that large, once-fertile areas in Kansas, Texas, Oklahoma, Colorado, and New Mexico had become a desolate dust bowl.[26] Such irreparable losses are particularly intolerable in view of the rapidly increasing need for food to sustain a burgeoning world population.

It takes anywhere from 300 to 1,000 years to produce one inch of topsoil under the most favorable conditions. Yet many areas of the earth are losing topsoil at the rate of several inches per year as poor management exposes it to wind and water erosion. In addition, we destroy the fertility of the land as a result of increasing mechanization and urbanization. Unlike horses, mules, and other beasts of burden, tractors do not fertilize the land they plow; and when food is shipped from farm to city, the organic wastes, instead of being returned to the land, are flushed away to become pollutants in the rivers, lakes, and oceans. Massive amounts of artificial fertilizers—phosphates and nitrates—have been used to supplement declining natural fertility, and to improve the productivity of land which is naturally deficient. But, as we have seen, a large quantity of these artificial fertilizers is washed into rivers and lakes, where it too contributes to pollution.

OTHER HAZARDS

In addition to the widely acknowledged environmental problems we have been considering thus far, a number of other threats to our well-being arise from the indiscriminate use of our incomplete technological knowledge. These include noise pollution, chemical hazards, and a variety of undesirable consequences associated with certain large-scale engineering projects.

Noise Pollution. Noise is a purely dysfunctional consequence of our technology. It is produced by airplanes, cars, buses, trucks, motorcycles, motorboats, factory machinery, dishwashers, garbage disposals, vacuum

[25] Ehrlich and Ehrlich, p. 202.
[26] Osborn, pp. 51–52.

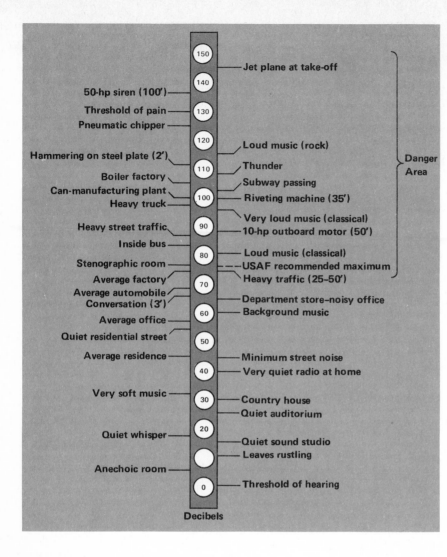

FIGURE 14-2
Decibel Values
of Common
Environmental
Sounds

Source: Richard H. Wagner,
Environment and Man. 2nd
ed. New York: Norton, 1974.

Figure contents:

150 — Jet plane at take-off
140
50-hp siren (100') — 130 — Threshold of pain
Pneumatic chipper —
120 — Loud music (rock)
Hammering on steel plate (2') — 110 — Thunder
Boiler factory — Subway passing
Can-manufacturing plant — 100 — Riveting machine (35')
Heavy truck —
— Very loud music (classical)
Heavy street traffic — 90 — 10-hp outboard motor (50')
Inside bus —
80 — Loud music (classical)
Stenographic room — USAF recommended maximum
Average factory — 70 — Heavy traffic (25–50')
Average automobile
Conversation (3') —
Average office — 60 — Department store–noisy office
— Background music
Quiet residential street — 50
Average residence — 40 — Minimum street noise
— Very quiet radio at home
Very soft music — 30 — Country house
— Quiet auditorium
Quiet whisper — 20 —
— Quiet sound studio
— Leaves rustling
Anechoic room —
0 — Threshold of hearing

Danger Area

Decibels

cleaners, television, radio, phonographs, air conditioners, jackhammers, bulldozers, and a hundred other tools of our social existence. Noise, which above a certain level can be harmful even when it is not consciously being heard, is directly affecting our physical and emotional well-being (see Figure 14-2). Thus studies have shown that we are suffering greater hearing losses with increasing age than in the past, and that noise is a significant contributor to the tension level of daily life, even sometimes precipitating a variety of stress-related illnesses such as peptic ulcer and hypertension.[27]

Chemicals. Pressure at all levels to get new products on the market has permitted the widespread use of various poisons (pesticides and

[27] Ehrlich and Ehrlich, p. 177; Rienow and Rienow, pp. 179–194.

herbicides) without adequate prior testing of their long-run cumulative effects—the introduction on a massive scale of synthetic materials, such as plastics, which create serious problems of disposal; the use of untested industrial chemicals such as vinyl chloride gas, which has been implicated in at least 20 deaths from cancer of the liver and in a higher incidence of miscarriages among the wives of men who work with vinyl chloride; [28] and an incredible proliferation in the variety and amount of what are called food "additives." There are over 2,500 food additives in current use in the United States; each individual has an average intake of over three pounds per year. Additives are used in the growing and processing of food. Yet there is little knowledge about the long-term effects of continuous ingestion of each such substance, and almost no knowledge regarding the possible synergistic effects on the body of the millions of possible combinations of substances.[29]

Large-Scale Engineering Projects. Perhaps because it gives them a sense of mastery over fate, people have always taken a great deal of pride in their ability to change the face of the earth in ways they have deemed

It may be natural for people to assert themselves by making noise, whether by hitting a stick against a tree or gunning the engine of a car. But beyond a certain point, noise adds to nervous strain and can cause injury to our hearing.
Geoffrey Gove

[28] *New York Times,* February 4, 1976, p. 23.
[29] Rienow and Rienow, pp. 197–198.

beneficial. Where they have frequently failed, however, is in properly anticipating and assessing the possible costs associated with such benefits. Thus the building of a new dam is hailed, both as an engineering masterpiece in its own right and because it opens up new lands for agriculture, settlement, and recreation (although sometimes there is a net loss of wilderness and recreational land). Less often recognized is the fact that while a dam may permit the controlled distribution of water to desired locations, it also "costs" a great deal of water through evaporation. Furthermore, large dams have caused significant earthquakes, even in geologically inactive areas, because of the tremendous pressures exerted by the billions of gallons of water they store. The giant Aswan Dam in Egypt epitomizes the potential of such large projects for producing other unwanted consequences. Although only a relatively few years old, the dam is already being blamed by ecologists for a rapid and dangerous increase in the incidence of schistosomiasis, a seriously debilitating disease, among the residents of the Nile valley, and for diminishing the once rich sardine fishing in the Nile delta through the silting up of nutrients behind the dam.

Another source of hazard to the environment is strip mining. Most coal in the United States lies deep within the earth, and in order to obtain it, underground mining is necessary. However, a large percentage of coal—particularly in Western states—lies close enough to the surface for strip mining, in which the top layers of soil are removed and the coal is excavated. While strip mining is much cheaper (and safer) than underground mining, it causes much greater harm to the environment.

This area of land in Tennessee was left completely barren by strip mining.
Kenneth Murray/
Nancy Palmer

Whole areas of land are left scarred by huge, ugly trenches and denuded of all life. Also, because the topsoil is removed from the earth's surface during the strip-mining process, healthy plant life can never return. Finally, because the delicate soil balance is disturbed, water supplies in the area are often damaged irreversibly: increased erosion at the mining site can cause both local and distant water sources to be contaminated by sediment, dissolved acids, and other pollutants.

Though some states have strict regulations governing strip mining—requiring, for example, that the topsoil be replaced when mining is completed—such regulations are not uniformly enforced. With oil supplies becoming depleted and the nation's energy needs growing, strip mining will probably become more widespread in the near future. Unless reclamation laws—requiring that a strip-mining site be returned to pre-mining condition—are passed and vigorously enforced, whole areas of land will be destroyed.

ORIGINS OF THE PROBLEM

An investigation of winter fish kills in Wisconsin lakes led to the unlikely conclusion that the use of snowmobiles was the cause. Heavy snowmobile use on a lake during the winter compacts the snow and makes the ice opaque. This reduces the amount of sunlight reaching the underwater plants, which require the sunlight for photosynthesis (the process whereby green plants transform carbon dioxide and water into carbohydrates and oxygen). The plants' oxygen production therefore declines, they die, and their decomposition consumes considerable amounts of what oxygen is left in the water. The fish then die because of the lack of oxygen.

As this example suggests, we can best view our environmental crisis as resulting from the interaction of three systems: the "natural" environment, our technological system, and our social system. The fish, ice, water, oxygen, plants, and the photosynthesis process are all elements of the natural system (see Figure 14-3). The snowmobile is an element of our technological system. That it is produced, marketed, bought, and used, and that there is no one to hold responsible for the fish kills, is a product of our social system. That the fish are indirectly and unintentionally killed by the snowmobiles illustrates the all too frequent dysfunctional consequences of the effects of our social and technological systems on the natural system.

Taking a broader perspective, we can define the natural system as containing these elements and their interrelationships: air, water, earth, solar energy, plants, animals, and mineral resources. Our technological system includes electricity-generating facilities, manufacturing processes and plants, various methods for extracting mineral resources, transportation, farming, and the actual consumption and residue disposal of the products of those processes. Our social system includes such elements as attitudes, beliefs and values, and institutional structures. And as with the fish and the snowmobiles, so too in larger matters we must look to our social and technological systems for the origins of the present crisis in our natural system.

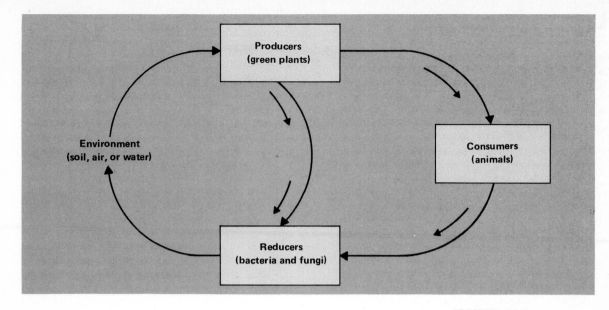

FIGURE 14-3
Circulation of
Materials in
the Ecosystem

Source: Robert Whittaker,
*Communities and Eco-
systems.* 2nd ed. New York:
Macmillan, 1975. Reprinted
by permission.

One element which transcends these systems' boundaries is that of numbers or population size (see Chapter 13). Quantitative increases in a system often result in qualitative changes in that system. Thus, as the number of people in a given society increases, societal relationships tend also to increase and to become more complex. To satisfy needs and desires, the technological system likewise increases in elaborateness and complexity. Finally, the needs of the swelling numbers make such demands on the natural system that they become an intolerable burden and the survival of the system is threatened. For as a system increases in complexity, it may become more fragile: small, tolerable changes in one element may be transformed through system dynamics into large, destructive changes in other elements.

Technology requires energy, and our basic source of energy is the sun. Through photosynthesis, plants produce, in addition to oxygen, both the carbohydrates which are the basis of our organic food supply and the fossil fuel deposits (coal and oil) from which we derive most of our electricity and heat and the power which runs our automobiles and airplanes. The electrical energy requirements of our society are enormous, and they are expected to double every ten years or less if the future recapitulates the past. One consequence of this projection has been government encouragement of the development of a nuclear power-generating technology and industry, which is intended to complement rather than replace fossil-fuel generating plants. However, both nuclear and fossil-fuel plants are major polluters, contributing massive amounts of sulfur oxides, hydrocarbons, and particulate matter to the air and heat to the water. With nuclear power plants, there is always the possibility of the release of enormous amounts of radioactivity in the event of an accident at the plant or, as was noted above, in the transportation, storage, or disposal of nuclear fuels. Also, in their daily operations these plants require enormous amounts of water which is returned polluted with both heat and radioactive waste.

Since the known sources of fossil fuels are rapidly being depleted, new sources must be discovered if we are to maintain and increase our level of energy production. Thus, despite many experiences with leaks, offshore drilling for oil continues and its importance is growing. And the quest for cheap coal has already led to the devastation of vast areas of West Virginia, Ohio, and Pennsylvania through strip mining.

Many of the dysfunctional aspects of the manufacturing and farming elements of our technological system were detailed in the previous section of this chapter. One element deserving further attention is that of transportation. There are some 200 million motor vehicles in the world, and half of them are in the United States. Automobiles consume almost half of the crude petroleum production in the United States, and do so very inefficiently. A private motorcar consumes about 4 gallons per 100 passenger miles, while a bus consumes around 0.8 gallons and a train 0.36. Automobiles are also major producers of air and noise pollution. Furthermore, we have given up millions of acres of land to provide the highways for automobile travel and seriously exacerbated the problem of insufficient space in and around our cities.[30]

So deep is our society's faith in the value of technology that despite the fact that every technological "advance" is accompanied by unwanted, unintended, and unanticipated consequences, we have failed to establish any comprehensive social control over the development or use of technology. In reaction to those consequences, many people have now become blindly antitechnology. The point must be emphasized that our environmental crisis is a function, not of technology *per se,* but of the failure of our social system to develop policies aimed at the development of a technology compatible with the requirements of environmental health. To correct that failure, we must first identify the attitudes, values, and beliefs which have permitted us to so befoul our environment and strain its resources.

One such belief is rooted in the very beginnings of our Judeo-Christian culture. That is the belief, expressed in the Old Testament of the Bible, that in creating the universe, God placed people at the apex of all living things, giving them domination over all other species. This anthropocentric view of the physical universe led to a belief that people did not belong to the natural world; rather, it belonged to them, to be exploited for their purposes.[31] The companion belief, that they were responsible for the way in which they used it, was too easily lost sight of.

When the first European settlers came to America, the land and its resources seemed limitless. No matter how rapidly colonization took place, it seemed that there would always be new land on which to settle. The coupling of the concept of an ever-expanding frontier with that of the supremacy of people over nature sent nineteenth-century America out

[30] Kenneth P. Cantor, "Warning: The automobile is dangerous to earth, air, fire, water, mind, and body." In Garrett de Bell, ed., *The Environmental Handbook.* New York: Ballantine, 1970, pp. 206–207.
[31] Lynn White, Jr., "The historical roots of our ecological crisis." In de Bell, pp. 12–26.

to "conquer the continent," much as today we speak of "conquering space." In the process, we exterminated or decimated much of our wildlife, and came near to committing genocide against the Indians.

We produce an incredible number and variety of goods in this country, ample evidence of the high value we place on material objects. Our materialism would appear to derive from three sources. One is the Calvinist doctrine of predestination, which asserted that each person was predestined before birth to go either to heaven or to hell. Although one could never be certain of his or her ultimate destination, it seemed reasonable to assume that those of whom God approved would be blessed with success in this world also, while those destined to be rejected later would be unsuccessful here as well. It thus became important to reassure oneself about salvation by the visible achievement of success; and what better way to demonstrate this than by the acquisition of economic goods, the personal possession of material objects?

A second possible source of our materialism is the fact that all societies establish status systems for differentiating their members, and in our society the acquisition of goods is an important factor in determining a person's status.[32]

Finally, there is our concept of life as progress. We take for granted that our standard of living should be constantly improved, and that this means growth in material wealth. This concept seems so natural to us that we tend to regard as primitive or backward those cultures, past and present, which advise people to be contented with what they have.

Given our belief that there are limitless resources available for our exploitation, and the value we place on the possession of material objects, it is no surprise that we have come to believe in the value of growth for growth's sake (what someone has termed "the ideology of the cancer cell"). Thus a government which was formed to promote the general welfare and ensure that each individual could enjoy "life, liberty, and the pursuit of happiness" has come to measure the former by gross national product and the latter by per capita income.

The primacy of economics over environment became a guiding principle in our system of law. Until recently, there was no basis for an action in law in which one could act as an advocate for the state of the environment itself; in order to bring suit against a despoiler, plaintiffs had to establish that they or their property had suffered economic injury. And now that we do have some laws specifically designed to protect the environment, the penalties for breaking them are also economic—larger or smaller fines. In most cases the fines have been relatively small, and the laws have not always been very energetically enforced.

The development of modern technology was made possible in large measure because of our economic structure, for the entrepreneurs of our "free-enterprise" system encouraged the development of labor-saving machinery. Capital came to replace property as the primary source of power in the society, and entrepreneurs were able to raise capital by demonstrating that they could make a profit on its investment. That meant minimizing costs, and the rivers and the air charged nothing for their services as waste disposal agents. The process of making free (ab)use of

[32] Campbell and Wade, p. 339.

the environment has now come to be recognized as in fact the "externalization" of costs which should properly be accounted for in the price of a given product, for when a steel plant, for example, discharges waste into a river at no cost to itself, it has artificially lowered the price of steel. When environmentalists and economists today say that we are going to have to spend tens of billions of dollars to restore (if we can) the quality of our environment, what they are really doing is presenting us with a bill long past due.

Having delineated some of the major attitudes and values which have led to our environmental crisis, we turn now to an examination of the behavior of some of our social institutions—government, corporations, and schools—to assess their role in creating the problem.

Prior to the recent creation of the Environmental Protection Agency (described later), governmental responsibility, at the federal level, for the state of the environment was divided among several departments. Air pollution control was the concern of the Department of Health, Education, and Welfare, which was also responsible for food and drug regulation. Water pollution control was assigned to the Department of the Interior, which also had responsibility for conservation of wildlife and natural resources and for the administration of the national parks, seashores, and forests. Responsibility for pesticides, which we have seen to be a significant source of air and water pollution and a danger to wildlife, was vested in the Department of Agriculture's Pesticide Regulation Division. Energy production, with the exception of nuclear power generation, which is licensed by the Atomic Energy Commission, is still under the regulation of the Federal Power Commission. The independent National Academy of Science is an important governmental advisory body on science policy, and the Department of Commerce has an Undersecretary for Science and Technology. Finally, Congress has various committees responsible for conducting hearings and developing legislation on different aspects of the environment, and the president has available a Science Advisory Council and a Council on Environmental Quality.

With such extensive federal concern for the environment, one might wonder why there should now be an environmental crisis at all. Unfortunately, conflicts of interest developed in the federal regulatory process. Too often, agencies which were set up to protect the public became advocates for the industries they were intended to regulate. Thus, as part of the Agriculture Department, the Pesticide Regulation Division performed more in the role of lobbyist for the pesticide industry than as protector of the environment. The Atomic Energy Commission is supposed to promote as well as to regulate the nuclear power industry. It has generally tended to stress the former function, and has given too little thought to the dangers inherent in the processing, handling, usage, transportation, and storage of nuclear fuels. The Department of the Interior is responsible for managing public lands so as to make maximum use of their recreational and natural resource potentials. Too frequently this has led to the exploitation of such lands for grazing, mining, and logging, and to their conversion from wilderness areas into what might be termed "nature-consumption packages." Finally, the administrative procedures specified by the major federal laws for the development and application of air- and water-quality standards are often cumbersome, time-consuming, and not sufficiently stringent. (We will discuss more recent federal environmental legislation later in this chapter.)

The federal government has also often been a direct contributor to the degradation of the environment. A number of projects of the Army Corps of Engineers can quite properly be called eco-catastrophes. These include the series of canals in Florida which have resulted in the lowering of the water table in the Everglades, with the resultant destruction of much of the area's wildlife, and a number of dam construction projects. Through its decision to invest heavily in highway construction while giving little support to mass transit, the federal government has contributed to air pollution, as well as to the other dysfunctions associated with our transportation system.

Until recently, the primary concern shown by state governments for the environment was in the areas of conservation and recreation. The past few years, however, have seen a marked increase in concern and action by the states in air and water pollution control, but their record of achievement thus far has not been good. There are several important reasons for this failure. First, state programs have been hampered by a lack of funds to build pollution-control facilities and to staff their regulatory agencies. Second, they have been cautious about prosecuting companies doing business in their states, for fear that the business would move elsewhere and that the state would get a reputation for "toughness" which would deter companies from opening facilities there in the future. Finally, water and air are not respecters of political boundaries: the sources of the pollution are often beyond a state's jurisdiction.

Municipalities and counties are the governmental bodies usually responsible for sewage and solid waste disposal. The record has been poor here also. Most sewage passes untreated into convenient waterways. Garbage is generally disposed of either by burning or by landfill; the former procedure causes air pollution and the latter—even when billed as "sanitary"—frequently produces stinking morasses. Coastal cities are particular offenders with respect to waste disposal. New York City has managed to destroy a portion of the Atlantic Ocean by its garbage dumping; San Francisco is filling in its bay with garbage, with potentially drastic consequences for its climate; Galveston pours millions of gallons of raw sewage into the Gulf of Mexico each day (see Table 14-2).

It would be easy to attribute the environmental failures of government to citizen apathy, as evidenced by an unwillingness to provide sufficient funds for control facilities and personnel, but the roots go much deeper. We have evolved an economy based on overconsumption,

TABLE 14-2
Ocean Dumping of Waste Materials

Coastal Area	Waste Type				Total
	Industrial	Sewage	Construction and Demolition	Solid Waste	
Atlantic	3,997,100	5,429,400	1,161,000	—	10,587,500
Gulf	1,408,000	—	—	—	1,408,000
Pacific	—	—	—	240	240

Source: Council on Environmental Quality.

coupled with a vast array of objects designed to be used once or for a brief time and then discarded. This brings us to a consideration of the role of the major corporations in the creation of our environmental problems.

The rapid growth of many companies after World War II, when the demand for consumer goods was particularly heavy, led to a number of significant changes in the nature of the American economy. The old idea of corporate stability as a virtue was replaced by a valuing of growth for the sake of growth, both in the economy as a whole and for each company in the economy. Thus it was no longer enough simply to satisfy customer needs; companies, through the use of advertising, began to create demand.[33] Individuals were no longer viewed as customers: they became consumers, to be manipulated into desiring products for which they had no real need—products which contributed to their standard of living but not always to the quality of their lives.

But the creation of consumer demand still did not satisfy the passion for growth. Corporations began to manufacture products designed to be replaced within a short time ("planned obsolescence"), or to be used once and then thrown away. Thus automobiles are now designed to last about three years (just long enough to finish the payments), paper diapers replace cotton, foods are double- and triple-packaged, bottles and cans are to be discarded after a single use (some companies have printed on the backs of their bottles "No deposit, no return—not to be refilled" and on the front, ever mindful of their image, "Please help fight litter—dispose of properly"). Annually, over $25 billion is spent on packaging alone in the United States. Most of the packaging materials are discarded, amounting to at least 13 percent of municipal solid wastes.[34] In this way do we drain our natural resources, befoul our air and water, and create mountains of solid waste.

It would be wrong to assume, however, that our environmental crisis is primarily a function of the "greedy rapaciousness" of the corporate leaders of our capitalist system. Communist countries too have been pre-eminently concerned with economic growth. The goals have been the same in both systems—only the means of organization have differed—and both are suffering the same unwanted consequences. If the Communists' environmental problems seem less severe thus far, it is only because their level of industrial production is not yet equal to ours. What should be understood, then, is that any materialist society lacking proper control is bound to produce an environmental crisis, and that our corporations have a vested interest in keeping our society on its present course. The automobile and petroleum companies traditionally head the *Fortune* magazine "500" list, and they make their money from the products which cause much of our pollution. Thus corporations will probably continue to oppose stringent environmental legislation, while seeking to represent themselves as nonpolluters.

[33] See, for example, Vance Packard, *The Hidden Persuaders.* New York: McKay, 1957; and John Kenneth Galbraith, *The Affluent Society.* Boston: Houghton Mifflin, 1971.

[34] U.S. Department of Commerce, *Containers and Packaging,* January 1974, pp. 3–4. See also William E. Small, *Third Pollution.* New York: Praeger, 1971, p. 21.

One argument corporations have used to try to block environmental legislation is that the costs of pollution-control efforts are too high—that the money spent on these efforts increases the costs of goods to consumers, which reduces sales and ultimately causes jobs to be lost. This argument of "jobs versus the environment" was used with particular effectiveness during the economic recession of the mid-1970s, when many deadlines for meeting air- and water-quality standards were postponed as a result of industry pressure. In fact, studies have found that federal environmental controls cost each citizen only about $47 annually, and that environmental programs—particularly the building of new sewage facilities—have already resulted in several hundred thousand new jobs.[35] The rehabilitation of waterways and the building of new, nonpolluting mass transit systems—to cite just two examples—would create many additional new jobs.

SOCIAL ACTION

Consideration of the nature and extent of our ecological crisis has led many to conclude that if we continue on our present course, we are going to have a future characterized by catastrophe. Scientists' projections and scenarios, based on current trends, all point to a future in which life would be like that of our forebears: "nasty, brutish and short." [36] The task before us, then, is to plan an alternative future. However, if we conceive that alternative merely as present society without present problems—no hunger, no pollution—we are unlikely to achieve it, for present problems, as we have seen, are largely outgrowths of past and present society. We must be prepared to make basic changes in our attitudes toward nature and the material world, and this is likely to mean changes in the organization of our social and economic life.

EDUCATING THE PUBLIC

Despite the attention focused on environmental problems in recent years, there is still need for a massive public education effort. People in general must know the facts about the state of the environment, how it got that way, and what can be expected to occur if we continue on our present course. They must also be persuaded to change their attitudes, which is likely to be more difficult to accomplish. Principally, they must learn that the resources of the earth are not limitless but finite. This entails a dual attack on our materialist and growth-valuing attitudes. If there are limits to the amount of goods we can produce, then we must get rid of the concept that "more is better," because at some point there can be no "more." In addition, we must manage some kind of relatively fair and equal distribution of our limited supply of life-supporting and life-enhancing goods among all the inhabitants of the planet. Such a redistribution is implicit in the concept of a finite environment, for the

---

[35] "Attacks on environmental rules blunted." *New York Times,* March 15, 1976, pp. 1 ff.
[36] See, for example, Paul Ehrlich, "Eco-catastrophe." In Campbell and Wade, pp. 269–280.

dwellers in that environment depend on one another and must be able to live in cooperation and reasonable harmony if they are to survive.[37]

In the schools, education in our ecologically sound alternative future would be based on a philosophy which views people as belonging to the world rather than it belonging to them. It would encourage students to concern themselves less with material acquisition and more with the quality of life as reflected in the individual's ability to live harmoniously with the environment. As part of this, children would be taught the value of cooperative rather than competitive behavior.

At the college level, science and engineering students would be required to study the social impact of science and the relation of their own disciplines to environmental health. Specialization and fragmentation of knowledge are probably unavoidable in an advanced technological society; but such training in "social accountability," coupled with the primary educational experience described above, should produce scientists and engineers who would regard the exercise of their knowledge in a framework of ecological awareness as a fundamental part of their jobs.

One of the great lessons to be learned from the study of the natural world is the concept of cyclical processing, for every natural process, as we have seen, forms one part of a cycle of constant renewal. Thus, once we recognize our environment as finite, we must restructure our life styles to allow for the recycling of what we use. There should be no problem of solid waste disposal, because there should be no solid waste. The recycling of all materials should be "programmed" in advance—what is output for a given system should be recycled as input, after usage, for the same or another system. There would be no "final use" for a product; it would always be in process. This would probably require legislation at the national level, regulating the distribution of goods in our society. Before manufacturers would be permitted to market a product, they would be required to demonstrate the adequacy of the recycling program for the product. Similarly, municipalities would not be permitted to discharge their solid wastes into waterways, but would be required to have effective recycling programs. Such programs could be developed on an industry-wide basis. They might rely on large deposits which would encourage the customer to return the used product (automobiles, bottles, cans); contracts with waste-collection agencies, municipal or private, which would directly return the product (paper, for example); or separation at centrally located trash reclamation sites.

In some areas of the country—and in some industries—successful recycling programs are already under way. For example, there are now 1,300 aluminum reclamation centers throughout the nation, which recycle over 17 percent of the country's aluminum cans. More than 100 cities have paper-collection programs; as a result, about 22 percent of all paper manufactured in the United States is recycled. In St. Louis, recycling has advanced to the point where a new plant has been built to recycle almost all of that city's refuse—almost 8,000 tons a day.

Such recycling not only helps save the environment, but is also profitable. It has been estimated that ordinary disposal of wastes costs

RECYCLING

[37] See Kenneth E. Boulding, "The economics of the coming spaceship earth." In de Bell, pp. 96–101.

this nation some $3.5 billion annually. Recycling wastes would enable companies and municipalities to save the energy needed to produce new materials and to use or even sell the materials derived from the waste. As one observer pointed out,

For every ton of steel produced from recycled municipal solid waste instead of ore, the following things happen:

Enough electricity is saved to power the average American home for eight months—a 74 percent saving in the amount of energy consumed to produce that one ton of steel.

Two hundred pounds of air pollutants, of the kind produced in making steel from ore, are not produced—an 86 percent decline in air pollution.

About 6,700 gallons of fresh water are not used—a 40 percent saving.

As the water that is used is returned to streams and sewers, 102 pounds of water pollutants are not discharged—a 76 percent reduction.

And 2.7 tons of mining wastes are not heaped on the landscape around the mine.[38]

Increasingly, it is becoming expensive *not* to recycle.

The concept of recycling also applies to industrial effluents; just as the final product must be recycled, so must the by-products of the manufacturing process. Much of what is effluent in one process can be used as input in other processes. A company should be required by law to return water at the same temperature and quality at which it was withdrawn and either to remove potential air pollutants at some early stage in the manufacturing process or to trap them in the stack. Again, the relevant legislation would probably have to be at the national level; otherwise "havens" of pollution would be created in states or municipalities which failed to pass the necessary laws. Penalties for violation might range from fines or plant shutdown to criminal charges against management personnel.

The recycling concept is directly applicable to another important cluster of environmental problems: urban sewage disposal, the stripping of nutrients from farm soil, and the runoff of artificial fertilizers from farms into waterways. Treated sewage makes excellent fertilizer, and if this were shipped from city to farm we would solve the disposal problem and considerably lessen the need for artificial fertilizers.

An important ramification of the recycling process is that it would require what are currently construed as "external" costs to be included, in addition to the current internal costs of production, in determining the price of the product. Thus the cost of environmental cleanliness would be borne by manufacturers (or their customers) rather than by the public as a whole. Presumably the burden of these costs would prove an incentive to the corporation to find ways of making the fullest possible use of waste products and effluents.

The "invisible hand" that Adam Smith, an eighteenth-century economist, said was guiding the free-enterprise system pulled out of the American economy in the early 1930s, and the federal government stepped in and announced that henceforth it would accept primary responsibility for the

Learning to recycle the resources we use will conserve these resources and reduce environmental pollution. Here, people are bringing their used bottles to a local recycling center.
Charles Gatewood

TECHNOLOGY ASSESSMENT

[38] Boyce Rensberger, "Coining trash." *New York Times Magazine,* December 7, 1975, pp. 31 ff.

state of the economy. We have engaged in a "free technology" system which closely parallels the free-enterprise system, and the quality of our environment is "crashing" today in a fashion not unlike that of the stock market in 1929. That is, a system which was generally believed to be stable has proved, in fact, to be unstable. Once again the government is having to intervene to restore balance and to regulate future activities. This time it will probably be necessary to devise ways of continually assessing the state of our technology and determining what present and new technologies we, as a society, shall utilize. Such assessment procedures will require a technological sophistication which we do not yet possess: the ability to predict accurately the probable indirect effects of a given technological innovation.[39] Only then could we be sure that any particular technological "advance" would be of greater benefit than cost to society. Even then, assessment must be coupled with regulation. For the government merely to publish assessment reports would accomplish little; the assessing body must also have the authority to prevent industry from disregarding them.

Three technological areas which especially require the attention of an assessing/regulating authority are energy production, transportation, and chemicals.

Energy Production. Our requirements for electric power are expected to double over the next decade—and to double again in the decade after that. This raises two important questions: How much of that demand should we satisfy (or allow to come into being, since much of it is created by the utility companies)? And how shall we generate the electricity? We currently employ three technologies for the generation of electrical power: fossil-fuel combustion, water power, and nuclear power. Each of them, as we have described above, generates its own brand of problems in addition to electricity. We need to support research and experimentation with other forms of power generation—particularly solar energy—and decide, first on an ecological basis and second on a cost/benefit basis, which is the most beneficial balance of generating capability. To do this, we must consider *all* the costs—the expense of eliminating pollution from fossil-fuel generation, the risks of nuclear power, and whatever else is involved.

If we are to avoid "blackouts" and "brownouts" and the waste of scarce resources, we need to develop a national energy policy which will assign priorities and/or a system of allocation for electricity consumption. Thus we might decide to limit automation and rely on human power, or to ration the amount of electricity each household and company may consume over a given period of time, or to restrict the production of household and office "labor-saving" devices, or to set general priorities on the types of products which should be made.

Transportation. The automobile is generally conceded to be a technological horror. It produces 60 percent of our urban air pollution; it is

<hr>

[39] See *Technology Assessment: Hearings Before the Subcommittee on Science, Research and Development* (no. 13). Washington, D.C.: U.S. Government Printing Office, 1970.

inefficient in comparison with other forms of transport; it is dangerous—about 50,000 people are killed each year in auto accidents; it requires ever-increasing amounts of public money and land for highway construction. Putting improved antipollution devices on cars will not begin to solve our transportation problems. We must also rebuild our declining railroad systems, probably through diversion of highway funds. Public transport systems in cities—buses and subways—must be updated and run for the convenience of their passengers. Cities are already considering the banning of private auotmobile traffic from some of their streets during certain hours of the day. They should also provide bikeways for the growing number of cyclists. We need to develop technologies which can deal with the needs of individual and mass transportation in ways that are in harmony with the capacities and resources of the environment.

Chemicals. Over 500 new chemicals are introduced into our environment each year. Yet we ordinarily have little or no knowledge about their biological consequences. Several classes of chemicals have proved to be seriously dysfunctional. These include the "killers" (pesticides such as DDT and the other chlorinated hydrocarbons; herbicides such as 2,4-D and 2,4,5-T, which were widely used in Vietnam), plastics, and food additives. We need to develop alternatives to the use of poisons for insect control, such as applied natural biological controls, and to develop new criteria for regulating the use of additives on the basis of biological and not marketing considerations.

LEGISLATION

The widespread concern about the earth's ecology that developed during the 1960s resulted in the passage of a number of laws designed to control or reduce the harm being done to our environment. The *National Environmental Policy Act* (NEPA) of 1970 required for the first time that before federal projects (or projects requiring federal approval) are undertaken, public hearings on possible environmental effects must be held and environmental impact studies must be filed. A major achievement of NEPA was to hold up the construction of the Alaskan oil pipeline until safeguards were established to ensure that the pipeline's environmental impact would be minimized. The *Clean Air Act* of 1970 established the federal Environmental Protection Agency (EPA) and empowered it to set and enforce standards of air quality. The EPA has since been given authority over most matters involving environmental quality. For example, the *Federal Water Pollution Control Act Amendments* of 1972 made it illegal to discharge pollutants into a water supply without a permit. The stated goal of the law, which is enforced by the EPA, is to eliminate all water pollution by the mid-1980s.

Unfortunately, despite such legislation, the battle against ecological disaster is still far from being won. The National Wildlife Federation publishes an annual environmental-quality index, which measures the environmental status of seven major categories: wildlife, living space, soil, timber, minerals, water, and air. According to the federation's seventh annual index,[40] the quality of all these categories has declined

[40] "Seventh environmental quality index." *National Wildlife Magazine,* February–March 1976.

since 1969, despite the environmental legislation of the intervening years. A large portion of the blame for this situation lies with industry, which has strongly resisted compliance with environmental laws. Enforcement of automobile emissions standards, for example, was delayed for many years because automobile company lobbyists claimed that the standards were unrealistic. The economic recession of the mid-1970s also set back environmental efforts: industry was able to convince Congress to postpone deadlines for meeting air- and water-quality standards on the basis that pollution-control devices were too expensive in a depressed economy. Finally, the EPA itself, either because it is understaffed or because it is sensitive to pressures from industry, or both, has been unable or unwilling in some instances to stringently enforce environmental laws.

Clearly, what is needed is a renewed commitment to the environmental legislation that already exists. As we have seen, the idea that pollution-control efforts cost too much money is a myth. In fact, quite the contrary is the case: it is pollution and waste that cost too much, depleting our resources, ravaging our environment, and ruining our health. A firm determination on the part of government, industry, and the individual citizen to see to it that environmental laws are obeyed and enforced would do much to begin to reduce the deterioration of our environment.

Additional legislation is required, however, in order to achieve the cleanest, healthiest environment possible. Prohibiting industrial land use in scenic or ecologically important areas; setting rigid controls on offshore drilling; limiting automobile size and weight, so that less fuel will be used and less pollution will be produced; providing additional funds for mass transit, so the reliance on automobiles will be reduced; making recycling mandatory; and setting new standards of air and water quality that will ultimately eliminate pollution almost completely—these are some of the additional steps that need to be taken before the environmental crisis can be solved.

POPULATION CONTROL

The goal of population control in a viable alternative future would be the stabilization of population size—sometimes known as "zero population growth." We must seek to achieve this by social regulation, as opposed to the "natural" or unsocial forms of regulation, such as famine, disease, and war, which kept population growth relatively stable until the last few centuries. (This was discussed more fully in Chapter 13.)

CREATING THE FUTURE

The alternative future we have been describing—an alternative to the creation of a septic world characterized by environmental crises—can only come into being if enough people want it strongly enough to make it happen. This requires organization and knowledge. There already exists a loose confederation of groups of concerned citizens, ranging from traditional conservationists to radical activists. They need to learn how to coordinate their activities and to develop positive programs for change —programs which should be concentrated in the two areas of education and regulation. We have already considered the former; environmental groups must continue to make information available and to press for the necessary new emphases in school curricula.

As for regulation, in our society law is the primary system employed for the regulation of behavior, and environmentalists must learn how to use it to gain their ends. In addition to direct lobbying for legislation to require recycling, population and pollution control, and technology assessment, environmental groups should apply pressure through the courts to ensure that public officials enforce laws already on the books.

They should also urge the Federal Trade Commission and the Federal Communications Commission to adopt more stringent regulations for radio and television advertisements. Such rules might provide that advertisements be limited to one minute of each broadcast hour, and that equal time be accorded free to recognized environmental groups; and they might prohibit the advertising of products which are directly destructive to the environment or which constitute a demonstrable hazard to human health, much as cigarette advertising has already been banned from television.

PROSPECTS

Given the proposition that the survival of any given species is dependent on the existence of a diversity of other life forms, we must seriously consider whether humanity will survive; for we have, within the past hundred years and at an increasing rate, caused the near or total extinction of a number of organisms and endangered many others. Several species of birds and fish have ceased to reproduce, as a consequence of high-level DDT concentrations in their bodies, and are thus as good as extinct. Some scientists fear that similar persistent poisons are also killing phytoplankton, the plants which provide oxygen in the oceans and serve as food for the animals at the bottom of the ocean food chains. One study found that 85 percent of the nation's larger lakes are already being choked by the proliferation of algae.[41]

As a test for air quality, miners used to carry a canary in a cage down into pits with them. When the canary sickened, the miners knew enough to leave the mine. But we cannot leave the earth. According to a number of experts, the question is only whether we will take corrective action before we succumb. The recommendations for such corrective action usually envision limiting both economic and population growth.

Other environmental scientists, along with researchers in related disciplines, are less apocalyptic in their views. Their arguments tend to center on two beliefs: first, that added economic growth is needed not only to satisfy present world demand for food and the artifacts of a high standard of living, but also to clean up the environmental mess we have already made; second, that the technology of the future will provide us with the means for restoring the environment while maintaining present life styles and improving the quality of life in poorer countries. Adherents of these views acknowledge that their predictions are based on the assumption that a means will be found to limit world population growth. One study concluded that the costs of environmental cleanup for 14 major industries

[41] "A turn in the tide—pollution battle being won?" *U.S. News & World Report,* August 4, 1975, p. 57.

would not be severe either for the industries involved or for the economy as a whole, and might, in fact, be more than balanced by the long-term savings which would accrue from the cessation of the damage caused by present pollution.[42]

The overall outlook is not encouraging, however. Our problems are numerous, varied, and complex. Educating the public is a lengthy, time-consuming process. Social change generally occurs slowly. Most of the power in any society is inevitably committed to maintaining the status quo, and we are running out of lead time. It will be difficult for a people intensely concerned with the acquisition of material objects voluntarily to limit such acquisition and renounce the goal of ever-increasing material wealth.

Beyond the question of change is the problem of incomplete knowledge. Our understanding of the natural system and how it functions is still very elementary, and we cannot always be sure what measures will be successful in rescuing the environment.

Of course, we need not be entirely pessimistic. Large numbers of people around the world are becoming aware of, and concerned about, the environment. The levels of some air pollutants (such as sulfur dioxide) in the United States have started to decline as a result of air pollution standards, though the levels of many other pollutants remain unchanged or are rising. There are some expectations that the nation's waters will be comparatively clean by the end of the twentieth century. The essential question remains to be resolved, however: Can we change our living habits and our social institutions before the harm we are doing to our environment—and to ourselves—becomes irreversible?

SUMMARY

Though all of us depend on the environment for our existence, we have been abusing the environment to the point where the quality of life has been reduced and our ability to survive is being threatened. The pollutants we pour into the air cause illness and even death; result in increased economic costs, due to deterioration of property and wasted resources; and may cause harm to the earth's entire ecosystem. The pollutants we pour into our waters render water useless for humans or for industry and kill essential fish and plant life. Many of these harmful pollutants accumulate in living species and ascend up the food chain, ultimately being ingested by people. Even the way we dispose of our solid and nuclear wastes is inefficient and potentially harmful. Add to this the wholesale degradation of land that is taking place, the growing amount of noise pollution, the proliferation of untested chemicals in our industries and in our food, and our fondness for large-scale engineering projects that cause damage, and it is clear that we are faced with an environmental crisis.

The origins of the crisis lie in our faith in the value of technology; our Judeo-Christian belief that we should dominate the earth; and our emphasis on materialism and progress. Though many laws exist to maintain standards of environmental quality, these laws have not been stringently enforced. Clearly, our style of life and our attitudes will have to change before the damage to the environment can be halted and reversed.

[42] *Business Week,* March 18, 1972, pp. 18–19.

Such a change will have to be effected in a number of ways: through public education programs to make people more ecologically aware; through implementation of recycling programs; through the development of less wasteful technologies; and through the passage and enforcement of environmental legislation. Only renewed dedication to saving the environment can save us from disaster and move us toward an ecologically sound alternative future.

BIBLIOGRAPHY

Campbell, Rex R., and Wade, Jerry L. *Society and Environment: The Coming Collision*. Boston: Allyn and Bacon, 1972.

Carson, Rachel. *Silent Spring*. Rev. ed. New York: Crest, 1973.

Commoner, Barry. *Science and Survival*. New York: Viking, 1967.

————. *The Closing Circle: Nature, Man and Technology*. New York: Knopf, 1971.

de Bell, Garrett. *The Environmental Handbook*. New York: Ballantine, 1970.

Falk, Richard A. *This Endangered Planet*. New York: Random House, 1971.

Goldman, Marshall I., ed. *Critical Issues in Controlling Pollution*. Englewood Cliffs, N.J.: Prentice-Hall, 1972.

Hefrich, Harold W., Jr. *The Environmental Crisis: Man's Struggle to Live with Himself*. New Haven, Conn.: Yale University Press, 1970.

Kormondy, E. *Concepts of Ecology*. Englewood Cliffs, N.J.: Prentice-Hall, 1969.

Love, Glen A., and Love, Rhoda A., eds. *Ecological Crisis: Readings for Survival*. New York: Harcourt Brace Jovanovich, 1970.

Meadows, Dennis, *et al*. *Dynamics of Growth in a Future World*. New York: Wiley, 1974.

Meadows, Donella H., *et al*. *The Limits to Growth: A Report for the Club of Rome's Project on the Predicament of Mankind*. New York: Universe, 1972.

Murdoch, William W., ed. *Environment: Resources, Pollution and Society*. Stamford, Conn.: Sinauer Associates, 1971.

Odum, Howard T. *Environment, Power and Society*. New York: 1970.

Rienow, Robert, and Rienow, Leona Train. *Moment in the Sun*. New York: Ballantine, 1967.

Wagner, Richard H. *Environment and Man*. 2nd ed. New York: Norton, 1974.

NAME INDEX

Abelson, H., 468n
Abrams, Charles, 527n
Adams, Stuart, 527n
Akers, Ronald L., 159–60
Alberts, Robert C., 372n
Albrecht, Gary L., 87n, 89
Alexander, Tom, 547n
Allen, Vernon L., 207n
Allison, Junius L., 253n
Alloway, Lawrence, 199n
Allport, Gordon, 277
Anthony, Susan B., 323
Antonovsky, Aaron, 29n, 30n, 40
Ardrey, Robert, 194
Ares, Charles E., 298n
Aristotle, 479
Aron, Raymond, 215
Ashley, Richard, 110, 111
Augustine, Saint, 432
Austin, Patricia Lee, 261n

Bagdikian, Ben, 237
Bahr, Howard M., 93
Bailey, Walter C., 173n
Baker, Susan S., 483n
Baratz, Joan C., 307
Baratz, Stephen S., 307
Barnett, Harold J., 527n
Bart, Pauline, 342, 343
Bartlett, Randall, 266
Beach, Frank A., 436
Beal, Frances M., 336
Bean, Lee L., 59
Beauvoir, Simone de, 363
Becker, Howard S., 101
Beers, Clifford W., 63
Belkaoui, Ahmed, 345n
Belkaoui, Janice M., 345n
Bell, Daniel, 483n, 491
Bell, Robert R., 317n, 325n, 342,
    344, 442n, 443n, 450n,
    451, 452n, 460, 463
Bem, Sandra L., 328n
Benn, Gloria J., 122
Berger, Alan S., 394
Berkanovic, Emil, 249n
Berkov, B., 402n, 403n
Berkowitz, Leonard, 194n
Berle, A. A., 233n
Bernard, Jessie, 342
Berns, Walter, 470
Besharov, Douglas, 395
Best, Fred, 505n, 507n
Bettelheim, Bruno, 343, 424, 425
Betz, George W., 521n
Bianchi, Eugene C., 196
Billet, Sanford L., 97

Björk, Lars E., 496n
Blakey, William A., 335
Blau, Zena Smith, 361, 367–68,
    376n, 379, 380, 382, 384
Blauner, Robert, 494n
Bloch, Donald, 418, 419
Block, Irving, 29n
Bloomberg, W., 500
Blum, Fred H., 499
Blum, Richard H., 100n, 113
Blum, Sam, 418
Blumberg, Rae Lesser, 390n
Blume, Marshall E., 229n
Boelkins, R. Charles, 193, 194
Bogart, Leo, 198, 211n, 212n
Bogue, Donald J., 528n
Borgatta, Edgar F., 175n
Boulding, Kenneth E., 518, 532,
    566n
Bradburn, Norman M., 392
Brady, James B., 413n
Braginsky, B. M., 488
Braginsky, D. D., 488
Brandwein, R. A., 410
Brecher, Edward M., 106n
Breughel, 471
Briedis, Catherine, 404
Brotman, Richard, 122n, 126n, 127
Brown, Barry S., 122
Brown, Bertram S., 127n
Brown, C. A., 410n
Brown, Richard Maxwell, 190
Brownmiller, Susan, 318–19
Bryan, James H., 462
Bryson, Rebecca B., 342n
Buell, John, 288n
Bultena, Gordon L., 382
Burack, Richard, 83n
Burgess, Robert L., 159–60
Burnette, Robert, 292
Burstein, Abraham C., 291
Butler, Robert N., 361n, 362n, 366,
    374, 379

Calendine, Jerry, 503n
Calvin, John, 480
Cameron, Juan, 288n, 292n, 293,
    295n, 296n
Campbell, Angus, 393n
Campbell, Arthur A., 529n
Campbell, Rex R., 561n
Cantor, David J., 412
Cantor, Kenneth P., 560n
Caplan, Gerald, 73–74
Carmichael, Stokely S., 292
Carr, Donald E., 546n, 549n,
    551n

Chafe, William H., 346n
Chafetz, Janet S., 339, 340n, 341,
    345n
Chafetz, Morris E., 81, 86n, 88,
    90n, 91n, 96n, 98n
Chamberlain, Neil W., 507n
Chambers, Marcia, 182n
Chambliss, William, 138, 139n,
    155–56
Chappell, Duncan, 438n, 441
Chaskell, Ruth, 405n
Chavez, Cesar, 304
Chesler, Phyllis, 61–62, 344n
Chinoy, Ely, 497
Clark, John R., 551n
Clark, Kenneth B., 250n, 301
Clark, Ramsey, 200n, 212
Clausen, John A., 52n
Clinard, Marshall B., 140, 200n,
    201n, 203n, 204n, 438n,
    457
Cline, Carolyn, 391
Coale, Ansley J., 518
Cohen, Albert K., 14
Cohen, David K., 288–89
Cohen, R., 468n
Coleman, James S., 287, 288
Coles, Robert, 300–1
Combs, Bob, 101
Commoner, Barry, 522
Conant, Ralph, 208
Connel, Philip H., 120n
Constantine, Barry L., 423n
Constantine, Joan M., 423n
Coolidge, Calvin, 233
Cooper, Barbara, 31n
Corrigan, Eileen, 404n
Coser, Lewis A., 239n
Costello, Mary, 42n
Cowen, Emory L., 72
Cowgill, Donald O., 375
Cox, Steven R., 243n
Cressey, Donald R., 142–43, 149n,
    171n
Crockett, Jean, 229n
Cuber, John F., 417
Curtis, Richard, 550n, 553n

Daly, Mary, 346
Damon, Allan L., 218n
D'Andrade, Roy G., 318n
Daniels, David N., 214n, 215,
    216n, 219n
Dank, Barry, 446–47
Davidson, Charles, 262n
Davis, Alan J., 445n
Davis, Catherine, 384n

Davis, Kingsley, 458–60, 515n, 531, 532
Davis, Nanette J., 460–62
de Beauvoir, Simone, 363
Della Fave, Richard L., 259, 268
deLuca, Tom, 288n
Demone, Harold W., Jr., 96n
Dickens, Charles, 67
Dickson, William J., 495n
Ditlea, Steve, 362, 376n, 383n
Dix, Dorothea, 63
Dowling, Harry F., 82n
Dunham, H. Warren, 55
DuPont, Robert L., 109, 119
Durand, John D., 515n
Durkheim, Emile, 13, 134, 154

Eagleton, Thomas, 47
Eaton, Joseph W., 59
Edwards, Michael D., 235n
Ehrenreich, Barbara, 29n, 39n
Ehrenreich, John, 29n, 39n
Ehrlich, Anne H., 518n, 522n, 525n, 535n, 544n, 546n, 547n, 549n, 552n, 553, 554n, 555n
Ehrlich, Paul R., 518n, 522n, 525n, 535n, 544n, 546n, 547n, 549n, 552n, 553, 554n, 555n, 565n
Ehrlichman, John, 142
Eichhorn, Robert L., 248n–50n
Eisenhower, Dwight D., 217, 236
Eisenstadt, S. N., 358, 373
Ellen, Mary, 397
Ellis, Albert, 423
Ellis, Havelock, 433
Elmer, Elizabeth, 396
Enke, Stephen, 518n
Epstein, Cynthia P., 325n
Epstein, Joseph, 252 n
Erikson, Erik, 344
Erikson, Kai T., 14
Erlanger, Howard S., 197
Etzioni, Amitai, 16n, 45n
Evans, John W., 306n

Fairfield, Richard, 421, 423
Fanon, Frantz, 192
Faris, Robert E. L., 55
Farrell, Warren, 315n, 325n, 341n, 343, 353n
Fasteau, Marc F., 328
Faunce, William, 506n
Feagin, Joe R., 208
Fein, Rashi, 296
Ferracuti, Franco, 196n
Ferriss, Abbott L., 407
Fichter, Joseph H., 345n
Finkelstein, M. M., 469n
Finsterbusch, Kurt, 216
Fisher, Peter, 455
Fogelson, Robert M., 207n
Foner, A., 415n

Fontana, Vincent, 400
Ford, Clellan S., 317n, 436
Ford, Gerald R., 347
Ford, Maurice deG., 287n, 289
Ford, Robert N., 496n
Foster, Henry H., Jr., 405n, 411n
Fox, E. M., 410n
Freed, Doris Jonas, 405n, 411n
Freedman, Jonathan, 60
Freeman, Jo, 323, 324
Freud, Sigmund, 64, 194, 319–20, 324, 343, 433–35, 473
Friedan, Betty, 316, 322, 323, 328
Friedenberg, Edgar A., 359, 360, 363–65, 374
Friend, Irwin, 229n
Fuchs, Victor R., 240–41, 331–32

Gagnon, John H., 431n–33n, 436, 439, 443n, 445, 446, 451, 453, 466, 473
Galbraith, John Kenneth, 240, 564n
Gallo, "Crazy Joe," 148
Galtung, Johan, 191
Gans, Herbert J., 256–57, 266n
Gardiner, John A., 152
Garson, Barbara, 495n
Garvey, Marcus, 302
Gaylin, Willard, 176n
Gebhard, Paul H., 440, 444
Geis, Gilbert, 460
Gerstl, J. E., 460
Geschwender, James A., 207, 208
Getty, J. Paul, 232
Giallombardo, Rose, 452
Gibbons, Don C., 139n
Gil, David, 396–98, 400
Gillin, Christian, 210n
Gilula, Marshall F., 214n, 215, 216n, 219n
Gitter, Max, 412
Glass, L., 49
Glasser, Lois N., 389, 415n
Glasser, Paul H., 389, 415n
Glick, Paul C., 406n, 413, 425n
Godman, Peter, 303n
Goetz, Charles M., 262n
Goffman, Erving, 69–71
Goldberg, Phillip, 328
Golding, William, 194
Goldstein, Joseph, 412
Goldstein, Michael J., 469
Goode, W. J., 321n, 322n, 325n
Gooding, Judson, 484n
Goodwin, Donald W., 85n
Goodwin, Leonard, 261
Gould, Robert E., 328n
Gould, William B., 294
Graham, Hugh Davis, 188, 191n, 273n
Graham, Saxon, 26, 29n
Greeley, Andrew, 530n
Greenley, James R., 54

Greisman, H. C., 216
Grier, Eunice, 291n
Grier, George, 291n
Griffin, C. W., Jr., 547n
Grinspoon, Leslie, 112n
Gross, Bertram M., 240n
Grupp, Stanley, 171n
Grutzner, Charles, 150n, 180n
Guevara, Che, 214n
Guggenheimer, Elinor C., 349n
Gurr, Ted Robert, 188, 189n, 191n, 196n, 273n
Gusfield, Joseph R., 81n
Guthrie, James W., 288n
Guttemacher, Manfred S., 441n
Guttentag, Marcia, 161n

Hahn, Harlan, 208
Haley, Alex, 301n
Hamer, John, 548n
Hamilton, Charles V., 292
Han, Wan Sang, 161
Hanchett, Arnold, 547n
Hardin, Garrett, 538n
Harrington, Michael, 248
Harris, Louis, 290, 304n
Harris, Marvin, 275
Hartjen, Clayton A., 137n
Hartley, Ruth E., 325
Hartley, Shirley F., 403, 404, 520n
Hartman, John J., 469n
Hartnagel, Timothy F., 198
Hauser, Philip M., 513n, 421n
Heaton, E., 468n
Hedbloom, Peter, 112n
Hedges, Janice Neipert, 504n–6n, 508n
Helser, John F., 193, 196
Henderson, Bruce, 431n–33n, 436
Henderson, Susan, 173n
Henry, Jeannette, 284
Herrick, Neal, 484
Herzberg, Frederick, 479, 494–95
Hicks, Nancy, 100n, 115n, 119n
Hills, Stuart L., 158n
Hirschi, Travis, 195n
Hogan, Elizabeth, 550n, 553n
Hole, Judith, 322n, 332n, 347
Hollingshead, August B., 55–59, 67
Hollister, Robinson, 371n, 381n
Hooker, Evelyn, 443n, 445n, 448, 449
Hoos, Ida Russakoff, 492
Hoover, J. Edgar, 469
Horner, Matina S., 328, 329
Horowitz, Irving L., 219n
Howard, Philip H., 547n
Howe, Florence, 250n, 341
Howe, Irving, 499n
Hughes, Howard, 232
Humphreys, Laud, 449
Hunt, H. L., 231
Hunt, Morton, 431, 435, 439–40, 442, 451, 459n, 472

Hunter, Charlayne, 213n
Hutton, S. P., 499

Ianni, Elizabeth, 148n
Ianni, Francis, 148n
Ilfed, Fred, 197, 219n
Isaacson, Pete, 250n
Iscoe, Ira, 73n

Jackman, Norman R., 460
Jackson, Joan K., 93n
Jacobs, Paul, 239n
Jacobson, Julius, 294n, 295n
Jaffee, Frederick S., 533n
Jerdee, Thomas H., 329n
Johnson, Elmer H., 172n
Johnson, Lyndon B., 240, 274, 337
Johnson, M., 415n
Johnson, Virginia, 434
Johnston, William, 288, 490n, 507n
Jones, Maxwell, 119
Jones, Wyatt C., 175n
Jorgensen, Christine, 431

Kalish, Richard M., 363, 380
Kallman, F. J., 448n
Kant, Harold S., 469n
Kanter, John, 472
Kanter, Rosabeth Moss, 424n
Kasindorf, Martin, 108n, 109–10, 119n, 125n
Katchadourian, Herant, 438
Kaufman, Richard F., 235n, 236n
Kempe, C. Henry, 399
Kendal, Denise, 106n
Kendall, Patricia L., 29n
Kennedy, Edward M., 44
Kennedy, John F., 291
Kennedy, Robert F., 148, 197
Kessel, R., 39n
Keyserling, Leon, 241n
King, Lourdes M., 337
King, Martin Luther, Jr., 15, 302
Kinsey, Alfred C., 431, 433–35, 437, 442, 451, 473
Kirk, Dudley, 535n
Klein, D. P., 487n, 488n
Klein, Malcolm, 160
Kleiner, Robert J., 57
Kobrin, Solomon, 174n
Koeppel, Barbara, 370n, 371n
Komisar, Lucy, 345
Kornhauser, Arthur, 497
Kramer, E. H., 115
Kraus, Harry D., 402n
Kreps, Juanita, 498n
Kristol, Irving, 470
Kübler-Ross, Elizabeth, 45–46
Kuhn, Maggie, 383

Lane, Robert E., 239n
Lang, Gladys Engel, 199

Lang, Kurt, 199
Langer, A., 56
Lansky, Meyer, 152–53
Lauter, Paul, 250n
Law, Sylvia A., 33n
Leinwand, Gerald, 546n, 547n
Lekachman, Robert, 333
Lenski, Gerhard, 317n
Lerman, Paul, 153n, 154n, 182n
Lerner, Monroe, 27, 30, 35n, 39n, 42n
Leventman, Seymour, 61
Levine, Adeline, 49
Levine, Ellen, 322n, 332n, 347
Levine, Murray, 49
Levine, Robert A., 265
Levinson, Richard M., 331
Levitan, Sar, 288, 306n, 490n, 507n
Lewis, Arthur, 226n
Lewis, Michael, 340
Lewis, Oscar, 254–55, 268
Leznoff, Maurice, 444n
Libman, Joan, 465n
Liebow, Elliot, 394n
Lilienthal, David, 553
Locke, John, 4
Lowenberg, Frank M., 503n
Lombroso, Cesare, 10
Long, C. D., 486
Lorenz, Konrad, 194
Lucas, Robert, 225n, 229n
Ludwig, Edward G., 248n, 249n, 250n
Lundberg, Ferdinand, 225, 230–34
Lunde, Donald T., 195n, 201–3, 438
Luther, Martin, 480, 508
Lynn, David B., 340
Lyons, Nancy, 228n

McCormack, Arthur, 530n
McDonald, Steve, 513n
McElroy, Wayne, 502n, 503n
McIntosh, Mary, 446
McIntyre, Jennie M., 198n
MacLeod, Celeste, 396n, 400n
Magargee, Ed, 195n
Majka, Linda, 235n
Malcolm X, 301
Malinche, 337
Malinowski, Bronislaw, 400
Mamdani, Mahmood, 534n
Mangum, Garth L., 263
Mankoff, Milton, 235n, 236
Mannheim, K., 376
Manson, Charles, 203
Marcuse, Herbert, 192
Marcussen, Jack, 503n
Marmor, Judd, 319, 322n
Marstom, Linda L., 211
Marx, Karl, 483, 498
Masters, William H., 434
Maudin, W. Parker, 530n

Mead, Margaret, 325, 374, 376, 379, 418, 419
Merton, Robert K., 160, 161, 277, 441
Meyer, Henry J., 175n
Meyer, Marshall W., 490, 491
Meyers, Frederick H., 81
Mill, John Stuart, 316
Miller, Herman P., 239, 528
Miller, Norman P., 506n
Miller, S. M., 56, 240
Miller, Walter B., 174n
Mills, Virginia K., 345n
Mishler, Elliot G., 56
Mix, Sheldon A., 552n
Money, John, 324
Moore, Wilbert E., 481
Moran, Patrick, 261n
Morgan, Theodore, 521n
Morse, Nancy C., 479n
Moynihan, Daniel, 393n, 394
Murray, Douglas R., 211
Mushkin, Selma, 108n, 117n
Myers, Jerome K., 58, 59
Myrdal, Gunnar, 267, 273, 274

Nader, Ralph, 234
Nagasawa, Richard H., 155–56
Nawy, H., 469
Nettler, Gwynn, 139n
Neugarten, Bernice L., 359, 361, 379, 380n, 384
Newfield, Jack, 176n, 179n
Nieburg, H. L., 106n
Nieto, Consuelo, 338
Nixon, R. A., 482n, 487, 488
Nixon, Richard M., 3, 27, 146
Noel, Donald L., 280n
Nordhoff, Charles, 420n
Northcott, Herbert C., 370n
Notestein, Frank W., 535n
Nowlis, Helen N., 100, 110n, 115–16

Ochberg, Frank, 210n
Ognibene, Peter J., 218n
O'Leary, K. Daniel, 325
Oppenheimer, Valerie K., 329n
Orden, Susan R., 392
Ornati, Oscar, 241
Orshansky, Mollie, 241
Osborn, Fairfield, 553n, 554n
O'Toole, Richard, 460
Owen, George C., 327

Packard, Vance, 564n
Palmore, Erdman, 380n
Parker, Seymour, 57
Parker, Stanley, 494, 499
Parks, Rosa, 15
Parlee, Mary B., 344n
Parrish, J. B., 315n
Parsons, Talcott, 360
Patterson, John E., 529n

Paul, Alice, 323
Paul VI, Pope, 429
Pearlin, Leonard I., 409
Penderglass, Virginia E., 335*n*, 336
Pepper, Max P., 59
Perrucci, Carolyn C., 325*n*
Peterson, Donald R., 68*n*
Peterson, James A., 407
Phelan, James R., 232*n*, 234*n*
Pinel, Philippe, 63, 66, 67
Pines, Maya, 306*n*
Pittman, David J., 455*n*
Piven, Frances Fox, 264*n*, 304
Plate, Thomas, 137
Platt, Gerald M., 360
Polansky, Norman, 396*n*
Pollock, Carl B., 399
Pope, Hallowell, 394*n*
Popovich, Marina, 326
Porter, Sylvia, 366*n*
Powers, Edwin, 175*n*

Quinney, Richard, 140, 141*n*, 142*n*, 146*n*, 147*n*, 152*n*, 155*n*, 200*n*, 201*n*, 203*n*, 204*n*

Rabkin, Leslie, 425*n*
Radbill, Samuel, 395*n*
Rains, Prudence, 404
Rainwater, Lee, 30*n*, 41, 257–58, 266
Ramirez, Efran, 120
Rankin, Anne, 298*n*
Raspberry, William, 286
Rausch, Charlotte L., 67*n*
Rausch, Harold L., 67*n*
Ray, Oakley S., 116*n*
Reader, George G., 29*n*
Reckless, Walter C., 139*n*
Redlich, Frederick C., 55–59, 67
Reeder, Leo G., 29*n*, 249*n*
Reiff, Robert, 72–73
Rein, Martin, 240*n*
Reiss, Albert J., Jr., 445, 446
Rensberger, Boyce, 567*n*
Richards, Louis G., 112*n*
Rienow, Leona Train, 545*n*, 546*n*, 551*n*, 552*n*, 555*n*, 556*n*
Rienow, Robert, 545*n*, 546*n*, 551*n*, 552*n*, 555*n*, 556*n*
Riesman, David, 499, 500
Riley, M., 415*n*
Rist, Ray, 307
Roberts, Ron E., 420*n*, 421
Robin, Gerlad D., 174*n*
Robinson, Duane, 506*n*
Roby, Pamela, 240
Rockefeller, John D., III, 228*n*
Rodman, Hyman, 258, 268
Roethlisberger, Fritz J., 495*n*
Rogers, Carl, 64
Röling, Bert V. A., 214*n*
Roosevelt, Franklin D., 47, 225
Roosevelt, Theodore, 144

Rosen, Benson, 329*n*
Rosenberg, B. G., 318*n*
Rosenberg, George S., 414*n*, 415, 416*n*
Rosenhan, D. L., 54, 71, 72
Rosenthal, Alan J., 219*n*
Ross, H. Laurence, 444
Rossi, Alice S., 343, 351
Rousseau, Jean-Jacques, 4
Rubington, Earl, 16*n*, 18*n*–20*n*
Rubenstein, Arthur, 379
Rushing, William, 56, 57
Ryan, William, 249*n*, 251*n*, 252*n*
Ryder, Norman B., 529*n*

Safilios-Rothschild, Constantina, 328*n*, 349*n*
Saghir, M. T., 448*n*
Salerno, Ralph F., 158, 179*n*
Samuels, Gertrude, 504*n*
Sartre, Jean-Paul, 193
Satir, Virginia, 418*n*
Sauber, Mignon, 404*n*
Sawyer, Jack, 327*n*
Scanzoni, John, 394*n*, 408, 409*n*
Schaffer, Leslie, 58
Scheff, Thomas J., 48, 49, 53, 76
Schelling, Thomas C., 218*n*
Schlegel, W. S., 447
Schoor, Alvin L., 251*n*, 252*n*
Schroeder, Richard S., 115*n*
Schulder, Diane B., 332
Schur, Edwin M., 142*n*, 143*n*, 157*n*, 177*n*, 178*n*
Schusshein, Morton J., 252*n*
Scott, Hilda, 326–27
Scott, William A., 60–61
Seeman, Melvin, 484
Segal, Sheldon, 535*n*
Seham, Max, 29, 30, 60*n*
Seligman, Ben B., 244, 245*n*, 486*n*, 490*n*
Selkin, James, 204*n*, 205*n*
Serbin, Lisa A., 325
Seward, Georgene H., 322*n*
Shakespeare, William, 359
Shanahan, Eileen, 487*n*
Shank, Paul C., 502*n*, 503*n*
Shaw, George Bernard, 248
Sheppard, Harold, 484
Siegel, Alberta E., 197*n*
Silver, Catherine B., 326*n*
Simms, Henry E., 83*n*
Simon, William, 394, 439, 443*n*, 445, 446, 451, 453, 466, 473
Skolnick, Jerome H., 190*n*, 192, 213
Small, William E., 564*n*
Smith, Adam, 233, 234, 432, 498, 567
Smith, Dwight S., 179*n*
Spengler, Joseph, 498*n*
Spitz, Mark, 226

Srole, Leo, 56
Stanton, Elizabeth Cady, 323
Steele, Brandt F., 399
Steinfeld, Jesse L., 212
Stewart, George Lee, 463*n*
Stoll, Clarice S., 324*n*, 325
Stolley, Paul D., 83*n*
Stone, Lucy, 323
Straus, Murray A., 319*n*
Straus, Robert, 85
Suffet, Fredric, 122*n*, 126*n*, 127
Sullivan, Harry Stack, 63
Sutherland, Edwin H., 141–42, 159–60
Sutton-Smith, Brian, 318*n*
Szasz, Thomas S., 50–52, 76

Taggart, Robert, 288
Targ, Dena B., 325*n*
Tausky, Kurt, 479*n*
Teevan, James J., Jr., 198*n*
Temerlin, Maurice K., 54
Thomas, Robert K., 282
Thomas, William E., 7
Thompson, Clara, 320
Thurow, Lester C., 225*n*, 229*n*
Tilgher, Adriano, 479*n*, 480, 501
Toby, Jackson, 166*n*, 169*n*
Trotter, Robert J., 505*n*
Tyler, Gus, 260*n*

Valentine, Charles A., 255–56, 268
Velarde, Albert J., 457, 458
Veysey, Laurence, 420*n*, 422*n*, 423
Vincent, Clark E., 404
von Clausewitz, Karl, 214

Wade, Jerry L., 561*n*
Wagley, Charles, 275
Wallace, George, 209
Warlick, Mark, 457, 458
Weber, Max, 482
Weil, Robert J., 59
Weinberg, Martin S., 16*n*, 18*n*–20*n*, 449*n*, 454
Weinberg, S. Kirkson, 439
Wice, Paul Bernard, 298, 309
Wicker, Tom, 156*n*
Wilkinson, Rupert, 98
Willard, Emma, 322
Williams, Colin J., 449*n*, 454
Williams, Robin H., Jr., 276*n*, 327
Wilson, James Q., 147–48
Wilson, W. Cody, 469, 470
Winick, Charles, 325, 464
Witt, Shirley, 337*n*, 338*n*
Wright, James D., 271

Yankelovich, Daniel, 88, 89, 100*n*, 115*n*

Zelnik, Melvin, 472
Zinn, Howard, 190
Znaniecki, Florian, 7

SUBJECT INDEX

AA (Alcoholics Anonymous), 65, 95–96, 119, 399

AARP (American Association of Retired Persons), 379

Adaptation approach to poverty, 257–58

Addiction, defined, 99; *see also* Drug abuse

Addiction Service Agency (NYC), 121

Adolescence, as concept, 359–60; *see also* Young, the

AEC (Atomic Energy Commission), 553, 562

AFDC (Aid to Families with Dependent Children), 244, 262, 264, 394, 405

Affluence, 229–40
 corporatism and, 233–36
 nature of, 229–32
 significance of, 237–40

Affluent, the, 225–32
 life style of, 225–27
 wealth accumulation by, 227–28

Age
 population by sex and, in developed and underdeveloped countries (figure), 523
 and sex composition of labor force, 482–83

Age Discrimination in Employment Act (1967), 368–69

Aged, the, *see* Elderly, the

Aging, stigma attached to term, 358; *see also* Elderly, the

Agism, 364–84
 consequences of, for the elderly, 374, 375 (table), 376
 consequences of, for the young, 372–76
 against the elderly, 366–68, 369 (figure), 370, 371 (table), 372; *see also* Elderly, the
 against the young, 364–65; *see also* Young, the
 social policy to fight, 362–64, 376, 377 (figure), 378–84

Aggression, prejudice, discrimination and, 278–79

Agrarian countries, *see* Developing countries

Agriculture, Department of, 241, 562

Aid to Families with Dependent Children (AFDC), 244, 262, 264, 394, 405

Air pollution, 542, 544–45, 546 (table), 547, 548 (figure)

Al-Anon, 96

Alateen, 96

Alcoholic psychoses, defined, 52

Alcoholics Anonymous (AA), 65, 95–96, 119, 399

Alcoholism, 84–99
 economic cost of, 80
 problem drinkers vs. alcoholics, 85–87
 social control of, 94–99
 social problems related to, 89, 90 (figure), 91 (figure), 92–94
 socioeconomic characteristics of drinkers, 87 (figure), 88 (figure)
 uses and abuses of alcohol, 84–86, 87 (figure), 88, 89

Alienation
 prostitution and, 461
 work, 483–85

Alimony payments, 413

AMA (American Medical Association), 27, 39, 44

American Association of Retired Persons (AARP), 379

American Bar Association, 454

American Hospital Association, 95

American Indians
 activism of, 304
 education of American Indian children, 283–84
 employment for, 294
 extermination of, 561
 housing of, 292
 institutionalized discrimination against, 282–83
 number of, on welfare, 261
 poverty of, 246
 sex discrimination against American Indian women, 337–38
 social equality for, 273
 stereotypes of, 281
 Tortured Americans, The (Burnette), 292
 voting rights of, 274
 See also Racial discrimination

American Lutheran Church, 353

American Management Associations, 504

American Medical Association (AMA), 27, 39, 44

American Psychiatric Association, 448

American Telephone and Telegraph (AT&T), 353

Amphetamines (speed, uppers, ups), 81, 111–13, 118

Anatomical destiny, Freudian theory of, 319–20

Animals, numbers of extinct species of, 542

Annual income
 percent distribution of families by (figure), 224
 of youth (table), 361

Anomie approach (goals and opportunities approach)
 to crime, 160–61
 to rape, 441

Antabuse programs, 96–97

Antidepressants, 66

Antitrust violations, 143–44

Appliances, cost of (table), 145

Arms race, 2–3; *see also* War

Army Corps of Engineers, 563

Arrests, *see* Crime

Asian Americans
 sex discrimination against Asian women, 338
 voting rights of, 274
 See also Racial discrimination

Asocial sex variance, as sexual social problem, 439–41; *see also* Rape

Assault and robbery, 203–4

Aswan Dam, 556

Atomic Energy Commission (AEC), 553, 562

AT&T (American Telephone and Telegraph), 353

Automation, 489–93
 areas of, 490
 impact of, 490–93

Automobiles
 drinking and automobile accidents, 90, 91 (figure)
 need to reassess function of, 568–69
 number of thefts (1975), 134
 role of, in environmental crisis, 560

Autonomy, as focal concern of lower-class culture, 164–65

Barbiturates (depressants), 81, 113–14
Battered child syndrome (child abuse), 156, 388, 395–400
Behavior modification, 66–67
Behavior patterns, social problems and acceptable, 5–6
BIA (Bureau of Indian Affairs), 282, 338
Biological perspective
    homosexuality in, 447–49
    social problems in, 10
    violence in, 193–94
Birth control, see Population control
Birthrate
    population explosion and, 515, 521–22
    social change and, 532
Black Muslim movement, 529
Black politicians, number of, 272
Black Power Conference, 529
Black separatism, 301–2
Blacks
    dilemma created by, 273
    education of black children, 283–84; see also Busing issue
    elderly, 375
    employment for, 294, 296
    family structure among, 393–95
    genocide feared by, 529
    health care for, 36
    housing for, 290–93
    income of, 272, 296, 297 (figure)
    institutionalized discrimination against, 282–83
    landmark Supreme Court decision affecting status of, 273–74
    mental disorders among, 60–61
    in 1960s civil disturbances, 205, 206 (figure), 207–8, 274, 302–4
    number of, on welfare, 261
    poverty among, 224, 244–46
    sex discrimination against black women, 335–36
    sexual stereotype of black males, 279–80
    social justice for, 299
    stereotypes of, 281
    unemployment among, 272, 296, 297 (figure)

Blacks (cont.)
    as victims of violence, 201–2, 204
    voting rights of, 276
    See also Racial discrimination
Blue Cross, 32, 34, 38, 39
Blue Shield, 32, 34, 39
Brown v. Board of Education (1954), 273–74
Buddhism, attitudes of, toward population control, 530
Burglaries, number of (1975), 134
Business-government crime, 144–46
Busing, 2, 285–90
    basic argument for, 285
    proponents and opponents of, 290
    racial tensions provoked by, 288
    reactions to, 286–87
    ways to make busing effective, 289

California Youth Authority, 167
Call girls
    characteristics of, 462
    defined, 454
Carbon dioxide, increase in artificially produced (figure), 548
Cash income programs, 260–62
Catholics
    attitudes of, toward abortions, 529–30
    as drinkers, 88
    promise of social equality and, 273
Census, Bureau of the, 240, 241, 295
Central Intelligence Agency (CIA), 3
Chemical pollution, 555–56
Chemicals, need to develop alternatives to, 569
Chemotherapy, 65–66
Chicago Area Project, 160, 174
Chicanos, see Mexican Americans
Child abuse, 156, 388, 395–400
Child Abuse Prevention and Treatment (Mondale Law; 1974), 396
Child molestation, 439–40, 469
Child-rearing practices, fighting sexism with changes in, 348–49
Child-support payments (table), 410
Children
    family happiness and, 392, 393 (figure)
    illegitimate, 388, 400–5
    See also Education
Children of Crisis (Coles), 300

Chinese Americans, see Asian Americans
Cities
    major city school systems with minority enrollment over 50 percent (figure), 285
    twelve fastest-growing, in the world (table), 525
Civil disturbances (1960s), 205, 206 (figure), 207–8, 274, 303–4
Civil rights, see specific forms of discrimination; for example: Agism; Racial discrimination
Civil Rights Act (1957), 274
Civil Rights Act (1960), 274
Civil Rights Act (1964), 274, 324, 331, 346, 347, 351
Civil Rights Act (1965), 274
Civil Rights Act (1968), 274
Civil Service Commission, 455
Civilian Conservation Corps, 94
Clean Air Act (1970), 569
Client-centered therapy (nondirective therapy), 64–65
Commission on Civil Rights (U.S.), 288, 289, 298
Commission on Human Rights (NYC), 294
Commission on Obscenity and Pornography, 467, 468
Common Cause, 234
Communes
    group marriage, 423
    hip, 422
    ideological, 422
    religious, 420, 422
    service, 422
    youth, 422
Community programs
    for drug addicts, 123
    for treatment of alcoholism, 97–98
Community psychology, treatment of mental disorders and, 72–74
Company programs for treatment of alcoholism, 98
Comprehensive Alcohol Abuse and Alcoholism Prevention, 95
Comprehensive Drug Abuse Prevention and Control Act (1970), 116
Comprehensive Employment Training Act (1973), 305
Compulsory education, 377–78
Comstock law (1873), 531
Conflict-habituated marriages, defined, 391
Conflict subculture, defined, 163
Conformity, culture and, 6

Consumer fraud, 144, 145 (table)
Contraception, *see* Population control
Contraculture, criminal world, as prostitute reference group, 460–61
Control theory of violence, 194–95
Conventional crimes, 147–48, 175–76
Corporate-military connections, affluence and, 235–37
Corporate-politician connections, affluence and, 233–35
Corporation executives, as members of the affluent class, 232
Corporatism, affluence and, 232–36
Corruption, organized crime and, 151–52
Costs
    annual, of crime (figure), 136
    of alcoholism, 80
    of appliances (table), 145
    of damages caused by air and water pollution, 542
    of health care, 26, 27, 30, 31 (figure), 32–35
    of health insurance, 34–35
    of national defense, 188, 218, 236–37
Council of Economic Advisers, 240
Crime, 134–85
    alcoholism and, 91–93
    conditions and causes of, 154–58
    drug abuse and, 117–18
    facts about, 134
    fraud as, 143, 144 (table), 145–46
    juvenile, 153–54; *see also* Juvenile delinquency
    legal definition of, 137
    nature of, 137–39
    occupational, 134, 141–44, 145 (table), 146, 156–57, 177–79
    organized, 148–52; *see also* Organized crime
    political, 3, 146
    professional, 152–53
    property, 134, 135 (figure), 141
    public order and conventional, 147–48, 175–76
    sex, *see* Sex crimes
    social control of, 165–67, 168 (figure), 169 (figure), 170–80
    sociological theories of, 158–65

Crime (*cont.*)
    statistics on, 135 (figure), 136 (figure)
    violent personal, 140–41
    See also Violence
Criminal justice system, need for reforms in, 175–80
Criminal violence, 200, 201 (table), 202 (table), 203–5
Criminal world contraculture, as prostitute reference group, 460–61
Criminalistic subculture, defined, 163
Crude birthrate, defined, 515
Cultural anthropological perspective, social problems in, 9–10
Cultural approach to poverty, 254–55
Cultural-situational approach to poverty, 256–57
Cultures
    child abuse and, 398–400
    conflict in, as manifestation of social disorganization, 18
    conformity, deviance and, 6
    criminal world contraculture, 460–61
    delinquency and lower-class, 164–65
    health and, 26–27
    heterogeneity of, crime and, 154–55
    sex roles and, 325
    See also Subcultures
Culture of poverty, 254–55

Daytop Village, 120
De facto segregation, defined, 285
De jure segregation, defined, 285
Death rate, defined, 515
Decibel values of common environmental sounds (figure), 555
Defense, Department of, 235
Defense budget (1977), 218
Defense contracts, 236–37
Delinquency, *see* Juvenile delinquency
Delinquent Boys (Cohen), 162–63
Demographic factors of crime, 155; *see also* Population explosion
Denver Child Abuse Center, 399
Depressants (barbiturates), 81, 113–14
Desensitization, 67
Deterrent
    retribution and deterrence,

Deterrent (*cont.*)
    crime control through, 165–67
    of violence, television as, 198
Developed countries (industrialized countries)
    effects of population explosion on, 512, 517–19
    food production in, 512
    gross national product of, 517
    population control in, 533–34
Developing countries (agrarian countries; underdeveloped countries)
    effects of population explosion in, 512, 519–27
    food production in, 512, 519, 520 (figure)
    gross national product of, 514–15
    population control in, 534–36
Deviance
    culture and, 6
    defined, 12–13
    as mental disorder, 48–50
    social change and useful, 14–15
    social problems in deviant behavior perspective, 18–19
Dictionary of Occupational Titles, 481
Differential association theory of occupational crime, 142, 159
Directive therapy, 65
Discrimination
    against homosexuals, 455
    nature of, 276–78
    See also Agism; Prejudice; Racial discrimination; Sexism
Diversity, as ecological concept, 543
Divorce
    explanations for trends in, 407–9, 410 (table), 411–14
    variations in rates of, 405, 406
Divorce Reform Law (1966; N.Y.), 411
Domestic violence, 199–213
    civil disturbances as, 205, 206 (figure), 207–8, 274, 303–4
    criminal, 200, 201 (table), 202 (table), 203–5
    social action and, 209 (figure), 210–13
Drinking, *see* Alcoholism
Drug abuse, 80–84, 114–31

Drug abuse (*cont.*)
    amphetamines, 81, 111–13, 118
    barbiturates, 81, 113–14
    hallucinogens, 110–11
    heroin, 81, 107–8, 109 (table), 110, 118
    of legal drugs, 82, 83 (figure), 84
    marijuana, 80, 81, 100–1, 106–7, 115–16
    social control of, 119–27
    social problems related to, 114–18
Drug Abuse Treatment Act (1972), 116
Drugs
    rationale determining acceptability of, 80–81
    what are, 81–82
Duration concept in differential association theory, 159

Ecology, *see* Environmental crisis
Economic growth
    crime and, 154
    in developing countries, population explosion and, 520–22, 523 (figure), 524
    to fight poverty, 263–64
    population explosion and, 517–18
    See also Gross national product
Economic Opportunity Act, 305
Economy, spaceman, defined, 518
Ecosystem, circulation of materials in (figure), 559
EDP, *see* Automation
Education
    Brown v. Board of Education, 273–74
    compulsory, 377–78
    divorce and, 408
    fighting sexism with changes in, 350–51
    Head Start, 274, 305–8
    poverty and, 250–51
    of public, to combat environmental crisis, 565–66
    racial discrimination in, 2, 283–84, 285 (figure), 286–90
    sex, 430, 472
    sexism in, 340–41
Education Amendments (1972), 351
Educational programs
    for drug addicts, 125–26
    treatment of alcoholism with, 98–9

EEOC (Equal Employment Opportunity Commission), 278, 331, 347, 351
Elderly, the, 358–84
    consequences of discrimination against, 374, 375 (table), 376
    discrimination against, 366–68, 369 (figure), 370, 371 (table), 372
    effects of retirement on, 367–68, 375 (table), 486
    facts about, 358
    family problems of, 414, 415 (table), 416
    isolation of, 2, 3, 388
    poverty among, 242–43, 358
    roleless role of, 359
    similarities between the young and, 362–64
    social policy, 378–84
    who are, 361–62
Embezzlement, 141–42
Employee Retirement Security Act (1974), 381
Employee society, defined, 482
Employment
    to fight poverty, 263–64
    discrimination in, *see* Job discrimination
    See also Unemployment
Encyclopedia of Social Work, 160
Energy consumption
    environmental crisis and, 559–60
    need to reassess, 568
Engineering projects, environmental crisis and large-scale, 556–57
Environmental crisis, 542–73
    air pollution in, 542, 544–45, 546 (table), 547, 548 (figure)
    chemical pollution in, 555–56
    dimensions of, 543–44
    exhaustion of natural resources in, 513, 542, 551–53, 561
    facts on, 542–43
    land degradation in, 542, 553–54
    large-scale engineering projects and, 556–57
    noise pollution in, 554, 555 (figure)
    origins of, 558, 559 (figure), 560–62, 563 (table), 564–65
    population explosion and, 513, 559

Environmental crisis (*cont.*)
    radioactive pollution in, 549–51
    social action to combat, 564–71
    solid waste disposal in, 551–53, 563 (table)
    thermal pollution in, 551
    water pollution in, 542, 547–51
Environmental Protection Agency (EPA), 562, 569, 570
Equal Credit Opportunity Act (1974), 353
Equal Employment Opportunity Commission (EEOC), 278, 331, 347, 351
Equal Pay Act (1963), 331, 351, 353
Equal Rights Amendment (ERA), 315, 351–52
Ethnicity, alcoholism and, 86
Excitement, as focal concern of lower-class culture, 164
Exhibitionism, 439, 440
    as asocial sex variance, 439, 441
Expectation in value-stretch concept, defined, 259
Experimenters of marijuana, defined, 100
Exploitation, prejudice, discrimination and, 280
Extended family, defined, 389; *see also* Family

Family, 388–95, 417–26
    adequately functioning, 388–91
    children and happiness of, 392, 393 (figure)
    communal, 419–25
    crime and disintegration of, 156
    effects of drinking on, 93
    effects of working women on, 391–92
    facts about, 338
    industrialization and changes in, 321 (table), 322
    sexism in, 342–43
    structure of, among the poor, 243, 244 (figure)
    two-partner, 417–19
    See also Family planning; Family problems; Female-headed households
Family planning, 531–32
Family problems
    child abuse as, 156, 388, 395–400

Family problems (*cont.*)
  of the elderly, 414, 415 (table), 416
  illegitimacy as, 400–5
  See also Divorce
Fate, as focal concern of lower-class culture, 164
FCC (Federal Communications Commission), 571
FDA (Food and Drug Administration), 113
Federal Bureau of Investigation (FBI), 3, 91, 135, 200
Federal Communications Commission (FCC), 571
Federal Gun-Control Act (1968), 211
Federal Housing Authority (FHA), 145–46, 291
Federal housing programs for the elderly, 382
Federal Trade Commission (FTC), 177, 571
Federal Water Pollution Control Act Amendments (1972), 569
Female-headed households
  black, 393–94
  number of, living under poverty line, 314
Females, *see* Sex roles; Sexism; Women
Feminine Mystique, The (Friedan), 323
Feminism, rise of, 320, 321 (table), 322–27
Fertility rate, defined, 515
FHA (Federal Housing Authority), 145–46, 291
Fifteenth Amendment (1870), 273
Financing systems for health care, 42–43
Firearms ownership, 188, 209–11
First Amendment (1791), 466
Fixed income approach to poverty, 240–41
Flexible work hours (flexitime), 505–6
Food and Drug Administration (FDA), 113
Food programs for the poor
  commodity distribution program, 263
  food stamp program, 263
Food production, 512, 519, 520, (figure)
Force, sex roles and threat and use of, by men, 318–19
Fortune Society, 156
Four-day work week, 503–5
Fourteenth Amendment (1868), 273, 323

Fraud, 143, 144 (table), 145–46
Frequency concept in differential association theory, 159
Frustration, as source of prejudice and discrimination, 278–79
Frustration-aggression theory of violence, 194–95
FTC (Federal Trade Commission), 177, 571
Full Employment Act (1948), 506

Gallup polls
  on busing, 290
  on crime, 136
  on population control, 528
Gangs, *see* Juvenile delinquency
Gault case (1967), 154
Gender identity, defined, 324
General Dynamics Corporation, 236
Genocide
  of American Indians, 561
  black fear of, 529
Goals and opportunities approach, *see* Anomie approach
Government
  as employer, to fight poverty, 264
  role of, in environmental crisis, 563 (figure), 564
  sexism in, 346–47
  See also Social control
Gray Panthers, 376, 379, 383
Great Britain, social control of drug addiction in, 123–25
Greenhouse effect, defined, 547
Gross National Product (GNP)
  of developed countries, 517
  of developing countries, 514–15
Group marriage communes, 422–24
Group-supported crime, 159–60
Group therapy, 65
Group values, value conflict and, 18
Gun control, 209 (figure), 210–11

Hallucinogens, 110–11
Harrad West (commune), 423
Harris polls
  on homosexuality, 442
  on status of women (1970; 1975), 315
Harrison Act (1914), 116, 117
Head Start, 274, 305–8
Health
  alcoholism and, 89–90
  culture and, 26–27
  See also Health care; Mental health; Mental illness

Health, Education, and Welfare, Department of (HEW), 37, 87, 261, 552, 562
Health care
  alternative financing systems for, 42–43
  alternative providers of, 41–42
  cost of, 26, 27, 30, 31 (figure), 32–35
  distribution of, 27–28
  inequality in distribution of, 29–30
  poverty and, 248, 249 (table), 250
  problems of unnecessary or harmful, 35–36, 37 (figure), 38
  social action to improve, 41–44
Health insurance
  cost of, 34–35
  Medicaid as, 35, 39, 42, 69, 249, 261, 263, 381
  Medicare as, 35, 39, 42, 43, 249, 263, 381
Health Maintenance Organization Act (1973), 42
Health Maintenance Organizations (HMO's), 41–42
Health Services and Mental Health Administration, 38
Heroin, 81, 107–8, 109 (table), 110, 118
Heterogeneous subsociety with variable and adapative subcultures, poverty as, 256
HEW (Department of Health, Education, and Welfare), 37, 87, 261, 552, 562
Hinduism, attitudes of, toward population control, 530
Historical perspective
  on feminist movement, 322–24
  on social problems, 8–9
  on technology, 560–62
  on treatment of mental disorders, 62–64
  on violence, 190–91
  on work, 479–80
HMO's (Health Maintenance Organizations), 41–42
Homemaker role, redefining, as prerequisite to sexual equality, 333
Homicides, 200, 201 (table), 202 (table), 203
  statistics on, 188
  by types of weapons used (figure), 208
Homosexuality, 430, 442–55

Homosexuality (*cont.*)
    biological and social factors in, 447–49
    defined, 442
    lesbianism, 450–53
    in prisons, 445
    social control of, 453–55
    subcultural aspects of, 449–50
Homosexuals
    married, 444
    recognizing oneself as, 446–47
    stable relationships of, 444–45
    stereotypes of, 443
Hospitals
    cost of, 31–33
    quality of, 26
Housing
    discrimination in, against the elderly, 369–70
    for the elderly, 382
    racial discrimination in, 290–93
    poverty and, 251 (table)
Housing and Urban Development Corporation (HUD), 308
Human Resources Administration (NYC), 291
Human Sexual Inadequacy (Masters and Johnson), 434
Human Sexual Response (Masters and Johnson), 434
Humanae Vitae (papal encyclical; On the Transmission of Human Life), 529, 530
Hunger in developing countries, 519, 520 (figure)
Hustlers (street walkers)
    characteristics of, 461–62
    defined, 457
    pimps and, 463–64
Hydrologic cycle, defined, 547
Hypnosis in treatment of mental disorders, 65

Ideological communes, 421–22
ILGWU (International Ladies Garment Workers Union), 336
Illegitimacy, 388, 400–5
Incest, 439–40
Income
    annual, of youth, 361 (table)
    of the elderly, 366 (figure), 369
    fixed income approach to poverty, 240–41
    job satisfaction and, 495
    median U.S. annual, 224
    percent distribution of families by annual (figure), 224

Income (*cont.*)
    percentage of total, received by each fifth and top five percent of affluent families (table), 228
    racial discrimination and, 272, 296, 297 (figure)
    relative income approach to poverty, 241–42
    of women, 314–15, 328–29, 330 (table), 331–32
Income-in-kind programs, 263
Income maintenance programs, 264–66
Income tax, negative, 265
Indian Affairs, Bureau of (BIA), 282, 338
Indian Historical Society, 284
Individual marriage, defined, 418
Industrial Revolution, 321
Industrialization
    effects of, on family, 321 (table), 322
    rise of feminism and, 321 (table), 322
    See also Automation; Developed countries; Technological system
Innovation concept in anomie approach, 160
Intensity concept in differential association theory, 159
Interdependence, as ecological concept, 543
Interior, Department of the, 562
Internal Revenue Service (IRS), 227, 486
International Ladies Garment Workers Union (ILGWU), 336
International Telephone and Telegraph Corporation (IT&T), 232
Institutionalized discrimination
    in administration of justice, 296–98
    in education, 2, 283–84, 285 (figure), 286–90
    in employment, 294–96, 297 (figures)
    in housing, 290–93
Integration, *see* School integration
Irish, the, alcohol consumption of, 86
IRS (Internal Revenue Service), 227, 486
Islam, attitudes of, toward population control, 530
Italians, alcohol consumption of, 86

Japanese Americans, *see* Asian Americans
Jews
    alcohol consumption of, 86, 88
    as members of the affluent class, 232
    social equality for, 273
    stereotypes of, 281
Job Corps, 262
Job discrimination
    against the elderly, 368, 369 (figure)
    racial, 294–96, 297 (figures)
    sexist, 314–15, 328–29, 330 (table), 331–32
    against the young, 378
Job satisfaction, 493 (table), 494–97
    income and, 495
    workers' participation and, 495–97
Joint Commission on Mental Health and Mental Illness, 73
Joint Legislative Committee on Crime, 179
Judaism
    attitudes of, toward population control, 530
    attitudes of, toward sex, 432
    See also Jews
Just Community of Niantic (Connecticut), 173
Justice
    need to reform criminal justice system, 175–80
    for the poor, 252–53
    racial discrimination in administration of, 296–98
Justice, Department of, 144, 145
"Justice in the Therapeutic State" (Szasz), 50
Juvenile delinquency, 153–54
    homosexual prostitution and, 445–46
    delinquent subcultures, 161–64
    lower-class culture and, 164–65
    lower-class youths as delinquents, 138–39
    social class and police behavior in cases of, 138
Juvenile Delinquency Prevention Act (1974), 182
Juvenile justice, need for reforms in, 175–80

Kennedy-Griffiths bill, 43
Kibbutz, 424–25

Kinship unit, *see* Family; Family problems

Labeling approach
classification of mental disorders and, 52–53
to social problems, 19–22
Labor, Department of, 481
Labor force
age and sex composition of, 482–83
women in, 314, 391–92, 478
See also Employment; Job discrimination; Unemployment; Work
Labor unions, employment discrimination and, 294–95
Lama Foundation, 422
Land degradation, 542, 553–54
Language, sexism in, 344–45
Larcenies, number of (1975), 134
Law Enforcement Assistance Administration, 136, 182
Laws
antiprostitution, 464–65
on contraception, 530
to curb domestic violence, 209 (figure), 210–12
discriminating against the young, 366, 378
divorce, 411–14
drug, 115–17, 126–27
environmental, 569–70
extending economic, to fight poverty, 264
homosexuality, 453–55
illegitimacy, 401–2
manpower training, 305
sexist, 332–34, 347–48, 351–52
sexuality, 430, 438
See also specific acts
Legal drugs, abuse of, 82–84
Legislation, *see* Laws; *and specific acts*
Leisure, 3, 497–501
fusing work and, 498–501
uses of, 498–99, 500 (figure), 506
Lesbianism, 450–53
Life satisfaction, job satisfaction and, 497
Limited functional autonomy of lower class, 257
Limits, concept of, as ecological concept, 543–44
Lockheed Aircraft Corporation, 146, 235, 236
Long-Ribicoff bill, 42–43
Lower class
crime among, 155–56

Lower class (*cont.*)
limited functional autonomy of, 257
See also Poor, the; Poverty; *and specific Minority groups; for example:* Blacks
Lower-class culture, delinquency and, 164–65
Lower-class youths, factors contributing to criminality of, 138–39
LSD (lysergic acid diethylamide), 110–11

Maladjustment, deviance vs., 48
Manic-depressive illness, defined, 52
Manpower Training and Development Act, 305
Manpower training programs to fight discrimination, 305
Manslaughter, defined, 200
Marijuana, 80, 81, 100–1, 106–7, 115–16
Marriage, 391
duration of average, 388
parental, 418
See also Family; Family problems
Masochism and passivity, sex roles and, 319
Mass advertising, as institutionalized deception, 157
Masturbation, as tolerated sex variance, 439
Media
as deterrent of violence, 198
regulating violence on, 211–12
sexism in, 344–45
stereotypes of elderly and, 370
television viewing by income and sex (figure), 500
violence on, 188, 197–99
Median income
U.S. annual, 224
of women (table), 330
Medicaid, 35, 39, 42, 69, 249, 261, 263, 381
Medical expenditures, 1975 (figure), 31
Medicare, 35, 39, 42, 43, 249, 263, 381
Medicine, paraprofessionals in, 502; *see also* Physicians
Mental health
facts about, 26
of women, behavior expressing, 344
Mental Health Facilities Act (1963), 73

Mental hospitals, organization of treatment in, 67–72
Mental illness, 26, 46–76
classification of, 51–54
model of, 51–52
nature of, 46–50
nonconformity to sex roles as, 314
social structure and, 54–56, 57 (figure), 58 (figure), 59–62
treatment of, 57, 58 (figure), 59, 62–74
what is, 47–48
Methadone, 120, 122
Mexican Americans
activism of, 304
education of Mexican-American children, 283–84
employment for, 296
institutionalized discrimination against, 282–83
poverty of, 245, 246
sex discrimination against Mexican-American women, 338
social justice for, 298
voting rights of, 274
See also Racial discrimination
Middle class, treatment of crime committed by, 138–39
Midtown Manhattan Study, 56–57, 59
Military-industrial complex, 217
Military personnel in private industry, 224, 235
Mind alteration; major substances used for (table) 103–4; *see also* Drug abuse
Mind That Found Itself, A (Beers), 63
Minorities
facts about, 272
meaning of term, 275–76
poverty among, 245–46
See also specific minority groups and specific forms of discrimination
Mobility orientation, mental disorder, social mobility and, 57
Modeling, as behavior modification technique, 67
Mondale Law (Child Abuse Prevention and Treatment; 1974), 396
Morality concept in social pathology perspective, 16, 20
Morning Star Ranch (commune), 422
Mother's Aid centers (Denmark), 405

Moynihan Report, 393, 394
Murder
    defined, 200
    murder rates (table), 202
"Myth of Mental Illness, The" (Szasz), 50

Narcotic antagonists, 122–23
Narcotics Division (Treasury Department), 116
National Academy of Science, 562
National Advisory Commission on Civil Disorders, 206, 274, 489
National Advisory Committee on Juvenile Problems, 182
National Advisory Council on Alcohol Abuse and Alcoholism, 95
National Alcohol, Drug Abuse and Mental Health Administration (Public Health Service), 117
National Caucus on the Black Aged, 379
National Center on Child Abuse and Neglect, 395
National Child Labor Committee, 365
National Commission on the Causes and Prevention of Violence, 203
    Task Force on Mass Media and Violence of, 198
National Commission on Marijuana and Drug Abuse, 81, 100, 118, 126
National Commission on the Reform of Secondary Education, 377–78
National Committee on the Employment of Youth, 378
National Committee for Mental Hygiene, 63
National Council on the Aging, 379
National Council on Crime and Delinquency, 181
National defense, cost of, 188, 218, 236–37
National Environmental Policy Act (NEPA; 1970), 569
National Gay Task Force, 450
National Health Service (British), 42, 125
National Institute on Alcohol Abuse and Alcoholism, 81, 88, 95, 97, 128
National Institute of Drug Abuse, 109, 116, 128

National Institute of Mental Health, 46, 63, 87, 106, 128, 396
    Task Force on Homosexuality of, 454
National Mental Health Act (1946), 63
National Organization for Women (NOW), 205, 323, 324
National Research Council, 241
National Rifle Association, 209, 211
National War Labor Board, 346
National Welfare Rights Organization (NWRO), 266
National Wildlife Federation, 569
Natural resources, exhaustion of, 513, 542, 551–53, 561
Natural system, elements making up, 558
Negative income tax, 265
Neighborhood Youth Corp, 262
NEPA (National Environmental Policy Act; 1970), 569
Neuroses
    defined, 51–52
    percentage of neurotics among total psychiatric patients (figure), 57
Nineteenth Amendment (1920), 323
No-fault divorces, 410–12
Noise pollution, 554, 555 (figure)
Nondirective therapy (client-centered therapy), 64–65
Normlessness, as manifestation of social disorganization, 18
NOW (National Organization for Women), 205, 323, 324
Nuclear family, defined, 389; see also Family; Family problems

Objective element of social problems, 3–4
Occupational crime (white-collar crime), 134, 141–44, 145 (table), 146, 156–57, 177–79
Old Age and Survivors Insurance, 372
Omnibus Crime Control and Safe Streets Act (1968), 181
On-demand divorces, 413
Opiates (heroin), 81, 107–8, 109 (table), 110, 118
Oral-genital sex, as tolerated sex variance, 439
Organic psychoses, defined, 52
Organized crime, 148–52
    combating, 179–80

Organized crime (cont.)
    as compatible with profit motive, 157–58
Organized religion, sexism in, 345–46
Orientals, see Asian Americans
Other People's Money (Cressey), 142
Outpatient treatment of mental disorders, 72–74
Overpopulation, see Population control

Paraprofessionals, 501–3
Parental marriage, purpose of, 418
Parents Anonymous, 399
Partial Nuclear Test Ban Treaty (1963), 219
Passive-congenial marriages, 391
Passivity
    masochism and, sex roles and, 344
    as sign of mental health of women, 344
Penis envy, sex roles and, 319, 320
Per capita income, U.S., 224
Personality structure
    of abusive parents, 399
    effects of racial discrimination on, 300–1
    homosexual and heterosexual, 430, 443, 446
Pesticide Regulation Division (Department of Agriculture), 562
Phoenix House, 120, 123
Photosynthesis, defined, 544–45, 559
Physical health, facts about, 26; see also Health care
Physicians
    cost of, 32–33
    incompetence of, 26, 27 (figure)
Pilot Intensive Counseling Organization Project (PICO), 167
Pimps, 460, 462–64
Plants, number of extinct species of, 542
Police
    crime and biases of, 137–39
    organized crime and corruption of, 151–52
Political crime, 3, 146
Politics (Aristotle), 479
Pollution, see Environmental crisis
Poor, the
    family structure among, 243, 244 (figure)

Poor, the (*cont.*)
    justice for, 252–53
    number of, 224
    unemployment among, 259–60
    on welfare, 260–62
    See also Lower class; Poverty; *and specific minority groups*
Population control
    compulsory, 532–33
    in developed countries, 533–34
    in developing countries, 534–36
    environmental crisis and, 570
    mixed attitudes toward, 527–29
    religious attitudes toward, 529–30
    voluntary approach to, 531–32
Population density, world patterns of (figure), 516
Population explosion, 2, 512–27
    daily rate of, 512
    in developed countries, 512, 517–19
    in developing countries, 512, 518, 520 (figure), 521–22, 523 (figure), 524, 525 (figure), 526–27
    environmental crisis and, 513, 559
    harmful effects of overpopulation, 512–13
    rate of growth of, defined, 517
    scope of problem, 513, 514 (figure), 515, 516 (figure), 517
Pornography, 465–71
    arguments against and for, 470–71
    commonality of exposure to, 468–69
    harmful effects of, 466–67
    sex crimes and, 469–70
Poverty, 237–69
    adaptation approach to, 257–58
    cultural explanation of, 254–55
    cultural-situational approach to, 256–57
    education and, 250–51
    among the elderly, 242–43, 358
    health care and, 248, 249 (table), 250
    housing and, 251 (table), 252
    nature of, 240–42
    physical health problems and, 39–41

Poverty (*cont.*)
    significance of, 237–40
    situational approach to, 255–56
    social action on, 262–66
    spatial distribution of, 246–48
    statistics on, 224
    value-stretch concept of, 258–59
    See also Lower class; *and specific groups affected by poverty; for example:* Blacks
Poverty-culture traits, 255–56
Poverty line
    number of blacks and Spanish-speaking Americans under, 272
    number of female-headed households under, 314
    number of people under, 224
Prejudice, 276–82
    consequences of, 299, 300 (table), 301–4
    nature of, 276–78
    psychological needs as source of, 278–80
    socialization, social structure and, 280–82
    See also Agism; Racial discrimination; Sexism
Premarital intercourse, as tolerated sex variance, 439
Presidential Panel on Youth, 364
President's Commission on Law Enforcement and Administration of Justice, 92, 128, 136, 150, 180, 182, 197
Prevention, crime control through, 173–75
Priority concept in differential association theory, 159
Prisons
    homosexuality in, 445
    lesbianism in, 452–53
    See also Criminal justice system
Private industry
    company programs for treatment of alcoholism, 98
    role of, in environmental crisis, 564–65
    stimulating, to fight poverty, 263–64
Professional crime, 152–53
Property crime, 134, 135 (figure), 141
Prostitution, 455–65
    defined, 455
    homosexual, 445–46

Prostitution (*cont.*)
    reasons for, 458–62
    social control of, 464–65
    as subculture, 463–64
Psychoanalysis, 64
Psychological perspective, social problems in, 10–11
Psychoses
    defined, 52
    percentage of psychotics among total psychiatric patients (figure), 57
Psychosomatic illness, defined, 52
Psychotherapy, 64–65
Puerto Ricans
    education of Puerto Rican children, 283–84
    employment for, 294–96
    institutionalized discrimination against, 282–83
    poverty of, 245
    sentences received by, 176
    sex discrimination against Puerto Rican women, 336–37
    stereotypes of, 281
    voting rights of, 274
    See also Racial discrimination
Puritanism, sexuality and, 432

Quality of life, population explosion and, 519

Race
    mental illness and, 60–61
    sexism and, 334, 335 (figure), 336–48
Racial discrimination, 278–311
    in administration of justice, 296–98
    consequences of, 299, 300 (table), 301–4
    in education, 2, 283–84, 285 (figure), 286–90
    employment, 294–96, 297 (figures)
    in housing, 290–93
    nature of, 276–78
    psychological needs as source of, 278–80
    roots of, 8–9
    social action against, 304–8
    socialization, social structure and, 280–82
Radioactive pollution, 549–51
Rape, 204–5, 318–19
    as asocial sex variance, 439–41
    exposure to pornography and, 469
    statistics on, 188
Recidivism, 168 (figure), 169
Recycling, 566–67

Regional health systems, 42
Rehabilitation
    of alcoholics, 95
    crime control through, 167, 168 (figure), 169 (figure), 170–3
    for drug addicts, 119–25
    for lower-class criminals, 139
Relative income approach to poverty, 241–42
Religion
    population control and, 529–30
    sexism in, 345–46
    See also specific religions and religious groups
Residual deviance, defined, 48–49
Resource equalization strategy, 258
Retirement, 367–68, 375 (table), 486
Retribution and deterrence, crime control through, 165–67
Rich, the, see Affluence; Affluent, the; Upper class
Robberies
    assault and, 203–4
    number of (1975), 134
Role exit, described, 367–68
Role relationships, importance of, in family functioning, 389–90
Roleless role of the elderly and the young, 359
Rural areas, poverty in, 246–48

Salaries, see Income
Schizophrenia, defined, 52
School integration, 2
    Brown v. Board of Education, 273–74
    See also Busing
Secondary deviance, defined, 20
Segregation, see Racial discrimination
Senile psychoses, defined, 52
Sex crimes
    pornography and, 469–70
    as sexual social problems, 437–38
    See also specific sex crimes; for example: Child molestation; Rape
Sex education, 430, 472
Sex roles
    facts about, 314
    homosexual, 445
    origins of traditional, 315–19
    rise of feminism and, 320, 321 (table), 322–27
Sexism, 327–55
    in education, 340–41

Sexism (cont.)
    in family, 342–43
    in government, 346–47
    job opportunities, income and, 314–15, 328–29, 330 (table), 331–32
    in language and media, 344–45
    legal, civil and economic rights and, 332–34
    in legal system, 347–48
    in organized religion, 345–46
    in psychiatry, 343–44
    social action to deal with, 348–52
    social class, race and, 334, 335 (figure), 336–38
    socialization process and, 325, 339–40
    stereotyping and, 314, 328–29
    See also Sex roles
Sexual social problems
    defining, 437
    sex crimes as, 437–38
    types of, 439–42
    See also Homosexuality; Pornography; Prostitution
Sexuality, 430–37
    facts about, 430
    origins of today's attitudes toward, 432–35
    present norms of, 430–31
    varieties of, 435–37
    See also Sexual social problems
Situational approach to poverty, 255–56
Social accountability, environmental crisis and training in, 566
Social action
    to combat environmental crisis, 564–71
    to control violence, 209 (figure), 210–13
    to deal with agism, 362–64, 376, 377 (figure), 378–84
    to deal with sexism, 348–52
    to fight poverty, 262–66
    on health care, 41–44
    against racial discrimination, 304–8
    on work-related problems, 501–6
Social change
    birthrate and, 532
    crime and, 154
    effects of, on family, 388
    useful deviance and, 14–15
Social class
    bias toward crime and, 138–39
    child abuse and, 398–400

Social class (cont.)
    drinking and, 87 (figure), 88 (figure)
    health care distribution, and, 28–30, 40–41
    mental disorder and, 55–56, 57 (figure)
    sexism and, 334, 335 (figure), 336–38
    understanding of social problems and, 7–8
    See also Affluence; Affluent, the; Lower class; Middle class; Upper class
Social control
    of alcoholism, 94–99
    of crime, 165–67, 168 (figure), 169 (figure), 170–80
    of drug abuse, 119–27
    of homosexuality, 453–55
    of prostitution, 464–65
    See also Laws
Social disorganization perspective, social problems in, 17–18
Social insurance programs, 262
Social pathology perspective, social problems, in 16–17
Social problems
    five perspectives on, 15–16, 17 (table), 18–20
    how social conditions become, 3–4
    premises for study of, 4–8
    in sociological perspective, 11–14
    studies of, in related disciplines, 8–11
Social Security Administration, 37–38, 241, 264, 333, 353, 368, 370–72, 381
Socialization
    as source of prejudice and discrimination, 280–82
    as source of sexism, 325, 339–40
Society
    conformity, deviance and, 6
    elements making up, 558
    mental disorder and, 54–56, 57 (figure), 58 (figure), 59–62
    prejudice, discrimination and, 280–82
Sociological perspective, social problems in, 11–14
Solid waste disposal, 551–53, 563
Specialization, 481–82
Speed (amphetamines; uppers; ups), 81, 111–13, 118
Status offense, defined, 153
Stereotypes
    of the elderly, 370, 371 (table)

Stereotypes (*cont.*)
    of homosexuals, 443
    of lesbians, 452
    prejudice, discrimination, and, 281–82
    sexist, 314, 328–29
    sexual, of black males, 279–80
Subcultures
    delinquent, 161–64
    homosexual, 449–50
    lesbian, 452
    prostitution as, 463–64
    of violence, 195–97
Supreme Court decisions
    on agism, 377, 378
    on busing, 289
    on homosexuality, 454
    on illegitimacy, 401–2
    on racial discrimination, 273–74, 285, 308
    on juvenile delinquency, 154, 397
    on mental disorders, 75
    on pornography, 467
    on sexuality, 435, 473
    on women's rights, 332–33, 347, 348
Synanon, 65, 119–20

Taxes
    negative income, 265
    paid by the affluent, 224, 227–28
    paid by the poor, 228
Thermal pollution, 551
Total institution concept, 69–70
Tranquilizers, 66
Transsexuality, 431
Two-partner family (serial monogamy; serial polygamy), 417–19

Underdeveloped countries, *see* Developing countries
Unemployment, 272, 484–89
    intermittent and chronic, 486–87
    invisible, 487–89
    involuntary retirement and, 486
    job discrimination and, 296, 297 (figure)
    among minorities, 272
    among the poor, 259–60
    youth, 358

United Farm Workers' Union, 304
Upper class, treatment of crime committed by, 139; *see also* Affluence; Affluent, the
Uppers (amphetamines; speed), 81, 111–13, 118
Urban areas, poverty in, 246–48

Value conflict perspective, social problems in, 18
Value-stretch concept of poverty, 258–59
Violence, 188–213
    biological explanation of, 193–94
    concepts of, 191–93
    domestic, *see* Domestic violence
    frustration-aggression and control theories of, 194–95
    historical perspective on, 190–91
    and media influence, 197–99
    subculture of, 195–97
    See also War
Voting
    by the elderly, 379
    by minorities, 274, 276
    by the young, 358
Voyeurism, as asocial sex variance, 439–41

Wages, *see* Income
War, 214–19
    arms race, 2–3
    explanations of, 215–17
    prevention of, 217–19
    statistics on casualties of, 188
War on Poverty, 305
Waste disposal, 551–53, 563 (table)
Water pollution, 542, 547–51
Wealth
    ownership of, 224, 229, 230
    perpetuation of, 229–31
    See also Affluence; Affluent, the
Welfare, 260–62
White-collar crime (occupational crime), 134, 141–44, 145 (table), 146, 156–57, 177–79
White Collar Crime (Sutherland), 141

White-collar workers, increase in, 481
Women
    alcohol consumption by, 87–88
    as criminals, 155
    income of, 314–15, 328–29, 330 (table), 331–32
    in labor force, 314, 391–92, 478
    lesbian, 450–53
    mental disorder among, 61–62
    as murderers, 201
    number of elderly, 358
    See also Prostitution; Sex roles; Sexism
Women's Bureau, 346
Women's Liberation Movement, 323, 338, 362
Work, 478–509
    facts about, 478
    in history, 479–80
    problem aspects of, *see* Automation; Job satisfaction; Leisure time; Unemployment
    social action on problems related to, 501–6
    trends in, 480–83
    See also Employment; Job discrimination; Labor force
Work hours, flexible, 505–6
Work week
    duration of average, 478
    four-day, 503–5
Workers' participation, 495–97
Workmen's compensation programs, 262

Young, the
    consequences of discrimination against, 372–76
    discrimination against, 364–65
    drinking among, 88–89
    facts about, 358
    roleless role of, 359
    similarities between the elderly and, 362–64
    social policy and prospects for, 376, 377 (figure), 378, 382–84
    who are, 359–60, 361 (table)
    See also Drug abuse; Juvenile delinquency
Youth communes, 422

Zero population growth, 517, 570